Children's Thinking

Third Edition

Robert S. Siegler

Carnegie Mellon University

Prentice Hall, Upper Saddle River, New Jersey 07458

Library of Congress Cataloging-in-Publication Data

SIEGLER, ROBERT S.
    Children's thinking / Robert S. Siegler. — 3rd ed.
        p.   cm.
    Includes bibliographical references and indexes.
    ISBN 0-13-397910-5
    1. Cognition in children.   I. Title.
BF723.C5S54   1998
155.4'13—dc21   97-9964
                                                 CIP

Editor in Chief: *Nancy Roberts*
Acquisition Editor: *Bill Webber*
Assistant Editor: *Jennifer Hood*
Editorial Assistant: *Emsal Hasan*
Production Liaison: *Fran Russello*
Editorial/Production Supervision: *Kim Gueterman*
Buyer: *Tricia Kenny*
Cover Designer: *Bruce Kenselaar*
Illustrator: *Asterisk Group*
Copyeditor: *Kathyrn Beck*
Marketing Manager: *Mike Alread*

This book was set in 10/12 Palatino by Pub–Set Inc.
and was printed and bound by Courier Companies, Inc.
The cover was printed by Phoenix Color Corp.

© 1998, 1991, 1986 by Prentice-Hall, Inc.
Upper Saddle River, New Jersey 07458

Printed in the United States of America
10   9   8   7

ISBN   0-13-397910-5

Prentice-Hall International (UK) Limited, *London*
Prentice-Hall of Australia Pty. Limited, *Sydney*
Prentice-Hall of Canada, Inc., *Toronto*
Prentice-Hall Hispanoamericana, S. A., *Mexico*
Prentice-Hall of India Private Limited, *New Delhi*
Prentice-Hall of Japan, Inc., *Tokyo*
Prentice-Hall Asia Pte. Ltd., *Singapore*
Editora Prentice-Hall do Brasil, Ltda., *Rio de Janeiro*

To Alice

Contents

5 LANGUAGE DEVELOPMENT 139

6 MEMORY DEVELOPMENT 173

Preface

Children's thinking is inherently fascinating. All of us were children once; most of us either have or expect to have our own children someday. The ways in which children think are both familiar and foreign. We remember some of the ways in which we thought at younger ages and have impressions of the thinking of many other children as well. As adults, we observe that children's thinking seems generally reasonable, and at times surprisingly insightful. At other times. though, children's reasoning leaves us flabbergasted. Why, for example, would an otherwise reasonable 5-year-old insist that pouring water into a differently shaped container changes the amount of water, even after an adult has just told the child that the amount of water is the same as before?

Until recently, many of the most intriguing aspects of children's thinking were inaccessible to our understanding. Philosophers have argued for hundreds of years about whether infants see the world as a "blooming, buzzing confusion" or in much the same way that older children and adults do. Only in the past few years, with the development of revealing experimental methods, has the answer become clear. Even newborns see certain aspects of the world quite clearly, and by 6 months of age, infants' perception resembles that of adults. This and other discoveries about children's thinking are the subject matter of this book.

Who would be interested in such a book? Anyone who is curious about children should find interesting observations and ideas in it. Anyone sufficiently motivated to take an undergraduate or graduate course in this area should find a great deal to intrigue the imagination and stimulate further interest in children's thinking.

One reason why writing about this area is so enjoyable is that understanding of many fundamental issues is rapidly increasing. This rapid growth has necessitated extensive updating of the book from its earlier editions. One major change has been a considerable increase in coverage of how development of the brain contributes to cognitive development. The weight of the brain increases fourfold between birth and adulthood; equally impressive changes are seen in the relative development of different parts of the brain and in the ability of the brain to change its functioning in response to experience. These neural changes influence perception, language, memory, and all other aspects of cognitive development.

A second major change involves increased discussion of contributions of the social world to children's thinking. In this book's previous edition, such coverage was limited largely to the "future trends" section of the final chapter. However, knowledge regarding the ways in which parents, siblings, other children, teachers, and the broader society influence cognitive development has grown to such an extent that the topic is now covered throughout the book. The social influences that are discussed include not only the direct effects of other people on children, but also effects of the tools that cultures provide (alphabets, number systems, calendars, and so on), the values and interests that they cultivate, and the basic human propensity to teach other people and to learn from them.

A third major change involves increased emphasis on practical contributions of research on children's thinking. This includes methods for diagnosing perceptual problems, such as blindness, during infancy; techniques for eliciting accurate recollections of events from children who need to testify in court cases; and instructional techniques for improving reading, writing, and mathematical skills.

Throughout the time that I've written the book, Carnegie Mellon University has provided a unique, exciting intellectual atmosphere in which to think and learn about cognitive development. One reflection of the intellectual atmosphere is the amount of high-quality suggestions and comments I received while writing the book. Zhe Chen, Bethany Johnson, and Doug Thompson offered especially helpful and constructive comments on part or all of the book. Of course, generous colleagues are not limited to any one university. Henry Wellman, Elyse Lehman, Eric Amsel, and Harriet Waters also provided useful comments, as did several anonymous reviewers. I am confident that their suggestions moved the book in the right direction; only readers can judge just how far in the right direction it evolved.

I would like to single out my secretary, Theresa Treasure, for special thanks. She worked with me throughout the writing process and did whatever it took to get the work done in a timely fashion. A different kind of thanks is due to my children, Aaron, Beth, and Todd, for greatly enriching my understanding of children's thinking, as well as for providing a number of colorful comments that I quoted at various places in the book. I also want to thank my wife, Alice, for keeping things going on the home front during the many times that I was preoccupied with the book. I hope that the text is worthy of all the confidence that she and the children have shown in me.

Robert S. Siegler

Acknowledgments

I would like to thank a number of individuals and publishing companies for permission to reproduce material in this book.

Figure 1.1 Aslin, R. N., & Dumais, S. T. (1980). Binocular vision in infants: A review and theoretical framework. In L. P. Lipsitt & H. W. Reese (Eds.), *Advances in child development and behavior*. New York: Academic Press.

Figure 2.7 Baillargeon, R. (1987). Object permanence in 3½- and 4½-month-old infants. *Developmental Psychology, 23*, 655–664.

Figure 3.6 MacWhinney, B., Leinbach, J., Taraban, R., & McDonald, J. (1989). Language learning: Cues or rules? *Journal of Memory and Language, 28*, 255–277.

Figure 4.5 Photograph courtesy of Dr. Martin Banks.

Figure 4.10 Photograph courtesy of Dr. Joseph Campos.

Figure 4.12 Photograph courtesy of Dr. G. Keith Humphrey.

Figure 6.1 Photograph courtesy of Dr. Carolyn Rovee-Collier.

Figure 6.3 Dempster, F. N. (1981). Memory span: Sources of individual and developmental differences. *Psychological Bulletin, 89*, 63–100.

Figure 6.5 Photograph courtesy of Dr. Patricia Miller.

Figure 6.6 Vurpillot, E. (1968). The development of scanning strategies and their relation to visual differentiation. *Journal of Experimental Child Psychology, 6*, 632–650.

Figure 7.2 Bomba, P. C., & Siqueland, E. R. (1983). The nature and structure of infant form categories. *Journal of Experimental Child Psychology, 35*, 294–328.

Figure 8.1 Vosniadou, S., & Brewer, W. (1992). Mental models of the earth: A study of conceptual change in childhood. *Cognitive Psychology, 24*, 535–585.

Figure 8.6 Karmiloff-Smith, A. (1986). Stage/structure versus phase/process in modelling linguistic and cognitive development. In I. Levin (Ed.), *Stage and structure: Reopening the debate*. Norwood, NJ: Ablex.

CHAPTER 1

An Introduction to Children's Thinking

When did the sun begin? **When people began living.** Who made it? **God.** How did God do this? **He put a real lot of light bulbs in it.** Are these light bulbs still in the sun? **No.** What happened to them? **They burnt out. No, they stay good a long time.** So are the light bulbs still in it? **No. I think he made it out of gold. And he lit it with fire.** (Conversation with my son, 1985)

I asked my younger son these questions one week before his fifth birthday. What do his answers tell us about how he viewed the world at that time? Do they reflect a simple lack of knowledge about astronomy and physics? Or do they indicate a fundamental difference between young children's reasoning and that of older children and adults? An adult who did not know the origins of the sun would never ascribe its origins to God putting light bulbs in it. Nor would an adult link the origins of the sun to the fact that people began to be alive. Do these differences mean that children generally reason in more literal and self-centered ways than adults? Or do they just reflect a child's grasping at straws when faced with a question for which he cannot even generate a plausible answer?

For hundreds of years, people have wondered about these and related questions. Do infants see the world in the same way as adults? Why do societies throughout the world first send children to school between the ages of 5 and 7? Why are adolescents so much more likely than 10-year-olds to fervently believe in causes such as vegetarianism or environmentalism? A century ago, people could only speculate about these issues. Now, however, we have concepts and methods that magnify our ability to observe, describe, and explain the process of development. As a result, our understanding of children's thinking is growing rapidly.

The goal of this chapter is to introduce some basic issues and ideas regarding children's thinking. The first section focuses on what children's thinking involves. The next section introduces some of the enduring questions that motivate people to study cognitive development. Finally, the last section provides an overview of the book's organization. An outline of the chapter is provided in Table 1.1.

WHAT IS CHILDREN'S THINKING?

Children's thinking refers to the thinking that takes place from the moment of birth through the end of adolescence. Defining what thinking is turns out to be quite difficult, because no sharp boundary divides activities that involve thinking from ones that do not. Thinking obviously involves the higher mental processes: problem solving, reasoning, creativity, conceptualizing, remembering, classifying, symbolizing, planning, and so on. Other examples of thinking involve more basic processes, processes at which even young children are skilled: using language and perceiving objects and events in the external environment, to name two. Still other activities might or might not be viewed as types of thinking. These include being socially skillful, having a keen moral sense, feeling appropriate emotions, and so on. The capabilities in this last group involve thought processes, but they also involve many other nonintellectual qualities. In this book, we give these boundary areas some attention, but the spotlight is on problem solving, conceptual understanding, reasoning, remembering, producing and comprehending language, and the other more purely intellectual, activities.

A particularly important characteristic of children's thinking is that it is constantly changing. How children think at particular points in development is

TABLE 1.1   Chapter Outline

  I. What Is Children's Thinking?
 II. Key Questions about Children's Thinking
      A. What Capabilities Are Innate?
      B. Does Development Progress through Stages?
      C. How Does Change Occur?
      D. How Do Individuals Differ?
      E. How Do Changes in the Brain Contribute to Cognitive Development?
      F. How Does the Social World Contribute to Cognitive Development?
III. The Book's Organization
      A. The Chapter-by-Chapter Organization
      B. The Central Themes
 IV. Summary

---

interesting in and of itself, but even more central for understanding cognitive development are the questions of what changes occur and how the changes occur. Comparing an infant to a 2-year-old, a 2-year-old to a 6-year-old, and a 6-year-old to an adolescent, it is easy to appreciate the magnitude of these changes. But what processes could transform the mind of a newborn baby into the mind of an adolescent? This is the central mystery of cognitive development.

Consider an example of the dramatic changes that occur with development. DeVries (1969) was interested in 3- to 6-year-olds' understanding of the difference between appearance and reality. She presented children of these ages with an unusually sweet-tempered cat named Maynard and allowed them to pet him. When the experimenter asked what Maynard was, all of the children knew that he was a cat. Then, as the children watched, the experimenter put a mask of a fierce dog on Maynard's face. The experimenter asked, "Look, it has a face like a dog. What is this animal now?"

Many of the 3-year-olds thought that Maynard had become a dog. They refused to pet him and said that under his skin he had a dog's bones and a dog's stomach. In contrast, most 6-year-olds knew that a cat could not turn into a dog, and that the mask did not change the animal's identity.

How can a human being, even a very young one, believe that a cat can turn into a dog? And how does the 3-year-old who has this belief turn into the 6-year-old who scoffs at such a silly notion? We know that the change happens; the issue is how it happens.

KEY QUESTIONS ABOUT CHILDREN'S THINKING

What are the most important questions in the study of children's thinking? Many answers are possible, but there is widespread agreement that the following six are among the most important. What capabilities are innate? Does children's thinking progress through qualitatively different stages? How do changes in children's thinking occur? Why do individual children differ so much from each other in their thinking? How does development of the brain contribute to cognitive development? How do the cultures within which children develop influence their thinking? These issues are introduced in the following sections.

What Capabilities Are Innate?

When infants are born, how do they experience the world? When they see a chair, or people talking to each other, or a dog barking, what exactly do they see? What do they know, what don't they know, and what learning capabilities do they possess? If we assume that infants come into the world poorly endowed with knowledge and learning capabilities, the question becomes "How can they develop as rapidly as they do?" If we assume that infants come into the world richly endowed, the question becomes "Why does development take so long?"

The question of infants' initial endowment has elicited many speculations. Three of the most prominent come from the *associationist perspective*, the *constructivist perspective*, and the *competent-infant perspective*.

The associationist perspective was developed by English philosophers of the 1700s and 1800s, such as John Locke, David Hume, and John Stuart Mill. They suggested that infants come into the world with only minimal capabilities, primarily the ability to associate experiences with each other. Therefore, the infants must acquire virtually all capacities and concepts through learning.

The constructivist perspective, developed by Jean Piaget between the 1920s and the 1970s, suggests that infants are born possessing not only these associative capabilities but also several important perceptual and motor capabilities. Although few in number and limited in scope, these capabilities allow infants to explore their environment and to construct increasingly sophisticated concepts and understandings. For example, infants in their first 6 months are said not to be able to form mental representations of objects and events, but through actively manipulating and investigating objects, they are said to become capable of forming such representations later in their first year.

The competent-infant perspective, based on more recent research (e.g., Carey & Gelman, 1991), suggests that both of the other approaches seriously underestimate infants' capabilities. Within this view, even young infants have a much wider range of perceptual skills and conceptual understandings than had previously been suspected. These capacities allow infants, in a rudimentary way, to perceive the world and to classify their experiences along many of the same dimensions that older children and adults use.

The impressive capabilities that recent investigations have uncovered can be illustrated in the context of infants' perception of distance. Philosophers have long speculated about how people can judge the distances of objects from themselves. Some, such as George Berkeley, an associationist philosopher of the eighteenth century, concluded that the only way in which infants could come to accurately perceive distance was by moving around the world and associating how objects looked with how much movement was required to reach them. Yet, the day after infants are born, they can already perceive which objects are closer and which are farther away (Granrud, 1987; Slater, Mattock, & Brown, 1990). Clearly, some degree of distance perception is present even before infants have experience crawling and walking around the environment.

Infants also possess surprising knowledge of the properties of objects. For example, by age 3 months, the earliest age at which such knowledge has been successfully measured, infants show some understanding that objects continue to exist even when they move behind other objects and cannot be seen; that without support, objects will fall; that objects move along spatially continuous paths; and that solid objects cannot move through each other (Baillargeon, 1994; Spelke, 1994). Such knowledge is not identical to that of adults; for example, 3-month-olds seem to believe that any contact between an object and a support is sufficient to hold the object up, even when only the right edge of a block on the bottom is under the left edge of a block on top of it. By 6 months, infants show the more advanced understanding that for a support to be effective, the block on the bottom must be under a substantial proportion of the block on the top (Baillargeon, 1994).

In addition to possessing primitive versions of fundamental concepts, infants also possess general learning mechanisms that help them acquire a wide range of new knowledge. One such learning mechanism is imitation. When 2-day-olds see an adult move his head in a certain way, they tend to move theirs in a similar fashion; when 2-week-olds see an adult stick out his tongue, they tend to stick out their tongues in response (Meltzoff, 1990; Meltzoff & Moore, 1983; 1989). Such repetitions provide a way for infants to learn new behaviors and also to strengthen their bond with those they imitate, particularly their parents.

Findings like these have given rise to the view that infants are quite cognitively competent. But like previous perspectives, the new view raises as many questions as it answers. If infants understand fundamental concepts, why do much older children experience such difficulty with the very same concepts? For example, if infants understand that a toy continues to exist even when a cover is placed on it, why do 3-year-olds still not understand that a cat cannot be turned into a dog simply by putting a mask on it? Reconciling the strengths that are present early in development with the weaknesses that are also present is one of the greatest challenges in understanding children's thinking.

Does Development Progress through Stages?

When a girl misbehaves, her parents might console each other by saying, "It's just a stage she's going through." When a boy fails utterly to learn something, his parents might lament, "I guess he just hasn't reached the stage where he can understand this." The idea that development, including cognitive development, occurs in stages is common among psychologists as well as parents. But what exactly does it mean to say that a child is in a stage, and do children in fact progress through qualitatively distinct stages of thinking? And, why might development be stagelike, rather than continuous?

The view of development as stagelike was in part inspired by the ideas of Charles Darwin (1877). Darwin is not usually thought of as a developmental psychologist, but in many ways he was one. In his book *The Descent of Man*, Darwin discussed the development of reason, curiosity, imitation, attention, imagination, language, and self-consciousness. Not surprisingly, he was most interested in the evolutionary course of these competencies, that is, in how they emerged in the course of the evolution from earlier-appearing animals to humans. However, many of his ideas could be and were translated into concepts about the development that occurs in an individual human lifetime.

Perhaps Darwin's most influential observation was his most basic: that over the vast period of time that living things have populated the earth, they have evolved through a series of qualitatively distinct forms. This observation suggested to some that development within a given lifetime also progresses through distinct forms or stages. Unlike Darwin himself, however, developmental theorists who adopted an evolutionary perspective further hypothesized that children would make the transition from one stage to the next quite suddenly. This stage approach directly contradicted speculations by associationist philosophers, such as John Locke, that children's thinking develops through the gradual accretion of innumerable particular experiences. Associationists compared the developmental process to a building being constructed brick by brick. Stage theorists compared it to the metamorphosis from caterpillar to butterfly.

In the early part of the twentieth century, James Mark Baldwin hypothesized a set of plausible stages of intellectual development. He suggested that children progressed from a sensorimotor stage, in which sensory observations and motor interactions with the physical environment were the dominant form of thought, to a quasi-logical, a logical, and, finally, a hyperlogical stage. The idea that children progress through these stages receives a certain amount of support from everyday observations of children. Infants' interactions with the world do seem, at least at first impression, to emphasize sensory input and motoric actions. And not until adolescence do children spend much time thinking about purely logical issues, such as whether laws that apply to them, such as those regarding driving, voting, and drinking, are logically consistent with each other. Baldwin's stage theory was ignored by most of his contemporaries, but it exerted a strong influence on at least one later thinker: Jean Piaget.

Piaget, without question, added more than any other individual to our understanding of children's thinking. He made a huge number of fascinating observations about the ways in which children think at different ages. For example, the reason that I asked my son about the origins of the sun (the anecdote at the beginning of this chapter) was that I was fascinated by Piaget's descriptions of the answers given by children in the 1920s when he asked this question, and I was curious as to whether children of today would respond similarly (they do). Among Piaget's other contributions were refining the theory of developmental stages to a much greater extent than Baldwin had and popularizing the idea of viewing intellectual development in terms of stages.

What exactly do we mean when we say that children's thinking progresses through certain stages? Flavell (1971) noted four key implications of the stage concept. First, stages imply *qualitative changes*. We do not say that a boy is in a new stage of understanding of arithmetic when he progresses from knowing 50 percent of the multiplication facts to knowing all of them. Instead, we reserve the term for situations where the child's thinking seems not only better but different in kind. For example, when a girl makes up her first genuinely amusing joke, after several years of telling stories that she may call jokes but that do not even make sense to adults, it seems like a qualitative change. Note the ambiguity of the term *seems like*, though. Perhaps the girl's efforts had been improving slowly for a long time but had not quite reached the threshold for what an adult recognizes as a joke. To some degree, what constitutes a qualitative change is in the eyes of the beholder.

A second implication of stage theories, which Flavell labeled the *concurrence assumption*, is that children make the transition from one stage to another on many concepts simultaneously. When they are in Stage 1, they show Stage 1 reasoning on all of these concepts; when they are in Stage 2, they show Stage 2 reasoning on all of them. As a result of these concurrent changes, children's thinking shows abstract similarities across many domains. When the parent in the above example said, "He's just not in a stage where he can understand this," the implication was that a general deficiency would keep the child from understanding not just the particular concept but also other concepts of comparable complexity.

Viewing children's thinking as progressing through a series of stages also has two additional implications. One, which Flavell called *the abruptness assumption*, is that children move from one stage to the next suddenly rather than gradually. Children are in Stage 1 for a prolonged period of time, enter briefly into a transition period, then are in Stage 2 for a prolonged period, and so on. The fourth assumption of stage theories is *coherent organization*. The child's understanding is viewed as being organized into a sensible whole, rather than being composed of many independent pieces of knowledge.

Thus, stage theories depict development as involving qualitative change, occurring simultaneously for many concepts, occurring suddenly, and involving a transition from one coherent way of thinking to a different coherent way of thinking. Without question, this is an elegant and appealing description. But how well does it fit the realities of children's thinking? This issue will be considered in greater depth in Chapter 2.

How Does Change Occur?

To develop is to change. Several types of change that occur during the course of development are illustrated in Figure 1.1. The depiction originally was formulated to describe changes in perceptual development (Aslin & Dumais, 1980), but the categories apply to all types of changes in children's thinking.

The left side of the figure illustrates three patterns of change that can occur in the *prenatal period* (before birth): a particular capability can develop fully, partially, or not at all. The right-hand side depicts changes occurring after birth. An already-developed ability either can be maintained or can decline; a partially developed ability can grow, stay the same, or decline; and an undeveloped ability can grow or stay undeveloped.

The variety of possible patterns expands further when we realize that any given ability involves many components that may follow quite different developmental courses. For example, regardless of where infants are born, they can produce all of the sounds that are used in any of the world's languages. Over the course of childhood, however, they lose the capability of producing many

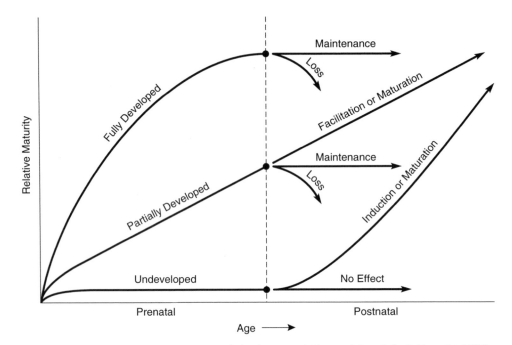

FIGURE 1.1   Illustration of several paths of developmental change (after Aslin & Dumais, 1980).

sounds that are not part of their native language. On the other hand, they gain increasing facility in producing at will the sounds that are part of their own language. Thus, after infancy, the ability to produce speech sounds both declines and grows, depending on which sounds we are talking about.

How can changes in children's thinking be explained? Two of the most influential efforts to answer this question are the Piagetian and the information processing perspectives. Piaget suggested that the basic mechanisms that produce all cognitive changes are *assimilation* and *accommodation*. Assimilation is the process through which people represent experiences in terms of their existing understanding. A 1-year-old girl who was given a round candle by her mother might think of it as a ball if she knew about balls but not candles. Accommodation is the opposite process; in it, people's existing understanding is altered by new knowledge. The 1-year-old who was given the round candle might notice that this "ball" was different from others in having a thin object (the wick) protruding from it. This discovery might lay the groundwork for later learning that the world included round candles.

Researchers who adopt the information processing approach to children's thinking have been particularly interested in the process of change. They have focused on four change mechanisms that seem to play large roles in cognitive development: *automatization, encoding, generalization,* and *strategy construction.*

Automatization involves executing mental processes increasingly efficiently so that they require less and less attention. With age and experience, processing becomes increasingly automatic on a great many tasks, allowing children to see connections among ideas and events that they otherwise would miss. For example, in the first few weeks of walking home from school, a 5-year-old girl might need to completely focus her attention on the task of finding her way. Later, the activity would become automatized, and she would find her way home despite paying attention to what other people were saying and doing while she walked with them.

Encoding involves identifying the most informative features of objects and events and using these features to form internal representations of them. The importance of improved encoding in children's increasing understanding of the world is evident in the context of their learning to solve story problems in arithmetic and algebra. Often such stories include irrelevant as well as relevant information. The trick to solving the problems is to encode the relevant information and to ignore the irrelevant parts.

The third and the fourth change mechanisms are generalization and strategy construction. Generalization is the extension of knowledge acquired in one context to other contexts. Strategy construction is the discovery of a new procedure for solving a problem. The workings of generalization and strategy construction can be illustrated through a single example. After repeated experience with suddenly nonfunctioning computers, lamps, toasters, and radios, a child might reach the generalization that when machines do not work, it often is due to their being unplugged. On drawing this generalization, the child might form a strategy of always checking the plug whenever pushing a machine's on-button has no effect.

The child's construction of this strategy illustrates that change processes work together rather than in isolation. Constructing the check-the-plug strategy depended on automatizing the perception of the machines sufficiently to encode the plug as a separate part of each machine and on drawing the generalization that machines that have plugs usually do not turn on when the plug is disconnected. As will be evident throughout the book, these four change processes—automatization, encoding, generalization, and strategy construction—play crucial roles in improvements in children's thinking in everything from 2-year-olds' language learning to adolescents' computer programming.

How Do Individuals Differ?

Just as children of different ages vary, so do children of any given age. Individual differences are present in all aspects of development, from height and weight to personality and creativity. However, they have received especially intense examination in the study of intelligence. This scrutiny began in earnest in the 1890s, when France initiated a program of universal public education. Recognizing that not all children would benefit from the same instruction, the French Minister of Education commissioned Alfred Binet and Theophile Simon to develop a test to identify children who would have difficulty learning from standard classroom procedures and who therefore would need special education.

The first Binet-Simon test was released in 1905. It included questions that were intuitively related to many aspects of intelligence: language, memory, reasoning, and problem solving. In 1916, Lewis Terman, a professor at Stanford, revised the test for use in the United States and labeled it the Stanford-Binet. Updated versions remain in wide use today.

The Stanford-Binet and other intelligence tests are based on the assumption that not all children of a given age think and reason at the same level. Some 7-year-olds reason as well as the average 9-year-old; others reason no better than the average 5-year-old. To capture these individual differences among children, intelligence tests distinguish between a child's *chronological age (CA)* and the child's *mental age (MA)*. Chronological age reflects the time since the child was born; if a girl was born 60 months ago, her chronological age is 5 years. Mental age is a more complex idea, in that it reflects the child's performance on an intelligence test relative to that of other children. Specifically, a child's mental age is defined as the age at which 50 percent of all children answer correctly as many items on the test as the particular child did. For example, if the average 5-year-old correctly answers 20 questions on a test, then a child who answered 20 items correctly would have a mental age of 5 years, regardless of whether the child is a 4-year-old, a 5-year-old, or a 6-year-old.

Terman saw that the implications of a 4-year-old, a 5-year-old, and a 6-year-old having a mental age of 5 are quite different. For a 4-year-old, this level of performance is precocious; for a 5-year-old, it is average; for a 6-year-old, it is slow. To express these implications numerically, Terman combined the concepts of mental and chronological age to form the concept of the *Intelligence Quotient*, or *IQ*. A child's IQ was the ratio between the child's mental and chronological ages. This ratio was multiplied by 100, so that the IQ could be expressed as an integer, as shown below:

$$IQ = \frac{\text{Mental Age}}{\text{Chronological Age}} \times 100$$

Thus, in Terman's example, the 6-year-old who had a mental age of 5 years would have an IQ of 83 ($5/6 \times 100$). The average IQ score is 100, since the average mental age for any age group is, by definition, that group's chronological age. Whether the IQ score is above or below 100 (that is, whether the child's mental age exceeds or falls below his or her chronological age) indicates whether the child scored above or below average for the age group; the distance of the score from 100 indicates how far above or below average the score was.

One reason that IQ scores have been used so widely is that they predict performance in school quite well. Another reason is their stability over long periods of time. For example, a 6-year-old's IQ quite accurately predicts the child's IQ at age 16. The relation is not perfect; some children show large increases in IQ over time, and others show large decreases. There is also considerable controversy about what intelligence is and how well these or other tests measure it. Clearly, however, test scores tend to be quite stable from first grade to adulthood, and they allow quite accurate prediction of school achievement.

Until recently, no comparable predictive relation between early and later performance had been established for very young children. Scores on intelligence tests developed for children younger than 4 years old were essentially unrelated to IQ scores of the same children when they were older. This suggested that individual differences in infant intelligence might be unrelated to individual differences in later intelligence.

Recently, however, a measure of infants' information processing has revealed considerable continuity between intelligence in infancy and intelligence in later childhood. The measure is surprisingly simple. When infants are repeatedly shown a stimulus, such as an object or a picture, they lose interest in it and look at it less and less. That is, they *habituate* to it. Individual infants habituate at varying rates; some reduce their looking quite quickly, whereas others take much longer to do so. The key finding is that the more rapidly that 7-month-olds habituate (stop looking), and the greater their preference for a new picture after they have habituated (often called "novelty preference"), the higher their IQ scores tend to be 4 to 10 years later (Colombo, 1993; Fagan & Singer, 1983; McCall & Carriger, 1993; Rose & Feldman, 1995; Rose, Feldman & Wallace, 1992; Sigman, Cohen, Beckwith, & Parmalee, 1986). The habituation rates also are related to later achievement test scores in reading and mathematics and to general language proficiency. Further, children whose habituation rates are slowest at 7 months have higher rates of learning disabilities when they are 6-year-olds (Rose et al., 1992).

Why should rate of habituation at 7 months predict IQ and achievement test scores years later? One explanation is that both the early and the later performance reflect the effectiveness of the child's encoding (Bornstein & Sigman, 1986; Columbo, 1993; 1995). In other words, more intelligent infants are quicker to encode everything of interest about the picture, leading them to be the first to lose interest in it. They perk up more when the new picture is shown because they more clearly encode the differences between it and the old one. Superior encoding has also been found to be related to the ability of gifted older children and adolescents to solve problems and learn quickly (Davidson, 1986). Thus, quality of encoding may link early and later intellectual capabilities.

The large majority of research on intelligence and other areas of cognitive development focuses on individual children's behavior. However, in trying to gain additional insights, researchers have recently been extending the search both inward and outward. The inward-looking efforts examine how development of the brain is related to changes in children's thinking. The outward-looking efforts consider not only the individual child but also the formative influences of other people and of cultural institutions. Thus, the first approach builds on findings and insights from the neighboring disciplines of biology and neuroscience, and the second builds on findings and insights from sociology and anthropology. These approaches to understanding children's thinking are introduced in the next two sections.

How Do Changes in the Brain Contribute to Cognitive Development?

In general, the bigger the brain of a species, the more intelligent animals of that species are likely to be. Without question, changes in the size, structure, and connection patterns of the brain during the course of a child's development profoundly contribute to changes in the child's thinking. These changes, which are both quantitative and qualitative, occur at three levels: (1) changes in the brain as a whole; (2) changes in particular structures within the brain; and (3) changes in the billions of cells that make up the brain (neurons).

Changes in the brain as a whole. The changes that occur in the brain as a whole are evident in large-scale increases in its weight from birth to adulthood. The brain weighs roughly 400 grams at birth; 850 grams at 11 months of age, 1,100 grams by age 3; and 1,450 grams by adulthood (Kolb & Whishaw, 1996). Thus, the brain of an adult weighs almost four times as much as the brain of a newborn. These changes in size make possible much more advanced thinking.

Changes in structures within the brain. The relative sizes and levels of activity of the main parts of the brain also change over the course of development. The brain can be divided into two main parts: *subcortical structures* and the *cortex*. The subcortical structures are areas atop the spinal cord, such as the thalamus, medulla, and pons (Figure 1.2). They are quite similar in the brains of humans and of other mammals, especially other primates such as apes and monkeys.

Like these subcortical areas, the cortex includes some structures that are similar in humans and other primates. Among them are the thalamus and the hypothalamus. In addition, however, the cortex includes a large structure that is far more highly developed in humans than in any other animal: the *cerebral cortex* (labeled as the "cortex" in Figure 1.2). Sitting atop the rest of the brain, this large structure is what makes possible the high-level cognitive skills that are unique to human beings, such as language and complex problem-solving.

At birth and for several years thereafter, the cerebral cortex is immature relative to other parts of the brain. This is evident both in its being a lower percentage of its adult weight and in its being less like its mature form in organization and patterns of electrical and chemical activity. The relative immaturity of the cerebral cortex has important consequences for cognitive function-

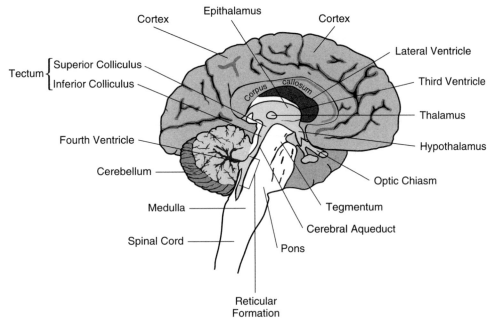

FIGURE 1.2   The structure of the brain. A number of subcortical areas are labeled; the convoluted area sitting atop them is the cortex.

ing. It leads to some types of cognition being impossible at early periods of development and to others being accomplished at first by more mature parts of the brain, even though the cortex will later play a dominant role in them.

As shown in Figure 1.3, the cerebral cortex includes four main lobes: the *frontal lobe*, at the front of the brain; the *parietal lobe*, at the top; the *occipital lobe*, at the back; and the *temporal lobe*, toward the bottom. Each area is particularly active in producing certain types of cognitive activity. For example, the occipital lobe is especially heavily involved in processing visual information, whereas the frontal lobe is especially involved in consciousness, planning, and the regulation of cognitive activity. As you might expect from the types of activities in which the frontal lobe is particularly active, it is especially immature at birth, relative to other parts of the brain and even other parts of the cerebral cortex. Its profound development during infancy and early childhood seems to be crucial to the rapid advances in cognitive capabilities that occur during that period. (For a good discussion of the different rates of maturation of different parts of the brain, see Chugani & Phelps, 1986.)

Changes in neurons.   The third, and most specific, level of change that occurs in the brain involves specific *neurons* (nerve cells). Neurons are present in vast numbers in all parts of the brain—a total of between 100 and 200 billion. All neurons that will ever be present are present from birth. The large changes that occur are a result of the neurons becoming increasingly interconnected.

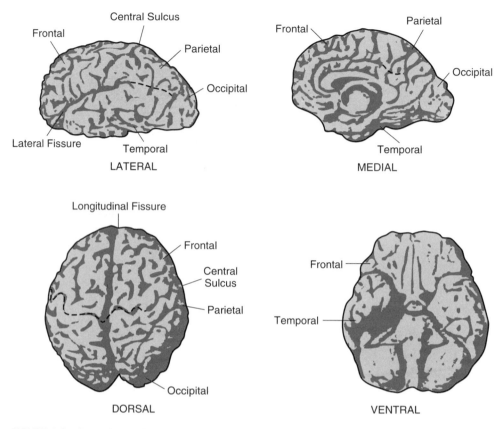

FIGURE 1.3   Four views of the cortex. The top-left view is from the left, the bottom-left view is from above, the top-right view is from the left looking at the inner surface of the right half of the brain, and the bottom-right view is from below.

Each neuron includes three main parts: a *cell nucleus*, which is the core of the nerve cell; a number of *dendrites*, which are fibers that bring information from other neurons to the cell nucleus; and one (or occasionally more) *axons*, which are larger fibers that transmit information from the cell nucleus to other neurons (Figure 1.4).

Neurons transmit information both electrically and chemically. Within a given neuron, the transmission is electrical. Electrical signals travel from the dendrites to the cell nucleus to the axon(s). Between neurons, the transmission is chemical. Neurons are not directly connected to each other; instead, there are tiny gaps, called *synapses*, separating the axon of one neuron from the dendrite of another. The electrical signal traveling along the axon leads to the release of chemical *neurotransmitters*, which flow across the synapse from the end of the axon to the beginnings of dendrites of adjacent neurons. When the neurotransmitters arrive at the dendrites of the receiving neurons, the information is converted back

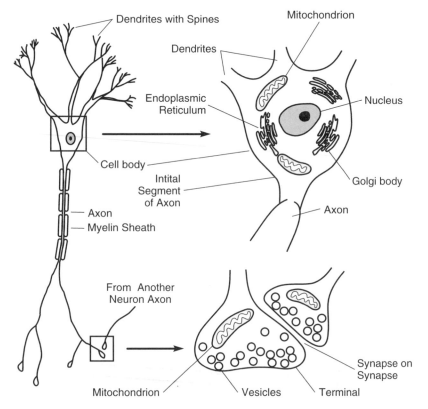

FIGURE 1.4   *Structure of a typical neuron (left) including dendrites at top, cell body in the square, and axon below the square. Note that the initial segment of the axon where it leaves the cell body is uncovered; the ovals around the axon below that are myelin, an insulator that improves the rate of electrical transmission. As shown in the drawing at the bottom right, synapses are where the ends of an axon from one neuron are adjacent to the beginning of a dendrite from another neuron. Chemicals known as neurotransmitters flow across the synapse from the end of the axon to the beginning of the dendrite or to another axon, thus transmitting information from neuron to neuron.*

into electrical impulses. In an adult, a single neuron often has more than 1,000 synapses with other neurons. These multiple connections allow information to be simultaneously transmitted to diverse areas of the brain (Thompson, 1985).

Synaptogenesis.   The formation of synapses between neurons (*synaptogenesis*), is far from complete at birth. Within many parts of the brain, it follows a distinctive developmental course of overproduction and pruning. Early in development, there is an explosive proliferation of synapses, causing the number of synapses in a toddler's brain to far exceed the number in an adult's. Then, over the course of childhood, the number of synapses decreases to adult levels. In one part of the frontal lobe, for example, the density of synaptic connections increases tenfold between birth and 12 months (Huttenlocher, 1979). By age 2, the density of connections there is almost twice as great as in adults. After this point, it gradually decreases, reaching adult levels by about age 7.

In other parts of the brain, the overproduction and pruning follows the same general pattern but with different timetables. For example, in the visual cortex, the peak density of synapses is generally reached earlier than in the frontal lobe—around 1 year—and the pruning continues longer—until age 11 (Huttenlocher, 1990). However, the basic cycle of rapid initial generation of synapses, followed by prolonged pruning of the synapses, seems to generally hold true.

What determines which synapses are maintained and which ones pruned? Experience seems to be a major determinant. If experiences lead to synapses firing so that neurotransmitters are released, the synapses tend to be maintained. If not, they tend to wither (Greenough, Black, & Wallace, 1987). Thus, in the brain as in behavior, development involves a complex interplay of genetics and experience.

Some researchers have proposed that the early surplus of synapses is re-lated to infants and toddlers acquiring certain kinds of capabilities more effec-tively than adults (e.g., Bjorklund & Green, 1992; Fischer, 1987). For example, toddlers and young children are especially apt at picking up the sounds and grammar of their native languages. They learn language far more effectively than those who immigrate to a new country as adults and try to learn its lan-guage then (Johnson & Newport, 1989). It is not just that the children are learn-ing their first language and the adults their second; young children also learn phonology and syntax more effectively when they are learning it in a second language (as when a 5-year-old comes to a new country). The extra synapses in the young children's brains may be especially useful for learning the extremely complex systems of contingencies embodied in the phonology and grammar of languages such as English.

How Does the Social World Contribute to Cognitive Development?

From the day they emerge from the womb, children live in a profoundly social environment. It is social not just in including other people who interact with the child—parents, siblings, other adults, and other children. It also is social in in-cluding many *artifacts*—the many objects that exist only because of people's ef-forts and ingenuity (books, television sets, computers, automobiles, etc.), the many skills that reflect our cultural heritage (reading, writing, mathematics, computer programming, video-game playing, etc.), and the many values that guide strategies and problem solving efforts in certain directions (speed, accu-racy, neatness, truthfulness, etc.). Clearly, all of these manifestations of the social world profoundly influence what children think about and how they think about it. As Gauvain (1995, p. 41) stated, culture provides "the overarching con-text of cognitive development."

Just as Piaget is the forefather of stage theories of development, so Lev Vygotsky is the forefather of sociocultural theories. These sociocultural theories emphasize the contribution of the social world to children's thinking. Although Piaget and Vygotsky were contemporaries, their theories pointed in different directions. Whereas Piaget depicted children as little scientists trying to understand the world largely on their own, Vygotsky portrayed them as living in the midst of other people eager to help them acquire the skills needed to live in their culture. Whereas Piaget was largely concerned with the aspects of development present among all children in all societies in all historical periods, Vygotsky emphasized factors that differ among children growing up at different times in different circumstances. The approaches are complementary, in the sense that understanding cognitive development requires understanding both the universal aspects and the variable ones.

Vygotskian concepts for thinking about development. Vygotsky introduced a number of key concepts for understanding the ways in which the social world contributes to children's thinking. Three of the most important are *zone of proximal development* (2PD), *social scaffolding*, and *cultural tools*.

The concept of a zone of proximal development (ZPD) was based on the insight that when other people guide and assist learners on parts of a difficult task, the learners can often think in more advanced ways than if they had to do the whole task themselves. For any given child, the ZPD is defined as the distance between what the child can accomplish through independent problem solving and what that child can do when given substantial help (Vygotsky, 1978). As illustrated in Figure 1.5, although two children may have identical abilities to deal with a task unaided, one may be able to do far more when helped, whereas the other may benefit from the help only slightly. Information about how well the child can do when given specific help yields a more com-

FIGURE 1.5 Two children's zones of proximal development (ZPD). The children's unaided performance is similar, but Child B can benefit more from another person's help.

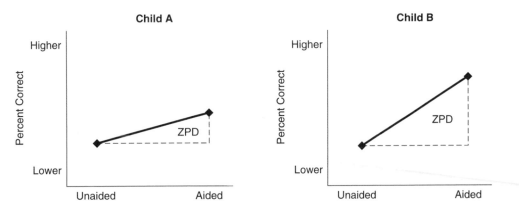

plete picture of the child's thinking than just examining the child's unsupported problem solving.

In drawing attention to the ZPD, the sociocultural approach focuses attention on the ways in which other people guide and support children in solving problems. One type of assistance they provide is social scaffolding, which includes helping children think about the task appropriately, modeling ways of solving problems, and giving hints that guide the child in useful directions. The idea of social scaffolding is based on an analogy to the process by which buildings are constructed. Scaffolds are metal frameworks that allow construction workers to work high above the ground while putting up the basic structures of buildings. Once the basic structure is built, it can support the workers; this allows the scaffolding to be removed. Similarly, in social scaffolding, the activities of more competent people provide a temporary framework that allows children to think in more advanced ways than they otherwise could. After working for awhile at this higher level, children can work at the level without the external support. Parents tend to teach their children in a way that fits the scaffolding model, playing active roles when children are just beginning to learn a skill, and progressively withdrawing to the background as the children show increasing mastery (Pratt, Kerig, Cowan, & Cowan, 1988; Wood, 1986).

Adults generally are better at providing scaffolding than are other children. They tend to involve children more in decision making and help them learn strategies for solving future problems. In contrast, other children, even ones as knowledgeable about the task as the adults, more often just tell the learners what to do, without much attention to helping them learn. Not surprisingly, children who have previously solved problems with their parents do better than ones who have previously solved them with peers (Ellis & Rogoff, 1986; Radiszewska & Rogoff, 1988).

The concept of cultural tools involves a far broader range of objects than the hammers, saws, and screwdrivers we usually think of as tools. It includes the entire range of objects and ideas that allow people to achieve their goals: machines such as calculators and computers; representational devices such as books and maps; ways of knowing about the world such as mathematics and science; notational systems such as numbers and letters; and ideas such as gravity and efficiency (Rogoff, 1990). Interacting with even the most mundane cultural tools helps children better understand the social and physical world. Think about calendars and clocks, for example. Learning about them involves much more than just telling time. It also involves learning the belief of our culture that it is useful to break up time into discrete units of years, months, days, hours, minutes, and seconds. The ways in which people use these tools also is revealing. We tell children to be home by 6:00 or 6:15, and to be at school at 8:05 or even 8:07, but never to be at home or at school by 8:07 and 30 seconds, much less at 8:07 and 30 and 7/10 seconds. We view it as useful to break up time to a certain level of precision, but not ordinarily beyond that. Countless such experiences shape the way in which children think about even concepts as basic as time.

The social world influences cognitive development not just through direct interactions with other people and by providing cultural tools, but by enabling children to participate in activities that are valued within the culture. Some of these activities, such as school and music lessons, are explicitly designed to teach particular skills and knowledge. However, a great many other activities teach valuable lessons despite not involving any formal instruction.

A good example of this latter type of activity is Girl Scout cookie sales. A main goal of such a sale is to raise money for a troop. However, in participating in them, the scouts learn a variety of values and skills (Rogoff, 1995). The learning occurs through direct interaction with troop leaders, parents, customers, and other children; through use of tools developed by other people, such as the color-coded order forms that are provided to indicate how much of each kind of cookie is being ordered and how much money is owed; through planning routes to deliver the cookies; through figuring out how much change is needed when customers pay for their orders; through trying various sales strategies; and so on. While engaging in these activities, children acquire not only skills but also values: responsibility, courtesy, efficiency, precision, and promptness, among others. As with the skills, these values are not explicit goals of the cookie sales. Rather, they are useful by-products, acquired in the course of pursuing the main goal of making money. Different cultures provide different learning activities, but in all cultures, children learn a wide range of values and skills through participation in activities that reflect the values of their respective societies.

Why don't apes sell cookies to each other?   Just as the cerebral cortex differentiates people from other animals, so does our propensity to develop culture. It is not easy to imagine monkeys selling cookies, or anything else, to each other. They simply do not develop such cultural institutions, nor the tools that underlie the institutions. What is it that leads humans to develop cultures so different from those of any other species?

Two basic human propensities seem crucial (Tomasello, 1995; Tomasello, Kruger, & Ratner, 1993). One is the propensity to teach; the other is the ability to learn from such teaching. People throughout the world teach to the young in their midst the traditions and discoveries that they and others in their group have made in the past. This enables the new generation to stand on the shoulders of their predecessors, rather than having to start anew. In contrast, apes in their natural habitats do not engage in even the rudimentary teaching that every 2-year-old child does. They do not spontaneously point to objects to call others' attention to them. Nor do they hold up objects to show them to others, much less engage in the elaborate kinds of scaffolding activities of human teachers.

Advanced social-learning ability is also critical to the human capacity for rapid cultural change. Even when people raise apes in their own families, the apes do not show anything like the social-learning abilities of children. Part of this is due to children having much more extensive language than the apes, which makes learning from others a great deal easier. Indeed, one of the greatest advantages of human language is that it allows us to socialize our young rapidly by transmitting the accumulated wisdom of the past to each new generation, and thus preparing them for a constantly changing future.

THE BOOK'S ORGANIZATION

The organization of this book can be viewed either on a chapter-by-chapter basis or in terms of the central themes that recur in many chapters. In the sections that follow, the book is described from each perspective.

The Chapter-by-Chapter Organization

The book is divided into three sections. The first section, which includes Chapters 1 through 3, explores broad perspectives on children's thinking, such as Piaget's theory and the information processing approach to development. The second section, which includes Chapters 4 through 9, focuses on more specific aspects of children's thinking, such as how they perceive the world, how they use language to communicate, and how they learn reading, writing, and mathematics. The third section includes only a single chapter, Chapter 10. It is a summary of what has gone before and a look forward toward the issues that promise to be most important in the future.

The first chapter, which you are just finishing, is an attempt to define the field that is considered in this book and to introduce ideas that are important within it. Chapter 2 is devoted to the work of Piaget, whose investigations into children's thinking can fairly be said to have created the modern field of cognitive development. On topics ranging from how children infer the origins of the sun to how they order the weights of different objects, Piaget saw much that other people had missed. In addition, Piaget observed children of an extremely wide age range, stretching from the first days of infancy into late adolescence. Thus, his observations provide a feel for many aspects of development in infancy, childhood, and adolescence.

Chapter 3 examines the other dominant theory of children's thinking, the information-processing approach. In some ways, this approach represents a modern extension of Piaget's theory; in other ways, it represents an alternative. The basic assumptions of the information-processing approach are that children's mental activities can be characterized in terms of processes that manipulate information; that processing capacities are limited; and that the interaction between the individual's processing system and the environment leads to cognitive growth (Klahr, 1989). The information-processing approach has proved especially useful for studying development, because it provides precise ideas about the mechanisms that produce cognitive change.

Chapter 4 begins the second main section of the book, which examines six specific aspects of children's thinking: perception, language, memory, conceptual understanding, problem solving, and academic skills. In Chapter 4, the focus is on perceptual development. The emphasis is on the surprising number of visual and auditory skills children possess from early in infancy. By the age of 6 months, their visual and auditory worlds seem to be largely similar to those of adults.

Chapter 5 examines language development. Here the discussion centers on what types of words children use first, when and how they learn grammar, how they acquire word meanings, and how they use their knowledge to communicate with others.

Chapter 6 is about the development of memory. It focuses on how the development of basic capacities, strategies, and content knowledge contribute to children's growing abilities to remember. The chapter also addresses the practical issue of whether in court cases, children's recall of what happened can be trusted, and how the accuracy of their testimony changes with age.

Chapter 7 concerns conceptual development. The early part of the chapter examines whether children internally represent concepts primarily in terms of dictionary-like definitions, in terms of loosely related characteristic features, or in terms of causally connected theories. The latter part of the chapter examines the development of several particularly important concepts: time, space, number, and mind.

Chapter 8 focuses on problem solving. All of us solve problems daily, but such activities play an especially large role in the lives of young children. The reason is that many tasks that older individuals find routine pose novel challenges for younger ones. Among the problem solving processes examined in the chapter are planning, causal inference, analogy, tool use, and logical deduction.

Chapter 9 concerns the development of reading, writing, and mathematics. The skills whose development is described in the preceding chapters—perception, language, memory, conceptual understanding, and problem solving—are all put to use in the classroom. Children's acquisition of these academic skills illustrates how different types of thought processes work together to allow learning of complex subjects.

The third main section of the book is Chapter 10. It summarizes the main conclusions that apply across the diverse areas of children's thinking and identifies key issues for future investigation.

The Central Themes

This chapter-by-chapter organization provides one way of thinking about the material the book covers. Another way is to consider the themes that arise in many chapters. The following are eight recurring themes.

1. The most basic issues about children's thinking are "What develops?" and "How does development occur?"

2. Four change processes that seem to be particularly large contributors to cognitive development are automatization, encoding, generalization, and strategy construction.
3. Infants and very young children are far more cognitively competent than they appear. They possess a rich set of abilities that enable them to learn rapidly.
4. Differences between age groups tend to be ones of degree rather than kind. Not only are young children more cognitively competent than they appear, but older children and adults are less competent than we might think.
5. Changes in children's thinking do not occur in a vacuum. What children already know about material that they encounter influences not only how much they learn but also what they learn.
6. The development of intelligence reflects changes in brain structure and functioning as well as increasingly effective deployment of cognitive resources.
7. Children's thinking develops within a social context. Parents, peers, teachers, and the overall society influence what children think about, as well as how and why they come to think in particular ways.
8. Increasing understanding of children's thinking is yielding practical benefits as well as theoretical insights.

A simple strategy for improving your understanding of the material in this book is to spend a few minutes now rereading and thinking about these eight themes. Then, as you read subsequent chapters, try to notice how they unite different aspects of children's thinking.

SUMMARY

For hundreds of years, people who have had contact with children have wondered about such questions as where the children's ideas came from and whether infants perceive the world in the same way as adults. Recent conceptual and methodological advances have greatly improved our ability to explore these and many other questions about children's thinking.

A number of the most important questions about children's thinking have long histories. What capacities are innate? Do children proceed through qualitatively different stages of thinking, or is development continuous? How do changes in children's thinking occur? How do individuals differ in qualities such as intelligence, and how much continuity is there between early and later abilities? How do the internal world of the maturing brain and the external world of other people shape development? These continue to be among the most basic questions about children's thinking.

A number of themes are identified that recur throughout the book. Among these are the surprising cognitive competence of infants and young children, the continuous growth of children's thinking beyond this initial competence, the challenge that children face of coping with complex tasks while having only limited processing resources, the ways in which existing knowledge influences learning, and the influence of brain development and of the social world on children's thinking.

RECOMMENDED READINGS

Flavell, J. H. (1971). Stage-related properties of cognitive development. *Cognitive Psychology 2*, 421–453. A classic analysis of stage theories of development.

Johnson, M. H. (Ed.). (1993). *Brain development and cognition: A reader*. Oxford, UK: Blackwell. This book includes a large number of the most important recent articles about the relation between development of the brain and children's thinking.

Meltzoff, A. (1990). Toward a developmental cognitive science. *Annals of the New York Academy of Sciences, 608*, 1–31. Infants in their first month out of the womb show some ability to imitate the actions of other people; this article summarizes some of the evidence for this surprising capability.

Tomasello, M., Kruger, A. C., & Ratner, H. H. (1993). Cultural learning. *Brain and Behavioral Sciences, 16*, 495–511. This article explores the fascinating issue of why people's thinking differs so much from that of even our closest primate relatives, apes and chimpanzees. It identifies people's propensity to teach and learn as critical sources of the differences.

CHAPTER 2

Piaget's Theory of Development

At age 7 months, 28 days, I offer him a little bell behind a cushion. So long as he sees the little bell, however small it may be, he tries to grasp it. But if the little bell disappears completely he stops all searching.

I then resume the experiment using my hand as a screen. Laurent's arm is outstretched and about to grasp the little bell at the moment I make it disappear behind my hand which is open and at a distance of about 15 cm. from him. He immediately withdraws his arm, as though the little bell no longer existed. I then shake my hand. . . . Laurent watches attentively, greatly surprised to rediscover the sound of the little bell, but he does not try to grasp it. I turn my hand over and he sees the little bell; he then stretches out his hand toward it. I hide the little bell again by changing the position of my hand; Laurent withdraws his hand. (Piaget, 1954, p. 39)

What does this infant's odd behavior tell us? Piaget (1954) advanced one provocative interpretation: that Laurent did not search for the bell because he did not know that it still existed. In other words, his failure to search was due to his inability to mentally represent the bell's existence. It was as if the infant's thinking embodied the strongest possible version of the adage "Out of sight, out of mind."

This chapter is the only one in the book whose title includes a person's name. This is no accident. Jean Piaget's contribution to the study of cognitive development is a testimony to how much one person can do. Before Piaget began his work, no recognizable field of cognitive development existed. Yet despite thousands of studies on children's thinking having been conducted in the interim, even Piaget's earliest research is still informative. What explains the longevity of Piaget's theory?

Perhaps the basic reason is that Piaget's theory communicates an almost tangible sense of what children's thinking is like. His descriptions feel right. Many of his individual observations are quite surprising, but the general trends he describes appeal to our intuitions and to our memories of childhood.

A second important reason is that the theory addresses topics that have been of interest to parents, teachers, scientists, and philosophers for hundreds of years. At the most general level, the theory speaks to such questions as "What is intelligence?" and "Where does knowledge come from?" At a more specific level, the theory examines development of the concepts of time, space, number, and other ideas that are among the basic intellectual acquisitions of humankind. Placing the development of such fundamental concepts into a single coherent framework has made Piaget's theory one of the significant intellectual achievements of our century.

A third reason for the theory's longevity is its exceptional breadth. It covers an unusually broad age span—the entire range from infancy through adolescence. Children's understanding of concepts such as cause and effect can be seen evolving from rudimentary forms in infancy to more complex forms in early childhood to yet more complex forms in middle childhood to even more complex forms in adolescence. The theory also encompasses an unusually broad variety of achievements at any given age. For example, it brings together 5-year-olds' scientific and mathematical reasoning, their moral judgments, their drawings, their idea of cause and effect, their use of language, and their memory for past events. One of the purposes of scientific theories is to point out the commonalities underlying seemingly unrelated facts. Piaget's theory is especially strong on this dimension.

A fourth reason for the theory's having endured is that Piaget had the equivalent of a gifted gardener's "green thumb," a knack for making interesting observations. One of these observations was quoted at the outset of this chapter: the one concerning infants' failure to search for objects if they cannot see them. Many of his other intriguing observations are described throughout this chapter.

Because of the range and complexity of Piaget's theory, it seems worthwhile to approach it first in general terms and then in greater depth. The first section of this chapter provides an overview of Piaget's theory. The second section describes children's thinking during each of his four stages of development. The third focuses on his description of the development of several especially important concepts from birth through adolescence. The fourth is an evaluation of the theory. Table 2.1 depicts this organization.

TABLE 2.1 Chapter Outline

I. An Overview of Piaget's Theory
  A. The Theory As a Whole
  B. The Stages of Development
  C. Developmental Processes
  D. Orienting Assumptions
II. The Stage Model
  A. The Sensorimotor Period (Birth to Roughly 2 Years)
  B. The Preoperational Period (Roughly 2 Years to 6 or 7 Years)
  C. The Concrete Operations Period (Roughly 6 or 7 Years to 11 or 12 Years)
  D. The Formal Operations Period (Roughly 11 or 12 Years Onward)
III. The Development of Some Critical Concepts
  A. Conservation
  B. Classes and Relations
IV. An Evaluation of Piaget's Theory
  A. How Accurately Does the Theory Describe Particular Aspects of Children's Thinking?
  B. How Stagelike Is Children's Thinking?
  C. How Well Do Piaget's General Characterizations Fit Children's Thinking?
  D. The Current Status of Piaget's Theory
V. Summary

AN OVERVIEW OF PIAGET'S THEORY

Piaget's theory is sufficiently broad and complex that it is easy to lose the forest for the trees. This section provides an overview of the forest.

The Theory As a Whole

To appreciate Piaget's theory, it is essential to understand his motivation for developing it. This motivation grew out of Piaget's early interest in biology and philosophy. When he was 11 years old, he published his first article, which described an albino sparrow he had observed. Between the ages of 15 and 18, he published several more articles, most of them about mollusks. The articles must have been impressive. When Piaget was 18, the head of a natural history museum, who had never met him but who had read his articles, wrote a letter offering him the position of curator of the mollusk collection at the museum. Piaget turned down the offer so that he could finish high school.

In addition to this early interest in biology, Piaget was keenly interested in philosophy. He was especially drawn to *epistemology*, the branch of philosophy concerned with the origins of knowledge. The theory of the eighteenth-century philosopher Immanuel Kant who, like Piaget, was most interested in the origins of knowledge, was a source of particular fascination for him.

The combination of philosophical and biological interests influenced Piaget's later theorizing in several ways. It led to the fundamental question underlying the theory: "Where does knowledge come from?" It also influenced the particular problems Piaget chose to study. He followed Kant in viewing space, time, classes, causality, and relations as basic categories of knowledge. At the same time, he opposed Kant's position that these basic categories of knowledge were innate to human beings. Instead, he believed that children came to understand the concepts increasingly deeply during infancy, childhood, and adolescence. Perhaps most important, the joint interest in philosophy and biology suggested to Piaget that longstanding philosophical controversies could be resolved by applying scientific methods. Just as Darwin attempted to answer the question "How did people evolve?" Piaget attempted to answer the question "How does knowledge evolve?"

Having this background, we can now consider the theory itself. At the most general level of analysis, Piaget was interested in intelligence. By this he meant a broader quality than what is measured on intelligence tests. He viewed intelligence as the ability to adapt to all aspects of reality. He also believed that within a person's lifetime, intelligence evolves through a series of qualitatively distinct stages. These stages, and the developmental processes that produce the transition from one stage to the next, are described in the next two sections.

The Stages of Development

As noted in Chapter 1, stage theorists such as Piaget make certain characteristic assumptions. They assume that children's reasoning in earlier stages differs qualitatively from their reasoning in later ones. They also assume that at a given point in development, children reason similarly on many problems. Finally, they assume that after spending a prolonged period of time "in" a stage, children abruptly make the transition to the next stage.

Piaget postulated that all children progress through four stages and that all do so in the same order: first the *sensorimotor period*, then the *preoperational period*, then the *concrete operational period*, and finally the *formal operational period*. The sensorimotor period typically spans the period from birth to about the second birthday, the preoperational period lasts roughly from age 2 to age 6 or 7, the concrete operational period extends from about age 6 or 7 to 11 or 12, and the formal operational period includes all of adolescence and adulthood.

First, consider Piaget's characterization of the sensorimotor period, lasting from birth through age 2. Piaget believed that at birth, a child's cognitive system is limited to motor reflexes. Within a few months, however, children build on these reflexes to develop more sophisticated procedures. They begin to repeat initially inadvertent behaviors systematically, to generalize their activities to a wider range of situations, and to coordinate them into increasingly lengthy chains of behavior. Children's physical interactions with objects provide the impetus for this development.

The second stage of development, the preoperational period, encompasses the age range from 2 to 6 or 7 years. The greatest achievement of this period is the acquisition of means for representing the world symbolically: mental imagery, drawing, and especially language. Vocabulary increases 100-fold between the ages of 18 and 60 months (McCarthy, 1954), and grammatical and sentence construction patterns move from one- and two-word phrases to sentences of indefinite length. In Piaget's view, however, preoperational children can use these representational skills only to view the world from their own perspective. They focus their attention too narrowly, often ignoring important information. They also cannot accurately represent transformations, instead only being able to represent static situations.

Concrete operational children (ages 6 or 7 to 11 or 12), who are in the third stage, can take other points of view, can simultaneously take into account more than one perspective, and can accurately represent transformations as well as static situations. This allows them to solve many problems involving concrete objects and physically possible situations. However, they do not consider all of the logically possible outcomes and do not understand highly abstract concepts.

The fourth stage of development, formal operations, is attained at roughly age 11 or 12. It is the crowning achievement of the stage progression. Children who attain it are said to reason in terms of theories and abstractions as well as concrete realities. This broader perspective brings with it the potential for solving many types of problems that are impossible for children in earlier stages. Although Piaget recognized that particular knowledge and beliefs continue to change, he believed that the basic mode of reasoning that characterizes the formal operational stage is sufficiently powerful to last a lifetime.

Developmental Processes

How do children progress from one stage to another? Piaget viewed three processes as crucial: *assimilation*, *accommodation*, and *equilibration*.

Assimilation. Assimilation refers to the way in which people transform incoming information so that it fits their existing way of thinking. To illustrate, when my older son was 2, he encountered a man who was bald on the top of his head and had long frizzy hair growing out from each side. To my embarrassment, on seeing the man, he gleefully shouted, "Clown, clown." (Actually, it sounded more like "Kown, kown".) The man apparently possessed the features that my son believed distinguished clowns from other people, and thus became a "kown."

Assimilation is important throughout life, not just in early childhood. Consider the experience of a music critic, Bernard Levin. Levin noted that when he heard the premiere performance of Bartok's *Concerto for Violin and Orchestra* early in Bartok's career, neither he nor other critics could make sense of it or later remember it in any detail. It was simply confusing and annoying to the ear. However, when he next heard the piece, almost 20 years later, it seemed eminently musical. Levin's explanation was that in the ensuing period, "I had come to hear the world with different ears" (*London Daily Telegraph*, June 8, 1977). In

Piaget's terms, he was initially unable to assimilate the Bartok piece to his understanding of music. Twenty years later, he was able to do so.

One interesting type of assimilation that Piaget described is *functional assimilation*, the tendency to use a mental structure as soon as it becomes available. Illustratively, when my older son was first learning to talk, he spent endless hours talking in his crib, even though no one else was present. A few years later, he would turn somersaults over and over again, despite encouragement from his parents to stop. Piaget contrasted this source of motivation with behaviorists' emphases on external reinforcers as motivators of behavior. In reinforcement, the reason for engaging in an activity is the external reward that is obtained. In functional assimilation, the reason for engaging in the activity is the sheer delight of mastering new skills.

Accommodation. Accommodation refers to the ways in which people adapt their thinking to new experiences. Returning to the "kown" incident, after biting my lip to suppress a smile, I told my son that the man we had seen was not a clown; that even though his hair was like a clown's, he wasn't wearing a funny costume and wasn't trying to make people laugh. My goal was to help him accommodate his idea of "clown" to the concept's standard meaning.

Assimilation and accommodation mutually influence each other; assimilation is never present without accommodation and vice versa. On seeing a new object, an infant might try to grasp it as he has grasped other objects (thus assimilating the new object to an existing approach). However, he would also have to adjust his grasp to conform to the shape of the new object (thus accommodating his approach as well). The extreme case of assimilation is fantasy play, in which children gloss over the physical characteristics of objects and treat them as if they were something else. The extreme case of accommodation is imitation, in which children minimize their interpretations and simply mimic what they see. Even at the extremes, elements of each process are present. Children at play do not totally ignore physical properties. (Beds are almost never assimilated as teacups, even in fantasy play.) Conversely, when we do not understand what we are doing, imitation often is imperfect. (Try to repeat verbatim a 10-word Arabic sentence.)

Equilibration. Equilibration is the process by which children integrate their many particular pieces of knowledge of the world into a unified whole. It thus requires balancing assimilation and accommodation. It is also the keystone of developmental change within Piaget's system. Piaget saw development as the formation of ever more stable equilibria between the child's cognitive system and the external world. That is, the child's model of the world would increasingly resemble reality.

Piaget also suggested that regardless of when in life it occurs, equilibration includes three phases. First, children are satisfied with their mode of thought and therefore are in a state of equilibrium. Then they become aware of shortcomings in their existing thinking and are dissatisfied. This constitutes a state of disequilibrium. Finally, they adopt a more sophisticated mode of thought that eliminates the shortcomings of the old one. That is, they reach a more stable equilibrium.

To illustrate the equilibration process, suppose a 6-year-old girl thought that animals were the only living things. (In fact, most 4- to-7-year-olds do think this; see Hatano, Siegler, Richards, Inagaki, Stavy, & Wax, 1993.) At some point, the girl might realize that plants, like animals, grow and die. This thought might create a state of disequilibrium, in which she was unsure if plants were alive and what it meant to be alive. Eventually she would learn that the critical attributes of life are growth and reproduction, that both plants and animals possess them, and that therefore, both are alive. The new understanding would constitute a more stable equilibrium, since further observations would not call it into question (unless the girl later became interested in certain viruses and bacteria whose status as living things continues to be debated by biologists).

This overview of assimilation, accommodation, and equilibration might create an impression that these change processes apply solely to specific, short-term cognitive changes. In fact, Piaget was especially interested in their capacity to produce far-reaching, longer-term changes, such as the change from one developmental stage to the next. Illustratively, the particular realizations that frizzy hair that looks like a clown's does not make its bearer a clown, that plants are alive even though they don't move, and that the sun's looking like gold does not mean it is gold are part of a more general trend from preoperational to concrete operational reasoning. Piaget believed that children generalize the assimilations, accommodations, and equilibrations involved in these particular changes into a broad shift from emphasizing external appearances to emphasizing deeper, enduring qualities.

Orienting Assumptions

The child as scientific problem solver. Piaget often likened children's thinking to that of scientists solving problems about the fundamental nature of the world. He applied the metaphor even to the thinking of infants. When an infant varied the height from which she dropped food from her high chair and observed how the results varied, Piaget detected the beginnings of scientific experimentation.

At least three considerations led Piaget to concentrate on scientific reasoning and problem solving. One was his view of what development was. Piaget viewed development as a form of adaptation to reality. A problem can be viewed as a miniature reality. The way children solved problems thus could lead to insights about how they adapted to all kinds of challenges that life posed.

A second reason for Piaget's emphasis on problem solving relates to his views about how and why development occurs. Equilibration only happens when some problem arises that disturbs a child's existing equilibrium. Thus, problems, which by their very nature challenge existing understandings, have the potential for stimulating cognitive growth. If encountering problems stimulates cognitive growth, then an interest in cognitive growth would naturally lead to an interest in problem solving.

A third reason for Piaget's focus on problem solving concerns the insights that can be gained by observing children's reactions to unfamiliar situations. Piaget noted that everyday activities may be performed by rote; when this is the case, they reveal little about children's reasoning. For example, if we ask a boy to name the capital of France, and he says "Paris," we learn little about his reasoning. We just learn that he knows the particular fact. By contrast, when children are unfamiliar with problems, their solution strategies reveal the child's own logic.

The role of activity. Piaget emphasized cognitive activity as the means through which development occurs. Assimilation, accommodation, and equilibration are all active processes by which the mind transforms, and is transformed by, incoming information. As Gruber and Voneche (1977) noted, it was significant that Piaget titled one of his most famous books *The Construction of Reality in the Child*. Within Piaget's approach, reality is not waiting to be found; children must construct it from their own mental and physical actions.

This distinction between a found reality and a constructed reality is analogous to the distinction between a picture of a bridge and an engineer's model of the forces operating on the bridge. A picture simply reflects the bridge's superficial appearance. In contrast, the engineer's model emphasizes the relations among components and how the structure distributes stresses. Piaget believed that children's mental representations, like the engineer's model, emphasize structural relations and causes. He also believed that the only way that children can form such representations is to assimilate their experience to their existing understandings; even when a relation is explained to them, they must actively integrate it with their own general understanding in order to remember it.

Methodological assumptions. Early in his career, Piaget perceived a trade-off between the precision and replicability that accompany standardized experimental procedures and the rich descriptions and insights that can emerge from methods that are tailored to the individual child. He also recognized the trade-off between the unexpected information that can emerge from talking with children and having them explain their reasoning and the possibility of underestimating the quality of their reasoning because of their inarticulateness.

Recognizing these trade-offs, Piaget used different methods to study different topics. His studies of infants, conducted early in his career, were based on observations of his own children, Jacqueline, Laurent, and Lucienne, in everyday situations and in simple informal experiments that he devised. His early studies of moral reasoning, causation, play, and dreams relied almost entirely on children's answers to hypothetical questions. His later studies of number, time, velocity, and proportionality relied on a combination of children's interactions with physical materials and their explanations of their reasoning.

Generally, when the choice was whether to follow standardized methods or to tailor tasks and questions flexibly to the individual child's actions and statements, Piaget opted for flexibility. This choice may have led him astray at times. Some of his conclusions may have been formed as a result of his methods' underestimating children's knowledge. However, the flexible methods also allowed him to follow up on unexpected observations, which resulted in remarkable discoveries and insights that might never have emerged had he used standardized procedures.

Possessing this overview of Piaget's theory, we now can examine the major trends that characterize his four hypothesized stages of development. To describe them as cleanly as possible, I will generally avoid phrases such as "Piaget said," "Piaget believed," and "Piaget argued." These qualifying phrases should be understood to be implicit, since many of the claims are controversial. Before getting into the controversies, however, we need to understand what Piaget was saying.

THE STAGE MODEL

The Sensorimotor Period (Birth to Roughly 2 Years)

Several years ago, at the first class meeting of a developmental psychology course I was teaching, I asked each student to name the five most important aspects of intelligence in infancy, early childhood, later childhood, and adolescence. A number of students commented that they found it odd to describe infants as having intelligence at all. By far the most frequently named characteristics of infants' intelligence were physical coordination, alertness, and ability to recognize people and objects. Part of Piaget's genius was that he perceived much more than this. He saw the beginnings of some of humankind's most sophisticated thought processes in infants' flailings and graspings.

Piaget's account of the development of sensorimotor intelligence constitutes a theory within a theory. Infants are said to progress through six stages of intellectual development within a two-year period. (For clarity, I will refer to these as "substages", to distinguish them from the broader stages such as the sensorimotor and preoperational stages.) This might seem like too large a number of substages for such a brief time span, but when we consider that the brain of a 2-year-old weighs almost three times as much as that of a newborn, the number does not seem unreasonable. As a general rule, cognitive competence, like brain size, grows especially rapidly in the first few years.

Substage 1: Modification of reflexes (birth to roughly 1 month). Newborn infants enter the world possessing many reflexes. They suck when objects are placed in their mouths, close their fingers around objects that come into contact with their hands, focus on the edges of objects with their eyes, turn their heads toward noises, and so on. Piaget believed that these reflexes are the building blocks of intelligence.

Even within the first month after birth, infants begin to modify the reflexes to make them more adaptive. In the first days, they suck quite similarly regardless of the type of object in their mouth. Later in the first month, however, they suck differently on a milk-bearing nipple than on a harder, drier finger, and they suck differently on both of them than on the side of their hand. Thus, accommodation can be seen even in the first month out of the womb.

Substage 2: Primary circular reactions (roughly 1 to 4 months).   By the second month, infants exhibit *primary circular reactions*. The term *circular* is used here in the sense of a repetitive cycle of events. The circles involve infants' actions, the effect of those actions on the environment, and the impact on the infants' subsequent actions of the effect of the earlier actions on the environment. Piaget (1954) provides the example of infants in their first few months trying to scratch and grasp all kinds of objects that they happen to touch: their mother's bare shoulder, the sheet folded over their blanket, their father's fist, and so on.

In primary circular reactions, if infants inadvertently produce some interesting effect, they attempt to duplicate it by repeating the action. If they are successful, the new instance of the interesting outcome triggers another similar cycle, which, in turn, can trigger another cycle, and so on.

These primary circular reactions are possible because Substage 2 infants begin to coordinate actions that originally were separate reflexes. In Substage 1, infants grasp objects that come into contact with their palms. They also suck on objects that come into their mouths. During Substage 2, infants put these actions together. They bring to their mouths objects that their hands grasp, and grasp objects with their hands that they are sucking on. Thus, the reflexes have already begun to serve as building blocks for more complex activities.

Primary circular reactions are more flexible than the earlier reflexes and allow infants to learn a great deal about the world. However, they also are limited in at least three ways. First, the 1- to 4-month-olds only try to reproduce the exact behavior that produced the original interesting event. Second, their actions are poorly integrated and have a large trial-and-error component. Third, they only try to repeat actions in which the outcome of the action involves their own bodies, as in sucking a finger.

Substage 3: Secondary circular reactions (roughly 4 to 8 months).   In this stage, infants become increasingly interested in outcomes occurring beyond their bodies. For example, they become interested in batting balls with their hands and watching them roll away. Piaget labeled the activities *secondary circular reactions*. Like all circular reactions, these activities are repeated over and over. Unlike the primary circular reactions, however, the interesting outcome (such as the ball rolling away) involves objects in the external world.

Between the ages of 4 and 8 months, infants also organize more efficiently the components of their circular reactions. Piaget described instances in which, after he started a mobile swinging, his children kicked their legs to continue the movement. As in the primary circular reactions, infants were only trying to reinstate the original interesting occurrence. However, they now could do so more efficiently. They reacted more quickly to the original event and wasted less motion.

At this point, it is tempting to conclude that infants understand the causal connection between their actions and the effects of their actions. Piaget was reluctant to credit them with this understanding, though. Rather, he thought that infants' activities were not sufficiently voluntary to say that they had independent goals. In his view, in the first month, they do not form any goals; and between 1 and 8 months, they only form goals directly suggested to them by the immediate situation. Not until after 8 months do they form true goals, independent of events in the immediate environment.

Substage 4: Coordination of secondary reactions (roughly 8 to 12 months). Infants approaching 1 year of age become able to coordinate two or more secondary circular reactions into an efficient routine. When Piaget (1952) put a pillow in front of a matchbox that his infant son Laurent liked, the boy pushed the pillow aside and grabbed the box. In earlier stages, the infant would not have been able to combine the two activities of pushing the barrier out of the way and getting the matchbox.

This example also illustrates another major development that occurs as children approach their first birthday. They realize that if they act in certain ways, particular effects will follow. Thus, Laurent now understood that removing the pillow would allow him to grab the matchbox.

Especially important, Substage 4 brings with it the ability to form relatively enduring internal representations of the world. Out of sight is no longer completely out of mind. Thus, when objects disappear from sight, as when they roll behind a chair, infants pursue them, rather than acting as if the objects had disappeared from the world. This ability to form mental representations is an especially important development, because it lays the foundation for all further cognitive growth.

Substage 5: Tertiary circular reactions (roughly 12 to 18 months). With the onset of tertiary circular reactions, shortly before 1 year of age, infants transcend the remaining limits on their circular reactions. They actively search for new ways to interact with objects and explore the potential uses to which objects can be put. As implied by the "circular reaction" label, they still repeat their actions again and again. Now, though, they deliberately vary both their own actions and the objects on which they act. Thus, the activities involve similar rather than identical behaviors. The following description of Piaget's son Laurent conveys a sense of these new competencies.

> He grasps in succession a celluloid swan, a box, etc., stretches out his arm,
> them fall. He distinctly varies the positions of the fall. Sometimes he stretc
> his arm vertically, sometimes he holds it obliquely, in front of or behind h
> etc. Then the object falls in a new position (for example on his pillow), he let ....
> two or three times more on the same place, as though to study the spatial relation;
> then he modifies the situation. (Piaget, 1951, p. 269)

These changes from primary to secondary to tertiary circular reactions show just how far infants come in their first 1½ years. As shown in Figure 2.1, primary circular reactions, first seen between the ages of 1 and 4 months, involve repetitions of events whose outcomes center on the infants' own bodies, such as putting their fingers into their mouths. Secondary circular reactions, first seen between the ages of 4 and 8 months, again involve repetition of an event that by chance produced an interesting outcome, but the interesting outcome is at least slightly removed from the infants' bodies (e.g., the ball rolling away from them). Tertiary circular reactions, first seen between the ages of 12 and 18 months, involve the infant deliberately varying the behavior that produced the interesting outcome.

The changes embodied in these three types of circular reactions are useful for thinking about a broad range of developments in infancy. At first, infants' activities center on their own bodies; later, they increasingly center on the external world. Goals begin at a concrete level (dropping an object) and become increasingly abstract (varying the heights from which objects are dropped). Correspondence between intentions and behaviors becomes increasingly precise, and exploration of the world becomes increasingly venturesome.

Substage 6: Beginnings of representational thought (roughly 18 to 24 months). Developments in this age range are transitional between the sensorimotor and preoperational periods. In the sensorimotor period, children can only act; they cannot form internal mental representations of objects and events. In the preoperational period, children can form such internal mental operations. Substage 6 is the transition point, in which internalized representations are first produced. Consider the following scenario involving Piaget playing with his daughter Lucienne. Piaget hides a watch chain inside an otherwise empty matchbox. Previously, he had left the matchbox open far enough that Lucienne could get the chain by turning over the matchbox, but now he closes it too completely for the chain to fall out. Lucienne

> looks at the slit [in the matchbox] with great attention; then, several times in
> succession, she opens and shuts her mouth, at first slightly, then wider and
> wider! Apparently, Lucienne understands the existence of a cavity subjacent to
> the slit [in the matchbox] and wishes to enlarge the cavity. The attempt at representation which she thus furnishes is expressed plastically, that is to say, due
> to inability to think out the situation in words or clear visual images, she uses
> a simple motor indication [her open mouth] as "signifier" or symbol. (Piaget,
> 1951, p. 338)

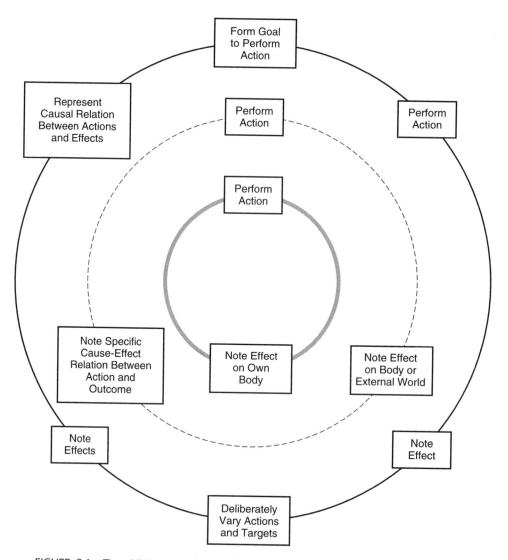

FIGURE 2.1   *The child's expanding universe: primary (═══), secondary (─ ─ ─), and tertiary (────) circular reactions. Diagram best read by starting at top of each circle and proceeding clockwise.*

As Lucienne opens her mouth, symbolizing her desire for the opening in the matchbox to become wider, we can almost see her internally representing the situation. That is, the representation is moving from her external actions to her mind. Such internalized representations are the hallmark of the preoperational period.

The Preoperational Period
(Roughly 2 Years to 6 or 7 Years)

Miller (1993) nicely captured children's position as they complete the sensorimotor period by likening them to mountain climbers who, after a hard trek, discover that what they have climbed is merely a foothill to Mt. Everest. By the end of the sensorimotor stage, infants have become toddlers. They interact smoothly with objects and people in their immediate environment. Their ability to form internal representations remains severely limited, however. The growth of representational ability is the key development of the preoperational period.

Early symbolic representations.   Piaget suggested that the earliest sign of internal representations is *deferred imitation*, the imitation of an activity hours or days after it occurred. For children to show such delayed imitation, they must have formed a durable representation of the original activity. How else could they imitate it so much later?

Children do not exhibit deferred imitation until late in the sensorimotor period. Consider the following description of Piaget's daughter Jacqueline kicking and screaming in her playpen.

> At 1;4(3) [Piaget's notation for 1 year, 4 months, and 3 days] Jacqueline had a visit from a little boy of 1;6 whom she used to see from time to time, and who, in the course of the afternoon, got into a terrible temper. He screamed as he tried to get out of a playpen and pushed it backward, stamping his feet. Jacqueline stood watching him in amazement, never having witnessed such a scene before. The next day, she herself screamed in her playpen and tried to move it, stamping her foot lightly several times in succession. (Piaget, 1951, p. 63)

Jacqueline had never before, to her father's knowledge, engaged in these behaviors. Thus, an internal representation of the playmate's tantrum must have helped her reproduce them.

Piaget distinguished between two types of internal representations: *symbols* and *signs*. The distinction is not identical to the standard English distinction between the two. Rather, it is the difference between idiosyncratic representations intended only for one's personal use (symbols) and conventional representations intended for communication (signs).

Early in their acquisition of internal representations, children frequently use symbols (the personal representations). They may choose a particular piece of cloth to represent their pillow or a popsicle stick to represent a gun. Typically, these personal symbols physically resemble the object they represent. The cloth's texture is similar to that of the pillow, and both are comforting; the popsicle's shape and texture are something like those of a gun barrel. Signs, by contrast, often do not resemble the objects or events they signify. The word *cow* does not look like a cow, nor does the numeral *6* have any inherent similarity to six objects.

As children develop, they make less use of the idiosyncratic symbols and more of the conventional signs. This shift is an important achievement, as it greatly expands their ability to communicate. The transition from personal to publicly accepted representations is not easy, however.

The difficulty is illustrated in Piaget's description of *egocentric communication*. Piaget applied the term *egocentric* to preschool-age children, not to castigate them for being inconsiderate, but rather in a more literal sense. Their thinking about the external world is always in terms of their own perspective. Their use of language reflects this egocentrism, particularly their use of idiosyncratic words that are meaningless to other people.

Although even very young children use signs as well as symbols, they at first do not use them consistently in a manner that other people can understand. Figure 2.2 portrays an instance of this aspect of young children's conversations. Preschoolers often speak right past each other, without appearing to pay any attention to what others are saying. Many times, even sympathetic adults cannot figure out what the children mean.

Between ages 4 and 7, speech becomes less egocentric. One of the earliest signs of progress can be seen in children's verbal quarrels. The fact that a child's verbal statements elicit a playmate's disagreement indicates that the playmate is at least paying attention to a perspective other than his own. Some children also are aware of the symbolization process and find it interesting in its own right. When my daughter was 4, she took great delight in saying such things as, "When I say 'chair', I'm going to mean 'milk'; could you give me a glass of chair?"

Piaget noted that mental imagery, like language, is a way of representing objects and events. He also suggested that the development of mental imagery resembles that of language. As children become able to describe situations ver-

FIGURE 2.2 *Two young children more or less having a conversation—an example of egocentric communication.*

bally, they also become able to represent them as images. Further, he believed that the initial representations in both domains are limited to the child's own perspective. That is, they are egocentric.

Although language, mental imagery, and many other skills grow greatly during the preoperational period, Piaget emphasized what preoperational children cannot do. He viewed them as unable to solve many problems that were critical indicators of logical reasoning. Even the name, "*pre*operational," suggests deficiencies rather than strengths.

One of the limits on preschoolers' thinking has already been mentioned: their egocentrism. This trait is evident in their ability to take different spatial perspectives, as well as in their conversations. Piaget had 4-year-olds sit or stand at a table in front of a model of three mountains of different sizes (Figure 2.3). The children's task was to choose which of several photographs corresponded to what children sitting at chairs at different points around the table would see. To solve the problem, children needed to recognize that their own perspective was not the only one possible and to mentally rotate the arrangement they saw to correspond to what the view would be elsewhere. This was impossible for most of the 4-year-olds; they could not imagine the view from other positions.

A second, related limit on preschoolers' thinking is that it centers on individual, perceptually striking features of objects, to the exclusion of other, less-striking features. A good example of this centration is found in Piaget's research on children's understanding of the concept of time.

Piaget's interest in this concept has an interesting history. In 1928, Albert Einstein posed a seemingly simple question to Piaget: In what order do children acquire the concepts of time and velocity? Einstein's question was prompted by an issue within physics. In Newtonian theory, time is a basic quality and velocity is defined in terms of it (velocity = distance/time). Within relativity theory,

FIGURE 2.3   The three-mountains problem. The child's task is to indicate how the display would look to someone viewing it from a perspective other than her own (after Piaget & Inhelder, 1969).

in contrast, time and velocity are defined in terms of each other, with neither concept more basic. Einstein wanted to know whether understanding of either or both concepts was present from birth or if children understood one before the other.

Almost 20 years later, Piaget (1946a, 1946b) published a two-volume, 500-page reply to Einstein's question. The gist of Piaget's answer was that mastery of all three concepts emerged simultaneously during the concrete operations period.

To test this view, Piaget presented a task involving two toy trains running along parallel tracks in the same direction. After the cars stopped moving, Piaget asked, "Which train traveled for the longer time (or the faster speed, or the farther distance)?"

Most 4- and 5-year-olds focused entirely on a single feature, usually the stopping point. They chose the train that stopped farther down the track as having traveled faster, for the longer time, and for the greater distance. Stated differently, they ignored when the trains started, when they stopped, and the total time for which they traveled. Not until roughly age 9 did they answer correctly.

The example illustrates another of the basic qualities of children's thinking in the preoperational period. They tend to focus on static states rather than transformations. The point at which each train ended constitutes a static position, readily perceivable and available for repeated inspection. The time, speed, and distance traveled are more transitory. The dimensions on which preoperational-period children focus usually are static states; the dimensions they ignore usually involve transformations.

Thus, Piaget viewed 2- to 6-year-olds as having difficulty taking perspectives other than their own, as paying too much attention to perceptually salient dimensions and ignoring less-salient ones, and as representing static states but not transformations. All of these descriptions suggest that such young children think about the world too simply and rigidly. They largely surmount these limitations in the next period of development.

The Concrete Operations Period
(Roughly 6 or 7 Years to 11 or 12 Years)

The central development in the concrete operations period is the acquisition of *operations*. These operations are mental representations of dynamic as well as static aspects of the environment. All development up to this time has been prelude to this achievement. In the sensorimotor period, children learned to operate physically on the environment. In the preoperational period, they learned to represent static states mentally. Finally, in the concrete operations period, they become able to represent transformations as well as static states.

The importance of operations can most easily be illustrated in the context of conservation problems. Consider children's understanding of three interesting types of conservation: liquid quantity, solid quantity, and number. Although these conservation problems differ among themselves in certain respects, all share a basic three-phase procedure (Figure 2.4). In the first phase, children see two or more identical objects or sets of objects: two identical rows of checkers, two identical glasses of water, two identical clay cylinders, and so on. Once the children agree that the two are equal on some dimension, such as the number of objects, the second phase begins. Here, one object or set of objects is transformed in a way that changes its appearance but does not affect the dimension of interest. Children might see the row of checkers lengthened, the water poured into a different-shaped glass, the clay cylinder remolded into a ball, and so on. Finally, in the third phase, children are asked whether the dimension of interest, which they earlier said was equal for the two choices, remains equal following the transformation of one of them. The correct answer invariably is "yes."

These problems seem trivially easy to adults and older children. However, almost all 5-year-olds answer them incorrectly. When shown number-conservation problems, they claim that the longer row has more checkers (regardless of the actual numbers in each row). When shown conservation-of-liquid-quantity problems, they claim that the glass with the taller column of liquid has more (regardless of the cross-sectional areas of the glasses). When shown conservation-

FIGURE 2.4   Procedures used to test children's understanding of conservation of number, solid quantity, and liquid quantity.

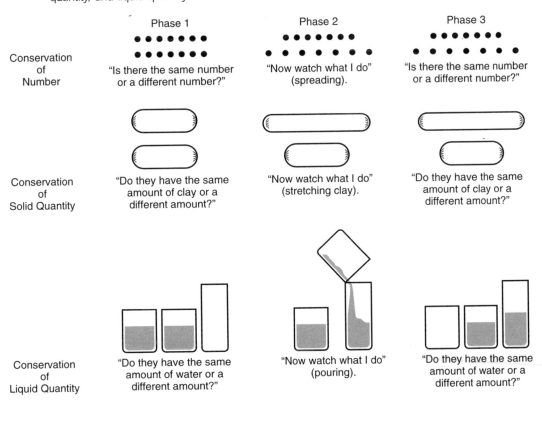

of-solid-quantity problems, they believe that the longer sausage has more clay (again regardless of the cross-sectional areas).

Considering what children need to do to solve conservation problems makes understandable the 5-year-olds' difficulty. They must mentally represent the spreading, pouring, or remolding transformation involved in the problem. And, they must not focus all their attention on the perceptually salient dimension of height or length; they need to consider cross-sectional area and density as well. Finally, they need to realize that even though the transformed object may seem to have more of the dimension in question, it might not. That is, they need to understand that their own perspective can be misleading. Each of these is difficult for 5-year-olds to do.

In the concrete operations stage, children master all three conservation problems. They also master the train problem that was used to measure understanding of time, distance, and velocity. Piaget explained their mastery of these and many other concepts in terms of the children's now possessing mental operations. These operations allow them to represent transformations as well as static states.

Children's explanations of their reasoning on conservation problems are especially revealing. When 5-year-olds are asked to explain why the amount of water has changed, they regularly say that the water in the new glass is higher. When 8-year-olds are asked to explain why the amount of water remains the same, they point to the nature of the transformation ("You just poured it"), to changes in the less-striking dimension offsetting the changes in the more-striking one "The water in this one is taller, but the water in that one is wider"), to the water looking different but really being the same, and to the reversible nature of the operation ("You could pour it back and it would be the same"). Interestingly, 5-year-olds will grant many of these points, but do not see them as implying that the two glasses have the same amount of water.

Although children in the concrete operations period become capable of solving many problems, certain types of abstract reasoning remain beyond them. Some of these problems require reasoning about contrary-to-fact propositions ("If people could know the future, would they be happier than they are now?"). Others involve treating their own thinking as something to be thought about. To quote one adolescent, "I was thinking about my future, and then I began to wonder why I was thinking about my future, and then I began to think about why I was thinking about why I was thinking about my future" (Mussen, Conger, Kagan, & Geiwitz, 1979). Still others involve thinking about abstract scientific concepts such as force, inertia, torque, and acceleration. These types of ideas become possible in the formal operations period.

The Formal Operations Period
(Roughly 11 or 12 Years Onward)

Perhaps the most striking development during the formal operations period is that adolescents begin to see the particular reality in which they live as only one of an infinite number of imaginable realities. This leads at least some of them to think about alternative organizations of the world and about deep questions concerning meaning, truth, justice, and morality. As Inhelder and Piaget (1958) put it, "Each one has his own ideas (and usually he believes they are his own) which liberate him from childhood and allow him to place himself as the equal of adults" (pp. 340–1). From this perspective, it is no coincidence that many people first acquire a taste for science fiction during adolescence.

Many of the differences between formal and concrete operational reasoners are evident in Inhelder and Piaget's (1958) descriptions of children's and adolescents' approaches to the chemical combinations problem. The task involved four beakers, each with a particular chemical solution, and a "special" beaker with an unknown mixture of one or more of the other chemicals in it. When another chemical was added to the special beaker, the solution turned yellow. The children were asked to determine which of the four chemicals were in the solution that turned yellow and what role each played.

Concrete operational children typically generated several pairs of the chemicals, then tried all four together, and then generated a few of the possible sets of three. They often repeated combinations they already had tried and left out other combinations altogether. In contrast, formal operational children first devised a plan for systematically generating all possible combinations of the chemicals. Then they used their plan to generate each combination without redundancies or omissions.

The formal operational reasoners' more systematic approach also helped them draw a more appropriate conclusion about when and why the yellow color appeared. Concrete operations children often stopped collecting evidence after they found a single combination that turned the solution yellow. They concluded that it must be the original solution and that all chemicals in it were necessary for the reaction to occur. In contrast, formal operations children, who tried all 16 possible combinations, eventually learned that 2 different combinations produced the yellow color. What these combinations had in common was the presence of two of the chemicals and the absence of a third. (The absence of the third chemical was what distinguished the two instances in which the solution turned yellow from two others that had both necessary chemicals in them but that did not turn yellow.) Therefore, the formal operational reasoners reached the correct conclusion that two of the chemicals were necessary to produce the change in color, that a third would prevent it from happening even if the first two were present, and that the fourth had no effect. Their focusing on the system of possible combinations allowed them to obtain the relevant data and to interpret it appropriately.

Some of the largest changes in thinking during the formal operations period involve logical and scientific reasoning (Moshman, in press). The abstract and systematic thinking that develop especially greatly during the formal operations period are particularly crucial in such contexts. Scientific and logical reasoning problems often require applying the most abstract ways of thinking to the most challenging problems. Not surprisingly, Piaget viewed such formal operations as the culmination of the process of cognitive development, the fruition of all that had developed before.

THE DEVELOPMENT OF SOME CRITICAL CONCEPTS

The broad sweep of Piaget's descriptions of children's thinking emerges most clearly in his accounts of the development of particular concepts. Some concepts where his descriptions are especially interesting are conservation, classes, and relations. He traced the development of each of these from the earliest origins in the sensorimotor period, through more refined versions in the preoperational and concrete operational periods, to the most sophisticated understandings in the formal operations period. People do not usually think of infants' thinking as having anything to do with that of teenagers. Part of Piaget's genius was that he saw the connection.

Conservation

Conservation in the sensorimotor period. During the sensorimotor period, children acquire a simple but crucial part of the conservation concept. This might be labeled "conservation of existence," though Piaget called it *object permanence.* Adults know that objects do not just disappear from the world (although they sometimes seem to). If we want a ball and it rolls behind another object, we search for it and remove barriers if necessary to get it. Piaget observed that infants younger than 8 months do not search like this; they simply turn their attention to something else. He did not attribute this to their losing interest or being too poorly coordinated to retrieve the object. Instead, he advanced the more radical view that they did not understand that the objects still existed. He further argued that full understanding of object permanence required the entire sensorimotor period.

In Substage 1, from birth to 1 month of age, infants look at objects directly in front of them. However, if an object moves away, they do not follow it with their eyes. Thus, an infant will look at her mother's face when it is directly above, but will stop looking if the mother moves aside. In Substage 2, between 1 and 4 months, infants prolong their looking at the place where an object disappeared, but do not follow its movement. If they are playing with a toy and drop it, they continue looking at their hand rather than at the floor. In Substage 3, between about 4 and 8 months of age, they anticipate where moving objects will go, and look for them there if they are partially visible. However, if the object is completely covered, they do not attempt to retrieve it (as illustrated in the quotation at the beginning of this chapter).

In Substage 4, between 8 and 12 months of age, infants begin to search for objects behind or under barriers. This indicates that they realize that objects have a permanent existence. Under certain circumstances, however, 8- to 12-month-olds make an interesting mistake. If they see an object hidden twice in succession under the same container, they retrieve the object from there each time. If they then see the same object hidden under a different container, however, they look under the container where they found it before, rather than under the one where it is now. It is as if this original container had assumed an independent status as a hiding place where the object can be found.

In Substage 5, roughly between 12 and 18 months of age, infants stop making this error and search wherever they last saw the object hidden. However, they remain unable to deal efficiently with transformations where the desired object cannot be directly perceived. When a toy is first hidden under a cover, and then the toy and cover together are hidden under a pillow, and then the cover is removed so that the toy remains under the pillow, 12- to 18-month-olds do not look under the pillow. By Substage 6, however, between the ages of 18 and 24 months, babies understand even this type of complex displacement and immediately search in the right place.

I remember when I first read about Piaget's theory of object permanence. I found his account fantastic, both in the sense of extremely interesting and in the sense of extremely improbable. It seemed to me much more likely that infants younger than 8 months old failed to search for objects either because they were not well enough coordinated to do so or because they had lost interest.

An experiment by Bower and Wishart (1972), however, rendered unlikely both of my initial suspicions. Five-month-olds saw a toy hidden under a transparent cup. The large majority of infants retrieved it. Then the infants saw the same toy hidden under an opaque cup. Only 2 of 16 retrieved it. This experiment ruled out both motoric immaturity and lack of motivation as explanations for the infants' failure to search under the opaque cup. If they lacked sufficient interest in the toy to retrieve it, or failed because they lacked the necessary coordination, why were they interested and coordinated enough to retrieve the same object when it was hidden under the transparent cup?

Conservation in the preoperational and concrete operational periods. In the sensorimotor period, infants come to realize that the existence of objects is conserved over certain types of transformations, specifically, ones where the object is hidden. In the preoperational and concrete operational periods, children come to realize that certain qualities of objects also are conserved even when transformations change their appearance. Spreading out objects increases the length of the row but leaves unchanged the number of objects. Pouring water from a typical glass to a tall thin one changes the height of the liquid column but leaves unchanged the amount of water. By the end of the concrete operational period, children realize that even when transformations alter appearances, a great many tangible dimensions are conserved: number, amount, length, weight, perimeter, area, and so on.

Conservation in the formal operational period. During the formal operations period, adolescents come to understand complex forms of conservation
that involve transformations of transformations. One such concept is conservation of motion. Inhelder and Piaget (1958) studied children's and adolescents'
understanding of this concept by presenting them with a spring-powered
plunger that shot balls of various sizes. The task was to predict where the balls
would stop, to explain why some balls stop earlier than others, and to explain
why balls stop at all.

Performance on this problem at various ages illustrates the types of reasoning that Piaget thought were fundamental at those ages. Preoperational children focus on only one dimension and take only one perspective. They might
consistently predict that a big ball will go farther because it is stronger. Concrete
operational children realize that multiple dimensions are important and take
multiple perspectives. They might realize the importance of qualities of the surface on which the ball rolls, as well as of the ball itself. They also might recognize that the problem can be thought of in terms of what makes the ball stop,
as well as what makes it go. Thus, they might believe that bigger balls go farther, but also that rougher surfaces lead to balls going less far.

By the formal operations stage, children think of the problem in terms of
sophisticated scientific concepts, such as conservation of motion. That is, they
conceptualize the problem in idealized terms ("If there were no air resistance or
friction..."). This way of thinking is a distinctive formal operations achievement, because it involves conservation of a dimension—motion—that itself involves a transformation—movement through space. In addition, it illustrates
how adolescents proceed from the actual to the possible, since no one has experienced an environment without air resistance or friction.

Classes and Relations

Another of Piaget's insights was seeing the connection between children's understanding of classes and relations. This connection can be illustrated with regard to numbers. What does it mean when we say that a girl understands the
concept "three"? One part of the understanding is seeing what three balls, three
cars, and three spoons have in common—that they are all members of the class
of three-member sets. She also should understand the relation of this class to
other classes—larger than sets with two members and smaller than sets with
four. Piaget viewed children as originally thinking of classes and relations as
separate ideas, but eventually integrating them into a unified understanding.

Understanding of classes and relations in the sensorimotor period. Piaget
contended that infants classify objects according to the objects' functions. He illustrated this point by describing his daughter Lucienne's reaction to a plastic
parrot that sat atop her bassinet. Lucienne liked to make the parrot move by
kicking her feet while lying in the bassinet. At 6 months of age, she made sim-

ilar kicking motions when she was out of the bassinet but still could see the parrot. Piaget interpreted this as Lucienne classifying the parrot as "something that swings when I kick my feet." Far more sophisticated categories are seen as evolving from such simple classifications.

Understanding of relations, like understanding of classes, is seen as developing out of sensorimotor actions. Piaget described his three children at 3 and 4 months as being greatly amused by the relation between the vigor of their actions and the strength of the reaction they produced. More vigorous kicking produced more vigorous swinging of objects on the bassinet; more vigorous shaking of a rattle produced louder noises; and so on. Thus, they understand the relation "the more vigorously I do something, the larger its effect."

Understanding of classes and relations in the preoperational period. Children progress considerably in classificatory ability during the preoperational period. This progress is evident when they are asked to put together a group of blocks varying in size, color, and shape. Early in the preoperational period, a boy might try to put together all of the small objects, and therefore choose a small red square, then a small blue square, then a small red triangle. However, the fact that the last object was a triangle might grab his attention, leading him to add a large red triangle and a large green triangle, thus creating a group without any unifying characteristic. Not until later in the preoperational period, around age 4 or 5 years, do children come to classify on a consistent basis. At this point, they put all small objects into one group and all big ones into another.

Although children learn to solve this type of problem during the preoperational period, other classification problems remain difficult. The limitations of their reasoning are most evident when they simultaneously need to consider competing bases of classification, as in Piaget's *class inclusion problem*. On such problems, children might be presented eight toy animals, six of them cats and two dogs. They then would be asked, "Are there more cats or more animals?" Most children below age 7 or 8 answer that there are more cats, despite the number of cats inherently being less than or equal to the number of animals.

Piaget saw this behavior as stemming from preoperational children's tendency to focus on a single dimension to the exclusion of others. To solve the problem, children need to keep in mind that an object (for example, Garfield) may simultaneously belong both to a subset (cats) and to a superset (animals). They find this difficult. Therefore, they reinterpret the question in a way that allows them to solve a problem that they do understand: whether there are more cats or more animals other than cats. This leads them to compare the number of cats to the number of dogs, and thus to say that there are more cats than animals.

Children's understanding of relations also grows considerably during the preoperational stage. However, their ability to focus on the relation that is relevant in the particular situation, and to screen out irrelevant ones, remains limited. To illustrate both the growth and the remaining deficiencies, Piaget (1952) presented preoperational children the type of *seriation problem* shown in Figure 2.5. He asked

1. Early in the Preoperational Stage
   If Asked to Seriate

Children Create

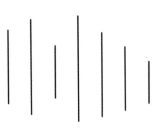
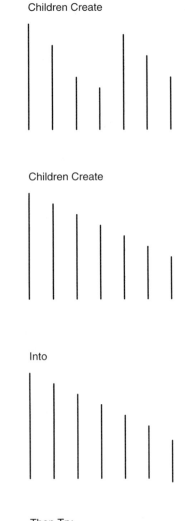

2. Later in the Preoperational Stage
   If Asked to Seriate

Children Create

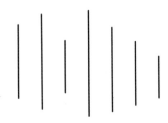

3. But: If Asked to Insert

Into

Children First Try

Then Try

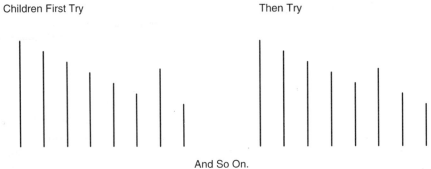

And So On.

FIGURE 2.5   Typical responses to seriation problems by children early and late in the preoperational stage.

them to arrange the sticks from shortest to longest in a single row. If they succeeded at this task, he presented them a second problem. Here they needed to insert a new stick of medium length at the appropriate point in the row they had made.

Early in the preoperational stage, between ages 2 and 4, children encounter great difficulty creating correct orderings. As in the first row of Figure 2.5, they might arrange two subsets of the sticks correctly, but not integrate the two into a single overall ordering. The shifting focus is similar to that shown when they first grouped together several small objects and then, after encountering a small triangle, started putting all triangles in the group.

Later in the preoperational stage, children can correctly order the lengths of the original set of sticks. However, they often fail to find the correct place to insert the additional stick without extensive trial and error. Piaget attributed this remaining difficulty to preoperational children's difficulty in simultaneously viewing the new stick as smaller than one stick and larger than another quite similar in size.

Understanding of classes and relations in the concrete operations period. Piaget contended that in the concrete operations period, children come to treat classes and relations as a single, unified system. Their attempts to solve *multiple classification problems* illustrate this development. Consider the problem in Figure 2.6. Children see intersecting rows of stimuli that vary along two dimensions, in this case shape (square, circular, or oblong) and color (black, white, or striped). The task is to choose an object to put in the blank space so that all nine objects are ordered along the two dimensions. This requires identifying the two relevant classes (shape and color) and choosing an object that maintains the relations among objects already established within the rows and columns of the matrix.

Inhelder and Piaget (1964) reported that 4- to 6-year-olds selected objects that included at least one of the desired dimensions on 85 percent of problems. However, they chose the single object that included both desired dimensions on only 15 percent. By 9 or 10 years of age, the large majority of children choose the object that maintains both dimensions, revealing an ability to consider classes and relations together.

Understanding of classes and relations in the formal operational period. Formal operational reasoning enables adolescents to think about relations among relations and about classes of classes. For example, they might first divide the students in their high school into a number of classes (nerds, jocks, skaters, preppies, druggies, etc.), and then construct higher order classes of the groups whose members tend to be friends with each other (e. g., preppies and jocks).

Formal operational reasoning also leads adolescents to interpret observed outcomes within the context of logically possible outcomes. This type of rea-

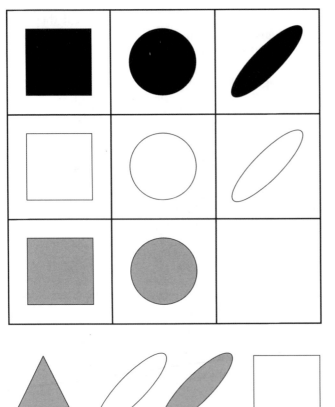

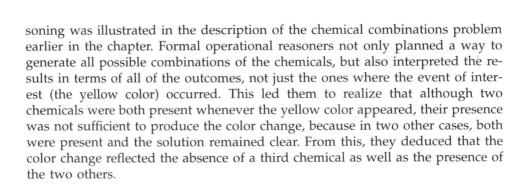

FIGURE 2.6   Type of matrix used to test children's understanding of multiple classification. The task was to decide which of the four objects at the bottom belonged in the empty square in the matrix (after Inhelder & Piaget, 1964).

soning was illustrated in the description of the chemical combinations problem earlier in the chapter. Formal operational reasoners not only planned a way to generate all possible combinations of the chemicals, but also interpreted the results in terms of all of the outcomes, not just the ones where the event of interest (the yellow color) occurred. This led them to realize that although two chemicals were both present whenever the yellow color appeared, their presence was not sufficient to produce the color change, because in two other cases, both were present and the solution remained clear. From this, they deduced that the color change reflected the absence of a third chemical as well as the presence of the two others.

A chronological summary.   It is easy to become confused among the numerous developmental changes Piaget described. Table 2.2 places some of the most important changes in relation to each other and may create a better feel for which types of changes occur when in development.

TABLE 2.2 Children's Thinking at Different Ages: The Piagetian Model

STAGE OF DEVELOPMENT	RELEVANT AGE RANGE	TYPICAL ACHIEVEMENTS AND LIMITATIONS
Sensorimotor Period (Birth to 2 years)	Birth to 1 month	Modification of reflexes to make them more adaptive.
	1 to 4 months	Primary circular reactions and coordination of actions.
	4 to 8 months	Secondary circular reactions. No searching for hidden objects.
	8 to 12 months	Coordination of secondary circular reactions. Baby retrieves hidden objects but continues searching where objects were previously found rather than where they were last hidden.
	12 to 18 months	Tertiary circular reactions. Baby systematically varies heights from which it drops things.
	18 to 24 months	Beginning of true mental representations. Deferred imitation.
Preoperational Period (2 to 7 years)	2 to 4 years	Developmental of symbolic capacities. Growth of language and mental imagery. Egocentric communication.
	4 to 7 years	Good language and mental imagery skills. Inability to represent transformations. Child focuses on single perceptual dimensions in conservation, class inclusion, time, seriation, and other problems.
Concrete Operational Period (7 to 12 years)	Whole period	Child can perform true mental operations, represent transformations as well as static states, and solve conservation, class inclusion, time, and many other problems. Child still has difficulty thinking of all possible combinations, as in the chemical problem, and of transformations of transformations.
Formal Operational Period (12 years through the rest of life)	Whole period	Adolescent can think about all possible outcomes, interpret particular events in terms of their relation to hypothetical events, and understand abstract concepts such as conservation of motion and chemical interactions.

AN EVALUATION OF PIAGET'S THEORY

How can we evaluate this rich and diverse theory of cognitive development? Some of the strengths of the theory were mentioned at the outset of the chapter. It provides us with a good feel for what children's thinking is like at different points in development. It addresses questions that have intrigued parents, teachers, philosophers, and scientists for hundreds of years. It surveys a remarkably broad spectrum of developments in children's thinking and covers the entire age span from infancy through adolescence. It includes countless surprising observations of how children think.

With these general virtues in mind, we can consider three more specific questions. How accurately does the theory describe the particulars of children's thinking at different ages? How useful are its stages as descriptions and explanations of children's thinking? How valid are its general trait characterizations of children's thinking, such as that preoperational children are egocentric?

How Accurately Does the Theory Describe Particular Aspects of Children's Thinking?

Piaget's theory makes many specific claims about how children think and reason at different ages. How have these claims held up in the face of subsequent research?

The most basic issue for any scientific theory is whether other people can replicate the findings on which the theory is based. Piaget's observations were so surprising that many early experiments were conducted simply to replicate them. These replication experiments used larger, more representative samples of children and more standardized versions of Piaget's tasks, but otherwise closely resembled his approach.

In general, the attempts to replicate were successful. Larger samples of American, British, Canadian, Australian aboriginal, and Chinese children tested in the 1960s and 1970s showed the same type of reasoning that Piaget's small samples of Swiss children had almost half a century earlier (Corman & Escalona, 1969; Dasen, 1973; Dodwell, 1960; Elkind, 1961a, 1961b; Goodnow, 1962; Lovell, 1961; Uzgiris, 1964). Children in non-Western societies reached the stages at older ages, but when they did, they showed the expected type of reasoning. This was especially true for the sensorimotor, preoperational, and concrete operational periods. Formal operational reasoning seems to be exhibited by some adolescents, but only by a minority of them, even in advanced societies, at least on the scientific reasoning problem typically used to assess formal operations (Byrnes, 1988; Kuhn, et al., 1995).

Can we accept these replications at face value? Perhaps the immature reasoning that children display in many situations is due not to their reasoning being immature, but rather to the verbal methods used by both Piaget and the replication studies underestimating their knowledge. Critics of such methods argue that young children's inarticulateness often creates a falsely pessimistic impression of their cognitive capabilities (e.g., Brainerd, 1978). Just because children cannot explain their reasoning does not mean that the reasoning itself is deficient.

It now is apparent, however, that young children show similar reasoning when tested with nonverbal versions of Piaget's tasks. I have been involved in one such series of experiments in which I employed a nonverbal method to examine a number of Piaget's tasks, among them balance scale problems; time, speed, and distance problems; and conservation of liquid quantity, solid quantity, and number problems (Siegler, 1976, 1978, 1981; Siegler & Richards, 1979). On each of these tasks, children reasoned much as would have been expected from Piaget's descriptions.

A third question is whether children possess conceptual understanding not revealed by Piaget's experiments. Here the situation is different. Throughout development, children seem to have basic understandings not evident in their performance on Piaget's problems. Many of the demonstrations of children's early understandings have been extremely clever.

Consider Baillargeon's (1987) experiment on object permanence. Piaget claimed that infants younger than 8 months do not realize that objects continue to exist when they disappear from view. Baillargeon developed a more sensitive measure that showed that even with infants as young as 4 months, out of sight does not mean totally out of mind. Her experiment involved placing a box behind a wooden board (Figure 2.7). An axle went horizontally through the middle of the board so that pushing the board made it swing. At first, the board was in a position where the box was clearly visible. Then, the experimenter set the

FIGURE 2.7 *Baillargeon's object permanence task. After being habituated to the drawbridge swinging through 180 degrees and seeing the barrier placed in its path, infants look longer at the impossible event, where the drawbridge seems to rotate through the space occupied by the now-hidden barrier than at the possible event, where it stops at the barrier's location (after Baillargeon, 1987). Copyright © 1987 by the American Psychological Association. Reprinted with permission.*

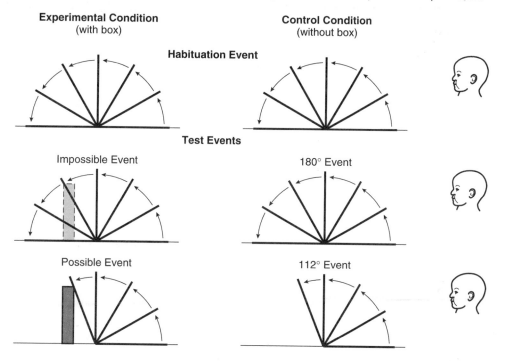

board swinging, which hid the box from the child's line of sight. In the physically possible condition, the swinging board reached the box, which was near
the apex of its swing anyway, and then swung the other way. In the physically
impossible condition, the board appeared to swing right through the place
where the box had been. (This effect was accomplished with trick lighting and
mirrors.) Despite the box's not being visible anymore, the 4-month-olds appeared surprised when they saw the seemingly impossible event. They looked
much longer than they did when the physically possible event occurred. They
apparently thought the board's swinging should be impeded by the box, even
when they could not see it.

The results are not unique to this particular method; Baillargeon (1993)
demonstrated that 3½-month-olds showed similar surprise when the upper half
of a rabbit seemed to disappear as the rabbit moved across a window where, if
not for trickery, it would have been visible. In other experiments, she has shown
that infants can represent as many as three hidden objects simultaneously, and
that they can represent not only the fact that an object continues to exist, but also
its approximate height and location. Thus, children as young as 4 months possess some understanding of object permanence.

The demonstrations of earlier-than-predicted cognitive competence are not
limited to sensorimotor acquisitions. Preschoolers also show rudimentary understanding of concepts that Piaget believed were too advanced for them. Consider conservation of taste and of weight, two concepts that Piaget believed were
too difficult for preoperational stage children. However, when 3- to 5-year-olds
see sugar dissolved in a cup of water, most believe that despite the sugar not
being visible, the water will taste sweet, that it will continue to taste sweet in
the future, and that it will weigh more than it did when no sugar was in the cup
(Au, Sidle, & Rollins, 1993). To explain their views, the 3- to 5-year-olds advanced explanations indicating that the sugar still exists in tiny invisible particles that influence the taste and weight of the solution even though it looks
identical to the solution with no sugar. Thus, children in the preoperational stage
do have some understanding of conservation of taste and of weight.

Discovery of unsuspected cognitive strengths in infants and young children has been one of *the* leading stories in the recent study of cognitive development. It is interesting to consider why these competencies are being
discovered now. One reason is the development of clever new methods for finding out what children understand. Another reason is that a broader range of
children's thinking is being considered. The research of Gelman and her colleagues illustrates this trend (Gelman, 1990; Gelman & Gallistel, 1978; Miller &
Gelman, 1983). Piaget focused on preschoolers' frequent failures on number
conservation tasks and concluded that they do not grasp the concept of number. Gelman's research indicated that whether or not preschoolers grasp the concept of number, they know a great deal about numbers. They count accurately,
and in a way that suggests understanding of the principles underlying counting; they know the effects that addition and subtraction have on small collec-

tions of objects; they know which numbers are bigger and which smaller; and so on. The number of insightful demonstrations of early competence is too large to review in any detail here. Examples include work on children's understanding of causality (Ahn, Kalish, Medin, & Gelman, 1995; Leslie, 1988; Oakes & Cohen, 1995), classification (Gelman & Coley, 1990; Waxman, 1990; Waxman & Hatch, 1992), space (Blades & Spencer, 1994; Huttenlocher, Newcombe, & Sandberg, 1994), time (Bauer & Mandler, 1992; Friedman, 1990; 1995; Levin, 1989), and properties of objects (Kotovsky & Baillargeon, 1994; Spelke, Breinlinger, Macomber, & Jacobson, 1992). In short, although Piaget's observations reveal a great deal about how young children think, and although they can be replicated using both verbal and nonverbal methods, they tend to underestimate the children's competence.

How Stagelike Is Children's Thinking?

Stage models such as Piaget's imply that children's thinking changes qualitatively from one stage to another; that within any one stage, their reasoning is similar across diverse problems; and that they are unable to learn to think in ways associated with the next higher stage until they are near that stage or in it (Brainerd, 1978; Flavell, 1971). How well do these characterizations fit what is known today about children's thinking?

Qualitative changes. Whether children's thinking undergoes qualitative change depends in large part on how closely you look at it. When viewed from afar, many changes in children's thinking appear discontinuous; when viewed from close up, the same changes often appear as part of a continuous, gradual progression. Again, development of object permanence can be used to illustrate the general point. As noted previously, infants younger than 7 or 8 months old often do not reach for objects when they see them hidden. Under the same conditions, older infants almost always do reach for the objects. Piaget interpreted these results to mean that the older infants understand that objects have a permanent existence and that the younger ones do not.

Newer evidence suggests a different interpretation: that the change is not as sudden as Piaget believed. Infants as young as 6 months old succeed on the classic Piagetian object permanence task if allowed to reach immediately after the object is hidden. The longer that infants must wait before trying to get the object, the older they must be before they reach for it (Diamond, 1985). Gradual improvements in memory for the locations of hidden objects, rather than a sudden insight that objects continue to exist, seems to underlie the change.

Even if we believe that infants experience some type of insight that elevates their understanding of the continued existence of hidden objects, it is still clear that after this insight, they continue to expand their ability to locate such objects. Reaching for objects that have been placed under opaque containers is part of a more general cognitive trend—improved skill in searching the physi-

cal environment for lost or hidden objects. These search skills develop over a long period; even 4-year-olds err on some hidden-object problems. Further, when older children err, their mistakes parallel those of younger children. When presented with three, rather than two, potential hiding places, infants, 1-year-olds, and 4-year-olds most often make the same type of errors. They look at locations where they have found the object previously, rather than locations where they never have found it. The frequency of errors declines, but the type of errors remains the same. (For interesting articles on young children's abilities to search physical environments and find missing objects, see Baker-Ward & Ornstein, 1988; DeLoache, 1987; 1991; 1993; Sophian, 1984; Wellman, 1988; Wellman, Cross, & Bartsch, 1986).

A branch of mathematics known as *catastrophe theory* provides justification for viewing development as both continuous and discontinuous. Catastrophe theory examines sudden changes such as the collapse of bridges. The forces that lead to bridges collapsing often build up slowly over a period of years. The visible collapse, however, can be breathtakingly sudden. Analogously, despite the seeming abruptness of cognitive progress when a boy solves a problem one day that he could not solve the day before, the progress may be based on years of gradually improving understanding. In the boy, as in the bridge, the change can be viewed as either a continuous process of small, invisible alterations or as a discontinuous shift from one state to another.

Similar reasoning on different problems.   Saying that children are in a certain stage of reasoning implies that their reasoning across many tasks shares that stage's characteristics. Within Piaget's theory, an 8-year-old ideally would grasp all concrete-operations-level concepts—conservation of liquid quantity, class inclusion, seriation, and so on—and would fail to grasp all formal-operations-level concepts—thinking in terms of all possible combinations, conservation of motion, and so on.

It has become increasingly clear that this view does not accurately characterize children's thinking. Consider three concrete-operations-level concepts: conservation of number, conservation of solid quantity, and conservation of weight. Theoretically, all of these should be mastered simultaneously; a child should understand either all or none of them. Actually, however, most children master Piaget's number conservation task at around age 6, his solid quantity conservation task at around age 8, and his weight conservation task at around age 10 (Elkind, 1961a; Katz & Beilin, 1976; Miller, 1976). These data do not support the idea of concurrent development, even within the concept of conservation.

Despite the evidence against the view that children generally reason similarly across many problems, consistencies of reasoning across tasks continue to be of great interest. The motivation is rooted in everyday observations of children's reasoning. There seems to be something characteristic in 2-year-olds' reasoning that distinguishes it from 5-year-olds'; something in 5-year-olds' reasoning that distinguishes it from 10-year-olds'; and so on. That is, children of a given age do seem to reason in a characteristic way in different contexts.

In one attempt to address the issue, Flavell (1982) hypothesized that the amount of consistency of reasoning across tasks may depend on when we observe the reasoning. Children seem to reason more similarly across different concepts when they are just beginning to understand them than when they understand them better. For example, 5-year-olds solve a large variety of problems that they are just beginning to understand by identifying a single relevant dimension of the problem and focusing on it. On conservation of liquid quantity, they predict that whichever glass has the taller liquid column also has more water, regardless of the cross-sectional areas. On conservation of solid quantity, they predict that whichever clay sausage is longer also has more clay, again regardless of the cross-sectional areas. In judging which side of a balance scale will tip, they rely entirely on relative amounts of weight, ignoring distance of the weights from the fulcrum. They exhibit similar reasoning with concepts as diverse as temperature, happiness, and morality (Case, 1985; 1992a; Ferretti, Butterfield, Cahn, & Kerkman, 1985; Levin, Wilkening, & Dembo, 1984; Siegler, 1981; Strauss, 1982).

In contrast, the ages at which children solve these problems correctly varies a great deal. Even 9-year-olds generally can solve conservation of liquid and solid quantity problems; even college students often cannot solve balance scale problems. Differing amounts of experience with the problems, differences in the ease of drawing analogies to better-understood problems, and differences in the complexity of the most advanced solution formulas contribute to these differences in age of mastery.

Another potential source of consistency in children's reasoning is the level of their most advanced reasoning (Fischer, 1980; Fischer & Bidell, 1991; Halford, 1982; 1993). For example, the most advanced thinking of 9-year-olds might involve single operations. This would mean that none of their thinking involves operations on operations (as in the formal operations period). However, it would not mean that they solve correctly all problems that can be solved using single operations. Whether they solve a given problem depends on how much experience they had had with it, whether they were familiar with related problems, whether it occurred in a familiar context, and so on. In sum, unities in children's reasoning may be most apparent in their early reasoning, when they have little knowledge of the concepts involved, and in the level of the most advanced reasoning of which they are capable.

Can development be accelerated? Piaget's views concerning the possibility of accelerating cognitive development through training are among his most controversial. Some of his comments indicate that no training could be successful. Others suggest that training might at times be effective, but only if the child already possesses some understanding of the concept and if the training procedure involves active interaction with materials.

In fact, young children can learn more than Piaget thought they could, and they can benefit from a greater variety of instructional techniques (Beilin, 1977; Field, 1987). The findings dovetail with the unsuspected early competence that children have been found to have even without training. Not only do children understand more than previously thought, they also can learn more.

It is important not to throw out the baby with the bathwater, however. Although young children can learn to solve these problems, they often find doing so exceptionally difficult. Older children who cannot yet solve the same problems typically learn them much more easily. It now is indisputable that young children can learn concepts once thought to be "too advanced" for their age group. What we still don't understand is why, when two children both don't understand a concept, the older child so often can learn it more easily.

(handwritten margin note: but can't understand why)

How Well Do Piaget's General Characterizations Fit Children's Thinking?

In addition to describing children's thinking in terms of particular examples of their reasoning at particular stages (e.g., "Preoperational stage children think that the glass with the taller liquid column must have more water"), Piaget also characterized children's thinking in terms of intellectual traits. For example, he described preoperational stage children as being egocentric, precausal, semilogical, and perceptually oriented. These terms fit in some ways, but not in all. The characterization of preoperational children as egocentric illustrates many of the issues.

Recall from the discussion of egocentric communication and the cartoon of the two children talking past each other that 2- to 4-year-olds are not very skilled communicators. They often ignore what other people say to them and have trouble understanding other people's viewpoints. These types of observations led Piaget to label their thinking "egocentric."

But in other situations, young children communicate nonegocentrically. If you ask 3-year-olds to show you their drawings, they hold the side with the artwork toward you. If they were completely egocentric, they would hold the coloring toward themselves, because they would assume that what they see is what you see. Similarly, even 2- and 3-year-olds practice deception. For example, Sullivan & Winner (1993) described a 2-year-old who feigned tears when his aunt would not play with him; when the aunt came over, the child said to his mother "I tricked her. I made her think I was sad" (p. 160). If the 2-year-old believed that the aunt knew exactly what he knew, how could he "trick" her?

Similar demonstrations have shown that preschoolers' representation of space also is not entirely egocentric. To measure spatial egocentrism, Piaget used tasks such as the three-mountains problem shown in Figure 2.3. Such problems require not only taking another perspective but also choosing between competing frames of reference: the one that children actually see and the one they are asked to imagine seeing from the other vantage point. Even adults find such choices between competing frames of reference to be difficult (Rieser & Garing, 1991). In contrast, when the competing frame of reference is eliminated (by covering the original arrangement), and children are given ways of expressing the concepts "left" and "right" (by putting a sticker on one of their hands and referring to the sticker side and the non-sticker side), even 3-year-olds can take spatial perspectives other than their own (Newcombe & Huttenlocher, 1992). This does not mean that they can take other people's perspectives as well as older children. After all, older children succeed on the three-mountain task even when a competing frame of reference is present. The finding does mean, however, that under less-demanding conditions, 3-year-olds can take perspectives other than their own.

Conversely, people well beyond the preoperational period continue to be "at risk" for egocentrism (Flavell, Miller, & Miller, 1993). A classic demonstration of this involved a situation analogous to a phone conversation. Two children were seated opposite each other at a table with a board between them; thus, they could not see each other. Each child was presented identical sets of pictures, with each picture containing an irregular design. The speaker had to describe one of the pictures so that the listener could figure out which one was being described (Krauss & Glucksberg, 1969).

Not surprisingly, older children communicate which picture they have in mind more effectively than do younger ones. More surprising, even 8- and 9-year-olds often have difficulty overcoming their knowledge of what they are describing to generate a description that will allow the other child to understand. Further, children well beyond the preoperational period experience difficulty knowing who is to blame for the missed communication—whether the message is inadequate or whether the listener simply failed to respond properly to it. (See Beal, 1988; Beal & Belgrad, 1990; Robinson & Robinson, 1981; Sodian, 1988; Waters & Tinsley, 1985; and Whitehurst & Sonnenschein, 1981; for detailed discussions of egocentric communication.) There seems little doubt that young children often behave more egocentrically than older ones. Labeling an age group "egocentric" is too strong, though. It leads us to ignore both the ways that younger children's thinking is not egocentric and the ways that older children's thinking is.

The Current Status of Piaget's Theory

If Piaget's theory underestimates young children's reasoning abilities, overestimates older children's reasoning abilities, and describes children's thinking in terms that are misleading as well as revealing, why pay so much attention to it? The simple reason is that with all of its shortcomings, the theory still gives us a good feel for how children think. It also points us in the right direction for learning more about children's thinking. Piaget recognized the intelligence in infants' early activities. In making these discoveries, he raised the issue of what additional capabilities infants might have, an issue that has led to many additional discoveries about infants' thinking. His estimate of the degree of unity in children's thinking was too high, but he discovered some important unities and pointed to the importance of searching for more of them. Finally, Piaget's basic questions are the right ones. What capabilities do infants possess at birth? What capabilities do they possess at later points in development? What processes lead to the remarkable increases in their understanding that occur with development? The remainder of this book is an attempt to answer these questions.

SUMMARY

Piaget's theory remains a dominant force in developmental psychology, despite the fact that much of it was formulated half a century ago. Some of the reasons for its lasting appeal are the important acquisitions it describes, the large span of childhood it encompasses, and the reliability and charm of many of its observations.

At the most general level, Piaget's theory focused on the development of intelligence. The purpose of intellectual development was to allow children to adapt to the environment. This adaptation was achieved through generating progressively more accurate and encompassing representations of reality.

Piaget's general depiction included four stages of development: the *sensorimotor, preoperational, concrete operational*, and *formal operational periods*. The sensorimotor period occupies the age range between birth and 2 years, the preoperational period between age 2 and age 6 or 7, the concrete operational period between age 6 or 7 and age 11 or 12, and the formal operational period from early adolescence to the end of life. Each period includes large changes in understanding of such important concepts as conservation, classification, and relations.

Piaget also identified three basic developmental processes: *assimilation, accommodation*, and *equilibration*. Assimilation refers to the means by which children interpret incoming information to make it understandable within their existing mental structures. Accommodation refers to the ways in which children's current understandings change in response to new experience. Equilibration is a three-step process that includes assimilation and accommodation. First, children are in a state of equilibrium. Then, inability to assimilate new information leads to their becoming aware of shortcomings in their current understanding. Finally, their mental structure accommodates to the new information in a way that creates a more advanced equilibrium.

During the sensorimotor period, infants acquire primary, secondary, and tertiary circular reactions, in which their actions become more deliberate and more systematic and extend beyond their bodies. They also acquire a precursor of conservation—the object permanence concept—in which they realize that objects continue to exist even if they move out of sight. They also form simple understandings of classes and relations.

In the preoperational period, children become able to represent their ideas through language and mental imagery. Despite this development, Piaget primarily emphasized what preoperational children cannot do. He noted that 5-year-olds usually fail conservation, class inclusion, and seriation problems. He attributed such failures to the children's focusing on perceptual appearances rather than transformations, to their being egocentric, and to their centering on a single dimension rather than considering multiple dimensions simultaneously.

In the concrete operations period, children master these concepts and many others. They become able to represent transformations and to integrate multiple sources of information. These advances allow children to master such concepts as conservation of liquid and solid quantity, time, seriation, and class inclusion.

The formal operations period, according to Piaget, brings the ability to think in terms of all possible outcomes and to view actual outcomes within this framework of logical possibilities. Children in this stage can perform systematic experiments, a skill made possible by sophisticated understanding of classes and relations. In sum, their reasoning comes to resemble that of scientists.

Piaget made a number of controversial statements about what children know at different points in development, about the stages of development that they pass through, and about general characteristics of their thinking. When given either the original or nonverbal versions of Piaget's problems, children typically reason much as he described. However, they appear to have important cognitive capabilities that he did not detect.

Piaget's stage descriptions predict that children think in qualitatively different ways in different periods of development, that they reason similarly about diverse concepts, and that they cannot learn modes of thought much more advanced than those that characterize their current stage. Each of these views contains a certain amount of truth, but also has certain problems. When viewed from a distance, many developments appear to represent qualitative changes. However, when examined closely, the same changes often appear to be part of a gradual progression, with important precursors developing earlier and refinements and extensions continuing for years after. In general, the consistency of reasoning across tasks that Piaget predicted has not been found. However, considerable consistency has been apparent in children's early conceptual understanding. Young children do not learn as rapidly as older children, but it is nonetheless possible for them to acquire a great many concepts that are well beyond the understanding typical of children their age.

Piaget also described children in terms of general intellectual traits such as egocentrism. These trait descriptions fit young children's thinking in many ways, but not in all. For example, although 5-year-olds are egocentric in some situations, they and even younger children behave nonegocentrically in other situations. Moreover, even older children and adults sometimes behave egocentrically. The trait descriptions thus seem to be in the right ballpark, but to gloss over exceptions. More generally, Piaget's theory continues to be of interest because it communicates a good feel for children's thinking and because it asks the right questions.

RECOMMENDED READINGS

Baillargeon, R. (1994). How do infants learn about the physical world? *Current Directions in Psychological Science*, 5, 133–39. This article provides a clear and interesting description of recent research on infants' impressive cognitive competence.

Carey, S., & Gelman, R. (Eds.) (1991). *The epigenesis of mind: Essays on biology and cognition*. Hillsdale, NJ: Erlbaum. A group of leading students of cognitive development explore one of the issues that motivated Piaget's research—how biology and experience interact to produce cognitive growth—but with much more emphasis on innate and early-developing knowledge than in Piaget's theory.

Flavell, J. H. (1963). *The developmental psychology of Jean Piaget*. New York: Van Nostrand. The classic summary of Piaget's work from 1925–1960.

Moshman, D. (in press). Cognitive development beyond childhood. To appear in D. Kuhn & R. S. Siegler (Eds.), W. Damon (Series Ed.) *Handbook of child psychology (5th ed.): Vol. 2: Cognition, perception, and language*. New York: Wiley. This article provides a comprehensive and up-to-date review of the many changes in scientific and logical reasoning that take place during adolescence and afterward.

Piaget, J. (1952). *The child's concept of number*. New York: W. W. Norton. In this book. Piaget describes his classic experiments on class inclusion, seriation, conservation of liquid quantity, and conservation of number.

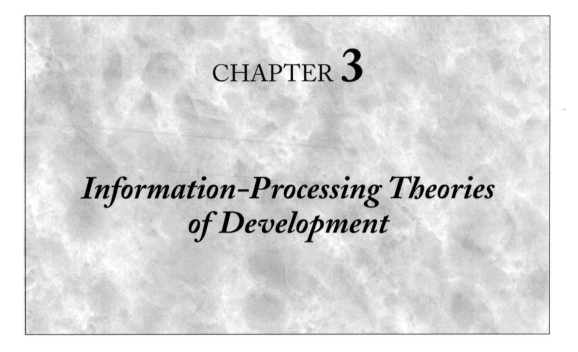

CHAPTER 3

Information-Processing Theories of Development

Scene: Daughter and father in their yard. A playmate rides in on a bike.
  Child: Daddy, would you unlock the basement door?
  Father: Why?
  C: 'Cause I want to ride my bike.
  F: Your bike is in the garage.
  C: But my socks are in the dryer. (Klahr, 1978, pp. 181–2)

What thinking underlay this child's enigmatic comments? Klahr, a prominent information-processing theorist, built the following model of the thinking that led to her initial request for him to unlock the basement door:

Top goal: I want to ride my bike.
  Constraint: I need shoes to ride comfortably.
  Fact: I'm barefoot.
    Subgoal 1: Get my sneakers.
    Fact: The sneakers are in the yard.
    Fact: They're uncomfortable on bare feet.
      Subgoal 2: Get my socks.
      Fact: The sock drawer was empty this morning.
      Inference: The socks probably are in the dryer.
        Subgoal 3: Get them from the dryer.
        Fact: The dryer is in the basement.

Subgoal 4: Go to the basement.
Fact: It's quicker to go through the yard entrance.
Fact: The yard entrance always is locked.
  Subgoal 5: Unlock the door to the basement.
  Fact: Daddies have the keys to everything.
  Subgoal 6: Ask daddy to unlock the door.

As this example suggests, the information-processing approach to development speaks to the essential tension within children's thinking, the tension produced by children ceaselessly striving to reach their goals despite patchy knowledge, limited processing capacity, and obstacles posed by the external world. The particular strategy used in the story was *means-ends analysis*, which involves repeatedly comparing one's current state with one's goal and then taking steps to reduce the distance between them. In other situations, children use other strategies. To overcome their limited memory capacities, they use strategies such as *rehearsal* (repeating material over and over before recalling it, as when trying to remember a phone number). To overcome their limited knowledge, they use the tools provided by the culture in which they live: older children and adults who will answer their questions, dictionaries, encyclopedias, calculators, and other devices.

Information-processing theories of development vary among themselves, but they all share several basic assumptions. The most fundamental assumption is that thinking is information processing. Rather than focusing on stages of development, they focus on the information that children represent, the processes that they apply to the information, and the memory limits that constrain the amount of information they can represent and process. Cognitive growth is analyzed in terms of age-related changes in these capabilities. Information-processing analyses generally are more precise than those of stage approaches; the detailed analysis of goals, subgoals, knowledge, and inferences within Klahr's model of his daughter's thinking is characteristic.

A second defining characteristic of information-processing theories of development is an emphasis on *precise analysis of change mechanisms*. Two critical goals are to identify the change mechanisms that contribute most to development and to specify exactly how these change mechanisms work together to produce cognitive growth. The flip side of this emphasis on how development occurs is an emphasis on the cognitive limits that prevent development from occurring more rapidly than it does. Thus, information-processing theories attempt to explain both how children of given ages have come as far as they have and why they have not gone further.

A third assumption of most information-processing approaches is that change is produced by a process of continuous *self-modification*. That is, the outcomes generated by the child's own activities change the way the child will think in the future. For example, in Siegler and Shipley's (1995) model of strategy choice, use of alternative strategies creates increasing knowledge concerning

the effectiveness of each strategy which, in turn, changes the strategies that are used. Such self-modifying processes eliminate the need to account for special age-defined transition periods, as in Piaget's proposed transition from the concrete operations to the formal operations stage around age 12. Instead, children's thinking is viewed as continuously changing at all ages.

What is the relation of information-processing approaches to alternative views, such as the Piagetian approach? The two approaches have quite a bit in common. Both are aimed at answering the same fundamental questions: "What develops?" and "How does development occur?" Both try to identify children's cognitive capabilities and limits at various points in development. Both try to explain how later, more-advanced understandings grow out of earlier, more-primitive ones.

The two approaches also differ in important ways, though. Information-processing approaches place greater emphasis on the role of processing limitations, strategies for overcoming the limitations, and knowledge about specific content. There also is a greater emphasis on precise analyses of change and on the contribution of ongoing cognitive activity to that change. These differences have led to a greater use of formalisms, such as computer simulations and flow diagrams, that allow information processing theorists to model in detail how thinking proceeds. A final difference is that information-processing theories assume that our understanding of how children think can be greatly enriched by knowledge of how adults think. The underlying belief is that just as we can more deeply understand our own adult thinking when we appreciate how it developed, we also can better understand the development of children's thinking when we know where the development is going.

This chapter is divided into two main sections. In the first, we examine the basic information-processing framework. This framework provides a way of thinking about the cognitive systems of both children and adults. In the second main section, we consider five information-processing theories that focus on development. No one of these theories covers the huge expanse of topics and ages encompassed by Piaget's theory. On the other hand, each provides more precise and complete characterizations of particular aspects of development than Piaget did. The chapter's organization is outlined in Table 3.1.

TABLE 3.1   Chapter Outline

I.   An Overview of the Information-Processing System
   A.   Structural Characteristics
   B.   Processes
II. Information-Processing Theories of Development
   A.   Neo-Piagetian Theories
   B.   Psychometric Theories
   C.   Production System Theories
   D.   Connectionist Theories
   E.   Theories of Cognitive Evolution
III. Summary

AN OVERVIEW OF THE INFORMATION-PROCESSING SYSTEM

Any cognitive theory must come to grips with two basic characteristics of human cognition. First, our thinking is limited, both in the amount of information that we can attend to simultaneously and in the speed with which we can process the information. Second, our thinking is flexible, capable of adapting to constantly changing goals, circumstances, and task demands. Information-processing theories have attempted to come to grips with this dual nature of cognition by focusing on both *structural characteristics*, which determine the limits within which thinking occurs, and *processes*, which provide the means for flexible adaptation to a constantly changing world.

Structural Characteristics

Structural characteristics of the information-processing system provide its basic organization. They sometimes are referred to as the *cognitive architecture*; the analogy is to the architectural plan for a building, which specifies its main characteristics, but not the more detailed features. Structural features of the cognitive system tend to be relatively enduring; the same basic organization is believed to be maintained throughout development. Structural features are also universal; all children have the same basic cognitive organization, though the efficiency with which the different parts operate varies across individuals and age groups. This basic organization is often viewed within a three-part framework: sensory memory, working memory, and long-term memory.

Sensory memory. People possess a special capacity for briefly retaining relatively large amounts of information that they have just encountered. This capacity is often labeled *sensory memory*. Sperling (1960) established several characteristics of sensory memory that influence processing of visual information. He presented college students a three-by-four matrix of letters for one-twentieth of a second. When asked immediately after the presentation to name the letters, the college students typically recalled four or five, about 40 percent of the list. Then Sperling changed the procedure in a small but important way. Rather than having the students recall all of the letters, he asked them to recall only the letters in one row. Since it was impossible to anticipate the identity of the row, the students needed to process all 12 letters, just as in the original task. However, requiring them to recite the contents of only one row eliminated their need to retain the information while they named the first few letters.

Sperling found that when the experimenter indicated which row to recall immediately after the display was shut off, the college students recalled 80 percent of the letters in the row. When the row's identity was indicated one-third of a second after the display was turned off, their recall declined to 55 percent. When it was indicated one second after, performance declined to the original 40 percent. Sperling's interpretation was that a one-twentieth-second exposure was sufficient for letters to create a visual *icon* (a literal copy of the original stimulus), but that the icon faded within one-third of a second and disappeared after a second. These estimates remain reasonable in light of subsequent research.

Sperling's clever method led to a surprising discovery about children's sensory memory: The sensory memory of a 5-year-old is as great as that of an adult. In one study (Morrison, Holmes, & Haith, 1974), 5-year-olds and adults were presented with an array of seven geometric figures. The screen then went blank, and after a one-twentieth-second delay, a marker pointed to one of the seven positions. The child or adult needed to name the object that had been in that position. The 5-year-olds' recall was as good as adults', suggesting that the capacity of their sensory memory is equivalent to adults'.

Working memory. Working memory is where active thinking occurs: constructing new strategies, computing solutions to arithmetic problems, comprehending what we read, and so on. Its operation involves combining information coming into sensory memory with information stored in long-term memory and transforming that information into new forms. For example, when we read a book, working memory combines the sensory information about the words on the page with long-term-memory representations of the meanings of the words and uses the data to represent the meaning of the text as a whole.

The operation of working memory is limited in several ways. The first is its capacity, the number of symbols it can operate on at one time. This number is not large; it is usually estimated to be between three and seven units. Being 7 ± 2 more precise than this is difficult, because the exact numbers depend on the particulars of the task on which the capacity is measured. For example, estimates of capacity tend to be larger when they are based on the number of numbers that can be maintained in memory than when based on the number of letters that can be maintained (Dempster, 1981).

The limit on working-memory capacity is a limit on the number of meaningful units (chunks) that can be operated on rather than on the number of physical units. A letter, a number, a word, or a familiar phrase can function as a single chunk, because each is a single unit of meaning. Thus, it is as easy to remember a set of three unrelated words with nine letters (e.g., *hit, red, foot*) as to remember three unrelated letters (e.g., *q, f, r*) (Miller, 1956).

The rate at which information is lost from working memory also limits cognitive functioning. Material ordinarily is lost within 15 to 30 seconds. However, at least with verbal information such as words or numbers, rehearsal can maintain the information in working memory for a longer time.

Older children can maintain considerably more information in working memory than can younger ones. A large part of the reason appears to be the older children's more rapid rate of rehearsal. In general, the faster that both adults and children can rehearse verbal material, the more material they can maintain in working memory (Baddeley & Hitch, 1974; Baddeley, 1986). Faster

Articulation
Rate.

rehearsal means less time between repetitions of a given word, and thus less likelihood that the word will be forgotten before it is rehearsed again. As shown in Figure 3.1, rate of pronunciation of words is closely related to number of words that can be maintained in working memory. Older children's greater speed of pronunciation appears to be a large part of the reason why they can maintain more material in working memory (Hitch & Towse, 1995).

Working memory appears to include separate storage capacities for verbal and spatial information, together with an executive processor that coordinates their operation and helps separate the two types of information (Baddeley, 1986). Development of working memory appears to involve both changes in the amount of information of each type that can be remembered and increasingly effective separation between the two. Evidence comes from a study in which 8-year-olds, 10-year-olds, and college students were presented either a series of digits, which would usually be coded verbally, or a series of locations of Xs on a tic-tac-toe grid, which would usually be coded spatially (Hale, Bronik, & Fry, 1996). The main task was to remember the digits or the locations of the Xs in the order they were presented. However, participants also needed to execute a secondary task, which required either a verbal response (naming the color of the digits or Xs) or a spatial one (pointing to the color of each digit or X within a spatial array of colors).

Not surprisingly, undergraduates recalled more information than 10-year-olds, and the 10-year-olds more than 8-year-olds. More interesting, at all ages, having to perform the spatial secondary task interfered to the greatest degree with recall of the spatial information and having to perform the verbal secondary task interfered most heavily with the verbal task. This finding supported the view that spatial and verbal information are represented separately in working memory. Especially interesting, at age 8 but not thereafter, having to do a spatial secondary task also interfered with ability to recall verbal material, and having to do a verbal secondary task interfered with ability to recall spatial material. This suggests that not until age 10 do children cleanly separate verbal from spatial information in working memory.

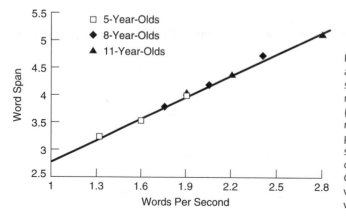

FIGURE 3.1   Memory spans of 5-, 8-, and 11-year-olds for unrelated, orally presented words as a function of articulation rate and number of syllables in words (numerals next to data points indicate number of syllables in word). For example, 11-year-olds could pronounce 2.8 single-syllable words per second and could remember about five such words. Older children tend both to pronounce words faster and to remember more words (from Hitch & Towse, 1995).

Long-term memory. Even young children are able to remember a vast assortment of experiences and facts about the world. Some of their knowledge is about specific episodes, such as their feelings when they wandered around the playground on their first day of school. Other knowledge is about enduring qualities of the world, such as that a nickel is worth five pennies. Yet other knowledge concerns procedures, such as how to ride a bicycle. These varied types of knowledge are the contents of long-term memory.

Unlike sensory and working memory, there are no limits on either how much information can be maintained in long-term memory or how long the information can stay there. Consider an experiment on recognition of faces in high school yearbooks (Bahrick, Bahrick, & Wittlinger, 1975). People were asked 35 years after graduation to recognize which yearbook pictures were of people in their high school class and which were of people from a different high school. In spite of all of the time that had passed, people correctly recognized 90 percent of the pictures. Thus, the name *long-term memory* is truly a fitting one.

An interesting property of the way people store information in long-term memory is that the storage is not in all-or-none form. Rather, people store information in separable units and can retrieve some units without retrieving others. This quality has been demonstrated in adults in experiments on the tip-of-the-tongue phenomenon. When adults can almost but not quite remember a word, they often can recall several of its characteristics: its first letter, its number of syllables, a word it sounds like, and so on (e.g., Brown & McNeil, 1966). I do not know of any formal research on the topic, but everyday observations of my own children lead me to suspect that the description applies to children's storage of information in long-term memory as well. For example, in trying to remember a friend who had moved away, my then 6-year-old daughter said, "She was from South America, she had black hair, she was just as silly as I am, why can't I remember her name?" A few minutes later, she succeeded in recalling the friend's name, Gabriella.

Processes

Processes are used to actively manipulate information in sensory, working, and long-term memory. Two processes that play particularly important roles in cognitive development are automatization and encoding.

The role of automatization. Processes vary considerably in how much attention they require. Those that require a great deal of attention are often labeled *controlled*, whereas those that require little if any attention are labeled *automatic*. The amount of attention required is influenced both by the type of information being processed and by the amount of experience the child has had processing that type of material. Some types of information inherently require less attention than others. However, even with processes that at first require a great deal of attention, practice reduces the amount that is needed.

Automatic processing is important in development in that it provides an initial basis for learning about the world. One example involves frequency information, that is, data on how often various objects and events have been encountered. People retain this information even when they are not trying to do so. Thus, we have a good sense of the relative frequency with which letters of the alphabet appear, although no one tries to remember such trivia. Recall of such information is influenced neither by instructions to remember nor by practice in trying to remember it. Level of recall also is equivalent over a wide age range. Children as young as 5-year-olds are as proficient as college students in retaining frequency information (Hasher & Zacks, 1984).

Children's automatic retention of information about frequencies seems to contribute to cognitive development in many ways. When children form concepts, they must learn which features go together most frequently. For example, learning the concept "bird" requires learning that the same animals tend to fly, have feathers, have beaks, and live in trees. More subtle learning, such as learning of sex roles, also may depend on automatic processing of frequency information. Only when children see a large difference in the frequency with which men and women engage in an activity do they imitate same-sex models more often than ones of the opposite sex (Perry & Bussey, 1979). Children are almost never conscious of gathering information about how often men engage in an activity and how often women do. Rather, they seem to acquire the information automatically and then base their behavior on what they have observed.

Thus, processing of frequency information appears to be automatic from early in development, perhaps from birth. Other processes, however, may change from controlled to automatic as people gain experience with them. This process is known as *automatization*.

The term *automatization* is well chosen. Once skills are learned to a sufficiently high degree, they are difficult to inhibit even when it is advantageous to do so. Learning of single-digit addition provides an example of this phenomenon, as illustrated in a study by LeFevre, Bisanz, and Mrkonjic (1988). Their experiment involved presentation of a problem such as 4 + 5 and then, a fraction of a second later, presentation of a single digit such as 9 slightly to the right of the first two numbers. The task was to say whether the number on the right was one of the addends in the problem. Thus, the answer for the above problem would be "no," because 9 was not one of the addends in 4 + 5. However, automatized knowledge of arithmetic facts would interfere with performance on this task, leading children either to say "yes" or to take longer to say "no" when the number to the right was the answer to the addition problem than when it was neither the answer to the problem nor one of the digits.

Studies of this task indicate that the easiest single-digit addition problems are automatized quite early in learning, but that it takes several years before harder ones are (LeFevre et al., 1991; LeFevre & Kulak, 1994; Lemaire, Barret, Fayol, & Abdi, 1994). Second graders show the interference effects associated with automatic processing only on small number problems (both addends of five or less). Third graders show the effects on both small and medium problems (one addend of six or more), but not on large number problems (both addends of six or more). Fourth and fifth graders and adults show automatic processing on all single-digit addition problems: small, medium, and large.

As suggested by this example, automatization generally is useful, because it frees mental resources for solving other problems. For example, automatizing the addition facts would make it easier to do long multiplication problems in one's head. However, when the situation looks like a typical problem but requires different processing, the automatization can be harmful.

The role of encoding. People cannot represent all features of the environment; the world is simply too complex. Children often fail to encode important features of objects and events, sometimes because they do not know what the important features are and sometimes because they do not know how to encode them efficiently. This failure to encode critical elements can limit the effects of potentially useful experiences; when children do not take in relevant information, they cannot benefit from it.

Kaiser, McCloskey, and Proffitt (1986) provided one demonstration of how inadequate encoding can hinder learning. They presented 4- to 11-year-olds and college students with a moving electric train carrying a ball on a flatcar. At a predesignated point, the ball dropped through a hole in the moving flatcar and fell several feet to the floor. The task was to predict the trajectory of the ball as it fell.

More than 70 percent of the children and a sizable minority of the college students predicted that the ball would fall straight down. After they advanced this hypothesis, the experimenter demonstrated what actually happened. (The ball moved in a curving path, going forward as well as down.) The children and the college students were faced with reconciling their predictions with the outcome they had seen. Their explanations revealed how expectations influenced their encoding of what they saw. Some said that the ball actually had fallen straight down but that it was released from the train later than the experimenter said it was. Others said that the train gave the ball a push forward just before it was released. Interestingly, a number of the college students who encoded the ball as having gone straight down had previously passed college physics courses that included the relevant concepts. However, this experience was insufficient to change either their expectations or their encoding of what they saw.

Encoding begins to play an important role in both developmental and individual differences in the first year of life (Colombo, 1993; 1995). Evidence for its importance comes from studies of the rate at which infants take in all of the relevant information and therefore become bored with looking at an object and look elsewhere. The length of time it takes before infants stop looking at a given object drops by more than half between the ages of 3 and 7 months. Recall also from Chapter 1 (p. 11) that the more rapidly 7-month-olds habituate to a repeatedly displayed object, the higher their IQs as much as 7 or 8 years later.

Presumably, more intelligent infants are quicker to encode everything of interest about the picture, leading them to be the first to lose interest in it. They perk up more when the new picture is shown, because they more clearly encode the differences between it and the old one.

INFORMATION-PROCESSING THEORIES OF DEVELOPMENT

In the remainder of this chapter, we consider five types of theories of how information-processing capabilities develop: neo-Piagetian theories, psychometric theories, production-system theories, connectionist theories, and evolutionary theories. Each of these is best viewed as a family of theories, with the individual theories of each type sharing basic principles but also having unique features. The discussion of each family of theories includes identification of the shared general principles and description of one particular realization of those principles. The hope is that this will convey the central features of the approach as well as a specific sense of how the approach is useful for understanding children's thinking.

All of these theories reflect the contributions of both Piaget's theory and adult information-processing approaches, as well as a number of other influences. Table 3.2 lists some of these. It also summarizes the goals of the theories and the mechanisms of development that they emphasize.

TABLE 3.2   Overview of Information-Processing Theories of Development

TYPE OF THEORY	REPRESENTATIVE THEORIST	GOAL OF THEORY	MAIN DEVELOPMENTAL MECHANISMS
Neo-Piagetian	Case	To unite Piagetian and information-porcessing theories of development.	Automatization, biologically based increases in working memory, and strategy construction.
Psychometric	Sternberg	To provide an information-processing analysis of the development of intelligence.	Strategy construction, encoding, and automatization.
Production System	Klahr	To demonstrate via computer simulation how the cognitive system modifies its own operation.	Generalization, based on the working of regularity detection, redundancy elimination, and the time line. Also encoding and strategy construction.
Connectionist	MacWhinney	To explain how children can learn language from the data available to them.	Associative competition among simple processing units. Also generalization.
Evolutionary	Siegler	To understand how the processes of variation and selection shape cognitive development.	Associative competition among strategies. Also strategy construction and generalization.

Neo-Piagetian Theories

The goal of neo-Piagetian theories is to maintain the strengths of Piaget's approach while adding the strengths of information-processing approaches. Typically, they incorporate stages much like Piaget's with the emphasis on goals, working memory limitations, and problem-solving strategies typical of information-processing approaches. Their greatest emphasis tends to be on how the biologically based growth of working memory and automatization of processing allow children to progressively overcome processing limits. Among the most prominent neo-Piagetian theories are those of Halford (1993), Fischer (e.g., Fischer & Farrar, 1988), van der Maas & Molenaar (1992), van Geert (1994), and Demetriou and Efklides (e.g., Demetriou, Efklides, & Platsidou, 1993).

Probably the most influential neo-Piagetian theory is that of Robbie Case. This theory can be divided into two main parts: the developmental stages themselves and the transition processes that produce progress between stages (Figure 3.2).

Like Piaget, Case (1985) hypothesized that children progress through four developmental stages. He characterized these stages in terms of the types of mental representations and operations children can form while they are in them. The first stage involved *sensorimotor operations*. Children's representations in this stage are composed of sensory input. The actions they produce in response to these representations are physical movements. In the *representational operations stage*, children's representations include concrete internal images, and their actions can produce additional internal representations. In the stage of

FIGURE 3.2   An outline of the main structures and processes in Case's theory.

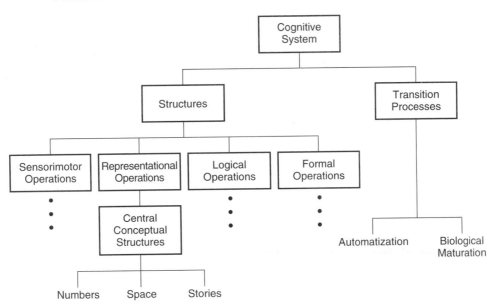

logical operations, children represent stimuli abstractly; they can act on these representations with simple transformations. In the *formal operations stage,* children also represent stimuli abstractly, but they are capable of performing complex transformations of the information. (Note: In all stages, children also produce representations and actions like those that were possible earlier.)

Examples may clarify the differences in the representations that become possible in each stage. A sensorimotor operation might involve a child's seeing a frightening face (the sensory representation) and then fleeing from the room (the motor action). A representational operation might involve the child's producing a mental image of the same frightening face (the internal representation) and using the image to draw a picture of the face (the representational action). A logical operation might involve a child's realizing that two of his friends did not like each other (the abstract representation) and telling them that they could have more fun if they all were friends (the simple transformation). A formal operation might involve the child's realizing that such direct attempts at producing friendships rarely succeed (the abstract representation) and therefore leading all three into a situation in which they would need to overcome some common obstacle, thus producing friendly feelings (the complex transformation). The resemblance to Piaget's stages of development seems clear.

Case's view of the developmental sequence by which children acquire understanding of particular concepts also resembled Piaget's views. Like Piaget, he postulates broad unities in the developmental sequence across different concepts. His views are more moderate, in that the postulated similarities of reasoning are limited to particular types of knowledge. However, even across these types of knowledge, substantial commonality in the developmental sequence is evident.

In particular, Case claims that much of children's thinking is organized into *central conceptual structures.* These are defined as "an internal network of concepts and conceptual relations which plays a central role in permitting children to think about a wide range (but not all) situations at a new epistemic level" (Case & Griffin, 1990, p. 224). Case and his colleagues (e.g., Case & Okamoto, 1996; Griffin, Case, & Sandieson, 1992; Marini, 1992; McKeough, 1992) have focused on three main central conceptual structures, one for thinking about numbers, one for thinking about space, and one for thinking about stories. All three have a general resemblance, based on overall structural limits of the cognitive system at that age, but all also reflect the particulars of the domain to which they apply. For example, Case and Okamoto (1996) proposed that at age 6, the central conceptual structures focus on a single dimension. In the structure dealing with numbers, this involves forming a mental number line, which allows children to perform such tasks as knowing which numbers are bigger than which other numbers. In the structure dealing with stories, the central conceptual structure at this age allows children to form mental story lines, that is, to represent the plot line of the story in terms of the sequence of events. In the structure dealing with space, 6-year-olds' thinking focuses either on the shape or location of objects, but not both. By age 8, central conceptual structures coordinating two dimensions are formed. In the domain of numbers, this allows children to coordinate two number lines, for example, to understand the base-10 system dealing with numbers below 100 by coordinating understanding of the concepts of tens and ones. In the domain of stories, it allows them to coordinate two story lines into a single plot. In the domain of space, it allows them to represent simultaneously the shapes and locations of objects.

Where Case differs most clearly from Piaget and shows the strongest influence of the information-processing approach is in his account of transition mechanisms. Case emphasizes working-memory capacity as a determinant of cognitive growth. His claim is not that the absolute capacity of working memory increases, but rather that it functions increasingly efficiently, and that it therefore can handle more information.

How might such increases in processing efficiency occur? Case (1985) proposed that one contributor is automatization. With practice, a cognitive operation that previously required all working-memory resources could be accomplished more efficiently. This would free up part of the working-memory capacity for other processing. It may be useful to think of this view of working memory in terms of an analogy to a car's trunk. The capacity of a car's trunk does not change as the owner acquires experience in packing luggage into it. Nonetheless, the amount of luggage that can be packed into the trunk does change. Whereas the trunk at first might hold three suitcases, it eventually come to hold four or five. With more efficient packing, trunk space is freed for additional cargo. Like knowledge of how to pack one's trunk, the central conceptual structures provide efficient ways of organizing goals and procedures for accomplishing the goals. Thus, they allow children to circumvent working memory limits.

Biological maturation was also assigned a role in explaining the increasing efficiency of working memory. Case (1992b) proposed that stage transitions arise from pervasive changes in electrical activity in the frontal lobes, a part of the brain particularly active in problem solving and reasoning. The specific proposal was that at the beginning of each stage, new short-distance connections develop between the frontal lobe on the left side of the brain and parts of the brain that had not previously been connected to them. During a second substage, longer-distance connections are formed within both left and right hemispheres of the brain. During a third substage, short-distance connections are formed within the right hemisphere. Then the brain is ready for a new stage to begin. Patterns of electrical activity in the brain at different ages lent some support to this proposal (Thatcher, 1992).

Case and his colleagues have applied this theory to an exceptional variety of tasks. They range from scientific reasoning (Marini, 1992) to musical sight reading (Capodilupo, 1992), solving arithmetic word problems (Okamoto, 1992), telling time (Case, Sandieson, & Dennis, 1987), handling money (Marini, 1984), drawing (Dennis, 1992), and understanding social phenomena such as moods and interpersonal conflict (Bruchkowsky, 1992; McKeough, 1992).

Another strength of Case's theory is its usefulness for designing effective instructional techniques. Consider his analysis of missing addend problems, of the form 4 + ? = 7 (Case, 1985). Although the task appears simple, first graders who are taught it in school find it a major obstacle.

After analyzing several correct and several commonly used incorrect strategies for solving missing addend problems, Case noted that most correct strategies required more working-term memory capacity than 6- and 7-year-olds usually possess. However, he also noted that the simplest correct strategy and the most-demanding incorrect strategy made the same memory demands. The least-demanding correct strategy, according to his analysis, was to count on from the one addend given in the problem and to note the number of counts required to reach the sum. For the problem 4 + ? = 7, this simplest correct strategy would involve counting from 4 to 7 and keeping track of the number of counts needed to get from one to the other. The most-demanding (and the most-common) incorrect strategy was to count up first to the addend that was given and then to count on from there the number of times indicated by the sum. Illustratively, on the problem 4 + ? = 7, children would first count to 4, then count up 7 more times to 11, and finally answer that the missing addend was 11. Case reasoned that if 6-year-olds could learn the incorrect strategy, they also could learn the correct one.

The instructional strategy that Case used was straightforward. As shown in Figure 3.3, the first step was to illustrate that the equal sign (=) meant that entities on each side of the sign were equivalent. The next step (the third pair of faces) was to illustrate that the plus sign (+) meant that the child should sum the entities adjacent to the sign. After the child finished working with the faces, the focus of the instruction shifted to direct consideration of problems involving numbers. In one part of this instruction, the experimenter demonstrated the incorrectness of children's existing strategy for solving missing addend problems involving numbers by having them compare the numbers on the two sides of the equal sign that their strategy yielded. This would allow them to see that on 4 + ? = 7, the 11 that their strategy yielded was not equivalent to the 7 on the other side of the equal sign. Following this, the simplest correct procedure for solving missing addend problems (the counting-on strategy described in the previous paragraph) was introduced, one step at a time.

Case (1978) reported that his teaching strategy allowed 80 percent of kindergarten children to learn missing addend problems. This percentage represented a considerable improvement over the 10 percent of children who were able to learn such problems from the standard state of California arithmetic workbook. Thus, Case's approach seems useful for applied as well as theoretical purposes.

Several criticisms of Case's theory have been voiced. Flavell (1984) noted that Case has not explicated the principles by which he determines how much working memory capacity a procedure requires. As a result, it is often difficult

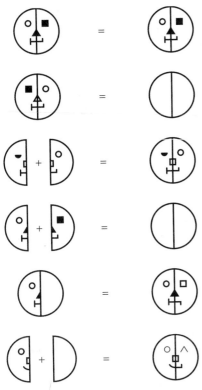

FIGURE 3.3 Faces used by Case (1978) to teach missing addend problem. The first pair of faces was used to demonstrate the meaning of the equal sign. The second pair was used to test whether the child could make the right-hand face equal to the left-hand face. The third pair was used to demonstrate that the whole on the right could be created from the parts on the left. The fourth pair was used to test whether the child could create a whole out of the parts. The fifth pair, like the missing addend problem, showed one part of the whole on the left and the whole on the right; the task was to fill in the other part of the whole on the left. The sixth pair included the plus sign, to make problem even more like standard missing addend problems with numbers.

to evaluate whether the estimates are comparable from one task to the next. Further, his ideas about the role of biological changes in producing stage changes are quite speculative; little relevant evidence is yet available. On the other hand, Case's theory is exceptional among information-processing approaches to development in its attempt to relate basic capacities, strategies, and learning. It has yielded compelling analyses of development on many tasks and has proved practically useful as well. And there is a strong intuition among many researchers that improved ability to surmount memory limits does underlie much of cognitive development, although it is difficult to provide evidence that unambiguously supports the position. Thus, it seems that Case has taken a difficult but potentially rewarding path. To the extent that the effort succeeds, it will be a grand achievement.

Psychometric Theories

Psychometric theories are aimed at clarifying the processes measured on tests of mental abilities, such as intelligence tests. Since the beginning of the twentieth century, intelligence has been characterized by a single number: the IQ score.

This practice has several drawbacks: A single number is inherently inadequate to capture a quality as rich and complex as intelligence, IQ tests may be culturally biased, and such tests do not directly measure the ability to learn and create. IQ tests also have unique virtues, however: Scores on them are closely related to school performance at the time they are given; they predict later school performance quite accurately; and they provide a solid base from which to examine individual differences in cognitive functioning.

A number of investigators have tried to preserve these virtues while reducing or eliminating the negative qualities (Anderson, 1992; Ceci, 1990; Gardner, 1983). Probably the most prominent such theory is Robert Sternberg's (1985) *triarchic theory of intelligence.* He has applied the analysis to diverse tasks and diverse groups of children and has related his results to those yielded by traditional intelligence tests.

As suggested by the name *triarchic,* Sternberg's theory divides intelligence into three types of information-processing components: performance components, knowledge acquisition components, and metacomponents (Figure 3.4). The metacomponents serve as a strategy construction mechanism, orchestrating the other two types of components into goal-oriented procedures. When the child already possesses sufficient understanding to solve a problem, only the metacomponents and the performance components are needed to construct a problem-solving strategy. The metacomponents select which performance components to use and the order in which to use them. The performance components do the work of actually solving the problem. When the child does not yet possess sufficient understanding to solve the problem, the knowledge-acquisition components also come into play. That is, the knowledge-acquisition components obtain new information relevant to solving the problem and communicate this information to the metacomponents.

FIGURE 3.4   A schematic diagram of Sternberg's theory of intelligence.

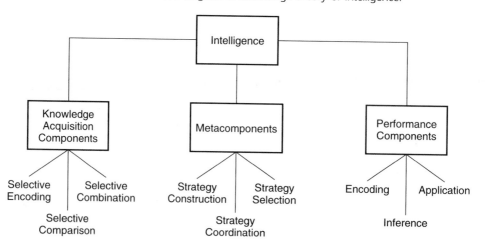

The metacomponents then combine the new and previous understanding to construct a problem-solving strategy.

Now we can analyze each type of component in greater detail. First consider *performance components*. These are the processes within problem-solving procedures. Sternberg has identified four performance components that people use to solve a great many problems: encoding, inference, mapping, and application.

The way in which these performance components work can be illustrated by thinking about analogy problems. Consider the problem:

Turkey : Cranberry sauce :: Eggs: (1) Corn (2) Ham

The task is to decide whether corn or ham has the same relation to eggs that cranberry sauce has to turkey.

Sternberg suggested that the first step in solving this problem is to encode the terms. This step involves identifying each term's attributes—for example, noting that turkey is a kind of food, that it is a meat, that it is a bird, that it is eaten on Thanksgiving, and so on. Next, inference is used to specify the relation between the first and second term, in this case that turkey is often eaten with cranberry sauce. Then, mapping is used to establish the relation between the first and third terms, that turkey and eggs are both foods. Finally, application involves inducing a relation between the third term and one of the possible answers that parallels the relation between the first and second terms. Here, eggs go with ham in much the same way that cranberry sauce goes with turkey.

Sternberg and Rifkin (1979) found that 7-year-olds use the same components as adults to solve analogy problems. However, they differ in their allocation of cognitive resources to the components. Adults spend more time encoding the terms but then move much more quickly through the remaining steps. Children encode only one or a few features of each term, try to solve the problem, and then encode more features if the initial approach does not work. The children's strategy reduces the initial memory load but ultimately lengthens the time needed to solve the problem.

The amount of time devoted to encoding correlated positively both with children's IQ and with success on the task. Although high-IQ children generally tend to be fast on intellectual tasks, they, like adults, spent an especially long time encoding (Marr & Sternberg, 1986). Thus, complete encoding of the critical information is associated both with high IQs and with success in solving analogy problems. This type of linking of the information-processing construct of encoding with the psychometric construct of IQ is representative of the kinds of bridges between psychometric theory and information processing that Sternberg's theory is intended to build.

The second part of Sternberg's theory involves *knowledge-acquisition components*. Sternberg has focused on three of these: selective encoding, selective combination, and selective comparison. Selective encoding involves distinguishing relevant from irrelevant information. Selective combination involves integrating information in a meaningful way. Selective comparison involves relating newly-encoded or combined information to previously stored information.

These constructs have proved especially useful for analyzing what processes distinguish children with high IQs. Davidson and Sternberg (1984) tested use of each of the three types of knowledge-acquisition components on insight problems—problems much like the brain teasers in puzzle books. They reasoned that knowledge-acquisition components would be especially important on these problems, because they are new to everyone. The following is an example of the insight problems Sternberg and Davidson used: "If you have black socks and brown socks in your drawer, mixed in the ratio of 4 to 5, how many socks will you have to take out to be sure of having a pair of socks of the same color?"

The basic assumption underlying the experiment was that high-IQ children execute knowledge-acquisition components more effectively than other children. They therefore would be expected not only to perform better on all problems but also to benefit less than children with average IQs from conditions that lessened the need for effective execution of knowledge-acquisition processes. The reason was that they would execute the processes effectively even without help.

The experimental procedures generated by this logic can be illustrated with regard to the selective-encoding component. Its role in the socks problem just cited was tested by either including or omitting the irrelevant information about the 4-to-5 ratio of the two colors. When this information was present, children needed to ignore it and selectively encode only the essentials of the problem. (If you had socks of two colors, how many socks would you need to look at to be sure that two would match?) When the irrelevant information was absent, skill in selective encoding was less important, because there was less distracting information.

Consistent with the view that high-IQ children's encoding is especially selective, such children did especially well relative to other children when it was necessary to ignore irrelevant information.

Then Davidson and Sternberg went a step further. They offered a Saturday-morning course designed to train children with high IQs and with average ones in executing the three processes. The course included 14 hours of instruction, distributed over a 7-week period. At the end, children were given a posttest. The posttest included mathematical-insight problems, hypothesized to require use of the knowledge-acquisition processes the children had been taught. It also included logical-deduction problems, hypothesized to require different processes that were not taught in the course and that therefore would not be expected to improve as a result of taking it.

On the mathematical-insight problems, the children with average IQs showed greater gains from before the course to after it than did the children with high IQs. This finding was consistent with the view that they were more in need of instruction in these components. Neither group showed gains on the logical-deduction task, in accord with the view that this task required skills that were not part of the training program. In sum, high-IQ children's superior knowledge-acquisition components contributed to their superior performance on the insight problems.

The third part of Sternberg's theory involves *metacomponents*, components used to construct strategies. Metacomponents govern the use of the other components. They also are responsible for most aspects of developmental change. As Sternberg (1984) commented "There can be no doubt that in the present conceptual scheme, that metacomponents form the major basis for the development of intelligence" (p. 172).

The importance of metacomponents is evident in people's transfer of knowledge from one context to another. Older children and people with greater expertise are generally better able to apply their knowledge to new problems than are younger people and people with less expertise (Campione & Brown, 1984; Gentner, Ratterman, Markman, & Kotovsky, 1995; Staszewski, 1988). Knowledge is especially important; 10-year-olds who are expert at chess more successfully solve novel chess problems than adults with little knowledge of chess but whose general memory capacities are higher (Chi, 1978). However, within a given level of knowledge, people with higher IQs generally can apply existing knowledge to acquire new knowledge more rapidly (e.g., Johnson & Mervis, 1994).

How should Sternberg's theory be evaluated? Two weaknesses can be noted. One is that the theory summarizes more than it predicts. It is not clear what types of evidence would be inconsistent with the approach. Another involves the role of metacomponents in the organization of the system. These are crucial parts of the overall theory, but their workings remain somewhat mysterious. On the other hand, the theory is exceptional in the breadth of phenomena and of populations to which it has proven applicable. It encompasses a large number of intuitively important aspects of development and organizes them in an easy-to-grasp way. It provides a plausible outline of how a strategy-construction mechanism would operate. In short, it constitutes a useful framework within which to view development.

Production-System Theories

Perhaps the most difficult challenge for theories of cognitive development has been to explain how development occurs. Piaget and many others have tried to generate such explanations, but they have not been entirely successful. Consider the following evaluation:

> For 40 years now we have had assimilation and accommodation, the mysterious and shadowy forces of equilibration, the Batman and Robin of the developmental processes. What are they? How do they do their thing? Why is it after all this time, we know no more about them than when they first sprang on the scene? What we

need is a way to get beyond vague verbal statements of the nature of the developmental process. (Klahr, 1982, p. 80)

One promising effort to provide more precise and satisfying explanations of change has been to model development through *production systems*. These are a class of computer-simulation languages that have proven useful for modeling cognitive development. Each production is a kind of if–then rule that indicates what the system would do in a particular situation. Together, the productions indicate what the system would do under a wide range of circumstances. The key properties of production systems are:

1. The basic organization consists of two interacting structures: a *production memory*, which is the system's enduring knowledge, and a *working memory*, which is the system's representation of the current situation.
2. The production memory includes a large number of specific productions, each of which includes a condition side and an action side.
3. The condition side of each production specifies the circumstances under which the production is applicable. The action side specifies the actions that are taken when these conditions are met. Such actions include both activities in the external world and manipulations of symbols in working memory.
4. The contents of working memory are constantly changing, because they reflect constantly changing situations. Information enters working memory both through perception of events in the external world and through taking the actions indicated by the action side of productions.
5. Thinking occurs through a cycle of (a) information being present in working memory, (b) the information matching the condition side of one or more productions, (c) this match resulting in the actions on the action side of those productions being taken, (d) the actions placing new information in working memory, thus starting the cycle anew.
6. Learning occurs through a process of *self-modification*, in which new productions are created and existing productions modified as a result of previous experience.

The basic organization of production systems is diagrammed in Figure 3.5.

An example of a simple production system that produces correct performance on Piaget's number conservation problem is shown in Table 3.3. The bottom part of the table indicates the sequence of working-memory states that the system produces while solving the problem. The particular production system always searches downward from the top of the list of productions until it finds a production whose condition side is matched by the contents of working memory. That production then fires, and the search begins anew from the top of the list.

In the experimental situation to which the Table 3.3 production system applies, the child has been shown two rows of objects, has been told that they have the same number of objects, has seen the objects in one of the rows spread out, and has been asked whether the two rows now have the same number of objects. This information is represented in the initial contents of working memory in the bottom part of Table 3.3. The initial state of working memory matches the condition side of P1 (Production 1), which therefore fires, putting into working

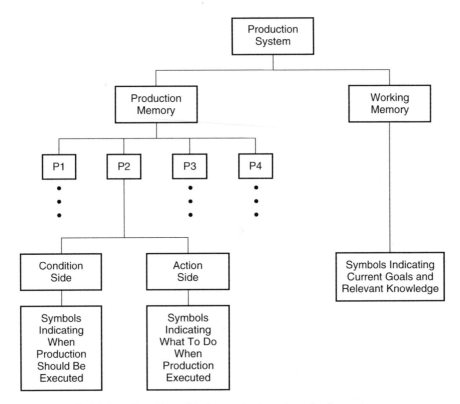

FIGURE 3.5   The hierarchical organization of production systems.

memory a goal of stating the numerical relation between the rows. When the system starts from the top again, the contents of working memory do not match P1 (because its second condition is not matched) nor P2 (because its second condition is not matched.) However, the contents of working memory do match the condition side of P3, which therefore fires. This places in working memory the information that the rows have the same number of objects. With this information, P2 can fire and the system states the correct answer.

David Klahr is probably the most prominent advocate of production systems as a tool for explaining how development occurs. The key developmental mechanism in Klahr's theory is generalization. Number conservation provides a convenient context for explaining how his theory works.

Klahr and Wallace (1976) divided the process of generalization into three components: the time line, regularity detection, and redundancy elimination. The *time line* contains the data on which generalizations are based. It is a record of all the situations the system has ever encountered, the responses produced in those situations, the outcomes of the actions, and the new situations that arose. Table 3.4 illustrates the type of information that might be included in the time line's record of a single event. A child saw a group of cookies and noticed that

TABLE 3.3   A simple production system for number conservation*

P1: **If** you are asked about the numerical relation between two collections **and** you do not have a goal of stating the relation, **then** set a goal of stating the relation.

P2: **If** you have a goal of stating the numerical relation between two collections **and** you know the relation, **then** state the relation.

P3: **If** you have a goal of stating the numerical relation between two collections, **and** the collections had the same number of objects before a transformation **and** the transformation did not involve adding or subtracting objects, **then** the rows still have the same number of objects.

Initial Working Memory (WM1): Rows had same number of objects before, one row then was spread, nothing added or subtracted, question is whether rows have same number of objects now.

P1 fires.

WM2: Goal is to state whether rows have same number of objects now, rows had same number of objects before, one row then was spread, nothing added or subtracted, question is whether rows have same number of objects now.

P3 fires.

WM3: Goal is to state whether rows have same number of objects now, rows have the same number of objects, rows had same number of objects before, one row then was spread, nothing added or subtracted, question is whether rows have same number of objects now.

P2 fires.

System answers: "The rows have the same number of objects."

Source: *Adapted from Klahr & Wallace, 1976.

there were three. This realization was made possible by *subitizing* (a process by which both children and adults can rapidly perceive the number of objects in sets ranging from one to four objects). Next, the child transformed the spatial position of the cookies by picking them up in his hand. Finally, the child again subitized the collection of cookies and found that there still were three.

Such detailed records of situations, responses, and outcomes might at first seem unnecessary. Why remember so much about each experience? In fact, the information could be invaluable. In many situations, children cannot know beforehand what will turn out to be relevant. If they retain detailed information that may or may not be relevant, they later may be able to draw unanticipated generalizations. If they retain only what they know to be relevant, however, they will miss much relevant information.

Is it realistic to think that children have a memory record similar to a time line? Observing the level of detail with which they remember certain information suggests that it is. Almost all parents have anecdotes to this effect. One of

TABLE 3.4   A Portion of a Child's Time Line

(PREVIOUS PROCESSING EPISODES)

_____	_____
_____	_____
_____	_____
87456.	Cookies on table.
87457.	I subitized.
87458.	There were three.
87459.	I heard a bird.
87460.	I picked up the cookies.
87461.	I subitized the cookies.
87462.	There were three again.
_____	_____
_____	_____
_____	_____

mine concerns a vacation on which my wife, our almost-2-year-old son, and I were staying in a motel. We wanted to go to dinner but could not find the room key. After 10 minutes of searching, I finally listened to my son long enough to understand what he was saying: "Under phone." As soon as I understood, I knew he was right. I had put it there (for reasons I no longer remember). It seems likely that if he remembered this relatively inconsequential detail, he probably was remembering many other details as well. Hasher and Zacks's (1984) ideas about automatic processing of frequency information and of several other aspects of experience, such as spatial locations and time of occurrence, suggest the types of content that might be entered into the time line. Thus, Klahr and Wallace's contention that children retain a detailed ledger of their experiences seems quite plausible.

The second key process, *regularity detection*, operates on the contents of the time line to produce generalizations about experience. This is accomplished by the system's noting places in the time line where many features are similar and where the same outcome occurs despite variations in one or more features. In number conservation, regularity detection could produce at least three types of generalizations. One would involve generalizing over different objects. Regardless of whether two checkers, two coins, two dolls, or two cookies were spread, there still would be two objects. Children also could generalize over equivalent transformations. Spreading, compressing, piling up, and putting in a circle all preserve the initial number of objects.

The third process in Klahr and Wallace's model, *redundancy elimination*, accomplishes a different type of generalization. It improves efficiency by identifying processing steps that are unnecessary, thus reaching the generalization that a shorter sequence can achieve the same goal. In the number-conservation example, children would eventually note that it is unnecessary to subitize after picking up the cookies. Since there were three cookies before, and since picking up objects never affects how many there are, the number still must be the same. Klahr and Wallace hypothesized that the information-processing system eliminates redundancy by examining procedures within the time line and checking if the same outcome always occurs even if one or more steps are deleted. If so, the simpler procedure is substituted for the more complex one.

When does the information-processing system have time to detect regularities and to eliminate redundancies? Klahr and Wallace (1976) advanced one intriguing possibility: Perhaps children do it in their sleep. Other possibilities are that moments of quiet play, relaxation, or daydreaming are when children accomplish these functions.

Klahr and Wallace's approach, unlike stage theories, implies that different children develop skills in different orders. In the cognitive system's attempts at self-modification, there is no reason why one type of regularity always should be detected before another type. Children learning about number conservation either could first detect that it does not matter if the rows of objects contain cookies or checkers or could first detect that it does not matter if the row of cookies is shortened or lengthened. Thus, there is less of a lock-step feel to the model than to stage approaches.

Another implication of Klahr and Wallace's theory relates to the idea of encoding. The way in which information is encoded in the time line shapes the learning that can later occur. Suppose, for example, that in a liquid-quantity-conservation experiment, a child encodes only the heights of the water in the glasses. Such a child would not be able to detect the regular relation between increments in the height of water and decrements in its cross-sectional area. The information about cross-sectional area simply would not be available in the time line.

Klahr has been in the forefront of investigators arguing for greater use of computer simulation as a tool for modeling development. He has noted that such simulations allow more explicit and precise models of how development occurs than would otherwise be possible (Klahr, 1989; 1992). Consistent with this stance, Simon and Klahr (1995) formulated a *self-modifying production system* that illustrated how children could come to understand conservation. At the outset, the model could not solve the number conservation problems it was presented. Through experience trying to solve them, it figured out how to do so. Of special interest, Simon and Klahr generated two versions of the model, one corresponding to 3-year-olds and one to 4-year-olds. Both models were able to learn when given relatively extensive experience with the problems, but only the model of 4-year-olds learned from limited experience with them. These data corresponded to the results obtained with real 3- and 4-year-olds who had been presented with these experiences by Gelman (1982).

The models of the younger and older children suggested hypotheses concerning why 3- and 4-year-olds showed the patterns of learning that they did. Both models contained learning mechanisms that allowed them to learn from the more extensive experience. However, two differences between them resulted in the model of 4-year-olds, but not the model of 3-year-olds, learning froi limited experience. The model of 4-year-olds more clearly remembered the tion between the sets before the transformation, and it was more likely to check whether the differences between the lengths of the rows after the transformation corresponded to a difference in numbers of objects. These differences in the models were consistent with what is known generally about 3- and 4-year-olds. The 4-year-olds are more likely to use counting to check whether their perceptions regarding numbers of objects are correct (Sophian, 1987) and also usually remember more about past states (Schneider & Bjorklund, in press). Thus, the differences between the models of 3- and 4-year-olds were both consistent with past observations of these age groups and suggested hypotheses regarding why the two age groups might learn as they did in this particular context.

Not everyone shares Klahr's enthusiasm for computer-simulation models, though. Critics note that people are not computers and that unlike computers, people develop. This leads them to the conclusion that development cannot be modeled appropriately on a computer (Beilin, 1983; Liben, 1987).

As Klahr (1989) pointed out, however, ideas about development are embodied in the computer *program*, not the computer on which the program runs. The computer is simply the device used to test whether these ideas account for the known phenomena. To illustrate the point, Klahr noted that computer simulations of cognitive development do not imply that children are computers any more than computer simulations of hurricanes imply that the atmosphere is a computer.

Several limitations of Klahr's theory should be mentioned. Although he has often proclaimed the virtues of self-modifying production systems, neither he nor other investigators interested in children's thinking has yet written many of them. In addition, such self-modifying production systems thus far has been more useful for explaining previous findings than for generating new ones. On the other hand, these shortcomings do not detract from the potential of self-modifying production systems as models of development. In addition, Klahr and Wallace's explanation of generalization in terms of the time line, regularity detection, and redundancy elimination is more precise and explicit than almost all other mechanisms of cognitive development that have been proposed. These are important virtues and may foreshadow additional breakthroughs.

Connectionist Theories

One especially "hot" approach to thinking about cognitive development (and to thinking about cognition in general) is *connectionism*. Like production systems, connectionist theories are computer simulations of how thinking occurs. Much of the reason for the rapidly-growing popularity of connectionist models is their general resemblance to the workings of the brain. This makes the approach a promising candidate for modeling how thinking is achieved within the brain. Connectionist models have several key characteristics (Plunkett, 1996):

1. They are made up of large numbers of simple processing units, akin to neurons in the brain.
2. The processing units are organized into two or more hierarchically-organized layers (Figure 3.6). Typically, these include an *input layer*, whose processing units encode the initial representation of the situation; one or more *hidden layers*, whose units combine information from the input units; and an *output layer*, whose units generate the system's response to the situation.
3. The individual processing units are connected to other processing units in different layers (and sometimes within the same layer as well). The strength of the connections varies with the system's experience and is crucial in determining the processing that is done.
4. As in the brain, a given processing unit fires when the amount of activation it is receiving from all of the other processing units that are connected to it exceeds a threshold. The amount of activation that a unit receives from each unit connected to it is determined by the degree of activation of the processing unit that is sending the activation and the strength of the connection between the units.
5. As in the brain, the activity of the many simple processing units occurs *in parallel* (simultaneously).
6. Knowledge is represented through the strengths of connections among all of the units in the system. There is no single location that corresponds to a particular piece of knowledge; rather, the knowledge is distributed over all of the units and their interconnections. Because of this, and because processing occurs over many units in parallel, these systems are often known as *parallel distributed processing (PDP)* systems.
7. Learning occurs through the system receiving input, generating a response, observing the discrepancy between it and the correct answer, and adjusting the strengths of connections among the processing units in ways that would have led to a better answer. The adjustments include strengthening some connections and weakening others. Through this process, the system implicitly learns the rules underlying correct responses to the problem, although there is no single place in which the rule is represented.
8. Generalization of the system's knowledge is based on similarity of new situations to ones the system has encountered previously. When the same types of implicit rules apply to new problems, connectionist systems are very effective in generalizing previous experience to them.

A number of researchers have advocated connectionist models of development: McClelland (1995); Shultz, Schmidt, Buckingham, and Mareschal (1995); Plunkett (1996); and Marchman (1992), among them. A particularly impressive connectionist model, and one that illustrates the strength of the approach for modeling development, is that of MacWhinney, Leinbach, Taraban, and McDonald (1989).

The model of MacWhinney et al. (Figure 3.6) depicted German children's learning of their language's system of definite articles. These definite articles are the multiple terms that in German serve the function that the single word *the* serves in English. The task was of interest precisely because the German article system is so difficult. Which article should be used to modify a given noun depends on the gender of the noun being modified (masculine, feminine, or neuter), its number (singular or plural), and its role within the sentence (subject,

FIGURE 3.6   The connectionist model of MacWhinney et al. (1989) of how children learn the German system of articles. Note that at the top (input) level, the model encodes five semantic features of the noun (corresponding to the "5" at the level just below the top on the extreme left), presence or absence of 11 phonological features at as many as 13 locations in the word (also represented at the level just below the top), and 17 explicit case cues, which indicate the function of the noun within the sentence. These input-level units transfer activation to hidden units at the next two levels below, and eventually to the six output units, which correspond to the six articles that accompany nouns in German. The article that goes with the most activated output unit is advanced as the response (after MacWhinney et al., 1989). Copyright © 1989 by Academic Press, Inc.

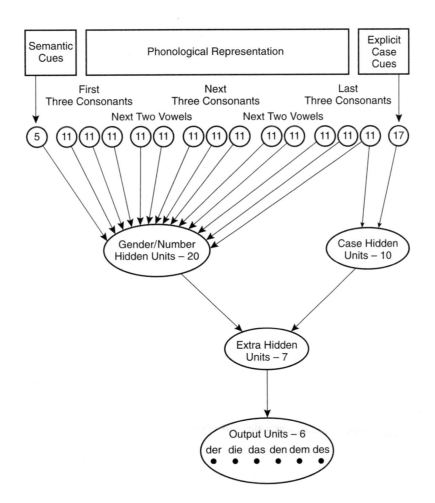

possessor, direct object, or indirect object). To make matters worse, assignment of nouns to gender categories is often nonintuitive. For example, the word for *fork* is feminine, the word for *spoon* is masculine, and the word for *knife* is neuter. The relations are so complex that they seem almost impossible to learn. However, MacWhinney et al. built a connectionist model that showed how children could learn them.

The model of MacWhinney et al., like most connectionist models, involves an *input layer*, several *hidden layers*, and an *output layer* (Figure 3.6). Each of these layers contains a number of discrete units. For example, in the model, the 35 units within the input layer represent features of the particular noun that the article modifies. Each of the hidden layers includes units that represent combinations of these input-level features. The six output units represent the six articles in German that correspond to *the* in English.

As noted above, a central feature of such connectionist models is the very large number of connections among processing units. In the model of MacWhinney et al., each input-layer unit is connected to first-level hidden units; each first-level hidden unit is connected to second-level hidden units; and each second-level hidden unit is connected to each of the six output units. Learning occurs through a cycle of the system (1) receiving initial input (in this case, a noun in a certain context); (2) projecting on the basis of the strengths of its various connections (which reflect past experience) what output to produce; (3) advancing that response; and (4) adjusting the strengths of connections between units so that connections that suggested the correct answer are strengthened and connections that suggested the wrong answer are weakened.

MacWhinney et al. tested this system's ability to master the German article system by repeatedly presenting it with 98 common German nouns. The simulation needed to choose which article to use with each noun in the particular context—that is, in the context of wanting to express a particular meaning with particular words. After it did this, the correct answer was presented, and the simulation adjusted connection strengths so as to optimize its accuracy in the future.

Following experience with this training set, the MacWhinney et al. simulation chose the correct article for more than 90 percent of the nouns in the original set. This could not be attributed simply to rote learning of which article accompanied each noun. When the simulation was presented a previously encountered noun in a novel context, it chose the correct article on more than 90 percent of trials, despite the noun's often taking a different article in the new context than it had in the previous ones. The simulation also proved able to generalize to novel nouns; even when it had never encountered the particular term, it could use the term's sound and meaning to make educated guesses as to what article would accompany it.

The simulation's learning paralleled children's learning in a number of ways. Early in the learning process, the simulation, like children whose first language is German, tended to overuse the articles that accompany feminine nouns. The reason appeared to be that this form of the articles is used most often within the language. Further, the same article–noun combinations that are the most difficult for German children to learn were the most difficult for the simulation to learn as well. The particular errors made by the simulation also resembled those of children.

Connectionist models have successfully depicted a number of other developmental acquisitions as well. These include object permanence (Munakata, McClelland, Johnson, & Siegler, in press), understanding of balance scales, time-speed-distance problems, and causal reasoning (Shultz, et al., 1995), early reading acquisition (Plaut, McClelland, Seidenberg, & Patterson, 1995), second language learning (MacWhinney, 1996), and acquisition of word meanings and grammatical understanding (Elman, 1993; MacWhinney & Chang, 1995; Marchman, 1992; Plunkett & Sinha, 1992).

As with all theories, connectionist approaches are open to criticism. One frequent criticism is that their claim to be "brain style cognition" is overstated. Nothing within them corresponds to the chemical activity that is crucial to brain functioning, and the functioning of their simple processing units bears only an abstract similarity to the functioning of neurons. Another limitation is that their learning is extremely slow and requires many more exposures than do human beings. They do not show the kind of sudden insight that people sometimes do (Raijmakers, Koten, & Molenaar, 1996). A third limit, related to the second one, is that they do not learn the symbolic rules, such as mathematical formulas, that people do, and may not be able to learn certain aspects of grammar (Pinker & Prince, 1988). On the other hand, connectionist models have proven useful for modeling the many developments that do not depend on acquisition of explicit rules. Although the operation of such systems clearly differs from that of the brain, it more closely resembles it than do other computer simulation approaches. Connectionist models have proven especially useful for modeling domains such as perception and language, in which numerous, partially valid sources of information must be integrated to produce successful performance. Given these advantages, it is not surprising that the popularity of connectionist models of development is growing rapidly.

Theories of Cognitive Evolution

One of the most-profound intellectual contributions of all time is Darwin's theory of evolution. Within evolutionary theory, competition among species is a basic aspect of existence. Species originate and change through two main processes: variation and selection. Genetic combination and mutation produce *variation*; survival of offspring is the basis of *selection*. Together, these processes have produced our planet's ever-changing mosaic of living things.

As in the biological context, competition seems to be a basic feature of cognition. Rather than species competing, however, the competitions are among ideas. The main challenges for evolutionary theories of cognitive development are to describe the competing entities within the human cognitive system, to describe how the competition among these entities leads to adaptive outcomes, and to identify the mechanisms that produce cognitive variation and selection.

A number of recent models of cognitive development are based on analogies between the functions that must be accomplished to produce evolutionary and developmental change (Changeux & Dehaene, 1989; Cziko, 1995; Edelman, 1987; Johnson & Gilmore, 1996). However, since I'm the one writing the book, I will use my own *overlapping waves approach* to illustrate the way in which the analogy to biological evolution can contribute to understanding of development.

The basic assumptions of this approach are that at any one time, children have a variety of ways of thinking about most topics; that these varied ways of thinking compete with each other for use; and that the more advanced ways of thinking gradually become increasingly prevalent. These assumptions are illustrated in Figure 3.7. At any given time, several ways of thinking (the strategies in the figure) are present in a child's thinking. (Strategies are procedures aimed at meeting particular goals.) These strategies compete with each other, and with experience, some become more frequent, some become less frequent, and some first become more frequent and later less frequent. Further, new strategies are introduced and old strategies stop being used. This overlapping waves model seems more in accord with what is known about cognitive development than do depictions that show children suddenly moving from one approach to another.

My colleagues and I have pursued this evolutionary model within a variety of areas: arithmetic, time telling, reading, spelling, problem solving, and memory tasks, among them (e.g., Crowley & Siegler, 1993; Siegler, 1996; Siegler & Shrager, 1984). In each of these areas, we have found that competition leads to adaptive consequences, and that basic strategy choice and discovery mechanisms produce the adaptation. The findings can be illustrated in the context of young children's learning of simple addition.

FIGURE 3.7   Siegler's overlapping waves model of cognitive development.

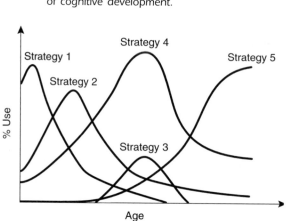

First consider the competing entities. Even 5-year-olds use a variety of strategies to solve basic addition problems such as 3 + 5. Sometimes they *count from one*; this typically involves putting up fingers on one hand to represent the first addend, putting up fingers on the other hand to represent the second addend, and then counting the raised fingers on both hands. Other times, they put up fingers but recognize the number of fingers that are up without counting. Yet other times, they retrieve an answer from memory. Some children also know another strategy, the *count-on strategy*. Children using this strategy choose the larger of the two addends and count on from that point the number of times indicated by the smaller addend. For example, for 3 + 9, children might think to themselves, "9, 10, 11, 12."

It is not the case that some 5-year-olds use one of these strategies and some use another. Rather, almost all use several different strategies. Similarly, on subtraction, multiplication, spelling, time telling, and memory tasks, the majority of children have been found to use at least three strategies. Even on individual problems, the outcomes of the competition vary, so that the same child will choose one strategy one day and a different one the next (Siegler, 1987a).

Children's choices among these strategies are adaptive in several different ways. One sense in which their choices are adaptive is that they use retrieval, the fastest strategy, predominantly on simple problems where it can yield accurate performance, and use more time-consuming and effortful strategies on more-difficult problems, where such strategies are necessary for accurate performance (Siegler, 1986).

Children also choose adaptively among strategies other than retrieval. In particular, they tend to use each strategy most often on problems where it works especially well compared to alternative approaches. In evolutionary terms, strategies find their niches. For example, the counting-on strategy is used most often on problems such as 2 + 9, where the smaller addend is quite small and the difference between addends is large. On such problems, counting-on is both easy to do and effective relative to alternative procedures such as counting-from-one (Siegler, 1987b).

Changes over time in strategy use also are adaptive. For example, in simple addition, children increasingly use the most efficient strategies, such as retrieval and counting on, and decrease their use of less-efficient strategies, such as guessing and counting from one. They also acquire new strategies, such as decomposition (e.g., solving 3 + 9 by thinking "3 + 10 = 13, 9 is 1 less than 10, so 3 + 9 = 12").

What type of selection mechanisms could produce such adaptive strategy choices? The model that I formulated divides the information-processing system into representations and processes. The representations include factual information and data; the processes operate on the representations to produce behavior. For example, in the context of arithmetic, the representation includes associations between problems and various possible answers to the problems. The processes are strategies such as counting from one, counting on, and retrieval that solve problems by operating on the data in the representation.

Figure 3.8 illustrates how this type of organization could yield effective choices among strategies at any one time and adaptive changes in strategy use over time. Within the model, the use of strategies to solve problems generates answers to the problems and also generates information about the speed and accuracy with which the problem was solved. This information feeds back to provide increasingly detailed knowledge about both the strategies and the problems. Subsequent choices among strategies are made on the basis of their past effectiveness in solving problems in general, in solving particular kinds of problems, and in solving specific problems. The more effective a strategy has been in solving problems in the past, the more often it will be chosen in the future. Further, the choices among strategies become increasingly refined as children learn that a strategy that in general is the most effective is not necessarily the most effective for a particular type of problem.

This view of development has provided the basis for computer simulations of the development of arithmetic (Siegler & Shrager, 1984; Siegler & Shipley, 1995). To illustrate how the general theoretical assumptions are realized within a specific simulation, I will describe Siegler and Shipley's (1995) model of the development of single-digit addition. This simulation modeled how children learn to choose among three approaches: counting from one, counting on from the larger addend, and retrieval. Its working can be illustrated by considering its strategy choices on 9 + 1. The simulation gradually learns that it is easier to solve this problem by counting on from the larger addend than by counting from one. It requires far fewer counts to say "9, 10" than "1, 2, 3, 4, 5, 6, 7, 8, 9, 10." This lesser amount of counting results in fewer errors and shorter solution times, which, in turn, leads to more frequent future choices of the counting-on strategy. The simulation uses this experience and similar experience with other

FIGURE 3.8   Overview of Siegler & Shipley's (1995) strategy choice model. The diagram is best read by starting at the top left.

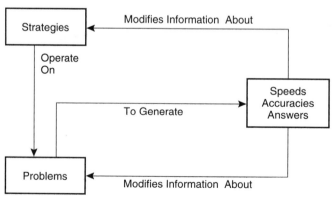

problems to draw the generalization that counting on works better than counting from one on related problems, such as 9 + 2 and 8 + 1 and uses the knowledge to generalize appropriately to unfamiliar problems.

As children increasingly choose strategies that correctly solve problems, they also increasingly associate the correct answers with the problems. For example, 9 + 1 becomes strongly associated with 10. This association allows them to retrieve 10 as the answer to the problem. Retrieving an answer is even faster than counting "9, 10" and is just as accurate. Thus, the very success of the counting-on strategy in producing correct answers leads to its own obsolescence, because it makes accurate retrieval possible.

The evolutionary perspective raises the further issue of the source of strategic variation. In particular, how are new strategies acquired? Sometimes children are taught a new strategy or imitate another person who is using it. However, the most interesting case is *strategy discovery*, in which children invent a strategy for themselves.

How do children discover new strategies? To find out, Siegler and Jenkins (1989) examined 4- and 5-year-olds' discovery of the counting-on strategy. Recall that this strategy involves solving problems such as 2 + 9 by thinking, "9, 10, 11." At the beginning of the study, children in the Siegler and Jenkins experiment knew how to add by counting from one, but did not yet know how to do so by counting on from the larger addend. The children practiced solving addition problems three times per week for 11 weeks. Because even young children can accurately report immediately after an addition problem how they solved the problem (Siegler, 1987b), it was possible to identify the exact trial on which each child first used the new strategy. This allowed us to examine what led up to the discovery, what the experience of discovering a new strategy was like for a child, and how children generalized the new strategy to other problems after making the discovery.

Almost all of the children discovered the new strategy during the course of the experiment. The time that they took to make the discovery varied widely; the first discovery came in the second session, whereas the last one did not come until the thirtieth session. The quality of the discoveries also varied widely. Some discoveries showed a great deal of insight, as exemplified by "Lauren's" protocol:

E: How much is 6 + 3?

L: (Long pause) Nine.

E: OK, how did you know that?

L: I think I said . . . I think I said . . . oops, um . . . I think he said . . . 8 was 1 and . . . um . . . I mean 7 was 1, 8 was 2, 9 was 3.

E: How did you know to do that? Why didn't you count 1, 2, 3, 4, 5, 6, 7, 8, 9?

L: Cause then you have to count all those numbers.

E: OK, well how did you know you didn't have to count all of those numbers?

L: Why didn't . . . well, I don't have to if I don't want to. (Siegler & Jenkins, 1989, p. 66)

Other children did not show nearly as much understanding. In fact, some claimed not to have counted at all, despite videotapes of their performance providing audible and visible evidence that they had used the new strategy.

What led up to the discoveries? Our expectation had been that difficult problems, or situations in which children failed to solve previous problems, would elicit them. This proved not to be the case, however. The problems on which discoveries were made, and the accuracy of performance just prior to discovery, did not differ from performance in the rest of the experiment. The only distinguishing characteristic of performance immediately before the discovery was solution times that greatly exceeded the usual amount. For example, Lauren, the child quoted above, took 67 seconds to generate the answer on the trial just before her discovery and 35 seconds on the trial where she first used the new strategy. Both trials were much longer than her average time of 11 seconds. These long times were accompanied by numerous false starts, pauses, odd statements (as in Lauren's comment referring to her own counting "I think *he* said"), and other indicators of cognitive ferment.

Another striking characteristic of the children's performance was how slowly they generalized the new strategy to other problems. For example, one girl used the new strategy on only 7 of the first 84 problems after her discovery; another girl did so on only 2 of the first 49. Temporarily, the children continued to rely heavily on the familiar counting-from-one approach, even though they knew the potentially more effective count-on strategy.

The amount of generalization increased dramatically, however, when *challenge problems* were presented to the children in the eighth week of the study. These were problems such as 24 + 2 that were easy to solve using counting on but almost impossible to solve using counting from one or retrieval. For children who had discovered the strategy of counting on from the larger addend, encountering these problems seemed to increase awareness both of the new strategy as constituting a different approach and of the goals that the new strategy could meet. In a sense, they rediscovered the strategy in a way that increased their understanding of how it served the goals of addition. After encountering the challenge problems, they generalized the counting-on strategy much more widely than they had before, on small as well as large number problems. On the other hand, children who had not used the counting-on strategy at all did not benefit from being presented the challenge problems; they simply became confused.

What are the main limitations of this theory? One problem is that the mechanisms that produce variation have not been spelled out in the same detail as the mechanisms that produce selection. Whereas the computer simulations of strategy choice indicate in detail how choices are made among existing strategies and how choices among the strategies change over time, no similarly detailed model exists for how new strategies are discovered. Also, the theory seems most applicable to domains in which children use clearly-defined strategies; its applicability to areas in which strategies are less well defined remains to be demonstrated. Still, it would be disingenuous of me to appear pessimistic about it. The basic observation that cognitive development resembles biological evolution is beginning to emerge in many areas: perceptual development (Johnson & Karmiloff-Smith, 1992), language development (MacWhinney & Chang, 1995), motor development (Thelen, 1995), and analogical reasoning (Gentner, 1989) among them. If the approach proves half as useful in understanding cognitive development as it has in understanding biological evolution, the effort to apply the idea will be well worthwhile.

Developmental mechanisms work together. In this chapter, contributions to cognitive development of the four mechanisms described earlier—automatization, encoding, generalization, and strategy construction—have been discussed in the contexts of different theories. This reflects the fact that different theories emphasize different mechanisms. However, all of the theories recognize that all of these mechanisms (and others) work together to produce cognitive change.

Consider an example of how all four mechanisms might contribute to a single development—a girl learning to attach "ed" to verbs to indicate that the action occurred in the past. Early in the process of language development, all of her mental resources would be needed just to perceive clearly words and phrases she heard. (Think of hearing a conversation in a foreign language that you don't know or are just starting to learn.) With greater experience listening to people talk, her processing of the words and phrases would become automatized, freeing up cognitive capacity for other types of processing. This extra capacity would allow her to notice that similar meanings were often expressed by words that ended with an *ed* sound. This realization, in turn, would lead her to encode the *ed* sound as a separate unit, to find out just what it meant. She then could note the regular connection between the *ed* sound and the action having occurred in the past. Finally, she could construct a new strategy based on the generalization: Whenever you want to indicate that an action occurred in the past, attach an *ed* to the end of the word describing the action. By working together in this way, automatization, encoding, generalization, and strategy construction may account for many improvements in children's thinking.

SUMMARY

Information-processing theories of development have several distinguishing characteristics. Their basic assumption is that thinking *is* information processing. They emphasize precise analysis of change mechanisms. They focus on the strategies that children devise to surmount the challenges posed by the environment and by their own limited processing capacity and knowledge.

Within information-processing approaches, cognition is viewed as reflecting both structure and process. Structure refers to relatively fixed aspects of the information-processing system, process to relatively variable and changeable ones. Among the most critical structures are sensory, working, and long-term memory. Sensory memory is devoted to holding a relatively large amount of unanalyzed information for about a second after the information is encountered. Working memory involves the information in the current situation and in long-term memory that is receiving attention at any given time. Without continuing attention, information is lost from working memory within 15 to 30 seconds. Long-term memory involves our enduring knowledge of procedures, facts, and specific events. It appears to be of unlimited capacity, and information remains in it indefinitely.

In contrast to this relatively small number of structures, each of which influences thinking in almost all situations, a much larger group of processes contributes in more delimited situations. These processes vary greatly with the particular circumstances, thus giving human cognition much of its flexibility. The same situation also elicits different processes in different people, depending on their past experience and abilities. Rules, concepts, and strategies are among the types of processes that people most often use.

Several information-processing theories of development have been formulated to make understandable how creatures as helpless and ignorant as infants eventually attain the power and flexibility of the adult information-processing system. Neo-Piagetian theories are aimed at uniting Piagetian and information-processing theories. Case's approach is a particularly influential example. It posits a series of stages much like Piaget's and a set of central conceptual structures that organize thinking in domains such as number, space, and narratives. It also suggests that limited working-memory capacity is a major obstacle to cognitive growth. By automatizing their processing, through biological maturation and through acquisition of more advanced central conceptual structures, children become able to perform increasingly difficult cognitive feats.

Psychometric theories are intended to reveal the processes underlying the individual differences that appear on intelligence tests. Sternberg's triarchic theory of intelligence illustrates how information-processing ideas can be used to pursue this goal. Sternberg divides intelligence into three types of components: metacomponents, performance components, and knowledge-acquisition components. Metacomponents function as a strategy-construction mechanism, arranging the other two types of components into goal-oriented procedures. Knowledge-acquisition components are used to obtain new information when no solution to a problem is immediately possible. Performance components do the work of solving the problem. The theory has been applied to diverse cognitive skills and to many populations, including gifted and retarded children.

Production-system theories are intended to explain how changes in problem solving occur. Klahr's theory explains particularly clearly how self-modifying production systems can advance understanding of development. It focuses on the developing system's capacity for generalization. In this analysis, generalization includes three components: the time line, regularity detection, and redundancy elimination. The time line is a record of all the situations the system has encountered, its responses to the situations, and the outcomes. Regularity detection operates on the data in the time line to detect repeated patterns. Redundancy elimination looks for parts of procedures that could be eliminated without changing the outcome of processing. Together, these mechanisms allow children to generalize their knowledge to new situations.

Connectionist theories are a class of computer simulation models based on an analogy to the workings of the brain. In them, numerous simple processing units, analogous to neurons, are connected to each other with varying strengths. When presented input, the processing units receive activation from each other, with the processing activity leading to a response. The response is compared to the correct answer, and the strengths of connections are adjusted in ways that would have led to more accurate responding. MacWhinney et al. demonstrated how such a model could learn the German language's complex system for determining whether given nouns are masculine, feminine, or neuter and which article should be attached to a given noun. The system's learning resembled that of children both in which nouns were hardest to learn and in the types of errors that it made.

Evolutionary theories are based on an analogy between biological and cognitive evolution. As emphasized in my own approach, the critical contributors to change in both cases are sources of variation and sources of selection. In children's thinking, strategy discovery provides one source of variation; strategy choice procedures provide a means of selection. The two types of processes work together to change not only how often children use different strategies, but also when they use each approach. The theory has stimulated observations of how children construct new strategies and of how use of existing strategies changes over time.

RECOMMENDED READINGS

Case, R., and Okamoto, Y. (1996). The role of central conceptual structures in the development of children's numerical, literacy, and spatial thought. *Monographs of the Society for Research in Child Development* (Serial No. 246). The most up-to-date presentation of Case's theory. Presents extensive evidence for Case's idea of central conceptual structures, together with a general model of how they develop.

Klahr, D. (1989). Information-processing approaches. In R. Vasta (Ed.), *Annals of Child Development, Vol. 6.* Greenwich, CT: JAI Press. A witty and insightful description of current information-processing approaches to development. In the article, the author characterizes Piaget as "a charter member of the soft-core information processing club." Klahr also describes his own work as a founder of the club's hard-core faction.

Plunkett, K. (1996). *Connectionism and development: Neural networks and the study of change*. A readable introduction to connectionist models and to their potential for enriching understanding of development.

Siegler, R. S. (1996). *Emerging minds: The process of change in children's thinking*. New York: Oxford University Press. The most recent statement of Siegler's theory, emphasizing how variability, choice, and a variety of change processes together shape cognitive development.

Sternberg, R. J. (1985). *Beyond IQ: A triarchic theory of human intelligence*. New York: Cambridge University Press. An articulate and persuasive presentation of Sternberg's influential theory of human intelligence.

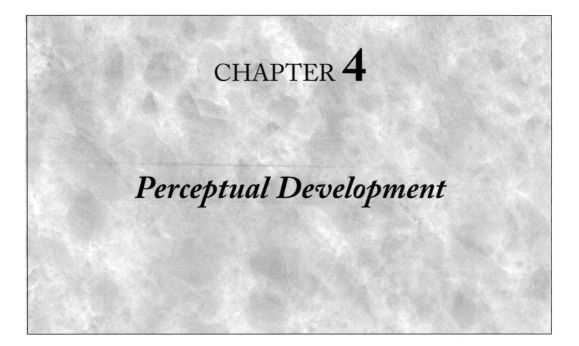

CHAPTER 4

Perceptual Development

A 4-month-old girl is shown two movies, with their screens side by side. In one movie, a woman is playing peekaboo. She repeatedly hides her face with her hands, uncovers it, and says "Hello baby, peekaboo." In the other film, a hand holds a stick and rhythmically strikes a wood block. The experimenter plays either the one sound track, with the woman saying "peekaboo," or the other, with the drum beat, but not both at the same time.

Somehow, the 4-month-old knows which sound track goes with which visual sequence. She demonstrates this knowledge by looking more at the screen that displays the movie that goes with the sound track than at the screen showing the other movie.

Spelke (1976) found that almost all 4-month-olds behave as the girl in this story did. Of the 24 infants she tested, 23 looked for more time at the screen with the appropriate video accompaniment than at the alternative. Apparently, even in their first half-year, infants connect sights and sounds in meaningful ways.

This example is representative of current findings about perceptual development in a number of ways. The children in the study were less than 6 months old. The investigator used a simple experimental procedure yet asked a fundamental question about human nature: Are infants able to integrate sights with sounds from very early in life? The results of the study showed greater perceptual abilities in young infants than might have been expected.

The central theme of this chapter is the remarkable rapidity with which perceptual functioning reaches adultlike or near-adultlike levels. By the age of 6 months, infants see and hear the world quite clearly. To put this in perspective, consider other facts about 6-month-olds. They ordinarily cannot say even one word. They do not appear to understand anything that is said to them. They can solve few problems. They do not search for toys that roll behind other objects. The advanced status of 6-month-olds' perception stands in marked contrast. Indeed, given the obvious value of skilled perception for remembering, solving problems, and learning language, perceptual development may function as a launching pad from which other aspects of cognitive development take off.

Perception and human nature.   One reason that perceptual development is such a fascinating topic is the questions it raises about human nature. Many of these center around the nature-nurture issue: How does people's biological inheritance contribute to the way in which they perceive the world? How does their experience contribute? Above all, how do the two interact?

Empiricist philosophers such as John Locke, David Hume, and George Berkeley suggested that perception might be a learned skill. Infants might at first experience the world in terms of isolated lines and angles. Gradually, they would learn that these lines and angles constitute objects. Later still, they would learn to infer properties of the objects, such as how far away they were, by noting the relation between how the objects look and how long it took to crawl or walk to them. The type of impoverished initial endowment that these philosophers envisioned led the great early psychologist William James (1890) to hypothesize that infants experienced the world as "one great blooming, buzzing, confusion."

Other theorists, such as J. J. and Eleanor Gibson (e.g., J. J. Gibson, 1979; E. Gibson, 1994), hypothesized that perceptual capabilities that are essential to survival are built into the infant. They noted that humans, like all animals, evolved in an environment of objects and events. Young, as well as older, animals needed to perceive these objects and events accurately to survive. The Gibsons also emphasized that survival depends on animals being able to act on their perceptions. For example, children need to perceive whether the terrain in front of them can be walked on (solid ground) or not (water or a cliff). Therefore, they hypothesized that perception and action were closely linked and that the linkage was already present in infancy.

Subsequent research has revealed a picture much more like that posited by the Gibsons than like that proposed by the empiricists. Even in the first months, infants seem to experience a world of objects and events that is in important ways similar to that experienced by adults (Kellman, 1988; Slater, et al., 1990). All current theories recognize that people are biologically prepared to perceive the world in certain ways, that many important perceptual capabilities are present at birth, and that other capabilities emerge in the first few months of infancy, as long as infants have normal experience and intact sensory systems.

Subsequent research also has supported the Gibsonian view that from the beginning of life, perception and action are closely connected (e.g., Bertenthal & Clifton, 1996; Goodale & Milner, 1992; Thelen, 1995). For example, when infants see a ball rolling in front of them, they sometimes move their hands to intercept it. Rather remarkably, they reach not where the object is when they begin the reach, but rather toward where it will be by the time their hands arrive (von Hofsten, 1982; 1993).

The linkage between perception and action also is evident at the neurophysiological level. The visual system appears to include two main subsystems. One, the *ventral system*, which carries information in large part to the temporal cortex of the brain (see p. 14), is specialized for recognizing and representing the visual world. The other, the *dorsal system*, which carries information largely to the parietal cortex, is specialized for using perceptual information to guide action (Goodale & Milner, 1992). The dorsal system, linking perception and action, seems to function from the first months (Bertenthal, in press).

When we think about why we perceive the environment at all, the centrality of the linkage between perception and action makes complete sense. For any organism that moves, perception provides the data needed to act effectively in the environment. It allows us to stay in touch with a constantly changing world. There is a reason why plants don't see anything; it would do them no good, because they cannot move around the environment anyway. In contrast, for animals that can move, sight, hearing, and the other senses help them meet the basic needs of obtaining food and avoiding predators.

The task of perception.   We perceive the world through a number of sensory systems: vision, audition (hearing), gustation (taste), olfaction (smell), and a few others. Regardless of the particular sense being considered, however, the task of perception can be thought of in terms of the need to accomplish three functions: attending, identifying, and locating.

Attending involves determining what in a situation is worthy of detailed processing. *Identifying* involves recognizing what we are perceiving. *Locating* involves specifying how far away the perceived object or event is and in what direction relative to the observer.

An example may make more meaningful the distinctions between the three functions. If you are in an Asian jungle and a tiger is charging, you need to orient your attention toward the tiger, to identify it as a tiger, and to locate how far away it is so that you can decide whether to climb a tree, hide, or pray. The example illustrates how attending, identifying, and locating are conceptually distinct, but also interrelated. A blur of motion in the periphery of the eye might stimulate initial attention to the tiger. More careful and focused attending would presumably follow identifying the moving object as a tiger. Yet more careful attention would follow locating the tiger as nearby and rapidly approaching.

Although people perceive the world through a number of senses, we rely most heavily on sights and sounds. Therefore, this chapter focuses on the

TABLE 4.1   Chapter Outline

I. Vision
   A.   Attending to Objects and Events
   B.   Identifying Objects and Events
   C.   Locating Objects
II. Hearing
   A.   Attending to Sounds
   B.   Identifying Sounds
   C.   Auditory Localization
III. Intersensory Integration
   A.   Attending
   B.   Identifying
   C.   Locating
IV. Summary

development of vision and audition (hearing), as well as on the way in which information from these and the other senses is integrated. The chapter's organization is outlined in Table 4.1.

VISION

As recently as 1960, many psychologists, pediatricians, and nurses believed that newborn infants were functionally blind (Lamb & Campos, 1982). A very different picture has emerged recently, however. The visual capabilities of newborns are not so great as they will be even a few months later, but the newborns definitely can see enough to start to learn about the world.

To understand visual development, it is essential to understand at least a little about the mature visual system. Visual perception ordinarily originates with light being reflected from, or emitted by, an object in the environment. The light impinges on the eye and progresses through the *cornea* and *pupil* to the *lens* (Figure 4.1). The lens bends the light rays to project a focused image on the light-sensitive retina behind it. Change in the shape of the lens that brings the object into focus is known as *accommodation*.

The retina includes two kinds of *photoreceptors* (receivers of light): *rods* and *cones*. The cones are concentrated in the *fovea*, which is a small, approximately circular area near the center of the retina. In contrast, the rods are absent from the fovea; they are in the *periphery* of the retina. In normal lighting, vision is most acute in the fovea, in large part because cones are very densely packed into it.

From the retina, information is relayed to the brain by way of the optic nerve. The *visual cortex* of the brain registers the information and integrates it with previous information to form a representation of the visual scene.

This description provides the framework within which visual development occurs. But it also leaves open many questions. For example, is the development of visual perception primarily due to changes in the eye or to changes in the parts of the brain that process input from the eyes? Does the early immaturity

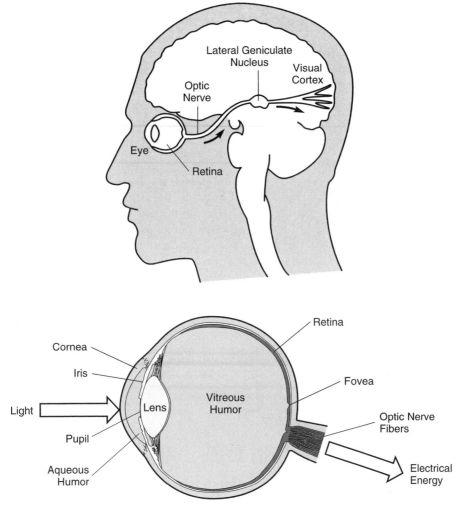

FIGURE 4.1   *Flow of information within human visual system (top), and more detailed de-piction of the eye (below).*

of the brain mean that *subcortical mechanisms* (the retina, optic nerve, midbrain, etc.) initially play a larger role in perception than they will later? Is perception direct, in the sense of depending only on currently perceivable stimuli, or do previously formed memories also influence it?

Although people have long wondered about these questions, only recently has substantial progress been made in answering them. Development of experimental methods that allow infants to demonstrate their visual competence has contributed crucially to this progress. Infants cannot verbally describe how they see the world. They also cannot follow instructions, thus ruling out almost all conventional methods for studying perception.

The key to learning about infants' perceptual capacities, then, was identifying some behavior that reflected the capacities. An incredibly mundane seeming behavior—eye movements—provided such a key to revealing the perceptual world of the infant. Infants move their eyes and turn their heads to look at what interests them. Such behavior reflects perception, because for an object to be of interest, it must be perceived.

Recognizing that infants turn their heads toward what interests them led researchers to devise two main methods for studying infant perception: the *preferential-looking paradigm* and the *habituation paradigm*. The preferential-looking paradigm typically involves displaying side by side two objects or events that differ in only one way. The question is whether infants consistently look more at one of them. If they do, they must be perceiving the difference. For example, if infants are repeatedly shown a red ball and an otherwise identical gray one, and each is sometimes on the left and sometimes on the right, and the infants consistently look at the red ball, they must perceive a difference in color.

The habituation paradigm is based both on infants' propensity to look more at objects that interest them and on the fact that they, like older individuals, grow bored with objects as the objects are presented repeatedly. The paradigm includes two phases. First is the familiarization phase, in which an object is presented repeatedly. When infants no longer look at it much, a new object or sound that differs in some specific way is introduced. If infants show renewed interest in the new object or sound, they must be perceiving a difference between the two. These simple methods have allowed researchers to make great progress in answering fundamental questions about how infants perceive the world.

Attending to Objects and Events

From the day of birth, infants look at some objects and events more than others. These preferences may be crucial to development. Cognitive growth will presumably be more rapid if infants orient to informative parts of the environment rather than to uninformative ones. But how informative should informative be? Objects and events that are too far beyond infants' current knowledge of the world may be impossible for them to understand.

Cohen (1972) made an important distinction between *attention-getting* and *attention-holding* properties of stimuli. The idea is that gross physical characteristics of objects attract initial attention, but the objects' meaningfulness determines whether the attention persists. Cohen suggested that the same attention-getting properties continue to influence perception throughout life, but that attention-holding properties change with age and experience. Movement grabs the attention of adults as well as infants, but infants and adults differ considerably in what they find interesting enough to continue looking at. In the next sections, we first consider attention-getting properties, and then attention-holding ones.

The orienting reflex.   When people see a bright flash of light or hear a sudden loud noise, they orient their attention to it even before they identify what it is. This *orienting reflex* seems to be present from birth. It is adaptive in helping people react quickly to events that call for immediate action.

The orienting reflex can be controlled by the cortex, but it more typically is controlled primarily by subcortical areas of the brain. This conclusion emerged from a study of an *anencephalic* infant (an infant born without a cortex) (Graham, Leavitt, Strock, & Brown, 1978). The anencephalic infant showed an orienting response when novel stimuli were presented. The infant also habituated to familiar stimuli. That is, as shown in Figure 4.2, the infant's heart rate, which initially showed a large decrement five to seven seconds after a speech sound (a typical orienting response), stopped showing this response after six exposures to the sound. Since this infant did not have a cortex, its abilities to orient and habituate prove that cortical activity is not needed for these processes to occur. Subcortical mechanisms must be sufficient for both.

Especially intriguing, the pattern of orienting and habituating in Graham et al.'s 1-month-old anencephalic infant actually was precocious. It was typical of a 2-month-old normal infant. Graham et al. concluded that very early in development, cortical activity may hinder rather than facilitate orienting,

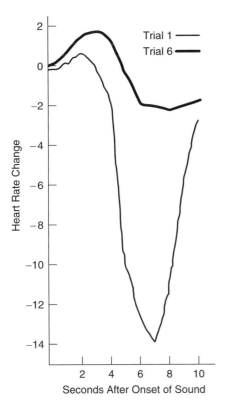

FIGURE 4.2   Orienting response of an infant born without a cortex. The curves indicate changes in the infant's heartbeat rate after he heard someone talk. On the first trial, there was a large decrease in the infant's heartbeat rate 5 to 7 seconds after the word was pronounced. This is a typical orienting-response pattern. By the sixth trial, there was little change in heartbeat rate. Thus, the infant habituated to the sound despite not having a cortex. (Adapted from Graham, Leavitt, Strock, & Brown, 1978.)

and that this was why the performance of the anencephalic infant was unusually advanced.

Overt and covert deployment of attention.   Quite often, when people's attention is attracted by an object or event, they turn to look at it. In these cases, attention is reflected in overt behavior. Other times, however, people look at one thing but their minds are on something else entirely. In these cases, attention is being deployed covertly.

Determining whether infants can attend to something different than what they are looking at has taken considerable ingenuity. However, Johnson, Posner, and Rothbart (1994) devised a way to find out. They exposed 4-month-olds to a training procedure in which the appearance of a diamond in the periphery of one side of their field of vision usually meant that an interesting beeping, rotating, multicolored wheel would appear a half second later on the other side. The diamond was on the screen too briefly for the infants to make an eye movement to look directly at it, and infants rarely looked at the side with the diamond before the wheel appeared. However, on some trials, the colorful wheel appeared just after the diamond had appeared on the opposite side. If infants were attending to the side with the diamond, but not looking there, they presumably would be especially quick to move their eyes to the opposite side where the wheel would appear. This is exactly what happened. Thus, even though the 4-month-olds were not looking directly at the diamond, they were attending to it, demonstrating that they were capable of covert as well as overt attention.

Rules for scanning the environment.   Even in their first days of life, infants do not just orient to attention-grabbing objects that appear in their visual fields; they actively seek out interesting stimulation. Haith (1980) suggested that newborns act as if they knew the following five rules for finding the interesting parts of their environments:

1. If you are awake and alert, and the light is not too bright, open your eyes.
2. If opening your eyes reveals darkness, scan the environment intensively.
3. If opening your eyes reveals light, scan the environment broadly.
4. If you find an edge, stop scanning broadly and continue scanning around the edge. Cross the edge and look at the other side if you can.
5. When you are scanning near an edge, reduce the range of fixations perpendicular to the edge if there are a lot of contours in the area.

Acting in accord with these rules helps infants find some interesting aspects of their environments, but may result in their missing others. In particular, it may lead to infants scanning the edges of objects to the exclusion of their interiors. For example, as shown in Figure 4.3, 1-month-olds scan the external contours of faces and the eyes, but not until 2 months do infants examine other internal features (Haith, Bergman, & Moore, 1977; Salapatek, 1975).

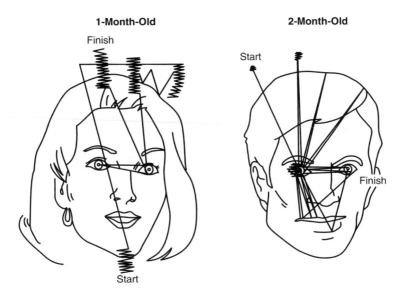

FIGURE 4.3   Visual scanning of a person's face by 1- and 2-month-olds (after Salapatek, 1975). The concentration of horizontal lines on the chin and hairline of the face on the left indicated that the 1-month-old focused on the external contours. The concentration of horizontal lines on the mouth and eye of the face on the right indicated that the 2-month-old focused on internal features as well.

These age-related changes in scanning patterns, as well as other changes in infants' attention, appear to be due in large part to the relative rate of maturation of the visual cortex of the brain and of subcortical visual structures (Bronson, 1974). Scanning can be controlled either by the visual cortex or by subcortical structures involved in vision, such as the retina and the lateral geniculate (page 105). The subcortical structures are more mature at birth and therefore seem to play a larger role in directing attention in the first months than they do later. This leads to the infants attending more to the outlines of objects, such as faces, and high-contrast areas, such as the eyes, because the subcortical mechanisms are especially sensitive to the visual information in these areas.

Several types of evidence support the view that subcortical mechanisms play an especially large role in directing attention in the first month or two. One is the anatomical immaturity of the visual cortex at birth. It is unclear that this part of a newborn's brain is sufficiently developed to direct choices of where to look. A second source of evidence is that in newborns, subcortical areas, in particular the midbrain, are known to be strongly involved in deploying attention so as to avoid returning to locations that were focused on immediately before (Valenza, Simon, & Umilta, 1994). Third, as the cortex matures during the first year, success on a variety of attentional tasks that would seem to require cortical involvement becomes possible, and analysis of brain activity during these tasks shows increasing metabolic activity in cortical areas such as the parietal lobe (Chugani, Phelps, & Mazziotta, 1987; Posner, Rothbart, Thomas-Thrapp, & Girardi, in press). Thus, the shift from initial subcortical dominance to later increasing cortical involvement in the deployment of attention seems likely to exert a major influence on where infants look.

Stimulus complexity. What qualities of objects and events hold an infant's attention beyond the initial attention-drawing occurrence? One attention-holding property appears to be moderate stimulation. Given a choice between a moderately bright object, a very dim object, and a very bright object, even 1- and 2-*day*-olds prefer the moderately bright one (Lewkowicz & Turkewitz, 1981). Even more striking, when the infants are stimulated by a loud noise just before such objects are presented, their preference shifts to the dim object. Maurer and Maurer (1988) suggested that this was due to the infants' trying to modulate the total amount of incoming stimulation; the loud noise and the dim light together provided a moderate level of stimulation. In keeping with this interpretation, Maurer found that simultaneously increasing by a small amount the amount of stimulation in each of three sensory modalities (sight, sound, and touch) had the same effect on infants' attention as increasing one of them (sound) by a large amount.

Infants cannot regulate the amount of incoming information by leaving a noisy room or telling other people to be quiet. However, they do have a powerful means for coping with overstimulation; they go to sleep. Maurer and Maurer (1988) documented a seemingly paradoxical phenomenon noted by many parents. In the first weeks of life, infants respond to increases in the amount of light and noise by sleeping *more*. Given less stimulation, they sleep less. The Maurers speculated that infants may use sleep as a strategy for regulating the amount of stimulation they receive. If given too much, they simply take a nap.

In addition to preferring moderate stimulation, infants also prefer to look at moderately complex objects, rather than at ones that are extremely simple or extremely complicated. Of course, the meaning of moderate complexity changes as the infant develops. Situations that seem moderately complex to a 2-month-old often seem simple to a 6-month-old. These observations have led to the formulation of the *moderate-discrepancy hypothesis:* that infants are most interested in looking at objects that are moderately discrepant from their existing capabilities and knowledge (Greenberg & O'Donnell, 1972; McCall, Kennedy, & Applebaum, 1977).

Several findings seem consistent with the moderate-discrepancy hypothesis. As infants grow older, they increasingly look at more complex stimuli. For example, in studies in which infants are shown checkerboards, 3-week-olds spend more time looking at 2-by-2 than at 8-by-8 boards; in contrast, 14-week-olds prefer the more-complex 8-by-8 checkerboards (Brennan, Ames, & Moore, 1966). The familiarity of the specific pattern also influences preferences. When initially shown 2-by-2 and 24-by-24 checkerboards, 4-month-olds initially preferred the simple 2-by-2 boards. After repeated exposure to both boards, however, the infants preferred the more-complex 24-by-24 patterns (DeLoache, Rissman, & Cohen, 1978). Again, as the children's ability to deal with complexity increased, they preferred more complexity.

Part of the appeal of the moderate-discrepancy hypothesis is that it suggests a mechanism of great potential importance for all aspects of cognitive development. If people are programmed to orient toward material that is just beyond their current understanding, they continually will be pulled toward more-sophisticated attainments. If there were 10 possible levels of understanding in an area, they would first attend to the material that could be grasped with the simplest level of understanding, then to the material that could be grasped with the next more complex understanding, and so on. They spontaneously would choose the optimal sequence of experiences for learning, and thus would effectively regulate their own development. Because it is difficult to measure infants' knowledge, however, it also is difficult to know what is moderately discrepant from it. Thus, at present, the moderate-discrepancy hypothesis has more the status of an intriguing possibility than of a scientifically validated law.

Expectations.   Infants are oriented toward the future, as well as the present, from the first days outside the womb. For example, expectations about the future state of the world are what allow them to reach for moving objects where the objects will be, rather than where the objects are when they begin reaching.

At least by the time infants are three months, they also form expectations about where interesting events will occur, and they use these expectations to guide their looking. This was learned in a series of studies in which the location at which an interesting picture would appear varied either in a regular alternating sequence (Left-right-left-right . . .) or in an unpredictable sequence (Canfield & Haith, 1991; Haith, 1993; Haith, Hazan, & Goodman, 1988). After less than a minute of exposure to a regular alternating pattern, 3-month-olds detected the pattern and used it to anticipate where the pictures would appear next. That is, they were more likely than infants who saw the irregular sequence of locations to look left after the picture appeared on the right, and vice versa.

Three-month-olds also form expectations about more complex patterns of events. For example, they were shown sequences in which the interesting picture's location varied in a 2/1 pattern (LLRLLR . . .) or in a 3/1 pattern (LLLR-LLLR . . .). The 3-month-olds detected these patterns and used them to guide their looking, just as they had with the alternating sequence. In contrast, 2-month-olds gave no evidence of forming expectancies about these patterns. Thus, the expectations that infants form depend on their age and cognitive level.

What, then, can we conclude about development of visual attention during infancy? Certain events, such as loud noises, bright lights, and changes in the environment, attract the attention of newborns, just as they do with adults. Even in the absence of such events, newborns scan the environment in ways that lead them to attend to the most important information. For example, their eyes focus on the contours of objects rather than on internal details. They can attend to locations covertly, even when their eyes are focused elsewhere. Infants' attention also is guided from early in life by a preference for moderate degrees of stimulation and by the expectations they form.

Next we turn from considering the determinants of infants' visual attention to considering how they identify the objects and actions that they see.

Identifying Objects and Events

Seeing clearly is one major determinant of infants' ability to identify objects and events. However, it is not the only one. Movement and color also contribute. Further, people seem to be equipped to identify especially well evolutionarily important stimuli, such as faces and human motion. This section focuses on how each of these factors contributes to our identification of objects and events.

Visual acuity.   The single capability that is most crucial for identifying objects and events is the ability to discriminate them from the ongoing flux of visual stimulation. This ability to discriminate stimuli—to see clearly their similarities and differences—is known as *visual acuity*. Typically, the Snellen chart, which hangs in every optometrist's office, is used to measure visual acuity. The letters you can read from 20 feet away are used as the reference point. If you can just read at 20 feet the letters that a person with "normal" vision can read at 150 feet, your vision is said to be 20/150.

Infants' visual acuity cannot be measured by asking them to read the letters on a chart. However, their preferences for looking at one object rather than another can yield similar information. Almost all infants would rather look at alternating black and white stripes than at undifferentiated gray fields. By showing infants a gray field on one side and a set of stripes on the other, and examining whether the infants look more toward the stripes, researchers have been able to determine how much space between stripes (*spatial frequency*) infants need in order to see the difference.

Results obtained via this technique indicate that newborns see objects at 20 feet as well as adults with 20/20 vision see them at about 660 feet (Courage & Adams, 1990). Their acuity therefore is about 20/660. Average acuity improves to about 20/300 for 2-month-olds, 20/160 for 4-month-olds, and 20/80 for 8-month-olds. The 20/80 acuity at 8 months is about as good as that of an adult who could see better if she wore glasses but would not usually bother to do so. To give a qualitative sense of what a young infant's vision is like, Figure 4.4 illustrates the finest level of stripes that most 1-week-olds can discriminate from a gray field at a distance of 1 foot (Maurer & Maurer, 1988). It is enough to see the outlines of objects, but not their details.

Differences between infants' and adults' visual acuity are present not just in absolute sensitivity, but in where the greatest sensitivity is. One-month-olds' sensitivity is greatest at very low spatial frequencies (widely separated stripes).

FIGURE: 4.4   Finest stripes that 1-week-olds can discriminate from gray field (after Maurer & Maurer, 1988).

Over the next few months, visual acuity becomes best at progressively higher spatial frequencies (stripes closer together). This means that 1-month-olds are maximally sensitive to very coarse outlines; after this, optimal vision is found with increasingly detailed patterns. What these changes mean for infants' ability to see a woman's face is illustrated in Figure 4.5.

A clinical application of visual-acuity research.   Above and beyond what they have revealed about normal development, methods developed to study visual acuity are proving useful for diagnosing infants suspected of having visual defects. One technique, described by Dobson (1983), involves showing infants cards divided into two halves. One half is an undifferentiated gray field; the other is a striped area with alternating black and white columns, like that in Figure 4.4. As noted earlier, infants strongly prefer looking at the striped area *if their visual acuity is sufficiently good that they do not see the striped area as just another gray field.* Presenting such cards to infants with known or suspected visual difficulties provides a means of assessing whether the infants' vision is sufficiently impaired to warrant corrective surgery. Because it does not demand any verbal skills, the procedure has proved useful with both normal and retarded infants ranging in age from 2 months upward (Teller, McDonald, Preston, Sebris, & Dobson, 1986).

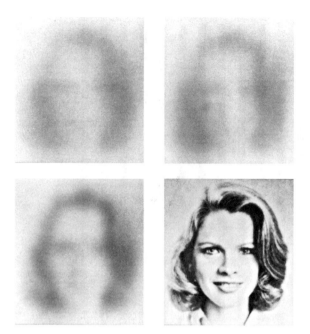

FIGURE: 4.5   A woman's face, as it would appear from a distance of 5 feet, to 1-, 2-, and 3-month-olds and adults (from Ginsburg, 1983).

Dobson (1983) described several case histories in which ophthalmologists referred infants with suspected visual problems to her. In one case, a 2-month-old boy, born four weeks prematurely, was suspected of being blind. During pediatric examinations, he seemed neither to fixate on stable objects nor to follow moving ones. However, the preferential looking procedure revealed that the boy's vision was well within normal limits; he consistently looked toward the striped area rather than the gray field, even when this required quite good acuity. By 4 months of age, the boy also was showing everyday evidence of appropriate looking. In this case, the technique saved the boy's parents several months of unnecessary worry, and saved him from being treated as a blind child.

The preferential-looking technique also has proved valuable for diagnosing whether children need corrective surgery for such maladies as cataracts, muscular weakness in the eyelids, and cross-eyedness. Even when infants have these problems, their visual acuity may still be sufficient to avoid surgery; in other cases, surgery is required. Given the inherently conflicting needs to correct many visual impairments as early as possible, while at the same time avoiding surgery that is not absolutely necessary, any technique that allows early accurate diagnosis of what an infant can see is welcome news to both parents and physicians.

Motion.   From the first day out of the womb, infants' attention is drawn to moving objects. Infants' ability to follow the movement, however, is limited by their imperfect control of their eyes. Typically, they fixate at the location where an object used to be for a second or two after it has moved away. Then, they jerk their eyes forward to a position roughly, but often not precisely, in line with the object's new location. Not until infants are about 4 months old do their eyes follow moving objects smoothly, and then only when the object moves slowly (Aslin, 1993).

People's propensity to attend to motion exemplifies the subtle and varied ways in which our perceptual system has evolved to help us adapt to our environment. In the world in which people evolved, moving objects could represent threatening predators, enticing prey, or any number of significant events. Attending to moving objects was, and continues to be, useful for survival.

The fact that motion attracts our attention also is useful in another way: It helps us identify objects. Intuitively, it might seem that identifying moving objects would be more difficult than identifying stationary ones. After analyzing the information available in the physical environment, however, Gibson (1966) noted that movement provides critical data about properties of objects that persist throughout the movement, such as that all parts of the object move together. Thus, infants might find it easier to perceive the unity of different parts of a single object (though not its details) if the object is moving.

Subsequent research supported this analysis. Infants' perception of objects as single entities often does appear to be based in large part on information provided by movement (Kellman & Short, 1987; Kellman and Spelke, 1983). For example, 3-month-olds perceive objects as separate if they move independently, but not if the same objects are stationary (Spelke & van de Walle, 1993). Thus, motion not only attracts infants' attention, it also helps them know what they are seeing.

Color vision. Adults can perceive wavelengths of light ranging from roughly 400 to 700 nanometers (nm). We see particular wavelengths as particular colors. For example, we perceive wavelengths of 450–480 nm as clearly blue, 510–540 as clearly green, 570–590 as yellow, and 615–650 as red. Although we see some wavelengths as mixtures (for example, 500 nm is perceived as bluish-green), we see most as unambiguously one color or another.

Anthropologists often have speculated that division of the wavelengths into colors is culturally relative; that is, people in different cultures would classify different wavelengths as different colors. Subsequent research in infant perception and other areas, however, has indicated that this view is false. Bornstein (1978) repeatedly presented 4-month-olds with a particular wavelength until they lost interest and stopped looking at it. Then he presented one of two alternative wavelengths. These alternatives were equally far from the original, now "uninteresting," wavelength in physical terms. However, at least to adults, one of the new wavelengths looked like a different color than the original wavelength, whereas the other looked like a slightly different shade of the same color.

Infants looked at the alternative that adults saw as the different color more than at the one adults saw as the slightly-different shade of the original, suggesting that they, too, saw the one wavelength as a different color. It has since been found that even newborns show such discriminations for some colors (Adams, 1987), and that 1-month-olds discriminate colors across the entire spectrum (Clavadetscher, Brown, Ankrum, & Teller, 1988). Thus, long before they learn color names, infants place the boundaries between colors at the same places that adults do. These results, together with identification of cells that respond differently to different colors (DeValois & DeValois, 1975) and observations that people all over the world classify the same wavelengths as being the best examples of particular colors (Berlin & Kaye, 1969), indicate that our biological makeup plays a critical role in color perception.

Social perception.   Attention to the faces of mothers, fathers, and other people has been hypothesized to play a unique role in infant development. Having your baby concentrate on your face is a gratifying experience, and having the baby show that he or she recognizes you is even better.

From the first months, infants prefer looking at faces over most other objects. Until recently, however, it was unclear whether this preference was due to the infants seeing the faces as faces or to other properties of the faces that attract infants' attention. Faces contain many characteristics that babies like; they are roughly symmetrical, have high contrast, make sounds, and move. Thus, liking for the individual features, rather than the perception that the faces are faces, might explain the fact that infants like looking at them.

A particularly clever study by Dannemiller and Stephens (1988), however, established that at least by 3 months of age, faces as such are special for infants. Groups of 6- and 12-week-olds saw the computer-generated stimuli depicted in Figure 4.6. Although stimuli A and B differ only in having their contrast reversed, adults see Figure *A* as much more facelike. At 6 weeks, infants looked at the two figures equally often; by 12 weeks, however, they strongly preferred the more face-like Figure A. They do not show any change toward preferring Figure 4.6C over 4.6D, thus demonstrating that the change toward preferring the face-like Figure 4.6A is not simply due to 12-week-olds preferring pictures with thick dark edges. Thus, 12-week-olds seem to identify faces as faces and to look at them at least in part for that reason. Younger infants also like looking at faces, but their attraction may be based on details such as motion and contrast rather than faceness as such.

How do infants learn so quickly about faces? Subcortical attentional mechanisms appear to contribute in critical ways to the rapidity of learning. In the first month after birth, infants follow moving faces with their eyes more than they do most other moving objects (Johnson & Morton, 1991). This attention to faces provides the input infants need to learn in detail what a face looks like. The faces do not need to have the detail of real faces to attract infants' attention. They just need two blobs approximately where the eyes would be and another blob where the mouth would be. Thus, newborns track both of the two leftmost faces in Figure 4.7 more than the two rightmost ones.

A

B

FIGURE: 4.6 *Stimuli presented to infants by Dannemiller and Stephens (1988). Despite A and B being identical except for the reversals of the black and white shading, A looks more facelike to adults and attracts more attention from 12-week-olds. The same infants had no preference between C and D, indicating that their preference for A was a result of their perceiving its facelike quality, rather than generally preferring stimuli with thick dark borders.*

C

D

The tendency to track moving faces declines sharply between 4 and 6 weeks after birth, a time when a number of subcortically based reflex-like behaviors decline in frequency. By the age of 3 months, infants track the four stimuli to equal extents. This led Johnson and Morton (1991) to suggest that subcortical mechanisms were responsible for the early visual tracking of faces. After this point, the visual cortex plays a large role in face recognition, particularly in distinguishing one face from another.

Distinctions among faces. In addition to liking to look at faces generally, infants prefer some faces to others. Even newborns look at photographs of their mother's face more than photographs of a female stranger (Bushnell, Sai, & Mullin, 1989; Walton, Bower, & Bower, 1992). The finding is the same regardless of whether the faces are seen in person, in a photograph, or on videotape.

Infants also have aesthetic preferences among faces. Quite remarkably, infants as young as 2 and 3 months look at faces that adults rate attractive more than faces that adults rate unattractive (Langlois, Roggman, Casey, Ritter, Reiser-Danner, & Jenkins, 1987). Roughly two-thirds of infants looked for a greater amount of time at photographs of attractive women than at photos of unattractive ones. The finding is the same regardless of raters' judgments of the attractiveness of the infants' own mothers. Infants' preference for faces that adults rate as attractive extends to the faces of women of different races, to the faces of men as

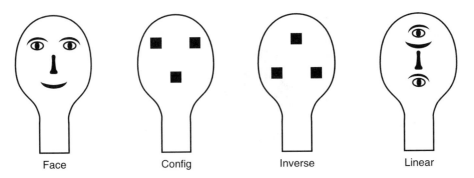

FIGURE: 4.7 *The four "faces" presented by Johnson and Morton (1991) to newborns.*

well as women, and to the faces of other babies as well as adults (Langlois, Ritter, Roggman, & Vaughn, 1991). Thus, as with division of wavelengths into colors, judgments of attractiveness cannot be attributed entirely to cultural conventions. Innate predispositions also play a role.

Why might infants (and adults) like the particular faces they do? A large part of the explanation seems to be that faces are perceived as attractive to the degree that they fit a prototype of an average face. This prototype can be approximated by taking black-and-white photos of a large number of faces, averaging the shadings of each pixel within the pictures, and using the averaged values to create a composite face. Rather than generating faces that are average in attractiveness, this procedure creates faces that adults rate as being more attractive than almost any actual face and that infants look at more than almost any actual face (Langlois, Roggman, & Musselman, 1994). These faces are average in their physical characteristics, but not in their attractiveness to infants or adults.

Human motion.   Infants also are attracted to human motion. Even 4-month-olds look longer at displays of lights that to adults look like a cartoon of a person walking than at an equally numerous, randomly placed set of lights showing similar individual motions (Bertenthal, 1993). The attraction appears to be fairly specific to human motion; 4-month-olds do not show similar interest in displays that to adults look like walking four-legged spiders (Bertenthal & Pinto, 1993).

Knowledge influences perception.   Computer chess programs compete with the greatest human chess champions, but no computer vision system recognizes objects as well as a typical 1-year-old. The reason is that recognizing what you are seeing, even in relatively simple situations, requires a surprising amount of knowledge.

Needham, Baillargeon, and Kaufman (in press) found that at least three types of knowledge influence infants' (and older individuals') perception of objects: configural knowledge, physical knowledge, and experiential knowledge. *Configural knowledge* is understanding of the type that enables us to know that Figure 4.8A probably depicts a single ball and box, rather than a ball and two separate shapes alongside the ball; the similar shapes on each side of the circle suggest that the circle is in front of a single object, rather than between two separate objects. *Physical knowledge* tells us that if the ball and box in Figure 4.8B depict real objects, the ball and box must be a single object; otherwise the ball could not stay suspended in midair. *Experiential knowledge* indicates that the ball and box in Figure 4.8C are probably two objects; we often encounter balls and often encounter boxes, but rarely see balls attached to boxes.

By 5 months of age, infants can use all three types of knowledge to determine what they are seeing (Needham et al., in press). For example, 2- to 4-month-olds understand that a solid object cannot fall through another solid object; this leads them to look usually long when an experimenter, using trickery, shows them a situation in which such an impossible event seems to happen (Spelke, Breinlinger, Macomber, & Jacobson, 1992). Thus, perception is influenced not only by action but also by knowledge.

Summary. Infants enter the world with some degree of visual acuity. They are far from blind, though their acuity increases considerably in the first 6 months and beyond. Even in the first month, infants see the outlines of objects quite clearly, as well as some high-contrast interior detail. They also seem to see the same qualitatively distinct colors as adults do. Both faces and human motion attract and hold infants' attention. Surprisingly, infants prefer to look more at faces that adults consider attractive than at other faces. Thus, preferences that were once thought of as purely the product of culture-specific values turn out to emerge so early in infancy that they almost certainly reflect biological predispositions as well.

In the next section, we examine how infants determine where objects are located relative to themselves.

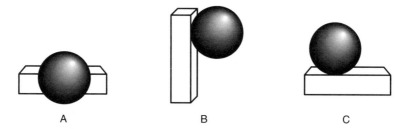

A   B   C

FIGURE: 4.8   A. Configural knowledge allows us to perceive the box as a single object, rather than as two shapes alongside a ball; B. Physical knowledge indicates that if this display depicts real objects, the ball must be attached to the box, because otherwise it would fall; C. Experiential knowledge, along with configural knowledge, suggests that a ball is on top of a box, rather than the two being part of a single object. (Example from Needham et al., in press.)

Locating Objects

Perceiving an object's location requires perceiving both its direction and its distance from oneself. When the object can be seen, perceiving its direction presents no special problem; determining its distance, however, is more problematic. At any one time, the display of light on the retina only specifies height and width, not depth; how can a three-dimensional world be represented in a two-dimensional retinal image? Yet, as noted in Chapter 1, even 1- and 2-day-olds solve the problem; they perceive distance with some accuracy (Slater, et al., 1990). In this section, we consider some of the *monocular cues* (cues available separately to each eye) and some of the *binocular cues* (cues available only when both eyes focus on an object) that make depth perception possible.

Monocular depth cues. The cues to depth that can be perceived through one eye working alone fall into two groups: those that rely on motion and those that are present even in stationary scenes. First, consider some cues that involve motion. As objects approach us, or we approach them, they fill an increasing portion of our visual field; this is known as *visual expansion*. Similarly, when a person moves his or her head, the retinal images of closer objects move faster than those of more distant objects; this is known as *motion parallax*. A third monocular cue based on motion is *occlusion*; when one object moves in front of another, the closer object occludes the overlapping parts of the more distant one. Infants seem to use all of these monocular cues based on motion in the first months of life (e.g., Arterberry, Craton, & Yonas, 1993).

In contrast, not until the age of 6 or 7 months do infants seem to infer depth on the basis of monocular depth cues that do not involve motion. These are frequently referred to as *pictorial depth cues*, since they were originally described by Leonardo da Vinci as ways of conveying distance within paintings. One such cue is *relative size*; other things equal, the closer object will cover more area on the retina. Another is *texture*; other things equal, the closer objects will have a more differentiated surface. A third cue is *interposition*, which is like occlusion, except that the objects are stationary. Five-month-olds do not appear to perceive depth from any of these pictorial cues, whereas each of them is effective in conveying information about depth to 7-month-olds (Arterberry et al., 1993). Thus, use of pictorial depth cues to infer relative distance seems to develop between 5 and 7 months of age.

Binocular cues to depth. Because people's eyes are several centimeters apart, the patterns of stimulation that impinge on the two retinas almost always differ. This retinal disparity is valuable for estimating the distance of objects from oneself. The value can be illustrated by going to an unfamiliar location, closing one eye, and trying to estimate which of two objects is farther away. Most people do much worse when they look with only one eye than when they use both.

Stereopsis, the ability to perceive depth solely on the basis of binocular cues, emerges suddenly at around 4 months. Individual infants consistently move within a week or two from clearly not having such binocular depth perception to clearly having it (Figure 4.9). The key change seems to be segregation of neural pathways from the eye to the brain (Held, 1993). Before the age of 4 months, information from both eyes arrives at the same cells in the visual cortex. Rather suddenly, the pathways are segregated so that information from the left eye arrives at some cells and information from the right eye at others. This makes it possible for the brain to detect disparities in the input from the two eyes and to infer depth based on the degree of the disparity (the farther the object, the less the disparity).

The fact that stereopsis develops so consistently and so quickly at around the age of 4 months might be interpreted as meaning that the development is only a result of maturation. It turns out, however, that visual experience also is crucial. Administering drugs that block the neural activity that would normally occur in response to visual experience results in the segregated neuronal pathways not forming at the usual time (Johnson, in press; Stryker & Harris, 1986). As often is the case, maturation does not occur in a vacuum. Even developments that are universal and that occur at a fixed age generally require normal experience as well as maturation.

The fact that both normal experience and maturation are involved in the development of stereopsis has important clinical consequences. Banks, Aslin, and Letson (1975) tested binocular functioning in children and adults who, because they were cross-eyed, did not focus bifoveally until the condition was corrected by surgery. After surgery, all of the children and adults focused both eyes on the same point in space. However, only those whose vision was corrected before age 3 had normal binocular depth perception. If the cross-eyedness was corrected before age 4 months, the time at which bifoveal fixation ordinarily becomes the rule, binocular depth perception was normal. After that age, the later the condition was corrected, the more harm was done, until about age 3, after which, unfortunately, surgery could not reduce the damage.

These clinical data suggest that in addition to the normal developmental period for binocular depth perception, birth to 4 months, there is a sensitive period within which the ability must be used if it is ever to function. This sensitive period seems to last for the first 3 years of life. The existence of such sensitive periods makes all the more valuable the development of techniques for testing suspected visual defects in infancy.

Using depth cues to avoid falling. How do infants know that they shouldn't crawl over the edges of supporting surfaces? This issue has been investigated through use of one of the true classics of psychological research, the visual cliff task (Figure 4.10). This task involves a clear plexiglass surface on which infants can crawl. One side has a tablecloth with a checkerboard pattern just below the surface; the other side has a tablecloth with the same pattern several

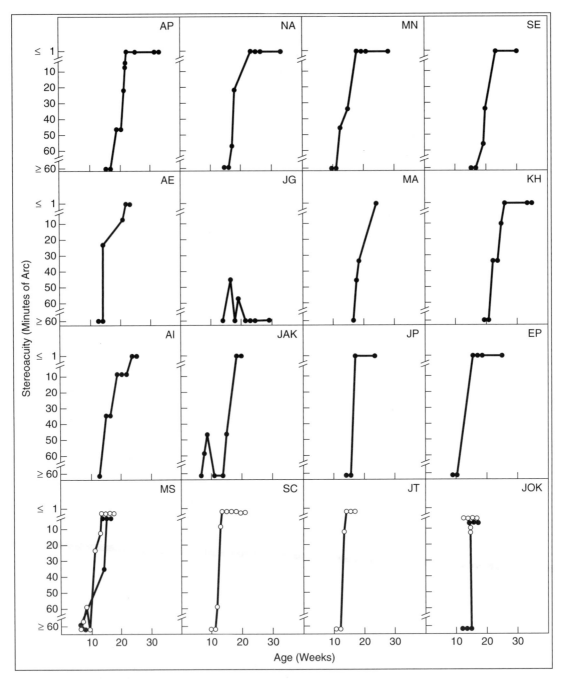

FIGURE: 4.9 Changes in 16 infants' stereoacuity between 10 and 30 weeks. Note the dramatic increases that occurred for most infants at around age 4 months (after Shimojo, Bauer, O'Connell, & Held, 1986).

feet below the surface. To adults, it looks like the surface falls off sharply at the boundary between the two parts. Infants able to crawl are placed on the "shallow" side, just before the boundary with the "deep" side, and their mothers beckon them to crawl across to them. Seven-month-olds who have been crawling for six to eight weeks often refuse, and their heart rates accelerate (a sign of fear) when they are urged to do so. In contrast, babies of the same age who are not yet crawling do not show similar signs of fear (Campos, Bertenthal, & Kermoian, 1992).

The key to this difference seems to be the experience of self-generated locomotion, rather than experience with crawling per se. In another experiment, a group of precrawling infants was given 40 hours of experience with a walker, which allowed them to move around independently by sitting in a seat and pushing with their feet on the floor. The infants given experience in the walker showed greater fear, as measured by accelerating heart rates, than infants of the same age who had not been given such experience (Bertenthal, Campos, & Kermoian, 1994).

Why would self-generated locomotion produce this effect? After all, the infants would often have experienced their parents carrying them from one place to another. However, Bertenthal et al. suggested that self-generated locomotion is different, in that it demands continuous updating of one's orientation relative

FIGURE: 4.10   An infant approaches the visual cliff (photo courtesy of Dr. Joseph Campos).

to the spatial layout. Consistent with this view, mammals that can locomote from birth shy away from cliffs from early in life. The difference between self-produced and other-produced locomotion may also account for adults learning so much more about locations when we drive to them than when someone else drives us.

Summary.   Infants use a variety of cues to determine the distances of objects from themselves. These include monocular cues, available to each eye individually, and binocular cues, available only when both eyes focus on the same point. Monocular cues can be divided into motion-based and pictorial cues. Even 1-month-olds seem to extract information about depth from motion-based monocular cues, but not until 6 or 7 months of age are the pictorial cues effective. This is one more illustration of motion aiding perception, especially young infants' perception.

The ability to perceive depth on the basis of binocular cues is called stereopsis. It arises quite suddenly at around 4 months of age, apparently based on segregation of the visual pathways connecting the eye and the brain. Humans, unlike many other mammals, do not shy away from cliffs from the time of birth. By the time they can locomote freely, however, they do avoid them. Experience with self-generated locomotion appears critical to this perceptual development.

HEARING

Attending to Sounds

Even before birth, infants demonstrate surprising auditory abilities. When babies in the uterus are exposed to loud sounds, they move around more and their hearts beat faster. By 1 week of age, infants hear and respond to a wide range of sounds. When presented with loud noises, they look startled, blink their eyes rapidly if they are open or squeeze them tightly shut if they are already closed, and jerk their limbs erratically. Quieter sounds elicit less-dramatic reactions. Thus, the newborns' auditory system is functional from the first days.

Infants are more attentive to some sounds than others. They appear especially attentive to speechlike sounds. Several general characteristics of their hearing predispose them in this direction. They react most noticeably to sounds in the frequency range (pitch) of 1,000 to 3,000 Hz, the range in which most speech occurs. They also react more to sounds that, like speech, include a range of frequencies, than to pure tones, in which all sound is at a single frequency. This is not due to their being able to hear these tones the most acutely. They detect sounds of higher frequencies at least as accurately (Schneider, Trehub, & Bull, 1979). Rather, these are the sounds that interest them enough to attract their attention. The auditory attention to frequencies in the speech range is reminiscent of the visual attention to faces and human motion—in both cases, infants are predisposed to attend to information that helps them learn about other people.

One type of sound that infants find especially attractive is that of their own names (Mandel, Jusczyk, & Pisoni, 1995). Already by 4 months of age, they attend for a greater amount of time to a loudspeaker that is saying their names than to a loudspeaker that is saying a different name with a similar stress pattern (e.g., Jojo versus Mimi).

Identifying Sounds

Infants show impressive ability to identify and discriminate between sounds that differ only subtly. Many of the most impressive demonstrations of this ability concern speech perception. However, infants also have keen abilities for identifying and discriminating among other sounds, such as musical tones.

Speech. First, consider speech perception. Two-month-olds discriminate between such similar sounds as *ba* and *pa*, *ma* and *na*, and *s* and *z*. Their perception of the differences between these sounds seems to be categorical, just as their perception of the differences between colors is. This was originally shown in experiments testing 1- and 2-month-olds' ability to discriminate *ba* from *pa* (Eimas, Siqueland, Jusczyk, & Vigorito, 1971). The two sounds differ only in *voice onset time (VOT)*, the time when speakers begin to vibrate their vocal cords to make a sound. Despite this dimension of timing being continuous, adults hear sounds with VOTs below a certain value as *ba*s and otherwise identical sounds with VOTs above the threshold as *pa*s—we do not hear any sound as a mixture of *ba* and *pa*. Apparently 1- and 2-month-olds also perceive the speech sounds categorically. After hearing *ba* repeatedly, they dishabituate more when they hear a *pa* than when they hear a different *ba*, one whose VOT is equally far from the original *ba* but in the opposite direction. Infants have shown similar abilities to discriminate syllables that differ only in the position of the speakers' lips (*ba* versus *ga*), their tongues (*a* versus *i*), and numerous other features of speech (Aslin, Jusczyk, & Pisoni, in press).

Might these discriminations be caused by the particular language infants hear? A study with Guatemalan infants between 4 and 6 months of age suggests not. The Guatemalan infants were of interest because the Spanish they hear places the VOT boundary between *ba* and *pa* at a different place than it is in English and most other languages. In spite of this linguistic experience, the infants dishabituated in a way that indicated that they placed the boundary between *ba* and *pa* where most languages do, rather than where their native language does (Lasky, Syrdal-Lasky, & Klein, 1975). Thus, infants may enter the world with sensitivities attuned to particular boundaries.

These predispositions do not persist forever. Although infants are sensitive to many contrasts not used in the language they hear, they later lose sensitivity to these features. Werker, Gilbert, Humphrey, and Tees (1981) demonstrated this phenomenon with English- and Hindi-speaking adults and 7-month-olds who were brought up in Canada. The task was one in which two sounds differed on a contrast that differentiates words in Hindi but not in English. After repeatedly presenting one sound, the experimenter abruptly switched to the other. To get a reward, subjects needed to turn their head to one side when the sound changed. Among the infants, 11 of 12 accurately perceived the change, as did all of the Hindi-speaking adults. However, only 1 of 10 English-speaking adults accurately perceived it.

The beginning of the decline in the ability to hear contrasts not used in one's native language coincides in time with beginning to speak the native language (Werker & Desjardins, 1995). Both occur at around the age of 10 months. Declines in ability to hear contrasts occur at this time for two different distinctions used in Hindi but not in English and for three different distinctions used in Zulu but not in English (Best, 1995; Werker, 1989). The decline continues for the next 8 to 10 years, at which time ability to discriminate the sounds has sunk to adult levels.

Why does this decline in phonemic discrimination abilities occur? The reason seems to be that in the course of acquiring their native language, children learn to group together sounds that differ physically but where the differences do not affect meaning (such as the physically different *ba* sounds studied by Eimas and his colleagues). Attesting to this interpretation, infants show considerably heightened sensitivity to the sound patterns of their native languages in the period just before they lose sensitivity to sound differences that do not matter in their language. Thus, 9-months-old, but not 6-month-olds: (1) prefer listening to words that have sequences of phonemes that are common in their language to ones that are uncommon (Jusczyk, Luce, & Chales Luce, 1994); (2) prefer listening to words that have stress patterns that are common in their language over ones that are uncommon (Jusczyk, Cutler, & Redanz, 1993); (3) are more likely to integrate novel 2-syllable sequences into a single unit (like a word) when the two syllables conform to the stress pattern typical of their language (Morgan, 1996). Thus, increasing sensitivity to the sound patterns of their native languages precedes, and may well cause, decreasing ability to discriminate among sounds that are not meaningfully different in their native language. As is often the case, developmental gains also involve losses (for a wide range of illustrations of this principle, see Baltes, 1997).

Speech perception involves much more than the ability to discriminate among sounds. Among the other skills that it requires is identifying the voices of different speakers. Infants as young as 3 days old can identify their mother's voice, and they prefer it to other voices. DeCasper and Fifer (1980) devised a procedure in which an infant's sucking was followed either by presentation of the mother's voice or by the voice of a female stranger. They found that the 3-day-olds sucked at a higher rate when the reward was their own mother's voice.

In DeCasper and Fifer's experiment, none of the infants had spent more than 12 postnatal hours with its mother. Although this experience may explain the preference for the mother's voice, another possibility is that the preference was based on familiarity with the voice obtained before birth. Evidence supporting this possibility was found in a study in which expectant mothers were asked to read aloud Dr. Seuss' story *The Cat in the Hat* each day during the last six weeks of their pregnancy. After the babies were born, an experimenter played a tape recording of the mother reading that story or an unfamiliar one. The babies sucked at a higher rate in response to the familiar story (DeCasper & Spence, 1986).

When adults talk to infants and young children, they often speak in a style known as *motherese*. This style is characterized by high pitch and exaggerated intonations. In a study of German mothers, Stern, Spieker, and MacKain (1982) found that 77 percent of the mothers' utterances to infants between birth and 6 months of age fell into the motherese category. Subsequent studies have shown that most men as well as women talk to infants in this way and that motherese is used in a wide variety of cultures and language communities (Fernald, Taescher, Dunn, Papousek, de Boysson-Bardies, & Fukui, 1989).

Adults have good reason to use motherese in talking to infants. Infants as young as 2 days old seem to prefer it. They look longer at a checkerboard pattern when the reward for looking is hearing a tape of a woman speaking simple sentences in motherese than when the reward is hearing the same woman saying the same sentences as she would to an adult (Cooper & Aslin, 1990). The extremely early age at which this preference for motherese is shown suggests that it does not depend on associating a way of talking with other rewards that the mother provides, such as food and comfort. Instead, it seems independent of postnatal experience. As with the preference for *The Cat in the Hat*, however, the liking for motherese could be influenced by experience hearing the mother talk that way while the baby is still in the womb.

In sum, infants are able to discriminate among speech sounds, voices, and intonation patterns. They also prefer their mother's voice to that of other women and prefer motherese to adult intonations.

Music. Infants perceive the distinctions between some types of musical sounds categorically, just as they perceive colors and speech sounds. In listening to the types of sounds made on a violin, adults perceive some as plucks and others as bows. The differences between plucks and bows can be reduced to a single physical dimension known as rise time. Two-month-olds discriminate between plucks and bows, but not between stimuli equally discrepant in *rise time* that adults hear as two types of plucks or two types of bows (Jusczyk, Rosner, Cutting, Foard, & Smith, 1977).

Although both speech and musical sounds are processed categorically, different parts of the brain predominate in processing them. The left hemisphere of the brain predominates in speech perception, whereas the right hemisphere dominates perception of other complex sounds such as music. Such *lateralization* (dominance of one hemisphere in processing a certain type of information), is evident in auditory evoked responses. To examine these *auditory evoked responses*, the experimenter places electrodes at specific points on the left and right sides of the head, presents a stimulus simultaneously to the two ears, and records the amount of electrical activity on each side of the brain. When the stimulus involves speech, the left hemisphere shows greater brain activity—that is, a greater auditory evoked response. When the stimulus involves music, the pattern is reversed, with the right hemisphere showing greater activity.

Some lateralization may be present even before most babies are born. Newborns born four to six weeks prematurely show greater left-hemisphere response to speech sounds, just as adults do (Molfese & Molfese, 1979). By the age of 2 months, infants also show greater right-hemisphere responses to musical sounds than they do to speech (Best, Hoffman, & Glanville, 1982). Thus, the beginnings of lateralization may be among the reasons that very young infants can identify both speech and musical sounds.

Just as speech discrimination abilities conform increasingly to those that are meaningful in the infant's native language, so do music perception abilities. Lynch and Eilers (1992) presented 6- and 12-month-olds with a brief melody either in the commonly used major scale or in the rarely used augmented scale. The melody was presented repeatedly through a stereo speaker until the infants were familiar with it. Then, they started hearing either the familiar melody or a version of it with one note somewhat off-key. The 6-month-olds discriminated the deviations in both cases; they turned toward the speaker more often when the off-scale note was played in either the familiar or unfamiliar scale. In contrast, 12-month-olds' discrimination skills, and also those of adults, were more limited. They noticed deviations within the familiar scale, but not in the rarely-heard one.

The finding raises an intriguing question: Is the similar timing of the narrowing of music- and speech-perception abilities a coincidence, or does it indicate a general reorganization of the auditory perception system? At present, no one knows.

Auditory Localization

After his daughter was born, an unusually single- ninded psychologist named Wertheimer entered the delivery room. Rather than basking in the experience, Wertheimer used his daughter's birth as an opportunity for an experiment. He sounded a clicker first on one side of the room and then on the other. From the first sounding of the clicker, the baby turned her head in the direction of the sound. Thus, at least a crude sense of *auditory localization* (the ability to locate sounds in space) seems to exist from birth (Wertheimer, 1961). The same result has been found in larger samples of newborns. The subsequent findings indicate some ability to localize the sounds within the side from which they came, as well as to locate them as being generally to the right or to the left (Morrongiello, Fenwick, Hillier, & Chance, 1994).

Surprisingly, newborns seem better able to localize sounds than 2- and 3-month-olds, although not better than 4-month-olds. This pattern of data, which appears in a number of contexts throughout the book, has been labeled a *U-shaped curve*. At first, performance is at a high level, then it drops, then it returns to a high level. The U-shaped pattern is of special interest, because it suggests that different mechanisms are responsible for the same behavior at different points in development. This seems to be the case in auditory localization.

Muir, Abraham, Forbes, and Harris (1979) conducted a longitudinal study in which they repeatedly examined four infants over the first 4 months of the infants' lives. They found that three infants showed a U-shaped pattern

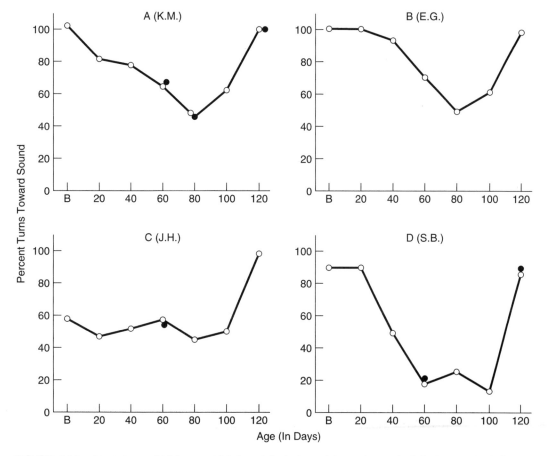

FIGURE: 4.11   *Percentage of trials on which four infants turned toward sounds. Infants were tested every 20 days from birth to 120 days (from Muir, Abraham, Forbes, & Harris, 1979).*

of auditory localization. As shown in Figure 4.11, the infants first showed high levels of head turning toward the side from which the sound came, then showed reduced levels, and then, by about the age of 4 months, returned to the prior high levels. The decline in the middle was not caused by lack of interest in the sounds. Even when an infant's mother or father called the child's name in the middle of a group of rattling sounds, the pattern of head turning did not change.

Muir et al. proposed an explanation much like those proposed by Bronson (1974) and Johnson (in press) to explain U-shaped patterns in infants' visual behavior. They suggested that auditory localization in the first month after birth reflects subcortical functioning. In the second and third months, cortical activity increases and it replaces subcortical activity as the dominant influence on infants' auditory localization. However, at this point, the cortical activity is not sufficiently developed to produce as accurate performance as the subcortical mechanisms had previously. Only in the fourth month does the cortical activity become sufficiently mature to reinstate accurate localization.

The precision of auditory localization improves rapidly between the ages of 2 and 5 months, and it continues to improve more slowly until infants are roughly 1½ years old (Ashmead, Davis, Whalen, & Odom, 1991). It is probably not coincidental that the rapid improvement occurs during the time when infants' ability to control their heads is also rapidly improving. Better control allows infants to move their heads more precisely to where they want them to go and allows them to learn how to move their heads to the optimal location for hearing (Bayley, 1969; Bertenthal & Clifton, 1996).

To summarize, infants enter the world with substantial auditory capabilities, and the capabilities develop further in the first few months. The capabilities are evident in which sounds attract infants' attention, in their ability to identify sounds, and in their ability to localize where sounds originate. Sounds with frequencies and other characteristics that resemble speech are especially likely to attract infants' attention. This seems to be more a result of the sounds interesting them than to the sounds being especially easy for them to detect. Infants, like adults, appear to process both speech and music sounds categorically. And, like adults, the left hemispheres of infants' brains seem to be most involved in processing speech sounds, and their brains' right hemispheres in processing musical tones. Development of both speech and music perception involves losses as well as gains; toward the end of the first year, infants' perceptual abilities narrow in a way that focuses them on the type of speech and music that are part of their culture. The ability to localize sounds shows a U-shaped pattern between birth and the age of 4 months. It is best at the two extremes, and is less good in between. A plausible explanation is that subcortical mechanisms produce the initial high level of skill, whereas cortical mechanisms produce similarly good localization beyond the age of 4 months.

INTERSENSORY INTEGRATION

How do infants integrate the information they receive from different sensory systems into a single coherent experience? One plausible developmental path would be that each sensory system first develops independently and then, when all have reached a degree of maturity, they become interconnected. Piaget (1971) proposed just such a theory. Recent investigations of infants' intersensory integration suggest a quite different picture, however. It now appears that sights and sounds are integrated from birth.

Demonstrations of intersensory integration have been presented under other headings throughout this chapter. These studies have shown that intersensory integration influences all three of the functions that have been examined: attending, identifying, and locating.

The orienting reflex exemplifies how intersensory integration influences infants' attention. Hearing loud noises cause infants to look toward the source of the sound. That is, they use auditory information to guide visual attention.

Both sights and sounds are also used to identify objects and events. Recall Spelke's (1976) study in which 4-month-olds looked more often at the movie whose visual images were in keeping with the sounds they were hearing (the mother playing peekaboo or the drum beat). If the infants were not trying to integrate visual and auditory information to understand the movie, they would have had no reason to act in this way.

Finally, vision and audition are clearly coordinated from birth when the purpose is to locate the source of a sound. All of the studies of auditory localization that were discussed used head turns toward the source of the sound as the primary measure of localization. Head turning would not be a useful measure if infants did not look toward the sources of sounds.

In this section, we consider in greater depth how infants integrate information from different senses to attend, identify, and locate.

Attending

Just as infants follow looking rules based on visual information, so do they follow rules based on auditory information (Mendelson & Haith, 1976). One such rule is that when you hear a sound, and you are looking somewhere else, look toward the source of the sound. Another rule concerns what to do when you already are looking at the apparent source of a sound. Under this condition, you should center attention closely on that source and shorten the length of your eye movements. The rules seem likely to promote attention to animate objects, such as people and other animals, that make noise. Consistent with this view, when 5- to 7-month-olds hear a voice, they increase their scanning of a face in front of them, particularly the eyes (Haith, Bergman, & Moore, 1977).

Identifying

Spelke (1976) demonstrated that 4-month-olds integrated auditory and visual information in identifying the events in the movie. More recently, she and a co-worker demonstrated that 4-month-olds also integrate *tactile* (touch) and visual information in identifying objects (Streri & Spelke, 1988). The infants first explored with their hands one of two objects: either two rings connected by a rigid stick, or the same rings connected by a flexible band. A thick cloth was placed so as to prevent the infants from seeing the object that their hands were exploring. After the infants habituated to handling the object, they were shown visually either the rigidly or the loosely connected rings.

The 4-month-olds looked more at the object with the type of connection they had not encountered previously. The demonstration was especially interesting because during the manual-exploration phase, most infants had not touched the connection; they only played with the rings. Thus, their visual identification seemed to be based on their making an inference about the type of object that would produce the observed reactions to their pushing and pulling the rings.

One question that follows from these findings is whether visual experience promotes or hinders ability to identify objects sheerly through manual exploration. To find out, Morrongiello, Humphrey, Timney, Choi, and Rocca (1994) contrasted the ability of congenitally blind 3- to 8-year-olds to identify objects through manual exploration with that of sighted children of the same ages who performed the task blindfolded. One possibility was that the sighted children would do better, because they had had the opportunity to learn what objects looked like when manual exploration revealed certain properties. Another line of reasoning suggested that the blind children would do better. They would have had to depend more on manual exploration, and might be more skilled at it.

In fact, blind and sighted children were equally skillful in identifying the objects through manual exploration. They were correct on an equal percentage of trials, took equally long to do the exploration, and were equally complete in their explorations. In contrast, the older children were better on all of these measures than the younger children. The findings indicate that manual exploration skills improve with age, but that the improvement is due to general cognitive improvements rather than specifically-visual experience or experience correlating manual and visual information.

Locating

Reaching in the dark. As noted earlier, visual information is used to guide reaching from the first days of infancy. Infants also can use auditory information to guide their attempts to get objects. By 3 months of age, infants in totally dark rooms will reach for objects that are making sounds (Clifton, Muir, Ashmead, & Clarkson, 1993). Interestingly, the first age at which they were able to make contact fairly consistently with the object in the dark is the same as the first age at which they were able to make contact fairly consistently with a moving object in a lighted room—12 weeks. Thus, although vision seems intuitively to be the primary sense that guides our reaching, hearing can exercise a comparable influence, at least early in infancy.

Sonar aids for blind children. Earlier, we discussed how research on visual acuity had proved useful for diagnosing infants suspected of having defective vision. The development of sonar aids for blind children indicates that knowledge of perceptual development may be useful for devising innovative treatments as well as diagnostic procedures. These sonar aids can be viewed as a kind of intersensory compensation, since they allow blind children to use their hearing to locate obstacles in their paths and thus to move around freely.

A scientist from New Zealand, Leslie Kay, invented the sonar aid in the early 1960s. The device provides people with the same types of information as that used by dolphins and bats to locate objects. It sends out and receives back ultrasonic waves and then transduces the reflected waves to frequencies that people can hear through earphones (Figure 4.12).

The sonar aid works by providing information about the distances, directions, and textures of objects. The frequency of the signal indicates the distance of the object. The closer the blind child comes to an object, the lower the tone that is reflected. The child can adjust the absolute frequencies depending on the type of distances of interest in a particular situation. If a girl wanted information about objects that were close by, as she might if playing indoors, the range could be set so that objects 6 feet away would make the highest sounds and closer objects proportionally lower sounds. If the girl were going to play with friends outside, she might set the sonar aid so that objects 20 feet away made the highest sounds.

The direction of objects is indicated by relative volumes in the two ears. An object on the right side produces a louder signal in the right ear than in the left. The degree of the discrepancy indicates the deviation of the object's location from directly in front of the child.

FIGURE: 4.12   A blind child wearing a sonic guide reaches for an object (photo courtesy of Dr. G. Keith Humphrey).

Information about an object's texture is provided by the purity of the tone. The waves reflected from smooth surfaces such as glass and metal approach pure tones. Rougher surfaces, such as bushes and trees, reflect more complex tones. In addition, rough surfaces give rise to characteristic patterns that can help in identifying the object.

If sonar aids can provide useful information to blind people, what is the optimal age for children to begin to wear them? To answer this question, some information about the typical development of blind children is essential. Much of their early development is like that of sighted children, including the ages at which they raise their heads and chests, sit, roll over, and stand. Walking, however, is considerably slower to develop in blind children. Fraiberg (1977) suggested that the sight of attractive objects provides a "lure" for walking, and that the absence of this lure among blind children was responsible for the delay. By this logic, the sonar aid's assignments of sounds to ordinarily-silent objects might motivate blind children to begin walking earlier. The argument suggests that the sonar aid might best be introduced at the time when children begin walking or shortly before, that is, at about 9 to 15 months of age.

Aitken and Bower (1982) examined four blind children in an effort to determine the optimal age for starting them with the sonar aid. Two children who began to wear the aid at 6 and 8 months of age, respectively, learned to use it effectively, but two whose use began at 13 and 14 months of age, respectively, did not. This led the investigators to hypothesize that children must begin wearing the aid in their first year for it to be helpful.

However, Humphrey and Humphrey (1985) found that older children also can learn to use the sonar aid effectively. The two children they studied began using the device when they were 19 and 31 months old, respectively. The 31-month-old, Eddy, made especially impressive progress. When the aid was on, Eddy's exploration of a new environment was described as "smilingly confident." He both avoided obstacles and skillfully sought objects to climb on. When the aid was removed, Eddy's steps became "slower, smaller, and more hesitant." He became unwilling to explore further following repeated collisions with chairs and tables.

After several years of experience with the aid, Eddy most often wore it to explore new surroundings, such as a house he had not visited before. He rarely wore it in familiar locales (Humphrey, Dodwell, Muir, & Humphrey, 1988). Thus, he seemed to use it to build an initial mental map of the new environment, but then discarded it when he possessed such a map (presumably so he could hear other sounds from the surrounding world).

Perhaps the most eloquent testimony for the value of the sonar aid comes from an individual introduced to the device as an adult.

> In the first few months the Sonicguide functions primarily as an obstacle detector. Slowly but surely one starts putting things together and over a period of time begins using it as an environmental sensor. I can't tell you enough how gratifying it is to be able to recognize the sound of a tree, a person, a picket fence, etc. With the

guide there is information which may help in not only mobility, but in providing a sense of what's "going on in the world around me."

After using the Sonicguide 5–10 hours a week for the past three years, I am at the point that I react very naturally to its signals. I no longer have to think about what each signal could mean; rather I react instinctively. I go around someone on the sidewalk without even realizing I've done it: that's how much a part of you it becomes. (Lepofsky, 1980)

A chronological summary.   We have considered infants' perceptual development from the perspective of how each sensory system develops. Also considering what capacities infants possess at different ages in the first year may convey a larger picture of perceptual development. Table 4.2 lists a number of the capabilities that we can be confident infants have developed by the ages listed. The estimates are deliberately conservative; infants may well possess some of these abilities earlier than indicated in the table.

The table reveals an interesting pattern: Hearing seems to develop considerably more rapidly than vision or intersensory integration. All the basic developments in hearing that are listed are achieved by age 3 months. This is not the whole story, of course. Infants' hearing is still improving quantitatively. For example, they are becoming able to hear softer sounds, especially in the lower frequencies. They also will later lose the ability to perceive some speech contrasts as their hearing becomes increasingly attuned to their own language. It also is possible that further research on infants' hearing will reveal some abilities they do not possess at all until after they are 3 months old, or that further research will reveal that all the visual and intersensory capabilities also develop by equally young ages. For the present, however, it is striking just how advanced hearing is in early infancy. The level of development seems even more impressive when we realize that we are viewing it against the backdrop of all these other extraordinarily early-developing capabilities.

SUMMARY

Perceptual functioning reaches adultlike or near-adultlike levels remarkably rapidly. Even newborns see, hear, and integrate information from different sensory systems. These abilities develop considerably further in the next 6 months, enabling infants to attend to, identify, and locate objects and events quite effectively. From the beginning, perception and action are closely connected.

The properties that attract visual attention differ from those that hold it. In general, the properties that attract attention remain the same throughout life. For example, the orienting reflex leads newborns, as well as adults, to attend to loud noises and bright lights, as well as to unfamiliar objects and to moving objects. Newborns as well as adults also respond to light, edges, and contours with characteristic scanning patterns that can be described as looking rules. Attention-holding properties, on the other hand, change greatly with age and experience.

TABLE 4.2 Perceptual Abilities Infants Clearly Have at Different Ages

AGE	CAPABILITY		
	VISION	HEARING	INTERSENSORY INTEGRATION
Birth	Orienting reflex. Looking rules. Color vision. Size constancy. Scan external contours of objects. Motion-based monocular depth cues.	Orienting reflex. Almost adultlike volume thresholds in medium- and high-frequency ranges. Prefer mother's voice.	Look toward source of sounds. Looking rules for responding to sounds. Visually guided reaching.
1 month		Categorical speech perception.	Sounds intensify visual scanning.
2 months	Scan interiors of objects.	Categorical perception of musical sounds.	
3 months	Form expectations. Eyes smoothly follow moving objects. Prefer mother's face.		
4 months	Prefer organized "biological" motion patterns. Binocular depth perception (stereopsis).		Integrate sights and sounds with similar rhythms. Integrate visual and tactile information.
5 months	Avoid visual cliffs.		
6 months 7 months	Pictorial depth cues are effective: interposition, relative size, etc. Use memory to infer distance.		Blind infants benefit from sonar aids.

Although the visual attention of both infants and adults is held by moderate degrees of stimulation, what constitutes moderate stimulation changes with development. Similarly, although expectations seem to guide attention at all ages, the expectations that can be formed change. In the first few months, subcortical brain mechanisms play an especially important role in guiding attention; after that, the increasing maturity of the cortex allows it to become increasingly important in controlling where infants look.

A number of abilities related to visual identification of objects and events show marked growth in the first eight months. Visual acuity improves from roughly 20/660 to 20/80. The improvement is especially marked at moderate spatial frequencies. The anatomical immaturity of the eye during the first months after birth seems responsible for many properties of vision in the first few months, such as infants preferring to scan contours rather than interiors and preferring to look at checkerboards with large checks. In addition to infants' general capabilities for identifying objects, they also have clear preferences for looking at certain objects rather than others. Among these preferred objects are human faces, particularly attractive ones and especially those of their own mothers.

Locating objects demands being able to identify how far away and in what direction the objects are. Infants locate the distance of objects from themselves by using both monocular cues (cues available to each eye, even if the other is closed) and binocular cues (cues to depth based on the difference in images on the two retinas when both eyes are used). Monocular depth cues based on motion are effective quite early, whereas the pictorial monocular cues are not effective before 6 or 7 months. Binocular depth perception (stereopsis) emerges quite suddenly at about age 4 months, apparently due to a combination of maturation of the visual pathways connecting the eye and the brain and normal visual experience.

The levels of auditory perception shown by young infants are at least as impressive as their achievements in visual perception. Infants are especially attentive to speechlike sounds. This appears due to their being interested in the speechlike sounds, rather than to their being able to detect them more easily than other sounds. By 4 months of age, they are also interested in some particular sounds, such as their own names.

Infants' identification of both speech and musical tones is categorical, much like their color perception. The categorical perception is not attributable to the particular language infants hear; infants may set categorical boundaries at points different from those that appear in their native language. In addition to being able to discriminate between specific sounds, newborns are also able to identify more general speech characteristics. For example, they can discriminate their mother's voices from those of other women. They also show a preference for motherese, a form of speech characterized by high-pitched sounds and exaggerated intonations.

Auditory localization shows a U-shaped function. At birth and after 4 months of age, localization is quite accurate. In the interim, the ability is less acute. The pattern, like infants' pattern of visual attention, may reflect a shift from subcortical to cortical dominance.

Perceptual development research also has yielded important discoveries for diagnosing and treating infants with perceptual defects. Research on visual acuity has led to techniques for diagnosing whether infants suspected of being blind can see well enough to avoid corrective surgery. On the treatment side, sonar aids show great potential for helping blind children navigate around their environments. These devices substitute sounds for the sights that blind people cannot experience. The sonar aids provide information about the distance of the objects, their direction, and the type of object involved. Some researchers have hypothesized that the aids should be introduced during the first year, but they seem to be effective even when introduced considerably later.

RECOMMENDED READINGS

Bertenthal, B. I. & Cliften, R. (1996). Origins and early development of perception, action, and representation. *Annual Review of Psychology, 47,* 431–459. This review of the development of perception and action during infancy provides an up-to-date discussion of important findings and issues in this rapidly evolving field.

Humphrey, G. K., Dodwell, P. C., Muir, D. W., & Humphrey, D. E. (1988). Can blind infants and children use sonar sensory aids? *Canadian Journal of Psychology, 42,* 94–119. Heartening descriptions of blind children's use of sonar aids to maneuver around their environments.

Langlois, J. H., Ritter, J. M., Roggman, L. A., & Vaughn, L. S. (1991). Facial diversity and infant preferences for attractive faces. *Developmental Psychology, 27,* 79–84. Why would an infant prefer to look at attractive faces, and how would she know which ones are attractive? This article provides plausible answers to these questions.

Maurer, D., & Maurer, C. (1988). *The world of the newborn.* New York: Basic Books. This book won the American Psychological Association book award for 1988. The award was well deserved, because the book is both readable and informative in describing how newborns see, hear, feel, and think.

Werker, J. F., & Desjardins, R. N. (1995). Listening to speech in the first year of life: Experiential influences on phoneme perception. *Current Directions in Psychological Science, 4,* 76–80. A brief and readable summary of what infants bring to the task of speech perception and what is gained—and lost—with age and experience.

CHAPTER 5

Language Development

Where you going?
I'm going.
Shoe fixed.
Talk to mommy.
Shoe fixed.
See Antho.
Anthony.
Good night.
See morrow morning. (Weir, 1962)

The preceding monologue was obtained from a tape recording of a 2½-year-old talking in his crib before going to sleep. The statements exemplify several key properties of children's use of language. First, they communicate meaning. It is easy to understand most of what is being said, even though the phrases are not the ones that older individuals would use. Second, the statements are cryptic. When children first learn to speak, they include only the essentials. They omit many of the prepositions, articles, adverbs, and adjectives that lend precision, color, and grammatical structure to the language of older individuals. Third, the language is internally motivated. No one else was in the room during Anthony's monologue. Nonetheless, he found talking sufficiently interesting that he spoke anyway.

Children's acquisition of language raises several fundamental questions. Perhaps the most basic parallels one alluded to in the previous chapter on perceptual development: How do children make sense of the blooming, buzzing, confusion of speech sounds? Simply dividing the flow of sound into distinct words is quite demanding; no computer program yet devised can do it very well. Comprehending other people's statements requires additional abilities: understanding not only the meanings expressed directly but also unspoken implications. Speaking correctly requires yet further abilities: enunciating the individual sounds, ordering words within sentences, and organizing sentences in ways that communicate coherent thoughts.

In response to these demands, children engage in a variety of mental activities that enable them to comprehend and produce speech. Their well-developed auditory perception system, described in the previous chapter, allows them to divide speech into individual words. This accurate perception of other people's speech, and children's early-developing ability to imitate, help them learn to pronounce words correctly. They pay attention to and remember the order of words that they hear in particular phrases, while also searching for generally applicable grammatical rules.

Above all, they attend to meanings, both the meanings they wish to convey and the meanings other people are trying to get across. Emphasizing meaning is an intelligent approach to language acquisition. Language is a tool for adapting to the social world. Sentences that express intended meanings will further that adaptation, even given serious shortcomings in pronunciation and grammar. Sentences that do not express intended meanings will not be adaptive, even if grammar and pronunciation are perfect.

In addition to children's own efforts to learn language, parents, siblings, other adults, and other children also help. They vary their intonations in ways that attract infants' and toddlers' attention, speak in short simple sentences that are easy to comprehend, and focus on objects and events that are present in the immediate environment. Cultural history is also on the language learner's side. Languages were constructed by human beings, and they have evolved so that children can learn them. The result is that despite the immense complexity of language, almost all children learn their native tongue quickly and painlessly.

Is language special? Everyone agrees that just about all children learn language rapidly and well, but there is enormous disagreement about why they are able to do so. The great linguist Noam Chomsky (e.g., 1972) proposed one answer: That people possess a "language organ" that allows them to acquire language especially easily. Chomsky thought that only a special mechanism such as a language organ could account for how young children so quickly learn the immensely complicated and abstract systems of rules characteristic of grammar. Just as organs such as the heart and lungs effortlessly perform complex, specialized tasks in the circulatory and pulmonary systems, so would the language organ perform the complex, specialized task of learning grammar.

Chomsky proposed that the language organ embodies innate knowledge of aspects of grammar that are consistent across all the world's languages ("*universal grammar*"). This innate knowledge would allow children to recognize which of a few possible types of grammar their native language used and thus to learn it quickly, despite its inherent complexity.

Several types of evidence support Chomsky's view that language learning is special, in the sense that it differs from learning in general (Maratsos, in press). One way in which language acquisition is special is its universality. It occurs, and occurs quickly, across a wide range of environments. Children learn in cultures in which adults converse with children on topics of special interest to the children, in cultures in which adults refuse to discuss such topics, and in cultures in which they discourage young children from talking to them at all (Snow, 1986). Acquisition of most complex cognitive skills is more dependent on favorable circumstances and direct instruction.

Another special characteristic of language acquisition is its self-motivating properties. Some children are interested in trucks, others in birds, yet others in dinosaurs. In contrast, all children are sufficiently interested in language to master a very complex system in a relatively short time. Part of this is due to a desire to communicate. This desire is so characteristic of human beings that it is tempting to think it must apply to other animals as well. Interest in communicating information of no direct importance for survival seems to be uniquely human, though. No other animal communicates in the wild with anything like the frequency that every normal 3-year-old does. Even chimpanzees that have learned to communicate quite well through sign language rarely communicate just for the sake of communicating (Tomasello, Kruger, & Ratner, 1993).

People's interest in language goes beyond communicating; we also try to speak grammatically. Beginning language users often ask question such as Anthony's "Where you going?" Other people understand such statements, respond appropriately to them, and rarely correct them. Yet children soon abandon such immature forms in favor of grammatically correct ones. This motivation cannot be attributed to a general desire to imitate adults and older children, as young children's special tastes in clothing, music, and food indicate. Instead, the desire to learn language, like the desire to be near other people and to understand the world around us, seems to be a basic part of people's makeup.

A third way in which language is special is its relation to mental abnormalities that affect thinking in general. This is especially apparent in comparing the linguistic skills of children with Down Syndrome and Williams Syndrome (Maratsos & Matheny, 1994; Mervis & Bertrand, 1993; Miller, 1992; Singer, Bellugi, Bates, Jones, & Rossen, 1995). Children with both syndromes tend to have IQs that are much lower than normal, usually between 50 and 70. However, the language skills of children with Williams Syndrome are better than would be expected from their IQs, whereas those of children with Down Syndrome are worse. Williams Syndrome children have both much greater vocabularies and much greater grammatical skills. In fact, some adolescents and adults with Williams Syndrome speak well enough that they could be mistaken for typical adults. This almost never happens for those with Down Syndrome. Then again, by adolescence, Down Syndrome children fairly often succeed on Piagetian tasks designed to measure reasoning, such as number conservation and class inclusion, that children with Williams Syndrome consistently fail. Thus, while language and thought are complexly interdependent, these syndromes indicate that they also are distinct.

As Chomsky theorized, then, language acquisition appears to be special in certain ways. However, his claim that children have innate knowledge of a universal grammar has fared less well. The problem is that there does not appear to be a universal grammar to be learned. Comparisons of the grammars of the world's languages reveal tremendous diversity (Slobin, 1986). Even simple grammatical distinctions, such as that between *a* and *the*, are made in remarkably varied ways. In English, *a* and *the* are separate words, though both words are placed before the noun. In Finnish, a single word, *en*, is attached to the front of the noun when it plays the role of *the* and to the back of the noun when it plays the role of *a*. In Hungarian, the distinction can be signaled through the order of the verb and the direct object. In some African languages, tone patterns are used to make the distinction. In Chinese and Japanese, the distinction is inferred purely from context. Thus, language learning is far more complex than simply recognizing which of a few possible types of grammar is being heard. It seems to require both general learning abilities and abilities specific to language acquisition (Maratsos, in press).

Does language have a special biological underpinning? The view that language acquisition differs from other kinds of learning suggests that language might have a special biological basis, such as a specific location in the brain or specific electrical patterns. Two concepts are especially important in thinking about this issue. One is *localization*, the idea that the brain activity that underlies a specific cognitive function is concentrated in a particular part of the brain. The other is *plasticity*, the idea that brain functioning changes in response to experience.

First, consider evidence regarding localization of language. Language has a distinct anatomical base. For the large majority of people, the dominant area in language processing is in the middle of the left hemisphere of the brain, in particular in Broca's Area and Wernicke's Area (Figure 5.1). Studies of patients with *brain lesions* (damaged or removed parts of the brain) indicate that damage to these areas harms language competence more than comparable amounts of damage to corresponding areas of the right hemisphere. This is true of sign language as well as spoken language, indicating that the critical processing in this area is not limited to speech or to the auditory modality.

In addition to language processing as a whole ordinarily being concentrated in the left hemisphere, particular linguistic functions tend to be located in

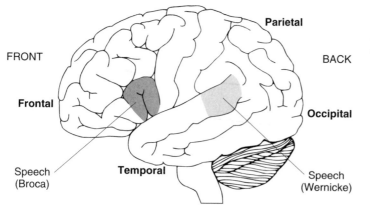

FIGURE 5.1. Side view of left hemisphere of brain, indicating locations of Broca's and Wernicke's Areas.

particular parts of the left hemisphere. For example, studies of brain-damaged patients indicate that naming of colors involves at least three areas. Lesions to an area toward the back of the brain (in the lower occipital lobe) cause loss of color vision. Lesions to Wernicke's Area (Figure 5.1) cause inability to say color names. Lesions to areas in between often leave intact the ability to see colors and to list the words used to label colors (for example, by saying "red, green, blue, brown . . ."), but they interfere with patients' ability to say which name goes with which color (Damasio & Damasio, 1989; 1992).

Localizing linguistic functions in particular parts of the brain often proves tricky, though. Even the best accepted finding, the dominance of the left hemisphere in language use, has exceptions. For one-third of left-handers, language processing occurs primarily in the right hemisphere (Kolb & Wishaw, 1996). The more specific the function, the more exceptions to the typical location in the brain.

Although the left hemisphere already dominates most people's language activity during infancy, damage to the left hemisphere before age 1 results in much less impairment to ability to understand and produce language than will similar damage later in development. That is, the brain's plasticity in the face of such damage decreases with age.

Evidence regarding this point comes from the experiences of infants born with brain abnormalities that cause life-threatening seizures. The only way known to correct these seizures is to remove the entire hemisphere that is causing the seizures, a surgical procedure known as a *hemispherectomy*. Usually, this procedure results in some degree of retardation (Huttenlocher, 1994), though at least one person who underwent a hemispherectomy attended and graduated from college and entered a professional career (Smith, 1984). Surprisingly, given the usual dominance of the left hemisphere in linguistic processing, people who have undergone left-side hemispherectomies before they are 1 year old develop quite normal language. The right hemisphere takes over much of the function that usually would be done by the left, and the people use language quite normally in most contexts (Stiles & Thal, 1993). One apparent cause of the recovery is that language processing takes over areas of the right hemisphere that usually support perceptual-spatial functioning. Thus, left-side hemispherectomies performed on infants sometimes result in more damage to perceptual and spatial functioning, in which right hemisphere functioning is usually dominant, than to language functioning, in which left-hemisphere functioning is. The pattern of results suggests the presence of a genetically based program that prefers to occupy tissue in the left hemisphere but which, if such tissue is unavailable, will commandeer tissue elsewhere (Maratsos & Matheny, 1994).

Even greater early plasticity is evident with more localized damage. If localized left-hemisphere lesions are incurred in the first year of life, children's prospects for close-to-normal linguistic development are good (Stiles & Thal, 1993). Their language learning in the first 3 years is slower (Marchman, Miller, and Bates, 1991), but by the time they are 4 or 5 years old, their linguistic ability is generally within the normal range. Left-hemisphere damage after this tends to produce more lasting damage, however. Thus, as is often the case, substantial plasticity in the location of processing is present early on, but the degree of plasticity decreases with development.

Organization of the chapter.   The discussion of language development in the rest of this chapter is divided into five main sections. The first four correspond to the four main aspects of language: phonology, meaning, grammar, and communication. *Phonology* concerns the ways in which people produce meaningful sounds, such as those within words. *Meaning* emphasizes the correspondences between particular words and phrases on the one hand and particular objects, properties of objects, events, and ideas on the other. *Grammar* focuses on the system of rules through which people form sentences. *Communication* involves the way that phonology, syntax, and semantics are used to convey messages to other people and to understand what they have in mind.

These four aspects of language first assume prominent roles at different points. Phonology begins to develop soon after birth, as infants increasingly make the sounds characteristic of their language. Around their first birthday, infants produce their first understandable words, which makes the meaning of those words an important issue. At roughly 18 months, toddlers begin to string together phrases of two or more words, so that their grammatical rules for constructing such phrases become an issue. Finally, communication is complexly related to all the other aspects of language and could reasonably be placed at any point in the ordering. Because it can best be understood in the context of the other aspects of language, however, we examine it after them. Finally, the discussion closes with brief consideration of an issue that affects all aspects of language: the relation between language and thought. The chapter's organization is outlined in Table 5.1.

TABLE 5.1   Chapter Outline

PHONOLOGY

How People Speak

When people are silent, air passes freely through the windpipe, nose, and mouth in the process of breathing. We speak by impeding the airflow. The two fundamental classes of speech sounds—vowels and consonants—are produced by different types of impediments. With vowels, the only impediment to the airflow comes in the vocal cords. There is no further blocking by the tongue, teeth, or lips. Consonants, on the other hand, involve impediments by the tongue, teeth, and lips, as well as by the vocal cords. The difference can be seen in pronouncing a vowel such as the *a* in *hat* and then making a consonant sound such as the *b* in *ball*. With the vowel, we do not use our lips; with the consonant, we do. All languages include both vowels and consonants.

Different vowels are distinguished primarily by the placement of the tongue. As shown in Table 5.2, the vowel sound in *meet* is produced with the tip of the tongue high and quite far forward in the mouth. In making the vowel sound in *mat*, however, the tongue is much lower. (Because people usually are unaware of their tongue's location within their mouth, it may be informative to use your fingers to determine its location when you make these sounds.)

Development of Phonology

Infants produce a wide variety of sounds. However, their assembly of the sounds into language is limited by difficulty in making the particular sound

TABLE 5.2   Placement of Tongue within Mouth for English Vowel Pronunciations

	FRONT OF MOUTH	MIDDLE OF MOUTH	BACK OF MOUTH
High in mouth	meet mitt		cooed could
Middle of mouth	mate met	glasses	code cawed
Low in mouth	mat	mutt	cod

they want to make. Development comes in increasing ability to produce the sounds at will.

How does ability to make these sounds develop? The following list gives a general sense of the progression (Kent & Miulo, 1995):

1. *Crying:* Infants cry from the day they are born. The crying communicates that they would like something to be different. Many parents believe that they can infer what their infant would like merely from the sound of the crying. Given tape recordings of their infants' cries, however, parents usually cannot tell what the infants want (Muller, Hollien, & Murray, 1974). Thus, parents must infer the cause of the crying from the context, rather than from the precise sound.
2. *Cooing:* Between the ages of 1 and 2 months, infants begin to make sounds other than cries. In particular, they coo by placing their tongue near the back of their mouth and rounding their lips. These coos resemble the *uh* sound that older individuals make in pronouncing the word *fun*.
3. *Simple articulation:* At around 3 months of age, infants substantially increase the number of consonant sounds they make.
4. *Babbling:* By 6 months of age, infants combine consonants and vowels, and thus produce syllables. These syllables are often repeated in sequences such as *bababababa*. The intonations of the babbling increasingly resemble those of speech.
5. *Patterned speech:* Toward the end of the first year of life, infants increase their production of sounds that appear in their language and decrease their production of sounds that do not. Near their first birthdays (give or take a few months), most say their first words.

Although hearing their infant's first word is a major milestone for parents, the infant's achievement is quite continuous with development of babbling before that point. The sounds of infants' babbling and of their first words tend to be similar. Summed across a set of 15 languages, the sounds *b, p, m, d,* and *n* are the most common sounds in infants' babbling (Locke, 1983). This tendency makes understandable why in extremely diverse languages, words with these sounds, such as *papa, mama,* and *dada,* are names for parents and are among the first words that children learn (Table 5.3). Babies are making the sounds anyway; languages may as well take advantage of the fact.

In Table 5.3, the consonants *m* and *n* are associated with the meaning "mother" but not "father." This pattern is typical; an examination of more than 1,000 terms drawn from the world's languages showed that 55 percent of the terms for "mother" included nasal sounds such as *m* and *n*, but only 15 percent

TABLE 5.3   Early Words for Mother and
Father in 10 Languages

	MOTHER	FATHER
English	mama	dada
German	mama	papa
Hebrew	eema	aba
Hungarian	anya	apa
Navajo	ama	ataa
Northern Chinese	mama	baba
Russian	mama	papa
Spanish	mama	papa
Southern Chinese	umma	baba
Taiwanese	amma	aba

of the terms for "father" did (Jakobson, 1981). Jakobson proposed an intriguing explanation for the difference. The only phonemes that can be produced when the lips are pressed to the breast are nasal sounds, such as *m* and *n*. Later, infants may reproduce these sounds at the mere sight of food, to express an interest in eating, or to ask for some other change. Thus, words including *m* and *n* are especially convenient for naming the person who most often provides food and fulfills desires, the baby's mother. The use of such easy-to-make sounds to name mothers is a particularly nice example of cultures adapting to children's natures in ways gratifying to parent and child alike.

Cultures also accommodate to the phonological limitations of slightly older children by not using difficult-to-pronounce words for the objects toddlers most want to talk about (people, animals, vehicles). For example, although *str* sequences are fairly common in English (e.g., *strong, strap, straight*), few are present in the names of objects that particularly interest young children.

Despite these accommodations of languages to infants' and toddlers' capabilities, achieving phonological competence requires a great deal of practice. The importance of such practice was illustrated in a case in which a birth defect required a cognitively normal infant to have a tube in her mouth between the ages of 5 and 20 months (Locke & Pearson, 1990). During this time, the infant heard a typical amount of speech, but the tube prevented her from making almost all sounds. When the tube was removed at 21 months of age, she immediately greatly increased the number of sounds she made, but very few were well-formed syllables. Her speech more closely resembled that of deaf children of the same age (Oller & Eilers, 1988) than that of hearing children. Only after a few months of being able to produce sounds freely did she gain normal phonological competence for her age.

Most children do not gain full phonological competence until roughly school age. Some of the problems that toddlers and preschoolers experience come from their failing to produce the sound they intend. Their pronunciation is inconsistent, in the sense that they sometimes mispronounce words that at other times they pronounce correctly. Another part of the problem stems from certain sounds simply being difficult to make. Producing sounds such as *sh*, *th*, *s*, and *r* requires precise coordination of vocal cords, tongue, teeth, and lips. Coping with other cognitive demands exacerbates the difficulty; mispronunciations increase when children try to produce grammatically-complex sentences (Panagos & Prelock, 1982).

Young children cope with such challenges by choosing their words carefully. When toddlers with vocabularies as small as 25 to 75 words know more than one term for a given meaning, they tend to select the term that is easier to pronounce (Leonard, 1995; Menn & Stoel-Gammon, 1995). Conversely, once they become able to produce a sound pattern, they increase their use of terms that make use of that phonological pattern (Vihman, 1992).

Young children seem to be quite conscious of their pronunciation difficulties. For example, in one experiment, a 3-year-old was presented a number of sentences ("I 'mell a 'kunk") and asked whether that was the way he would say it or the way his father would. On all 30 trials, the boy was correct in identifying the person who would use that pronunciation (Kuczaj, 1983). Such knowledge is an early example of *metalinguistic awareness*—awareness of what you know, and don't know, about language. To make concrete this metalinguistic awareness, consider the following conversation between a psycholinguist and his 2½-year-old son:

FATHER: *Say "jump."*
SON: *Dup.*
FATHER: *No, "jump."*
SON: *Dup.*
FATHER: *No. "Jummmp."*
SON: *Only Daddy can say "Dup!"* (Smith, 1973, p. 10)

MEANING

Learning the meaning of even a single word is far from simple. For example, if a parent points to a dog and says, "That's a dog," the lesson is unclear. Should the child conclude that the word *dog* means animal, collie, mammal, four-legged object, furry object, or any number of other possibilities? And, that's about the simplest case. Often, children hear words in the context of rapidly spoken sentences addressed to other people and referring to objects and events that are not even present. Yet somehow they figure out the words' meanings. The question is how they do so. In this section, we first describe the relatively slow course of children's learning of words and word meanings up to about 18 months of age, and then the much-faster acquisition that occurs thereafter.

Early Words and Word Meanings

A child's first words.   The similarity between children's babbling and their early words makes it difficult to identify just when they produce their first word. Parents often discern words months before even sympathetic friends and relatives can. It is unclear whether the discrepancy reflects parental hopes and pride or whether the parents are simply more skilled in understanding their child. In any case, most uninvolved observers place the typical age of the eagerly awaited first word between the ages of 10 and 13 months, although deviations in both directions are common.

By 18 months of age, a vocabulary of 3 to 100 words is typical. These words seem to many observers to have a characteristically childlike favor. One-year-olds use words like *ball*, *doggie*, and *more*; they almost never use words like *stove*, *animal*, and *less*. In general, they refer to objects and actions that interest them, that are relatively concrete, and that they want.

Children throughout the world refer to the same types of objects with their earliest terms. They talk about people: *dada*, *papa*, *mama*. They talk about vehicles: *car*, *truck*, *train*. They also talk about food, clothing, and household implements, such as keys and clocks. Table 5.4 lists the 50 most common words of children in the United States (Nelson, 1973). The first words spoken by children in Italy and other countries are highly similar (Caselli, Bates, Casadio, Fenson, Fenson, Sanderl, & Weir, 1995). This similarity is not limited to spoken languages; the first 50 sign-language words of deaf children of deaf parents are comparable, including such terms as *Mommy*, *Daddy*, *cookie*, *baby*, *shoes*, *milk*, *dog*, *bye*, and *ball* (Bonvillian, Orlansky, & Novack, 1983).

One-word phrases.   In children's first half-year of speech (roughly 12 to 18 months), they usually speak in single words. The demands of producing even a single word stress their cognitive resources, as evidenced by their frequent reduction of multisyllabic words to a single syllable (saying *po* for *piano*) and by their frequently pausing between syllables within a word (Echols, 1993; Johnson, Lewis, & Hogan, 1995). Thus, the cognitive demands of phonology appear to limit the meanings that toddlers can express.

Toddlers partially compensate for these limitations by choosing single words that convey larger meanings. These single words are often called *holophrases*, because they express the meaning of an entire phrase. When 1-year-olds say *ball*, the word seems to imply an entire thought such as "Give me the ball," "That is a ball," or "The dog took the ball." Both context and the particular words toddlers choose make these one-word statements understandable. For example, children in the one-word stage who want a banana usually say *banana* rather than *want* (Greenfield & Smith, 1976). Because of the many things the child could want, and the relatively few aspects of bananas about which the child could be commenting, *banana* is the more informative term. However,

TABLE 5.4 Words Most Commonly Appearing in the First 50 Words Children Use

CATEGORY AND WORD*	FREQUENCY†	CATEGORY AND WORD	FREQUENCY
FOOD AND DRINK:		VEHICLES:	
Juice	12	Car	13
Milk	10	Boat	6
Cookie	10	Truck	6
Water	8	FURNITURE AND HOUSEHOLD ITEMS:	
Toast	7	Clock	7
Apple	5	Light	6
Cake	5	Blanket	4
Banana	3	Chair	3
Drink	3	Door	3
ANIMALS:		PERSONAL ITEMS:	
Dog (variants)	16	Key	6
Cat (variants)	14	Book	5
Duck	8	Watch	3
Horse	5	EATING AND DRINKING UTENSILS:	
Bear	4	Bottle	8
Bird	4	Cup	4
Cow (variants)	4	OUTDOOR OBJECTS:	
CLOTHES:		Snow	4
Shoes	11	PLACES:	
Socks	4	Pool	3
TOYS AND PLAY EQUIPMENT:			
Ball	13		
Blocks	7		
Doll	4		

Source: Adapted from Nelson, 1973.

*Adult form of word used. Many words had several variant forms, in particular the animal words.

†Number of children (of 18) who used the word in the 50-word acquisition sequence.

when offered a banana they do not want, 1-year-olds generally say *no* rather than *banana*, presumably because saying *banana* could be misinterpreted.

Overextensions, underextensions, and overlaps.   The fact that young children use a word does not guarantee that they mean the same thing by it that older individuals do. Clear deviations from standard meanings are quite common up to about age 2, and more subtle ones continue for years thereafter.

Children's deviations from standard meanings fall into three categories: overextensions, underextensions, and overlaps. Anglin (1986) observed each of these in the speech of his oldest daughter, Emmy. *Overextensions* involve using a word to refer not only to the standard referents but to others as well. For example, Emmy used the term *doggie* not just to refer to dogs, but to refer to lambs, cats, wolves, and cows. *Underextensions* involve limiting the use of a word to a subset of its standard referents. For example, Emmy used *bottle* to refer only to her plastic drinking bottles; she would not use it with other bottles, such as Coke bottles. *Overlaps* involve overextending a term in some ways and underextending it in others. Emmy underextended the term *brella* by refusing to apply it to a folded umbrella, but simultaneously overextended it to kites and to a leaf used to keep off rain by a monkey in her storybook.

Overextensions are the most dramatic of these errors; almost everyone notices when a child calls a cat *doggie*. Underextensions are less dramatic; in everyday situations, it is often impossible to know whether a child who does not say *doggie* upon seeing a dog underextends the term or simply does not feel like talking about the dog. This created an initial impression that overextensions were more common than underextensions. Testing 1- and 2-year-olds' word meanings more directly (by showing them objects and asking "What's this?" or "Is this a _____?") has revealed a different picture, though. These studies have shown that underextensions actually are more common than overextensions (Kay & Anglin, 1982). Beginning language learners tend to be conservative in extending newly acquired words to novel referents (MacWhinney, 1989).

Form and function.   What features play the largest roles in early word meanings? Two that appear to be especially important are *forms* (the perceptual appearances of objects) and *functions* (the purposes that they serve). The role of form is evident in children's overextension errors (Clark, 1973). For example, children throughout the world call round things, such as walnuts, stones, and oranges, *balls*. These objects share few functions with balls, but they do share a similar appearance. The importance of function in early word meanings is evident in the earliest words that children use (Nelson, 1973). These words tend to refer to things that children want (e.g., *more, up, cookie*), or objects or activities that interest them (e.g., *doggie, car, keys*).

Form, function, and other properties *can* dominate early word meanings, but no one of them always does. Bowerman (1980) illustrated this point with observations of her daughters, Eve and Christy. Both overextended many of their early words. Typically, their overextensions were consistent with the particular instance from which they first learned the term. The overextensions emphasized a variety of notable features of the objects and actions they named, although form and function were the most common.

Table 5.5 presents a good example. Eve learned the term *kick* in the context of kicking a ball. She later overextended the term to describe activities with similar forms and functions, even though many of the events she referred to are not ordinarily labeled *kicks* in English. For example, she used *kick* to refer to sudden sharp contact between her arm and an object, to an object being propelled, and to the waving of a limb (Bowerman, 1982).

This example illustrates the demands of learning word meanings. When children hear an unfamiliar word, they cannot be sure which aspect of the situation it labels. Some words refer mainly to functions (e.g., *helps*), others to form (e.g., *big*), others to actions (e.g., *hits*). Interesting forms and functions increase the likelihood of children being sufficiently intrigued by an object or action to try to guess the right word for it and to use the word early on. Thus, both figure prominently in the meanings they assign to those words.

Development beyond the Earliest Words and Word Meaning

The course of vocabulary acquisition. Until about 18 months, word learning proceeds very slowly. At this point, however, there is a "language explosion" during which vocabulary learning accelerates. As shown in Table 5.6, average vocabulary size more than doubles between the ages of 18 and 21 months and again between the ages of 21 and 24 months. The rapid growth continues for years (Smith, 1926). Current estimates indicate that by first grade, a typical child understands at least 10,000 words, and, by fifth grade, 40,000 (Anglin, 1993). This means that from age 1½ to 10, children add an average of more than 10 words per day to the set of words they understand. The number of words that

TABLE 5.5   *Some Early Words and Their Referents*

1.   Eva, kick.
     Prototype: kicking a ball with the foot so that it is propelled forward.
     Features: (a) waving limb; (b) sudden sharp contact (especially between body parts and other object); (c) an object propelled.
     Selected samples. Eighteen month: (first use) as kicks a floor fan (Features a, b); looking at picture of a kitten with ball near its paw (all features, in anticipated event?); watching moth fluttering on a table (a), watching a row of cartoon turtles on television doing can-can (a). Nineteenth month: just before throwing something (a, c); "kick bottle," after pushing bottle with her feet, making it roll (all features). Twenty-first month: as makes ball roll by bumping it with front wheel or kiddicar (b, c); pushing teddy bear's stomach against Christy's chest (b), pushing her stomach against a mirror (b); pushing her chest against a sink (b), etc.

Source: Bowerman, 1982, p. 284.

TABLE 5.6   Size of Vocabulary at Various Ages

AGE		NUMBER OF WORDS	GAIN
YEARS	MONTHS		
	8	0	
	10	1	1
1	0	3	2
1	3	19	16
1	6	22	3
1	9	118	96
2	0	272	154
2	6	446	174
3	0	896	450
4	0	1,540	318
5	0	2,072	202

Source: Adapted from M. E. Smith, 1926.

children produce in their own speech increases at a similarly rapid rate (Dromi, 1986; Goldfield & Reznick, 1990).

This torrid pace suggests that children must infer the meanings of new words from a few exposures. Studies of acquistion of word meanings support this conclusion. Despite the many possible meanings a word might have, 1-year-olds often can identify a new word's meaning (or at least a good approximation) from fewer than 10 exposures to it (Woodward, Markman, & Fitzsimmons, 1994). Two- and 3-year-olds often can approximate the correct meaning after a single exposure (Carey, 1978; Heibeck & Markman, 1987). But how is such "fast mapping" between a word and its meaning possible, when, as pointed out earlier, even pointing to a dog and saying "This is a dog" allows so many interpretations? The philosopher Quine (1960) labeled this question "the riddle of induction."

Markman (1989; 1992) proposed that children solve this riddle by never considering the vast majority of logically possible hypotheses about word meanings. Instead, they focus on the meanings that adults are most likely to have in mind. This does not mean that they are mind readers. Rather, as Markman suggested, their hypotheses about word meanings are constrained in ways that narrow the range of possibilities and that often lead to their first guesses being correct. She suggested that three constraints on the guesses are especially important: the *whole-object constraint*, the *taxonomic constraint*, and the *mutual-exclusivity constraint*.

The whole-object constraint.   When someone points to an object and says its name, even young children tend to assume that the word refers to the object as a whole, rather than to one of its parts or properties. Thus, when an adult points to a novel object and says, "This is my blicket," 2-year-olds assume that *blicket* is the name of the novel object, rather than its color or texture (Soja, Carey,

& Spelke, 1991). Given the same situation, adults make the same assumption (Imai & Gentner, 1993).

When children are told "This is an *X*," their guesses about what *X* means are particularly influenced by the shape of the object being labeled. Both preschoolers and adults will use a newly introduced word to refer to objects that have the same shape as the original example but that differ in color, texture, and size (Baldwin, 1992; Landau, Smith, & Jones, 1992; Smith, Jones, & Landau, 1992). They are much less likely to use the new word to refer to objects that have different shapes but that are similar in color, texture, or size.

The taxonomic constraint. The taxonomic constraint refers to children's tendency to guess that when a new word is used to label an object, the word can also be used to refer to other objects in the same class. For example, when children as young as 18 months are shown a picture of a dog chewing a bone and told "This is a sud," they assume that *sud* refers to dogs as a class, rather than to the dog's nose, body, or coat or to dogs chewing bones (Markman, 1989).

Even if children assume that words that are used to describe objects refer to the category of which the objects are members, they still must determine the level of generality of the category. In the previous example, in which children were told "This is a sud," how can children know whether *sud* means a general term such as *animal*, a more specific term such as *dog*, or a yet more specific term such as *German shepherd*? Part of the answer is that children tend to assume, unless given evidence to the contrary, that unfamiliar words involve a *basic level* of description—that is, a level that conveys the main perceptual and functional properties of the object without being extremely specific (Golinkoff, Shuff-Bailey, Olguin, & Ruan, 1995). In the above example, children would assume that *sud* means *dog*, because knowing that an object is a dog tells us its main characteristics without getting into detailed distinctions among types of dogs. This assumption works well, because language addressed to young children includes many more basic-level terms, such as *dog*, than more abstract or more specific ones (Anglin, 1977; Blewitt, 1983).

Another issue raised by the taxonomic constraint is how children learn words that refer to properties if they assume that words name classes of objects. For example, if a mom says "Winnie the Pooh is sad," how does her child figure out what "sad" means? One way is for the person introducing the new term to contrast it explicitly with already-known terms within the same category. Twice saying "It's not gray, it's celadon" is sufficient for 3-year-olds to realize that *celadon* is the color of the object being described, as long as the contrastive term (gray in this example) is the one that children themselves would have used (Au & Laframboise, 1990).

Sometimes the taxonomic constraint conflicts with the tendency to extend novel terms to objects of the same shape. For example, in one experiment, children were shown a birthday cake, told that puppets call it a *fep*, and then asked whether two other objects are also feps: a pie shaped differently than the birthday cake and a hat shaped like it. When faced with such conflicts, 3-year-olds are more likely than 5-year-olds to choose the similarly shaped object as a fep, whereas 5-year-olds are more likely to choose the object from the same class (Imai, Gentner, & Uchida, 1994; Merriman, Scott, & Marazita, 1993). As suggested by this example, appearance is particularly important in very young children's guesses about word meanings. With age, belonging to the same category (e.g., sweets) and serving the same function (e.g., being good to eat) become more important.

The mutual-exclusivity constraint. When children encounter an unfamiliar word in a context in which the word might refer to one of two objects, and they already know a name for one of them, their first guess is usually that the unfamiliar word refers to the object whose name they do not know. The term *mutual-exclusivity constraint* is based on the view that children assume that an object's having a name makes it unlikely that a new term will refer to it. For example, if 3-year-olds who already know the word *spoon* but not the word *tongs* are shown a spoon and a tongs and are told "Show me the gug," they generally choose the tongs (Golinkoff, Hirsh-Pasek, Lavallee, & Baduini, 1985; Markman & Wachtel, 1988).

The mutual-exclusivity constraint seems especially important for reducing overextensions of word meanings. Recall that young children sometimes use words too broadly; for example, a child might call all four-legged mammals *doggie*. If such a child also followed the mutual-exclusivity constraint, hearing an adult say "See the cat" would lead the child to narrow the previous definition of doggie so that it no longer included cats and other animals that were more like cats than dogs. In this way, *doggie* would eventually be restricted to dogs. Mutual exclusivity does not only apply to names of objects; preschoolers also assume that novel verbs refer to actions for which they do not know a term rather than to actions for which they do know a term (Clark, 1993; Golinkoff, Hirsh-Pasek, Mervis, Frawley, & Parillo, 1995; Merriman, Marazita, & Jarvis, 1993).

The mutual-exclusivity constraint appears to be present by the time children are 1½ years old (Liitschwager & Markman, 1994). In particular, 16-month-olds more quickly learn a new label for an object for which they lack an existing word than for one for which they have one. However, the consistency with which they rely on the constraint increases considerably over the next few years (Merriman & Bowman, 1989).

What accounts for children's increasingly consistent reliance on the mutual-exclusivity constraint? One source of development may be an increasing ability to simultaneously keep in mind the apparent meanings of both previously known and new words, and thus to perceive the implications of a new word's apparent meaning for the likely meaning of an old one (Merriman & Bowman, 1989). Another likely source of development is a desire among children to fill gaps in their mental dictionaries (Clark, 1993). If you encounter an unfamiliar word and two objects to which the word might refer, why not guess that the new word refers to the object whose name you do not know rather than the one that you can already talk about?

These constraints are not the only factors that help children home in on word meanings without much trial and error. Grammatical cues also contribute, at least by the time children are 2 or 3 years old (Fisher, Hall, Rakowitz, & Gleitman, 1994; Naigles & Kako, 1993). For example, very young children know that words introduced by saying "This is *X*" are usually proper names (e.g., "This is *Robert*"), that words introduced by saying "This is some *X*" usually refer to undifferentiated masses (e.g., "This is *some silly putty*"), and that words introduced by saying "This is an *X*" usually refer to specific objects (e.g., "This is a *truck*") (Gelman & Taylor, 1984; Macnamara, 1982). Adults also provide corrective feedback when word meanings are incorrect (Bohannon & Stanowicz, 1988). Further, not only are young children quite conservative in extending words beyond the contexts in which they have heard them, they also spontaneously stop overgeneralizing terms if they do not hear them used by others in the way that they themselves use them (Merriman & Bowman, 1989). These are some of the devices that allow children to learn so many word meanings so quickly.

Linguistic creativity.   Young children also show considerable creativity in inventing words to express meanings for which they do not know any appropriate term. Clark (1995) cited such examples as a 24-month-old saying "There comes the rat-man" and a 25-month-old saying "Mommy just fixed this spear-page." The *rat-man* was a colleague of her father's who worked with rats in a psychology laboratory; the *spear-page* was a torn picture of a jungle tribe holding spears that her mother had taped together. Clark also cited the example of a 28-month-old saying "You're the sworder and I'm the gunner." As these examples suggest, children's innovative uses of language are far from random. They reflect rules for forming new words, such as combining words or other components that are meaningful in their own right and that, when put together, have an unambiguous meaning. Such linguistic creativity allows children to express meanings that are well beyond what their limited vocabularies would otherwise allow.

Linguistic analysis.   What of more complex word meanings? Do children ever reorganize their initial knowledge of word meanings to reflect a more mature general level of thinking, as might be suggested by a Piagetian analysis of cognitive development?

Apparently they do. Consider how 2- to 6-year-olds learn when the prefix *un* can be attached to a verb. At first glance, terms such as *uncover, undress, unlock,* and *unstaple* would not seem to have anything in common that distinguishes them from nonwords such as *unbreak* and *unspill*. Careful analysis of these words, however, suggests a pattern (Bowerman, 1982; Clark, 1995). *Un* often can be attached to verbs that involve contact between objects (*unlock, unfasten*, and *unstaple*) or covering (*undress*, *unveil*, and *uncover*). In contrast, *un* almost never can be attached to other verbs.

Bowerman found that children's first use of these terms involved correct repetition of words that they had heard other people use, such as *unbuckled* and *untangled*. Later, children began to attach the prefix in new and often incorrect ways. For example, one child said to her mother, "I hate you! And I'll never un-hate you or nothing!" Such errors indicate that the child realized that *un* was a distinct part of the verbs she had heard it with, and that it could be attached to other verbs, but had not figured out when it could be used. Later errors show greater understanding that *un* usually can be attached only to verbs that involve covering or contact. For example, the same child who vowed never to unhate her mother recited a ghost story eight months later and said, "He tippitoed to the graveyard and *unburied* her." Although *unburied* does not happen to be a word in English, it does conform to the rule that *un* can often be attached to terms involving covering. The subtlety of the distinction reflects how remarkable children's learning of meaning is: How many adults could tell you the rule governing when *un* can be attached to a verb?

GRAMMAR

All human languages have *grammar*—that is, rules for forming sentences. As noted earlier, young children are motivated to learn grammar, even when they can communicate well without learning them and are not corrected for grammatical errors. This interest in learning grammar differentiates people from apes, who, even when taught to express meanings through symbols, show no interest whatsoever in learning the grammar of the languages they are taught.

The grammars of many of the world's languages are extremely complex. Children's ability to learn such complex systems at young ages has led some students of language development to propose that people's brains have special capabilities for learning and using grammar. Consistent with this view, observation of the brain's electrical activity in response to spoken language suggests that terms with specifically grammatical functions are processed at different locations than other terms (Neville, 1995a; Neville, Mills, & Lawson, 1992). When people read a word whose main function is grammatical (e.g., *the*), the brain's electrical response reaches its peak about one-quarter of a second after the word is read, and the reaction is maximal toward the front of the temporal lobe in the left hemisphere. In contrast, when people read a word with a specific meaning (e.g., *dog*), the electrical response reaches its peak after about one-third of a second, and the maximal response is seen toward the rear of both hemispheres.

The electrical activity elicited by the grammatical terms depends on having mastered the grammar of one's language. Among 8- to 13-year-olds and among deaf adults, those with greater grammatical knowledge tend to show the distinctive response to the grammatical terms, whereas those with less grammatical knowledge do not (Neville, 1995a). No one knows why grammatical terms are processed primarily at the front of the left temporal lobe, but the fact that they are suggests that this area of the brain is specialized for learning grammar. Below, we consider grammatical development in the first two years of life, then grammatical development at later ages, and then several explanations of how children learn grammar.

Early Grammatical Understanding

Sentences are the basic unit of grammar. They are more than simple strings of words. Instead, they are cohesive units that express meaning and that follow conventions regarding word order, intonation, and stress. So basic are they that Anisfeld (1984) commented, "In a real sense, sounds and words exist to be used in sentences" (p. 113).

Even before toddlers begin to produce sentences in their own speech, their understanding of other people's statements reflects knowledge of some grammatical conventions (Hirsh-Pasek & Golinkoff, 1996). For example, children who are mainly producing one-word phrases already show some understanding of the role of word order within sentences. In one set of studies, 17-month-olds were simultaneously shown two films that differed only in who was doing what to whom. Thus, Big Bird would be washing Cookie Monster in one film, and Cookie Monster would be washing Big Bird in the other. When asked questions such as "Where is Big Bird washing Cookie Monster," the toddlers usually looked at the film where that was occurring. This pattern suggests that the 17-month-olds knew that the character mentioned first in the sentence probably was doing the action, which corresponds to the usual grammatical pattern in English.

Turning to children's own speech, their earliest two-word phrases seem somewhere between pairings of individual words and true sentences. The two words in each phrase tend to express related meanings, but they are not very cohesive and often are separated by long pauses. Sometimes, they are referred to as *sequences* (of words), to distinguish them from true sentences. Thus, one 20-month-old boy produced such phrases as *train/bump*, *cow/moo*, and *beep/beep/trucks* (Anisfeld, 1984; the slashes indicate pauses between words). These expressions seemed to indicate meanings comparable to those of simple sentences ("The train bumped." "Cows say moo." "Trucks beep."). However, they lacked the intentional patterns and cohesion of sentences.

Along with these sequences, children begin to produce true sentences. At first, the sentences are rare, but within a few months, they become dominant. The cognitive effort needed to construct them is evident in the halting way in which young children talk. Braine (1971) estimated that 30 to 40 percent of 24- to 30-month-olds' statements are "replacement sequences," in which children build on earlier statements until they succeed in producing the desired form and meaning. Thus, Braine described a 25-month-old saying in succession, "Want more. Some more. Want some more." and a 26-month-old saying, "Stand up. Cat stand up. Cat stand up table."

Early in language learning, grammatical knowledge is often interwoven with knowledge of meanings (Corrigan, 1988; Corrigan & Odya-Weis, 1985). Children from different language backgrounds emphasize the same meaningful relations in their two-word phrases: agent-action ("Mommy hit"), possessor-possessed ("Adam checker"), attribute-object ("big car"), recurrence ("more juice"), and disappearance ("juice allgone") (Anisfeld, 1984; Bloom, 1990; Braine, 1976). Within each relation, children order words in a regular fashion. Thus, when describing an object that has disappeared, a child who said "juice allgone" would rarely if ever say "allgone juice" or "allgone milk." However, the consistency of the word ordering is specific to the meaning being expressed.

At first, children are very conservative about generalizing from the islands of grammatical competence that they have established. For example, Kuczaj (1986) observed that one of his two children initially used *are* only in declarative sentences starting with *these* or *those* ("Those are good toys."). His other child at first used *is* only at the end of sentences ("There they is."). This reluctance to extend newly-acquired grammatical forms to novel contexts parallels children's conservatism about extending newly acquired word meanings to new referents and their avoidance of words that they have trouble pronouncing.

Later Grammatical Development

Once children produce true sentences, they begin to acquire many of the grammatical conventions used in adult language. For example, English-speaking children learn to indicate that an event happened in the past by appending *ed* to the verb. They learn to indicate that more than one individual was involved in an event by appending *s* or *es* to the noun. They learn to use *am*, *is*, and *are* in the full range of circumstances to which they apply. Acquisition of two grammatical conventions, those used to form past tenses and to ask questions, illustrate grammatical development particularly clearly.

Past-tense forms. In English, the past-tense forms of most verbs are produced by adding *ed* to the infinitive (e.g., adding *ed* to *help* to produce *helped*). However, the past-tense forms of a number of the most common verbs are exceptions to this rule; for example, *came*, *went*, *hit*, and *ate*. To indicate that events occurred in the past thus requires mastering both the rules and the exceptions.

Children appear to begin learning by treating each word as a separate case. This leads to their first past-tense verbs being correct repetitions of forms they have heard, both regular (e.g., *jumped*) and irregular (e.g., *ran*). However, once they have learned a fairly large number of verbs (roughly 60 to 70 in most cases) and abstracted the *ed* rule, they impose it not only in cases where it fits but also in cases where it does not (Marchman & Bates, 1994). The rule helps them to infer the correct past-tense form for the many regular verbs whose past-tense forms they never have heard, but it also leads to *overregularized forms* such as *runned* and *eated*. These overregularized forms are not the only ones that they produce at any given time. The same child who says *runned* in one sentence will say *ran* in the next, and may occasionally say *ranned* as well (Marcus, Pinker, Ullman, Hollander, Rosen, & Xu, 1992). However, the overregularizations persist for a long time, being produced occasionally by most children from around age 2 into the school years (Marcus et al., 1992). They also cannot be dismissed as accidents. When 5- and 6-year-olds are asked to judge whether particular forms are "ok" or "silly," most indicate that both *ate* and *ated* are ok, though most judge *eated* to be silly (Kuczaj, 1978). Not until age 7 do they judge only the correct past-tense form to be correct.

Questions.   Soon after children begin to use two-word phrases, they start to learn a common, but surprisingly complex, set of grammatical forms: those involved in asking questions. Quite often, the first question they ask is "What dat" (Reich, 1986). This is soon followed by questions involving "where" ("Where Mommy boot"), yes-no questions ("Go now"), and questions involving doing ("What Billy doing").

Plainly, it is a long way from these abbreviated questions to fully grammatical ones. It takes several years of experience before children consistently ask questions grammatically. For example, consider the process of learning to ask *wh* questions. Initially, children often maintain the basic subject-verb-object order that is typical of English and just attach a *wh*-term to a sentence that they have just heard (de Villiers, 1995). A child who was told "Billy hates Mary" might ask "Why Billy hates Mary?" Later, children realize that auxiliary verbs such as *does* must be added. Sometimes they produce forms with the auxilliary verb in the wrong place ("Why Billy does hate Mary"). Other times, they produce forms with the auxilliary verb in the right place but with the *s* not removed from the verb ("Why does Billy hates Mary"). Yet other times, the same child will produce the correct form. Not until roughly age 5 do children ask such questions consistently correctly. Their persistence in learning this complicated set of forms again illustrates their high motivation to speak grammatically.

Critical periods in grammar learning.   Why are such grammatical forms learned when they are, rather than earlier or later? Lenneberg (1967) raised one intriguing possibility: that the time between 18 months and puberty is a critical period, during which the brain is especially receptive to learning grammar.

Initial explanations of grammatical acquisition seemed to contradict Lenneberg's hypothesis. For example, comparisons of adults and preschoolers who were completing their first year of living in Holland indicated that the adults' mastery of Dutch grammar was superior (Snow & Hoefnagel-Hohle, 1978).

However, studies that have focused on the end point of grammatical acquisition, rather than knowledge after one or a few years of exposure to the language, suggest that learning of grammar reaches higher levels if the learning begins early. Johnson and Newport (1989) examined knowledge of English grammar among Korean and Chinese immigrants who had come to the United States when they were between 3 and 39 years old and who had lived in the United States for between 3 and 26 years. Because age of arrival and number of years in the United States were only moderately correlated in the group they studied, the investigators could separate the influences of the age at which the immigrants began to learn English from the amount of time they had spent learning it.

Age of arrival was closely related to ultimate level of grammatical mastery. In contrast, number of years in the United States had little relation to it. Immigrants who came before age 7 knew grammar as well as native-born adults; those who came between age 8 and 10 knew it slightly less well; those who came between age 11 and 15 knew it somewhat less well. Most striking, hardly any of those who came after age 15 mastered English grammar very well at all (Figure 5.2). Only 1 of the 22 people who arrived that late showed as much grammatical knowledge as the least-knowledgeable of the 15 people who arrived before age 11. Further, among those who arrived after age 15, neither age at arrival nor number of years in the United States correlated highly with degree of mastery. Unlike the universal mastery of the basics of English grammar seen among native speakers, some adult learners mastered English grammar to a moderate degree, others very poorly.

FIGURE 5.2. Performance on test of grammatical competence as a function of age of immigration from East Asia to U. S. (Data from Johnson & Newport, 1989.)

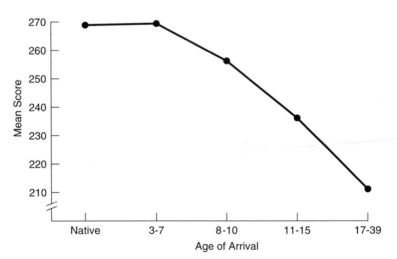

The grammars of English and Chinese are drastically different. What of people who learn a second language with a more similar grammar? A study of native speakers of Spanish who learned English as adults (Johnson, in press) showed that the native Spanish speakers mastered English grammar to a higher degree than did the native Chinese speakers. However, their mastery was still well below that of native English speakers. This held true even for native Spanish speakers who had been in the U.S. for many years, far more time than a child takes to master these basic grammatical devices.

On a somewhat more optimistic note, other studies have shown that some adults who learn English as a second language do acquire grammatical proficiency comparable to that of native speakers (Bialystok & Hakuta, 1994; White & Genesee, 1992). Even these studies, however, show that those exposed to the second language at younger ages are much more likely to fully master its grammar.

Explanations of Grammatical Development

Currently, there is no generally accepted theory of grammatical development. However, several accounts seem to tell parts of the story.

Basic child grammar. Slobin (1986) proposed that children impose a basic child grammar on whatever language input they receive. This view is a first cousin of the constraints approach to word meaning and a second cousin of Piaget's general concept of assimilation. Within Slobin's view, children expect that certain meanings are sufficiently important that they should be reflected in grammar. They also expect that particular meanings should be expressed in particular places within phrases. When the grammar of the language marks the meanings children believe are important in the places children believe they should be, children learn the grammatical conventions quickly. When the grammatical markings are in different places, or when children do not expect the meaning to be important at all, they learn more slowly.

Use of negative terms illustrates Slobin's general idea. Negatives affect the meaning of the entire clause they modify. When we say, "He didn't run to the store," the term *didn't* modifies the entire clause *run to the store.* Children's errors indicate that they try to keep the negative outside of the clause, even when the language they hear places it inside the clause. In Turkish, correct sentences specify the verb, then indicate whether the meaning is negative, and then complete the verb phrase (as in "He run didn't to the store"). Turkish children often err, however, by moving "didn't" outside the verb phrase (as in "He didn't run to the store"). Thus, children's expectations can, for a time, override the language to which they are exposed, leading to grammatical errors. More generally, the fit between children's expectations and the grammatical conventions of the language they hear influences how quickly they learn the grammar.

Semantic bootstrapping. Children's early sentences usually follow standard orders of meanings such as agent-action-recipient (e.g., "Billy hit me."). Eventually, however, children also produce sentences that deviate from such standard sequences. For example, when a child says "Going to school sure is fun," the grammatical subject (*going to school*) is not an agent, the verb (*is*) is not an action, and the grammatical object (*fun*) is not a recipient of any action. As children's grammatical competence grows, they also recognize that a meaningless sentence can still be grammatically correct (e.g., "Frequent exercise prevents restless windows."). A full account of grammatical understanding must explain how people reach such abstract understanding of grammar and what role their initial understanding of meaning plays in the process.

Pinker (1984) proposed that early learning of grammar is based on *semantic bootstrapping*. The key idea is that children first identify the most common categories of meanings in the sentences they hear (for example, the person or thing that produces the action, the name of the action, and the person or thing affected by the action). They then use these meanings to form meaning-based categories and rules for ordering words in sentences. Finally, they use these meaning-based categories and rules to pull themselves up to purely grammatical categories and rules.

Such a learning process is possible because grammatical categories tend to be correlated with meanings. In English, names of persons or things usually function as nouns, actions as verbs, and attributes of persons or things as adjectives. These relations provide a basis for early analysis of sentences. For example, from frequent exposure to sentences such as "Babar jumped on the bed" children can learn that in English, the agent who engaged in the action is typically named at the beginning of the sentence, that the action itself is typically in the middle, and that the recipient of the action is typically at the end. This provides a basis for the child to order words within sentences according to the agent-action-recipient framework.

These early sentence frames do not only allow children to produce grammatical sentences; they also provide a basis for learning grammatical rules that are not based on meaning. Within Pinker's theory, grammatical categories such as noun, verb, subject, and predicate are innate to human beings. Children's learning task is to identify how these grammatical categories function within their particular language. They do this by establishing correspondences between the meanings they initially represent and the innately known grammatical categories. For example, they map the grammatical category *subject* onto the meaning-based concept *agent* and the grammatical category *verb* onto the meaning-based category *action*. Once they code the language they hear in terms of these grammatical categories, they note regularities of ordering, phrasing, and intonation that allow them to extend the grammatical categories to cases where the grammatical subject is not an agent and the verb is not an action. In doing this, they create the purely grammatical categories that characterize mature grammatical competence.

Connectionist accounts. As discussed in Chapter 3, several connectionist models of development have focused on learning of grammar (e.g., Elman, 1992; MacWhinney & Leinbach, 1991; MacWhinney & Chang, 1995; Plunkett & Marchman, 1993). They have demonstrated that computer simulations that encode features of phonology, meaning, and word ordering can learn complex grammatical systems such as English past tense forms and German gender markings. These systems operate by detecting patterns of correlations in the language that the system is presented and using these correlational patterns to predict what the form should be in new cases. All of the connectionist models learn grammar quite slowly, as a result of exposure to thousands and thousands of instances. This fits children's learning quite well. As Maratsos (in press) has noted, grammatical systems are so complex that children's acquisition of them is by necessity more like a process of "grinding through" than like a process of testing a few hypotheses to see how the system works.

Evaluation. How can we evaluate these alternative accounts of children's acquisition of grammar? In many ways, they resemble the proverbial story of the blind men feeling different parts of the elephant. Each explanation incorporates part of the truth, but none the totality. Slobin's and Pinker's emphasis on the role of meaning in formation of early grammatical categories seems well founded. Pinker's semantic bootstrapping idea is an attractive transition mechanism. The connectionist idea that grammatical competence is based on detection of complex patterns of correlations within the language also is clearly a large part of the story. Yet the views are sufficiently different that it is unclear how they could be integrated into a single theory. In sum, the task of explaining grammatical development continues to challenge the best minds in the field.

COMMUNICATION

The ultimate purpose of language is communication. Such communication can be accomplished either verbally or through gestures. Each of these modes of communication is considered in the following section.

Communication through Spoken Language

Communication to and from infants. Rudimentary communication skills are present even in the first months after birth. Already by the age of 3 or 4 months, infants act in ways that motivate adults to speak to them. They tend to be quiet when an adult talks to them and to vocalize more when the adult stops talking (Ginsburg & Kilbourne, 1988). In the first few months after birth, infants' and mothers' vocalizations frequently clash, in the sense of occurring simultaneously. By the age of 3 or 4 months, however, the interactions evolve into a smooth turn-taking process, akin to that of the conversations of older children and adults. Infants of this age also tend to reproduce the general intonational pattern that their mothers just produced (Masataka, 1992). The infants' turn taking and reproduction of intonational patterns encourages adults to talk more with them than if they remained silent or behaved in ways uncorrelated with what the adult was saying (Locke, 1995).

Adults, in turn, speak to infants in ways that encourage them to listen and respond. Just as infants imitate their mothers' intonational patterns, mothers imitate the speech sounds that infants make. When mothers imitate their infants' speechlike sounds, but not other vocalizations, the infants' proportion of speech-like sounds increases (Bloom, Russell, & Wassnberg, 1987). As noted in the previous chapter, adults and older children in many cultures also use a form of speech known as motherese, in which they speak in high registers, exaggerated intonations, short, simple sentences, and elongated vowels (as when saying *Wheeee*). This style of speech increases infants' attention to what is being said and to the mother's activities more generally (Fernald, 1992).

Motherese is very common among the world's cultures, but it is not universal. For example, on the island of Java, parts of Guatamala, and parts of Western Samoa, parents rarely talk to babies (Ochs & Schieffelin, 1995; Pye, 1992; Smith-Heffner, 1988). When Kaluli adults in New Guinea saw Westerners speaking in motherese to babies, they wondered how the babies ever learned to speak proper language (Schieffelin, 1990). In these societies, infants and toddlers learn language primarily by observing adults speaking. These cases cannot be dismissed as oddities of small tribes; 100 million people live on Java. The practices may not seem very conducive to language learning, but children still master the grammars of their native language quite efficiently (Ochs & Schieffelin, 1995).

Communication to and from toddlers and older children. When babies begin to produce words, they add new strategies for communicating. Some of these strategies are unique to beginning language users. For example, some toddlers repeat entire phrases with only minimal grammatical alterations (Billman & Shatz, 1981; Keenan, 1977). When I once asked my then 2-year-old son, "Are you a great big boy?" he responded, "I are a great big boy." The early responses to *wh* questions that were described previously provide another example of such imitations. The imitations often are considerably longer than the child's typical sentences at that time. Thus, they may provide a steppingstone for constructing longer and more complex sentences than the child previously generated (Schlesinger, 1982).

By their second year, babies appear to have a basic understanding that greatly facilitates their learning of language. They realize that speech generally refers to what the speaker is attending to, even if it is not what they are attending to. To demonstrate that infants have this understanding, Baldwin (1991; 1993a) created a situation in which an adult was looking at one novel object and an 18-month-old at another. When the adult said "A modi!" The babies responded by shifting their attention to the object that the adult was looking at.

When later asked to get the modi, they were more likely to choose the toy that the adult had been looking at when she used the term than the one that they had been looking at.

Other types of understanding of intentions and attention also aid toddlers' language learning. If an adult appears to perform a novel action accidentally while saying a word, toddlers do not associate the action with the word, whereas they do associate the word with the action if the adult appears to perform the same action intentionally (Tomasello & Barton, 1994). Further, when they are told, "Let's find a toma," and then see the experimenter pick up and put down two objects before gleefully saying "Ah" after picking up a third object, they later choose the third object as the toma. Thus, understanding of communication, and of the social world more generally, influences children's learning of word meanings.

Although infants and toddlers bring a great deal to the task of communication, understanding some of the finer points requires direct parental effort. Learning of politeness conventions is one prominent example, as illustrated in the following conversation (cited in Ely & Gleason, 1995, p. 252):

CHILD: *Mommy, I want more milk.*
  MOM: *Is that the way to ask?*
    C: *Please.*
    M: *Please what?*
    C: *Please gimme milky.*
    M: *No.*
    C: *Please gimme milk.*
    M: *No.*
    C: *Please . . .*
    M: *Please may I have more milk?*
    C: *Please may I have more milk?*

Communication through Gestural Language

The development of gestural language among deaf children illustrates that many features of language do not depend on being able to communicate through speech. Consider one study of the language development of 10 deaf children, all of whom had hearing parents who did not know sign language (Goldin-Meadow & Morford, 1985). Despite this unpromising-sounding language environment, all 10 children invented signing systems to express themselves. Not only did the children convey meanings; most also developed simple rules of grammar for ordering the signs. For example, when transferring an object to a person, they consistently named the object being transferred before the recipient (e.g., "Coke Johnny").

The meanings expressed in these first gestures closely resembled the meanings expressed in the first words of hearing children. Both referred to toys, animals, clothing, vehicles, and people. Both also seemed to reflect the same goals: to note the existence of objects and to comment on or request actions relevant to the objects. Further, older deaf children, like older hearing children, use considerable amounts of nonliteral language such as metaphor, simile, and invented words (Marschark & West, 1985; Marschark, West, Nall, & Everhart, 1986).

In addition to the signs that they invent, deaf children also often learn formal gestural systems, such as American Sign Language (ASL). Stokoe (1960) described three dimensions that determine meaning within ASL. One is the location at which a sign is made. The most common locations, in order of frequency, are the area in front of the body where the hands ordinarily move, the chin, the trunk, the cheek, the elbow, and the forehead. These also are the locations at which young children find it easiest to produce signs, one more instance of languages' having evolved to facilitate learning (Bonvillian, Orlansky, & Novack, 1983). A second dimension that distinguishes signs is hand shape. Several common hand shapes are shown in Figure 5.3. The third

FIGURE 5.3.   *Some signs used in American Sign Language (from Newport, 1982).*

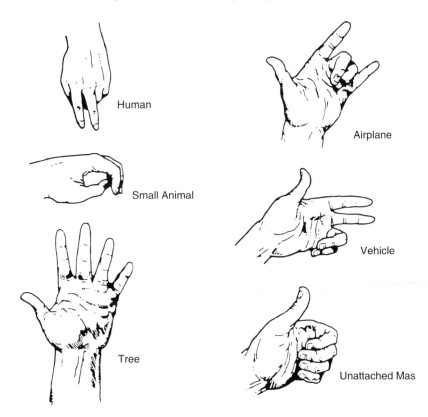

Human

Airplane

Small Animal

Vehicle

Tree

Unattached Mas

dimension of variation among signs is hand movement. For example, in the "vehicle moving upward" sign, the active hand moves upward in a winding pattern (Newport, 1982).

The degree to which children master ASL varies greatly. One influential factor is whether the child comes from a home with hearing parents or deaf parents. The large majority of deaf children are born to hearing parents. In such homes, children and adults often invent simple gestural languages for communicating before they are exposed to any formal sign language. Such "home sign" languages typically lack grammatical markings. Even when these children of hearing parents later are taught ASL, they often fail to learn much of its grammar (Newport, 1982).

The people who most frequently acquire the more elaborate features of ASL, including a sophisticated grammar, are deaf children born to deaf parents. They are exposed to a formal sign language from infancy onward. Interestingly, though, the sign language that they usually see their parents use is the relatively simple form used by first-generation deaf people. How these children progress beyond the language they see their parents use is unknown.

Deaf children who acquire sign languages from birth and hearing children who acquire spoken languages from birth, show closely parallel acquisition paths (Petitto, 1992; 1995). Both groups babble, produce one-word phrases, and produce two-word phrases at similar ages; they produce grammatical forms such as past tenses, negatives, and questions at similar ages; and they acquire similar meanings and similar communciative competence at similar ages.

These similarities led Petitto (1995) to suggest that the same language acquisition mechanism leads to learning of both spoken and signed language. She hypothesized that this mechanism recognizes input that is structured in the way that both spoken and signed language is, and that once it recognizes relevant input, it stimulates motor activity (speech or gesture) that responds to that structure, regardless of whether the structured input is seen or heard. A similar view is reflected in Goldin-Meadow and Morford's (1985) comment "Communication in humans is a resilient phenomenon; when prevented from coming out of the mouth, it emanates almost irrepressibly from the fingers" (p. 146).

Language and Thought

Many Westerners know that Japanese society is technologically very advanced. Many also know that Japanese students score very highly on mathematics achievement tests. However, far fewer know that the Japanese language has an unusually extensive system of number words. As shown in Table 5.7, Japanese includes separate words for counting people; birds; four-legged animals; long, thin objects such as pencils; and broad, thin objects such as sheets of paper. On rainy days, Japanese mothers and their young children will play games such as "Let's count birds" (Hatano, 1989). Perhaps the many terms for numbers within Japanese encourages children to think that numbers are important and to pay close attention to them.

TABLE 5.7   Japanese Words for Counting Different Types of Objects

NUMBER	PEOPLE	BIRDS	FOUR-LEGGED ANIMALS	PLANAR OBJECTS	LONG, THIN OBJECTS
1	hitori	ichiwa	ippiti	ichimai	ippon
2	futari	niwa	nihiti	nimai	nihon
3	sannin	samba	sambiki	sanmai	samhon
4	yonin	yonwa	yonhiki	yonmai	yonhon
5	gonin	gowa	gohiki	gomai	gohon

Observations and speculations such as these have stimulated considerable controversy about the relation between language and thought. Everyone agrees that people have concepts within which they categorize objects and events. Everyone also agrees that they have words for describing the objects and events. But how are the words and concepts related? The issue is absolutely essential for understanding cognition. Do people throughout the world think in basically similar ways? Or, are languages a sufficiently strong lens that people who speak different languages see the world differently? Similarly, does children's learning of new words trigger the formation of new concepts, or does ability to understand new terms demand that the relevant concepts already be in place? Consider three possible relations:

1. Language shapes thought.   This position, known as the Whorf Hypothesis (after its leading proponent), is based on the view that language shapes thought so profoundly that "the 'real world' is to a large extent unconsciously built up by the language habits of the group" (Sapir, 1951, p. 164). The basic assumptions of the Whorf Hypothesis are that a culture's language shapes the way members of the culture interpret information about the world, and that differences among languages produce parallel differences in the way that members of each culture view the world.

2. Thought shapes language.   As noted in Chapter 2, Piaget believed that development of representational abilities at the end of the sensorimotor period makes possible development of language, as well as other forms of representation, such as drawing and mental imagery. Thus, he saw language development as awaiting the relevant cognitive development (development of representational ability), rather than causing it. Within this view, "the linguistic input received by the child appears to have little importance either in determining that a category will be established or in determining the composition of a category" (Mervis, 1987, p. 225).

3. Language and thought influence each other.   The Russian theorist Vygotsky is especially identified with this position. According to Vygotsky (1962), language and thought begin developing independently. By age 2, however, their development becomes intertwined, and they mutually influence each other thereafter. The child's thinking about the world is expressed increasingly precisely in language, and language becomes increasingly effective in directing thought and action. Eventually much of thought becomes internalized language.

A great deal of evidence has been collected on all sides of the issue. First, consider evidence that thought influences language. As noted above, infants and toddlers throughout the world seem most interested in certain types of objects and events (animals, people, food, etc.). The names of these objects and events become their first words regardless of the particulars of their language. Thus, the topics children like to think and talk about dictate which words they learn first.

Another type of evidence for the influence of thought on language comes from the meanings that young children assign to the first words they learn. These meanings differ in characteristic ways from the meanings of the same words for adults. For example, when children are first learning to speak, they often refer to trucks and buses as *cars*. These uses reflect children's classification of the objects overwhelming the influence of the language that they hear.

The influence is by no means all in one direction, however; language also influences children's thinking. When adults apply a word to an unfamiliar object, the labeling pushes children thereafter to think of the object as a member of the category referred to by the word (Mervis, 1987). Similarly, adults' use of a word to label an object for which a child does not know a word may lead the child to form a new category that includes objects like that one (Markman, 1987). Learning a label for a category can also result in children becoming more consistent in assigning objects with that label to the category and not assigning other objects to it, thus stabilizing the membership of the category (Schlesinger, 1982).

Together, these findings support the conclusion that language and thought mutually influence each other. Direct evidence supporting this position was provided by a study of the effects of labeling unfamiliar objects and sorting them into categories (Kuczaj, Borys, & Jones, 1989). Teaching 3- , 4- , and 5-year-olds names for objects improved the children's ability to sort the objects into categories. Thus, learning language that was relevant to the objects influenced children's thinking about them. Conversely, experience sorting the objects into categories led to more effective later learning of their names. Here, thinking about the objects promoted the learning of language relevant to them. As Vygotsky suggested, language and thought may at first develop separately. By the second year of life, however, the development of thought and language seem inextricably intertwined.

SUMMARY

The acquisition of language in the first few years of life is one of children's greatest achievements. They quickly learn phonology, meanings, grammar, and communication. Phonology refers to the production and comprehension of speech sounds. Meaning refers to relations between words and what they describe. Grammar involves the ordering of words into sentences, as well as the specification of tense and number. Communication is the way phonology, grammar, and meaning are used together to express desires and intentions, elicit reactions, and provide information.

Phonologies of all languages involve production of vowels and consonants. Impeding the usual flow of air is critical to both. However, they differ in the particular type of impediment that produces them. With vowels, the only impediments are produced by the vocal cords; with consonants, the tongue, teeth, and lips produce additional ones. Phonological development proceeds in a regular sequence. First infants cry, then they coo, then they produce consonant sounds, then they babble, and then they produce words. Languages throughout the world take advantage of the types of syllables that babies babble most often by making these names of caretakers: *mama*, *papa*, *dada*, and so on. The ease of understanding what beginning speakers say is improved both by their avoidance of words with difficult-to-make sounds and by the tendencies of languages to use relatively easy-to-pronounce words to name objects that young children wish to discuss. Later phonological development occurs in ability to control the sounds that are made and in the clarity of pronunciation.

Throughout the world, children's first words express similar meanings. The words refer to people, animals, toys, vehicles, and other objects that interest children, that are relatively concrete, and that the children want. Even when beginning language users say the same words as adults, they may not assign the same meanings to them. At first, children underextend some meanings, overextend others, and develop some meanings that are underextended in some ways and overextended in others. The rate of acquisition of new words is at first gradual, but it speeds up greatly at about age 18 months. Assumptions that unknown words label whole objects rather than parts of them (the whole object constraint), that words refer to classes of objects (the taxonomic constraint) and that their referents are distinct from those of already-known words (the mutual-exclusivity constraint) may facilitate this language explosion. Children also use a variety of clever strategies to invent words for expressing meanings when they do not know any appropriate standard word.

Grammatical development begins when children first produce two-word phrases, because doing so creates a need to order words within statements. At first, children base their ordering of words on the words' meanings. The orders follow standard patterns such as agent-action and possessor-possessed object. After the two-word period, children learn to form a wide variety of grammatical constructions, many of them based on categories that have no clear correspondence to meanings. Among the factors that contribute to formation of purely grammatical categories and rules are children's expectations about the forms grammars should take, bootstrapping from early meaning-based categories to later grammar-based ones, and detection of regular patterns within the language. Although adults at first learn new grammars more rapidly than children, the children overtake them and eventually learn the new languages' grammar more completely.

Children communicate both through verbal language and through gestures. Long before infants say words, they motivate older people to talk to them by moving in synchrony with speech intonations and making sounds when the other person stops talking. Adults and older children motivate young children to listen by adopting the conversational style known as motherese, involving high pitches, exaggerated intonations, and simple sentences. Deaf children use gestures as well as verbal language to communicate; they invent informal sign languages and also learn formal languages such as ASL. There are notable parallels in the order and timing of linguistic development between children who are learning spoken languages and children who are learning signed ones. These parallels suggest that there may be a general motivation to communicate and to find regular structures in communicative input, regardless of whether that input arrives through the eye or the ear.

Language and thought are intertwined from early in language learning. Each affects the other's development. Learning names for objects facilitates grouping them into categories, and categorizing objects makes it easier to learn their names. Language also influences thought by stabilizing the membership of categories, and thought influences language by making it easier to learn words that correspond to preexisting categories.

RECOMMENDED READINGS

Johnson, J. S., & Newport, E. L. (1989). Critical period effects in second language learning: The influence of maturational state on the acquisition of English as a second language. *Cognitive Psychology, 21,* 60–99. Unusual study that examines the relation between age at onset of immersion in a language and the degree to which people master the language's grammar. Makes a strong case for a critical period in grammatical acquisition.

Kuczaj, S. A., II, Borys, R. H., & Jones, M. (1989). On the interaction of language and thought: Some thoughts on the developmental data. In A. Gellatly, D. Rogers, & J. A. Sloboda (Eds.), *Cognition and the social world*. New York: Oxford University Press. Kuczaj and his colleagues present an intriguing consideration of the relation between language and thought.

Maratsos, M. (In press). Grammatical development. In D. Kuhn & R. S. Siegler (Eds.) *Handbook of child development: Volume 2: Cognition, perception, and language*. (5th ed.).

New York: Wiley. Insightful discussion of the challenge of learning grammar and of how children meet the challenge.

Markman, E. M. (1992). Constraints on word learning: Speculations about their nature, origins, and domain specificity. In M. R. Gunnar and M. Maratsos (Eds.) *Modularity and constraints in language and cognition: The Minnesota Symposia on Child Psychology, Volume 25*. Hillsdale, NJ: Erlbaum. This chapter provides a current perspective on Markman's important and influential work on constraints on language learning and categorization.

Pettito, L. A. (1992). Modularity and constraints in early lexical acquisition: Evidence from children's early language and gesture. In M. R. Gunnar and M. Maratsos (Eds.) *Modularity and constraints in language and cognition: The Minnesota Symposia on Child Psychology, Volume 25*. Hillsdale, NJ: Erlbaum. Intriguing evidence regarding similarities and differences in 1-year-olds' learning of gestures and oral language.

CHAPTER 6

Memory Development

> My brother Colin was trying to get Blowtorch [an action figure] from me, and I wouldn't let him take it from me, so he pushed me into the wood pile where the mouse trap was. And then my finger got caught in it. And then we went to the hospital, and my mommy, daddy, and Colin drove me there, to the hospital in our van, because it was far away. And the doctor put the bandage on this finger. (Billy, a 4-year-old) (Ceci & Bruck, in press)

There was only one problem with Billy's detailed recollection of this slightly traumatic event—the event never happened!

The 4-year-old who delivered this utterly convincing rendition of his "memory" of catching his finger in a mousetrap was part of an experiment. The purpose of the experiment was to determine when children's testimony about abuse and injuries to themselves can be believed. The situation was somewhat unusual—once a week for 10 weeks, children in the experiment were asked leading questions about events that had never happened to them. For example, Billy had been asked such questions as "Tell me if this has ever happened to you. Do you remember going to the hospital with a mousetrap on your finger?" "Can you tell me more?" "What happened next?" The quotation was of Billy telling a different adult about his experience.

Although the situation may seem contrived, it is not very different than that which children frequently face in child-abuse cases. It has been estimated that child witnesses are interviewed an average of 10 times before their cases come to trial (Whitecomb, 1992). Nor are the questions asked of child witnesses any less leading. Consider the following sequence from a highly publicized 1989 trial in which the head of a day-care center was charged with abusing the children who attended the center. Some of the abuse was believed to involve kitchen utensils:

PROSECUTOR: *Did she touch you with a spoon?*
     CHILD: *No.*
        P: *No? OK. Did you like it when she touched you with a spoon?*
        C: *No.*
        P: *No? Why not?*
        C: *I don't know.*
        P: *You don't know?*
        C: *No.*
        P: *What did you say to Kelly when she touched you?*
        C: *I don't like that.*

What makes the reliability of children's memory in such cases so critical is that mistakes in either direction are disastrous. If a jury does not believe a child who accurately reports abuse, the perpetrator may abuse other children. If the jury believes a child who falsely reports abuse, an innocent person may spend years in jail. So how can we know when children should be believed? Are younger children, who may not distinguish as clearly between their imaginations and reality, more likely than older children to report events that never happened? Or, are older children, who can imagine a greater range of events, more likely to do so? What kind of questioning is needed to get children to testify about events that are uncomfortable for them to discuss, without leading them to report events that never happened? With more than 100,000 children testifying in legal cases each year (Ceci & Bruck, 1993) and more than 40 percent of children who testify in sexual abuse cases being younger than 5 (Gray, 1993), answering these questions about children's memory becomes critically important.

Psychological research is especially useful for determining the reliability of children's eyewitness testimony. In experiments, unlike in court cases, we can know for sure what really happened and use that as a comparison point for children's reports. The answers that are starting to emerge from such experiments tell us a great deal about memory development in general and about children's eyewitness testimony in particular.

CHILDREN'S EYEWITNESS TESTIMONY

People often think of memory as a series of photographs, or a movie, of our experiences. If this were the case, eyewitness testimony would not be a problem; the witness would simply recount what happened. However, at no age is memory nearly this complete or this accurate. Adults, like children, fail to remember what they saw, "remember" events that never happened, and combine separate experiences into a single composite. Preschoolers' memories are somewhat less accurate than those of older individuals, but the difference is one of degree rather than kind—everyone has memory problems.

A good way of thinking about memory is to divide it into three phases, ordered along the dimension of time: *encoding, storage,* and *retrieval.* Memory for any event requires encoding the important information when the event occurs, then storing the information in memory for later use, and, finally, retrieving it when it is needed. Each step offers potential pitfalls. People may not take in all of the important information at the time when the event occurs; they may take in the information but store it in a form that is vulnerable to forgetting; or they may encode and store it effectively, but be unable to retrieve it when it is needed.

Encoding

When people encode information, they form two types of representations: *verbatim* and *gist* (Brainerd, Reyna, Howe, & Kingma, 1990). Verbatim representations include the literal details of the situation: the exact words spoken, the expressions on the people's faces, the color of the walls, and so on. Gist involves the meaning or essence of the events: Who did what to whom. People encode both types of information, but the representations of gist last much longer than the verbatim information. Everyday experience illustrates the difference; when you read a story, you remember the exact words only briefly, but you may remember the basic plot for years.

Part of the reason for young children remembering somewhat less well than older individuals is that their encoding places greater emphasis on verbatim information, relative to gist (Brainerd, et al., 1990). Since everyone forgets verbatim information more quickly than the gist of what happened, the young children's emphasis on verbatim information leads to more forgetting. Like older children, younger ones encode the gist of events; however, their relative emphasis on it is not as great. They also fail to encode some important parts of events altogether.

A large part of the reason for younger children's less-complete encoding of gist concerns their lesser knowledge. Memory for an event does not occur in a vacuum; it reflects people's prior knowledge about what is important, and what is plausible in the situation. For example, in a study in which 3- to 7-year-olds were asked about a visit to a doctor, 7-year-olds very rarely said "yes" when asked such outlandish questions as "Did the nurse lick your knee?" In contrast, 3-year-olds quite often answered such questions affirmatively, especially when questioned a long time (three months) after the visit (Gordon, Ornstein, Clubb, Nida, & Baker-Ward, 1991). Older children's greater knowledge of what does and does not go on during visits to the doctor's office presumably helped them both to encode what actually occurred during the visit and to rule out the possibility that a nurse could have licked their knee there.

Prior knowledge is a two-edged sword, though. It generally leads to more accurate recall, but it can also produce distortions. Stereotypes about other people are one source of such distortions. Consider what happened when a group of preschoolers heard stories that depicted a character named Sam Stone as a clumsy oaf (Leichtman & Ceci, 1995). After four such stories, a man introduced as Sam Stone visited the classroom for two minutes; the visit was pleasant but uneventful. The following day, it was "discovered" that a teddy bear was dirty and a book was torn; the question was who was responsible.

The children's prior knowledge about Sam Stone by itself did not lead to many claims that he was responsible for the damage. However, when the stereotype was paired with leading questions that suggested that Stone was the culprit, 72 percent of 3- and 4-year-olds claimed that Stone had done it, 44 percent claimed they had seen him do it, and 21 percent maintained their claim even when asked, "You didn't really see him do it, did you?" Children who had not heard the stories before the visit were less likely to make these claims, as were older preschoolers (5- and 6-year-olds) who had heard them.

As illustrated by this example, people's memories are not limited to what actually happened. Instead, memories are a mixture of what people see, what they know, and what they infer. Children's inferences are frequently correct, but sometimes they are mistaken. Thus, in the Sam Stone experiment, some children reported seeing him soak the teddy bear with water and smear crayon on it (which matched the condition they found it in the next day). These plausible inferences are much of what make it so difficult even for experts to discern when children's testimony is accurate and when it is not. When more than 100 clinicians and researchers who specialize in issues regarding children's eyewitness testimony were shown videotapes of children talking about what Sam Stone had done, they were unable to identify which children were reporting accurately and which were not (Leichtman & Ceci, 1995).

Storage

Better storage of information also contributes to older children's more accurate memory. One aspect of this phenomenon that is particularly relevant for eyewitness testimony involves *suggestibility*. Children below age 6, in particular, tend to be more suggestible than older children, in the sense that their recall of events can be greatly influenced by experiences that occur after the original event but before the time of retrieval. Thus, when asked leading questions after the relevant events occurred, preschoolers often change their recall in directions consistent with the implications of the questions they are asked (Clarke-Stewart, Thompson, & Lepore, 1989; Goodman & Clarke-Stewart, 1991). Suggestive questions can lead children to "recall" not just unimportant events but also events affecting their bodies, such as nurses blowing in their ears (Ornstein, Gordon, &

Larus, 1992), pediatricians sticking fingers or sticks into their genitals (Bruck, Ceci, Francoeur, & Renick, 1995), and strangers putting yuckie things in their mouths (Poole & Lindsay, 1995). Older children and adults are also suggestible, but less so than preschoolers.

Another technique that is commonly used in legal cases but that can distort children's memories is asking them to imagine events and then asking them to report whether the imagined event occurred. Such imaging often leads to children reporting the imagined event as real and continuing to do so thereafter (Foley, Harris, & Herman, 1994; Parker, 1995). Preschoolers are especially likely to show difficulties in *reality monitoring*—distinguishing what they imagined from what really happened.

A final influence on the quality of stored information is time. As time passes, people forget. The forgetting is especially marked in young children. Even when they remember as much as older children immediately after the event, they forget the material more rapidly (Brainerd & Reyna, 1995). Much of the forgetting occurs relatively soon after the event, but forgetting continues for a prolonged period of time. Over periods of one to two years, periods that are comparable to those that often elapse between the original abuse and trial dates, the accuracy of children's recall deteriorates considerably. Relative to their recollections immediately after the event, children become more likely to omit important information and to include information that is plausible but that did not happen (Goodman, Hirschman, Hepps, & Rudy, 1991; Poole & White, 1993).

Retrieval

When asked to retrieve general information about events (e.g., "What happened at school today"), children tend to underreport what happened. Most of what they say is accurate and relevant to the question, but preschoolers especially leave out a great deal of important information. Asking more specific questions leads to greater reporting of events that actually happened. For example, when 5- and 7-year-old girls were questioned following a genital examination, they did not admit any genital contact unless asked such specific questions as "Did the doctor touch you here" (Saywitz, Goodman, Nichols, & Moan, 1991). As long as the questions do not indicate that the questioner prefers a certain answer, asking specific questions soon after an initial event seems to protect memories from decaying more than it produces false recollections (Ceci & Bruck, in press).

The conditions under which children are asked to retrieve information greatly influence what and how much they remember. One important influence is whether they need to *recall* the information from memory ("Where did the doctor touch you") or just recognize it ("Did the doctor touch your tongue"). People of all ages find recognition much easier than recall. Another influence is the amount of encouragement to think deeply about the event. For example, when 5- and 6-year-olds were asked to draw as well as tell that happened when they visited a fire station, they recalled more than when they were simply asked to talk about the visit (Butler, Gross, & Hayne, 1995). Presumably, needing to draw the fire station caused them to think about the visit more deeply. Another influence is the expectations of the person asking the questions. When the questionner believes that certain events happened, preschoolers are more likely to report those events (Ceci, Loftus, Leichtman, & Brock, 1994; Goodman & Clarke-Stewart, 1991). A final influence is how often the question is asked. Asking the same question twice fairly often elicits different answers. This is not all attributable to forgetting; not infrequently, a child will not remember an important detail at an earlier time but will remember it later.

Conclusions about Children's Eyewitness Testimony

Studies of children's memory for events lead to the following four conclusions about their eyewitness testimony:

1. Children's recounting of events reflects what they encoded initially, their experiences during the storage interval, and the conditions under which they retrieved the information.
2. In the absence of biased questions and stereotypes, even preschoolers accurately recall much that is relevant to legal cases. The testimony may be lacking in detail, but what they say is generally accurate.
3. Preschoolers are especially vulnerable to the effects of misleading questions and stereotypes. Everyone is vulnerable to these influences, but preschoolers are more influenced by them than older children or adults.
4. The vulnerability is present with events that involve children's own bodies and events with sexual overtones, as well as with less personal experiences.
5. To obtain the most accurate recall, questions should be asked in a neutral fashion, they should be sufficiently specific to elicit memories that might otherwise not be reported, and the questioning should not be repeated more often than necessary.

What Develops in Memory Development?

As suggested by the data concerning eyewitness testimony, older children generally remember more accurately than younger ones. But why is this the case? Four types of explanations seem most likely.

One explanation is that older children have superior *basic processes and capacities.* Translated into terms of a computer analogy, this view suggests that development occurs in the hardware of memory—its absolute capacity or speed of operation. A second explanation emphasizes *strategies.* Older children know a greater variety of memory strategies than younger children and use them more often, more efficiently, and more flexibly. A third explanation highlights *metacognition*—knowledge about one's own cognitive activities. Older children better understand how memory works; they may use this knowledge to choose strategies and allocate memory resources more effectively. Finally, older children have greater prior knowledge of the types of content they need to remember; this greater *content knowledge* may be a major source of their superior memory. Of course, these four hypotheses are not mutually exclusive; all of them, or any combination of them, could contribute to the superiority of older children's memory (Brown & DeLoache, 1978).

In the remainder of this chapter we consider the contributions to memory development of these four sources of change (Table 6.1). Just to preview what will emerge, it appears that some of the sources of development contribute more than others, and that some play large roles in certain periods of childhood but not others. It may be worthwhile to apply what you have learned about eyewitness testimony and about children's thinking in general to predict which of these sources of memory development will be most influential in infancy and early childhood, in middle childhood, and in late childhood and adolescence.

TABLE 6.1   Chapter Outline

I.   Children's Eyewitness Testimony
    A.   Encoding
    B.   Storage
    C.   Retrieval
    D.   Conclusions about Children's Eyewitness Testimony
    E.   What Develops in Memory Development?
II.   Basic Processes and Capacities
    A.   Explicit and Implicit Memory
    B.   Association
    C.   Recognition
    D.   Imitation and Recall
    E.   Insight, Generalization, and Integration of Experiences
    F.   Inhibition and Resistance to Interference
    G.   Infantile Amnesia
    H.   Processing Capacity
    I.   Processing Speed
    J.   Evaluation
III.   Strategies
    A.   Searching for Objects
    B.   Rehearsing
    C.   Organizing
    D.   Selective Attention
    E.   Alternative Explanations of Strategic Changes
    F.   Evaluation
IV.   Metacognition
    A.   Explicit Metacognitive Knowledge
    B.   Implicit Metacognitive Knowledge
    C.   Evaluation
V.   Content Knowledge
    A.   Effects on How Much Children Remember
    B.   Effects on What Children Remember
    C.   Scripts
    D.   Content Knowledge as an Explanation for Other Memory Changes
    E.   How Does Content Knowledge Aid Memory?
    F.   Evaluation
VI.   What Develops When in Memory Development?
VII.   Summary

BASIC PROCESSES AND CAPACITIES

Basic processes are frequently used, rapidly executed, memory activities such as association, generalization, recognition, and recall. They are among the building blocks of cognition, in the sense that all more complex cognitive activities are built by combining them in different ways. Because they are used so frequently, age-related differences in them could account for an enormous number of other differences in memory.

The role of basic processes in memory functioning is especially dominant early in life. Infants do not possess memory strategies, are ignorant about the workings of their own memory, and lack knowledge of the world. Still, they manage to learn and remember a great deal. Their relatively skillful execution of basic processes is what makes this possible.

Explicit and Implicit Memory

Basic processes allow children to form both *explicit memories* and *implicit memories*. Explicit memories are ones that can be described verbally, that are conscious, or that can be visualized as a mental image (Nelson, 1995). Implicit memories are ones that are not evident in these ways but that can be detected in other, less direct ways, such as patterns of solution times or physiological responses. A study by Newcombe and Fox (1994) illustrates the difference. They showed 9-year-olds pictures of preschool classmates from five years earlier and pictures taken at the same time of children who went to another preschool. Roughly half of the 9-year-olds showed some explicit recognition of their preschool classmates; they were more likely to say that a child who attended preschool with them was in their class than to say that a child who did not was. The other half of the 9-year-olds did not show such explicit recognition. Regardless of whether the children showed such explicit memory, however, they showed physiological reactions characteristic of memory more often when they saw pictures of children from their original class than when they saw pictures of other children. These physiological responses indicated implicit recognition, regardless of whether the children consciously recognized their former classmates.

Implicit memory is not limited to physiological responses; it is also evident in behavior. Thus, when children have seen pictures previously, they can recognize blurry versions of them more often than when they have not seen the pictures, even though they have no conscious awareness of having seen the picture previously (Drummey & Newcombe, 1995).

Infants form implicit memories from birth onward, but they may not form explicit ones until 6 to 8 months of age (Nadel & Zola-Morgan, 1984; Nelson, 1995). The evidence for this view includes both behavioral and physiological data. Behaviors indicative of memory that infants show before this age, such as looking at novel objects more than familiar ones, elicit especially active processing in parts of the brain associated with implicit processing, such as the striatum and the cerebellum. The types of memory that are evident after this age but not before it, such as reproducing sequences of events after an extended delay, draw heavily on brain structures associated with explicit processing, such as the prefrontal cortex and the amygdala. Some of the structures associated with explicit memory, especially the prefrontal cortex, mature very late, which may explain why young infants do not appear to form such memories. Yet other structures—in particular, the hypothalamus—are sufficiently mature in the first few months after birth to support implicit processing, but they seem to require further maturation to support explicit processing. Thus, substantial postnatal brain maturation may be necessary before infants can form explicit memories.

Next, we consider some specific processes that produce memories: association, generalization, recognition, and recall.

Association

Association is one of the most basic of basic processes. It is difficult to even imagine cognitive development taking place without the ability to associate stimuli with responses. Not surprisingly, given its centrality, ability to associate stimuli and responses is present from birth. In one demonstration of this fact, whenever a buzzer sounded, newborns received a sweet solution for turning to the right (Siqueland & Lipsitt, 1966). Whenever a tone sounded, they received the solution for turning to the left. The newborns quickly learned to turn to the correct side, indicating that they associated one sound with turning left and the other with turning right.

Recognition

As with association, recognition is present from birth. This is apparent in newborns' patterns of habituation and dishabituation. When newborn *preterm* infants are presented a picture repeatedly, their looking at it gradually falls off; when they are shown a different picture, their looking immediately increases (Werner & Siqueland, 1978). Thus, they implicitly recognize the old picture as familiar, and reduce the time they spend looking at it, and then recognize the new picture as unfamiliar, and look longer at it.

Infants' recognition of objects is surprisingly durable. Even two weeks after they are habituated to a particular form, 2-month-olds continue to prefer to look at other forms that they have not seen previously (Fantz, Fagan, & Miranda, 1975). Further, as noted in Chapter 1, the rate at which 7-month-olds habituate to stimuli predicts their later IQs quite accurately (Rose et al., 1992). This may be because infants and children who quickly recognize objects have more time and energy to learn about other aspects of the world, or it may be because rapid habituation in infancy is indicative of generally more efficient information processing.

On what basis do infants recognize objects as familiar? To answer this question, Strauss and Cohen (1978) habituated 5-month-olds to an object with a particular size, color, form, and orientation (for example, a large, black arrow pointing down). Later, the infants were shown the original object plus another one that varied in one or more of these attributes. The alternative object could be a large, white arrow pointing down. In the example, for the infants to prefer the new object, they would need to remember the color of the original, for this is the only dimension that differentiates the new object from the old one.

Immediately after 5-month-olds were shown the original stimulus, they remembered all four attributes. Fifteen minutes later, they remembered only form and color. Twenty-four hours later, they remembered only the form. Thus, infants' recognition of the type of object they saw (e.g., an arrow) is quite durable, but their memory for its properties, such as size, orientation, and color, is less enduring. This enduring importance of form in infants' memory is reminiscent of their reliance on shape in inferring early word meanings (Chapter 5).

Recognition is strikingly accurate even at young ages; 2-year-olds recognize pictures more accurately than adults recall them (Perlmutter & Lange, 1978). By the age of 4 years, the accuracy of recognition is truly remarkable. In one study, 4-year-olds answered correctly 100 percent of questions concerning whether they had seen a picture earlier, despite their having seen as many as 25 other pictures between their two exposures to the repeated one (Brown & Scott, 1971). Even when preschoolers were asked to recognize small differences—for example, when the only difference between two pictures was whether a dog they had seen was sitting or standing—they still recognized correctly on 95 percent of the trials (Brown & Campione, 1972). Ability to recognize subtle distinctions improves further beyond the preschool period (Sophian & Stigler, 1981), but, in general, recognition is excellent from early in development.

Imitation and Recall

Soon after birth, infants recall some actions well enough to imitate them later. For example, when 6-week-olds see adults engage in activities that the infants sometimes do on their own, such as sticking out their tongues or opening and closing their mouths, they do that activity more often 24 hours later than do infants who did not see the adult engage in the activity (Meltzoff & Moore, 1994). The imitation is specific to the activity the infant saw. Infants who saw tongue protrusions increased their frequency of tongue protrusions but not their frequency of opening and closing their mouths. Infants who saw the adult open and close his mouth showed the opposite pattern. To imitate these actions, infants must recall what they earlier saw.

The range of activities that infants imitate and the length of time over which they imitate them expand considerably over the next year. By 9 months of age, infants are capable of recalling and imitating 24 hours later not only naturally occurring actions, but arbitrary ones such as pressing a button to trigger a beeping sound (Meltzoff, 1988). By the age of 14 months, infants will repeat even more unusual actions after more time has passed. For example, they will press their foreheads against a panel to make a light go on four months after they saw an adult do it (Meltzoff, 1995). The sequence of activities that infants will imitate is reminiscent of Piaget's hypothesized circular reactions, in which infants first only repeat activities that involve their own bodies and later repeatedly engage in activities involving external objects. Such early imitation provides infants a way of learning from other people, as well as demonstrating that infants are capable of recalling activities months after they saw them.

Insight, Generalization, and Integration of Experiences

Several of infants' basic capabilities have been revealed in a series of experiments involving mobiles (Rovee-Collier, 1995). In these experiments, a mobile is placed above an infant's crib, and a string is tied to the infant's ankle and to the mobile so that the mobile moves and makes noise when the infant kicks that leg (Figure 6.1). Three-month-olds' learning on this task often comes quite abruptly. At a certain point in the session, they suddenly begin kicking

FIGURE 6.1   An infant making a mobile move by kicking his leg (photograph courtesy of Carolyn Rovee-Collier).

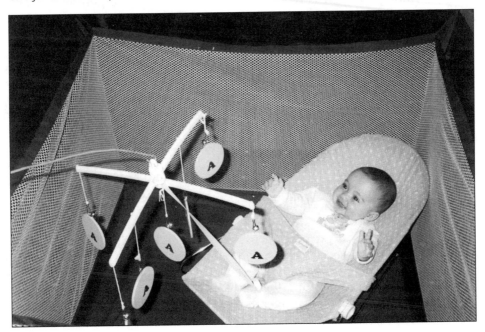

much more often (Rovee & Fagen, 1976). The abruptness of the change suggests that infants, like adults, may from time to time have insights about how things work.

Three-month-olds' encoding of the relation between their kicking and the mobile's moving is often surprisingly literal, however. Even differences that seem totally irrelevant, such as having a different color cloth on their cribs on the second occasion, lead 3-month-olds not to generalize their earlier learning to a new mobile. However, given exposure to several similar mobiles, they learn to generalize to new ones (Rovee-Collier, 1989). Thus, 3-month-olds have the capacity to generalize, but display it only under highly facilitative circumstances.

Infants also are able to integrate related experiences that occur fairly close in time. If 3-month-olds encounter the mobile a second time within three days of the initial exposure, they will better recall the relation five to seven days later than if they encountered the mobile only once or if they encountered it on two occasions separated by four days or more (Rovee-Collier, Evancio, & Earley, 1995).

To explain such integration of memories over time, Rovee-Collier (1995) proposed the construct of a *time window*. The basic idea is that there is a certain period during which children can integrate information and strengthen initial memories (the time when the window is open). Once this period ends, the window is closed, and even highly similar occurrences are stored separately and not integrated with the original one. The duration for which the time window is open is determined in large part by forgetting of the initial information; once information is forgotten, the time window is closed. Since older children generally forget more slowly, their time windows tend to be longer for any given task.

Presenting the second, similar event toward the end of the time window, when memory for the details of the original event are less strong than they were originally but not yet forgotten, is especially effective in preserving initial memories. This is true not only for infants, but also for older children and adults (Rovee-Collier, 1995; Rovee-Collier, Adler, & Borza, 1994). The finding has an interesting implication for eyewitness testimony. Asking a child questions toward the end of his or her time window for the original event may be especially effective for preserving the original memory (Brainerd & Ornstein, 1990).

Inhibition and Resistance to Interference

To think well, we must prevent irrelevant ideas from intruding. Because concepts tend to be associated both with ideas that are relevant and ones that are irrelevant in the particular situation, efficient use of memory and other cognitive processes involves inhibiting the ideas that are not useful. Illustratively, if you are trying to master a new algebra concept, it is helpful to inhibit thoughts of how much you hate algebra.

The frontal lobe seems to play a crucial role in inhibition. It is one of the last areas of the brain to develop, showing substantial development toward the end of the first year, and also between 4 and 7 years (Luria, 1973). The effects of this neural development during infancy can be seen on ability to perform tasks that require inhibition of response tendencies, such as Piaget's *A-not-B* task. On this task, infants see an object hidden and retrieve it several times at Location *B*; then they see it hidden at Location *A*. To succeed, the infants must inhibit the tendency to reach where the reward was obtained in the past, and instead reach where it is now. Adult monkeys can perform this task; however, if their frontal cortex is removed or frozen, they lose the ability and instead reach to the former hiding place (Diamond, 1985; Goldman-Rakic, 1987). Such experiments cannot be performed on human infants. However, it has been learned that between the ages of 6 and 12 months, the time when human infants become able to perform the task, they show increasing electrical activity in the frontal lobe while performing it (Bell & Fox, 1992). The improved inhibitory capabilities allow more enduring memory for the new location. Thus, Diamond (1985) found a steady increase in the delay that infants could tolerate and still search where the object was most recently hidden. At 7 months of age, infants would search at the correct location with delays as long as 2 seconds; at 9 months, with delays as long as 6 seconds; and at 11 months, with delays as long as 10 seconds (Figure 6.2).

FIGURE 6.2   Delays at which infants between 7 and 12 months can succeed on the A-not-B task (after Diamond, 1985).

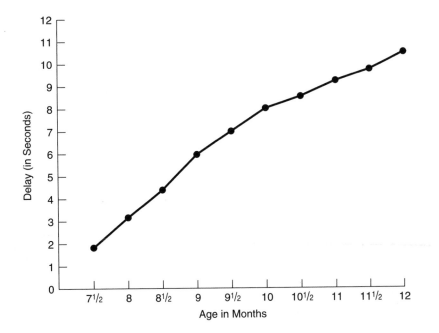

Further parallel developments between ability to inhibit responses and frontal lobe functioning are present between the ages of 4 and 7. An everyday example of this development is the ability to play "Simon Says." When the adult has been saying "Simon Says" but then fails to say it, 4-year-olds find it difficult to inhibit the inclination to execute the command. Seven-year-olds find it much easier to show the needed inhibition. Many similar changes occur between ages 4 and 7 on tasks that require inhibition (Dempster, 1992). For example, to remember lists of words, children must focus on words on the most recent list and inhibit associated terms and words from other lists. Part of 4- and 5-year-olds' difficulty on such tasks is that they fail to inhibit such related terms and recall them as being on the new list (Harnishfeger & Bjorklund, 1994). Similarly, to exhibit conservation of liquid quantity, children must inhibit the perceptual information that the tall, thin glass *looks* like it has more water and focus on the fact that nothing was added or subtracted (Dempster, 1992). Again, 4- and 5-year-olds have difficulty doing this. Supporting the view that young children's difficulty on the conservation task lies in ignoring interfering information, if the misleading cues are removed—for example, by putting a shield in front of the glasses containing the liquid—4-year-olds consistently succeed on the task (Bruner, 1966). Thus, growing ability to inhibit inappropriate responses and to block out interfering information seem to contribute considerably to cognitive development during infancy and early childhood.

Infantile Amnesia

If infants can recognize, associate, and learn, why are adults almost never able to remember anything that happened to them in their early years? Think about it: What do you remember about your life before you were 3? Few people can remember anything (Pillemer & White, 1989). Adults' memories of the next few years also tend to be scanty. Most people remember only a few events, usually ones that were extremely meaningful and distinctive, such as a trip to Disneyland, being in a hospital, or a sibling being born. The phenomenon is not limited to human beings; rats and many other mammals also show little recall of events that occurred early in their lives (Spear, 1984).

How might this inability to recall early experiences be explained? The sheer passage of time does not account for it; recall from Chapter 3 adults' excellent recognition of pictures of people who attended high school with them 35 years earlier. Another seemingly plausible explanation, that infants do not form enduring memories at this point in development, also is incorrect. Children between 2½ and 3 years old remember experiences that occurred in their first year (Myers, Clifton, & Clarkson, 1987), and 11-month-olds remember some events a year later (McDonough & Mandler, 1994). Nor does Freud's (1905/1953) hypothesis that infantile amnesia reflects repression of sexually charged episodes explain the phenomenon. While such repression may occur, people cannot remember ordinary events from the infant and toddler periods, either.

Three other explanations seem more promising. One involves physiologi-cal changes relevant to memory. Maturation of the frontal lobes of the brain con-tinues throughout early childhood, and this part of the brain may be critical for remembering particular episodes in ways that can later be retrieved (Diamond, 1990; Schacter, 1987). Demonstrations of infants' and toddlers' long-term mem-ory have involved their repeating motor activities that they had earlier seen or done, such as reaching in the dark for objects, putting a bottle in a doll's mouth, or pulling apart two pieces of a toy. The brain's level of physiological matura-tion may support these types of memories, but not ones requiring explicit ver-bal descriptions.

A second explanation involves the influence of the social world on chil-dren's language use. Hearing and telling stories about events may help children store information in ways that will endure into later childhood and adulthood (Fivush & Hammond, 1990; Hudson, 1990). Through hearing stories with a clear beginning, middle, and ending, children may learn to extract the gist of events in ways that they will be able to describe many years later. Consistent with this view, parents and children increasingly engage in discussions of past events when children are around 3 years old. However, hearing such stories is not sufficient for younger children to form enduring memories. Telling such stories to 2-year-olds does not seem to produce long-lasting verbalizable mem-ories (Goleman, 1993).

A third likely explanation for infantile amnesia involves incompatibilities between the ways in which infants encode information and the ways in which older children and adults retrieve it. Whether people can remember an event de-pends critically on the fit between the way in which they earlier encoded the in-formation and the way in which they later attempt to retrieve it. The better able the person is to reconstruct the perspective from which the material was en-coded, the more likely that recall will be successful.

Supporting this view are the variety of factors that can create mismatches between very young children's encoding and older children's and adults' re-trieval efforts. The world looks very different to a person whose head is only 2 or 3 feet above the ground than to one whose head is 5 or 6 feet above it. Older children and adults often try to retrieve the names of things they saw, but in-fants would not have encoded the information verbally. General knowledge of categories of events (e.g., birthday party, visit to the doctor's office, baseball game) help older individuals encode their experiences ("I remember the base-ball game I went to on my seventh birthday"), but again infants and toddlers are unlikely to encode many experiences within such knowledge structures (Nelson, 1993).

These three explanations of infantile amnesia are not mutually exclusive; indeed, they support each other. Physiological immaturity may be part of why infants and toddlers do not form extremely enduring memories, even when they hear stories that promote such remembering in preschoolers. Hearing the stories may lead preschoolers to encode aspects of events that allow them to form memories they can access as adults. Conversely, improved encoding of what they hear may help them better understand and remember stories and thus make the stories more useful for remembering future events. Thus, all three explanations—physiological maturation, hearing and producing stories about past events, and improved encoding of key aspects of events—seem likely to be involved in overcoming infantile amnesia.

Processing Capacity

One of the most controversial issues about children's thinking is whether the amount of information that they can actively process at one time (their working-memory capacity) changes with age. There is no question about the potential importance of such changes. If young children cannot simultaneously process as much information as older ones, their ability to learn and remember would be seriously impaired. But does working-memory capacity in fact expand?

This question has been addressed by examining how many randomly selected letters or single-digit numbers children of different ages can remember. Figure 6.3 illustrates that the number increases steadily with age. Most 5-year-olds can correctly recall lists of four digits, but not longer ones, whereas most adults can recall lists with seven digits. Such data have led a number of investigators, among them Pascual-Leone (1970, 1989), to propose that the absolute number of symbols that people can hold in working memory more than doubles from infancy to adulthood.

Although the data are clear, the implications for whether working-memory capacity changes with age are not so obvious. The demand on cognitive resources that a task imposes reflects both the child's resources and the task.

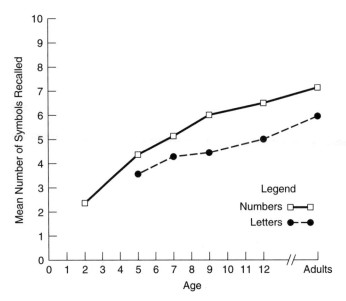

FIGURE 6.3 Improvement with age in memory span for numbers and letters (after Dempster, 1981). Copyright © 1981 by the American Psychological Association. Adapted by permission.

Developmental improvements in performance can be produced either by an increase in the child's resources or by a decrease in the resources the child expends in doing the task. Consider some reasons why older children might remember longer lists of numbers, even if the absolute capacity of their working memory did not differ from that of younger children. The older children know more about numbers. This greater familiarity could help them remember the numbers more efficiently. They also know more strategies, such as rehearsal, for enhancing their recall. They also are more skillful in choosing when to use the strategies they know. Thus, it is clear that older children can store more material in working memory, but it remains unknown (and perhaps unknowable) whether this is because of a change in the actual capacity of working memory or because of changes in knowledge and strategies that allow more material to be stored within the same capacity (as in the car trunk analogy in Chapter 3).

Processing Speed

Speed of information processing, like the number of numbers that can be held in memory, increases greatly with age. This has been found for immediate processing (Hoving, Spencer, Robb, & Schulte, 1978; LeBlanc, Muise, & Blanchard, 1992), processing of information in working memory (Hale, 1990; Hale, Bronik, & Fry, 1997; Hitch & Towse, 1995; Miller & Vernon, in press), and retrieval of information from long-term memory (Hale, 1990; Kail, 1986, 1988; Whitney, 1986). The general form of the improvement is not in dispute. As shown in Figure 6.4,

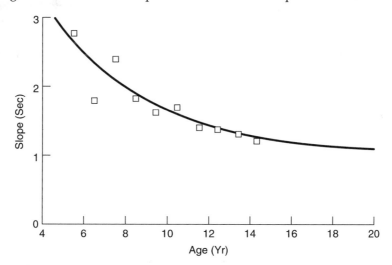

FIGURE 6.4   *Change in estimated processing speed as a function of age. The values indicate times to perform basic operations; thus, 5-year-olds take roughly three seconds per operation, but 14-year-olds take only slightly more than one second per operation. The estimates are based on performance of children and college students in 72 experiments, published over a 30-year period (after Kail, 1991).*

processing speed increases most rapidly at young ages, with the rate of change slowing thereafter, though speed continues to increase well into adolescence (Kail, 1991). However, considerable controversy has arisen over whether the increased speed is due to greater use of more efficient strategies, to greater familiarity with the items being processed, or to increases in speed per se.

Recent evidence suggests that speed of processing per se increases with maturation. At a given age, children who are more physically mature (i.e., a greater percentage of the height that would be expected from their parents' heights) process information more quickly (Eaton & Ritchot, 1995). Although practice also produces faster information processing, the relation between age and processing speed does not seem to be reducible to older children having more practice at the tasks. The best-fitting mathematical function for describing the increase in processing speed with age is different from the one that best describes the improvements that come with practice (Kail, 1991; Miller & Vernon, in press). Further, similar increases in processing speed are present for tasks that children rarely encounter (e.g., mental rotation) as for ones they encounter daily (reading and arithmetic). Thus, speed of processing increases with age, above and beyond increases attributable to practice and superior strategies. The faster processing leads to improved performance on many tasks.

Evaluation

Basic processes are large and direct contributors to memory development from the first days out of the womb. Even very young infants associate, recognize, recall, generalize, and perform other basic processes. These capacities allow them to remember a tremendous amount before they possess strategies, understanding of memory, or content knowledge. Further, without basic capacities, all other memory activities would be futile. For example, rehearsing a phone number would be pointless if we could not associate the phone number with the person whose number it was. The number of associations that are made, the length of time over which experiences are recalled, the time window within which experiences are integrated, the variety of circumstances over which generalizations are drawn, and the speed with which all of these processes are executed, increase substantially during and after infancy. However, basic processes allow infants to learn and remember from the earliest days of life.

STRATEGIES

A 9-year-old boy memorized the license plate number of a getaway car following an armed robbery, a court was told Monday. . . . The boy and his friend . . . looked in the drug store window and saw a man grab a 14-year-old cashier's neck. . . . After the robbery, the boys mentally repeated the license number until they gave it to police. (*Edmonton Journal*, January 13, 1981, cited in Kail, 1984)

Without using this memory strategy, known as *rehearsal*, the boys almost certainly would have forgotten the license number before they could tell the police. But what are memory strategies, how do children acquire them, and how do they choose when to use them?

Strategies are "cognitive or behavioral activities that are under the deliberate control of the subject and are employed so as to enhance memory performance" (Naus & Ornstein, 1983, p. 12). Children employ strategies in all phases of memorization: when they encode material, when they store it, and when they retrieve it. Many age-related improvements in memory reflect acquisition of new strategies, refinement of existing ones, and application of existing strategies to additional situations.

Although many particulars vary with the strategy, certain features characterize the development of all strategies (Waters & Andreassen, 1983). When children first acquire a memory strategy, they use it in only some of the situations in which it is applicable. They limit it to materials with which the strategy is easy to use and to situations that are relatively undemanding. They also are quite rigid in applying the strategy and often fail to adapt to shifting task demands. All of this changes with development. Older children use strategies in more diverse situations, including ones that make them difficult to execute. They also use higher-quality versions of strategies, tailor them to the particulars of the situation, and derive greater benefits from using the strategies.

Another general feature of strategy use is that it varies with children's experience. For example, German second and third graders use certain strategies for organizing material more often than do their American age peers (Kurtz, Schneider, Carr, Borkowski, & Rellinger, 1990). Why is this the case? It does not appear to reflect any inherent difference between German and American children. After children of both nationalities receive brief training in the organizational strategy, they use it equally often. Instead, the source seems to be differences in adults' approaches. When asked whether they teach children such strategies, German parents and teachers reported doing so considerably more often than did American parents and teachers (Kurtz et al., 1990).

We next consider some of the specific strategies that children use, how their use changes with age, and why the changes occur.

Searching for Objects

Even before their second birthday, children begin to use rudimentary strategies. Several of these strategies are evident in the way they search for hidden objects. In one study (DeLoache, Cassidy, & Brown, 1985), 18- to 24-month-olds saw a Big Bird doll hidden under various objects such as pillows. They then had to wait three or four minutes until the experimenter asked them to find the doll. The toddlers engaged in a variety of strategic activities to keep alive their memories of the doll's location. While waiting, they looked at the hiding place, pointed to it, and named the hidden object. They did not engage in these activities nearly as frequently when Big Bird was in plain sight, thus indicating that the strategies were limited to situations in which they were needed.

Very young children's use of such strategies is fragile; they use them only under the most favorable circumstances. Thus, when an object was hidden under one of three identical cups, rather than under a more distinctive object such as a pillow, 2-year-olds did not engage in strategic activities such as watching or touching the correct cup. In contrast, 3-year-olds extended to these confusable objects the types of strategic activities, such as naming and pointing, that younger children applied only to more distinctive objects (Wellman, Ritter, & Flavell, 1975). In general, familiarity with the task setting leads to more consistent and efficient searching (Schneider & Sodian, 1988).

Development of strategies for finding hidden objects continues for a number of years. For example, when asked to find an object hidden under one of six identical cups placed on a spinning turntable, 8-year-olds spontaneously used the strategy of picking up from the table a gold star or a paper clip and placing the marker on the relevant cup; 5-year-olds usually required hints from the experimenter to use this strategy; 3-year-olds either did not use the strategy at all or did so only after a great deal of prompting (Beal & Fleisig, 1987; Ritter, 1978).

Rehearsing

When verbatim recall is essential, repeating information over and over can be very helpful. School-age children often use this strategy to good advantage, as was illustrated in the license plate anecdote at the beginning of this section. However, children younger than age 6 or 7 would have been considerably less likely to rehearse the numbers in the license. In one study of the uses of such rehearsal, 5- and 10-year-olds were shown seven pictures and saw the experimenter point to three of them. The children knew they would need to point to the same three pictures in the same order, but they had to wait 15 seconds before doing so. Far more 10- than 5-year-olds moved their lips or audibly repeated the pictures' names over and over in the 15 seconds between when the pictures were presented and when the children were asked to name them. Those children who rehearsed in this way recalled more than those who did not (Flavell, Beach, & Chinsky, 1966).

Sometimes these results are interpreted to mean that 5-year-olds do not rehearse and that older children do. The reality is more complex, though. Trial-by-trial examination of children's serial recall has shown that on some trials, most 5-year-olds rehearse in the same way as older children (McGilly & Siegler, 1989; 1990). They also recall correctly more often on trials in which they rehearsed than on trials in which they did not.

Teaching rehearsal strategies leads 5-year-olds to use them more and to recall more than they did previously. However, the levels of recall do not rise to the levels of older children, and the young children often do not continue rehearsing more often in new situations (Hagen, Hargrove, & Ross, 1973).

Organizing

When people need to recall material, but not necessarily in the original order, they often reorganize it into easier-to-remember forms. For example, when 10-year-olds are asked to remember the terms "couch, banana, dog, chair, apple, rat, table, cow, orange," they often organize the terms into three categories—furniture, fruit, and animals. Then they try to remember by thinking to themselves something like, "Furniture, let's see, was there a table, yes, 'table;' was there a lamp, no; was there a chair, yes 'chair';" and so on.

The development of such organizational strategies parallels the development of rehearsal. As with rehearsal, 5- and 6-year-olds use the strategy less often than 9- and 10-year-olds (Carr, Kurtz, Schneider, Turner, & Borkowski, 1989). However, younger children, like older ones sometimes do use organizational strategies (Bjorklund & Coyle, 1995), and children who use such strategies tend to remember more than those who do not (Schneider, 1986). The same type of trial-to-trial variability that is present in rehearsal strategies is also evident in use of organizational strategies (Coyle & Bjorklund, 1997).

A final parallel involves learning new strategies. Children as young as 4 or 5 years old can learn organizational strategies, and learning the strategies helps them remember more (Lange & Pierce, 1992). On the other hand, they often do not transfer the learning to new situations, even to ones that resemble the original one (Williams & Goulet, 1975).

Selective Attention

As noted in the discussion in Chapter 4 on the attention-drawing properties of stimuli, much of infants' attention has an elicited, involuntary feel to it. Children soon begin to attend more selectively, though. For example, 4-year-olds who are told that they will later need to remember some toys tend to name those toys more often during the waiting period (Baker-Ward, Ornstein, & Holden, 1984). This suggests that they selectively attend to the toys they need to remember.

As with rehearsal and organization, selective-attention strategies become considerably more prevalent between preschool and middle childhood. The increasing selectivity is particularly tangible in the task shown in Figure 6.5. Children see two rows of boxes, with six boxes in each row. Inside each box is a toy animal or household object; the boxes with animals have a picture of a cage on top, and those with household objects have a picture of a house. Some children are told that they will need to remember where each animal is, others that they will need to remember where each household object is. Then they are given a study period, during which they can open any boxes they want to help them remember the location of the relevant objects. A sensible strategy for a child who needed to remember the animals would be to open each box marked with a cage, to find out which animal was in each one.

FIGURE 6.5   *Apparatus used by Miller and her colleagues (e.g., DeMarie-Dreblow and Miller, 1988) in selective-attention experiments. During the study period, children could open any of the 12 boxes to see what was inside, but on the test, they would be asked only about the content of the six boxes with the marking they had been told was relevant (cage or house). Photo courtesy of Patricia Miller.*

The selectivity with which children focus their attention on the relevant category increases greatly between the ages of 3 and 8 (DeMarie-Dreblow & Miller, 1988; Miller & Seier, 1994). The least-advanced children, who also tend to be the youngest children, look indiscriminately in both types of boxes during the study period. Somewhat more-advanced children look more often in the boxes of the relevant category, but still also look fairly often in the boxes in the other category. Yet more-advanced children look almost exclusively in the boxes of the relevant category but do not recall more than those children who also look at some irrelevant boxes. Only the most advanced children both limit their attention completely to the relevant boxes and remember more than children who deploy their attention less selectively.

Part of older children's superior deployment of attention involves its greater systematicity. This was demonstrated in an analysis of 4- to 8-year-olds' eye movements (Vurpillot, 1968). The children were shown pictures of houses with six windows, like those in Figure 6.6. They needed to determine whether the house on the left was identical to that on the right, and if not, where they differed. Ideally, children would scan a window in the house on the left, then the corresponding window in the house on the right, then another window in the first house, then the corresponding window in the second house, and so on until they either found a difference or had examined all of the windows. Systematically proceeding through the different windows—for example from top to bottom and left to right—also seemed a desirable way to deploy attention, because it would assure that all windows would be compared without repetition.

With age, children's scanning became increasingly systematic. Older children more often looked back and forth between corresponding windows in the two houses and more often proceeded down a column or across a row within a

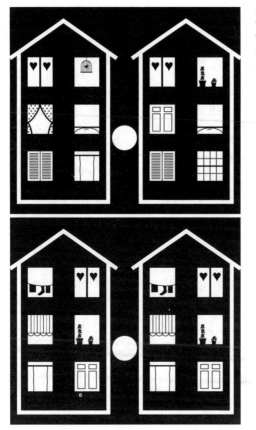

FIGURE 6.6   Stimuli used by Vurpillot (1968) to study development of visual attention. Children needed to find whether houses were different (as in the top pair) or identical (as in the bottom pair) (after Vurpillot, 1968). Copyright © 1968 by Academic Press, Inc.

house. They also more often examined all windows before answering that the houses were identical. To summarize, with age, children's attention becomes more focused on relevant information and more systematic.

Alternative Explanations of Strategic Change

These findings raise the question: Why would children not use a helpful strategy? Initial attempts to account for this phenomenon focused on two reasons why preschoolers might not use rehearsal. One was that they have a *mediational deficiency* (Reese, 1962). In this view, the young children do not use strategies such as rehearsal because the strategies do not lead to them recalling more than if they do not use them. The other proposed explanation was that young children's infrequent use of such strategies was due to a *production deficiency* (Flavell, 1970). Within this view, the problem was children not choosing to use the strategy, even though using it would have aided their memory.

Today, neither of these positions seems to provide an adequate explanation. The mediation-deficiency hypothesis fails to explain why young children's recall usually increases when they are taught strategies. The production deficiency hypothesis does not explain why most 5-year-olds sometimes rehearse, nor why they sometimes would choose to rehearse and other times not.

What seems necessary to understand preschoolers' limited use of rehearsal and other memory strategies is a deeper appreciation of the costs as well as the benefits of using a strategy. In many cases, young children both realize fewer benefits from using strategies and incur greater costs. When people first learn a strategy, the costs in mental effort required to use it are greater than they will be later. For example, rehearsing a set of numbers while simultaneously performing another task (such as tapping one's index finger on a table as fast as possible) produces greater decrements in performance on the other task for younger than for older children (Guttentag, 1984, 1985; Kee & Howell, 1988). The greater decrease in young children's tapping rate seems to be due to the greater mental resources they need to expend to rehearse.

This analysis suggests that young children's use of a strategy can be raised either by increasing the benefits or decreasing the cost of using it. Consistent with this prediction, children more often rehearse, and rehearse in more sophisticated ways, when the benefits to them of using a strategy are increased; for example, by paying them money for successful recall (Kunzinger & Wittryol, 1984). Strategy use also increases when costs of using the strategy are decreased; for example, by presenting material that is relatively easy to rehearse (Ornstein, Medlin, Stone, & Naus, 1985; Ornstein & Naus, 1985). Children's use of a strategy thus is sensitive to both its costs and its benefits. Increases with age in strategy use reflect both greater benefits and lower costs to the older children.

The concepts of mediation and production deficiencies were proposed to explain why children often do not use strategies that would improve their recall if they used them. Recently, the construct of a *utilization deficiency* has been proposed to account for the opposite phenomenon: Fairly often, children use strategies that do not initially help them remember better (Bjorklund & Coyle, 1995; Miller, 1990; Miller & Seier, 1994). The lack of improved recall seems to reflect the cost in mental resources of using the strategies negating the benefits that the strategies convey. Consistent with this analysis, when an experimenter reduces the mental effort needed to use a strategy by executing part of it for the child, younger children benefit from strategies that otherwise would not increase their recall (DeMarie-Dreblow & Miller, 1988; Miller, Woody-Ramsey, & Aloise, 1991).

The existence of utilization deficiencies raises the question of why children would use strategies that do not help their recall. A key to answering the question may lie in the fact that utilization deficiencies generally occur with newly acquired strategies. The efficiency of executing any procedure increases with practice; this finding is so consistent that it is referred to as the "law of practice" (Newell & Rosenbloom, 1981). Thus, if a newly learned strategy already yields performance as successful, or even almost as successful, as a well-practiced strategy, the odds are excellent that with practice, the new strategy will yield more successful performance. Why not use it? Utilization deficiencies thus may reflect the cognitive system acting as if it implicitly knew the law of practice.

Evaluation

Age-related improvements in the frequency of use and quality of children's strategies play a large role in memory development between the preschool years and adolescence. During this time, frequency and quality of rehearsal, organization, and selective attention improve greatly. Development of memory strategies is not limited to changes in how often the strategies are used. Older children also use more effective versions of the strategies, use them in difficult as well as easy contexts, and generally increase their recall more substantially when they use them.

One intriguing phenomenon related to memory strategies is that training children to use such strategies is no guarantee of their continued use. This raises the question, "How do children decide which strategy to use?" One possibility is that children rely on their *metacognitive knowledge* (knowledge of relevant strategies, task difficulty, and their own cognitive capacities) to make such decisions.

METACOGNITION

Metacognition can be divided into two types of knowledge: (1) explicit, conscious, factual knowledge and (2) implicit, unconscious knowledge (Brown, Bransford, Ferrara, & Campione, 1983). As an example of explicit metacognitive knowledge, even preschoolers are consciously aware that it is easier to remember a few items than many. However, much metacognitive knowledge is unconscious; the knowledge influences behavior without our being aware of it. Such implicit metacognitive knowledge is apparent when good readers slow down their reading when a book becomes difficult, without even knowing they are doing so. In this section, we examine the development of both explicit and implicit metacognitive knowledge and how they affect children's ability to remember.

Explicit Metacognitive Knowledge

Children beyond preschool age and adults possess a large fund of explicit knowledge about thinking in general and memory in particular. This knowledge includes information about tasks ("It's easier to remember the main point of a passage than to remember the passage verbatim"), about strategies ("Rehearsing a telephone number is useful for remembering it"), and about people ("Older children usually remember more than younger ones"). Much of this information seems to be acquired between ages 5 and 10.

Probably our most basic knowledge of memory is that it is fallible. Almost all children beyond age 6 know that they forget, but a substantial minority of 5-year-olds (30 percent) deny that they ever do (Kreutzer, Leonard, & Flavell, 1975). Young children's overoptimism about their memory capacities can be seen in other contexts as well. For example, when 4-year-olds were asked how many of 10 pictures they would remember, most thought they would remember all 10 (Flavell, Friedrichs, & Hoyt, 1970). Their estimates of what they would remember were higher than those of older children, even though they actually remembered less. The preschoolers' overoptimism may reflect wishful thinking as well as lesser abstract knowledge; when asked to predict how much other children would remember, they were less overoptimistic than in predicting their own performance (Stipek, 1984).

During elementary school and beyond, children and adolescents acquire a wide range of knowledge about how tasks, strategies, and characteristics of learners affect memory (Schneider & Pressley, 1989; Weinert, 1986). Approximately half of first graders know that it is easier to remember the gist of a story than it is to remember the story verbatim; virtually all fifth graders do (Kreutzer et al., 1975). Similarly, approximately half of first graders know that recognition is easier than recall, whereas virtually all fifth graders do (Speer & Flavell, 1979). The growth in metacognitive knowledge during this period may be stimulated by the increasing amount of remembering children need to do at school.

Much research on this type of explicit factual knowledge of cognition has been motivated by the plausible assumption that children's increasing knowledge about memory and about the general cognitive system leads them to choose better strategies and to remember more effectively. Evidence for this intuitively reasonable position has been surprisingly hard to obtain. Early investigations revealed only weak relations (Cavanaugh & Perlmutter, 1982). More recent analyses of the results of many studies have yielded evidence of somewhat stronger relations between metamnemonic knowledge and memory performance (Schneider, 1985). Still, the relation is not as strong as many people's intuitions would suggest.

Implicit Metacognitive Knowledge

In contrast to their limited explicit, factual knowledge about memory, toddlers and preschoolers show impressive implicit knowledge. This is especially evident in their monitoring of their own cognitive activities. For example, 2-year-olds show that they monitor their use of language when they spontaneously correct their mistakes in pronunciation, grammar, and naming of objects. They also show such monitoring in comments on their own and others' use of language, and in their adjusting what they say to listeners' knowledge and general cognitive level (Clark, 1978). For example, my then 2½-year-old daughter once told me, "You're a 'he,' Todd's a 'he,' and girls are 'she's.'" Two weeks later, she encountered difficulty pronouncing the word *hippopotamus* and explained, "I can't say it because I can't make my mouth move the right way."

Such self-monitoring enables even young children to experience a *feeling of knowing* that can help them anticipate how well they will later remember. Illustratively, in one study, 4- and 5-year-olds were shown photographs of children whom they knew to varying degrees. Even when 4- and 5-year-olds did not remember the name that went with a photo, they accurately predicted whether they would be able to remember the name if given the set of names of all of the children in the photos (Cultice, Somerville, & Wellman, 1983).

Despite this early ability to monitor thought processes well enough to experience feelings of knowing, and despite the fact that such monitoring improves further during the elementary school period (Zabrucky & Ratner, 1986), the skill is far from perfectly developed even among older students (Pressley, 1995; Zabrucky & Ratner, 1986) and adults (Baker & Anderson, 1982; Glenberg & Epstein, 1987). Problems are especially persistent in monitoring one's understanding well enough to detect a lack of understanding of what other people are saying. For example, even a fairly large percentage of college students failed to detect the blatant contradictions in the following paragraph:

> Some snakes have a poisonous bite, but some snakes are harmless and even help us. The garter snake, for example, helps us by keeping bad insects away from our gardens. Garter snakes eat these insects. They find the insects by listening for them. The insects make a special noise. Garter snakes do not have ears. They cannot hear the insects. They can hear the sounds of the insects. That is how they are able to find the insects. (Elliott-Faust, 1984; cited in Schneider & Pressley, 1989, p. 167)

Good readers and poor ones differ greatly in ability to monitor their comprehension. Older and better readers slow down and often return to the place in the text where comprehension difficulties began. In contrast, younger and poorer readers rarely return to problem spots (Garner & Reis, 1981; Whimbey, 1975). The situation is paradoxical; the younger and less-skilled readers have more reason to reread (because they typically understand less well on the first reading), but they do so less often.

Self-monitoring skills are especially critical for choosing what and how much to study. Not surprisingly, older children more effectively monitor their knowledge and more effectively adapt their study strategies to how well they know the material. The amount of time children study before saying that they know material increases steadily from age 4 at least through age 12 or 13, presumably because older children's monitoring of their knowledge reveals that they have not mastered the material until later in the studying process (Dufresne & Kobasigawa, 1989; Flavell, Friedrichs, & Hoyt, 1970). Older children also focus more of their attention on material they have not yet mastered, again presumably because their monitoring suggests that this material needs the greatest attention (Bisanz, Vesonder, & Voss, 1978).

Allocating study time is a tricky business, though. Consider just the dilemma posed in studying for later tests after receiving the results of earlier tests on the same material. Is the best strategy to concentrate primarily on the topics that caused the most errors earlier, or is it better to devote study time to other topics as well? Focusing on the sections that you didn't remember should help performance on that material but might lead to worse performance on the material you correctly recalled the first time. On the other hand, reviewing the better-learned portions might be a waste of time.

Not surprisingly, children who are just learning to study have difficulty making these choices. In one experiment in which children were given a chance to study after performing partially correctly on an initial memory test (Masur, McIntyre, & Flavell, 1973), 7- and 9-year-olds took different paths. The 9-year-olds focused on the items they had not remembered; the 7-year-olds distributed their attention more widely. The 9-year-olds' strategy sounds more sophisticated, but it was no more helpful than that of the 7-year-olds. The two strategies led to equal improvements in recall on the second test. The items children forgot between the first and second testings canceled out the items that they previously had not remembered but later did. Some problems just do not have good solutions.

Evaluation

Metacognition is at the same time intriguing and frustrating as an explanation of memory development. Part of the appeal resides in the plausibility of its central premise—that what children know about memory influences how they attempt to remember. Another part lies in the potential generality of the influence of metacognitive skills and knowledge. For example, knowing the relative usefulness of strategies could improve children's strategy choices. Yet another part of the appeal resides in the potential benefits of teaching metacognitive knowledge and skills. Metacognitive knowledge and skills are potentially both instructible and broadly applicable. This makes them a better candidate for instruction than basic processes, which are difficult if not impossible to change. It also offers an advantage over teaching specific strategies that can only be used in narrow circumstances (for example, rehearsal can only be used for rote memorization). In contrast, teaching children metacognitive skills, such as how to monitor their comprehension, can have broadly beneficial effects on their learning (Baker, 1994; Borkowski, Johnston, & Reid, 1987; Palincsar & Brown, 1984; Pressley, 1995).

The frustrating aspect of metacognition becomes apparent when we try to determine whether children's increasing metacognitive knowledge helps them remember better. Both memory performance and knowledge about memory improve with age. However, the relation between which children remember best and which know the most about memory is not especially strong. This raises the question of how much impact metacognition actually has on memory development.

One useful way of thinking about the issue is summarized in the proverb, "Many a slip 'twixt the cup and the lip." Metacognitive knowledge may influence memory performance only when each of a relatively long series of conditions is met. Consider what might be involved in a girl's using metacognitive knowledge to choose a strategy for remembering verbatim a long list of numbers. The girl would need to know that her memory was not perfect and that she might not remember all of the numbers. When she heard the particular list of numbers, she would need to monitor her own memory well enough to recognize that her storage of the numbers was insufficient to hold them in memory without using some strategy. She also would need to know a relevant strategy, such as rehearsal, and would need to choose it rather than a less effective alternative. Finally, for her to use the relevant strategy more often in the future, she would need to attribute whatever benefit she derived to using the strategy rather than to some other factor, such as trying harder.

This perspective makes understandable both the considerable success that can be gained from teaching children metacognitive skills and the frequent findings of weak relations in the everyday environment between metacognitive knowledge and memory performance. If all links in the chain are present, as would often occur in carefully planned instructional programs, metacognitive knowledge can considerably aid memory performance. If even one link is missing, however, as would often occur in the everyday environment, the relation can disappear.

Consider how this seems to operate in one area—transfer of strategies to new situations. Even if children know a strategy, use it, and witness improved memory as a result, they rarely transfer the strategy to new situations unless they also attribute the improvement in memory to use of the strategy (Borkowski, Carr, & Pressley, 1987; Fabricius & Hagen, 1984; Pressley, Levin, & Ghatala, 1984). Children and adults who have been taught to use a strategy that improves their memory often attribute the improvement to factors other than the strategy. For example, Fabricius and Hagen (1984) created a situation in which 6- and 7-year-olds sometimes used an organizational strategy and sometimes did not. The children recalled considerably more when they used the strategy. Although all children had the opportunity to make this observation, only some attributed the difference to using the strategy. Others attributed the successes to looking longer, using their brain more, or slowing down. The children's attributions concerning the cause of their success predicted whether they employed the strategy a week later in a slightly different situation. Fully 99 percent of children who earlier attributed their success to the use of the new strategy used it on the second occasion, compared with 32 percent of those who thought other factors responsible.

Whatever the theoretical status of metacognitive knowledge, its practical importance is clear. In the discussion of children's reading in Chapter 9, we will encounter a remarkably successful training program initiated by Palincsar and Brown (1984) to teach poor readers to understand better what they are reading. The program teaches them to effectively monitor their comprehension of the text they are reading and also supplies strategies for dealing with failures to comprehend. Anything that works as well as this program is well worth learning more about.

CONTENT KNOWLEDGE

Older children know more than younger ones about almost everything. In general, the more that people know about a topic, the better they learn and remember new information about it. Therefore, greater content knowledge would lead older children to remember more even if there were no other differences between them and younger children.

Prior knowledge of related content affects memory in several ways. It influences how much and what children recall. It influences their execution of basic processes and strategies, their metacognitive knowledge, and their acquisition of new strategies. Under some circumstances, it exerts a greater influence than all other factors combined. Evidence concerning each of these points is discussed next.

Effects on How Much Children Remember

The fact that older children regularly recall more than younger ones is due in large part to the older children's knowing more about the material they are trying to remember. Content knowledge exerts such a large impact that more-knowledgeable children can remember more than less-knowledgeable adults. For example, when shown chess positions on a board and then asked to reconstruct them from memory on an empty board, 10-year-old chess experts outperformed adults who were novices at the game (Chi, 1978). This finding was not attributable to the children being smarter or possessing better memories. When the children and adults were given a standard digit-span task, the adults remembered more (Figure 6.7). Later comparisons of child chess experts with equally proficient adult experts showed that the children recalled chess configurations just as well (Schneider, Gruber, Gold, & Opwis, 1993). Children remember even more than adults about types of content that they know better, such as titles of children's TV programs and books (Lindberg, 1980; 1991). Thus, differences in content knowledge can outweigh all of adults' other memory advantages.

Differences in content knowledge can also influence memory for that type of content more than the child's overall IQ does. Schneider, Korkel, and Weinert (1989) examined German children's memory for a story about a fictitious

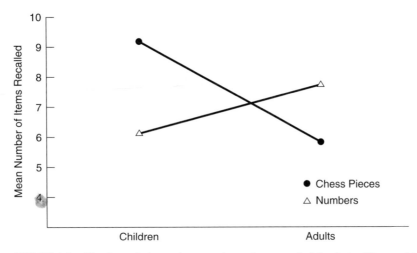

FIGURE 6.7   Number of chess pieces and numbers recalled by 8- to 10-year-old chess experts and adult chess novices immediately after presentation (after Chi, 1978). The child chess experts recalled the positions of more chess pieces, but not more numbers, than did the adults.

young soccer player and his experiences in "the big game." The children who heard the story included equal numbers of children with high soccer knowledge and above-average IQs, high soccer knowledge and below-average IQs, low soccer knowledge and above-average IQs, and low soccer knowledge and below-average IQs.

As might be expected, children with high soccer knowledge remembered more about the stories, drew a greater number of correct inferences, and noticed more inconsistencies within the story than those with lower knowledge. Surprisingly, however, at each level of expertise, higher-IQ children did not remember any more about the soccer game than did lower-IQ children. High-IQ children acquire expertise faster (Johnson & Mervis, 1994), and this may lead to their becoming expert on a greater range of topics. When knowledge is equivalent, however, memory for new information also tends to be equal.

Effects on What Children Remember

As noted in the discussion of children's eyewitness testimony, what children know before an experience greatly influence what they remember about it. Thus, preschoolers who already knew that Sam Stone was a clumsy oaf "remembered" that he was the one who had soiled the teddy bear during his visit to the classroom. Similarly, the "knowledge" children gain through misleading questions ("Did you like it when she touched you with the spoon") may cause them to later recall that the implied event happened.

Although these examples illustrate how knowledge can lead children to remember incorrectly, it more often helps them remember correctly. Much of this benefit comes from the knowledge allowing children to draw correct inferences. Thus, young children who hear a story about a helpless creature with a broken wing remember that the story was about a bird, even when that fact is not explicitly mentioned (Paris, 1975). Similarly, knowledge helps children remember what did not happen. Recall how the 7-year-olds, but not the 3-year-olds, knew that the nurse at the doctor's office had not licked their knees. Thus, content knowledge helps people remember both what happened and what did not.

Scripts

Many events recur frequently in similar forms. When children bake cookies, attend birthday parties, eat meals, or go to a doctor's appointment, the particulars vary from occasion to occasion, but the basic structure is the same. For example, going to a doctor's office generally involves going to the office, telling the receptionist that you are there, sitting in the waiting room, getting up when your name is called, going with the nurse to another room, and waiting for the doctor or nurse to come and do whatever they're going to do.

By the age of 3, children represent such routine activities in the form of *scripts*, which are knowledge structures that describe the way that events usually go. Even preschoolers possess scripts for eating at their day-care center and at restaurants (Nelson, 1978), attending birthday parties (Nelson & Hudson, 1988), going about their daily routine (Fivush & Hammond, 1990), and engaging in other familiar activities. The scripts are especially apparent in children's mistakes in remembering events that for the most part conform to the script but that deviate in certain particulars (Fivush & Hammond, 1990; Nelson & Hudson, 1988). For example, when preschoolers eat at a nice restaurant, they often recall paying before eating, as they would have done at a fast-food restaurant. Such confusions between the script and particular events are particularly prevalent in the preschool period. By the age of 7, children discriminate more clearly between what usually happens and what happened on the particular occasion (Farrar & Goodman, 1992).

Which experiences lead children to form scripts? One influence seems to be the stories that parents tell them and the questions that the parents ask about past events. For example, Hudson (1990) observed that in most families, parents' requests for young children to recall information largely center on recalling past events. Parents tend to ask the questions in an order that parallels the usual order of activities: "How did we get to the birthday party?" "What did you give Billy when you got there?" "Did you have something to eat at the party?" The sequence of questions helps children realize both what is important and the order in which the important events usually occur (Nelson, 1993).

Children use scripts not only to recall their own experiences but also to remember stories about other people, such as fairy tales. Many stories that are told or read to children follow a standard form in which the setting is described, an event happens, characters have an internal response, they set a goal, they attempt to reach the goal, and they obtain (or fail to obtain) the goal (Trabasso, van den Broek, & Suh, 1989). Often several such sequences occur, in which earlier outcomes create new goals and attempts by the characters to meet the goals.

Typically, 3-year-olds' retellings of such stories omit the characters' main goals and internal reactions, and they include details that are unrelated to the main sequence (Trabasso & Nickels, 1992; Trabasso & Stein, 1995). The retellings of 4-year-olds focus more exclusively on relevant actions, but they still often omit the characters' goals and intentions. Not until age 5 do children's retellings consistently include all of the key parts of the story. Thus, between the ages of 3 and 5, children both narrow their scripts for fairy tales so that the scripts focus on the most important events and broaden them to include the psychological states that impel the characters' actions.

Content Knowledge As an Explanation for Other Memory Changes

Changes in basic capacities, strategies, and metacognition contribute to age-related improvements in children's memory for specific content. The inverse is also true, however: Increasing content knowledge improves efficiency of basic processes, acquisition and execution of strategies, and metacognitive knowledge.

First, consider the effect of increasing content knowledge on efficiency of execution of basic processes. At least from age 5, children automatically encode the relative frequency of events, and do so very accurately. However, 5-year-olds' encoding of frequency information is even more accurate when the content is familiar (pictures of classmates) than when it is not (pictures of children who are strangers) (Harris, Durso, Mergler, & Jones, 1990). Similarly, the more that people know about the content they are trying to remember, the more material they can maintain in working memory (Huttenlocher & Burke, 1976).

Next, consider how content knowledge influences the use and efficiency of memory strategies. Children use strategies such as organization more often for remembering groups of familiar items than for remembering groups of less familiar ones (Bjorklund, Muir-Broaddus, & Schneider, 1990). Moreover, the greater efficiency when strategies are executed with familiar content is sufficient so that 8-year-olds who rehearse familiar items subsequently remember as much as 11-year-olds who rehearse unfamiliar ones (Zember & Naus, 1985).

Familiar content also facilitates learning of new strategies. Chi (1981) examined a 5-year-old's learning of an alphabetic retrieval strategy for her classmates' names. (First, think if any names start with A; then think if any names start with B, etc.) Although the strategy was novel, the girl learned it and applied it to recalling her classmates' names rather easily. However, the same girl could not then apply the alphabetic strategy she had already learned in the familiar context to remembering a new set of names of people she had never met.

These results may hold an important implication for how children learn new strategies. Early in the acquisition process, they may employ strategies effectively only on familiar content. Practice using the strategies with the familiar content may lead to execution of the strategies becoming automatized and making fewer demands on the children's processing resources. This automatization, in turn, allows children to apply the strategies to more-demanding, unfamiliar content. Thus, the familiar content may serve as a kind of practice field upon which children exercise emerging memory strategies.

Finally, content knowledge influences metacognition. Child chess experts not only remember more than adult novices about chess positions they see, they also more accurately predict the relatively large number of viewings required before they will be able to perfectly reconstruct from memory the positions on the board. Clearly, all aspects of memory are influenced by content knowledge.

How Does Content Knowledge Aid Memory?

Content knowledge aids memory through a number of mechanisms. One is *encoding of distinctive features.* By focusing attention on distinctive features, content knowledge helps children remember different entities. For example, part of the way that scripts aid memory is by indicating what children should encode. When they go to a birthday party, the script indicates that they should be sure to note the present they gave to the birthday child, the presents that other children gave, the games that were played, the type of cake that was served, and any favors that they brought home. Similarly, much of the benefit of expertise is knowing which information should be encoded. Chess experts can so accurately recall board configurations primarily because they encode groups of pieces that have certain functions—protecting the king, attacking the bishop, and so on—and relate them to the overall situation. When presented a random configuration of chess pieces, experts are no better than novices at recalling the arrangement (Chi, 1978). Thus, part of how content knowledge helps memory is by enhancing encoding.

Another key mechanism through which content knowledge exercises its effects is *spreading activation.* When people think about a topic, the topic becomes activated, in the sense that people can quickly retrieve information about it. The activation automatically spreads from topics that are receiving attention to others that are associated with it, thus facilitating retrieval of information about them. For example, when children think about their summer vacation, they may remember eating lobster there, which may remind them of eating lobster on other occasions, eating mussels and clams on other occasions, and so on. If someone asked them just after they had this thought whether mussels have shells, they probably would be able to answer "yes" more quickly than usual.

As children learn about a topic, spreading activation helps them remember increasingly effectively. Consider why children who are knowledgeable about a topic might use organizational strategies more effectively and more often (Rabinowitz & Chi, 1987). Suppose two 8-year-old boys, differing in knowledge of birds, both needed to remember a set of words, including *hawk*, *penguin*, and *chicken*. The more-knowledgeable boy probably would know that all three are birds, whereas the less-knowledgeable one would probably know only that hawks are. For the more-knowledgeable boy, activation would spread among all three terms and the general category of birds, whereas for the less-knowledgeable one, activation would spread only between *bird* and *hawk*. This would lead to the more-knowledgeable boy being more likely to use *birds* as a category for organizing his memory of the three examples, and it would help his recall to a greater extent if he did so (since the *bird* category would activate all three original terms). Thus, spreading activation may lead knowledgeable children to use strategies more often and to the strategies aiding their recall to a greater extent.

Evaluation

Any explanation of memory development must reserve a large place for increasing knowledge of specific content. Content knowledge increases steadily from infancy through adulthood. It is clearly related to how well children remember, as was evident in the studies of memory for chess positions, for soccer, and for fairy tales. It provides scripts within which children can organize new information, allows them to check on the plausibility of their memories, facilitates their drawing of inferences, and helps them encode distinctive features of objects and events. It also contributes to the development of other competencies that have been proposed as explanations of memory development, such as basic capacities, strategies, and metacognition. Without question, increasing content knowledge is a large part of the reason why older children remember more than younger ones.

WHAT DEVELOPS WHEN IN MEMORY DEVELOPMENT?

Different aspects of memory not only contribute different amounts to memory development, but also make their greatest contributions at different times. Table 6.2 summarizes the contributions of basic processes and capacities, strategies, metacognition, and content knowledge during several periods of life.

TABLE 6.2 Contributions of Four Aspects of Memory During Several Periods of Development

SOURCE OF DEVELOPMENT	AGE		
	0–5	5–10	10–ADULTHOOD
Basic Capacities	Many capacities present: association, generalization, recognition, etc. By age 5, if not earlier, absolute capacity of sensory memory at adult-like levels.	Speed of processing increases.	Speed of processing continues to increase.
Strategies	A few rudimentary strategies such as naming, pointing, and selective attention.	Acquisition and increasing use of many strategies: rehearsal, organization, etc.	Continuing improvement in quality of all strategies.
Metamemory	Little factual knowledge about memory. Some monitoring of ongoing performance.	Increasing factual knowledge about memory. Improved monitoring of ongoing performance.	Continued improvements in explicit and implicit knowledge.
Content Knowledge	Steadily increasing content knowledge helps memory in areas in which the knowledge exists.	Steadily increasing content knowledge helps memory in areas in which the knowledge exists. Also helps in learning of new strategies.	Continuing improvements.

Many basic processes, such as ability to associate objects with each other and to recognize familiar objects, are present at birth. These processes are crucial in enabling children to learn and remember from the first days of life. It is unknown whether the absolute capacity of memory increases with age. However, speed of processing increases from birth through late adolescence, and this helps the functional capacity of memory to increase regardless of whether the absolute capacity increases.

Memory strategies begin to contribute to memory development somewhat later than basic capacities. The earliest known strategies appear in the second year of life, but many other important strategies, such as rehearsal, organization, and elaboration, become prominent between the ages of 5 and 7. The quality of the strategies, the frequency of their use, and the flexibility with which they are tailored to the demands of specific situations continue to develop well into later childhood and adolescence.

Two types of metacognitive skills, explicit factual knowledge about memory and implicit procedural knowledge, seem to have different developmental courses. Implicit metacognitive knowledge is evident quite early. Even toddlers sometimes monitor their comprehension and develop feelings of knowing, although the range of situations in which they do so continues to grow for many years thereafter. In contrast, explicit knowledge about memory appears to develop primarily between the ages of 5 and 15, perhaps in response to attending school and needing to remember a great deal of arbitrary information.

Content knowledge contributes to memory development from infancy onward. It influences both how much and what children remember. It also affects the efficiency of execution of basic processes, the learning of new strategies, and metacognitive knowledge about memory. Together, basic capacities, strategies, metacognition, and content knowledge account for the two essential features of memory development: first, that even infants in the first two weeks of life have the ability to learn and to remember what they learned; and second, that the effectiveness of memory continues to improve throughout early childhood, middle childhood, and adolescence.

SUMMARY

Children are being called increasingly often to testify in court cases. Research on the accuracy of their testimony indicates that when they are asked unbiased questions, even preschoolers' recall is accurate and relevant. However, asking biased questions and inducing stereotypes may lead children, especially preschoolers, to report events that never happened. For this reason, obtaining the most accurate recall requires asking specific questions and phrasing them neutrally.

Memory development has been attributed to four types of causes: changes in basic processes and capacities, in strategies, in metacognition, and in content knowledge. Basic capacities and processes, such as the abilities to associate and recognize, are already present in newborns. By the age of 3 months, infants display many other basic processes. They generalize, remember the gist of events, and even show insight. Processing speed increases throughout childhood and adolescence. The number of symbols that can be held in working memory also improves gradually over this period, but it is unclear whether this is because of changes in the absolute capacity of memory or because of other improvements.

The use of broadly applicable strategies such as rehearsal, organization, and selective attention increases rapidly between age 5 and adolescence. Children who use such strategies typically remember more than those who do not. Changes in the quality of strategies and the range of situations in which they are used continue well beyond the ages at which they are first adopted. Strategies can be taught to children earlier than the age at which children would ordinarily use them. However, children who have received such training often fail to use the strategies in subsequent situations, and they use them less effectively than older children. This may be because children derive lesser benefits and incur greater costs from using the strategies and because they fail to perceive the connection between using the strategy and remembering better. Overall, learning of these strategies seems to account for an important part of memory development, particularly in middle childhood and beyond.

Metacognition includes two distinct types of knowledge: explicit and implicit. Explicit knowledge about memory is conscious and verbalizable. It usually involves factual knowledge about strategies, tasks, and capacities. Implicit knowledge, in contrast, is not conscious or verbalizable; it involves such processes as monitoring one's comprehension and feelings of knowing. Implicit knowledge of memory is already evident among toddlers. Explicit knowledge is not evident as early, but between the ages of 5 and 10, it, too, becomes quite extensive. Development of both types of metacognitive knowledge continues throughout life.

Knowledge of related content greatly affects children's memory at all ages. Content knowledge allows children to remember more than they otherwise would, influences their ability to learn strategies, helps them make plausible inferences, and allows them to form scripts for remembering sequences of events. Under some circumstances, differences in content knowledge can outweigh all other changes in memory that come with age and experience. Children who are experts on topics such as chess and soccer exhibit truly impressive memory in their areas of expertise, although their memory in other areas is unexceptional. Encoding of distinctive features and spreading activation appear to be two of the mechanisms that help children with high content knowledge to remember new information better.

RECOMMENDED READINGS

Ceci, S. J., & Bruck, M. (1993). The suggestibility of the child witness: An historical review and synthesis. *Psychological Bulletin, 113,* 403–39. A readable review of research on the accuracy of children's eyewitness testimony and the conditions that make it more and less accurate.

Kail, R. (1991). Developmental changes in speed of processing during childhood and adolescence. *Psychological Bulletin, 109,* 490–501. Intriguing evidence is presented that the basic speed of information processing increases with age over the entire period from early childhood through adolescence.

Miller, P. & Seier, W. (1994). Strategy utilization deficiencies in children: When, where, and why. In H. Reese (Ed.) *Advances in child development and behavior.* (Vol. 25, pp. 107–56). New York: Academic Press. This review presents a large body of evidence documenting the surprising finding that children often use strategies before their recall benefits from them, and suggests several explanations for why they do so.

Rovee-Collier, C. (1995). Time windows in cognitive development. *Developmental Psychology, 31,* 147–69. In this article, Rovee-Collier introduces the construct of the time window, the period during which experiences can be integrated so as to improve memory of the original experience. She illustrates the applicability of the time-window construct to language development, eyewitness testimony, and other areas.

Schneider, W., & Pressley, M. (1989). *Memory development between 2 and 20.* New York: Springer-Verlag. This book provides a comprehensive summary of what is known about memory development, particularly about strategies and metacognition.

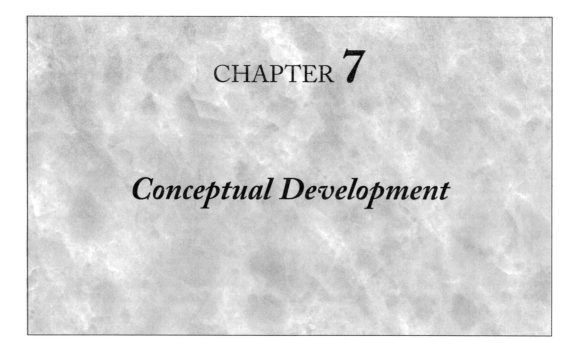

CHAPTER 7

Conceptual Development

Experimenter: It's twelve o'clock in the afternoon and the sun is shining really bright. You already ate something today, but you're still very hungry, so you decide to eat pancakes with syrup, orange juice, cereal, and milk. Could that be lunch?

Kindergartner: No . . . because lunch you have to have sandwiches and stuff like that.

E: Can you have cereal for lunch?

K: No.

E: Can you have pancakes for lunch?

K: No . . . No.

E: Well, how do you know if something is lunch or not?

K: If the time says 12:00.

E: This was 12:00.

K: Well, I don't think so.

E: (Repeats story.) Is that lunch?

K: I know . . . that one is not lunch . . . you have to eat sandwiches at lunch.

E: Can you have anything else?

K: You can have drinks, but not breakfast. (Keil, 1989, pp. 77, 291)

This child's concept of lunch clearly differs from that of older children and adults. But what can we conclude from the difference? Is it simply an isolated confusion between typical and essential characteristics of lunch? Or is it symptomatic of a more general tendency of younger children to understand concepts superficially and not to grasp their core meaning?

Concepts involve grouping together different entities on the basis of some similarity. The similarity can either be quite concrete (a concept of balls) or quite abstract (a concept of justice). Concepts allow us to organize our experience into coherent patterns and to draw inferences in situations in which we lack direct experience. If told that malamutes are dogs, a child immediately also knows that they have four legs, a tail, fur; that they are animals; that they probably are friendly to people; and so on. Concepts also save us mental effort by allowing us to apply previous knowledge to new situations. Once we have the concept "kitten," we do not need to think hard about this particular scrawny, taffy-colored kitten to guess what she would like to eat.

The tendency to form concepts is a basic part of human beings. Infants form them even during their first months (Haith & Benson, in press; Quinn & Eimas, 1995). Within a few years, children acquire a huge number of them. Consider a few concepts that most 5-year-olds in the United States possess: tables, gold, animals, trees, Nintendo, dirt bikes, running, birthdays, winter, fairness, time, and number. Some of these concepts involve objects, others events, others ideas, others activities, and yet others dimensions of existence. Some of the objects are part of nature; others are artifacts made by people to serve a specific purpose. Some of the concepts are possessed by children throughout the world and have been throughout history. Others are specific to children living in advanced industrial societies of the late twentieth century. Some are broadly applicable; others are quite narrow.

In this chapter, we look at conceptual development from two perspectives. One focuses on conceptual representations in general; the other focuses on the development of a few particularly important concepts (Table 7.1).

TABLE 7.1 Chapter Outline

I. Conceptual Representations in General
   A. Defining-Features Representations
   B. Probabilistic Representations
   C. Theory-Based Representations
   D. Summary
II. Development of Some Particularly Important Concepts
   A. Time
   B. Space
   C. Number
   D. Mind
III. Summary

The approach that emphasizes the development of conceptual representations in general is based on the assumption that the nature of people's minds leads them to represent most or all concepts in a particular way. The nature of this representation is of primary interest; the details of the particular concepts are secondary. This approach has been most common in studying object concepts such as tools, furniture, and vehicles, where the particulars of the concept are less important than the concept's representativeness.

If the nature of people's minds leads them to impose a certain type of representation, and if young minds differ fundamentally from older ones, then young children's concepts may also differ fundamentally. For example, their concepts may be concrete, whereas those of older children may be abstract. Many of the most prominent developmental theorists have subscribed to this *representational development hypothesis*. Table 7.2 lists some of the contrasts between younger and older children's concepts that they have proposed.

The other main approach has been to focus on the development of a few inherently important concepts. Certain concepts, such as time, space, number, and mind, are so basic to our understanding of the world that their development is important in its own right. These concepts have played central roles in the theories of philosophers such as Kant and psychologists such as Piaget. They also may develop differently than other concepts. Unlike most concepts, they are universal across cultures and historical periods, are present in rudimentary form in infancy, and are constantly used. It is hard to imagine how people could learn such concepts if there were not some relatively specific biological basis for them. For example, if people did not encode events as occurring before or after each other, what experiences could lead to their doing so? Understanding of these basic concepts often changes dramatically during development, but their core seems to be part of our inheritance as human beings (Spelke, 1994). In the sections that follow, we first consider the development of conceptual representations in general, and then the development of a few particularly important concepts.

TABLE 7.2 Classic Characterizations of Older and Younger Children's Concepts

DESCRIPTION OF YOUNG CHILDREN'S CONCEPTS	DESCRIPTION OF OLDER CHILDREN'S CONCEPTS	THEORIST(S)
Concrete	Abstract	Piaget (1951)
Perceptual	Conceptual	Brunner, Goodnow, & Austin (1956)
Holistic	Analytic	Werner & Kaplan (1963)
Thematic	Taxonomic	Vygotsky (1934, 1962)
Global	Specific	Inhelder & Piaget (1964)

CONCEPTUAL REPRESENTATIONS IN GENERAL

How do people represent concepts? Three main possibilities have been proposed: defining-features representations, probabilistic representations, and theory-based representations. The differences among the proposed representations can be seen in the Figure 7.1 depictions of the concept "uncle." *Defining-features representations* are like dictionary definitions. They include only the necessary and sufficient features that determine whether an example is or is not an instance of the concept. *Probabilistic representations* are more like the articles in encyclopedias. Rather than just representing a few features that must always be present, people may represent concepts in terms of a large number of properties that are somewhat, but not perfectly, correlated with the concept. Thus, uncles tend to be nice to their nieces and nephews, though they are not necessarily so. Finally, *theory-based representations* are akin to chapters in a science textbook, in that they emphasize causal relations among elements of a system. Children's conceptual representations may include explanations for why their uncles tend to be nice, why they tend to be about as old as their parents, and so on.

FIGURE 7.1   *Ways in which the concept "uncle" might be represented within defining features, probabilistic, and theory-based approaches.*

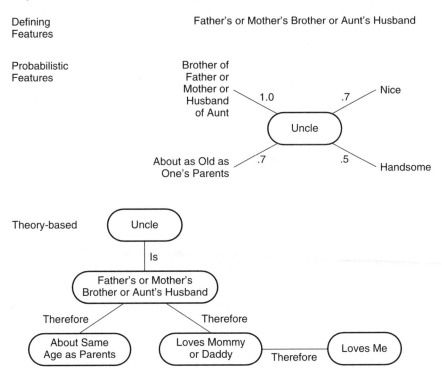

Are young children capable of generating all of these types of representations? As previously noted, some of the most eminent developmental theorists—Piaget, Vygotsky, Werner, and Bruner, among others—thought not. Although they used different terminology, all hypothesized that young children cannot form what we are calling defining-features representations. We next consider the evidence on which they based this view and whether they were right.

Defining-Features Representations

What would it mean for people to represent concepts in terms of defining features? First, they would know the concepts' necessary and sufficient features. Second, they would use these features to determine whether particular examples were instances of the concept.

Piaget, Bruner, and others largely based their view that young children could not form defining-features representations on observations of children playing with objects. They presented children several types of objects, such as toy animals, vehicles, and furniture, and observed which ones children put together. They found that older children typically divide the objects into categories with a defining feature: They put animals with animals, vehicles with vehicles, and so forth. In contrast, a typical preschooler might put together a dog and a car (because dogs like to ride in cars), a cat and a chair (because cats like to curl up in chairs), and a game and a shelf (because games belong on shelves). Such groupings led Inhelder and Piaget (1964) to conclude that preoperational stage children's concepts were *thematic* (organized in terms of a common activity or theme), whereas concrete operations stage children's were *taxonomic* (organized in terms of hierarchically organized categories, like those used to classify plants and animals in biology).

Vygotsky (1934, 1962) used a similar task. He presented children a number of blocks that differed in size, color, and shape, and asked them to group together those that went together. Children 6 years of age and older who were given this sorting task typically chose a single quality as the defining feature. For example, they might choose color as necessary and sufficient for membership in a group, and put all the red blocks together, all the green blocks together, and so on. Preschoolers, however, seemed to form what Vygotsky called *chain concepts*. These were concepts in which the basis of classification changed from example to example. They might put together a few red blocks; then put a few triangles, green as well as red, together; and then put a few green blocks together.

These types of observations led Vygotsky to hypothesize that children pass through three stages of conceptual development. Very early, they form thematic concepts, stressing relations between particular pairs of objects. Later, they form chain concepts by momentarily classifying on the basis of abstract dimensions such as color or shape, but often forgetting what they were doing and switching their basis of categorization. Still later, during the elementary school period, they form true concepts, based on stable necessary-and-sufficient features.

Evaluation.   The defining-features view of concepts has led to a number of discoveries about preschoolers' conceptual understanding: that they often do not sort objects along a single consistent dimension; that they tend to arrange objects according to how the objects interact, rather than according to their categorical relations; and that they find different relations of interest than do adults.

But should we believe the broader theoretical claim that young children's concepts differ fundamentally from those of older children and adults? Probably not. Research conducted to test whether young children can form types of concepts typical of older children has consistently shown that they can. For example, Bauer and Mandler (1989a) found that even 1-year-olds form taxonomic concepts. They presented children of this age with sets of three objects. The target object was placed in the middle, and children were asked, "See this one? Can you find another object just like this one?" Of the remaining two objects, one was related to the target object thematically and the other taxonomically. For example, in one problem, the object in the middle was a monkey, the object related to it taxonomically was a bear, and the object related to it thematically was a banana. The 1-year-olds chose the taxonomically related objects (the monkey and the bear) as being the similar ones on more than 85 percent of trials.

If even 1-year-olds understand taxonomic relations, why would the impression have arisen that 4- and 5-year-olds cannot understand them? Confusing children's interests with their capabilities may be the reason. Young children may put dogs and frisbees together, rather than dogs and bears, because they find the relation between dogs and frisbees more interesting. Supporting this interpretation, Smiley and Brown (1979) found that preschoolers who sorted objects thematically could, when asked, explain perfectly the taxonomic relations as well. Cole and Scribner (1974) reported similar findings with tribespeople in Africa. Experimenters could elicit the ostensibly more-sophisticated taxonomic sortings from the tribespeople only by asking, "How would a stupid man do it?" Both the children and the tribespeople possessed the relevant concepts, but they chose not to apply them in the particular situation.

Another contributor to the misimpression has been underestimating the role of specific content knowledge in conceptual understanding. Although young children represent some concepts in terms of defining features, they do not know what the defining features are for many other concepts. Consider an experiment in which 5- and 9-year-olds heard two stories describing a particular object and then were asked whether that object could be an example of the concept (Keil & Batterman, 1984). As shown in Table 7.3, one story indicated that the object included many features people associate with the concept, but it also

TABLE 7.3 *Stories from Keil and Batterman (1984)*

CHARACTERISTIC FEATURES BUT NOT DEFINING FEATURES

Island

There is this place that sticks out of the land like a finger. Coconut trees and palm trees grow there, and the girls sometimes wear flowers in their hair because it's so warm all the time. There is water on all sides except one. Could that be an island?

DEFINING FEATURES BUT NOT CHARACTERISTIC FEATURES

On this piece of land, there are apartment houses, snow, and no green things growing. This piece of land is surrounded by water on all sides. Could that be an island?

indicated that it lacked the defining feature. The other story indicated that the object included the defining feature, but lacked many associated features.

The 9-year-olds generally emphasized the defining features; they usually said that the story at the top of Table 7.3 did not describe an island, but that the story at the bottom did. The performance of the 5-year-olds was in some ways different and in other ways similar. The 5-year-olds did not rely on the defining feature on as many concepts as the 9-year-olds. However, on familiar concepts, such as "robbers," the 5-year-olds did rely on defining features. And, on relatively unfamiliar concepts, such as "taxis," the 9-year-olds did not consistently do so. (The fact that the study was conducted in a small town probably had a lot to do with the concept "taxi" being unfamiliar.) Thus, both younger and older children can form defining-features representations, but knowledge about the defining features of particular concepts increases with age.

Probabilistic Representations

From the time of Aristotle until relatively recently, most concepts have been viewed as having defining features. Children and adults might or might not know the defining features, but they were there to be known. Today, however, the prevailing view among philosophers is that most concepts do not have defining features. Consider the term *chair*. At first glance, a chair would seem to have the defining attributes, "an object with four legs, intended to be used for sitting." But what about beanbag chairs, that have no legs? What about chairs in modern museums, that never were intended for sitting? The situation is more extreme for complex terms, such as *game* and *mercy*. It is difficult to even imagine what the defining attributes might be for such concepts.

These difficulties with identifying defining features open the possibility that all of us, adults as well as children, represent most concepts in terms of probabilistic relations between the concept and various features, rather than in terms of a few defining features. Eleanor Rosch, Carolyn Mervis, and their colleagues have developed an appealing theory based on this view of concepts. The central theme is that instances of most concepts are united by family resemblances rather than by defining features. The instances resemble each other to varying degrees and in varying ways, much like different family members do, but there is no set of features that all of them possess. Rosch and Mervis' theory is built around four powerful ideas: cue validities, basic-level categories, nonrandom distributions of features, and prototypes.

Cue validities.   How might children decide whether objects are examples of one concept or another? Rosch and Mervis (1975) suggested that they do so by comparing *cue validities*. The basic idea is that the degree to which the presence of a feature makes it likely that an object is an example of a concept depends on the frequency with which the feature accompanies that concept and on the infrequency with which the feature accompanies other concepts. For example, the feature "capable of flight" makes it likely that an object is a bird in proportion to the frequency with which birds can fly and in proportion to the infrequency with which other things can. Because most (though not all) birds can fly, and because most (though not all) other things cannot fly, flight is a highly valid cue for an object's being a bird.

The idea of cue validities helps the probabilistic approach explain a phenomenon that proved troublesome for the defining-features approach: that some instances of a concept seem like better examples of it than others. Within the defining-features approach, if a robin and an ostrich both have the necessary and sufficient features for birds, why would robins seem like better examples of birds than ostriches? The probabilistic approach suggests that objects perceived as better examples are ones whose features have higher cue validities for that concept. Thus, people view robins as better examples of birds than ostriches, because the robins' color, size, and ability to fly are more valid cues to their being birds.

The cues that people consider in forming concepts change considerably over the course of development. Infants in the first few months are already sensitive to cue validities, but the types of cues on which they focus change with age and experience. Infants initially pay greatest attention to visible and audible features, but, with experience, they pay increasing attention to more abstract ones (e.g. Eimas & Quinn, 1994; Madole & Cohen, 1995). There is a reason why infants form categories such as dogs and running, but not ones such as tools or fairness.

Basic-level categories.   Rosch, Mervis, Gray, Johnson, and Boyes-Braem (1976) noted that many categories are hierarchical, in the sense that all instances of one category are necessarily instances of another. They proposed that these hierarchies typically include at least three levels (Table 7.4): a general one (*the superordinate level*), a specific one (*the subordinate level*), and one of middling generality (*the basic level*). The basic level is the level at which cue validities are maximized. For example, "chair" is a basic-level category, because it has parts with very high cue validities, among them legs, a back, and a seat. Superordinate categories, such as "furniture," do not have features with comparably high cue validities. Some pieces of furniture have legs and others do not; some are for sitting and others are not. Conversely, subordinate categories, such as "kitchen chairs," share all features of the basic level category, but lack features that clearly discriminate them from other instances of the basic-level category. What features cleanly discriminate kitchen chairs from dining room chairs? Rosch et al. concluded that basic-level categories are more fundamental classifications than either superordinate or subordinate categories.

If basic-level categories are indeed basic, children should learn them before they learn superordinate or subordinate categories. This implication has been tested by presenting infants with a habituation procedure. First, the infants are repeatedly shown members of a basic category until they reduce their looking at the objects. Then they are presented either a novel member of the same basic-level category or a member of a different basic-level category within the same superordinate category. For example, they might repeatedly be shown horses, and then be shown either a giraffe or another horse.

Results with 3- to 9-month-olds have consistently shown that infants dishabituate when shown members of a different basic-level category (Columbo, O'Brien, Mitchell, Roberts, & Horowitz, 1987; Quinn, Eimas, & Rosenkrantz, 1993; Roberts, 1988). For example, after repeatedly being presented pictures of horses, infants dishabituated when shown similar-size pictures of giraffes, zebras, or cats (Eimas & Quinn, 1994). However, using the same methods, infants have recently been shown to form more general categories as well (Behl-Chadha, in press). For example, when shown several different mammals, 3- and 4-month-olds dishabituated when shown birds, fish, or furniture, but not when shown other animals. Thus, infants are able to form basic-level categories but also more general ones.

Although basic-level categories play prominent roles in early conceptual understanding, some of the particular categories differ considerably from those that adults consider basic. Illustratively, the objects that 1-year-olds label "balls" often include such objects as round candles, round coin banks, and multisided beads. Their "ball" category seems to correspond to the adult category "things that can roll." Mervis (1987) labeled such notions *child-basic categories*. The particulars of "child-basic" and standard-basic categories often differ, but Mervis argued that the principles by which they are formed are the same. Both young children and adults include in their basic categories objects that can be used to

TABLE 7.4 Examples of Superordinate, Basic, and Subordinate Category Members

SUPERORDINATE LEVEL	BASIC LEVEL	SUBORDINATE LEVEL
Furniture	Table	End table
Animal	Bird	Canary
Food	Vegetable	Asparagus
Tool	Hammer	Tack hammer
Vehicle	Car	Miata

achieve similar functions and that have similar appearances. Differing perspectives on what constitutes an interesting function lead to the differences in the categories that are produced at different ages.

How do children move from child-basic to standard-basic categories? Grasping the role of perceptually insignificant but functionally important attributes may be critical for making the transition (Tversky & Hemenway, 1984). For example, young children initially ignore the slots in round coin banks and the wicks on round candles and focus on the more perceptually striking round shape. Once the child understands the purpose of the slots and wicks, the conceptual distinctions become easier to understand. In keeping with this interpretation, 2-year-olds can move from child-basic to standard-basic categories if an experimenter identifies perceptually subtle attributes that are critical to category membership, and explains the importance of those attributes (Banigan & Mervis, 1988).

Correlations among features. Conceptual understanding involves more than knowing cue validities of individual features. Correlations among features are at least as essential. Features of objects in the world are not randomly distributed, but rather tend to cluster together. Things that slither along the ground also tend to have scales, to be long and thin, to be difficult to see in their natural environments, and so on. Fortunately, even 10-month-olds are adept at noting correlations among features and at using the correlations to form new concepts (Younger, 1990; 1993).

Prototypes. A fourth concept introduced by Rosch and her colleagues was that of prototypes. Prototypes are the most representative instances of concepts—that is, the examples that have the highest cue validities. Lassie was a prototypical dog because she had qualities (e.g., size, shape, bark) representative of dogs in general.

Infants as young as 3 months old abstract prototypical forms. Bomba and Siqueland (1983) showed 3- and 4-month-olds a variety of dot patterns generated by randomly transforming an original "prototype" shape, such as an equilateral triangle (Figure 7.2). During this initial phase of the experiment, infants never saw the prototype. However, exposure to examples derived from the prototype (such as the shapes in the rightmost three columns of Figure 7.2) led infants later to act as if they had seen the prototype as well. When they were shown the prototype along with an unfamiliar pattern, they preferred looking at the other pattern; they acted as if they had seen the prototype often and were bored with it. Over time, as memory for the particular dot patterns decreased but the general concept remained, the 3- and 4-month-olds actually showed more interest in shapes they had seen but apparently did not remember, than in the prototype, which they had not seen but did "remember." Older children and adults show similar patterns of being more confident that they have seen prototypes, which actually have never been shown, than forms derived from the prototypes, which they have seen (Bransford, 1979).

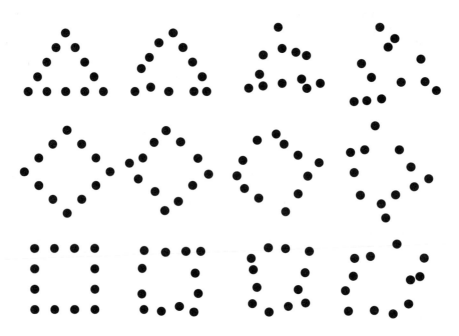

FIGURE 7.2 On the extreme left, from top to bottom, the prototypic triangle, diamond, and square are displayed. In each row, increasingly distorted versions of the prototypes are displayed from left to right (after
Bomba & Siqueland, 1983). Copyright © 1983 by Academic Press, Inc.

Evaluation. Viewing conceptual representations in terms of probabilistically related features has much to recommend it. Even in the first year of life,
infants abstract prototypical patterns, form basic-level categories, and notice cue
validities and correlations among features. With development, they form increasing numbers of superordinate and subordinate level categories, move from
child-basic to standard-basic categories for those concepts on which they started
with child-basic categories, and become sensitive to more complex and subtle
correlational patterns.

The probabilistic-features approach also has some weaknesses, though.
One that it shares with the defining-features approach is vagueness about what
constitutes a feature. For example, what features make up the concept "a beautiful face"? The features clearly are more complex than hair of a certain color,
eyes of a certain shape, lips curved at a certain angle, a nose of a certain form,
and so on. Much more important than these tangible attributes are relations
among the features, how they fit together. Yet it is unclear whether relations
such as "fitting together" can usefully be viewed as features; given that many of
the most beautiful faces strike us as unique, it also is unclear whether they are
based on probabilistic relations at all.

Another weakness, related to the previous one, is that the approach does not specify how children determine which features of unfamiliar objects and events they should encode and which they should ignore. As discussed in Chapter 3, determining which features to encode is often quite difficult. Yet, unless children encode the important features and relations, they cannot learn their cue validities.

Some researchers have proposed that infants and children are guided toward encoding relevant features through implicit theories of what is important (Wellman & S. Gelman, 1992; in press). The role of such theories is explored in the next section.

Theory-Based Representations

What concept has the following members: children, portable TVs, jewelry, and photo albums? The question seems bizarre until we hear the answer: things we would take out of the house first in case of a fire. Suddenly, the strangeness of the concept disappears (Barsalou, 1985).

As this example suggests, there is more to concepts than correlations among features and defining features. Concepts also embody theoretical beliefs about the world and the relations of entities to each other. These theoretical beliefs influence our reaction to new information. To understand this influence, contrast your reaction to the statement "Today, I saw a car with orange wheels" with that to the statement "Today, I saw a car with square wheels." Both situations are novel; people would not have had an opportunity to calculate cue validities or feature correlations for either the orange wheels or the square ones. Neither is in the least prototypical. Yet our theoretical beliefs lead us to react differently to the two statements. When we hear that a car has orange wheels, we infer that the owner may be a prankster or a hippie, that the rest of the car may also be brightly painted, and that the car probably functions normally. When we hear that a car has square wheels, we infer that it cannot move, that it was not intended to function normally, and that it may be a sculpture intended to elicit surprise. Such inferences reflect our informal theories about how cars work and why people do strange things.

Keil (1989; 1994) proposed an insightful theory regarding the role that such informal theories play in conceptual development. The following are among the main principles he suggested:

1. Most concepts are partial theories, in that they include explanations of relations among their parts and of their relations to other concepts.
2. Theories are complexly tied to people's associative knowledge; they do not stand apart from it.
3. Causal relations are basic within these theories; they are more useful than other types of relations.
4. Hierarchical relations also are especially informative.

The import of these assumptions can be illustrated with regard to a hypo-thetical situation. Suppose a girl was asked, "Why do yaks have four legs rather than three or five?" She might answer that four legs can be moved in pairs, which allows yaks to run relatively fast and still maintain their balance. This an-swer suggests that the child possesses theoretical understanding that allowed her to go beyond defining features and probabilistically-related features to ex-plain *why* the world is the way it is. The answer also illustrates the relation be-tween associative knowledge and theoretical beliefs, in that it reflects both specific memories of the running of other four-legged animals and an informal theory of how running works. The role of causal relations is evident in the child's explaining fourleggedness in terms of what it allows yaks to do. Finally, the fact that the child knew that she could reason from her knowledge of ani-mals in general to a particular animal—yaks—attests to the usefulness of orga-nizing concepts into hierarchies.

Theoretical understanding is present in concepts of very young children, as well as in those of older children and adults. This is not to say that the under-standing is the same at all ages. The accuracy and interconnectedness of the the-oretical beliefs, as well as the frequency with which they are relied on, increase with development. Keil (1989) hypothesized that at all ages, concepts include both theoretical connections and isolated factual information. However, as theo-ries become increasingly sophisticated, they explain an increasingly broad range of the factual knowledge.

Although people generate many informal theories, a few "core theories" may be especially important (Wellman & S. Gelman, 1992; in press). In particu-lar, Wellman and Gelman hypothesized that children are predisposed to develop three core theories: one concerning inanimate objects (*naive physics*), one con-cerning living things (*naive biology*), and one concerning the human mind (*naive psychology*). These core theories are said to organize a great deal of their knowl-edge about the world and help them in acquiring additional knowledge. As Wellman and Gelman (in press) noted,

> Conceptually, these domains encompass much of the external world with which we interact. Consider early humans. It is hard to imagine any more fundamental cog-nitive tasks than knowing about people, about plants and animals, and about the world of physical objects. Knowledge about other humans enables negotiating so-cial interactions and managing important tasks of mating and childrearing; knowl-edge about plants and animals fosters food-gathering, avoiding predators, and maintaining health; knowledge about physical objects allows prediction of the ef-fects of one's own and others' physical actions, the creation and use of tools, and so on. (Wellman & Gelman, in press)

One of the distinctive characteristics of these core theories is that they dif-fer in the type of causal relations that operate. Consider how we would answer a single question—"Why did X move?"—depending on whether we were talk-ing about a pebble, a fish, or a person. With the pebble or any other inanimate object, we would explain the movement by citing physical contact with another moving object, as in "The pebble shot across the road because a truck ran over it." With a fish or other biological entity, we would usually explain movement with regard to the function it serves for the species, as in "Birds fly South to stay warm in winter." With a person, we would explain the movement in terms of the individual's goals, such as "The boy went to the store to buy a CD."

Children as young as 7 months old differentiate among the actions of objects from these categories. For example, they will imitate the movements of people in a cartoon, but not the same movement executed by an inanimate object in a cartoon (Legerstee, 1991). They also show surprise if inanimate objects begin moving without any force being applied to them, but not if people do (Spelke, Phillips, & Woodward, 1995).

When do children first possess such core theories? Spelke (1994) speculated that infants begin life with a primitive theory of inanimate objects, which she labeled a theory of physics. This theory includes the knowledge that the world is composed of physical objects that are cohesive, have boundaries, have substance, move only when touched by another object, and move in continuous ways through space and time. As one source of evidence, she cited Baillargeon's (1987; 1994) finding that 4-months-olds show surprise when the drawbridge appears to move through another solid object (Chapter 2). She also cited her own findings (Spelke, Breinlinger, Macomber & Jacobson, 1992) that 4-month-olds show surprise when objects seem to jump from one point to another without passing through intermediate positions or when seemingly independent objects start moving and stop moving in tandem.

Wellman and Gelman (in press) suggested that the first theory of psychology may emerge at around 18 months and the first theory of biology at around 2 or 3 years. Even infants, however, have some sense of the differences among inanimate objects, people, and other living things, as the studies of infants' reactions to the movement of people and inanimate objects suggest (Legerstee, 1991; Spelke et al., 1995).

Evaluation.   The theory-oriented approach to conceptual development is bold and promising. Concepts are at their heart relational; causal relations are often especially critical. Children seem to focus on these causal relations from early in life. Knowing the causal relations helps children encode the most relevant information in a situation. The causal knowledge also helps them to draw inferences, to generalize, and to understand their experience.

The approach raises at least as many questions as it answers, however. One of its limitations is vague definition of what qualifies as a theory. A physicist's theory of matter differs profoundly from that of a typical adult, much less from that of an infant. Within scientific theories, internal consistency, parsimony, and formalization are important qualities. None of these qualities is shared by the concepts of infants and young children. Similar problems arise in trying to distinguish core theories from noncore ones.

This vagueness about what qualifies as a theory, and what qualifies as a core theory, has led to people using the term *theory* in very different ways. Carey (1985) proposed that very young children possess only two theories: a theory of physics and a theory of psychology. She suggested that they eventually differentiate these two into roughly a dozen theories, corresponding to major disciplines taught at universities: physics, chemistry, biology, psychology, economics, and so on. In contrast, Keil (1989) argued that concepts in general are theoretical and that young children may have innumerable theories. Without clearer specification of when understanding counts as a theory, and when it counts as a core theory, such disagreements are inevitable.

Despite these difficulties, viewing concepts in terms of theory-based representations is a promising approach to conceptual development. Many issues remain to be resolved, but the approach's emphasis on the role of causal relations within conceptual understanding seems an especially important insight. The propensity to explain the causes of our experiences is a basic property of human beings; it plays a central role in many of the concepts we form, both large and small.

Summary

What can we conclude about children's conceptual representations? From very young ages, children seem to be capable of representing concepts in all three ways that have been discussed: defining features, probabilistically related features, and informal theories. The prominence of the representations within children's conceptual understanding may change, however. In particular, when children are just beginning to form a concept, probabilistic relations between features and the concept may play an especially large role. Early on for some concepts and later on for others, children form simple theories that indicate causal relations, both among different aspects of the concept and between the concept and related ideas. Eventually, for concepts that fit the defining features model, children distinguish between those features that are definitional and those that are only characteristic.

DEVELOPMENT OF SOME PARTICULARLY IMPORTANT CONCEPTS

Some concepts are so important, and so pervasive, that they merit special attention. These concepts develop among children in all cultures, and probably at all times in history. All have their origins early in development. All also develop in ways that reflect the influence of the surrounding culture. Among these especially important concepts are time, space, number, and mind.

Time

The concept of time includes both experiential and logical aspects. *Experiential time* refers to our subjective experience of the order and duration of events. *Logical time* involves properties that can be deduced through reasoning. An event that starts later and ends earlier than another must have taken a shorter time.

   Experiential time. Without a sense of the order in which events occur, the world would be an extremely difficult place to understand. It should not be surprising, therefore, that infants in their first year of life already notice such order. For example, when interesting photos are repeatedly shown in the order "photo on right; photo on right; photo on left," 3-month-olds detect the pattern and begin to look to the appropriate side even before the photo appears (Haith, Wentworth, & Canfield, 1993). They would not know where to look if they did not encode the order of events. Similarly, 8-month-olds (though not 4-month-olds) discriminate between movies run forward and backward that show a block being dropped and falling to the floor (Friedman, 1995). Since the events in the movie are identical except for the order in which they occur, the infants must be encoding that blocks typically are higher at the earlier time and lower at the later time, rather than vice versa. By 12 months of age, infants usually imitate sequences of two actions in the correct order (Bauer, 1995).
   A later-developing aspect of experiential time is the ability to estimate the durations of events (how long they take). By age 5, children can estimate durations of 3 to 30 seconds quite accurately, especially if given feedback about the true durations (Fraisse, 1982). Older children become increasingly adept at using counting to help them estimate the intervals. However, counting only produces accurate estimates if the units of time being counted are equal; counting quickly to 10 does not take the same amount of time as counting slowly to 10. Many 5- to 7-year-olds count with units of varying length, which results in their inaccurately estimating the passage of time when they use counting strategies (Levin, 1989).
   Still later developing is a sense of durations stretching over weeks or months. By age 4, children begin to gain such competence; they consistently judge an event that happened one week ago to have occurred more recently than one that happened 7 weeks ago (Friedman, 1991). Children of this age also accurately judge whether their birthday or Christmas was more recent if one occurred in the recent past (the last 60 days) and the other did not (Friedman, Gardner, & Zubin, 1995). However, not until age 9 do children judge accurately which event was more recent when both occurred more than 60 days earlier.

   Logical time. To measure logical understanding of time, Piaget (1969) presented children two trains that ran in the same direction along parallel tracks;

the question was which train traveled for the longer time. Although the two trains started and stopped at the same times, children younger than 6 or 7 years old generally said that the train that stopped farther down the track traveled the longer time, as well as the longer distance and the faster speed. Piaget concluded that preoperational children lacked a logical understanding of time, speed, and distance.

Subsequent studies have replicated Piaget's observations but cast doubt on his interpretation. For example, when 5-year-olds observe cars moving in circular paths, rather than along straight lines, they have little difficulty deducing from the starting and ending times which car traveled for the greater total time (Levin, 1977). They also show understanding of these logical properties in comparing the sleeping times of two dolls that were said to fall asleep and wake up at the same or different times (Levin, 1982). In these cases, there were no strongly interfering cues, such as unequal stopping points, on which children could base incorrect judgments. It thus appears that 5-year-olds understand the logical relations among beginning, ending, and total time, but that their grasp is sufficiently fragile that interfering cues can lead to their not relying on it.

Young children are not the only ones who do not always use the logical understanding of time, speed, and distance that they possess. Older children and adults have the same problem. Think about this situation: When a race car travels around an oval track, do both its doors move at the same speed? Most adults' believe that they do, but in fact they do not. The door toward the outside of the track is covering a greater distance in the same time, and therefore is moving faster.

The reason that the problem is so difficult is that it flies in the face of what Levin, Siegler, and Druyan (1990) labeled the *single-object/single-motion intuition*. This is the belief that all parts of a single object must move at the same speed. Young children, older children, and college students share this intuition. They all consistently say that all parts of a single object travel at the same speed.

Despite the single-object/single-motion intuition ordinarily persisting at least from third grade through college, it can be overcome through physical experiences that dramatically contradict it. Levin et al. presented sixth graders a 6-foot-long rod, one end of which was attached to a pivot. The child and the experimenter both held the rod while walking around the pivot on four trials. On two of the trials, the child held the rod near the pivot, and the experimenter held it at the far end; on the other two trials, their positions were reversed. The difference in the speed at which children needed to walk while holding the inner and outer parts of the rod was sufficiently dramatic for them not only to learn that the outer part moved faster, but also to generalize the insight to other problems in which different parts of a single object moved at different speeds. The physical experience accomplished what years of informal experience and formal science instruction usually fail to do. As one boy said, "Before, I hadn't experienced it. I didn't think about it. Now that I have had that experience, I know that when I was on the outer circle, I had to walk faster to be at the same place as you" (Levin et al., 1990). Such physical experiences may help children understand concepts at a deeper level than classroom instruction usually does.

Space

From early in life, people, like other animals, encode not just when events occur but also where they occur. Under ideal circumstances, these encodings are very accurate from early in life. For example, as shown in Figure 7.3, when 1-year-olds see a Sesame Street toy buried in a long, thin, sandbox directly in front of them, and then wait while the experimenter smoothes the sand, they are very accurate in choosing where to dig for the toy (Huttenlocher, Newcombe, & Sandberg, 1994).

This basic ability to code space gets us started, but it does not overcome the many complex problems posed by the need to locate ourselves and objects in space. We can represent spatial locations and distances in at least three ways: in relation to our own position, in relation to landmarks, or in relation to an abstract framework (Huttenlocher & Newcombe, 1984). *Egocentric representations* involve locating objects in relation to ourselves. Thus, a target's position can be represented as "10 paces to my left." *Landmark-based representations* locate targets relative to other objects in the environment. Thus, we could represent a location by thinking, "I parked the car on the yellow level near the Section B sign." *Allocentric representations* locate targets relative to an abstract frame of reference, such as that provided by a map or coordinate system. The name allocentric reflects the fact that within such representations, any position can serve as the center or reference point for thinking about the surrounding space.

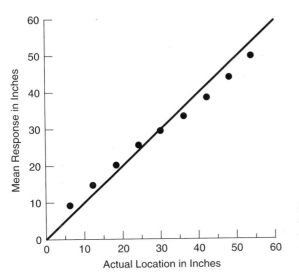

FIGURE 7.3   Mean location at which 1-year-olds searched for objects that had been buried within a sandbox, graphed against the objects' true locations. Note how close the searches were to the true locations (after Huttenlocher et al., 1994).

Egocentric representations.   Piaget (1971) suggested that infants in their first year of life exhibit a kind of sensorimotor egocentrism. Recall from Chapter 2 that egocentrism refers to young children's tendency to view the world solely from their own perspective. Piaget claimed that in infancy, the egocentrism is quite literal, and that infants represent locations of objects only in relation to themselves. For example, they might continue to represent an object as being a right turn away from themselves even after they moved to the opposite side of the object, resulting in its now being on their left.

Piaget's hypothesis was supported by subsequent findings that 6- and 11-month-olds frequently fail to compensate for changes in their own spatial position relative to a toy (Acredolo, 1978). In these experiments, a child is placed in a T-shaped maze and repeatedly finds a toy by crawling straight and then turning in a particular direction (e. g., to the left) at the intersection. Then the child is moved to the other end of the T-shaped maze and turned back toward the middle, thus requiring a turn in the opposite direction (e.g., to the right) to find the toy. Most 6- to 11-month-olds continue to turn in the direction that previously led to the toy. Not until the age of 16 months do they compensate for the change in their position.

This sensorimotor egocentrism is not absolute, even at such young ages. Infants' difficulty in adjusting to changes in spatial position can be mitigated if distinctive landmarks provide cues to the object's location (Rieser, 1979). Under such conditions, 6-month-olds usually turn in the appropriate direction, even when it differs from the direction that previously led to the toy.

How do infants learn to represent space in a way not tied to their own position within it? Just as experience with self-produced motion helps infants perceive depth well enough to avoid going over the visual cliff (Chapter 4, pp. 121–24), so it appears crucial for learning about space more generally. Eight-month-olds who crawl or who have had extensive experience in a walker succeed considerably more often in locating objects' spatial positions than infants of the same age who neither crawl well nor have experience with walkers (Bai & Bertenthal, 1992; Bertenthal, Campos, & Kermoian, 1994). The longer children have been locomoting, the greater their advantage (Kermoian & Campos, 1988).

What is it about self-produced locomotion that leads to this ability to overcome the egocentric perspective? Bertenthal et al. (1994) suggested that when infants crawl, they must continuously update their representation of where they are relative to the surrounding environment. Consistent with this view, when 12-month-olds walk to the other side of a layout and have the opportunity to look at all times at the location of a prize, they both look at it more than children who are carried and subsequently do better in turning toward the object from the new position (Acredolo, Adams, & Goodwyn, 1984).

Self-produced movement can enhance children's representation of space even when the space they are representing is not the one through which they are walking. This was learned in a clever experiment on the spatial imagery of

5-year-olds (Rieser, Garing, & Young, 1994). The children were classmates in the same kindergarten, but were studied while they were at their homes. Some children were asked to imagine being in their classroom, walking to the teacher's chair, and turning around to face the class. Then they were asked to point to where various objects in the room would be from that vantage point. Few could do so accurately. However, when children from the same class were asked to imagine the same actions while they actually walked and turned around, their pointing was very accurate. The fact that the walking was in their homes, a location far removed from the place they were imagining, did not prevent the actions from aiding their imagery. Similar findings were obtained with 4-year-olds and 9-year-olds, and in a location other than the children's home (a research laboratory). The findings indicate that self-produced movement activates people's representation of space, even if they are not in the particular space being imagined. More generally, it suggests that the systems that produce motor activity and spatial representations are closely linked (Rieser et al., 1994).

Landmarks.   We often give directions in terms of landmarks, as in "You go through the Fort Pitt Tunnel, turn off at the Banksville Road exit, and go south until you hit MacFarlane Road." We do this because landmarks provide a way of dividing the environment into manageable segments. In a sense, they allow people to apply a divide-and-conquer strategy to solving the perennial problem of how to get from here to there.

Representation of spatial locations in terms of landmarks begins in the first year of life. As noted previously, 6-month-olds' representations of an object's position survive a change in perspective if a distinctive landmark is near the object (Rieser, 1979). People as well as objects can provide such landmarks; 9-month-olds at times use their mothers' location as landmarks for locating interesting objects near her (Presson & Ihrig, 1982).

The use of landmarks undergoes considerable refinement beyond this initial period (Huttenlocher & Newcombe, 1984; Newcombe, 1989). Before a child's first birthday, only landmarks immediately adjacent to the target lead to accurate location of targets. By the time the child is 2 years old, landmarks that are more distant from the target also help. By age 5, children can represent an object's position relative to multiple landmarks, a much more powerful procedure for establishing exact locations. For example, they can represent an object as being midway between two other objects.

Although landmarks help young children locate objects in space, they can also distort their representations of the distances separating objects. Piaget, Inhelder, and Szeminska (1960) reported that preoperational stage children estimate the distance separating objects as smaller when a landmark (another object) is between them than when no such landmark is present. Subsequent studies have confirmed that most 4-year-olds, and about half of 5- and 6-year-olds, show this pattern (Fabricius & Wellman, 1993; Miller & Baillargeon, 1990).

Their main difficulty, as Piaget suggested, is that they focus on only one of the segments, and mistake the distance within it for the entire distance.

Allocentric representations. Frequently, barriers or sheer distance prevent us from seeing our intended destination. Such situations demand integration of spatial information from multiple perspectives into a common abstract representation. Such representations are perhaps the most purely spatial of the three types. Egocentric and landmark-based representations can be easily reduced to a verbal form (e.g., the restaurant is to my left; the restaurant is near DuPont Circle). In contrast, allocentric representations, which include all relations among the entities within the space, are very difficult to describe verbally.

Although intuition suggests that forming such allocentric representations is more challenging than relying on landmarks, 1-year-olds rely on allocentric representations in some situations in which they do not use landmarks. This was demonstrated in a study by Hermer and Spelke (1994), using the rooms diagrammed in Figure 7.4. Participants were in a rectangular room, with a red barrier in front of each corner. They saw a toy hidden in one corner of the room, were blindfolded and turned around 10 times, and then needed to locate the hidden object. Sometimes all four walls of the room were white; in this condition, participants needed to rely on allocentric representations, since no landmarks were present, and twirling blindfolded and stopping at an unknown point would have disrupted their initial egocentric orientation. Under these conditions, the best performance possible was to form a representation equivalent to "the toy is in a corner with a long wall on the left and a short wall on the right." Use of such a representation would lead to equal numbers of searches at the two corners that fit the description (Fig 7.4). This is what both 1-year-olds and adults do.

FIGURE 7.4 *Diagram of room used to study infants' searching in Hermer and Spelke (1994). The **X** marks the spot at which the object was hidden; the only difference between the conditions was that in the room diagrammed on the right, one wall adjoining the hiding location was blue, thus providing a landmark for locating the hidden object.*

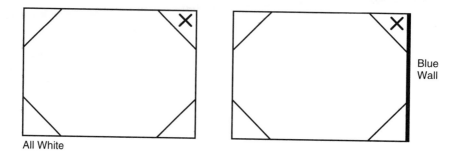

All White

Blue Wall

In another condition, a landmark was established, either by putting a blue cloth on one of the walls next to where the object was hidden or by putting a teddy bear there. Adults used these landmarks to guide their search consistently to the corner where the object was hidden. In contrast, the 1-year-olds were oblivious to the landmark. As previously, they searched predominantly in one of the two corners with the long and short wall in the proper positions, but they searched equally often in the two corners that fit that description. The finding suggests that from early in development, babies have a basic allocentric sense of space and use it to orient themselves, even in situations in which they cannot use landmarks to supplement it.

Studies of the spatial representations of visually impaired people illustrate the long-term consequences of self-produced movement in refining this basic allocentric sense (Rieser, Hill, Talor, Bradfield, and Rosen, 1992). Rieser et al. contrasted the spatial representations of adults who developed severe visual impairments either early in life (almost always before birth) or later in life (usually after age 10). The task was to imagine standing at a particular landmark facing in a particular direction in a familiar part of one's neighborhood and to point toward where other imagined landmarks would be.

Those whose visual impairments began early in life and whose peripheral vision was impaired represented the spatial layout much less accurately than those whose impairments started later or whose peripheral vision was intact. The finding suggested that early perceptual learning is critical for accurate spatial representations.

The centrality of spatial knowledge within one's culture also influences the degree to which children develop spatial skills. Evidence of this role came from a unique study of aborigines living in the western desert of Australia (Kearins, 1981). These aborigines have followed a nomadic hunting and gathering lifestyle for thousands of years. Their children do not attend formal schools. On most tests of cognitive functioning, the children do far less well than children of the same ages in Europe and North America.

Kearins reasoned, however, that a different picture might emerge if the focus was on types of thinking that were important in the aboriginal culture. Spatial thinking fits this criterion. Much of aboriginal life is spent trekking between widely spaced wells and creeks. Whether a particular location has water depends on capricious rainfall patterns. Few obvious landmarks exist in the stony desert to indicate the wells' and creeks' locations; thus, high-quality spatial thinking is important for survival.

This reasoning led Kearins to contrast the spatial memory of aboriginal children raised in the desert with those of white Australian children raised in the city. An experimenter presented 20 objects arranged in a 5-by-4 rectangle. After 30 seconds, she picked up the objects and then asked children to rearrange them as they were before.

The aboriginal children's memory for the spatial location proved superior. They also differed from the urban children in their strategies for remembering.

The aboriginal children studied in silence. When subsequently asked how they remembered where objects had been, they often said they remembered "the look of it." In contrast, the city-dwelling children used verbal rehearsal; they could be heard whispering and saying aloud the names of the objects while they studied them. The urban children's strategy is effective for remembering verbal material of the types needed to do well in school, but the aboriginal children's strategy is more useful for remembering spatial information. Thus, each group relied on strategies that were useful for the tasks of greatest importance in their everyday lives.

Number

Understanding of numbers involves two basic types of knowledge: understanding of cardinality and understanding of ordinality. *Cardinality* refers to absolute numerical size. A common property of people's arms, legs, eyes, and feet is that there are two of them. The cardinal property of two-ness is what these sets share. *Ordinality* refers to relational properties of numbers. That someone is the third-tallest girl in the class and that five is the fifth number of the counting string are ordinal properties.

Understanding of cardinal properties. Understanding of cardinality begins early in infancy. In the first half-year of life, infants can discriminate one object from two, and two objects from three (Antell & Keating, 1983; Starkey, Spelke & Gelman, 1990; van Loosbroek & Smitsman, 1990). This was learned through the use of the habituation paradigm. Infants were shown a sequence of pictures, each of which contained a small set of objects, such as three circles. The sets differed from trial to trial in size of the objects, brightness, distance apart, and other properties, but they always had the same number of objects. Once the infants habituated to displays with this number of objects, they were shown a set that was comparable in other ways to the displays they had seen but that had a different number of objects. Their renewed looking testified to their having abstracted the number of objects in the previous sets.

Discriminating among larger numbers of objects poses much greater difficulty. Not until 3 or 4 years of age do children discriminate four objects from five or six (Starkey & Cooper, 1980; Strauss & Curtis, 1984). This finding suggests that infants identify cardinalities through *subitizing*, a quick and effortless perceptual process that people can apply only to sets of one to three or four objects. When we see a row of between one and four objects, we feel like we immediately know how many there are; in contrast, with larger numbers of objects, we usually feel less sure and often need to count. Adults and 5-year-olds are similar to infants in being able to identify very rapidly the cardinal value of one to three or four objects, but not larger sets, through subitizing (Chi & Klahr, 1975).

The ability to discriminate among small quantities extends to sequences of events as well as static arrays of objects (Canfield & Smith, 1996; Starkey, Spelke,

& Gelman, 1990). For example, when 6-month-olds see a puppet repeatedly jump twice until they grow bored, and then see the puppet jump three times or one time, they show renewed interest, indicating that they discriminated among the number of jumps (Wynn, 1995).

These nascent understandings of cardinality also make it possible for infants to realize the consequences of adding and subtracting small numbers of objects (Simon, Hespos, & Rochat, 1995; Wynn, 1992a). In one task, 5-month-olds saw one or two objects, then saw a screen come down in front of them, then saw a hand place another object behind the screen, and then saw the screen rise. Sometimes the result was what would be expected by adding the one new object to the one or two that were already behind the screen; other times (through trickery) it was not. The infants looked for a longer time when the number of objects was not what it should have been.

Despite this strong beginning, children do not understand the consequences of adding even slightly larger numbers, such as 2 + 2, until they are 4 or 5 years old (Huttenlocher, Jordan, & Levine, 1994; Starkey, 1992). The reason is that the only process that infants can use to determine the number of objects is subitizing. This process is effective with very small sets, but not for dealing with sets of four or more objects. The case illustrates an important general lesson. Understanding children's thinking requires understanding the process they are using to solve the problems. The findings with infants might lead to the conclusion that infants "understand" addition. This is true in a sense, but it leaves totally unclear why they can apply it only to sets of one to three objects. Realizing that infants solve the small-number problems with a process that cannot be applied to larger sets, and that the process that can be applied to larger sets (counting) develops considerably later, makes understandable both their competence and their incompetence. _2 separate processes_
Subitizing vs counting

Counting. At 3 or 4 years of age, children become proficient in another means of establishing the cardinal value of a set—*counting*. This allows them to assign numbers to larger sets than can be subitized. Gelman and Gallistel (1978) noted the rapidity with which children learn to count and hypothesized that the rapid learning was possible because it was guided by knowledge of *counting principles*. In particular, they hypothesized that young children know

1. The *one-one principle*: Assign one and only one number word to each object.
2. The *stable order principle*: Always assign the numbers in the same order.
3. The *cardinal principle*: The last count indicates the number of objects in the set.
4. The *order irrelevance principle*: The order in which objects are counted is irrelevant.
5. The *abstraction principle*: The other principles apply to any set of objects.

Several types of evidence indicate that children understand all of these principles by age 5, and some of them by age 3 (Gelman & Gallistel, 1978). Even when children err in their counting, they show knowledge of the one-one principle, since they assign exactly one number word to most of the objects. For instance, they might count all but one object once, either skipping or counting twice the single miscounted object. These errors seem to be ones of execution rather than of misguided intent. Children demonstrate knowledge of the stable order principle by almost always saying the number words in a constant order. Usually this is the conventional order, but occasionally it is an idiosyncratic order such as "1, 3, 6." The important phenomenon is that even when children use an idiosyncratic order, they use the same idiosyncratic order on each count. Preschoolers demonstrate knowledge of the cardinal principle by saying the last number with special emphasis. They show understanding of the abstraction principle by not hesitating to count sets that include different types of objects. Finally, the order irrelevance principle seems to be the most difficult, but even here, 5-year-olds demonstrate understanding. Many of them recognize that counting can start in the middle of a row of objects, as long as each object is eventually counted. Although few children can state the principles, their counting suggests that they know them.

Gelman and Gallistel (1978) argued that one reason the principles are important is that understanding of them guides children's acquisition of counting skill. This argument rests on the assumption that children understand the principles before they count accurately. However, a variety of subsequent findings have indicated that children actually count skillfully *before* they understand the principles that underlie counting (Bermejo, 1996; Briars & Siegler, 1984; Frye, Braisby, Lowe, Maroudas, & Nicholls, 1989; Wynn, 1992b). Experience with counting may provide a data base from which children can distinguish essential features of the usual counting procedure (e.g., counting each object once and only once) from incidental ones (e.g., starting at the leftmost or rightmost end of a row).

In addition to learning the principles involved in counting objects, children also must learn the principles underlying the number system of their native language. Cross-cultural studies indicate that learning of counting varies with the number system being learned (Miller, Smith, Zhu, & Zhang, 1995; Miller & Zhu, 1991). For example, Chinese, like many East Asian languages, has a more regular sequence of number words than does English. In both languages, the numbers 1 through 10 are arbitrary, and the numbers after 20 follow a regular pattern of naming the decade name and then the digit name (e.g., "twenty-one"). However, in Chinese, the numbers from 11 to 20 also follow a regular pattern (comparable to 10-1, 10-2, etc.), whereas in English they do not. The apparent effect of this difference in the number systems is llustrated in Figure 7.5. Through age 3, when most learning is focused on acquiring the arbitrary set of the digits 1 through 10, performance of children in the two cultures is comparable. After this, however, the counting of children learning the rule-governed Chinese system takes off, whereas that children learning the arbitrary English terms for 11 through 20 continues slowly. The complexity of the English number system plainly is not the only reason that mathematics learning of children in the U.S. lags behind that of children in China and other East Asian

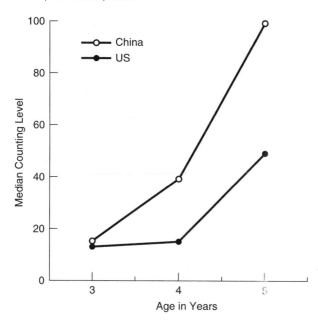

FIGURE 7.5 Counting performance of 3-, 4-, and 5-year-old children in China and the U. S. (Miller et al., 1995). Data indicate the median of the highest number reached at each age. Counting was comparable in the two countries at age 3, when children in both were mastering the first 10 numbers. However, it diverged at age 4, when children needed to master numbers in the teens.

countries, but it is one factor that slows early learning of counting. Given the importance of counting in learning subsequent skills such as addition and subtraction, the complexity of the number system may slow learning in those areas as well (Miller et al., 1995).

Ordinal properties of numbers. *Ordinality* refers to the relative positions or magnitudes of numbers. A number may be first or second in an order, or it may be greater or less than another number. Mastery of ordinal properties of numbers, like mastery of cardinal properties, begins in infancy. However, it seems to begin later, between 12 and 18 months of age.

The most basic ordinal concepts are *more* and *less*. To test when infants understand these concepts as they apply to numbers, Strauss and Curtis (1984) repeatedly presented 16- to 18-month-olds with two squares, one containing one dot, the other containing two. They reinforced the babies for selecting the square with two dots regardless of which side it was on and regardless how big or bright the dots were. Then they presented two new squares (e.g., squares with four dots and three dots). The babies more often chose the square with more dots, thus indicating understanding of the ordinal property "more numerous."

As with cardinality, extension of these early understandings of ordinality beyond sets with a few objects takes a number of years. The task most often used to examine later understandings of ordinality involve asking such questions as "Which is more: 6 oranges or 4 oranges?" Not until age 4 or 5 can children solve these ordinality problems consistently correctly for the numbers from

1 to 9 (Siegler & Robinson, 1982). Their difficulty in determining the larger number is greatest with numbers that are relatively large and close together (e.g., 7 versus 8). Counting skills may be important in development of this ordinal knowledge as well as in arithmetic; the number that occurs later in the counting string is always the larger number, and it is easier to remember which number comes later when the numbers are farther apart.

Mind

We live in a world not only of inanimate objects, plants, and animals, but also of other people. To understand these other people, and to predict what they will do next, we need to have a basic grasp of how their minds work. How could we have any idea what people would do if we did not realize that they have goals, intentions, and and expectations; that they know some things and not others; and that the fact that we know something does not mean that they do? Simply put, it is hard to imagine understanding other people without understanding basic properties of their minds.

Consciousness helps us gain this understanding; we are aware of some of the workings of our own minds, and this provides a basis for generalizing to the minds of others (Harris, 1992; Johnson, 1988; Smiley & Huttenlocher, 1989). How is it, though, that we come to understand that we have purposes, beliefs, knowledge, intentions, and desires? After all, no one has ever seen a purpose or a belief, and we do not attribute purposes or beliefs to cars, trees, or most other animals. Yet even toddlers are aware of such mental processes, as indicated by their everyday language (Bartsch & Wellman, 1995):

> Ross (2; 10) *Mommy can't sing it. She doesn't know it. She doesn't understand.* (p. 41)
> Naomi (2; 11) *I'm dreaming flowers and doggies.* (p. 41)
> Adam (2; 11) *I think it's gum drops . . . Nope.* (p. 46)

As these snippets of toddlers' conversations reveal, by age 3, children already are thinking about what they and other people *think, know, dream,* and *understand*. But how do they develop such knowledge so quickly, especially when the mind's contents are so elusive?

Children's theories of mind.   As noted earlier in this chapter, some investigators hypothesize that psychology is a core domain and that children come to life predisposed to form reasonable theories about how the mind works (Gopnik & Meltzoff, 1994; Leslie, 1994; Wellman & S. Gelman, 1992; in press). Wellman and his collaborators have formulated a particularly influential version of this idea They proposed that from roughly 3 years onward, children have a naive theory of how the mind works. They labeled it a *belief-desire theory* because its central tenet is that internal beliefs and desires lead to actions. The theory's basic organization is outlined in Figure 7.6.

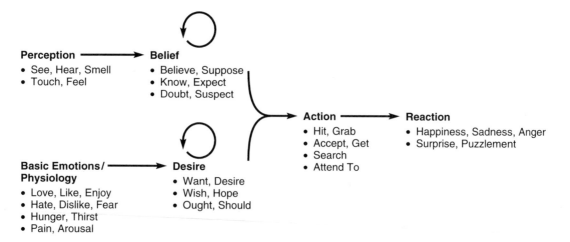

FIGURE 7.6   Wellman's (1990) depiction of children's belief-desire theory of mind.

Wellman (1990) hypothesized that 3-year-olds' theory of mind was built on a foundation of three types of understanding:

1. Understanding of the difference between the mind and other entities in the world.
2. Understanding that the contents of the mind represent those in the world.
3. Understanding of relations among mental entities, in particular beliefs and desires, and of their relation to actions.

With regard to the first of these understandings, the distinction between the mind and external objects, most 3-year-olds realize that thoughts, dreams, and memories differ both from typical physical objects, such as chairs and tables, and from insubstantial physical entities, such as smoke and sounds. When asked to explain why it is impossible to touch thoughts and dreams, 3-year-olds advance mental explanations ("Cause it's her imagination; Cause it's in his mind"). In contrast, they rarely advance such explanations in accounting for why they cannot touch sounds or smoke (Bartsch & Wellman, 1995; Woolley, 1995).

With regard to the second type of understanding, that the contents of the mind represent those in the world, 3-year-olds know that mental images can be representations of objects that exist in tangible form in the outside world (Woolley & Bruell, 1996; Woolley & Wellman, 1993). Their knowledge is not perfect; they often believe that such mental images are accurate reflections of reality, even when they are purely imaginary. Nonetheless, even 3-year-olds have considerable knowledge about the relation between their thoughts and the external world.

With regard to the third type of understanding, that of the relations among mental processes and between mental processes and actions, 3-year-olds again exhibit some understanding. They know that other people's beliefs and desires determine their actions, even when those beliefs and desires differ from the child's own (Wellman & Bartsch, 1988). They also have some knowledge of how beliefs and desires come to be; for example, they realize that perceiving something directly produces beliefs about the perceived object, and that merely being near the perceiver does not (Pillow, 1988; Pratt & Bryant, 1990).

Infants' and toddlers' understandings of the mind. Three-year-olds' understanding of beliefs and desires provides a convenient place to start thinking about development of understanding of the mind, but it marks neither the beginning nor the end of the process. First consider what leads up to the 3-year-olds' knowledge. Wellman (1990) hypothesized that the belief-desire theory is not children's first concept of mind, though it is the first, in his view, that is sufficiently elaborate to qualify for the title "theory." Preceding the belief-desire theory is an understanding of the role of desire without an understanding of the role of belief (Astington, 1993; Bartsch & Wellman, 1995; Gopnik & Slaughter, 1991; Lillard & Flavell, 1992). Two-year-olds consistently predict that characters in stories will act in accord with their desires (what they want), even when the child would make a different choice. However, 2-year-olds are considerably less likely to predict that characters will act in accord with their beliefs, for example, beliefs about where a hidden object is located, when those beliefs differ from those of the child (Wellman & Woolley, 1990).

The origins of the concept of mind can be traced back even farther. Between 12 and 18 months of age, children begin to engage in pretend play. For example, they pretend that a banana is a telephone and hold one end to their ear and talk into the other. Such pretending requires at least an implicit understanding that one object can represent another, a likely precursor of the realization that objects also can be represented by thoughts and mental images (Bretherton, 1984; Leslie, 1987). At first, the pretend object must resemble to some degree the real object to which it corresponds; thus, an 18-month-old would be much more likely to choose a banana than a toy car to represent the telephone (Lillard, 1993). By about 3 years, such resemblance is unnecessary, though children still often spontaneously choose objects with plausible forms to represent other objects.

An even earlier-developing understanding about the mind involves the concept of *intentionality*—the idea that people's actions are motivated by goals, and that the actions can be used to infer their goals and other mental states. Such a concept of intentionality appears to develop around 10 to 18 months of age (Bretherton, McNew, & Beeghly-Smith, 1981). Recall from Chapter 5 that toddlers associate the word an adult uses with a simultaneously performed action if the action appears to have been performed intentionally, but not if it appears to have been inadvertent (Tomasello & Barton, 1994). Thus, they distinguish between intentional and unintentional acts.

Development beyond age three: Understanding of appearance-reality and false belief. Development of understanding of the mind continues well beyond age 3. One key development is understanding of the appearance-reality distinction, the knowledge that looks can be deceiving. To examine development of this distinction, Flavell, Flavell, and Green (1983) presented 3-, 4-, and 5-year-olds with imitation objects, such as sponges that looked like rocks. The children were encouraged to play with the objects so that they could learn that the objects were not what they appeared to be. Then they were asked questions about what the objects looked like and what they "really really were." Similarly, they examined objects through a magnifying glass and then were asked about how big the objects looked and how big they "really really were."

Most 4- and 5-year-olds could answer these questions correctly. However, most 3-year-olds claimed not only that the sponge looked like a rock but also that it was a rock. When they looked at an object through a magnifying glass, the 4- and 5-year-olds again differentiated appearance from reality, but the 3-year-olds thought both that the object looked big when viewed through the magnifying glass and that it really was big. The finding is not unique to children growing up in Western societies; children growing up in China have similar views (Flavell, Zhang, Zou, Dong, & Qi, 1983). The shaky understanding of reality also is not limited to these tasks; for example, 3-year-olds quite often believe that the images on television screens represent tangible people and objects inside the set (Flavell, Flavell, Green, & Korfmacher, 1990). Further, teaching 3-year-olds the difference between appearance and reality is extremely difficult (Flavell, Green, & Flavell, 1986).

A cousin of these appearance-reality problems, the *false-belief task*, has generated especially great interest. A child might be shown a box of Smarties (a type of candy) with pictures of the Smarties on it. When asked what the box contains, both 3-year-olds and older children say "candy." Then the box is opened, and to the children's surprise, the box contains something else, such as pencils. Most 5-year-olds find this amusing, admit that they were surprised, and predict that other children who had not looked into the box would also expect it to contain candies. In contrast, most 3-year-olds miss the humor, claim that they always knew that the box contained pencils, and predict that other children also would know from the beginning that pencils were in the box (Flavell & Miller, in press; Gopnik & Astington, 1988; Wimmer & Perner, 1983). The following illustrates the response of a typical 3-year-old:

ADULT: *Look, here's a box . . . What's inside it?*

3-YEAR-OLD: *Smarties!*

A: *Let's look inside . . .*

3: *Oh . . . holey moley . . . pencils.*

A: *. . . When you first saw the box . . . what did you think was inside it?*

3: *Pencils.*

A: *Nicky* (child's friend) *hasn't seen inside this box . . . When Nicky sees the box, what will he think is inside it?*

3: *Pencils.* (Astington & Gopnik, 1988, p. 195)

As with the sponge-rock problems, this developmental pattern is not limited to children growing up in Western societies. For example, pygmy children from a hunter-gatherer tribe that lives in the African rainforest answer false-belief questions much like children do in the U. S. and in Europe (Avis & Harris, 1991).

Performance on the false-belief task has given rise to a decade of vociferous controversy. The controversy does not involve the findings themselves—they are easy to replicate—but rather their proper interpretation. In many ways, the arguments are reminiscent of those surrounding Piaget's findings regarding such concepts as conservation (Chapter 2). One group of researchers argues that 3-year-olds fail the false-belief task because they lack the basic competence—in this case, a theory of mind that recognizes that other people's minds include representations that may be different than one's own (Astington & Gopnik, 1991; Flavell & Miller, in press; Perner, 1991). Another group argues that 3-year-olds possess the competence in question but fail the false-belief task because of the demands that the task places on information-processing capacity and understanding of conversational conventions (Baron-Cohen, 1994; Fodor, 1992; Leslie, 1994; Siegal & Peterson, 1994). A third group also emphasizes the general information-processing demands of the task but argues that because such demands are inherent to understanding other people's minds, children do not understand mental representation until age 4 or 5 (Case, 1989; Frye, Zelazo, Brooks, & Samuels, 1996; Halford, 1993; Lewis, 1994; Olson, 1993; Russell, Jarrold, & Potel, 1994).

What can be concluded about 3-year-olds' understanding that people's minds include representations different than their own? After reviewing the voluminous literature on this issue, Flavell and Miller (in press) reached the following, reasonable conclusion:

> Many young 3-year-olds probably do have some beginning understanding, but this understanding is severely limited in several respects. It is fragile, with its expression easily impeded by information processing and other limitations. . . . It is probably rarely accessed spontaneously in the child's everyday, extralaboratory life. . . . Finally, the understanding itself may be different from what the older child possesses—more implicit, more procedural, less accessible to reflection and verbal expression.

The same conclusions could be drawn about many other aspects of children's understanding of the mind, as well as for conceptual development in general. Even concepts that appear in rudimentary form well before age 3 continue to grow more sophisticated for years thereafter. Consider the concept of intention. As noted above, 1-year-olds use their reading of an adult's intention to determine the object to which she is referring. However, 3-year-olds often confuse mistakes and accidents with intentional behavior (Abbott & Flavell, 1995, Astington, 1991; 1993). If the outcome is good, they assume that the action was intended to produce it. Four- and 5-year-olds are much better at distinguishing intentions from fortunate accidents. Thus, identifying an age at which children understand a concept is always difficult.

There is as much disagreement about the sources of development of understanding of false beliefs as there is about the meaning of the original findings. In many ways, the two debates parallel each other. Some researchers have emphasized maturation of processes specifically useful for understanding social information as the main source of development (Fodor, 1992; Baron-Cohen, 1991; Leslie, 1994). They have emphasized that the large majority of 5-year-olds have no trouble with false-belief tasks, whereas equally large majorities of 3-year-olds do. They also have emphasized findings regarding autistic children's especially great difficulty with appearance-reality, false-belief, and other tasks that measure understanding of how people's minds work. Autism is a rare deficit, affecting roughly 4 in 10,000 children. It is characterized by the inability to form relationships with other people; a lack of normal communicative skills; and strange, repetitive movements, such as rocking back and forth for long periods of time. Autistic children generally score poorly on IQ tests, but their performance on tasks requiring understanding of other people's minds, including the false-belief task, is worse than would be expected on the basis of their general intelligence. Even when compared to retarded children who answer fewer questions correctly on IQ tests, autistic children do worse on the false-belief task and related problems that require understanding of other people's thinking (Baron-Cohen, 1991; Baron-Cohen, Leslie & Frith, 1985). Autistic children also use mental verbs such as *think* and *know* less often than do other children of similar degrees of retardation (Tager-Flusberg, 1992). They do not even engage in pretend play, which is seen in typical 1-year-olds. Such findings have been used to argue that the mechanisms that allow understanding of the mind are partially independent from those used to understand other phenomena, and that autistic children suffer from a specific impairment to the mechanisms that allow understanding of their own and other people's minds (Frith, 1989; Leslie, 1991).

Other researchers have emphasized the growth of more general abilities, such as information-processing capacities, as the main source of development on the false-belief task and related problems (Case, 1989; Halford, 1993; Olson, 1993). The false-belief task imposes a considerable information-processing load. It requires children to remember not only what the other person saw but to inhibit what they themselves know to be true (Harris, 1991). Consistent with this interpretation that inhibiting vivid impressions is part of the problem, 3-year-olds do better on the false-belief task when they are just told what the true situation is, rather than seeing it with their own eyes (Zaitchik, 1991). Another line of evidence supporting the importance of general information-processing mechanisms is that other tasks that have nothing to do with understanding of the mind, but that require children to keep straight two sources of information, also are difficult for 3-year-olds and much less difficult for 4- and 5-year-olds (Frye, Zelazo, Brooks, & Samuels, 1996). Similarly, 3-year-olds do much better on the false-belief task when the information-processing requirements are reduced; for example, by having the child thoroughly learn the premises of the original problem (Lewis, Freeman, Hagestadt, & Douglas, 1994) or by actively engaging the child in deceiving the target person (Sullivan & Winner, 1993). Thus, development of general information-processing capacities may underlie improvements between ages 3 and 5 on the false-belief task and related problems.

A third approach to explaining development of ability to solve these kinds of problems has emphasized experience with other people (Dunn, 1988; Perner, Ruffman, & Leekam, 1994; Siegal, 1991). Supporting this view, children who as 2-year-olds talked about their feelings relatively often with their parents do better as 3-year-olds on the false-belief task, even when verbal ability is controlled for statistically (Dunn, Brown, Slomkowski, Tesla, & Youngblade, 1991). Preschoolers with greater numbers of brothers and sisters also do better on the false-belief task than ones with fewer siblings, presumably because they have more chances to learn about other people's thinking (Jenkins & Astington, 1996).

Fortunately, there is no need to choose among these explanations. Probably, all are correct: Development of understanding of the mind certainly reflects growth of general cognitive capacities, and experience with parents, siblings, and other people that provide opportunities to learn about their minds. It may also involve specialized mechanisms. The challenge is to understand how cognitive mechanisms and relevant experiences together produce the pattern of conceptual development that emerges so consistently in early childhood.

SUMMARY

Conceptual development can be approached either by considering conceptual representation in general or by focusing on particular concepts of special importance. Conceptual representation in general can assume at least three forms. Defining-features representations depict concepts in terms of a few necessary and sufficient features. Probabilistic representations include many features that are associated with the concept to varying degrees, but no feature that is necessary and sufficient for category membership. Theory-based representations focus on causal relations among different aspects of conceptual understanding.

A number of prominent developmental theorists, including Piaget, Vygotsky, Werner, and Bruner, have formulated versions of the representational development hypothesis. Within this view, young children cannot form representations based on defining features. However, even 1-year-olds have proved capable of relying on such features with familiar concepts. Young children do appear to rely on defining-features representations less often than do older individuals, but they clearly can form them.

Both children's and adults' representations often emphasize probabilistic relations rather than defining features. Beginning in infancy, children abstract prototypical forms, detect cue validities, note correlations among features, and generate basic-level categories. Within a relatively short time, children also begin to form subordinate and superordinate concepts, move from child-basic to standard-basic concepts, and abstract increasingly complex correlational patterns.

Theory-based representations emphasize the role of causal and hierarchical relations. Many of children's concepts seem to have theoretical aspects that facilitate inferences, explanations, and generalizations and that help children overcome the influence of superficial perceptual similarity. There may also be certain core theories, such as theories of biology and of the mind, that have different qualities than concepts in general; the ways in which such theories differ from others, however, are not yet clear. Some concepts have theoretical aspects from early in life, but the depth and scope of theory-based concepts clearly increases greatly with development.

Another perspective on conceptual development is provided by focusing on the particulars of the development of concepts of special importance. Among these central concepts are time, space, number, and mind. These concepts are worthy of unusual attention because they are used to represent a vast range of experiences, because they are present in some form from infancy to old age in all of the world's cultures, and because understanding the world would be impossible without them.

Time has both experiential and logical aspects. Infants as young as 3 months old encode the order in which events occur, thus showing a sense of experiential time. By age 5, children can estimate reasonably well the durations of relatively brief events. By the same age, children have some knowledge of the logical relations among beginning, ending, and total time, although their grasp is tenuous and can easily be disrupted by misleading cues.

Locations and distances within space can be represented in terms of relations to oneself, in terms of relations to landmarks, or in terms of an abstract system. Egocentric representations lead infants younger than 1 year old to continue turning in the direction that previously led to a goal, even when their position relative to the goal changes. Self-produced locomotion—in particular, crawling and walking—appears critical to infants overcoming the tendency to represent space egocentrically. Landmarks close to objects help infants locate objects in space even during their first year of life. Similarly, even in their first year, infants can form allocentric representations, in which they represent space in terms of the entire spatial layout. Early experience correlating the flow of visual information with one's own movements may be critical for forming such allocentric representations of space.

To understand numbers, children must possess both cardinal and ordinal information. Infants understand certain cardinal and ordinal properties of numbers. This is evident in their habituating to sets with a given number of objects and in their learning to choose the set with the larger number of objects. By the end of the preschool period, children supplement their early understanding of cardinality with understanding of counting and number conservation. They also supplement their understanding of ordinality with knowledge of numerical magnitudes. The number systems that children learn influence their facility in learning to count, which, in turn, appears to influence their learning of arithmetic and of numerical magnitudes.

Understanding of other people's minds seems to begin by late in the first year of life, when children show some appreciation of other people's intentions as a guide to which objects their words label. By age 2, they understand that other people possess desires that may not be the same as their own but that nonetheless govern the other people's behavior. By age 3, they understand the mind in terms of a system of desires and beliefs that lead to actions. After age 3, children come to understand increasingly deeply the distinction between appearance and reality and the fact that even when other people's beliefs are false, the other people will act in accord with them. Improvements in general information-processing capacities and experience with other people clearly contribute to this growing understanding of the mind; maturation of specific mechanisms for learning about other people's minds also may.

RECOMMENDED READINGS

Astington, J. W. (1993). *The child's discovery of the mind.* Cambridge, MA: Harvard University Press. A readable introduction to the immensely popular area of what children understand about their own and other people's minds.

Kearins, J. M. (1981). Visual-spatial memory in Australian aboriginal children of desert regions. *Cognitive Psychology, 13,* 434–60. An unusual study documenting the superior spatial skills that Australian aboriginal children develop in the course of their long treks through the desert.

Miller, K. F., Smith, C. M., Zhu, J., & Zhang, H. (1995). Preschool origins of cross-national differences in mathematical competence: The role of number-naming systems. *Psychological Science, 6,* 56–60. One aspect of cultures that influences cognitive development is the tools that they provide for thinking. As this article demonstrates, the greater regularity of East Asian languages' number

systems contributes to the greater rapidity of math learning among children growing up in these societies.

Rieser, J. J., Garing, A. E., & Young, M. F. (1994). Imagery, action, and young children's spatial orientation: It's not being there that counts, it's what one has in mind. *Child Development, 65,* 1262–78. Action, perception, and imagery are linked in complex and surprising ways. This study demonstrates that walking through one space improves children's representations of other spaces, if children are thinking about those other spaces while they are walking.

Wellman, H. M., & Gelman, S. A. (1992). Cognitive development: Foundational theories in core domains. *Annual Review of Psychology, 43,* 337–75. This chapter describes the theory-theory approach to conceptual development and argues articulately for the existence of a small number of key theories laying the foundation for a great deal of further development.

CHAPTER 8

Problem Solving

Georgie (a 2-year-old) wants to throw rocks out the kitchen window. The lawnmower is outside. Dad says that Georgie can't throw rocks out the window because he'll break the lawnmower with the rocks. Georgie says "I got an idea." He goes outside, brings in some green peaches that he had been playing with, and says: "They won't break the lawnmower." (Waters, 1989, p. 7)

Georgie's triumph over those who would spoil his fun illustrates the essence of problem solving: a goal, an obstacle, and a strategy for circumventing the obstacle and reaching the goal. In Georgie's case, the goal was to throw things out the window; the obstacle was his father's disapproval; the solution strategy was "throw peaches, not stones." Not bad for a 2-year-old.

Problem solving is a central part of all of our lives. Deciding what courses to take next semester, what word will complete a crossword puzzle, how to find misplaced keys, and how to answer a brain teaser all demand problem solving. Probably not a day goes by without our trying to solve some problem.

Problem solving also provides much of the purpose of other cognitive processes such as perception, language, memory, and conceptual understanding. If we ask why evolution would result in people's being able to perform these processes, a large part of the answer must be that they enhance people's ability to solve problems that the environment presents. That is, they help people adapt to challenging circumstances.

As pervasive as problem solving is in adults' lives, it probably is even more pervasive in the lives of children. With age and experience, people learn ways of circumventing obstacles so that situations that once posed problems no longer do. For example, when a child first goes to a friend's house a few blocks away, figuring out the best way to walk home represents a real problem. With repeated visits, however, it poses no problem at all. Because children encounter so many situations that are new to them, they constantly need to solve problems.

How do children cope with these challenges? DeLoache, Miller, and Pier-routsaks (in press) suggested the apt metaphor of the child as *bricoleur. Bricoleur* is a French term for a kind of tinkerer, someone who uses any materials at hand to solve whatever problem arises. As suggested by this metaphor, children combine reasoning, conceptual understanding, strategies, content knowledge, other people, and any other available resources for reaching their goals. Their solutions may not always be elegant, but they usually get the job done.

Organization of the chapter. This chapter includes two main sections (Table 8.1). The first provides an overview of children's problem solving. The initial part of the overview describes several general themes that have emerged from research on children's problem solving. Then, a number of these themes are illustrated in the context of development of problem solving on a single task: the balance scale.

The second section of the chapter focuses on specific problem-solving processes: planning, causal inference, analogy, tool use, and scientific and deductive reasoning. These processes were chosen for special attention because children frequently use them and because changes in their effectiveness have much to do with changes in the overall effectiveness of problem solving. They are not the only problem-solving processes that children use—they use far too many for all of them to be discussed in a single chapter—but they do seem to be among the most important ones. The section ends with a discussion of collaborative problem solving—how children work with other people to solve problems.

TABLE 8.1   Chapter Outline

I.   An Overview of Problem Solving
A.   Central Themes
B.   An Example of the Development of Problem Solving
II.   Some Important Problem-Solving Processes
A.   Planning
B.   Casual Inference
C.   Analogy
D.   Tool Use
E.   Scientific and Logical Reasoning
F.   Collaborative Problem Solving
III.   Summary

AN OVERVIEW OF PROBLEM SOLVING

Central Themes

Task analysis. Task analyses are careful examinations of problems, intended to identify the processes needed to solve them. For example, a task analysis of the standard algorithm for multidigit addition (e.g., 375 + 536) would involve such components as adding the numbers in the rightmost column, writing the 1s digit of the resulting sum as part of the answer, carrying the 10s digit of the initial sum (if there is one) to the tens column of the original problem, adding the carried number to the other numbers in the tens column, and so on. In situations in which people solve problems efficiently, task analyses can indicate what they are doing. In situations in which people cannot solve problems efficiently, task analyses can indicate where they are having difficulty and what the source of difficulty might be.

Consider how task analyses can lead to insights about children's problem solving. Klahr (1985) presented 5-year-olds a puzzle in which a dog, a cat, and a mouse needed to find their way to a bone, a piece of fish, and a hunk of cheese, respectively. To solve the puzzle, children needed to move all three animals to the locations with the appropriate food. Superficially, the greater the number of moves needed to reach the goal, the harder the problem would seem.

Klahr's task analysis, however, indicated that different problems created varying degrees of conflict between the child's immediate goal of getting a given animal to its desired food and the child's higher goal of getting all three animals to the right positions. Some problems required children to move an animal already at its goal away from the goal temporarily, so that another animal could reach its goal. These problems were more difficult for the preschoolers than problems that required more moves but did not entail any conflict among the different animals' goals. Other problems required children to resist the temptation to move an animal to its destination when it was one move away and instead to make a different move. These problems were even more difficult than the problems that required moving an animal away from a goal it had already reached. The detailed analysis of the task and the conflicts it created between immediate and longer-term goals enabled Klahr to identify the approach that many children used: trying on each move to increase the fit between the current and the desired arrangement of pieces. This approach, called *means-ends analysis,* is a widely-used problem-solving strategy.

Encoding. As discussed in Chapter 3, encoding involves identifying the critical information in a situation and using it to build an internal representation. Children often fail to encode important features of a task because they do not know what the important features are, because they cannot comprehend them, or because they do not know how to encode them efficiently. This failure to encode critical information can prevent children from learning from potentially useful experiences. If they are not taking in the relevant information, they cannot benefit from it.

Misencoding often dooms problem-solving efforts to failure. In one such case, 4- to 11-year-olds and college students watched a moving electric train carrying a ball on a flatcar. At a predesignated point, the ball dropped through a hole in the moving flatcar and fell several feet to the floor. The task was to predict the trajectory of the ball as it fell (McCloskey & Kaiser, 1984).

More than 70 percent of the 4- to 11-year-olds, and a sizable minority of the college students, predicted the ball would fall straight down. After they advanced this hypothesis, the experimenter ran the trains so that subjects could see what actually happened. (The ball fell in a parabolic trajectory.) The children and the college students were faced with reconciling their predictions with the outcome they saw.

Their explanations revealed how misencoding can influence problem solving and reasoning. Some said that the ball fell straight down, just as they thought it would. Others said that the train gave the ball a push forward just before it was released. Interestingly, a number of the college students who encoded the ball as having fallen straight down had previously taken and passed college physics courses. Apparently, this experience was insufficient to change either their expectations or their encoding of what they saw. As will be demonstrated in this chapter, changes in encoding play a critical role in the development of a variety of types of problem solving.

Mental models. To solve problems, children often construct *mental models* of the task and what they need to do to solve it (Gentner & Stevens, 1983; Johnson-Laird, 1983). Even young children form models of how complex systems work, as reflected in a 3-year-old's question, "Why doesn't my blood come out when I open my mouth?" (DeLoache, Miller, & Pierroutsakos, in press). The comment suggests a mental model of the circulatory system in which blood moves around the inside of the body, but in which it is everywhere rather than being limited to veins, arteries, and capillaries.

Halford (1993) identified several central characteristics of good mental models. The most important is that the model accurately represent the structure of the problem. That is, relations among components of the mental model should parallel the essential relations in the problem. When the model's structure parallels that of the situation depicted in the problem, people feel that they understand; otherwise, they feel they do not, even if they can generate a solution by other means, such as by remembering it. The structure depicted within a mental model includes not only static features but also dynamic ones, such as the moves and operations that are possible. The mental modeling process also involves abstraction, in which nonessential features of the problem are stripped away and not represented. This stripping away of incidental features facilitates generalization from the mental model of the original problem to related problems with different superficial characteristics but a parallel structure.

Forming mental models often requires children to reconcile what they are told by other people with their own experience. For example, children must wonder what adults mean when they say that the earth is round, when everyone can see that it is flat. In trying to solve this problem, 6- to 11-year-olds devise at least five mental models (Vosniadou & Brewer, 1992). Some children conceive of the earth as a disk, thus reconciling the statement that it is round with the observation that it looks flat (Figure 8.1). Others hold a dual-earth model, in which there are two earths, a round one up in the sky (perhaps derived from seeing models of the solar system) and a flat one on the ground where they live. Yet others conceive of the earth as a hollow sphere, with people living on flat ground inside the sphere, and the top part, the sky, covering the ground like a dome. Still others think of the earth as a flattened sphere, with people living on the flat part. Finally, some understand it as a complete sphere. Between first and fifth grade, the percentage of children thinking of the earth as a complete sphere increases, and the number adopting the other models decreases. Even in fifth grade, however, 40 percent of children rely on mental models other than the completely spherical one.

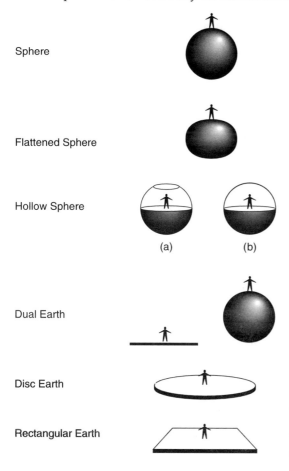

Sphere

Flattened Sphere

Hollow Sphere

(a)   (b)

Dual Earth

Disc Earth

Rectangular Earth

FIGURE 8.1   Mental models of the earth of 6- to 11-year-olds (from Vosniadou & Brewer, 1992). All but the rectangular earth represent children's efforts to reconcile adults' claim that the earth is round with the flatness that they observe around them (especially in Champaign-Urbana, Illinois, where the study was conducted). Copyright © 1992 by Academic Press, Inc.

Domain-general and domain-specific knowledge.   Problem-solving processes vary in the range of situations to which they can be applied. As the names suggest, domain-general processes can be applied relatively broadly, whereas the range of applicability of domain-specific processes is narrower.

At first, it might sound like domain-general processes must make a larger contribution than domain-specific ones; after all, they are more broadly applicable. The issue is not so simple, however, because there is a trade-off between the breadth of applicability of a process and its efficiency in solving any particular type of problem. Processes that are broadly-applicable tend not to be as efficient in solving a specific class of problems as are processes precisely tailored to fit a particular class of problems. Thus, even though the general problem-solving skills of adults are greater than those of children, the specific chess strategies of child chess experts studied by Chi (1978) allowed them to solve chess problems more effectively than inexperienced adult players who needed to rely more on general problem-solving processes to generate their moves.

Although the relative importance of domain-specific and domain-general processes has often been debated, it almost certainly is more useful to think about how the two work together than to compare their independent contribution (Ceci, 1989; Sternberg, 1989). The reason can be understood by returning to the anecdote about Georgie and the peaches. Without the specific knowledge that peaches are softer than stones, Georgie could not have generated his solution. Without general problem-solving skills, such as understanding that there may be different routes to the same goal, he also could not have done so. Problem solving relies on knowledge and processes of many levels of generality. The real issue is how children integrate such diverse information into efficient problem-solving procedures, rather than whether specific or general knowledge is more important.

Developmental differences.   Many of the best-known claims regarding cognitive development involve problem-solving processes that young children supposedly cannot perform. For example, Piaget (1970) and Inhelder and Piaget (1964) claimed that preoperational children were incapable of scientific and deductive reasoning. In contrast, they depicted formal-operational adolescents as excelling in these types of reasoning (Inhelder & Piaget, 1958).

More recent investigations, however, have not supported these categorical distinctions. Indeed, perhaps the most frequent theme of this chapter might be given the paradoxical title "young children's competence and older children's incompetence." Numerous studies have shown that young children are far more competent problem solvers than they had been given credit for being. The key to revealing these competencies has been simplifying problems by eliminating sources of difficulty extraneous to the process being examined. Complementarily, numerous other studies have shown that adolescents (and adults) are far less logical and rational than once was believed. Their planning, scientific reasoning, and powers of deduction all fall short of the ideal of the formal-operational reasoner.

These findings do not imply that problem solving is similar in early childhood and adolescence. In fact, it differs profoundly. The change, however, is not
typically from being absolutely unable to execute a process to being able to do
so. Instead, most changes involve the range of situations in which children successfully execute the problem-solving processes. Older children can fight their
way through thickets of memory demands, linguistic subtleties, and misleading
cues that utterly defeat younger children. They also learn how to solve new
problems much more quickly. Thus, although young children are more competent and older ones less so than was once thought, plenty of development still
is evident.

An Example of the Development of Problem Solving

To obtain a feel for the development of problem solving, it is helpful to consider
changes from infancy to adulthood on a single task. The balance scale provides
a useful context for considering these changes. Even infants in their first half-
year of life can solve some balance-scale problems; even college-educated adults
usually fail to solve others. Changes occur along a wide variety of dimensions
relevant to problem solving: children's untutored rules for solving the problem,
their ability to learn from experience with it, and their encoding of the problem,
among them. Development of problem solving on this task exemplifies a number of properties of problem solving in general.

Rules for solving problems. Figure 8.2 illustrates a type of balance scale
that has been used to examine children's problem solving. The scale includes a
fulcrum and an arm that can rotate around it. The arm can tip left or right or remain level, depending on how weights (metal disks with holes in them) are
arranged on the pegs on each side of the fulcrum. However, a lever (not shown
in the figure) is typically set to hold the arm motionless. The child's task is to
predict which (if either) side would go down if the lever were released.

A task analysis of this problem indicated that two variables influence this
outcome—amount of weight on each side of the fulcrum and distance of the
weight from the fulcrum. Thus, the keys to solving such problems are to attend
to both of the relevant dimensions and to combine them appropriately. This
analysis, together with the known tendency of young children to focus on a

FIGURE 8.2   *The balance scale. Metal disks are placed on a peg on each side of the fulcrum.
Children need to decide which side of the balance will go down, given the particular configuration of weights on pegs (from Siegler, 1976).*

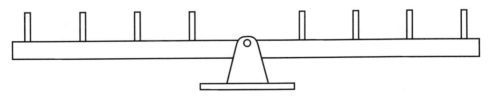

single relevant dimension, led Siegler (1976) to hypothesize that children would solve such problems by using one of the four rules depicted in Figure 8.3:

> *Rule I:* If the weight is the same on both sides, predict that the scale will balance. If the weight differs, predict that the side with more weight will go down.
> *Rule II:* If one side has more weight, predict that it will go down. If the weights on the two sides are equal, choose the side with the greater distance (i. e., the side that has the weight farther from the fulcrum).
> *Rule III:* If both weight and distance are equal, predict that the scale will balance. If one side has more weight or distance, and the two sides are equal on the other dimension, predict that the side with the greater value on the unequal dimension will go down. If one side has more weight and the other side more distance, muddle through or guess.
> *Rule IV:* Proceed as in Rule III, unless one side has more weight and the other more distance. In that case, calculate torques by multiplying weight times distance on each side. Then predict that the side with the greater torque will go down.

But how could it be determined whether children use these rules to solve balance-scale problems? Asking children how they solved the problems would be the simplest strategy, but answers to such questions could either overestimate or underestimate their knowledge. The answers would give a misleadingly positive impression if children simply parroted information they heard at home or in school. The answers would give a misleadingly negative impression if children were too inarticulate to communicate knowledge they in fact possessed.

In light of these difficulties, I formulated the *rule assessment method* to determine which, if any, rule a given child used. This rule assessment method involved generating problems for which different rules yielded specific patterns of correct answers and errors. As shown in Table 8.2, the types of problems used to assess children's rules were:

1. *Balance problems:* The same configuration of weights on pegs on each side of the fulcrum.
2. *Weight problems:* Unequal amounts of weights, equidistant from the fulcrum.
3. *Distance problems:* Equal amounts of weights, different distances from the fulcrum.
4. *Conflict-weight problems:* One side with more weight, the other side with its weight farther from the fulcrum, and the side with more weight goes down.
5. *Conflict-distance problems:* One side with more weight, the other side with "more distance," and the side with more distance goes down.
6. *Conflict-balance problems:* The usual conflict between weight and distance, and the two sides balance.

Children who used different rules would produce different patterns of responses on these problems (Table 8.2). Those using Rule I would always predict correctly on balance, weight, and conflict-weight problems and would always predict incorrectly on the other three problem types. Children using Rule II would behave similarly, except that they would answer correctly on distance problems. Those adopting Rule III invariably would be correct on all three types

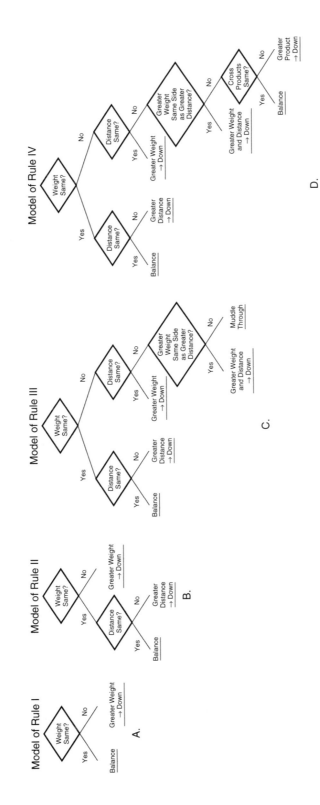

FIGURE 8.3   Rules for solving balance-scale problems (from Siegler, 1976).

TABLE 8.2 Predicted Percentage of Correct Answers on Each Problem Type for Children Using Each Rule

PROBLEM TYPE	RULE			
	I	II	III	IV
Balance	100	100	100	100
Weight	100	100	100	100
Distance	0 (Should say "Balance")	100	100	100
Conflict-Weight	100	100	33 (Chance Responding)	100
Conflict-Distance	0 (Should say "Right Down")	0 (Should say "Right Down")	33 (Chance Responding)	100
Conflict-Balance	0 (Should say "Right Down")	0 (Should say "Right Down")	33 (Chance Responding)	100

of nonconflict problems and perform at a chance level (33 percent correct) on the three types of conflict problems. Those using Rule IV would solve all problems.

When presented the types of problems shown in Table 8.2, more than 80 percent of 5- to 17 year-olds consistently used one of the four rules (Siegler, 1976). Five-year-olds most often used Rule I, 9-year-olds most often used Rule II or III, and 13- and 17-year-olds usually used Rule III. Few children of any age used Rule IV. Similar sequences of rules on the balance-scale task have been observed in a number of subsequent studies (Amsel, Goodman, Savoie, & Clark, 1996; Damon & Phelps, 1988; Ferretti & Butterfield, 1986; Marini, 1992; McFadden, Dufrense, & Kobasigawa, 1986; Surber & Gzesh, 1984; Zelazo & Shultz, 1989).

The expected developmental changes in performance on the six problem types also emerged. For example, consider performance on conflict-weight problems. As shown in Table 8.2, children using Rule I consistently solve such problems correctly. They predict that the side with more weight goes down, which, as previously noted, is by definition correct on conflict-weight problems. In contrast, children using Rule III, who realize that both weight and distance are important, muddle through or guess on all types of conflict problems. They therefore would not usually solve conflict-weight problems correctly. Consistent with this analysis, the 5-year-olds in Siegler (1976), most of whom used Rule I, were correct on 89 percent of conflict-weight problems, but 17-year-olds, most of whom used Rule III, were correct on only 51 percent. Developmental decrements in performance are sufficiently rare that this data pattern has strong support for the rule analysis that predicted that it would occur.

Development of the ability to solve balance-scale problems actually begins well before age 5. Some such ability emerges in infancy. Case (1985) presented infants a balance scale with a bell beneath one end. Pushing down on that end made the bell ring. By 4 to 8 *months* of age, infants who saw an experimenter produce the ringing sound by hitting that end of the arm responded by reaching to strike or touch that end themselves. By 12 to 18 months of age, infants imitated the experimenter's solution to a harder problem: depressing one end of the beam so that the other end would go up and ring a bell above it. By age 2 to 3½, children could figure out the solution to this problem without seeing the experimenter solve it first. By age 4 or 5, children could even make the bell ring when they were given a heavy and a light block and needed to put a block on each end of the scale in such a way that the bell above one would ring.

Turning to much older children, an anecdote may convey just how specific problem-solving skills often are. In the original Siegler (1976) study, I almost decided not to include the 16- and 17-year-olds. The headmistress of the school told me that the students would perform perfectly, since they had learned about balance scales in *two* previous science courses. She and I were both surprised when less than 20 percent of the students used Rule IV.

A later conversation with a science teacher in the school proved revealing. The teacher pointed out that the balance scale in the experiment was an arm balance, whereas the balance scale used in the classroom was a pan balance, in which pans with varying amounts of weight could be suspended from hooks at varying distances from the fulcrum. Retesting a few students indicated that they indeed could solve comparable problems presented on a pan balance! This limited generalization is, unfortunately, the rule rather than the exception in problem solving.

Learning and encoding. One reason for identifying both the typical development sequence of rules and the rules used by individual children is to predict which instructional experiences will help particular children learn. To illustrate this point, Siegler (1976) identified 5- and 8-year-olds who used Rule I on the balance-scale task. The children were then presented feedback experience. In this feedback experience, children first were given a problem and asked which side of the balance would go down. Then the lever that had held the arm motionless was released, and children saw whether their prediction was correct. Each child received such feedback on one of three types of problems. Some received balance and weight problems, problems that their existing approach (Rule I) would solve correctly. Others received distance problems, which their existing rule would not solve but which they would be able to solve when they acquired the next rule in the typical developmental sequence. Yet others received conflict problems, which they would not understand even qualitatively until they reached Rule III.

The moderate-discrepancy hypothesis (p. 110) suggested that the most effective problems for promoting learning would be somewhat, but not greatly, beyond the child's initial level. Thus, for children who used Rule I, distance problems would be most helpful, because they were solvable by Rule II, the next rule that Rule I children typically would acquire.

Consistent with this hypothesis, both 5- and 8-year-olds who were presented distance problems usually advanced to Rule II. Also as expected, both 5- and 8-year-olds who were presented feedback on weight problems, which their existing approach (Rule I) already solved, continued to use Rule I. Reactions to the conflict problems, however, differed somewhat from the prediction. As expected, most 5-year-olds made no progress. Unexpectedly, however, most 8-year-olds benefited greatly from experience with them. The 8-year-olds often advanced to Rule III, which entailed qualitative understanding of the roles of weight and distance on all problems.

Why might 5- and 8-year-olds, all of whom used Rule I initially, have reacted differently to experience with the conflict problems? Examination of videotapes of a few children solving conflict problems suggested that encoding of the balance-scale configuration played a critical role in determining learning. The 8-year-olds seemed to encode information about both weight on each side of the fulcrum and the distance between each pile of weight and the fulcrum. In contrast, 5-year-olds seemed to see each configuration solely in terms of two piles of weights, one on each side of the fulcrum. They did not appear to encode distances of the weights from the fulcrum. If 5-year-olds' encoding was limited in this way, their failure to learn from the conflict problems would not be surprising. They simply would not be taking in the relevant information about distance.

To test whether improved encoding was in fact related to learning, 5- and 8-year-olds who used Rule I were presented an encoding test. They were shown an arrangement of weights on pegs for 10 seconds. Then the arrangement was hidden behind a board, and they were asked to "make the same problem" on an identical balance scale that did not have any weights on it. Putting the right number of weights on the two sides indicated encoding of weight; putting the weights on the appropriate pegs indicated encoding of distance.

The 8-year-olds usually placed the correct number of weights on the correct peg, showing that they encoded both weight and distance. The 5-year-olds, in contrast, usually put the right number of weights on each side of the fulcrum, but generally put them on the wrong peg. They showed little if any encoding of the weights' distance from the fulcrum.

To further test whether limited encoding was related to 5-year-olds' not benefitting from experience with conflict problems, other 5-year-olds who used Rule I were taught to encode distance as well as weight. Then they were given feedback on the same conflict problems that previously had not produced learning in children of this age. The instruction in encoding made a big difference. Although none of the untrained 5-year-olds had benefited from feedback on such conflict problems, 70 percent who received encoding training did. Thus, encoding seems to be strongly related to learning.

Generality. Children approach a variety of problems in ways similar to those they use on the balance scale. Consider development of ability to solve projection of shadows problems (Siegler, 1981). On this task (Figure 8.4), each of two T-shaped bars was located between a light source and a screen. The question was which object would cast the larger shadow on the screen if the light sources were turned on. Typically, 5-year-olds based their judgments on a single dimension; they judged that the larger object always cast the larger shadow. This parallels their basing all of their balance-scale judgments on the single dimension of the amount of weight on each side. Among 8- and 9-year-olds, the most common approach was Rule II, in which children relied on the dominant dimension (here the size of the objects) unless its value for the two choices was equal; if so, they considered a second dimension, the distance of the objects from the light source. Among 12- and 13-year-olds and adults, Rule III predominated; they consistently considered both dimensions, but did not know the proportionality formula for integrating them. Finally, as with the balance scale, few people of any age knew Rule IV, the proportionality rule that solves all problems correctly. Similar sequences of rules have been found on a wide variety of problems, among them problems involving temperature and sweetness (Strauss, 1982), happiness and fairness (Marini, 1992), personality diagnosis (Marini & Case, 1994), fullness (Bruner & Kenney, 1966), and inclined planes (Ferretti et al., 1985; Zelazo & Shultz, 1989).

FIGURE 8.4   *Projection of shadows apparatus used by Siegler (1981). Turning on the point light sources led to different-size shadows on the screen, with the shadows' sizes depending on the length of the T-shaped bars and their distances from the light sources and the screen.*

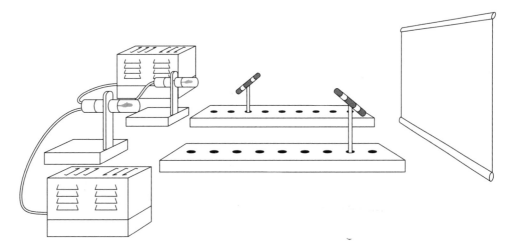

One especially common finding has been that 4- to 6-year-olds base many of their problem-solving approaches on only a single dimension on problems where two or more dimensions are relevant. This is the case not only with the problems just listed but also with liquid- and solid-quantity conservation problems; time, speed, and distance problems; probability problems; spatial reasoning problems; understanding of narratives, social dilemmas, monetary value, emotional reactions; musical sight reading; and use of quantitative adjectives (Bruchkowsky, 1992; Capodilupo, 1992; Case & Okamoto, 1996; Dean, Chabaud, & Bridges, 1981; Dennis, 1992; Griffin, Case, & Sandieson, 1992; Levin, Wilkening, & Dembo 1984; Marini & Case, 1989; McKeough, 1992; Siegler, 1981; Siegler & Richards, 1979; Surber & Gzesh, 1984).

These findings do not mean that 4- to 6-year-olds cannot consider more than one dimension in solving a problem. They can, and often do. Nor is it the case that young children are the only ones who rely on unidimensional rules in situations where more than one dimension is relevant. Adults also often do this (e.g., Neisser & Weene, 1962). However, children of this age do appear to have especially strong preferences for unidimensional rules; persuading them that such rules are incorrect can be very difficult.

The finding of developmental differences in learning on the balance scale also is typical of learning in many situations. A number of the most venerable constructs regarding cognitive development have been based on observations of developmental differences in learning: stages, critical periods, the problem of the match, and readiness, among them. For example, consider the following observation from the first decade of this century about *reading readiness:*

> Much that is now strenuously struggled for and methodized over in these early years of primary reading will come of themselves with growth, and when the child's sense organs and nervous system are stronger. . . . Reading will be learned fast when the time comes. Valuable time is wasted on it in the early years. (Huey, 1908, pp. 303, 309)

The language is quaint, but the basic observation—that older children learn faster than younger ones—remains true. How can we explain such differences in learning, which emerge even when younger and older children's initial performance is identical? We already have seen how differences in one problem-solving process, encoding, contribute to older children's greater facility in learning about balance scales. We now examine the contributions of a number of other critical processes to many other types of problem solving.

SOME IMPORTANT PROBLEM-SOLVING PROCESSES

Planning

Planning is future-oriented problem solving (Haith, 1994). It is used most often in complex and novel situations, in which we lack well-trodden paths to follow and are likely to make mistakes if we do not plan. Even in such novel situations, however, people often act without planning, at times to their regret (Friedman, Scholnick, & Cocking, 1987). Such failures to plan have often been lamented, but are understandable. Consider just a few of the reasons why children might not plan when doing so would help them solve problems (Ellis & Siegler, 1997):

1. Planning requires inhibiting the tendency to act immediately. Ability to inhibit actions develops slowly over the course of childhood (Dempster, 1993).
2. Children often are overoptimistic about the likelihood of succeeding without planning (Stipek, 1984).
3. Planning entails a risk of wasted effort; for example, if the child fails to execute the plan correctly or the problem is beyond the child's ability to solve (Berg, 1989).
4. Planning often requires coordination with other people; this is challenging for everyone, but especially so for children, who frequently bicker, lose track of the original task, and refuse to cooperate (Baker-Sennet, Matusov, & Rogoff, 1992).
5. If children don't plan, other people, especially parents, may save them from the consequences of their failure to do so. For example, if they do not allocate sufficient time for homework, parents may help them (Ellis, Dowdy, Graham & Jones, 1992).

With all of these obstacles and reasons not to plan, it is a little surprising that children ever do so. Yet quite often they do, from infancy onward.

Means-ends analysis. Means-ends analysis is an especially useful and widely applicable form of planning. As discussed in the socks-in-the-dryer episode in Chapter 3 (p. 63), it involves comparing the goal we would like to attain with the current situation, and reducing differences between the two until the goal can be met. The process demands simultaneously keeping in mind subgoals, procedures for meeting the subgoals, and discrepancies between the current state and the overall goal.

Infants near the end of their first year already use means-ends analysis. Willatts (1990) presented 12-month-olds with a foam rubber barrier, behind which was a cloth with a string attached to it and a toy that sometimes was attached to the string and other times was just nearby. When the toy was attached to the string, rather than just being nearby, babies were quicker to remove the barrier, to touch the cloth, and to reel in the string. Thus, the 12-month-olds appeared to form and execute a three-step plan: move the barrier, reel in the cloth, and pull the string to get the toy.

The development of means-ends analysis in subsequent years involves large changes in the number and complexity of subgoals that children can keep in mind at once and in their ability to resist the lure of short-term goals to pursue longer-term ones. The changes can be seen in 3- to 6-year-olds' approaches to the Tower of Hanoi problem (Figure 8.5). The game is to make one's own stack of cans into the same configuration as the experimenter's stack in as few moves as possible. There are only two rules: Move only one can at a time, and never place a smaller can on a larger one (because it would fall off). To appreciate the planning that is necessary to solve such problems, try to find the optimal (seven-move) solution to the problem in Figure 8.5.

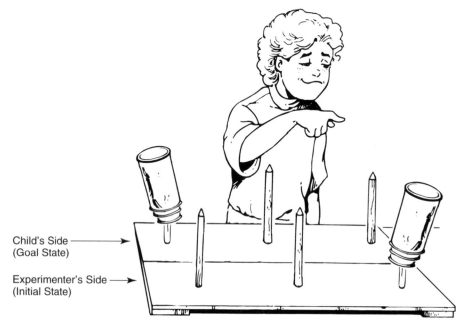

Child's Side ⟶
(Goal State)

Experimenter's Side ⟶
(Initial State)

FIGURE 8.5   Three-disk Tower of Hanoi problem. The goal is to have the three cans on the child's side match the three on the experimenter's top of larger ones. The problem can be solved in seven moves (from Klahr, 1989).

Not surprisingly, older children can solve longer problems. Most 3-year-olds solve two-move problems (i.e., problems that require two moves to progress from the initial arrangement to the goal); most 4-year-olds solve four-move problems; and most 5- and 6-year-olds solve five- or six-move problems (Klahr & Robinson, 1981; Welsh, 1991). More interesting than these changes in the length of problems that children can solve are changes in the strategies they use in planning which moves to make. The 3-year-olds' strategies are limited to direct efforts to move disks to their goal. When they cannot move a can to its goal because another can is on top of the one they want to move, they often break the rules and put the can there anyway. The older children react to such situations by planning subgoals that move them in promising directions for fulfilling their original goals. They also look further ahead in planning their moves. Even at age 6, however, children have difficulty solving problems that require them to make a move away from attaining a short-term goal, the same difficulty that children of this age encountered on the dog-cat-mouse problem described earlier in this chapter (p. 249).

Route planning.   One use of planning is to choose the most efficient route for reaching a destination. For example, when children are told to put away possessions that they have strewn about the house, they try to minimize the distance they must travel. They might pile up the clothes, games, books, and cassettes scattered around the first floor before hauling the heap to their bed-room on the second floor.

The ability to plan routes starts early. Children near their first birthday often journey to rooms they cannot see at the beginning of the trip in order to get toys they also cannot see at the beginning (Benson, Arehart, Jennings, Boley, & Kearns, 1989).

Not surprisingly, considerable development in route-planning skills occurs beyond this early period. Even in the short time between ages 4 and 5, children's skill at planning increases considerably. The 5-year-olds consider more alterna-tive routes before starting, do less backtracking, and correct errors more quickly than do 4-year-olds (Fabricius, 1988).

Older children also fit strategies to circumstances more precisely. In one study of 4- to 10-year-olds (Gardner & Rogoff, 1990), some children were told that they needed to plan how to get from one point to another, and that both speed and avoiding wrong turns were important. Other 4- to 10-year-olds were told that the only important consideration was avoiding wrong turns. Under both conditions, 4- to 7-year-olds planned some of the route in advance and the rest as they came to choice points. The 7- to 10-year-olds did the same when both speed and avoiding wrong turns mattered. However, when only choosing the most direct route mattered, the older children often planned the entire se-quence of choices before they began, which led to their reducing their number of wrong turns. The older children thus realized the benefits of planning when speed was unimportant and avoided the time cost of planning when speed was important. In contrast, the younger children's failure to plan in the condition in which speed was irrelevant led to their making as many errors there as when speed did matter.

Causal Inference

As mentioned in the last chapter, those who view concepts as implicit theories emphasize knowledge of causal relations as central to conceptual understand-ing. So important are causal relations for unifying our understanding that the philosopher David Hume described them as "the cement of the universe." Not surprisingly, then, problem solving is often an effort to determine the causes of events. For example, when a child takes a clock apart to see how it works, the child is trying to find out what causes each part to move. Two-year-olds' endless "Why" questions, such as "Why do dogs bark?" also are sometimes ef-forts to understand causes. (At other times, they are simply efforts to annoy their parents.)

Why people infer causal connections among events has long intrigued philosophers and psychologists. There is nothing in the external world that forces such inferences. It might seem obvious to us that when one pool ball hits another and the second ball begins to roll, that the rolling of the first ball caused that of the second. But is this inference logical? Couldn't the second ball simply have begun rolling for some other reason? Would we draw the same inference if we opened the trunk of a car and the car's radio suddenly turned on?

The Humean variables. British philosopher David Hume (1739–1740/1911) hypothesized that three features lead people to infer that events are causally related: The events occurred close together in time and space (*contiguity*); the event labeled the "cause" preceded the event labeled the "effect" (*precedence*); and the cause and effect consistently occurred together on past occasions (*covariation*). In line with Hume's hypothesis, each of these variables influences children's (and adults') causal inferences.

Infants in their first year of life already use both temporal and spatial contiguity to infer causal connections. In the experiments that established this point (Leslie, 1982; Oakes, 1994; Oakes & Cohen, 1990; 1995), 6- to 10-month-olds were repeatedly shown films of a moving object colliding with a stationary one and the stationary object then starting to move. Then the infants saw sequences that either violated spatial contiguity (the second object moved despite the first not reaching it) or that violated temporal contiguity (the first object struck the second but the second did not move until three-fourths of a second after the collision). Events that violated spatial and temporal contiguity elicited longer looking than events that maintained them, suggesting that the violations surprised the infants.

By age 5, perhaps earlier, children also use the order of events to infer that one event caused the other. When 3- and 4-year-olds are shown three events in the order *A-B-C* and then asked, "What made *B* happen?" they tend to choose Event *A*, which preceded Event *B*, rather than Event *C*, which followed it (Bullock & Gelman, 1979; Kun, 1978). It should be noted, however, that 3-year-olds show this understanding of precedence in fewer situations than do older children. In a variety of situations, as many 3-year-olds say that the second event caused the first as say the reverse (Corrigan, 1975; Kuhn & Phelps, 1976; Shultz, Altmann, & Asselin, 1986; Sophian & Huber, 1984). All studies, however, find that by age 5, children consistently choose the earlier event as the cause.

The importance of consistent covariation of events seems to be the last of the three Humean variables to be understood. Young children are especially likely to ignore this variable when it conflicts with contiguity. For example, 5-year-olds rarely attribute a causal connection to a sequence in which one event always follows five seconds after another event (Mendelson & Shultz, 1976). In contrast, 8-year-olds and adults do see the delayed but consistent relation as indicating that the two events are causally connected. To summarize, contiguity is influential even in infancy; precedence is sometimes considered in attributing causes by age 3 and consistently by age 5; and covariation becomes increasingly influential after age 5.

Beyond the Humean variables. Children's causal inferences extend beyond Hume's analysis in several respects. From infancy, they grasp that the size of an effect is related to the size of the cause. In one experiment, 11-month-olds were habituated to a medium-size object colliding with a stationary object and causing it to move a certain distance (Kotovsky & Baillargeon, 1994). Then they saw either a larger moving object cause the stationary object to move further or saw a smaller moving object cause the stationary object to move further. They looked for a longer time when the smaller object caused the larger movement, suggesting that they expected the smaller object to exert the smaller effect.

Children also understand from early in development that different types of causal explanations are appropriate for different types of entities. Even preschoolers realize that something inside of animals causes them to move when they want to do so (Simons & Keil, 1995: Gelman & Kremer, 1991). They are not too clear about what that something is, but they do not have similar causal beliefs about the causes of motion of inanimate objects. This general distinction probably leads them to look in different directions for the specific causes of motion of animate and inanimate objects.

These two examples illustrate a larger principle: From early in life, children emphasize the importance of causal mechanisms over all other clues to the causes of events. When they understand a causal mechanism, they expect events to be consistent with it. For example, the causal mechanism relevant to colliding objects is force. Other things equal, a smaller moving object will exert a smaller force on a stationary object, resulting in a smaller movement. Even infants appear to see violations of this relation as surprising.

Different situations present varying types of information for inferring what caused the event to occur. Sometimes these sources of information point to the same conclusion; other times they do not. Much of the challenge in deciding among alternative potential causes of events is deciding which type of information to weigh most heavily. At least from age 3 onward, children seem to use a set of strategy-choice rules for making these decisions (Shultz, Fisher, Pratt, & Rulf, 1986). When information about causal mechanisms is available, children use it. When it is not, they tend to rely on temporal and spatial contiguity and other perceptually striking events. Only when neither of these types of information is available do children consider less striking factors that are correlated with the effect's occurrence, such as delayed but regular covariation between cause and effect.

Analogy

Analogical reasoning is a pervasive and powerful process. It involves solving problems by identifying corresponding structures or functions in the objects or events being compared (Gentner, Ratterman, Markman, & Kotovsky, 1995; Halford, 1993). For example, understanding the metaphorical statement "a camera is like a tape recorder" requires understanding the function that each device serves—to record the present for future examination.

The development of analogical reasoning resembles that of causal inference. The range of analogies that children understand and generate increases greatly with age. For example, when presented the camera/tape-recorder analogy, 6-year-olds tend to cite such superficial similarities as that both are black, whereas 9-year-olds focus on their common functions (Gentner et al., 1995). On the other hand, even infants and toddlers draw successful analogies under some circumstances, and under other circumstances, even college-educated adults fail to do so. This resemblance between causal and analogical reasoning is no coincidence. Drawing appropriate analogies often depends critically on understanding and identifying parallels in the causal relations being compared (for example, why people use tape recorders and cameras).

Developmental similarities in analogical reasoning. A nascent ability to form analogies is present by the end of the first year of life. Chen, Campbell, and Polley (in press) presented 10- and 13-month-olds a series of three problems in which appealing toys were behind a barrier. The problems were like those presented by Willatts (1990); infants needed to remove a barrier and pull the towel with the string attached to the toy, rather than the towel with the string that was not attached to the toy. In Chen et al., however, children first tried to solve the problem on their own, then saw their parent model how to solve the problem, and then were presented conceptually identical problems that varied in superficial features such as the particular objects involved, their colors and sizes, and whether the child tried to obtain the toy from a sitting or standing position. After seeing their parent's solution to the first problem, 13-month-olds were able to solve subsequent problems increasingly efficiently, even when the problems did not look very similar to the original one. The 10-month-olds also could draw appropriate analogies, but only when the subsequent problems looked more like the one they had seen solved.

By preschool age, children form more complex analogies. In one study, 3- to 5-year-olds heard a story in which a genie needed to transport jewels across a wall and into a bottle (Brown, Kane, & Echols, 1986). The genie solved the problem by rolling up a piece of posterboard so that it formed a tube, placing the tube so that it led into the mouth of the bottle, and then rolling the jewels down through the tube and into the bottle. After hearing this story, children were presented a problem about an Easter bunny who needed to transport eggs across a river and into a basket on the other side. Children needed to show how they could use a piece of posterboard to transfer the eggs into a basket that was on the other side of a river that was drawn on the floor. Some 5-year-olds, but few 3-year-olds, solved the Easter bunny problem by using a strategy analogous to that in the genie story. Asked questions about the central facts of each story (what goal the main character was trying to achieve, what obstacle made it difficult to do so, what the main character did to overcome the obstacle), both 3- and 5-year-olds consistently solved the problem. Thus 3-year-olds could draw the relevant analogy, but they needed to be reminded of the key components to draw the relevant parallels.

Although infants and preschoolers can form some analogies, older children and adults fail to see many others. Like the 3-year-olds in Brown et al. (1986), college students often fail to recognize analogies that they readily understand when the parallel is called to their attention (Holyoak & Thagard, 1995).

As this example suggests, the same variables generally influence young children's, older children's, and adults' analogical reasoning. People of all ages are more likely to recognize analogies between situations when superficial characteristics (such as the characters' names) as well as deep characteristics (such as goals, obstacles, and potential solutions) are similar (Goswami, 1992; 1995a). They also are more likely to analogize when they have encountered several previous problems with the same solution principle, rather than just one (Crisafi & Brown 1986; Gholson, Emyard, Morgan, & Kamhi 1987). Complete encoding of relevant structural features is similarly important to analogical problem solving at all ages (Chen et al., in press; Gentner et al., 1995). The likelihood of drawing analogies changes with age, but the variables that increase or decrease that likelihood tend to be the same.

Developmental differences. These similarities in the variables that influence the likelihood of generating relevant analogies should not obscure the profound changes that occur with age in this domain. Young children require explicit hints to draw analogies that older children draw without such hints (Crisafi & Brown, 1986; Brown et al., 1986). Their analogizing is also hindered by superficial perceptual dissimilarities and associations that exert much less influence on the analogizing of older children and adults (Chen, 1996; Chen, Yanowitz, & Daehler, 1995; Goswami & Brown, 1990).

Comparable developmental trends are evident in interpretation of metaphors (Gentner, 1988; Winner, 1988). When presented the metaphor "The prison guard was a hard rock," 6- and 7-year-olds most often produce literal or magical interpretations, such as "the guard worked in a prison that had hard rock walls" or "the guard had hard, tough muscles" (Winner, Rosenstiel, & Gardner, 1976, p. 293). In contrast, 13- and 14-year-olds consistently emphasize the relation between psychological and physical characteristics, as in the explanation "The guard was mean and did not care about the feelings of the prisoners" (Winner et al., 1976; p. 293). In general, children correctly interpret metaphors based on appearances of the objects being compared before they correctly interpret metaphors where only relational structures are parallel. Further, with age, children become increasingly likely to interpret relationally those metaphors that can be viewed either in terms of similarities between objects or similarities between relations (Gentner, 1988).

Why does analogical reasoning improve with age? One reason is increasing content knowledge. As children acquire greater knowledge, they increasingly understand the centrality of properties that are not superficially striking. Returning to the tape-recorder/camera example, children learn that the key feature of these devices is information preservation, rather than color, size, or other obvious characteristics. A second source of development of analogical reasoning is language (Gentner et al., 1995). As discussed in Chapter 5, language influences thought by providing names for abstract relations that otherwise might not be recognized as similar. Thus, referring to both cameras and tape recorders as "information-preservation devices" calls attention to a similarity they share with each other and with other superficially different objects such as books and portraits.

Tool Use

Children do not solve problems in a vacuum. They use available tools to help them. Given the right problem, almost anything can serve as a tool: canes, rakes, spoken and written language, maps, mathematical notation, even other people. Tools vary in their breadth of applicability and in how directly they lead to solutions, but all provide ways for children to solve problems that otherwise would exceed their capabilities.

Among the first tools that children use are their mothers (Mosier & Rogoff, 1994). When attractive toys are placed out of reach, 6- to 13-month-olds use their mothers instrumentally to obtain the toys. They look back and forth beseechingly between the mother and the toy, make "gimme" gestures with their hands and fingers, lean toward the toys, and vocalize. As with any good tool, other people greatly expand the range of problems children can solve.

Children do not wait long to begin using inanimate objects as tools as well. In one study, 1½- and 2-year-olds saw an experimenter reel in an attractive toy by using a rake (Brown, 1989). Then the toddlers were asked to get the toy themselves. They were strapped into a seat so that they could not move, but had available a variety of potential tools. For example, a child who had seen the toy reeled in with a long rake might have within reach a long cane, a short rake, a long straight stick that was the same color as the original rake, and a long, squiggly, flexible object. The toddlers were quick to choose, and their choices were almost always good ones. They chose tools that were rigid, that had an end that was appropriate for pulling, and that were long enough to reach the toy. They were indifferent to whether the tool was the same color as the one they had seen used originally. They also were perfectly willing to substitute canes for rakes. Thus, they understood the causal properties that led to the tools being appropriate for solving the problem.

Symbolic representations as tools. Symbolic representations, such as maps, scale models, and pictures, also are widely useful problem-solving tools. By 3-years, children demonstrate considerable facility in using this type of tool. In a classic demonstration of this skill, DeLoache (1987) showed 30- and 36-month-olds a small toy being hidden in a scale model of a room. Then the child was asked to find the toy in a room that was a life-size version of the scale model. If the toy in the scale model was hidden under a miniature chair, it could be found under the corresponding life-size chair in the room. The experimenter would give instructions such as, "Watch! I'm hiding Little Snoopy here. I'm going to hide Big Snoopy in the same place in his big room!" (DeLoache, 1994, p. 110).

Despite the small (7-month) difference in average age of children in the two groups, they differed greatly in ability to use the scale model. The 3-year-olds found the hidden object without error on more than 70 percent of trials; the 2½-year-olds found it without error on fewer than 20 percent. This was not attributable to failure to understand the situation or failure to remember the demonstration with the model. Children of both ages consistently recalled where the miniature object was hidden within the model when they were asked about it. Rather, the difference was inability to use the scale model to infer the object's location in the larger room.

Why would 2½-year-olds encounter such difficulties in using the scale model to solve the problems? One possibility was that they did not understand how any type of representation could be used as a tool to solve such problems. To test this interpretation, DeLoache (1987) showed 2½-year-olds line drawings or photographs of the larger room, and told the toddlers to use them to find the object. The same children who failed with the scale model succeeded with the line drawings and photographs. Thus, they could use some symbolic representations as tools for solving problems.

DeLoache suggested that the source of the 2-year-olds' difficulty with scale models was a conflict between viewing them as interesting objects in their own right and as representations of another object. Consistent with this interpretation, having children first play with a scale model—which would lead them to think of the model more as an object in itself—decreased their later success in using it to find hidden objects. Conversely, eliminating any potential interaction with the model—by putting it in a glass case where it could be seen but not touched—allowed 2½-year-olds to find the hidden objects more successfully than usual (DeLoache, 1989). This interpretation also makes understandable why pictures and photographs can be used as problem-solving devices earlier than scale models: they are not very interesting as objects, and thus the conflict does not arise (DeLoache & Burns, 1994; Troseth & De-Loache, 1996).

It is fortunate that children can use symbolic representations as tools from early in life, because so many of the tools that are important in modern life involve symbols: spoken and written language, counting systems, measuring instruments, and, of course, computers. Children are not content to use the symbolic tools that the culture provides for them, however; they also create new ones of their own.

Self-created tools. One type of tool that children generate to solve problems is informal maps. In Karmiloff-Smith (1979; 1986; 1992), 7- to 11-year-olds played the part of ambulance drivers who needed to transport a sick patient to the hospital. The patient's home was a picture at one end of a 40-foot roll of paper; the hospital was a picture at the other end. In between were 20 choice points. Each choice point involved two choices, one of which led to a dead end. Children were told to make the trip once without the patient, so that they could find the fastest route. They were also encouraged to mark up the paper to help them remember which route to take later.

Within the one-hour session, children often changed the types of marks they made, even when the original marks were optimally informative. One 7-year-old's marks are depicted in Figure 8.6. At first, she indicated the dead end simply by placing a bar perpendicular to the path. Then she began augmenting this representation by putting both the bar and an X on the wrong path and an arrow on the right one. Finally, she returned to the original, leaner notation.

Why would children abandon a correct approach that allowed them to perform effectively? The issue is not unique to map drawing; the same phenomenon is present in children's number-conservation and class inclusion strategies and in their use of past-tense and causal verbs (Bowerman, 1982; Markman, 1979). Karmiloff-Smith (1986; 1992) suggested that the process reflects a drive that children have to understand *why* their strategies work. Children's first goal seems to be to perform correctly. Attaining that goal does not satisfy them forever, though. If they do not understand why an approach works, or suspect that another approach might be more effective, efficient, or elegant, they may abandon the original method, at least temporarily. Understanding this type of cognitive motivation, and the way in which children decide when to experiment with alternative approaches, is one of the deeper challenges confronting current theories of cognitive development.

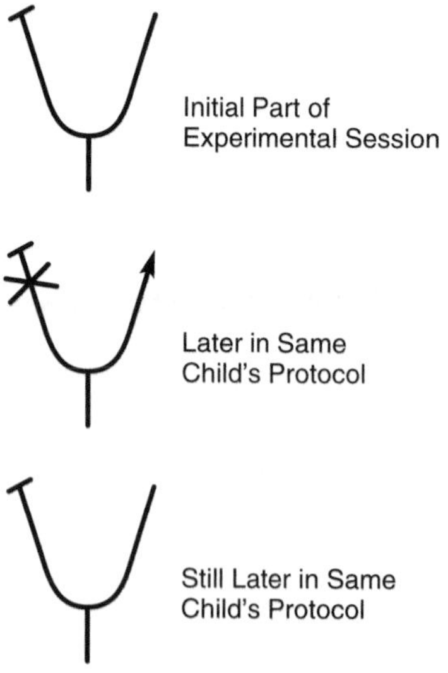

Initial Part of
Experimental Session

Later in Same
Child's Protocol

Still Later in Same
Child's Protocol

FIGURE 8.6   Maps drawn by a 7-year-old at three points during a session. Note how redundant features are added in the second representation but eliminated in the third (after Karmiloff-Smith, 1986; 1992).

Tools for measuring.   Measurement procedures such as counting, weighing, and using rulers are especially useful tools for solving many problems. Like all of the other problem-solving techniques, however, they are two-edged swords. Used appropriately, they enhance problem solving. Used inappropriately, they lead it down erroneous paths.

Consider how inappropriate use of measurement techniques—in particular, inappropriate use of counting—can lead children astray. Miller (1989) asked 3- to 10-year-olds to give two turtles equal amounts of food (the food was represented by pieces of clay of varying size). Most children used a counting strategy, in which they gave one piece to one turtle, the next piece to the other turtle, and so on. This resulted in an equal division of the number of pieces of food, but not usually of the amount of food, since some pieces were bigger than others. Belief in the effectiveness of the counting procedure ran sufficiently deep that when several preschoolers found they had given one more piece of food to one of the turtles, they simply cut in half a piece that belonged to the other turtle, and gave one piece to each, thus equalizing the numbers. With age, children more often attempted to create equal-size pieces, but they still counted out equal numbers for each turtle, even when the attempt to standardize their size failed. Not until age 9 did most children divide the food into equal amounts, rather than equal numbers of pieces. The difficulty is reminiscent of 5- to 9-year-olds inaccurately estimating the passage of time because they did not count in units of equal duration (Levin, 1989). Measurement tools expand children's capabilities, but they also can seduce them into making mistakes.

Scientific and Logical Reasoning

Scientific thinking.   Children have often been likened to scientists. Both ask fundamental questions about the nature of the universe. Both also ask innumerable questions that seem utterly trivial to others. Finally, both are granted by society the time to pursue their musings. This "child as scientist" metaphor has motivated a great deal of examination of how children form hypotheses, generate experiments, and interpret their data.

Despite some global resemblances between children's problem solving and that of scientists, there also are large differences. Some of these involve the quality of experiments. Children are less likely than adults to design experiments that hold constant all variables except the one whose effect is being examined; thus their experiments often have multiple interpretations (Klahr, Fay, & Dunbar, 1993; Kuhn, Schauble, & Garcia-Mila, 1992). They also often conduct too few experiments to generate the evidence they need (Klahr et al., 1993; Kuhn, Garcia-Mila, Zohar, & Andersen, 1995). Understanding of the logic of experimentation is not entirely lacking in childhood. When presented two potential experiments for deciding a simple question, first and second graders prefer the experiment that would yield conclusive evidence over the one that would not (Sodian, Zaitchik, & Carey, 1991). However, children's ability to generate experiments for testing an hypothesis, and to devise ways of deciding between alternative hypotheses, is quite limited.

Another important weakness in children's scientific reasoning is in separating theory and evidence. Children often fail to distinguish conclusions based on observations from conclusions based on their prior beliefs (Dunbar & Klahr, 1988; Kuhn, Amsel & O'Loughlin, 1988; Kuhn, et al., 1992; Metz, 1985). They have special difficulty in interpreting experiments that yield results inconsistent with their prior beliefs. Ability to change beliefs in response to unexpected observations is particularly important in scientific contexts, because new evidence frequently suggests unexpected conclusions.

Schauble (1990) performed a particularly interesting study of the interplay of prior beliefs, experimentation, and interpretation of data. Children aged 9 to 11 were presented a computer game involving toy race cars. The task was to determine the causal impact on the race cars' speed of five factors: engine size, wheel size, presence of tailfins, presence of a muffler, and color. In the game, a large engine and medium-sized wheels made the car go faster, muffler and color were irrelevant, and absence of tailfins increased the car's speed when the engine was large and had no effect when the engine was small.

The children had eight sessions in which to learn about the effects of the five features. In each session, they could equip cars with any features they chose, and then compare the speeds of cars with those features. The task was not inherently difficult. By varying one feature and holding all others constant, children could quickly establish the effect of each variable. An adult scientist who was presented the task identified the causal roles of all features in a single session.

The 9- to 11-year-olds were much slower to identify the causal relations. One reason was that more than half of their experiments were invalid. In such invalid experiments, the cars that children designed often varied in two or more ways, so that it was impossible to determine which factor caused the difference in their speeds. Even when children performed valid experiments, they often drew conclusions inconsistent with the evidence but consistent with their prior beliefs. Further, even after they first hypothesized a correct role for a variable and obtained evidence consistent with the hypothesis, they vacillated between the correct new hypothesis and the incorrect expectation produced by their prior view.

The picture of the 9- to 11-year-olds' scientific reasoning was not entirely bleak. The children showed substantial learning over the eight sessions. The percentage of their experiments that were valid increased, they drew appropriate conclusions increasingly often, and their predictions of the race cars' speeds became more accurate. Thus, with practice in scientific reasoning, children's experimental methods and their ability to draw appropriate conclusions both improve considerably.

Adults also often fall short of the ideals of scientific problem solving. They bias interpretations of data so that if fits their prior beliefs, continue to rely on incorrect old hypotheses after they have generated correct new ones, and vary more than one variable when performing experiments (Kuhn et al., 1995; Oaksford & Chater, 1994; Shaklee & Elek, 1988). They also rarely organize their experiments into overall plans, which results in the experiments often not yielding a clear conclusion (Schauble, 1996). The adults' experiments are better crafted, though, and their interpretations of data are somewhat less biased. For example, in one study that presented tasks similar to the race car problem, adults varied one variable at a time in 56 percent of their experiments, versus 34 percent for 11-year-olds, and the adults drew valid inferences in 72 percent of cases, versus 43 percent for the 11-year-olds (Schauble, 1996). Thus, scientific reasoning improves substantially with age, but identifying causes through valid experimentation and data interpretation remains a challenge for adults as well as children.

Deductive reasoning.   Consider the following impeccable logic of a 4-year-old: "If it doesn't break when I drop it, it's a rock. . . . It didn't break. It must be a rock" (Scholnick & Wing, 1995, p. 342). And, consider a 3-year-old's comment to her mother upon getting an already-opened can of soda from the refrigerator, "Whose is this? It's not yours, 'cause it doesn't have lipstick" (DeLoache, Miller, & Pierroutsakos, in press). The 3-year-old's reasoning seems to be: "My mother always gets lipstick on cans when she drinks from them; there's no lipstick on this can; therefore she didn't drink from it."

These statements are everyday examples of *deductive reasoning*, a process that can be used to solve problems whenever the information provided in the initial statement of a problem is sufficient to ensure that a particular solution is correct. In deductive reasoning, if the premises are true, the conclusions that follow from it are logically necessary. Deduction is often contrasted with *inductive reasoning*, which involves generalizing from observations. Conclusions produced via inductive reasoning may be highly probable, but they are not certain. The following examples, devised by Galotti, Komatsu, and Voelz (1997), illustrate the difference:

Deductive Problem	**Inductive Problem**
All poggops wear blue boots. Tombor is a poggop. Does Tombor wear blue boots?	Tombor is a poggop. Tombor wears blue boots. Do all poggops wear blue boots?

In the deductive problem, we can conclude with 100 percent certainty that Tombor wears blue boots. After all, he is a poggop and all poggops wear blue boots. In the inductive problem, we cannot conclude with certainty that all poggops wear blue boots. We cannot draw this conclusion even if we have seen 1,000 poggops and all wore blue boots. There always may be a poggop somewhere who we have not seen and who wears red boots; if so, not all poggops wear blue boots. Therefore, the best answer to the inductive problem is that we cannot tell whether all poggops wear blue boots.

Although young children use both deductive and inductive reasoning, it is unclear that they understand the difference between them (Cauley, 1985; Gellatly, 1987; Markovits, 1993; Murray, 1987; Murray & Armstrong, 1976). Consider kindergartners' and fourth graders' responses to the Tombor questions and others like them. Kindergartners responded similarly to the inductive and deductive problems; they thought both types of statements were equally likely to be true. In contrast, fourth graders more often thought that the deductive conclusions were true, were more confident that they were true, and reached their conclusions more quickly than on the inductive problems. These data suggested that the fourth graders, unlike the kindergartners, understood that deductive and inductive reasoning were different (Galotti, Komatsu, & Voelz, 1997).

These and other examples suggest that young children, such as the kindergartners in Galotti et al., may view their deductive inferences as not differing from other inferences, such as lunch not including cereal and orange juice. Such failure to distinguish between logically necessary and empirically likely outcomes would explain young children's eagerness to verify by empirical means relations that older children and adults view as purely logical relations (Effklides, Demetriou, & Metallidou, 1994; Galotti & Komatsu, 1989; Kuhn, 1989; Overton, Ward, Noveck, Black, & O'Brien, 1987). For example, 7-year-olds frequently insist that the experimenter open her hand before accepting as true the statement, "Either the chip I am holding in my hand is blue or it is not blue" (Osherson & Markman, 1975).

Failure to distinguish between empirically likely and logically necessary outcomes also would make more understandable the seemingly opposite tendency of young children to reach conclusions when the evidence does not logically allow them to do so (Acredolo & Horobin, 1987; Byrnes & Overton, 1986). For example, in a game in which four boxes were opened in succession, and children needed to say after each box was opened whether they could tell for sure which box a red chip had come from, most 5-year-olds chose the first box they saw that contained red chips, even in the face of the question "Could it have been one of the other (unopened) boxes?" (Fay & Klahr, 1996).

Why does it take children so long to understand the difference between deductive and inductive reasoning, even though they reason deductively from quite young ages? Halford (1993) proposed that three factors are influential: understanding of the basic logic of deduction, choices among alternative strategies, and information-processing limits.

Within Halford's theory, deductive reasoning originates in understanding of concrete situations. This can be illustrated in the context of *transitive inference* (If $A > B$, and $B > C$, then $A > C$.) Halford suggested that children might first exhibit such reasoning in the context of everyday activities, such as playing with blocks. In particular, they might notice that if Block A was bigger than Block B, and Block B bigger than Block C, then Block A invariably was also bigger than Block C. This initial understanding could serve as a mental model, useful for deciding how to represent other orderings. Consistent with this view, 4-year-olds can analogize from the story of *Goldilocks and the Three Bears*—in which Daddy Bear's attributes are always the largest, Baby Bear's the smallest, and Mommy Bear's in between—to solve transitive inference problems that they otherwise would be unlikely to solve (Goswami, 1995b).

Within Halford's model, a second source of development of logical deduction involves better choices among alternative strategies. Children typically know several strategies for solving problems, and young children may choose strategies other than deduction even when they understand the basic logic of deduction. Transitive inference again can be used as an illustration. Under some circumstances, even 5-year-olds solve these problems by logical means (Trabasso, Riley, & Wilson, 1975), but they also know and use alternative strategies for solving them. One such alternative is to simply assume that the most recently mentioned object is the largest on whichever property is being compared (Halford, 1984). This simplification strategy reduces the information-processing load, but it does so at the risk of a wrong guess about the ordering (as illustrated in Figure 8.7). Another strategy that accomplishes the same goals—and has the same drawbacks—is remembering the gist of the premises but not their details; for example, by forming an impression that a given stick is usually referred to as being longer than others (Brainerd & Reyna, 1990). Because these strategies often lead to wrong answers, children increasingly rely on the alternative approach of deduction.

The final development involves increases in information-processing capacity. Such increases allow children to hold all of the relevant information in memory in more-complex situations, and thus allows them to reason deductively in those situations as well as in less-demanding ones.

One implication of Halford's theory is that teaching children strategies that accurately represent the logical relations among the premises but that reduce the information-processing load should improve their performance on deductive problems. For syllogism problems (e.g., "All *A*s are *B*s, All *C*s are *B*s, Are all *A*s also *C*s?"), Venn Diagrams provide one such strategy. Adults frequently use Venn Diagrams spontaneously on such problems (Oakhill, 1988), but children rarely know how to do so. However, teaching sixth and eighth graders to use Venn Diagrams helps them avoid such logical errors as concluding that in summer, there are more tanned women at the beach than there are women at the beach (Agnoli, 1991). Thus, at least four improvements contribute to the development of deductive reasoning: improved understanding of the basic logic of deduction, better choices among alternative strategies, greater information processing capability, and learning new ways to represent the premises within deductive problems.

Collaborative Problem Solving

The previous sections of this chapter have described children solving problems on their own. Much of children's (and adults') problem solving, however, is conducted with other people: peers, younger and older children, and adults. In this

Hypothesized Representation:

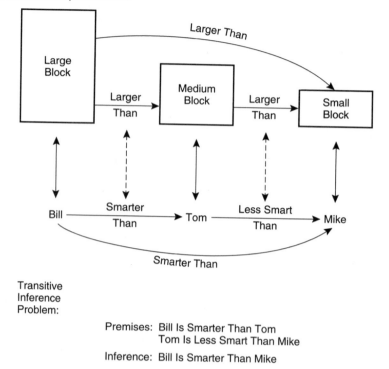

Transitive
Inference
Problem:

Premises: Bill Is Smarter Than Tom
Tom Is Less Smart Than Mike

Inference: Bill Is Smarter Than Mike

FIGURE 8.7   Halford's (1990) analysis of how a child might err on a transitive inference problem through analogizing to prior knowledge about blocks. Bill actually might or might not be smarter than Mike.

section, we examine the developing ability to solve problems with other people and the factors that determine the success of such collaborations.

Adults provide most of the opportunities that young children have for collaborative problem solving. This is not a bad thing, because adults are generally more effective than children in helping other children learn to solve problems. The adults' superiority as teachers is not just due to their knowing more about the problems that are being solved; even when child and adult teachers understand a task equally well, the adults still teach more effectively (Ellis & Rogoff, 1986; Lacasa & Villuendas, 1989; Radziszewska & Rogoff, 1988). This superiority appears due in large part to their style of interaction. Adults are more likely to outline the goals of the task, discuss strategies for meeting the goals, and involve learners in making decisions. In contrast, when 5- to 9-year-olds teach, they rely more on just telling learners what to do without explaining the reasons. Consistent with this interpretation of why adults are more effective, adults who share responsibility with learners to a greater extent promote more effective learning than adults who do not involve the child as much (Gauvain & Rogoff, 1989).

What of collaborations among peers? Having children collaborate with each other to solve problems has many potential advantages. It can motivate them to try difficult tasks, provide opportunities to imitate and learn each other's skills, fine tune their understanding by explaining what they know, and participate in discussions that increase their and their partners' understanding (Azmitia, 1996). These potential advantages have led to collaborative learning being widely used in many school systems.

But does peer collaboration have the desired effects on learning? The answer seems to be "sometimes yes, sometimes no." Some studies have found that solving problems with other children produces greater learning than solving problems alone (Blaye, Light, Joiner, & Sheldon, 1991; Perret-Clermont & Schubauer-Leoni, 1981). Others have not (Russell, 1982; Tudge, 1992). Yet others have found that depending on task instructions and on the nature of the interaction between the children, either result can occur (Glachan & Light, 1982; Levin & Druyan, 1993). The effectiveness of collaborations varies with the ages of the children, their relative expertise, their cultural backgrounds, and the problems being solved.

First, consider how the effects of collaboration vary with age. Ability to collaborate effectively with peers is a relatively late achievement. Even 5-year-olds, competent problem solvers in many circumstances, have difficulty working together to solve any but the simplest and most familiar problems (Tomasello, Kruger, & Ratner, 1993). Limited ability to ignore distractions, to coordinate attention so that both partners are thinking about the same aspect of the problem, to use language sufficiently precisely to communicate ideas, and to cooperate all contribute to the difficulties. Cooperating is often especially difficult for young children. Consider the following episode involving two preschoolers, one of whom had been taught how to build a copy of a Lego house and therefore was an "expert" at it. The children had been told to build a new copy of the Lego house together, but the expert was less than eager to let the novice help:

NOVICE: *You gotta let me help. You said you would.*

EXPERT: *I will, after I finish this* (the door).

N: (Sighs, sits back, crosses arms around chest and frowns. Twenty-two seconds later, takes some blocks and begins building a section of the model—correctly. After the section is completed, he hands it to the expert.) *I built this for our house.*

E: *I'm the builder, you find Legos when I tell you, OK? Give me a yellow two-dot.*

N: *I wanna be a builder too. She* (the experimenter) *said work together. My window is good . . .*

E: *Well, it's not going on my house* (moves copy of house out of reach of novice).

N: (Starts shaking the table, making it impossible for the expert to continue building.)

E: *Stop it! If you don't quit it we won't get finished. I'm almost done with the door.*

N: (Stops shaking the table, observes the expert until he finishes the door.) *My turn! My turn!* (Azmitia, 1996, p. 142)

The novice eventually avenged the indignities done to him. When the expert continued to resist his requests for a larger role, he started pelting him with Legos. When the expert lifted his hands to protect himself, the novice smashed the copy of the Lego house. This ended the collaboration.

Even after children are able to cooperate well enough to not attack each other during collaborations, the degree to which they become engaged in each other's thinking varies considerably. The amount of engagement greatly influences the effectiveness of collaborations. Children who understand and discuss each other's reasoning are more likely to solve problems and to learn from the experience than ones who pay each other's reasoning less heed (Azmitia, 1996; Azmitia & Montgomery, 1993; Berkowitz & Gibbs, 1985; Forman & MacPhail, 1993; Kruger, 1992; Tolmie, Howe, Mackenzie, & Greer, 1993). Those who simultaneously focus on the same issues are more likely to combine each others' ideas into new theories or rules, to identify the strengths and weaknesses in each approach, and to use the other person's ideas to identify weaknesses in their own. Such *transactive dialogues* are produced by both elementary school children and adolescents, but the adolescents' discussions are more likely to include analyses of the partner's reasoning and challenges to it (Berkowitz & Gibbs, 1985; Dimant & Bearison, 1991). Just talking does not improve problem solving by itself; thus, when children solve problems alone, having them talk aloud about what they are doing is not beneficial (Teasley, 1995). Rather, the key seems to be the extent to which the participants are actively thinking about each other's ideas.

Another influence on the effectiveness of peer collaborations is the relative expertise of the collaborators. In situations in which the peer collaboration is not acompanied by external feedback, three findings have consistently emerged (Ellis & Siegler, 1994): (1) when neither peer understands the relevant concept before the collaboration, little learning occurs; (2) when relative novices are paired with relative experts, the relative novices often acquire more advanced rules but the relative experts continue to use the same approaches as before; and (3) when relative novices are paired with relative experts, the highest rule that either partner is likely to attain is that with which the more expert child begins. On the other hand, when external feedback is presented, one or both partners fairly often learn rules more advanced than either used at the outset (Ellis, Klahr & Siegler, 1993).

The difficulty of the task also influences the effects of collaboration. On tasks that are either already understood by one of the collaborators or that they would be expected to master relatively soon, collaboration tends to promote successful problem solving and learning (Ames & Murray, 1982; Perret-Clermont & Schubauer-Leoni, 1981). On tasks that neither child understands and that are well beyond either of their existing knowledge, collaboration often produces regression or no improvement in understanding (Levin & Druyan, 1993; Tudge, 1992). The partners' relative confidence in their reasoning seems to be related to this effect. On the simpler tasks, children who are answering correctly tend to be more confident than ones answering incorrectly. This may encourage the partner who is answering incorrectly to follow their lead. In contrast, on hard problems, children whose reasoning is less advanced tend to be more confident because they fail to realize the plausibility of alternative perspectives (Levin & Druyan, 1993). This sometimes has the unfortunate effect of leading children whose reasoning is more advanced to shift toward the less-advanced reasoning of their confident collaborators.

Cultural norms further influence children's collaborative styles and outcomes. One study that documented this phenomenon contrasted collaborative problem solving of Navajo and Euro-American children (Ellis & Schneiders, 1989). The task involved a board-game maze. Because the maze included many dead ends, it was useful to plan a route before trying to move through it. Children who had been taught part of the problem (the "teachers") worked with younger children who had not received any instruction in it (the "learners"). Since Navajo culture does not value speed as highly as mainstream American culture, and because Navajo culture values both individual autonomy and cooperation, it was expected that the Navajo teachers and learners would interact in a way that led to the learners spending more time planning without the teachers pushing them to make moves. Both of these predictions proved accurate. Particularly on the most difficult problems (which required the most planning) the Navajo children planned for a longer time than did their Euro-American counterparts. They also made fewer errors in solving the maze problems. Thus, cultural values, as well as age, expertise, degree of engagement in the task, and task difficulty, influence collaborative problem solving.

SUMMARY

Problem solving involves children's efforts to orchestrate a large number of processes to overcome obstacles and attain goals. It is influenced greatly by the structure of the task; this makes accurate task analyses essential for understanding both successful and unsuccessful attempts to solve problems. Encoding of the critical information in the task, forming appropriate mental models from the encoded information, integration of general and specific knowledge, and selection of appropriate problem-solving strategies are among the main determinants of success in solving problems. Recent research has indicated that younger children are more competent, and older children less competent, problem solvers than was once believed. However, substantial development in the range of problems that children can solve also is present.

These general patterns are evident in performance on the balance scale. Task analyses suggested that children would use one of four solution rules to solve balance-scale problems, ranging from basing all judgments on the amount of weight on each side to computing torques when necessary. Application of the rule-assessment approach indicated that children used these rules. Some of the approaches, particularly 4- to 6-year-olds' tendency to base judgments on a single, salient dimension, have proved general across many tasks. Developmental differences in learning about balance-scale problems are due in large part to limitations of young children's encoding. Helping children encode relevant information helps them learn more effectively.

Among the most prominent problem-solving processes are planning, analogical reasoning, causal inference, tool use, scientific reasoning, and deductive reasoning. Planning is future-oriented problem solving. It is used most often in complex and novel situations. One frequent type of planning is means-end analysis, which involves progressively reducing differences between the current state and the goal. Simple forms of it are evident in a child's first year of life, both in solving balance-scale problems and in obtaining distant toys. Development of planning occurs primarily in the number and complexity of subgoals children can maintain in memory, and in their ability to avoid the temptation of meeting short-term goals at the expense of longer-term ones.

Many causal inferences are based on three variables whose importance was identified by the eighteenth-century philosopher David Hume: contiguity, precedence, and covariation. Even infants are influenced by contiguity. Precedence sometimes exerts an influence by age 3 and consistently does so by age 5. Covariation in the absence of contiguity becomes increasingly important beyond age 5. However, a fourth variable is given even greater weight than these three: the presence of mechanisms that could plausibly cause the effect. Preschoolers' choices among alternative potential causes reflect primary attention to mechanisms that could produce the effects, secondary attention to perceptually striking information such as contiguity, and tertiary attention to other cues such as consistent covariation.

Very young children can form analogies in simple situations, yet even adults often fail to recognize other, potentially useful analogies. Many of the same variables influence children's and adults' success in analogizing. However, older children and adults recognize many more analogies than do young children, especially when superficial features of problems obscure the relation between the old and new situations.

The use of tools to solve problems is also evident among very young children. Some of these tools, such as canes and rakes, can be used to attain goals directly. Others, such as maps and scale models, are effective in less direct ways. Tools are not always advantageous, however. Their availability can lure children into mistakes, as well as helping them solve otherwise difficult problems.

Scientific and logical reasoning are both relatively late-developing competencies. Children find it particularly difficult to design experiments that yield clear conclusions regarding their hypotheses. They also find it difficult to separate theory from evidence; often, their initial assumptions influence both the experiments they design and the conclusions they draw from the evidence. Adults also have these kinds of difficulty, but to a lesser degree. With regard to logical deduction, even young children deduce some conclusions, but the distinction between inductive and deductive reasoning is not usually understood until late childhood or adolescence, and sometimes not even then. Much of the difficulty is in distinguishing conclusions that are necessary, given the premises, from ones that are simply probable.

Much problem solving is performed collaboratively with other people. Before age 5, most such collaborations involve adults helping children learn. This has advantages, because children learn better how to solve problems from working with adults than with other children. The adults involve them more in the problem-solving process, as well as often knowing more about the problems. In later childhood and adolescence, children become increasingly able to collaborate effectively with each other. Such collaborations are most likely to be successful when the partners focus on, and actively analyze, each other's reasoning. Other factors that influence peer collaborations include the participants' ages, expertise, cultural backgrounds, and the difficulty of the problems.

RECOMMENDED READINGS

DeLoache, J. S. (1994). Early understanding and use of symbols: The model model. *Current Directions in Psychological Science, 4,* 109–13. DeLoache briefly summarizes her charming research on changes during early childhood in the ability to use symbolic representations to solve problems.

Halford, G. S. (1993). *Children's understanding: The development of mental models.* Hillsdale, NJ: Erlbaum. This book presents an integrative account of how changes in mental models, working-memory capacity, and problem-solving experience shape cognitive development.

Kuhn, D., Garcia-Mila, M., Zohar, A., & Andersen, C. (1995). Strategies of knowledge acquisition. *Monographs of the Society for Research in Child Development, 60,* (Whole No. 245.) Unusually precise descriptions of children and adults in the process of acquiring new knowledge.

Rogoff, B. (1990) *Apprenticeship in thinking.* New York: Oxford University Press. Perhaps the most sophisticated treatment to date of how children and adults together create the conditions under which cognitive growth occurs.

Vosniadou, S., & Brewer, W. (1992). Mental models of the earth: A study of conceptual change in childhood. *Cognitive Psychology, 24,* 535–85. Interpreting what adults mean is not easy, especially when their claims contradict seemingly obvious truths. Children's mental models of the earth's shape illustrate both the children's ingenuity and the ambiguity of even simple statements that we make to them, such as "The earth is round."

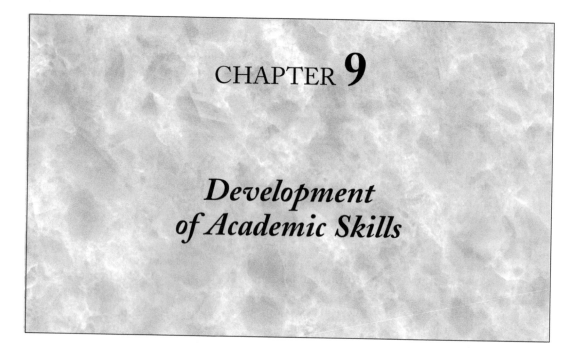

CHAPTER **9**

Development of Academic Skills

> I struggled through the alphabet as if it had been a bramble-bush; getting considerable worried and scratched by every letter. After that, I fell among those thieves, the nine figures, who seemed every evening to do something new to disguise themselves and baffle recognition. But, at last I began, in a purblind groping way, to read, write, and cipher, on the very smallest scale. (Pip, in Dickens's **Great Expectations**)

Cognitive development does not go into suspended animation while children are at school. What they learn there influences their general cognitive capabilities, as well as their specific knowledge and skills. The influence works in the other direction as well; children's general cognitive capabilities greatly influence what they learn in the classroom.

Practical decisions concerning children's educations, as well as theories of cognitive development, depend on the mutual influence of intra- and extra-classroom factors. For example, parents need to decide whether to start their children in school as soon as they are eligible or to hold them back and have them start the next year. In many communities in the U.S., it has become common to hold children, especially boys, back for a year. The logic is that they will be more mature, and able to learn more, when they are older.

To test whether the year of waiting leads to children learning more in first grade, a team of investigators examined children in a locality in which 95 percent of children still start school as soon as they are eligible (Bisanz, Morrison, & Dunn, 1995; Morrison, Smith, & Dow-Ehrenberger, 1995; Varnhagen, Morrison, & Everall, 1994). The studies used the *cutoff design*, which involves comparing children whose birth dates fell just before their district's cutoff for entrance into kindergarten with those whose birth dates fell slightly after it and who therefore were slightly too young to be admitted that year. The groups being compared were within one month of each other in average age, but one group entered first grade a full year before the other. The question was whether attending first grade at the older age would result in more learning.

The results were clear: Despite the 11-month difference in age, children who barely made the cutoff progressed just as much in reading and math during first grade as children who barely missed it. When the two groups finished first grade, their performance was indistinguishable. The pattern of results was not due to the children who just made or just missed the deadline being unusual. On tasks such as number conservation, in which schooling would not be expected to be influential but where age would be, the children who were almost a year older at the end of first grade did considerably better (Bisanz et al., 1995). Further, the IQs and parental backgrounds of children in the different groups were similar. There may be other reasons to hold children back from starting school, such as manual dexterity, skill in athletics, and social maturity. In terms of learning to read and do math, however, there seems to be no good reason to do so.

Organization of the chapter.   This chapter focuses on children's learning of the 3 Rs: reading, 'riting, and 'rithmetic. The first section begins by examining the arithmetic skills that are acquired in the preschool period and early in elementary school, and then progresses to more complex arithmetic, algebra, and computer programming. The next section begins by examining reading skills that children acquire prior to formal instruction, then the process of reading individual words, and finally the development of comprehension of larger units, such as stories. The final section describes how children write their first drafts of essays and stories and then proceeds to how they revise (or fail to revise) their work. Table 9.1 summarizes the organization.

Basic questions about academic skills.   When people think of school and psychology, the first thoughts that typically come to mind are of standardized tests. Educators use scores on IQ and achievement tests to help make a variety of important decisions, including placement in gifted programs, provision of special education, and college admissions.

Such tests are useful for predicting future school achievement and as an index of how much children know about given subjects. However, they tell us relatively little about the processes through which children learn, nor about how to teach children more effectively. Because of the great importance of these latter topics, both for understanding children and for helping them,

TABLE 9.1   Chapter Outline

research on children's thinking has focused increasingly on the specific processes involved in learning. These learning processes are the focus of this chapter.

Regardless of whether we are talking about math, reading, or writing, several questions about specific learning processes and instructional issues are central:

1. How do children allocate attentional resources to cope with competing processing demands?
2. How do children choose which strategy to use from among the approaches that they know?
3. Should instructors directly teach the techniques used by experts in an area, or are indirect teaching approaches more effective?
4. What causes individual differences in knowledge and learning?

These questions have led to discovery of some striking unities in children's thinking in different subject areas. Consider, for instance, children's strategy choices in arithmetic, reading, and spelling. In all three areas, children need to choose whether to state answers from memory or revert to more time-consuming alternatives. To add numbers, children need to decide whether to retrieve an answer and say it or to generate an answer by counting. To read words, they need to decide whether to state a pronunciation that they have retrieved from memory or to sound out the word. To spell, they need to decide whether to write a retrieved sequence of letters or to look for the word in a dictionary. Despite the differences among the subject areas, children seem to make all these decisions through the same strategy-choice process. In this chapter, we consider both specific findings in mathematics, reading, and writing, and general patterns across them.

MATHEMATICS

As discussed in Chapter 7 (pp. 234), by the time children enter school, they have a basic understanding of numbers. Most 5-year-olds can count at least to 20, know that counting involves assigning one and only one number word to each object, recognize that different sets of N objects have their numerosity in common, and know the relative sizes of the numbers 1 through 10. This leaves a great deal to learn, though: arithmetic, algebra, geometry, and so on.

Single-Digit Arithmetic

Single-digit arithmetic seems like the simplest of skills, calling only for retrieval of answers from memory. This impression is misleading, though. In the first few years of elementary school, children use a wide variety of strategies to solve problems such as 3 + 6 and 8 + 5. They not only retrieve answers from memory, but also count on their fingers from one, count from the larger of the two addends (on 3 + 6, counting "6, 7, 8, 9"), and infer answers from knowledge of related problems (e.g., "6 + 5, hmm, I know, 5 + 5 = 10, so 6 + 5 must be 11") (Fuson & Kwon, 1992; Geary, Fan, & Bow-Thomas, 1992). Even college students use strategies other than retrieval surprisingly often—on about 30 percent of single-digit addition problems (Geary, 1996; LeFevre, Sadesky, & Bisanz, 1996). In particular, they count on from the larger addend and break down difficult problems into two simpler ones (e.g., 9 + 6 = 10 + 6 − 1). Arithmetic also requires use of diverse parts of the brain. Magnetic resonance imaging (MRI) studies of people performing arithmetic problems indicate that the prefrontal cortex, the motor cortex, the parietal lobe, and a number of other areas in both hemispheres of the brain are involved (Rueckert, et al., 1996). Thus, arithmetic is more complex than it looks.

The development of single-digit arithmetic. Most contemporary children start to learn arithmetic quite early. By the time they enter kindergarten, many can solve a number of single-digit addition and subtraction problems. Their learning of these problems may be accelerated by educational television programs such as *Sesame Street*. Studies before the television era (e.g., Ilg & Ames, 1951) did not find similar competence until children were in first grade.

Use of varied arithmetic strategies is not limited to addition. For example, to multiply, second through fourth graders sometimes repeatedly add one of the multiplicands the number of times indicated by the other (solving 6 × 8 by adding eight 6s or six 8s), sometimes make hatchmarks and count or add them (solving 3 × 4 by drawing three groups of four hatchmarks each and counting or adding them), sometimes retrieve answers from memory, and sometimes base answers on those of related problems (Cooney, Swanson, & Ladd, 1988; Lemaire & Siegler, 1995).

As children gain experience, their strategies change. The most striking change is toward increasing use of retrieval. After a few years of adding and subtracting, and after about a year of multiplying and dividing, most children retrieve answers to most of the basic arithmetic facts. Their use of strategies other than retrieval also changes. When children begin to add, they rely most often on putting up their fingers and counting from one. As they gain skill and understanding, they increasingly use more sophisticated strategies, such as counting from the larger addend or decomposing a relatively hard problem into two easier ones (e.g., solving $9 + 7$ by thinking, "$10 + 7 = 17; 17 - 1 = 16$").

During the same period, children also come to solve arithmetic problems increasingly quickly and accurately. The changes in speed and accuracy come about both because of changes in which strategies are used and because of changes in how efficiently each strategy is executed. The strategies that predominate in later use, such as retrieval and counting from the larger addend, are inherently faster than the strategies used most often initially, such as counting from 1. Within any given strategy, speed and accuracy also increase.

The same developments are seen among children in Europe, North America, and East Asia, despite striking differences in their school systems (Fuson & Kwon, 1992; Geary, Bow-Thomas, Fan, & Siegler, 1993; Lemaire & Siegler, 1995). However, children in Europe and East Asia use more advanced strategies earlier than children in the U.S. and increase their speed and accuracy more rapidly. For example, East Asian children usually retrieve answers from memory, count from the larger addend, or rely on related arithmetic facts at ages when children in the U.S. still usually count from one (Geary, et al., 1993).

Choices among strategies.   One of the most striking characteristics of children's arithmetic is how adaptively they choose among alternative strategies. This adaptiveness is evident in children's choices of whether to state a retrieved answer or to use a *backup strategy* (a strategy other than retrieval). Even among 4- and 5-year-olds, the harder an addition problem (measured either by large numbers of errors or long solution times on the problem), the more often children solve it via a backup strategy, such as counting from one or the larger addend (Siegler & Shrager, 1984).

Using backup strategies most often on the hardest problems is adaptive because it helps children balance concerns of speed and accuracy. Consider a first grader's choice between solving an addition problem by stating a retrieved answer or by counting. Retrieval is faster, but counting tends to be more accurate on difficult problems. Young children reconcile these goals by using retrieval primarily on the easier problems, where it can yield accurate answers, and by using backup strategies primarily on the more difficult problems, where such strategies are necessary for accurate performance. In other words, children tend to choose the fastest approach that they can execute accurately. As shown in Figure 9.1, children make similarly adaptive strategy choices between backup strategies and retrieval in subtraction and multiplication (Siegler, 1986).

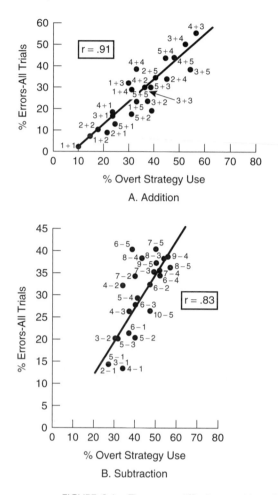

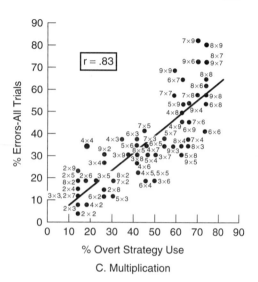

FIGURE 9.1   *The more difficult an arithmetic problem, as measured by percentage of errors on it, the more often children use overt strategies (data from Siegler & Shrager, 1984; Siegler, 1987a; 1988b). The label "% overt strategy" use in the figure is used because in these experiments, backup strategy use was assessed through videotapes of children's overt behavior while solving the problems.*

    A model of strategy choice.   How do children choose so adaptively among the alternative strategies that they know? The Siegler and Shipley (1995) strategy-choice model that was described in Chapter 3 focuses on this question. Here, we examine the way that the model makes the choice that was just described: whether to state a retrieved answer or to use a backup strategy to solve an addition problem.

    The mechanism by which the model makes this choice involves two interacting parts: a representation of knowledge about particular problems, and a process that operates on the representation to produce performance. The representation involves associations of varying strengths between each problem and potential answers, both correct and incorrect, to that problem. For example, in Figure 9.2, the answer 6 is connected to the problem "3 + 4" with a strength of .12, the answer 7 is connected to it with a strength of .29, and so on.[1]

Representations of different problems can be thought of as varying along a dimension of peakedness. In Figure 9.2, the representation of 2 + 1 is a *peaked* distribution, because most associative strength is concentrated in a single answer (the peak of the distribution). The representation of 3 + 4, in contrast, is a *flat* distribution because associative strength is distributed among a number of answers, with no one of them constituting a strong peak.

The process operates on this representation in the following way. First, the child sets a *confidence criterion*. This confidence criterion is a threshold that must be exceeded by the associative strength of a retrieved answer for that answer to be stated.

Once the confidence criterion is set, the child retrieves an answer. The probability of any given answer being retrieved on a particular retrieval effort is proportional to the associative strength of that answer relative to the associative strengths of all answers to the problem. Thus, because the associative strength connecting 2 + 1 and 3 is .79, and because the total associative strength connecting 2 + 1 with all answers is 1.00, the probability of retrieving 3 as the answer to 2 + 1 is .79.

If the associative strength of whatever answer is retrieved exceeds the confidence criterion, the child states that answer. Otherwise, the child may either again retrieve an answer and see if it exceeds the confidence criterion or abandon efforts to retrieve and instead use a backup strategy to solve the problem.

Within this model, the more peaked the distribution for a problem, the more often that retrieval, rather than a backup strategy, will be used on the problem (because the greater the concentration of associative strength in one answer, the higher the probability that the most strongly associated answer will be retrieved, and the higher the probability that that answer's associative strength will exceed the confidence criterion and thus allow the retrieved answer to be stated). Similarly, because the answer with the greatest associative strength ordinarily is the correct answer, the greater the concentration of associative strength in that answer, the more probable that the retrieved answer will be correct. Thus, the high correlations between percentage of errors on a problem and

[1]These estimated associative strengths are based on children's performance in a separate experiment. Four-year-olds received simple addition problems and were asked to "just say what you think the right answer is as quick as possible without putting up your fingers or counting." The purpose of these instructions was to obtain the purest possible estimate of the strengths of associations between problems and answers. The values in Figure 9.2 indicate the proportion of trials on which children advanced a given answer to a given problem in this retrieval-only experiment. Thus, when presented the problem 3 + 4, children advanced 6 as the answer on 12 percent of trials. Similar estimates for individual children emerged in a study in which individual children were presented the same problems on 10 occasions.

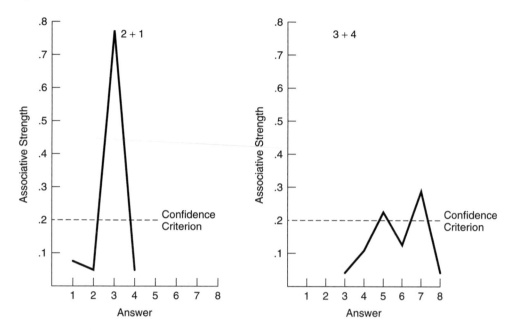

FIGURE 9.2 A peaked and a flat distribution of associations. The peaked distribution would lead to less frequent need for children to use overt strategies, fewer errors, and shorter solution times (from Siegler, 1986).

percentage of backup strategies on the problem (Figure 9.1) emerge because both errors and strategy choices on each problem reflect the peakedness of that problem's distribution of associations.

How do some problems come to have peaked distributions and others flat ones? A basic assumption of the strategy choice model is that children associate the answers they state with the problems on which they state them. Because children have at different times stated different answers to a problem, they will associate all of these answers to some degree with the problem. The more often an answer is stated on a problem, the more likely that the problem will elicit that answer on future presentations. Thus, a problem such as 2 + 1 comes to have a more peaked distribution of associations than 3 + 4 because children are more likely to correctly count three fingers, and thus to associate the answer 3 with 2 + 1, than they are to correctly count seven fingers and associate the answer 7 with 3 + 4. Consistent with this view, children who execute backup strategies the most accurately in first grade use retrieval the most often by second grade (Kerkman & Siegler, 1993).

This last finding, and the model as a whole, have an interesting instructional implication: The common policy of discouraging children from using their fingers to add is misguided. Many teachers repeatedly instruct children not to use their fingers. They have a certain logic on their side. One of the goals of education is to make younger and less skillful children more like older and more skillful ones. Older and more skillful children do not use their fingers; therefore, by this logic, neither should younger and less advanced ones.

The strategy-choice model, however, suggests that pushing children not to use their fingers may actually retard learning. Children with greater knowledge of arithmetic possess more peaked distributions of associations; they do not use their fingers because they can accurately retrieve answers to the problems. Younger and less knowledgeable children, however, use backup strategies precisely because they lack peaked distributions of associations. Forcing them to retrieve answers will lead to many errors, which, since each response adds to the associative strength of that answer, will strengthen wrong answers to the problem. Thus, paradoxically, pressuring children not to use their fingers may lead to their needing to use them for a longer time than if they were not pressured. As is often the case, the most direct method for pursuing an instructional goal is not necessarily the most effective one.

Individual differences.   One of the uses of this model has been in making understandable the ways in which children differ from each other. The model suggested two dimensions along which children could differ: the peakedness of their distributions of associations and the stringency of the confidence criteria that they set. The first would reflect differences in how well children know correct answers to the problems. The second would reflect differences in how sure children needed to be before they would state a retrieved answer.

Examination of first graders' addition and subtraction indicated that their performance differed along both dimensions (Kerkman & Siegler, 1993; Siegler, 1988). The children could be classified into three groups: good students, not-so-good students, and perfectionists.

The contrast between the performance of good and not-so-good students was evident along all of the dimensions that might be expected from the names. The good students were faster and more accurate on both retrieval and backup strategy trials and used retrieval more often. They also scored far higher on standardized achievement tests.

The differences between the performance of good students and perfectionists were more interesting. The two groups were equally accurate and scored similarly well on achievement tests. However, they differed in strategy use. Good students retrieved answers to more problems than either of the other two groups; perfectionists used retrieval less often than the other two groups, less even than the not-so-good students.

In terms of the model, good students were children who possessed peaked distributions of associations and set moderately stringent confidence criteria. Not-so-good students were children who possessed flat distributions and who set low confidence criteria. Perfectionists were children who possessed peaked distributions but who set very stringent confidence criteria.

To test this interpretation, three variants of the Siegler and Shipley (1995) model were created. The variants were identical except in the two variables hypothesized to distinguish the three groups: peakedness of distributions of associations and stringency of confidence criteria. The simulations produced the strategy choices and accuracy patterns characteristic of each group, thus indicating that the variables hypothesized to be important had the predicted effects.

The example illustrates a point made in the beginning of this chapter—that today's research creates a deeper understanding of thinking because specific cognitive processes, rather than standardized test scores, are being studied. The difference between the good students and perfectionists on the one hand and the not-so-good students on the other was evident in standardized achievement test performance. This difference reflected better and worse knowledge of arithmetic. However, the difference between the good students and perfectionists was not, and could not, be detected by achievement tests. These children were comparably knowledgeable but differed in cognitive style. Their patterns of performance represented different ways of being good at arithmetic, rather than a better way and a worse way. By predicting that children would differ along these dimensions, the model contributed to understanding of early individual differences beyond what could be learned from achievement tests.

Mathematical disabilities.   Based on poor performance in class and poor standardized test scores, approximately 6 percent of children in the U.S. are labeled as having mathematical disabilities (Badian, 1983). Like the not-so-good students in the previous description, these children have difficulty both in executing backup strategies and in retrieving correct answers (Geary, 1994). As first graders, they frequently use immature counting procedures (counting from one rather than from the larger addend), execute backup strategies slowly and inaccurately, and use retrieval rarely and inaccurately. By second grade, they use somewhat more sophisticated counting procedures, such as counting from the larger addend, and their speed and accuracy improve. However, they continue to have difficulty retrieving correct answers then and for years after (Geary, 1990; Geary & Brown, 1991; Goldman, Pellegrino, & Mertz, 1988; Jordan, Levine, & Huttenlocher, 1995). As they progress through school, these children encounter further problems in the many skills that build on basic arithmetic, such as multidigit arithmetic and algebra (Zawaiza & Gerber, 1993; Zentall & Ferkis, 1993).

Why do some children encounter such large problems with arithmetic? One reason is limited exposure to numbers before entering school. Many children labeled "mathematically disabled" come from poor families with little formal education. By the time children from such backgrounds enter school, they already are far behind other children in counting skill, knowledge of numerical magnitudes, and knowledge of arithmetic facts. Another key difference involves working-memory capacity. Learning of arithmetic requires sufficient working-memory capacity to hold the original problem in memory while computing the answer so that the problem and answer can be associated. However, children labeled as mathematically disabled cannot hold as much numerical information in memory as age peers (Geary, Bow-Thomas, & Yao, 1992; Koontz & Berch, 1996). Limited conceptual understanding of arithmetic operations and counting adds further obstacles to these children's learning of arithmetic (Hitch & McAuley, 1991; Geary, 1994). Thus, mathematical disabilities reflect a combination of limited background knowledge, limited processing capacity, and limited conceptual understanding.

Understanding of principles. As skill in arithmetic increases, so does understanding of the principles on which arithmetic is based. One such understanding is the *inversion principle*—the idea that adding and subtracting the same number leaves the original quantity unchanged. Development of understanding of this principle can be seen in performance on problems of the form $a + b - b = ?$ (e.g., $5 + 8 - 8 = ?$). Children who solve such problems through applying the inversion principle would answer in the same amount of time regardless of the size of b, because they would not need to add and subtract it. In contrast, children who solve the problem by adding and subtracting b would take longer when b was large than when it was small, because adding and subtracting large numbers takes longer than adding and subtracting small ones.

Between the ages of 6 and 9, performance on all $a + b - b$ problems becomes faster. However, 9-year-olds, like 6-year-olds, take longer on problems where b is large than on ones where it is small (Bisanz & LeFevre, 1990; Stern, 1992). The improved speed on all problems appears to be a result of improved procedural competence in addition and subtraction. The continuing difference between times when b is large and when it is small suggests that neither 6- nor 9-year-olds have sufficient conceptual competence (i.e., understanding of the inversion principle) to answer such problems consistently without adding and subtracting. Not until age 11 do most children, like almost all adults, ignore the particular value of b and solve all problems equally quickly, thus demonstrating the conceptual competence.

A related concept that takes surprisingly long for children to understand is that of *mathematical equality*. Even third and fourth graders frequently do not understand that the equal sign means that the values on each side of it must be equal. Instead, they believe that the equal sign is simply a signal to execute an arithmetic operation. On typical problems such as $3 + 4 + 5 = $ ____ , this misinterpretation does not cause any difficulty. However, on atypical problems, such as $3 + 4 + 5 = $ ____ $ + 5$, it causes most third and fourth graders either to just add the numbers to the left of the equal sign, and answer 12, or to add all numbers on both sides of it, and answer 17 (Alibali & Goldin-Meadow, 1993; Goldin-Meadow, Alibali, & Church, 1993; Perry, Church, & Goldin-Meadow, 1988; 1992).

On problems such as $3 + 4 + 5 = $ ____ $ + 5$, children frequently make hand gestures that indicate knowledge that is not evident in their verbal statements. For example, some children who answer 12 and explain that they just added

3 + 4 + 5 also motion with their hands toward the number to the right of the equal sign. Children who on a pretest show such discrepancies between their speech and their gestures subsequently learn more from instruction in how to solve these problems than do children whose gestures and speech on the pretest reflect the same understanding (Alibali & Goldin-Meadow, 1993; Goldin-Meadow, et al., 1993; Perry et al., 1988; 1992). Similarly, children whose pretest verbal explanations are vague as well as incorrect learn more from instruction than those whose explanations are clear but incorrect (Graham & Perry, 1993). The finding exemplifies a result that has been obtained in many contexts: Heightened variability of thought and action tends to accompany readiness to learn (Goldin-Meadow et al., 1993; Siegler, 1994; Thelen, 1992).

Effects of context. Gary Larson spoke for many when, in a "Far Side" cartoon, he depicted Hell's Library as stocked entirely with books of arithmetic and algebra word problems. Much of the difficulty presented by such problems is caused by their convoluted wording (e.g., Joe has 23 marbles; he has 7 more than Bill had yesterday before he gave Joe half of his marbles; has Bill lost all of his marbles?). Such phrasings burden working memory, and children often cannot interpret them (Mayer, Lewis, & Hegarty, 1992; Stern, 1993; Verschaffel, De Corte, & Pauwels, 1992).

Recognition of the memory burden that such wordings impose has led to recommendations that small numbers be used when word problems are first taught (e.g., Lesgold, Ivill-Friel, & Bonar, 1989). The logic is that simpler numbers will reduce the memory load. The flaw in this logic, however, is that people usually interpret the problem before they begin doing the arithmetic; thus, the two processes operate at different times. Probably for this reason, using simpler numbers does not help children interpret the word problems (Rabinowitz & Wooley, 1995).

Even when story wordings are not convoluted, unfamiliar contexts often lead children not to apply procedures that they use successfully in other contexts. This was illustrated in a study of 9- to 15-year-old Brazilian children who were the sons and daughters of poor families in a large city (Carraher, Carraher, & Schliemann, 1985). The children contributed financially to their families by selling coconuts, popcorn, corn-on-the-cob, and other foods at street stands. Their work required them to add, subtract, multiply, and occasionally divide in their heads. (One coconut costs x dollars; five coconuts cost. . . .) Despite having little formal education, the children could tell customers how much purchases cost and how much change they should get.

Carraher et al.'s study of these children involved presenting them with three types of problems. Some were problems that could arise in the context of customer-vendor transactions. ("How much do I owe for a coconut that costs 85 cruzeiros and a corn-on-the-cob that costs 63?") Other problems involved similar situations but with goods not carried by the child's stand. ("If a banana costs 85 cruzeiros and a lemon costs 63 cruzeiros, how much do the two cost together?") Yet others were numerically identical problems but presented without a sales context (e.g., "How much is 85 + 63?"). The children solved almost all of the problems involving goods sold at their stand and most of the problems that involved selling unfamiliar goods. However, they solved less than half of the problems without the sales context. The children clearly knew how to add, but did not always know when the skill should be used.

Complex Arithmetic

Once children have mastered basic arithmetic facts, they learn algorithms for solving multidigit problems. However, many children fail to grasp the relation between the procedures for solving these problems and the concepts that underlie the procedures. The resulting memorization-without-understanding creates fertile ground for misconceptions to grow. These misconceptions are exemplified by the "bugs" that show up in children's learning of the long subtraction algorithm.

Buggy subtraction algorithms. Brown and Burton (1978) investigated acquisition of multidigit subtraction skills. They used an error analysis method, much like the rule-assessment approach that was used to study balance-scale problems (pp. 254–56). It involved first presenting problems on which particular incorrect rules ("bugs") would lead to specific errors, and then examining individual children's pattern of correct answers and errors to see if they fit the pattern that would be produced by a buggy rule.

Many of children's errors reflected such bugs. Consider the pattern in Table 9.2. At first glance, it is difficult to draw any conclusion about this boy's performance, except that he is not very good at subtraction. With closer analysis, however, his performance becomes understandable. All three of his errors arose on problems in which the *minuend* (the top number) included a zero. This suggests that his difficulty was caused by his not understanding how to subtract from zero.

Analysis of the problems on which the boy erred (the first, third, and fourth problems from the left) and the answers he advanced suggests the existence of two bugs that would produce these particular answers. Whenever a problem required subtraction from zero, he simply flipped the two numbers in the column with the zero. For example, in the problem 307 − 182, he treated 0 − 8 as 8 − 0, and wrote 8 as the answer. The boy's second bug involved not decrementing the

TABLE 9.2   Example of a Subtraction "Bug"

307	856	606	308	835
−182	−699	−568	−287	−217
285	157	168	181	618

number to the left of the zero (not reducing the 3 to 2 in 307 − 182). This lack of decrementing is not surprising because, as indicated in the first bug, the boy did not borrow anything from this column. Thus, the three wrong answers, as well as the two right ones, can be explained by assuming a basically correct subtraction procedure with two particular bugs.

Although such bugs are common among American children, they are far less common among Koreans (Fuson & Kwon, 1992). A major reason appears to be that Korean children have a firmer grasp of the base-10 system and its relation to borrowing. The more transparent relation within East Asian languages between the names of multidigit numbers and their place in the base-10 system, noted in Chapter 7, may make it easier for them to acquire the relevant understanding (Miller et al., 1995). Thus, the Korean term for 57 is "5 10s and 7 1s). This phrasing makes it easier to see why, on problems such as 57 − 29, it is reasonable to change 5 10s and 7 1s into 4 10s and 17 1s. Such understanding makes it more likely that children's borrowing will maintain the value of the original number.

Fractions.   When presented the problem 1/2 + 1/3, many children answer 2/5. They generate such answers by adding the two numerators to form the sum's numerator and by adding the two denominators to form its denominator. The misunderstanding is far from transitory. Many adults enrolled in community college math courses make the same mistake (Silver, 1983).

Much of children's difficulty in fractional arithmetic arises from their not thinking of the magnitude represented by each fraction. This is evident in children's errors in estimating the answer to 12/13 + 7/8 (Table 9.3). On a national achievement test, fewer than one-third of U. S. 13- and 17-year-olds accurately estimated the answer to this simple problem (Carpenter, et al., 1981). Yet how could adding two numbers that were each close to 1 result in a sum of 1, 19, or 21?

A similar misunderstanding of the relation of symbols to magnitudes is evident in children's attempts to deal with decimal fractions. Consider how they judge the relative size of two numbers, such as 2.86 and 2.357. The most common approach of fourth and fifth graders on such problems is to say that the larger number is the one with more digits to the right of the decimal point (Ellis, et al., 1993; Resnick, et al., 1989). Thus, they would judge 2.357 larger than 2.86. Such choices appear to be based on an analogy between decimal fractions and whole numbers. Since a whole number with more digits is always larger than one with fewer digits, some children assume that the same is true of decimal fractions.

Another group of children made the opposite responses. They consistently judged that the larger number was the one that had fewer digits to the right of the decimal. Thus, 2.43 would be larger than 2.897. Many of these children reasoned that .897 involves thousandths, .43 involves hundredths, hundredths are bigger than thousandths, so .43 must be bigger than .897.

TABLE 9.3 *Estimating the Sum of Two Fractions**

ESTIMATE the answer to 12/13 + 7/8. You will not have time to solve the problem using paper and pencil.

	PERCENTAGE CHOOSING ANSWER	
ANSWER	AGE 13	AGE 17
1	7	8
2	24	37
19	28	21
21	27	15
I don't know	14	16

*From National Assessment of Educational Progress (Carpenter, Corbitt, Kepner, Lindquist, & Reys, 1981).

The difficulty in understanding decimal fractions does not quickly disappear. Zuker (1985; cited in Resnick et al., 1989) found that one-third of Israeli seventh and ninth graders continued to make one of the two errors described above. Thus, with decimal fractions as with long subtraction, children's failure to understand the number system leads to systematic and persistent errors.

Algebra

Learning algebra greatly increases the power of children's mathematical reasoning. A single algebraic equation can be used to represent and reason about an infinite number of situations. This power is frequently not realized, however. Even students who do well in algebra classes often do so by treating the equations as exercises in symbol manipulation, without any connection to real-world contexts.

This superficial understanding creates a situation in which misunderstandings often arise. Many such misunderstandings arise from incorrect extensions of correct rules (Matz, 1982; Sleeman, 1985). For example:

Since the distributive principle indicates that

$$a \cdot (b + c) = (a \cdot b) + (a \cdot c),$$

some students draw superficially similar conclusions, such as

$$a + (b \cdot c) = (a + b) \cdot (a + c).$$

Students use a variety of procedures to determine whether transformations of algebraic equations are appropriate. Among 11- to 14-year-olds, the most frequent strategy is to insert numbers into the original and transformed equations to see if they yield the same result (Resnick, Cauzinille-Marmeche, & Mathieu, 1987). This procedure reveals whether the transformation is allowable, though it rarely indicates why. Another common approach is to justify the transformation by citing a rule. Some students cite appropriate rules, but many others cite distorted versions of rules, such as the incorrect version of the distributive law cited above.

These problems are not quickly overcome. Even college students encounter difficulty with them. For example, 37 percent of freshman engineering students at a major state university could not write the correct equation to represent the simple statement "There are six times as many students as professors at this university" (Clement, 1982). Most wrote $6S = P$. At first glance, this seems logical. The impression crumbles, however, when one realizes that $6S = P$ means that multiplying the larger value (the number of students) by 6 yields a product equal to the smaller value (the number of professors).

As with long subtraction and decimal fractions, difficulties on these algebra problems stem from not connecting procedures (in this case procedures for writing equations) with underlying principles. Without such connections, algebra collapses into a meaningless exercise in remembering which arbitrary symbol manipulations are permitted and which are not. Thus, although the power of algebra ultimately comes from equations allowing abstraction over particular situations, learning to translate from particular situations to equations and from equations to particular situations is essential for mastery of the subject.

Computer Programming

Students currently attending school receive far more computer programming experience than those in any previous generation. Advocates of providing such experience have contended that it would produce not only skill at programming, but also enhanced general problem-solving ability. In one notable effort in this direction, Papert (1980) designed the LOGO language with the goal of helping children acquire such broadly useful skills as dividing problems into their main components, identifying logical flaws in one's thinking, and generating well-thought-out plans.

When learned in standard ways, LOGO has proved insufficient to meet these goals. However, *mediated instruction*, in which LOGO is taught with an eye toward building transferable skills, has been quite successful in producing them (Carver & Klahr, 1987; Klahr & Carver, 1988; Lehrer & Littlefield, 1991; 1993; Littlefield, Delclos, Bransford, Clayton, & Franks, 1989). Like conventional instruction in computer programming, mediated instruction involves teachers demonstrating to students how to use commands and concepts and providing them with feedback on their attempts to use them.

However, mediated instruction also involves teachers explicitly noting when particular commands and programs illustrate general programming concepts and drawing explicit analogies between the reasoning used to program and to solve problems in other contexts.

Such mediated instruction has produced a variety of kinds of desirable transfer. For example, Klahr and Carver (1988) demonstrated that mediated instruction in LOGO can create debugging skills that are useful outside as well as inside the LOGO context. Their instructional program was based on a task analysis of debugging. Within this analysis, the debugging process begins with the debugger determining the outcome that a procedure yields and observing if and how its results deviate from what was planned (for example, by running a computer program and examining its output). Following this, the debugger describes the discrepancy between desired and actual outcomes and hypothesizes types of bugs that might be responsible. The next step is to identify parts of the program that could conceivably produce the observed bug. This step demands dividing the program into components, so that specific parts of the program are identified with specific functions. Following this, the debugger checks the relevant parts of the program to see which, if any, fail to produce the intended results; rewrites the faulty component; and runs the debugged program to determine if it now produces the desired output.

The 8- to 11-year-olds who received this instruction took barely half as long to solve LOGO debugging problems as children who had not encountered it. They also improved their debugging of standard English instructions for accomplishing such tasks as traveling to a destination. The improvement seemed to occur as a result of the children applying the skills taught in the program: analyzing the nature of the original discrepancy from the anticipated results, hypothesizing possible causes, and focusing their search on relevant parts of the instructions, rather than simply checking them line by line.

Younger children also can gain problem-solving skills from mediated instruction in LOGO. Presenting such instruction to second graders led to better performance on standardized tests of analogical reasoning and also enhanced ability to analyze geometric shapes in terms of their similarities and differences (Lehrer & Littlefield, 1993). These results show that when taught via mediated instruction, LOGO can produce the type of transferrable problem-solving skills envisioned by its originators.

READING

Development of reading can be viewed either chronologically (what happens at particular ages) or topically (how does competency X develop). This section first provides a brief chronological summary of reading acquisition; then it focuses at greater length on some particularly important topics in the area, such as prereading skills, word identification, and comprehension.

The Typical Chronological Progression

Chall (1979) hypothesized that reading develops in five stages. The stages make reading acquisition seem neater and tidier than it really is, but they do convey an overview of the main achievements and the sequence in which they occur.

In Stage 0, lasting from birth to the beginning of first grade, children master several prerequisites for reading. Many learn to identify the letters of the alphabet, to write their names, and to read a few words. As with arithmetic, young children's knowledge of reading seems to be considerably greater today than it was 50 years ago. The improvement may be due to educational programs such as *Sesame Street* and to often-repeated, attention-grabbing television commercials.

In Stage 1, which usually occupies first and second grade, children acquire *phonological recoding skill*; that is, the ability to translate letters into sounds and to blend the sounds into words. Children also complete their learning of the letter names and sounds in this stage.

In Stage 2, most commonly occurring in second and third grade, children begin to read fluently. They identify individual words more quickly. However, Chall indicated that at this stage, reading is still not for learning. The demands of word identification on children's processing resources remain sufficiently great that acquiring new information through reading is difficult.

In Stage 3, which Chall identified with fourth through eighth grade, children become capable of obtaining new information from print. To quote her, "In the primary grades, children learn to read; in the higher grades, they read to learn" (p. 24). At this point, however, most readers only can comprehend information presented from a single perspective.

In Stage 4, which occupies the high school years, children come to comprehend written information presented from multiple viewpoints. This makes possible more sophisticated understanding of history, economics, and politics than was previously possible. It also allows appreciation of the subtleties of great works of fiction, which are presented much more often in high school than earlier.

This chronology points to two major themes in children's acquisition of reading skills: the centrality of comprehension as the ultimate purpose of reading, and the need for efficient word identification so that comprehension of difficult material is possible. Before children can acquire word-identification skills, however, they need certain prior capabilities. These are discussed in the next section.

Prereading Skills

Children acquire some prereading skills effortlessly—for example, the knowledge that (in English) text proceeds from left to right, that it proceeds from the extreme right on one line to the extreme left on the next, and that spaces between letter sequences signal separations between words. This knowledge is evident in their imitation writing; even before they know how to write the letters, their "writing" goes across horizontal lines and is segmented into scribbles of roughly the length of a word separated by small spaces (Levin & Korat, 1993; Teale & Sulzby, 1986). Two other prerequisites for reading are considerably more challenging, though: identifying letters and distinguishing the separate sounds within words.

Letter Perception.   To read, children must learn the unique combination of horizontal segments, vertical segments, curves, and diagonals that define each letter. Even after this initial learning, children still often confuse letters that differ only in orientation—*b* and *d*, and *p* and *q*, for example (Adams, 1990). Such confusions may arise because in contexts other than reading, orientation rarely affects identity. A boy's dog is his dog regardless of the direction in which it faces. In any case, by second or third grade, the large majority of children no longer confuse letters.

Many parents and teachers, as well as researchers, have wondered whether learning letter names before beginning school helps children learn to read. The picture is complex, but at least a preliminary conclusion is possible. Kindergarteners' ability to name letters predicts their later reading achievement scores, at least as late as seventh grade (Vellutino & Scanlon, 1987). At first glance, this would seem to indicate that early learning of letter names causes children to read better. However, teaching letter names to randomly selected young children does not facilitate their reading (Adams, 1990; Venezky, 1978). Together, the two facts suggest that learning the letter names does not cause better reading. Rather, other variables, such as interest in print, general intelligence, perceptual skills, and parental interest in their children's reading, probably are responsible both for some children learning the letter names early and for those children later tending to read well.

Phonemic awareness.   Another prerequisite for reading is realizing that words consist of separable sounds. This realization has been labeled *phonemic awareness*. Even after several years of speaking a language, most children seem unaware that they are combining separate sounds to make words. Liberman, Shankweiler, Fischer, and Carter (1974) illustrated this point with 4- and 5-year-olds. The children were told to tap once for each sound in a short word. Thus, they were supposed to tap twice for *it* and three times for *hit*. Performance on this and other measures of phonemic awareness proved to be an excellent predictor of reading achievement in the early grades (Bruck, 1992; Olson, Forsberg, & Wise, 1994). Especially important, training 4- and 5-year-olds in phonemic-awareness skills (for example, identifying which of three words does not contain the same sound) leads to improved reading and spelling performance as much as four years later (Bradley & Bryant, 1983; Byrne & Fielding-Barnsley, 1995; Vellutino & Scanlon, 1987).

Why should phonemic awareness enhance reading achievement? Thinking about the process by which children learn to read suggests an answer. When children are taught to read, they learn the sounds that typically accompany each letter. Unless they can blend these sounds into a word, however, the knowledge of sound-symbol correspondences does little good. Being able to distinguish the component sounds within words, the skill measured on phonemic-awareness tasks, seems critical to being able to blend sounds together to form words, and thus to read.

Phonemic awareness may have its origins in a quite charming source: parents reading nursery rhymes to their children. How well children know nursery rhymes at age 3 predicts their later phonemic awareness and reading readiness, even when the contributions of the mother's educational level and of the child's age and IQ are statistically controlled (Maclean, Bryant, & Bradley, 1987). The minimal contrasts that often occur between words at the ends of lines within nursery rhymes (e.g., *horn* and *corn*, *muffet* and *tuffet*) may help children isolate the individual sounds that are present within each syllable and recognize that words are made up of such separable sounds. School-based reading instruction also promotes such skill; children who barely made the cutoff for entrance into school show greater phonemic awareness at the end of first grade than do children of almost identical age who just missed the cutoff and therefore spent the year in kindergarten (Bentin, Hammer, & Cahan, 1991). Thus, phonemic awareness both promotes reading and is promoted by it.

Precocious readers.   Some 2- and 3-year-olds can read. They usually have not received any special instruction; instead, they crack the alphabetic code on their own.

What distinguishes these precocious readers from other children? As a group, they tend to be of above-average IQs, but their scores are usually not exceptional (Jackson, 1988). Conversely, although about half of children with very high IQs start reading by age 5, the other half do not (Roedell, Jackson, & Robinson, 1980).

Precocious readers differ from most other children in several ways (Jackson, Donaldson, & Cleland, 1988; Jackson, Donaldson, & Mills, 1993). Some have to do with intellectual capacities. Early readers tend to have unusually great verbal knowledge and large working-memory spans. Other distinctive characteristics involve early mastery of prereading skills. Most such children can recite the alphabet and identify some capital letters before age 3. Yet other unusual features involve interest in reading. Such children tend to be more interested in reading than most.

Contrary to the fears of a number of educators, precocious reading does not adversely affect later school performance. Children who know how to read when they enter school remain superior readers through at least sixth grade (Durkin, 1966; Jackson et al., 1993). It cannot be concluded that the early reading causes the later superiority. Exposing randomly selected children to two years of reading instruction prior to first grade did not result in their reading better at the end of third grade (Durkin, 1974/75). At minimum, though, precocious reading does children no harm and foreshadows good later reading.

Identifying Individual Words

Rapid and effortless word identification is essential not only for good comprehension but also for making reading enjoyable. The consequences of not having these skills are evident in a remarkable statistic reported by Juel (1988): 40 percent of fourth graders who were poor at word identification said that they preferred cleaning their room to reading. One said, "I'd rather clean the mold around the bathtub than read." Such attitudes are not only disastrous for reading per se, they also pull down achievement in other subjects, since all demand skillful reading to master the material (Stanovich, 1986). Poor word-identification skills also lead to children not reading more than the minimum required for class, which exacerbates the problem. As Adams (1990, p. 5) noted, "If we want to induce children to read lots, we must teach them to read well."

Children use two main word-identification procedures: *phonological recoding* (sometimes called *decoding*) and *visually based retrieval*. In both, children first look at a printed word and then locate the entry for the word in long-term memory. The difference concerns what happens in between. When children phonologically recode a word, they translate the visual form into a speechlike one, and use this speechlike representation to identify the word. When they visually retrieve a word, they do not take this intermediate step. The two approaches are not quite as distinct as the description suggests; for example, children sometimes phonologically recode the first letter or two and then retrieve the word's identity. Despite these mixed cases, the distinction still seems to correspond to a genuine difference in word-identification strategies.

The difference between the two word-identification processes is echoed in the difference between the two main approaches to reading instruction. The *whole-word approach* emphasizes visual retrieval; the *phonetic approach* emphasizes phonological recoding. Historically, educational practice has gyrated erratically between the two. At the beginning of this century, most teachers in the United States emphasized phonics. Between the 1920s and the 1950s, most emphasized visual retrieval. In the past 40 years, most again emphasized phonics. Two likely reasons for the switches are that both methods do eventually succeed in teaching most children to read, and that neither method succeeds in teaching every child to read well. In addition, neither approach has to be pursued in pure form. Most teachers use both. The issue is not whether children need to learn letter-sound relations or whether they need to retrieve words rapidly, but how early and to what extent each skill should be emphasized.

Another reason the debate has not been resolved is that plausible arguments can be made for each position. The whole-word argument: Skilled readers rely on visually based retrieval; the goal of reading instruction is to produce skilled readers; therefore, beginning readers should be taught to read like skilled ones. The phonics argument: For children to learn to read, they must be able to identify unfamiliar words; phonological recoding skills allow them to do this; therefore, beginning readers should be taught in a way that will allow them to read independently.

Understanding the processes by which children learn to read provides an informed basis for choosing between these arguments. In the next section, we examine the two word-identification processes and how children choose which to use to identify a particular word. The analysis suggests an explanation for why one of the instructional approaches has proved more effective than the other.

Phonological recoding. Phonological recoding allows children to read words that they otherwise would not know. An analysis of a basal reader makes evident why this skill is so important for beginning readers. Firth (1972) examined almost 3,000 words that occurred in a basal reader for first and second graders. More than 70 percent of the words were presented five times or fewer, and more than 40 percent of the words only once. Some basal readers repeat words more frequently, but more repetitive material tends to degenerate into the mind-numbing "Look, look, see Spot" style, so memorable to those who encountered it. Thus, early attainment of phonological recoding skill is essential for enabling beginning readers to identify the many words that they have rarely if ever encountered.

Beyond allowing children to read independently, skillful phonological recoding also contributes to efficient visually based retrieval. Jorm and Share (1983) and Share and Stanovich (1995) described how this might occur. Their basic assumption was that children learn the answers that they state; this was the same assumption made by Siegler and Shipley (1995) about arithmetic learning. If children lack good phonological recoding skills, they will be forced to rely more often on context to infer words' identities. Context, however, is often an undependable guide, relying on it will lead to many errors. In contrast, accurate sounding out will increase the association between the printed and the spoken word, thus increasing the likelihood of the child's being able to retrieve the word's identity through visual retrieval.

Visually based retrieval. It is tempting to describe the development of word-identification skills by saying that at first children sound out words and that later they use visually based retrieval. In fact, the progression is more complex. Many children can retrieve the identities of a few words even before they know any sound-symbol correspondences. Gough and Hillinger (1980) provided the example of a preschooler who learned to read two words: *Budweiser* and *Stop*. The boy learned the first word from beer cans, the second from road signs. Context provided clues to these words' identities. Many preschoolers, however, can also read a few words without contextual clues, for example, when they are typed on an index card. A girl might know that she knows two words and that *Budweiser* is the long one and *Stop* is the short one. Next, she might learn the word *Coke*. Since *Coke* and *Stop* both have four letters, she would need some feature other than length to discriminate between them. Perhaps she would notice the difference in their first letters and conclude that if the word is short and starts with a letter that has one curve, it is *Coke*, but if it is short and starts with a letter that has two curves, it is *Stop*.

Although the first uses of visually-based retrieval may rely on one or two features, the retrieval process eventually incorporates parallel processing of a great many sources of information (Seidenberg & McClelland, 1989). Among them are information from the particular letters, from the word as a whole, and from the surrounding context. Use of multiple cues, including the letters in the word and the surrounding context, begins as early as first grade. When first graders substitute one word for another, the word they choose usually has the same first letter as the word that is present and is also consistent with the surrounding context (Weber, 1970). Thus, multiple sources of information influence visually-based retrieval from the beginning of reading.

Strategy choices in word identification. As in arithmetic, children choose adaptively among reading strategies. They use the fast retrieval approach when it can yield correct answers and resort to backup strategies, such as sounding out, on the more difficult words (Figure 9.3). This observation raises the issue of how children know whether to use phonological recoding or visually based retrieval to identify a particular word.

The decision process seems to be the same as the one they use in arithmetic. Through experience, they associate each word's visual appearance and its identity (which word it is). When they encounter a word, they try to retrieve its identity. If the alternative they retrieve has sufficient associative strength, they say it. Otherwise, they resort to a backup strategy, such as sounding out the word or asking an older child or adult what it is.

This perspective, combined with Jorm and Share's (1983) position that children become able to use visually based retrieval through prior accurate use of phonological recoding, implies that phonics-based instruction should be superior to the whole-word approach in helping children identify words quickly and accurately. The logic is that accurate use of backup strategies will build strong associations between words and their printed forms, thus making possible fast and accurate retrieval. This prediction has proven correct. In both classroom and laboratory tests, phonics-based approaches have been found to be superior in promoting reading achievement (Adams, 1990).

Dyslexia. Some children, despite being of normal intelligence, have extraordinary difficulty learning to read. Two distinct problems have been identified, which correspond to the two main word-identification processes described in this section. The more common problem, *phonological dyslexia*, involves particular

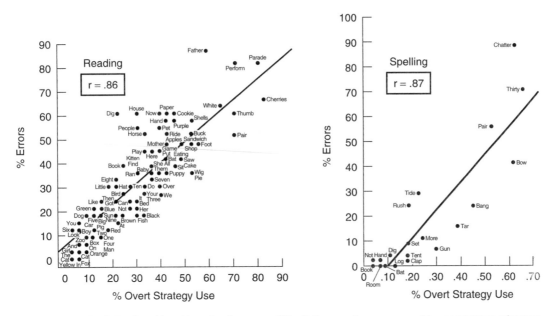

FIGURE 9.3   As with arithmetic, the more difficult the word, as measured by percentage of errors, the more likely that children will use overt strategies to read or spell it (from Siegler, 1986).

difficulty in phonological recoding. The less common one, *surface dyslexia*, involves difficulty in visually based retrieval (Rack, Snowling, & Olson, 1992; Wagner & Torgeson, 1987).

These forms of dyslexia can be distinguished by asking children to read *exception words* (words with irregular symbol-sound correspondences, such as *yacht*) and *pronounceable nonwords* (strings of letters that are not words but that can be sounded out, such as *thack*). Surface dyslexics, whose main difficulty is with visually based retrieval, have greater problems with the exception words, which other people can retrieve from memory (Castles & Coltheart, 1993; Manis, Seidenberg, Doi, McBride-Chang, & Peterson, 1996). Phonological dyslexics, whose main problem is with sounding out, have greater difficulty with the pronounceable nonwords, which, since they are novel, require phonological decoding.

Consistent with the Jorm and Share (1983) and the Share and Stanovich (1995) models, most children who have problems with pronounceable nonwords also have trouble with exception words, and vice versa. Thus, the distinction between phonological and surface dyslexia is usually one of degree of impairment in the two skills. However, about 25 percent of children are within the normal range on one task but below it on the other (Manis et al., 1996).

Children diagnosed as dyslexics tend to continue to be poor readers as adults. Even in those cases in which children's reading reaches near-normal levels, they continue to have difficulty reading nonwords where they must rely on their phonological recoding skills, and their phonemic awareness continues to be poor (Bruck, 1990; 1992). Presumably, experience with reading allows them to often use retrieval, but the difficulty with sounding out unfamiliar words remains (Manis, Custodio, & Szeszulski, 1993).

Fortunately, the situation is not hopeless. Teaching poor readers strategies for circumventing phonological-recoding difficulties, or intensively working to improve the phonological recoding skills themselves, can have substantial positive effects. For example, Lovett, at al. (1994) examined the effects of strategy training that taught poor readers to draw analogies between new and already-known words, to try alternative vowel pronunciations when their first guess does not work, and to identify parts of words that are known and then focus attention on the rest of the word. Given 35 hours of instruction in these strategies, the children made significant improvements in standardized tests of word identification and spelling relative to other poor readers who were given similar amounts of instruction in problem solving and study skills. Thus, although dyslexia is a persistent and difficult-to-remedy problem, training that illustrates ways around it can help.

Comprehension

Among the many academic skills that children acquire, reading comprehension may be the most important. It allows them to learn, to pursue interests, and to escape boredom.

The reading comprehension process can be divided into four components: lexical access, proposition assembly, proposition integration, and text modeling (Perfetti, 1984). *Lexical access* is another name for word identification. It is the process by which children retrieve the meaning of a printed word from long-term memory. *Proposition assembly* involves relating words to each other to form meaningful units. For example, in the sentence "The sick boy went home," the reader would construct the propositions "There was a boy," "The boy was sick," and so on. *Proposition integration* involves combining individual propositions into larger units of meaning. Finally, *text modeling* refers to the processes by which children draw inferences and relate what they are reading to what they already know. For example, readers could draw on knowledge about sick children and distances between schools and homes to infer that one of the boy's parents may have picked him up and driven him home, even though the sentence did not mention this happening.

Perfetti's analysis helps to clarify the relation between reading comprehension and listening comprehension. Both require forming propositions, integrating them, and constructing a general model of the situation. However, the lexical access processes differ. In reading, lexical access requires a translation between written words and meanings; in listening, lexical access requires a translation between spoken words and meanings. Beginning readers' greater competence in translating spoken words into meanings accounts for their listening comprehension exceeding their reading comprehension. Not until seventh or eighth grade do most children eliminate this gap, so that their reading and listening comprehension are similar (Sticht & James, 1984).

What develops in reading comprehension? What we comprehend is closely related to what we remember. Thus, it is not surprising that the main influences on memory development—basic processes, strategies, metacognitive understanding, and content knowledge—also influence reading comprehension.

Two basic processes whose development contributes to improvement in reading comprehension are automatization of word identification and increasingly efficient operation of working memory. Automatizing word identification helps reading comprehension in the same way that automatizing arithmetic helps learning of more advanced mathematics: it frees cognitive resources. Consistent with this view, degree of automaticity of word identification early in first grade is predictive of reading comprehension not only then but through the end of third grade (Lesgold, Resnick, & Hammond, 1985). The increasingly efficient operation of working memory helps comprehension for similar reasons. Children who can maintain more material in memory have a better chance to integrate previous and new ideas and to understand connections among them. Large working-memory capacity seems especially helpful in coping with ambiguous wordings, where comprehension requires maintaining more than one interpretation until the ambiguity is resolved (Daneman & Tardif, 1987).

Acquisition of strategies also influences the development of reading comprehension. Often, such strategies involve adjusting the speed and carefulness of reading to the difficulty of the material and one's goals in reading it. For example, good readers go through trash novels much faster than textbooks. However, this type of flexible strategy use develops surprisingly late. For example, 10-year-olds show little use of skimming when detailed understanding is unnecessary for answering the question; not until age 14 is such skimming common (Kobasigawa, Ransom, & Holland, 1980).

Reading comprehension is also influenced by metacognitive understanding of the reading process. At all ages between first grade and adulthood, better readers monitor their understanding of what they are reading more accurately than do poor readers (Baker, 1994). The comprehension monitoring of both good and poor readers improves with age, but the difference between good and poor readers also remains. Such comprehension monitoring leads older and better readers to adopt a variety of strategies for dealing with comprehension difficulties: returning to the source of the confusion, slowing down until comprehension is restored, trying to visualize the scene, and reducing abstractions to concrete examples.

A final source of age-related improvements in reading comprehension is increasing content knowledge. Children who have such knowledge can check the plausibility of their interpretations of what they are reading against what they already know. They can also draw reasonable inferences about motivations, events, and consequences that are implicit rather than stated. Although any relevant prior knowledge can aid comprehension, knowledge of causal connections is especially helpful. The more that readers focus on causal relations, the higher their recall (Trabasso, Suh, Payton, & Jain, 1994). With age, children represent a wider range of causal links, which improves their comprehension. For example, 8-year-olds focus mainly on causal links within an episode, whereas 14-year-olds emphasize links across episodes as well (van den Broek, 1989). In sum, improvements in the efficiency of execution of basic processes, in strategy use, in metacognition, and in content knowledge all contribute to age-related improvements in reading comprehension.

Instructional Implications

Importance of adequate background knowledge.   One implication of these findings for the teaching of reading is that teachers should ensure that all students have the prior knowledge needed to understand what they read. The problems that arise when children lack such content knowledge are evident in the saga of "The Raccoon and Mrs. McGinnis," a story that appeared in a second-grade textbook.

Mrs. McGinnis, a poor but good-hearted farmer, wishes on a star for a barn in which to house her animals. Instead, bandits come and steal the animals. A raccoon, who habitually looks for food at night on Mrs. McGinnis' doorstep, follows the bandits and then climbs a tree to be safe from them. The bandits see the raccoon's masked face and mistake it for another bandit. Frightened, they release the animals and inadvertently drop a bag of money they had stolen from someone else. The raccoon picks up the bag of money, returns to Mrs. McGinnis' doorstep to continue looking for food, and drops the bag on the doorstep. The next morning, Mrs. McGinnis finds the money and attributes the good fortune to her wish of the night before.

Although most adults find this story quite charming, the charm was lost on the second graders who read it. It simply confused them. Beck and McKeown (1984) hypothesized that the problem was that the children lacked two critical concepts needed to understand the sequence of events: coincidence and habit. Therefore, before another group of second graders read the story, an experimenter told them that coincidences involve two events just happening to occur together, with neither causing the other, and that habits often lead people and animals to engage repeatedly in the same activities. The experimenter also introduced several useful background facts: that the dark circles around raccoons' eyes look like masks, that raccoons habitually hunt for food at night, and that raccoons often pick up objects and carry them to other locations.

This background knowledge helped children understand the story. The explanation of the concept of coincidence increased the number of children who contrasted what Mrs. McGinnis thought had happened with what actually had. Moreover, children who received the background information, unlike many of their peers, did not conclude that the raccoon tried to help Mrs. McGinnis. Thus, possession of relevant background knowledge seems essential for good reading comprehension.

Importance of metacognition for comprehension.   Another effective instructional approach, *reciprocal instruction*, is based on findings regarding the role of metacognition in reading comprehension. This approach, developed by Palincsar and Brown (1984), was originally designed to improve the reading of a group of seventh graders from disadvantaged backgrounds. Although these students' word-identification skills were at their grade level, their comprehension was two to three years behind. Palincsar and Brown hypothesized that the heart of the students' difficulty was inadequate comprehension monitoring. In particular, they posited that the students needed to improve their execution of four processes involved in comprehension monitoring: summarizing, clarifying, questioning, and anticipating future questions.

To inculcate these skills, the teacher worked with small groups of students. After both the students and the teacher read a paragraph, the teacher would summarize it, point to sentences that needed clarification, anticipate likely questions, and predict what would happen next in the story. On the next paragraph, one or more students would carry out these activities. Then it would be the teacher's turn. This turn taking was essential, because at first, students were quite inept at the skills. For example, at the beginning of the training, only 11 percent of students' summary statements captured the main idea of the paragraph. By the end of the more than 20 sessions, 60 percent of their statements did so.

The instruction had many positive effects on the seventh graders' reading comprehension. After each day's instruction, they read new paragraphs and answered from memory 10 questions about them. On a pretest before the program began, the children averaged 20 percent correct on the test. At the end of the program, they averaged more than 80 percent correct. The improved comprehension for such paragraphs was still evident when the seventh graders were retested six months after the program ended. Even more impressive, on tests that were part of regular classwork in science and social studies, the trained children improved from the twentieth percentile of their school to the fifty-sixth percentile.

Subsequent findings have also been encouraging. A review of 16 studies of reciprocal instruction revealed positive effects with students from fourth grade to adulthood, with both low-achieving and average students, with groups ranging from 2 to 23 students, and with either experimenters or classroom teachers providing the instruction (Rosenshine & Meister, 1994). The gains also have been maintained for at least six months to a year after the instruction (Palincsar, Brown, & Campione, 1993).

What lessons can we draw from this success story? One lesson is the value of teaching skills in contexts that match as closely as possible the contexts in which the skills will be used. In reciprocal instruction, comprehension monitoring skills are taught in the context of reading meaningful material, the same context as that in which comprehension monitoring is used in the classroom. Another lesson involves the importance of actively engaging students in learning. Recall from Chapter 8 that the effectiveness of collaboration depends on the more-expert partner actively involving the less-expert one in the problem-solving process. Such engagement is integral to reciprocal instruction. From the beginning, students are encouraged to attempt the relevant processes (summarizing, questioning, etc.), and their roles progressively increase as their competence grows. Thus, the effectiveness of reciprocal instruction stems at least partially from its teaching skills in a context similar to the one in which they will be used and to the instructional process actively engaging students in learning.

WRITING

A venerable sorrow of teachers is how badly students write. The difficulty does not end in childhood. Computer companies produce machines capable of executing millions of instructions per second but rarely produce a manual that explains clearly how to operate them. Lack of writing skills is particularly unfortunate because of the huge role of writing in modern life. For example, business personnel spend an estimated 19 percent of their working hours writing memos, letters, and technical reports (Klemmer & Snyder, 1972).

Writing can be divided into two processes: initial drafting and revision. Both demand that writers surmount a variety of challenges: the formal demands imposed by punctuation, spelling, and grammar; the organizational demands needed to make the content comprehensible; and the demands of meeting the author's purpose, whether that purpose be persuading, describing, or conveying a point of view (Boscolo, 1995). Given how many goals must be considered simultaneously, it is no wonder that most people find writing difficult.

The Initial Drafting Process

Few people other than teachers have a good sense of what children's compositions are like. The following essay, a better-than-average effort for an 8-year-old, communicates the flavor:

> I have not got a bird but I know some things about them. They have tow nostrils and They clean Ther feather and They eat seeds, worms, bread, cuddle firs, and lots of other things. and they drink water. When he drinks he Puts his head up and it gose down. A budgie (birdie) cage gets very dirty and peopel clean it. (Kress, 1982, pp. 59–60)

This story reflects three sources of difficulty that children face in writing: the kinds of topics that are discussed, the need to simultaneously pursue multiple goals, and the mechanical demands of writing (Bereiter & Scardamalia, 1987).

Demands of unfamiliar topics. To write a story, children must first activate relevant information in long-term memory. In many cases, this is difficult because the topics are ones that children would never ordinarily think about (e.g. "What I know about birds"). Under such conditions, they must pull together material from diverse parts of their memory and generate an organization for thinking about them. The 8-year-old's essay about birds exemplifies what often happens: a list of facts about a topic, rather than an organized discussion of it.

Demands of multiple goals. People write to pursue a variety of goals: to amuse, to intrigue, to inform, to arouse, and to generate enough material to satisfy teachers. Intonations and nonverbal gestures, which can achieve some of these purposes in speech, are unavailable in writing. Further, the feedback that writers receive during the initial drafting process is ordinarily limited to their own reactions to what they have written. This is quite different from the situation in conversations, where other people's questions and comments often suggest new goals and paths to pursue. Thus, writing requires formulating goals with little outside stimulation, keeping them in mind for long periods, and independently judging when they have been met.

How do children cope with the need to pursue multiple goals? Scardamalia and Bereiter (1984) labeled children's typical approach the *knowledge-telling strategy*. This strategy simplifies the writing task to the point where only one goal at a time needs to be considered. The strategy can be summarized in terms of two commandments: (1) answer directly the question that was asked, and (2) write down relevant information as it is retrieved from memory. The "budgie" story exemplifies the results of using this approach. Initially, the child answered the basic question: "I do not have a bird, but I know some things about them." Then she listed several facts she remembered about birds. The simplicity of this organization accounts for one of the most striking features of children's compositions: their brevity. In the elementary school years, compositions typically are half of a typed page or less.

With experience in writing, children come to sequence goals into standard organizations that help them cope with the memory demands of writing. An unusual natural experiment reported by Waters (1980) demonstrated how skill in coordinating multiple goals develops with practice. Waters analyzed 120 essays written by a girl (herself) during second grade. All the essays were written in response to a "class news" assignment. Each day, students were to write about that day's events.

Waters intensively examined five essays she had written on consecutive days at the beginning of the year, five in the middle, and five at the end. As shown in Table 9.4, story contents at first were limited to the date, weather, and class activities. Later, they also included information about peers, duties, and materials brought to school.

More generally, the later stories showed a greater number and variety of goals than the earlier ones. In many of the later essays, each time Waters recalled an event, she seemed to form the goal of noting the time at which the event occurred and then describing her reaction to the event. This prearranged sequence of goals reduced processing demands by suggesting content beyond the sheer occurrence of events. Still, even her longer essays were less than one-third of a typed page long.

Helping young elementary school children to consider two or more goals simultaneously, and to relate these goals to each other, may improve their writing. Bereiter and Scardamalia (1987) found that a surprisingly simple instructional device promoted this objective. They gave children a deck of cards with common sentence openings: "Similarly," "For example," "On the other hand," and so on. Children were asked to choose one of these prompts when they could not think of what to say next. The logic was that these sentence openings would lead children to consider relations among previous sentences and to take into account the readers' perspective as well as what they as authors wanted to say. The prompts led to children writing essays with more content, and more richly interconnected content, even though the prompts did not specify what the content should be.

TABLE 9.4   Stories Written at Beginning, Middle, and End of Year for Class News Assignment

SEPTEMBER 24, 1956
Today is Monday, September 24, 1956. It is a rainy day. We hope the sun will shine.
We got new spelling books. We had our pictures taken. We sang Happy Birthday to Barbara
JANUARY 22, 1957
Today is Tuesday, January 22, 1957. It is a foggy day. We must be careful crossing the road.
This morning, we had music. We learned a new song.
Linda is absent. We hope she come back soon.
We had arithmetic. We made believe that we were buying candy. We had fun.
We work in our English books. We learned when to use *is* and **are**.
MAY 27, 1957
Today is Monday, May 27, 1957. It is a warm, cloudy day. We hope the sun comes out.
This afternoon, we had music. We enjoyed it. We went out to play.
Carole is absent. We hope she comes back soon.
We had a spelling lesson, we learned about a **dozen**.
Tomorrow we shall have show and tell.
Some of us have spelling sentences to do for homework.
Danny brought in a cocoon. It will turn into a butterfly.

Source: Waters, 1980.

As people develop expertise in writing, they progress from the knowledge-telling strategy to the *knowledge-transforming strategy* (Bereiter & Scardamalia, 1987). This strategy is defined by the writer trying to simultaneously meet two goals: deciding what information to convey and deciding how to convey it in a way that the anticipated audience will understand. Professional writers consistently use this strategy; many other adults use it on those occasions when they are knowledgeable about the topic of their essay. The strategy begins with an analysis of the subject of the essay and adoption of a point of view. Subsequent cognitive activities include moving back and forth between knowledge of the content area being discussed and knowledge of rhetorical devices that can be used to translate content into the desired form. The approach also involves frequent comparisons between what the writer would like to say and what he or she has written on the page. A useful by-product of the knowledge-transforming strategy is that the process of writing often increases the writer's knowledge. Trying to communicate a position to readers forces them to recognize gaps and contradictions in their own thinking. Resolving these gaps and contradictions often leads writers to deepen their understanding of the topic.

The trend toward greater use of the knowledge-transforming strategy can be seen in the amount of time spent planning before beginning to write. In general, college students take *more* time before they start writing than do fifth graders (Zbrodoff; 1984). They spend this time planning what their position will be, how they will argue for it, and what rhetorical devices they will use to do so.

The flexibility with which writers adapt to task constraints also increases with age. Fifth graders take the same (minimal) amount of time to start, regardless of time and length constraints. This is what would be expected from use of the knowledge-telling strategy; writing begins as soon as a direct response to the question can be generated. In contrast, college students increase their planning time when the assignment requires a longer essay and when they have more time to complete it (Bereiter & Scardamalia, 1987).

Mechanical requirements. A third type of difficulty involved in writing involves the mechanical requirements of forming letters, spelling words correctly, and putting capital letters and punctuation marks in the right places. These mechanical demands force many children to proceed so slowly that they forget what they are trying to say.

To test how mechanical demands and slow rate of production affect children's writing, Bereiter and Scardamalia (1982) asked fourth and sixth graders to compose essays under one of three conditions. In the typical-writing condition, children wrote as they ordinarily would, thus encountering both the mechanical demands and the slow rate of writing. In the slow-dictation condition, they dictated their essays to a scribe who had been trained to write at the child's writing speed. This released children from the mechanical requirements of writing but not from its slow pace. In the standard-dictation condition, children dictated into a tape recorder at their normal speaking rate. This released them from both the mechanical requirements and the slow pace of ordinary writing.

Children in the standard-dictation condition, burdened by neither mechanical demands nor slow rate, produced the best essays. Children in the slow-dictation condition, burdened by slow rate but not by mechanical demands, produced the next-best essays. Children in the typical-writing condition, burdened by both slow rate and mechanical demands, produced the worst essays.

These findings suggest that teaching children to type and use word processors might improve the quality of their writing, since it would allow them to go faster, not worry about handwriting, and reduce their attention to spelling. A recent analysis of 32 studies on the effects of word processing indicated that it has the desired effect. Access to word processing usually resulted in higher-quality writing (Bangert-Downs, 1993). The effects were largest with students who were not good writers under other circumstances. Positive effects continued to be found when students who previously wrote essays on the word processor returned to writing them by hand. The improvements in writing quality were not huge, but they were quite consistent. Thus, by removing mechanical demands of writing by hand, word processors can help students improve their writing.

The Process of Revision

Few first drafts are well written. Unfortunately, even students whose initial drafts cry out for changes rarely revise them; they just hand in the first draft. Worse yet, when students make revisions, the changes do not consistently result in improved quality (Fitzgerald, 1987). This raises the question of why revisions tend to be so inadequate.

Revision can be divided into two main processes: identification of weaknesses and their correction (Baker & Brown, 1984). To identify weaknesses, people must compare a unit of text, such as a sentence or paragraph, with an internal representation of the text's intended properties. Such a comparison requires the writer to be clear about the goals that the writing was intended to serve, even when the words on the page are confusing or distracting.

Children, as well as many adults, have difficulty identifying weaknesses in texts. For example, in a study by Beal (1990), children needed to correct essays presented to them that included missing sentences, impossible-to-interpret sentences, and direct contradictions. Fourth graders detected only 25 percent of these glaring problems, sixth graders only 60 percent.

In the more typical case in which children need to revise their own compositions, egocentrism exacerbates the difficulty. Children have trouble separating what they themselves know from what their readers could reasonably be expected to know. To illustrate this point, Bartlett (1982) asked children to revise either their own essay or an essay written by a classmate. The focus was on how well children detected two types of errors: grammatical errors and ambiguous references (e.g., "The policeman and the robber fought. He was killed."). If egocentrism contributed to the problem of recognizing weaknesses, children presumably would have more difficulty correcting ambiguous references in their own stories, where they knew the intended references, than in those of other children. On the other hand, egocentrism would not lead to their having more difficulty correcting their own grammatical errors than those of other children.

As anticipated, children were quite good at noticing other children's referential ambiguities but much less good at recognizing their own. Detection of grammatical errors, where egocentrism was not as much an issue, was more similar for their own and other children's essays. A major part of the development of revision skills, then, is ability to separate one's own perspective from that of the reader.

One inference that might be drawn from this finding is that writers should wait before revising. The logic is that psychological and temporal closeness to the composition increase egocentrism in the period immediately after the piece is written, and thus interfere with efforts at revision. With time, greater objectivity might be possible.

Such advice, however, does not get at the heart of the problem. The quality of fourth to twelfth graders' revisions is no better when they revise an essay a week after writing it than when they revise immediately (Bereiter & Scardamalia, 1982). It appears, therefore, that students may as well begin revising as soon after writing as is convenient. Waiting, in and of itself, does not help.

Even when children detect a problem in their writing, they still must repair it. Fortunately, children make such repairs quite effectively, at least when they recognize the problem spontaneously. For example, both fourth and sixth graders in Beal (1990) effectively corrected those problems that they detected themselves. The case was different, though, with weaknesses that adults pointed out after the children had missed them. The older students were fairly effective in fixing these problems, but the younger children were quite ineffective. Again, the key to success seems to be ability to adopt multiple perspectives. This helps both in perceiving problems with the original draft and in correcting problems that other people note. Thus, in writing, as in reading and mathematics, coordinating diverse types of knowledge, and shifting attention flexibly among them, is essential for successful performance.

SUMMARY

When they go to school, children build on their earlier understanding of numbers to acquire many new skills and concepts: simple and complex integer arithmetic, fractions, algebra, and computer programming among them. Development of simple arithmetic involves acquisition of more advanced strategies and in-creased speed and accuracy. The same pattern of development is found in North America, Europe, and East Asia, though the rate of development of arithmetic is faster among East Asian children. Individual differences among children are evident both in amount of knowledge and in the types of strategies that are preferred.

Children often do not understand the underlying concepts in mathemat-ics beyond simple arithmetic. This creates a variety of misconceptions and distortions, among them buggy subtraction rules, misunderstanding of deci-mal fractions and of the equal sign, and generation of nonsensical algebraic formulas. Mediated instruction, emphasizing not only computer program-ming concepts and commands but also their applicability to other situations, can improve general problem-solving competence as well as programming skill.

Learning to read involves acquisition of prereading skills, word-identifica-tion procedures, and comprehension. Among the most important prereading skills are letter perception and phonemic awareness. Teaching phonemic aware-ness skills to preschoolers leads to lasting increases in reading achievement.

Children use two main word-identification methods: phonological recod-ing and visually based retrieval. Both methods begin with examination of the printed word and end with access to the word's meaning and pronunciation in long-term memory. Phonological recoding also involves an intermediate step in which print is translated into sounds. The two skills are related in that accurate phonological recoding may aid development of strong associations between the printed word and its long-term memory entry and thus aid visu-ally based retrieval.

Reading comprehension is influenced by the same factors as influence memory development: improvements in basic processes, strategies, content knowledge, and metacognitive understanding. Helping children understand critical background content and improving their metacognitive processing has resulted in substantial improvements in reading comprehension.

Writing is a challenging task for most children. They have difficulty es-tablishing clear goals in the absence of the prompts and feedback that conver-sation provides. They also have difficulty reconciling the competing demands of executing the mechanics of writing, forming grammatical sentences, express-ing meanings, and anticipating the reader's reaction. In response, they first adopt the knowledge-telling strategy, which involves stating a reaction to the question that was posed and then listing supporting evidence in the order in which it is retrieved from memory. The strategy produces brief, listlike com-positions. A major change that occurs with age and experience in writing is im-proved ability to coordinate goals, to produce more extensive and interesting essays. This eventually enables writers to progress to the knowledge-transforming strategy, a strategy that demands more planning but that pays off in higher-quality products.

Skill at revising also improves with age and experience. The largest gains come in recognizing problems in the text. Once children recognize problems, they are reasonably skillful at fixing them. Underlying the improvement in identifying problems is growing ability to separate one's own knowledge from that of readers.

RECOMMENDED READINGS

Adams, M. J. (1990). *Beginning to read: Thinking and learning about print.* Cambridge, MA: MIT Books. A lively, well-written, and comprehensive presentation of issues regarding reading acquisition.

Bereiter, C., & Scardamalia, M. (1987). *The psychology of written composition.* Hillsdale, NJ: Erlbaum. An excellent summary of what is known about how children write and how their writing can be improved.

Geary, D. C. (1994). *Children's mathematical development: Research and practical implications.* Washington, DC: American Psychological Association. This book integrates issues ranging from what mathematical competencies are inherent to human beings to how mathematical disabilities arise.

Goldin-Meadow, S., Alibali, M. W., & Church, R. B. (1993). Transitions in concept acquisition: Using the hand to read the mind. *Psychological Review, 100,* 279–97. An intriguing description of how watching children's hand gestures, as well as listening to what they say, can help us understand their thinking.

Palincsar, A. S. & Brown, A. L. (1984). Reciprocal teaching of comprehension-monitoring activities. *Cognition and Instruction, 1,* 117–75. One of the most successful applications of psychological principles to the task of improving learning in the schools. Seventh graders with serious reading-comprehension problems became able to comprehend at an above-average level through participation in this program.

CHAPTER 10

Conclusions for the Present;
Challenges for the Future

"So how do children think?" (A 7-year-old, reacting to her father's description of what this book is about)

Previous chapters have focused on perception, language, memory, conceptual understanding, problem solving, and academic skills separately. The division has made it easier to consider the unique properties of children's thinking in each area. However, such divisions can obscure the continuing themes that unite different aspects of cognitive development. The two main goals of this concluding chapter are to discuss these unifying themes and to identify issues that seem likely to be central in the future.

In the opening chapter of the book, eight themes were listed that apply to children's thinking in general. These themes also provide the framework for this final chapter. The chapter is divided into eight sections, with each section focusing on a particular theme. The first part of each discussion summarizes current knowledge relevant to the theme. The second part introduces issues that are just beginning to be addressed. Among these "challenges for the future" are some of the largest and most interesting issues about children's thinking, such as whether learning and development are the same or different and why children think about what they think about. The chapter's organization is summarized in Table 10.1.

TABLE 10.1   Chapter Outline

I.   The most basic issues about children's thinking are "What develops?" and "How does development occur?"
   A.   Current Knowledge about What Develops and How Development Occurs
   B.   Future Issues

II.   Four change processes that seem to be particularly large contributors to cognitive development are automatization, encoding, generalization, and strategy construction.
   A.   Current Knowledge about Change Processes
   B.   Future issues

III.   Infants and very young children are far more cognitively competent than they appear. They possess a rich set of abilities that enable them to learn rapidly.
   A.   Current Knowledge about Early Competence
   B.   Future issues

IV.   Differences between age groups tend to be ones of degree rather than kind. Not only are young children more cognitively competent than they appear, but older children and adults are less competent than we might think.
   A.   Current Knowledge about Differences among Age Groups
   B.   Future issues

V.   Changes in children's thinking do not occur in a vacuum. What children already know about material that they encounter influences not only how much they learn but also what they learn.
   A.   Current Knowledge about Effects of Existing Knowledge
   B.   Future Issues

VI.   The development of intelligence reflects changes in brain structure and functioning as well as increasingly effective deployment of cognitive resources.
   A.   Current Knowledge about Development of Intelligence
   B.   Future Issues

VII.   Children's thinking develops within a social context. Parents. peers, teachers, and the overall society influence what children think about, as well as how and why they come to think in particular ways.
   A.   Current Knowledge about Social Influences on Children's Thinking
   B.   Future Issues

VIII.   Increasing understanding of children's thinking is yielding practical benefits as well as theoretical insights.
   A.   Current Practical Contributions of Research on Children's Thinking
   B.   Future Issues

IX.   Summary

---

1. The most basic issues about children's thinking are "What develops?" and "How does development occur?"

When investigators of children's thinking write in journal articles, "The purpose of this investigation is . . . ," they almost never complete the sentence with "to find out what develops" or "to find out how development occurs." Modesty, and the realization that no one study is likely to meet these goals, prevents researchers from mentioning them. Yet they are the deepest motivations of research on children's thinking. Always keeping them in mind is critical to understanding what the research is all about.

Current Knowledge about What Develops
and How Development Occurs

On one of the rare occasions when investigators stated their views about "what develops," Brown and DeLoache (1978) suggested that in the domain of memory development, there are four major sources of growth: basic processes, strategies, metacognition, and content knowledge. These sources of memory development provide a useful guide for thinking about what develops in other areas of cognitive development as well.

Many examples from previous chapters attest to the pervasive contribution to cognitive development of changes in these four types of capabilities. Improvements in basic processes were not only invoked to explain improved functioning of immediate, short-term, and long-term memory (e.g., Hale, et al., in press; Kail, 1991). They also were used to explain changes in the complexity of the stimuli infants prefer to look at (McCall et al., 1977), in the consistency of reliance on the mutual exclusivity constraint in toddlers' vocabulary acquisition (Markman, 1989), in preschoolers' success in making transitive inferences (Halford, 1993), and in school-age children's reading and arithmetic (Adams, 1990; Geary, 1994). Similarly, changes in strategies were seen in contexts other than rehearsal, organization, and the other mnemonic strategies. Improved strategies also helped children solve increasing numbers of class inclusion and measurement problems (Miller, 1989; Trabasso et al., 1978), to use the *ed* ending to generate past-tense verbs (Marcus et al., 1992), to allocate attention increasingly systematically (Miller & Seier, 1994), and to write more elaborate descriptions of the day's events on "class news" assignments (Waters, 1980). Improved metacognition not only aided memory functioning (Schneider & Pressley, 1989), it also allowed 1-year-olds to understand that their mother's words referred to what she was looking at (Baldwin, 1993a; Tomasello & Barton, 1994), 4-year-olds to understand that other people could believe something that the child knew was not true (Astington & Gopnik, 1991), school-age children to monitor their reading comprehension increasingly accurately (Baker, 1994), and adults to teach route planning more effectively than fourth graders because they more deeply realized the need to engage children in the learning process (Gauvain & Rogoff, 1989). Finally, superior content knowledge did not only lead to more accurate memory for visits to doctors' offices, fairy tales, and soccer games. It also led 4-month-olds who had played with two separate objects to be surprised when they later saw them move in tandem (Needham & Baillargeon, 1995); 3- and 4-year-olds from larger families to understand other people's thinking better than age-peers from smaller families (Jenkins & Astington, 1996); 5-year-olds to solve transitive inference problems better when they concerned relations among the bear family in *Goldilocks and the Three Bears* (Goswami, 1995); and 14-year-olds to comprehend stories better because they form links between episodes as well as between them (van den Broek, 1989).

Hypotheses about how development occurs, like hypotheses about what develops, reflect the interconnectedness of cognitive development. Recall some of the diverse contexts in which changes in children's thinking appeared due to improved encoding: infants' increasing tendencies to form categories based on abstract features (Eimas & Quinn, 1994; Madole & Cohen, 1995), toddlers' movement from child-basic to standard-basic categories once they begin to encode functionally important features such as the the wicks on round candles (Tversky & Hemenway, 1984), preschoolers' reading of words such as *Coke* and *Budweiser* on the basis of encoding distinctive features of their lengths and initial letters (Gough & Hillinger, 1980), and school-age children's improved ability to learn about balance scales once they encode distance as well as weight (Siegler, 1976).

Future Issues

To make substantial progress on such difficult issues as what develops and how development occurs will require advances in both theories and methods for studying development. One need is for theories that are both broadly applicable and precisely stated. Such theories could focus attention on critical issues, raise questions that have not been considered before, and serve as a point of departure from which to formulate ideas.

For many years, Piaget's theory served these integrative and agenda-setting functions. Arguments between "pro-Piagetians" and "anti-Piagetians" dominated journals, books, and conferences. But those days are past. Very few people would argue today that infants below 8 months of age have no understanding of object permanence, that 5-year-olds are completely incapable of understanding transformations, or that cognitive development can be divided into neat, orderly stages. Equally few people would argue that the difficulty that children have with the standard versions of the Piagetian tasks are just due to methodological artifacts, or that there is no unity in children's thinking at given ages. Instead, most students of cognitive development would subscribe to the more moderate positions that infants and young children encounter genuine difficulty understanding the skills and concepts emphasized by Piaget, but that they have some early understanding of them, gradually acquire greater understanding, and organize their thinking in coherent, but complex, ways.

Moderation has its virtues, but also its costs. Piaget was right in some of his views and wrong in others, but right or wrong, his theory lent coherence to findings about many aspects of children's thinking. What is needed now is a successor that has the virtues of Piaget's theory while surmounting at least some of its drawbacks. That is, a theory is needed that, like Piaget's, includes the entire age range from infancy to adolescence; addresses areas as diverse as problem solving, conceptual understanding, memory, and moral judgments; and uncovers heretofore unknown changes in children's thinking.

In previous chapters, we encountered a number of efforts at formulating such broad yet detailed theories. Each of them has added to our understanding of cognitive development, but none has captured the imagination of the field as Piaget's theory did. The question now is how can we work toward such a theory.

One way to promote such theoretical progress is to study children's thinking using methods that examine changes as they are occurring. Providing a precise and plausible account of change has been the weakpoint of both Piaget's theory and more recent theories of cognitive development. Explaining change is inherently difficult, but the difficulty appears to have been exacerbated by the methods traditionally used to study children's thinking. These methods contrast performance of children at relatively widely spaced ages; if differences between age groups are observed, the researcher attempts to infer what happened between the younger and older age. Unfortunately, this strategy of inferring how changes must have occurred from observations widely spaced in time leaves open many possible paths to change, especially since changes in children's thinking often do not proceed by the most direct route we can imagine.

The indirect path that change often takes was evident in one of the few studies that have examined changes while they were occurring: Karmiloff-Smith's (1992) study of children drawing maps for an ambulance driver to follow while delivering a patient to the hospital (p. 269). By examining the sequence of maps that the children drew, Karmiloff-Smith discovered that the maps often regressed from efficient and informative notations to ones with considerable redundancy, before returning to the earlier efficient and informative formats. Without examining the changes in drawing from one map to the next to the next, Karmiloff-Smith would have been unlikely to detect these regressions. More generally, such detailed data about change indicate to theorists what exactly they need to explain.

This study of map drawing exemplifies the *microgenetic method*, an approach that is just beginning to be commonly used, but that has the potential to increase understanding of change. The key characteristic of the microgenetic method is obtaining frequent samples of children's thinking as the thinking is changing. These frequent samples provide more precise data about the change process than could otherwise have been obtained.

An encouraging feature of microgenetic studies that have been run is that they have yielded similar findings regarding change, despite the studies having been performed by researchers with diverse theoretical orientations. One consistent finding is that change does not ordinarily involve a simple substitution of a more advanced approach for a less advanced one (Kuhn, 1995). Older, less adequate approaches continue to be used, often for prolonged periods of time, after new, better approaches are generated. This is true even in cases in which children can explain why the new approach is superior (Siegler & Jenkins, 1989). Thus, application of new ways of thinking tends to be halting and piecemeal, rather than sudden and complete.

A second consistent finding is related to the first. Children generally think about a problem in multiple ways at a given time. This cognitive variability is evident before periods of rapid change, during them, and after them, though it may be most apparent during them (Alibali & Goldin-Meadow, 1993). It is evident in populations and domains as varied as infants' strategies for deciding how to descend down ramps (Adolph, 1995), toddlers' language use (Kuczaj, 1977), preschoolers' beliefs about conservation (Acredolo & O'Connor, 1991), older children's memory and problem-solving strategies (Alibali & Goldin-Meadow, 1993; Coyle & Bjorklund, 1997), and adults' attempts to understand novel technologies (Grannott, 1993).

A third generalization is that innovations follow success as well as failure. Failure is not necessary to motivate discoveries; children generate new ways of thinking when older approaches have been yielding correct solutions as well as when they have not (Karmiloff-Smith, 1992). At times, children discover new strategies on the same problem that they shortly before solved correctly using an older approach (Siegler & Jenkins, 1989).

In summary, by yielding detailed data about change, microgenetic methods may help provide the foundation for formulating new broad and encompassing theories that indicate what develops and how development occurs.

> 2. Four change processes that seem to be particularly large contributors to cognitive development are automatization, encoding, generalization, and strategy construction.

Current Knowledge about Change Processes

Although understanding of change processes in children's thinking is just beginning to accelerate, we do know that large contributions are made by four families of processes: automatization, encoding, generalization, and strategy construction. *Automatization* refers to a procedure coming to be executed whenever the relevant stimulus conditions appear and with minimal or no expenditure of cognitive resources. Related concepts include freeing cognitive resources, shifting from controlled to automatic processing, and shifting from serial to parallel processing. *Encoding* involves representing objects and events in terms of sets of features and their relations. Ideas that overlap with encoding include assimilation, discrimination, differentiation, identification of critical features, and formation of mental models. *Generalization* refers to extrapolating known relations to new cases. Similar constructs include induction, abstraction, transfer, regularity detection, and analogical reasoning. Finally, *strategy construction* involves integrating the other processes to adapt to task demands. Related mechanisms include accommodation, strategy discovery, and the operations of metacomponents and central conceptual structures.

Although understanding of these mechanisms is far from complete, each undoubtedly contributes to a wide range of developments. A few of these are listed in Table 10.2.

TABLE 10.2   Some Demonstrations of the Importance of Automatization, Encoding, Generalization, and Strategy Construction

PROCESS	DOMAIN	INVESTIGATOR
Automatization	Mechanics of writing essays	Bereiter & Scardamalia (1987)
	Execution of memory strategies	Guttentag (1985)
	Basic arithmetic	Lemaire et al. (1994)
	General theory of development	Case (1992)
Encoding	Individual differences in infants' intelligence	Rose et al. (1992)
	Preschoolers' focus on gist of stories	Brainerd et al. (1990)
	Older children's linguistic reanalysis	Bowerman (1982)
	General theory of development	Sternberg (1985)
Generalization	Infants' learning about mobiles	Rovee-Collier (1996)
	Toddlers' overregularization of **ed** endings	Marcus et al. (1992)
	Uses of causal concepts	Keil (1989)
	General theory of development	MacWhinney et al. (1989)
Strategy Construction	Infants' means-ends analysis	Willatts (1990)
	Young children's route planning	Ellis & Schneiders (1989)
	Older children's scientific experimentation	Kuhn et al. (1995)
	General theory of development	Siegler (1996)

The four processes are important for their joint contribution to development, as well as for each process's individual contribution. To get a feel for how they might together produce development in a particular area, think about the counting-on strategy for adding numbers (Chapter 3). This strategy involves first identifying the larger addend and then counting up from it the number of times indicated by the smaller addend. On 2 + 5 and 5 + 2, for example, a child using the counting-on strategy would note that 5 was the larger addend, count "5, 6, 7," and answer, "7."

Now consider how the four processes might work together to generate this strategy. Constructing the strategy depends on having previously formed the generalization that adding $a + b$ always yields the same answer as adding $b + a$. Otherwise, there would be no basis for always counting from the larger addend, regardless of the order of addends in the problem. This generalization, in turn, depends on appropriate encoding. To learn that addend order is irrelevant, children need to encode the features "first addend" and "second addend," as well as the particular addends within each problem. Finally, encoding not only the particular addends but also the categories "first addend" and "second addend" probably requires automatizing other processes, such as counting, so that they do not require all of the child's processing resources.

Future Issues

The influence of automatization, encoding, generalization, and strategy construction is not unique to cognitive development. All are essential to learning in general, regardless of when in life the learning occurs. This leaves a major unanswered question, though: Are there change mechanisms that are uniquely developmental, that is, mechanisms that only operate during certain periods of life?

A common way of addressing this issue is to ask whether learning and development are the same or different (Feldman, 1995; Fischer & Grannott, 1995; Halford, 1995). The terms are certainly used differently. Acquisitions tend to be labeled "development" when they consistently occur at a particular age, when they are universal across cultures, and when they are universal among individuals within a culture. Acquisitions tend to be labeled "learning" when they are acquired at a variety of ages, in some cultures but not others, and by some but not other individuals within a culture. These linguistic distinctions, however, leave open the basic question of whether the same or different processes give rise to the outcomes labeled "development" and "learning."

Developmental neuroscientists have distinguished between two types of processes that give rise to changes in the brain: experience-expectant and experience-dependent (Greenough et al., 1987). This distinction also seems useful for thinking about the neural substrates of learning and development and also about how the processes might differ.

Experience-expectant processes correspond to the "development" end of the development-learning continuum. Such processes are hypothesized to be based on the early synaptic overproduction and pruning over broad areas of the brain that was described in Chapter 1 (pp. 15–16). In experience-expectant processes, the initial overproduction of synapses is maturationally regulated, but which ones are pruned depends on experience. Normal experience at the normal time results in neural activity that maintains typical connections; lack of such experience at the usual time results in atypical connections. Thus, there is a sensitive period (Bornstein, 1989) in which relevant experience must occur for the experience to have the usual effect on brain development. The type of experience that is relevant to such experience-expectant processes is experience that has been widely available throughout the evolutionary history of the species.

Greenough et al. suggested that one advantage of such experience-expectant processes is that they allow both efficient acquisition in normal environments and reasonable adaptation to abnormal ones. In particular, the genes provide a rough outline of the eventual form of the process, thus facilitating acquisition under normal circumstances. Unusual environments or physical deficiencies, however, lead to different neural activity, which creates alternative organizations of brain activity that are adaptive given the atypical circumstances.

Direct support for this account comes from observations of the brains of deaf and blind children (Neville, 1995b). Children who are completely deaf do not receive any auditory experience. As a result, certain areas of the brain that would be devoted to auditory processing if the brain were receiving both auditory and visual stimulation instead come to be devoted to visual processing. Conversely, blind children do not receive any visual experience. As a result, some areas of their brains that would be devoted to visual processing if they were receiving both auditory and visual stimulation come to be devoted to auditory processing. The brains of deaf and blind children do not show these unusual processing patterns at birth. They emerge only after the children's brains do not receive the typical input in the months after birth (the sensitive period). Thus, the brain is predisposed to devote certain areas to processing certain types of stimuli, but if the expected pattern of stimulation is not present, the brain uses the area to process signals from other senses.

The other side of Greenough et al.'s dichotomy involves *experience-dependent* processes. These are the neural substrate of what is usually thought of as learning. With experience-dependent processes, formation of synaptic connections depends on experiences that vary widely among individuals in whether and when they occur. The experience-dependent processes appear to operate through the formation of synapses in response to specific neural activity, caused by partially or totally unsuccessful attempts to process information. Such synapses can be generated as rapidly as 10 to 15 minutes after a new experience (Chang & Greenough, 1984). Synapse production under such circumstances appears to be localized to the site of the previous information processing. However, as with experience-expectant processes, more synapses are produced than will later be present. The synapses that are maintained are those involved in subsequent neural activity.

This analysis suggests both similarities and differences between experience-expectant and experience-dependent processes. In both cases, the change mechanism involves a cycle of synaptic overproduction and pruning. Also in both, neural activity determines which synapses are maintained. However, the events that trigger the production of synapses and its degree of localization within the brain distinguish the two types of processes. The challenge now is to provide similarly precise descriptions of change mechanisms at the cognitive level, so as to better understand the similarities and differences between learning and development.

> 3. Infants and very young children are far more cognitively competent than they appear. They possess a rich set of abilities that allow them to learn rapidly.

Current Knowledge about Early Competence

Literally from the day they emerge from the womb, infants possess a variety of perceptual capabilities. They see the world in color (Adams, 1987) and accurately perceive the relative distance of objects from themselves (Slater et al., 1990). They look in the direction from which sounds come (Morrongiello et al., 1994) and prefer listening to tape recordings of stories read to them before birth (DeCasper & Spence, 1986). By 4 months of age, their seeing and hearing become considerably more acute. They also prefer looking at faces over other types of objects (Danemiller & Stevens, 1988), prefer looking at attractive faces over unattractive ones (Langlois et al., 1994), and prefer listening to their own name over that of other people (Mandel et al., 1995). Integration of information from different senses also is evident from birth and even more so by the age of 4 months. Infants use sounds to guide their looking (Haith, 1980), sights to guide their reaching (von Hofsten, 1993), and knowledge gained from manual exploration of objects to guide their looking (Needham & Baillargeon, 1995; Streri & Spelke, 1988).

The early competence is not restricted to perception. Infants less than 1-year-old possess rudimentary understanding of a variety of concepts, including time (Friedman et al., 1995; Haith et al., 1993), space (Bai & Bertenthal, 1992), number (Wynn, 1992a), and causality (Oakes & Cohen, 1995). They can solve problems via means-ends analysis (Willatts, 1990), analogical reasoning (Chen et al., in press), and letting their mothers know what they want (Mosier & Rogoff, 1994).

One reason that infants are able to do so much so quickly is that they possess a variety of generally applicable learning processes. From the first days outside the womb, infants orient their attention toward bright lights, loud noises, moving objects, and other potentially informative stimuli (Aslin, 1993; Cohen, 1972). They form associations, recognize familiar objects, generalize what they have learned to similar objects, and imitate some actions of other people (Meltzoff & Moore, 1989; Rovee-Collier, 1995; Siqueland & Lipsitt, 1966). By 2 to 4 months of age, they form expectations and abstract prototypical patterns (Bomba & Siqueland, 1983; Haith et al., 1993). By 10 months of age, they detect correlations among features and use them to form new concepts (Younger, 1993).

These general learning processes are not the only reason for children's early cognitive competence. Infants' and toddlers' thinking also seems to be biased in certain directions that help them learn. Perceptual and conceptual development seem to be aided by valid assumptions about the nature of physical objects. Infants less than 6 months old already seem to expect that all parts of a physical object will move together, that objects cannot move through spaces occupied by other objects, and that objects must move in continuous paths (Baillargeon, 1994; Kellman & Spelke, 1983; Spelke et al., 1992). By 18 months of age, children seem to expect that new words will refer to all objects within a given class (the taxonomic constraint) and that they will not mean the same thing as existing words (the mutual exclusivity constraint) (Markman, 1989; Merriman & Bowman, 1989). Infants and toddlers also are biased toward assigning causal relations a central position in their concepts (Leslie, 1982) and toward using the causal relations to guide their memories of events (Bauer & Mandler, 1989b).

It is important to remember that these early competencies are part of the story of cognitive development, but only part. Infants' and toddlers' understandings and capacities almost always differ greatly from those of older children. Taken together, however, the early competencies, the generally applicable learning mechanisms, and the more specific biases to think of the world in certain ways result in exceptionally rapid cognitive growth in the first few years.

Future Issues

Probably the single largest issue regarding infants' cognition concerns how to reconcile the competence they show under some circumstances with the incompetence they show under others. A recent model by Munakata et al. (in press) provides a start in this direction. The model concerns development of object permanence. Recall from Chapter 2 that Piaget (1954) hypothesized that infants younger than 8 months old do not understand that objects continue to exist when they can no longer be seen. He supported this interpretation with evidence that 6- and 7-month-olds do not reach for toys that are taken from them and placed under an opaque container. However, subsequent experiments by Baillargeon (1987) and others demonstrated nascent understanding of object permanence at 3 months of age. When 3-month-olds are shown a stationary object on a table, then have their view of it occluded, and then see a moving object appear to go through the space where the stationary object had been, they look longer than when they see the same motion but without having seen the stationary object earlier. This finding suggested that the 3-month-olds represented the unseen object and looked for a long time because they were surprised to see another object appear to go through it. The question was why infants would show knowledge of object permanence in their looking so long before they show it in their reaching.

One possibility was that infants understand the principle of object permanence by the age of 3 months but that they do not know until considerably later that they can act on one object (the opaque container) to retrieve another (Baillargeon, 1994; Diamond, 1991). Arguing against this possibility, and the related possibility that the infants did not want to retrieve the toy, the same infants who do not remove an opaque container to get a toy will remove an otherwise-identical transparent container to get it (Bower & Wishart, 1972; Munakata et al., in press). They also will press a button to get a toy they can see but not to get a toy they cannot see (Munakata et al., in press).

Munakata et al. suggested a different explanation: that infants in their first half-year of life possess representations of the continuing existence of hidden objects that are strong enough to elicit looking but not strong enough to elicit reaching. Studies of brain-damaged adults indicate that the damage often results in visual representations that are strong enough to maintain behaviors that are not too demanding on the representations but not ones that place greater demands on them (Farah, Monheit, & Wallace, 1991). Reaching may well be more demanding than looking; not only does it require a greater expenditure of energy, but infants do not consistently reach for interesting objects until about 4 months of age, whereas they look at them from birth (von Hofsten, 1993). Thus, infants' representations of hidden objects, like the representations of brain-damaged people, may be strong enough to produce success in favorable situations but not in more challenging ones.

To test whether this idea could explain infants' competence on some object permanence tasks and incompetence on others, Munakata et al. (in press) formulated a connectionist model. Like the MacWhinney et al. (1989) connectionist model of the development of the German article system (p. 88), Munakata's model of object permanence included an input layer, a hidden layer, and an output layer. Also as in the other connectionist model, each layer included a number of processing units, and there were many connections between processing units in different layers.

The experience received by the Munakata et al. model involved codes corresponding to a barrier and a ball. Sometimes the barrier moved in front of the ball and occluded it, and then moved away to reveal it again (Figure 10.1). This corresponded to infants seeing objects disappear behind other objects and then reappear when the other objects moved.

As the network gained experience with these situations, it learned to represent the continued existence of the ball and to predict that the ball would reappear where it had been earlier when the barrier moved away. At first, the model maintained such representations only over brief periods of occlusion; it gradually learned to maintain them over longer and longer periods. This corresponded to Diamond's (1985) finding that between 6 and 12 months of age, infants gradually extend the periods of occlusion over which they show object permanence.

Especially important in the present context, the model demonstrated how looking measures could reveal representations of occluded objects long before reaching measures revealed comparable knowledge. Within the model, the same representation of the object motivated looking and reaching. However, the process of strengthening connections between the representation and the reaching system was programmed to start later and to proceed more slowly than learning the connections that led to looking. Because of this slower strengthening of connections between the representation of the object and the reaching system, at any given point in development, a stronger representation of an object was needed to elicit reaching than to elicit looking.

This simulation has interesting implications for the general issue of how to reconcile infants' competence in some situations with their incompetence in others. When infants show competence in a situation, it is tempting to ascribe to

FIGURE 10.1 Representation of ball and barrier presented to Munakata et al. model. At first, (Time 0) the barrier is to the left of the ball. Then it moves rightward until it is in front of the ball (Times 4–6). Then it moves leftward, revealing that the ball is still present (Time 7). After encountering a number of episodes like this, the model learns that the ball continues to exist even though it cannot be seen.

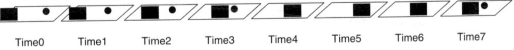

Time0   Time1   Time2   Time3   Time4   Time5   Time6   Time7

them the kind of high-level understanding that would lead adults to engage in the behavior. Adults know as a general principle that objects continue to exist even when they cannot be seen. Perhaps infants' longer looking times when objects seem to disappear reflects the same type of surprise an adult would feel. However, the longer looking times may just imply a tendency to look at unusual events. After moving unusually slowly in a traffic jam, we are not surprised when we drive past the scene of an accident, but we tend to look anyway. The Munakata et al. model illustrates how detection of an unusual event could trigger longer looking times without surprise and without understanding of principles. It also indicates how experience seeing objects disappear behind barriers and then reappear when the barriers moved could eventually lead to competence via reaching as well as looking measures. Thus, the model provides a way of reconciling infants' competence and incompetence, as well as a perspective on what they know about object permanence and how they come to know it.

> 4. Differences between age groups tend to be ones of degree rather than kind. Not only are young children more cognitively competent than they appear, but older children and adults are often less competent than we might think.

Current Knowledge about Differences between Age Groups

As discussed in the previous section, infants and toddlers have a much richer cognitive life than was suspected until recently. The same is true of preschoolers. Consider just Piagetian tasks and concepts that were once thought impossible for children below age 7. Placing distinctive stickers on the left and right side of the three-mountains apparatus allows 3-year-olds to distinguish between their own spatial perspective and that of someone sitting on the other side of the mountains; thus, they are not always egocentric (Newcombe & Huttenlocher, 1992). When 3- to 5-year-olds see sugar dissolved in a cup of water, they believe that the water will weigh more than it did before, despite no change being visible; this indicates some understanding of conservation of weight (Au et al., 1993). Preschoolers also possess greater understanding of numbers than Piaget recognized; they can add and subtract small numbers, identify the larger of two numbers, and count in a way that reflects understanding of the structure of the number system (Geary, 1994).

At the other end of the age spectrum, adults' reasoning has turned out to be less rational than once thought. Without training, even high school and college students rarely solve Piagetian formal operations tasks, such as balance-scale and shadow-projection problems (Byrnes, 1988; Kuhn, et al., 1995). Even after taking college physics courses, many students believe that when a car circles an oval, the door toward the outside moves at the same speed as the door toward the inside, despite the door toward the outside moving farther in the same time (Levin et al., 1990). Such difficulties are not limited to scientific reasoning. Shaklee (1979) reviewed a host of irrational aspects of adults' thinking. Adults will bet more on a cut of a deck of cards when playing against a nervous opponent than when playing against a relaxed one. They become more confident of their ability to win a game of pure chance after having time to practice it. When asked to judge which of two sequences of random events is more likely, they ignore the randomness if one sequence sounds more representative. (They say a married couple is less likely to have six children in the order "girl, girl, girl, boy, boy, boy" than to have them in the order "girl, boy, boy, girl, boy, girl.") In short, although young children act like budding scientists in some contexts, educated adults ignore the most basic logical considerations in others.

As implied by these findings of cognitive competence in early childhood and of illogical thinking in adulthood, development generally is an incremental process, occurring gradually over many years. Consider findings regarding children's understanding of the mind. Around their first birthday, infants show some understanding that other people have intentions; when an adult says, "That's a *dax*," they interpret *dax* as referring to the object at which the adult is looking, even if they themselves are looking at something else (Baldwin, 1993a). Two-year-olds understand that other people's desires influence their behavior, but not ordinarily that other people's beliefs are also influential (Wellman & Woolley, 1990). Four-year-olds understand that beliefs as well as desires influence people's behavior, and also distinguish between appearance and reality (Astington & Gopnik, 1991; Flavell, et al., 1983). However, they believe that they can remember far more than they really can (Flavell et al., 1970) and often do not see the necessity of using strategies to help them remember (Schneider & Pressley, 1989). Understanding of how to monitor one's reading comprehension, how to allocate study time among tasks, and how to assess other people's intentions continue to develop through adolescence, and adulthood (Baker, 1994; Pressley, 1995). Lengthy and complex sequences of development, such as that involved in learning about our own and other people's minds, are the rule rather than the exception.

Future Issues

Discoveries of young children's previously unsuspected competence, and of adults' previously-unsuspected incompetence, have doomed many explanations of development. It is no longer tenable to believe that preschoolers' inherent egocentrism makes it impossible for them to take other people's perspectives. Nor is it tenable to believe that their mediation deficiencies makes it impossible for them to benefit from using memory strategies or that their holistic thinking precludes them from forming concepts with defining features. These falling dominos, in turn, have made increasingly indefensible a more general belief about children's thinking: that it is possible to state a single age at which children acquire a particular concept.

The age at which children understand a concept often has been equated with the age at which most children succeed on a particular task that involves the concept. For example, for many years, children were said to understand the concept of number when they could solve Piaget's number conservation task. As investigators devised additional tasks corresponding to the same concept, however, it became clear that the ages at which different numerical tasks could be solved varied dramatically. At what age, then, do they understand the concept?

One plausible approach to answering this question is to identify understanding with the earliest form of understanding. Braine (1959) argued for this view when he wrote, "If one seeks to state an age at which a particular type of response develops, the only age that is not completely arbitrary is the earliest age at which this type of response can be elicited" (p.16).

Braine's statement is entirely reasonable, as far as it goes. When one considers the many years that often separate initial from mature understanding, however, a paradox becomes evident. Adopting the initial-competence criterion puts us in the position of saying that many concepts are understood at young ages yet also of saying that children fail many reasonable indexes of understanding for years thereafter. Stated another way, if we adopt the initial-competence criterion, most understanding develops after the concept is understood.

Brown (1976) advocated an alternative criterion for conceptual understanding: that of *stable usage*. Children would not be viewed as understanding a concept until they could use it in most or all situations to which it applies. The problem here is evident in Braine's comment. What exactly does a child understand when he or she can use a concept in some situations but not in most? It does seem arbitrary to identify understanding with anything other than the earliest form of understanding. However, it seems misleading to identify it with the earliest understanding.

The object permanence data cited in the previous section illustrate the difficulty. Do infants understand object permanence at 3 months of age, when their looking times suggest such understanding? Or, do they understand it at 9 months of age, when they begin to reach for hidden objects? Or, do they not understand it until sometime later, when they know as a general principle that an object must continue to exist somewhere, even if they have no idea where it is (as when older children misplace their keys)? Given the complexity of cognitive development, it almost always will prove impossible to provide a meaningful statement about *the* age at which children acquire a cognitive capability. Models that specify how children think under various conditions, and how they come to think in those ways, are needed to deal with this complexity.

> 5. Changes in children's thinking do not occur in a vacuum. What children already know about material that they encounter influences not only how much they learn but also what they learn.

Current Knowledge about the Effects
of Existing Knowledge

People almost always find it easier to understand, learn, and remember in areas where they already have some knowledge. With experience looking at checkerboards, infants come to prefer looking at more complex arrangements (DeLoache et al., 1978). Toddlers use knowledge of word meanings to help them learn grammar (Corrigan, 1988). Preschoolers use scripts that they have abstracted from their experiences with birthday parties and eating at restaurants to remember new parties and meals (Hudson, 1990; Nelson, 1993). School-age children with some knowledge of conservation and class inclusion more easily master the concepts than do less knowledgeable children (Inhelder et al., 1974; Strauss, 1972).

Prior content knowledge influences what people learn as well as how much they learn. Such effects are especially evident in the relatively rare cases where knowledge interferes with learning and remembering. Learning the sounds of their native language leads infants and young children to progressively lose the ability to discriminate sounds that are not differentiated within it (Werker & Desjardins, 1995) and leads children past age 7 to progressively lose the ability to fully master the grammar of another language (Johnson & Newport, 1989). Knowledge of typical eating patterns leads preschoolers to reject the possibility that lunch could consist of cereal and orange juice (Keil, 1989). Negative stereotypes, based on previous tales of a person's clumsiness, lead children to incorrectly "remember" that the person engaged in other misdeeds (Leichtman & Ceci, 1995). School-age children filter adults' statements that the earth is round through their knowledge that it looks flat, and conclude that the earth is a flattened disk, perhaps with a dome over it (Vosniadou & Brewer, 1992).

Prior knowledge does not operate as a mechanism apart from the previously-mentioned change processes. Rather, the prior knowledge, along with incoming information, provides data on which the change processes operate. Put another way, prior knowledge helps determine what the change processes do: what features children encode, what generalizations they draw, what strategies they construct, and what operations they automatize. The nature of the change processes, however, determines how they do it.

Future Issues

Some of the most controversial issues about children's thinking concern hypothesized high-level knowledge structures, such as theories of physics and mind. Do such high-level structures exist, do they differ from other types of knowledge, and what do they imply about cognitive development in general?

The issue can be illustrated in the context of children's knowledge of biology. Wellman and Gelman (1992; in press) hypothesized that biology, like physics and mind, is a core theory. Substantial evidence supported their view that preschoolers' understanding of biology met the four criteria that they proposed for core theories: fundamental categories unique to the domain, causal explanations unique to the domain, unobservable explanatory constructs, and coherent organization.

Consider some of the evidence for knowledge of fundamental categories unique to biology. Two such categories are animals and plants. By their first birthday, infants know that animals differ from other types of objects in being able to move independently, to drink, and to sleep (Mandler & McDonough, 1996; Woodward, 1995). Three- and 4-year-olds know that plants are also a separate category and that they, like animals, grow (Hatano et al., 1993; Hickling & Gelman, 1995), heal after injuries (Backscheider, Shatz, & Gelman, 1993), and decompose after death (Springer, Ngyuen, & Samaniego, 1995). Children remain unsure for several years after this whether plants should be grouped with animals as living things (Hatano et al., 1993), but they are aware from preschool age that plants and animals share many basic properties that no other objects possess.

Preschoolers also understand that the actions of biological entities reflect causal processes unique to the domain, such as growth and inheritance, and invisible entities unique to the domain, such as germs. For example, they know that biological growth is essentially unidirectional, with organisms growing from smaller to bigger but not the reverse (Rosengren, Gelman, Kalish, & McCormick, 1991). They also know that inheritance leads baby animals to grow into beings that resemble adults of their species, even if they do not look like them at birth, whereas the same will not happen with dolls or other inanimate objects (Gelman & Wellman, 1991). With regard to unobservable entities, they understand that germs lead to illness and believe that an unobservable and unchanging essence leads to organisms of a given type having similar internal parts and behavioral properties, even if they look different (Kalish, 1996; Gelman, Coley & Gottfried, 1994). Together, these findings suggest that preschoolers have a coherent understanding of biology.

Whether these four properties differentiate children's understanding of biology from their understanding of innumerable other domains, however, is open to question. All four properties also characterize such obviously noncore domains as baseball. Knowledge of baseball includes categories unique to the domain (e.g., pitcher, catcher, home run), a specific kind of causality (centered on the goal of having scored a greater number of runs after nine innings), invisible explanatory constructs (e.g., baseball savvy, clutch hitting), and a coherent organization. Yet if knowledge of baseball qualifies as a core theory, there must be thousands of them. As Wellman and Gelman noted, "It is not yet clear how many domains children distinguish in all nor which analytic criteria identify foundational domains of thought." (p. 66 in manuscript). Similarly, despite many claims that theories are produced by domain-specific learning mechanisms (e.g., Keil, 1989; Leslie, 1994; Spelke et al., 1992; Wellman & Gelman, in press), no such mechanisms have been described in any detail.

Paradoxically, although proponents of viewing conceptual understanding in terms of theories have emphasized the domain specificity of knowledge and of learning mechanisms, their most important long-term contribution may be an insight that applies to all domains. Traditionally, almost all analyses of development have assumed that knowledge proceeds from concrete to abstract. In this view, children first learn about aspects of the world that they can see, hear, and touch, and later learn about invisible aspects, such as causal relations, that link these tangible objects, events, and qualities. Proponents of the core-theory approach, however, have emphasized that in foundational domains, even infants and young children think in terms of underlying causes and invisible entities: momentum, force, intentions, deceptions, germs, inheritance, and so on. Such thinking has been viewed as distinguishing knowledge of core domains from knowledge of other areas (Wellman & Gelman, in press).

However, the tendency to emphasize causes and other unobservable explanatory constructs from early in learning may not be limited to core domains: It may apply to all domains (Simons & Keil, 1995). Toddlers' non-stop "why" questions are not limited to a small set of core domains; they ask about the causes of all kinds of phenomena. Similarly, young children's frequent use of the term "because" extends to all kinds of topics, not just a few special ones. Perhaps in recognition of children's constant search for explanations, when adults explain a new game or concept, they usually begin by describing the basic goals and causality. When they describe tic tac toe, for example, they usually start by saying that the idea of the game is to win and that you win by getting three Xs or three Os in a row. This understanding of causality is useful; returning to tic tac toe, children have been found to possess abstract understanding of the causal structure of the game that allows them to recognize the value of advanced strategies even before they use them (Siegler & Crowley, 1994). Thus, the predisposition to search for causes may not be limited to core domains: It may be a key characteristic of knowledge acquisition in all domains.

This analysis does not rule out the possibility that learning proceeds differently in the areas labeled "core domains" than in other areas. In their first few years of life, children certainly acquire a great deal of knowledge about inanimate objects, people, and plants and animals. This rapid learning suggests that children might use specialized mechanisms to learn about them. Then again, young children also have innumerable opportunities to observe and learn about inanimate objects, people, and plants and animals. Maybe the number of learning opportunities is what distinguishes these domains from others where children acquire knowledge more slowly. As with many developmental questions, resolving this issue will require detailed observations of learning as it occurs, so that knowledge acquisition in different domains can be compared. It also will require well-specified models of the mechanisms that produce learning in different areas.

6. The development of intelligence reflects changes in brain structure and functioning as well as increasingly effective deployment of cognitive resources.

Current Knowledge About the Development of Intelligence

Intelligence develops through the interaction of brain maturation and experience. Changes in the size of the brain alone convey a sense of how much maturation occurs. The brain of an adult weighs four times as much as that of a newborn, with almost half of the increase occurring after age 5 (Lemire et al., 1975). Parts of the cortex grow to 10 times their size at birth. Not all of the changes are from less to more, though. The density of synapses in many parts of the cortex reaches levels during early childhood greater than those in the adult brain. For example, in the frontal lobe, the density of synapses reaches twice the adult level by age 2, and it does not decline to adult levels until age 7 (Huttenlocher, 1979). This high density may allow superior learning of language and motor skills during this early period (Bjorklund & Green, 1992; Fischer, 1987).

The uneven maturation of different parts of the brain leads to a given cognitive function sometimes having different neural bases at different ages. In the first months after birth, subcortical areas, which are relatively mature, play large roles in vision, hearing, and deployment of attention (Bronson, 1974; Johnson, in press; Muir et al., 1979; Posner et al., in press). By 4 to 10 months of age, cortical areas, which develop later, assume major roles in all of these functions. The early subcortical dominance leads to the cognitive system obtaining useful early input; the later cortical role provides more effective processing once the relevant areas are sufficiently mature (Johnson & Morton, 1991).

Brain development involves a mix of anatomical specificity and plasticity. For example, for almost all right-handed people and most left-handed people, language processing occurs predominantly in the middle of the left side of the brain. The specificity is sufficiently great that words whose main function is grammatical, such as *the*, primarily activate different areas of the left hemisphere than content words such as *dog* (Neville, 1995a). However, if the left side of the brain is damaged or surgically removed during the first year of life, language becomes localized on the right side of the brain and develops to near-normal levels (Stiles & Thal, 1993). If the damage occurs after the first year, language also is represented in the right hemisphere, but the later the damage, the less effective that language processing will be (Maratsos & Matheney, 1994).

These changes in the structure and functioning of the brain, however, are only part of the story of the development of intelligence. Another large part involves experience leading to increasingly effective use of available cognitive resources. For example, even in the first few months of life, infants show some ability to deploy processing resources effectively. They orient to the most informative parts of the environment, track moving objects with their eyes, and form expectations of where interesting stimuli will appear (Aslin, 1993; Haith et al., 1993). It should not be surprising, however, that considerable growth occurs beyond these initial bases. With experience, children form representations that are increasingly complete, increasingly flexible, and increasingly robust.

Consider the trend toward representations becoming increasingly complete. When 1-month-olds examine objects, they only scan the contours; 2- and 3-month-olds scan the interiors as well (Salapatek, 1975). When 5-year-olds are presented conservation, class-inclusion, and balance-scale problems, they only represent a single important dimension; by age 8, children represent multiple relevant dimensions on these tasks (e.g., Case, 1992a; Halford, 1993). When 8-year-olds read stories, they focus on causal links within an episode; 14-year-olds also focus on causal links across episodes (van den Broek, 1989).

Examples of the trend toward children forming increasingly flexible representations also come from many areas and age groups. On false belief tasks, 4-year-olds shift more flexibly than 3-year-olds between what they know about a situation and what they know other people know about it (Astington & Gopnik, 1991; Perner, 1991). As they gain experience in arithmetic, elementary school age children choose strategies in ways that fit the demands of problems increasingly precisely (Lemaire & Siegler, 1995). Preadolescents and adolescents adjust their reading and writing strategies in response to instructions and time demands that have no effects on younger children's reading and writing (Kobasigawa et al., 1980; Zbrodoff, 1984).

The third sense in which adaptations to task environments become increasingly successful is robustness. Young children's understanding is often displayed only under ideal circumstances (Sophian, 1984). With age and experience, children come to use their competencies in demanding as well as facilitative situations. Thus, infants and toddlers, like older children, can find hidden objects in space after their own orientation relative to the objects has changed, but unlike the older children, they require nearby landmarks to do so (Acredolo, 1978; Huttenlocher & Newcombe, 1984). Two-year-olds can use a scale model to locate objects in rooms if the model is in a glass case, but not if they handle it, whereas 3-year-olds can use the model appropriately under either condition (DeLoache, 1994). Five-year-olds solve transitive inference, syllogistic reasoning, and analogical reasoning problems if misleading visual cues are not present or if facilitative wording is used. Not until years later, however, do children solve such problems under more challenging circumstances (Brown, et al., 1986; Byrnes & Overton, 1986; Goswami, 1995a).

Future Issues

Increasing understanding of brain maturation and deployment of cognitive resources raise the issue of how these factors interact to create individual differences in intelligence. Two views of individual differences in intelligence have already been discussed. The psychometric approach emphasizes differences along a single dimension—general intelligence. Differences in people's intelligence quotient (IQ) are viewed as reflecting differences in their general intelligence. A second view is Sternberg's (1985) triarchic theory. Here, individual differences in intelligence are viewed as deriving from differences in the efficiency of three classes of information-processing components: performance components, learning components, and metacomponents. Although these two approaches differ in many ways, they share the assumption that there is a common core to intelligence that manifests itself across domains.

One type of evidence for the existence of general intelligence is positive correlations in performance among items on different parts of intelligence tests. For example, children who perform successfully on items measuring vocabulary also tend to do well on items measuring spatial reasoning, arithmetic, and interpretation of proverbs. Another key piece of evidence is that IQ test scores are quite stable over long age periods. A third important piece of evidence is that scores on IQ tests predict grades in school quite accurately. Thus, knowing a first grader's score on an IQ test allows fairly accurate estimates of the child's future grades in high school. A fourth type of evidence is that children with higher IQs tend to learn new material more quickly (Johnson & Mervis, 1994). These types of evidence have led many people to conclude that some children are higher in general intelligence than others and that intelligence is stable over long periods of time.

A number of critics have questioned these interpretations, however (e.g., Ceci, 1990; Gardner, Kornhaber, & Wake, 1996; Resnick, Levine, & Teasley, 1991). The positive correlations among the items on IQ tests may reflect the way in which items are chosen rather than the existence of a general intelligence. New IQ test items are chosen in part for correlating positively with existing IQ test items. Whole areas, such as art and music, in which performance does not tend to correlate with performance on existing IQ test items, are excluded.

With regard to the arguments concerning stability of IQ scores over long periods of time, the relations of early IQ scores to later school performance, and the relation between IQ and learning, one important issue is whether the stability involves intelligence, motivation, or both. Motivation to succeed in intellectual domains may influence performance on IQ test items, performance in school, and learning in laboratory situations. If so, and if such motivation is stable over time, it could lead to the observed relations among IQ test scores, learning of new material, and later intellectual performance.

More general criticisms of IQ tests also have been raised. One criticism focuses on the oversimplification inherent in characterizing individual differences in intelligence as ranks along a single dimension (the IQ score). Children's thinking differs along many dimensions, not just one. The tests also have been criticized for the inegalitarian implications of viewing some children as generally less intelligent than others and for confusing the products of intellectual activity with the processes that produced them. The fact that one child does better than another on an IQ test may reflect different amounts of prior relevant experience, or different skill in taking multiple-choice tests, rather than differences in any inborn quality.

These and other considerations led Gardner (1983; Gardner, Kornhaber, & Wake, 1996) to formulate the *multiple intelligences approach*. Gardner's basic idea is that what is usually called *intelligence* might better be thought of in terms of seven *intelligences*: linguistic, musical, logical-mathematical, spatial, bodily-kinesthetic, self-understanding, and social-understanding. He proposed that each intelligence applies to separate (though overlapping) domains, is based on a distinct symbol system, and includes separate change mechanisms.

Gardner specified several criteria for deciding whether a type of thinking is a separate intelligence. One involves localization within the brain. If a type of thinking is a separate intelligence, then damage to some specific area of the brain should have much more adverse effects on that type of thinking than on others. A second criterion is the existence of idiot savants or prodigies in the area—individuals whose excellence in the domain far exceeds what would be expected from other aspects of their intelligence. Thus, the existence of a Mozart—composing music at age 5, though not being especially smart in other ways—is evidence for a separate musical intelligence. A third criterion is a distinct system for representing the domain, such as mathematical notation, oral language, or choreographers' representations of dance movements. A fourth is similar performance in different aspects of the domain; children good at one skill within a domain should be good at others as well.

Consider evidence that musical intelligence is a distinctive ability. As noted in Chapter 4, musical stimuli elicit activity primarily on the right side of the brain, unlike speech stimuli, which elicit activity primarily on the left side. Consistent with this analysis, Gardner (1983) noted that damage to the right-side temporal and frontal lobes usually interferes with music perception while leaving language perception relatively intact, whereas the reverse occurs when the damage is to the corresponding areas on the left side of the brain. Gardner also cited cases of severely retarded children who had had no formal instruction in music being able to play on the piano pieces that they had just heard for the first time. The same children exhibited only the most primitive learning abilities in other domains, suggesting that they learned music through different mechanisms than they used to learn other skills. Music clearly has its own notational system, and people who are musically gifted often are skilled at numerous instruments and modes of musical expression.

Gardner also saw evidence for the operation of distinct intelligences in the exceptionally strong motivation that some children have to exercise particular talents. When the great mathematician Pascal was a child, his father forbade him to talk about mathematics and severely discouraged him from reading about it. In spite of this harsh reaction, Pascal marked the walls of his room with charcoal, trying to find ways of constructing triangles with equal sides and angles. He invented names for mathematical concepts, since he did not know the conventional words. He developed an axiomatic system for geometry and, in so doing, reinvented much of Euclid. He even dreamed of theorems and axioms—all of this in the face of a hostile environment.

The idea of separate intelligences has problematic aspects. Several of the abilities that Gardner classified as separate intelligences seem to be related. Children's performance on tests of verbal, logical-mathematical, and spatial reasoning consistently correlate positively. This may be due to motivation to achieve in these areas being similar, but it could also be due to general intelligence influencing performance in all of these areas. Further, the existence of prodigies and idiot savants in an area may reflect the isolation of the area from other aspects of life rather than whether the ability is a separate intelligence. There are idiot savants who can quickly calculate what the day of the week will be on January 19, 6593, yet it would be hard to argue that calendar calculation is a separate intelligence.

Despite such problems, the idea of separate intelligences is intriguing. Children's performance often differs dramatically across domains, particularly when we consider types of intelligence not measured by IQ tests, such as artistic, athletic, and social intelligence. Viewing intellect as a set of distinct capacities could yield more precise descriptions of the ways that children's thinking differs than is possible in a single number. Thus, it may lead to a more nuanced understanding of the thinking of individual children.

> 7. Children's thinking develops within a social context. Parents, peers, teachers, and the overall society influence what children think about, as well as how and why they come to think in particular ways.

Current Knowledge of Social Influences on Children's Thinking

People are profoundly social animals. Parents in every society, but not adults of any other species, teach their children the skills, attitudes, and values that they believe are important for succeeding in that culture. Children in every society, but not the young of any other species, constantly point out events of interest to anyone who will listen. These teaching and learning propensities are essential for cognitive development (Tomasello et al., 1993). A child who ignored other people, or who grew up in a world in which other people had no desire to communicate, could not develop normally. Fortunately, such situations almost never occur.

The prototypic example of social influences on children's thinking is parent-child interactions. When talking to infants, parents usually use the high-pitched, sing-song intonations known as motherese, a form of communication particularly effective in attracting and holding infants' attention (Fernald, 1992; Stern et al., 1982). When trying to help toddlers and preschoolers remember past events, parents ask questions in sequences that suggest scripts for organizing the activities into memorable forms (Hudson, 1990). When teaching problem-solving skills to school-age children, parents engage the children in the learning process by encouraging them to identify the goals that need to be met, discuss strategies for meeting them, and execute the strategies (Azmitia, 1996; Ellis & Rogoff, 1986).

Parents are not the only adults who influence the course of cognitive development. When Girl Scout leaders conduct cookie sales, they help children acquire not only skills such as salesmanship and record keeping but also values such as politeness and promptness (Rogoff, 1995). Similarly, when teachers engage in reciprocal instruction, they provide scaffolding, in which they initially give children a great deal of support and gradually transfer responsibility to them (Palincsar & Brown, 1984).

Children are not passive recipients of these efforts; from day 1, they actively shape adults' interactions with them. Much of the reason that adults speak in motherese is that even newborns pay more attention when they do (Cooper & Aslin, 1990). By 4 months of age, infants verbalize more after adults talk to them; this leads to a simple form of turn-taking, which encourages both adults and infants to "talk" to each other (Ginsburg & Kilbourne, 1988). The reciprocal influence extends well beyond language. Through expressions of interest and boredom, tugs on sleeves, dragging of feet, and demands of "Want it," children exercise considerable control over their elders. Older children and adolescents also have a nasty tendency to remember perfectly reasonable points that parents and teachers earlier made to them and turn the points against their originators in totally unreasonable ways. In short, children and adults learn from each other.

Children also influence each other's development. One-year-olds imitate each other's behaviors well after the behaviors occur (Piaget, 1951). Four-year-olds adjust their language so that 2-year-olds can understand them (Shatz & Gelman, 1973). School-age children and adolescents collaborate effectively when they attend to and discuss each other's ideas (Berkowitz & Gibbs, 1985).

In addition to these person-to-person interactions, the social world also influences cognitive development through providing a variety of tools for solving problems. One-year-olds can use rakes to obtain toys (Brown, 1989). Three-year-olds can use scale models to find hidden objects (DeLoache, 1994). Seven- to 11-year-olds can use maps to indicate how an ambulance should go to a destination (Karmiloff-Smith, 1979). And then there are such omnipresent tools as spoken and written language and mathematical notation.

Finally, the culture as a whole communicates attitudes and values that influence cognitive development. East Asian languages make the base-10 system particularly easy to learn and thus enhance learning of early mathematics (Fuson & Kwon, 1992; Miller et al., 1995). Navajo society prizes thinking for oneself; probably not coincidentally, Navajo children both plan longer than Euro-American children before attempting to solve puzzles and allow less-knowledgeable children more time to plan before showing them what to do (Ellis & Schneiders, 1989). German society values organization, German teachers provide more instruction in organizational strategies than do teachers in the U.S., and German children use such organizational strategies more often (Kurtz et al., 1990). In sum, parents, other adults, other children, and society as a whole all shape cognitive development.

Future Issues

A key issue that has only begun to be addressed involves children's motivation for thinking. Why do children think about the things they do?

Part of the motivation to acquire skills and knowledge of one type rather than another comes from what is important in the society in which children grow up. Children's learning about abacuses illustrates this point. Abacuses are commonly used in East Asia to solve arithmetic problems. Although the advent of calculators and computers might seem to have made them obsolete, their popularity among children as well as adults remains great. In several Asian countries, abacus training is a part of every schoolchild's curriculum. Many children take lessons after school to gain extra proficiency. Winners of national abacus competitions become quite famous and are greatly respected.

Figure 10.2 illustrates the type of abacus most commonly used. Its columns represent a base-10 notation, like that used in standard computation. The column at one end (it can be either end) is the ones column, the next column inward is the tens column, the next column inward is the hundreds column, and so on. Each column is divided into the single bead above the divider and the four beads below. The bead above the divider represents a value of 5; each of the four beads below it represents a value of 1.

When the value of a column is zero, the 5 bead is at the top of the abacus and the four 1 beads are at the bottom. To represent numbers greater than 0, the operator moves beads toward the divider in the middle. Thus, if a girl wanted

FIGURE 10.2   *The number 123,456,789 as represented on an abacus. The number 1 is represented on the leftmost bar and the number 9 on the rightmost one (from Stigler, 1984).*

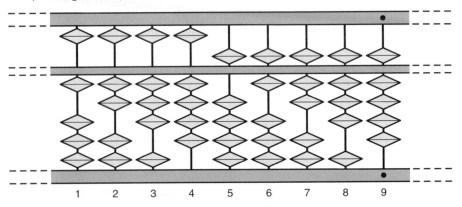

to add 4 + 3, she would first push four 1 beads from below the divider up toward the middle with an upward finger motion (to represent the 4). When her finger reached the top of the column, she would make a downward motion, pushing the 5 bead down toward the middle and returning two of the 1 beads that had been pushed up near the divider to their original position. This would leave the 5 bead and two 1 beads in the middle, indicating the answer, 7.

Learning abacus skills may influence the way in which children represent numbers as well. To examine this influence, Stigler (1984) presented 11-year-old Taiwanese abacus experts with problems ranging from quite simple (adding two numbers, each having two digits) to quite demanding (adding five numbers, each having five digits). The children needed to solve the problems on one occasion in their heads and on another occasion on their abacuses.

It was no surprise that the 11-year-olds' addition on the abacus was quick and accurate. After all, they were practicing abacus arithmetic in school every day and after school at least three days a week. Their mental arithmetic performance was surprising, though. They correctly solved more than 90 percent of problems. Further, they actually added more rapidly in their heads than on the abacus.

What might the children's abacus expertise have to do with their exceptionally skillful mental arithmetic? Following a hypothesis advanced by Hatano, Miyake, and Binks (1977), Stigler argued persuasively that the children formed a mental image of the abacus and imagined carrying out the same finger movements on it that they would on a real abacus. The children's error patterns supported this interpretation. Many errors were off by exactly five in one of the columns. This type of error is easy to make on the abacus, because only the single 5 bead discriminates between 2 and 7, 3 and 8, and so on. Second, the Taiwanese children were three times as likely as American undergraduate and graduate students to err by leaving out a column altogether. If an answer to a problem was 43,296, a common type of error for the Taiwanese was 4,396. This type of error would occur if the Taiwanese children read their answers from a mental image in which a column of the abacus had faded.

Hatano and Osawa (1983) studied Japanese abacus experts and demonstrated another benefit of expertise of this type. Abacus experts possess digit spans far beyond those of nonexperts. Again, they seem to represent the digits in terms of a mental image of an abacus. Asking them to simultaneously remember digits and perform another visual-imagery task lowered their digit span markedly. The same visual-imagery task did not interfere with the digit span of other people, who followed the typical strategy of auditorially rehearsing the digits. Conversely, asking the abacus experts to simultaneously remember digits and perform a task that taxed auditory memory did not lower the abacus experts' digit span. It did reduce the digit span of the other people, who used verbal rehearsal rather than visual imagery to maintain the digits in memory.

Children also think about some topics rather than others because the topics interest them (Renninger, Hidi, & Krapp, 1992). In one study of the effects of interest on memory, 3-year-olds were observed playing at their preschool (Renninger & Wozniak, 1985). The goal was to learn which toy was each child's favorite. Later, the experimenter presented the children with cards that contained a colored dot in the middle and pictures of two objects on the sides, and asked them to identify the dot's color. What the experimenter was really interested in was which object the child looked at after identifying the color. When a picture of their favorite toy was on the card, children consistently looked at it.

Next, the children were shown a set of pictures that they were told depicted the presents another child received at his birthday party. Then the experimenter gave them a pile of pictures, and asked them to separate the pictures of the birthday presents from the others. Children more often remembered whether their favorite toy had been a birthday present than whether other toys had.

These findings suggest a means by which even small initial differences in interest can have large repercussions. Children pay more attention to objects that interest them and remember more about them. Greater attention and memory lead to greater knowledge about these objects, which is likely to be intrinsically rewarding. The greater knowledge also may attract praise, and will facilitate further learning about the subject. Thus, early-developing interests, formed for idiosyncratic reasons, may snowball into significant factors in children's lives.

Motivations to avoid, as well as motivations to approach, influence cognitive development. An extreme example of motivation to avoid is "math phobia." Many people dread having to do anything mathematical. This fear is especially common among women. At a time of increasing need for mathematical and scientific expertise, such fears are important societally as well as personally.

Analyses of why children avoid activities indicate that the aversion often grows out of initial failures. When given a series of unsolvable problems, many people react by giving up (Dweck, 1991). Even after the series of unsolvable problems ends, they often are unable to solve easier problems that ordinarily would cause no special difficulty.

Some children (and adults) defy this pattern, however. They react to failure by maintaining their efforts or trying even harder. Their problem solving remains at least as successful as previously.

What differentiates these resilient children from others? It is not their IQs, which are similar to those of other children (Dweck & Goetz, 1978). Instead, they differ most dramatically in their attributions of failure. When they fail, they believe the reason was that they did not try hard enough, and that greater effort probably would have brought success. Children who become helpless in the face of failure, on the other hand, tend to attribute their failures to a lack of ability. With this attribution, they see greater effort as being of limited value.

Girls and boys differ in their typical reactions to failure. Girls tend to blame their own ability. Boys tend to blame bad luck and other people, such as unfair teachers.

The types of feedback that girls and boys receive in classrooms may contribute to the differing reactions. Girls and boys receive the same amount of negative comments, but the particular comments differ (Dweck & Licht, 1980). Teachers' criticisms of girls' performance focuses consistently on the intellectual quality of the work. Their criticisms of boys' performance sometimes focuses on intellectual quality and sometimes on neatness, conduct, or effort.

Dweck and Licht suggested that these differing criticisms might lead girls to attribute failures to their limited abilities and boys to attribute them to factors that do not reflect negatively on their abilities. Boys can attribute teachers' negative reactions to sloppiness, bad conduct, or lack of effort, since teachers fault them for all of these. Girls, on the other hand, cannot easily blame such factors, since teachers rarely criticize them for these reasons. Adding to the imbalance, both girls and boys view teachers as liking girls better. This adds another attribution for failure that boys can make but girls cannot.

These differing attributions of failure may especially influence reactions to mathematics. In reading, social studies, and most other subjects, children progress steadily toward mastery. From the beginning, children understand some of the information being presented, and the amount they understand steadily increases. Thus, they rarely encounter failure. Math is different. People's first reaction to a new mathematical concept or procedure often is total bewilderment. This may lead those children who react to failure by feeling helpless to give up on mathematics.

Licht and Dweck (1984) tested the interpretation that it was the tendency to feel helpless that led girls to do badly following initial failures. They presented 10-year-old girls and boys with a questionnaire concerning their likely reactions to failures, and classified them as helpless or mastery-oriented depending on their answers. The children were then presented one of two conditions. Some children first received a confusing task, designed to elicit reactions like those that accompany presentation of a new math concept. The other children did not receive this initial task. Then children in both groups were presented a set of eminently solvable problems.

As illustrated in Figure 10.3, mastery-oriented children's problem solving was not adversely affected by prior exposure to the confusing task. However, children who reacted to failure by feeling helpless solved problems much less effectively following exposure to the confusing task. The findings were similar for children classified as helpless regardless of their sex, and were similar for children classified as mastery-oriented regardless of their sex. The difference between the sexes was in the percentage of children who fit each pattern.

In the face of failure, why do some children react with resignation where others respond with renewed effort? One reason may be that the children's goals

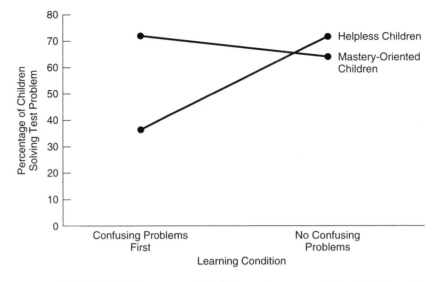

FIGURE 10.3   *Percentage of helpless and mastery-oriented children who solved the test problem in Licht and Dweck (1984) after encountering the impossible problem or before encountering it. Encountering the impossible problem adversely affected the helpless children's subsequent performance, but not that of the mastery-oriented children.*

differ. Dweck and Leggett (1988) suggested that the helpless reaction is based on *performance goals*, in which the child's main objective is to secure favorable judgments of his or her competence from others. Mastery-oriented children, in contrast, were viewed as emphasizing *learning goals*, where the major objective is to increase competence. The difference in goals, in turn, was viewed as reflecting different underlying theories of intelligence. Performance goals reflected a view in which intelligence is basically fixed. Learning goals reflected a view in which intelligence changes with increasing competence. These perspectives result in different attitudes toward having to work hard to solve problems (Elliott & Dweck, 1988). To children with performance goals, the need to work hard reflects negatively on their ability; they view themselves as lacking the intelligence to succeed without great effort. To children with learning goals, working hard reflects positively on their ability, because by working hard, they are increasing their intelligence. The one set of beliefs encourages hard work, the other discourages it.

The view that math phobia among women is attributable to motivational factors received indirect support from a comparison between gifted East Asian and Caucasian children. As a group, East Asians within the United States are unusually strong in mathematics and science achievement. For example, although the population of New York was less than 2 percent East Asian in the 1970s and early 1980s, the group accounted for almost 20 percent of the region's Westinghouse Science Contest winners during that period (Campbell, Connolly, Bologh,

& Primavera, 1984). Of special interest in the present context, the percentage of female winners differed for the ethnic groups. Among Caucasians, 27 percent of the winners were female; among East Asians, 46 percent were.

Why are East Asian girls more likely than their Caucasian counterparts to achieve at a superior level in mathematics and science? Cultural attitudes about mathematics may be critical. All cultures view some knowledge and skills as essential for everyone to acquire, and other knowledge and skills as optional. For example, most people in the U.S. view reading as an essential skill for everyone, and they view playing a musical instrument as valuable if the child is interested or talented but not essential for everyone. Similar views are prevalent in East Asian cultures. However, attitudes toward math differ markedly. In East Asian cultures, extensive knowledge of math beyond arithmetic is viewed as essential for everyone, in the same category as reading. In contrast, most people in the U.S. seem to view math beyond arithmetic as being like music, desirable if the child is interested or talented, but not essential for everyone (Hatano, 1990). The East Asian view that advanced knowledge of math is essential for everyone buttresses the general emphasis in those cultures on effort, rather than ability, as the key to intellectual success (Lee, Stigler, & Stevenson, 1984). The overall message is that mathematics is important for everyone to learn, and that with effort, everyone can learn it. These attitudes seem integral to the outstanding performance of children from East Asian countries on international tests of mathematics achievement, as well as to the high math and science performance of East Asian children of both sexes in the U.S. Thus, cultural beliefs and values about what is important and what is attainable, as well as individual differences in interests and abilities, influence what children think about and how well they think about it.

> 8. Increasing understanding of children's thinking is yielding practical benefits as well as theoretical insights.

Current Practical Contributions of Research on Children's Thinking

Research on children's thinking is already yielding a variety of practical benefits. Most of the benefits with infants and toddlers have involved diagnosis and treatment of perceptual problems. Infants' preference for looking at stripes rather than gray surfaces provides a means to diagnose blindness in infancy (Dobson, 1983). Analyses of the timing of corrective surgery for cross-eyedness has shown that the surgery should be conducted before the age of 4 months, if possible, and definitely before age 3 (Banks, Aslin, & Letson, 1975). Sonar aids have been shown effective for helping blind children walk around their neighborhoods (Humphrey & Humphrey, 1985).

Another large class of practical contributions involves conclusions about how to obtain valid testimony from children in court cases. These studies indicate that children as young as 4 years old provide accurate, if incomplete, testimony when asked specific questions that do not indicate the questionner's preferred answer (Ceci & Bruck, in press). However, the memories of children this young are especially vulnerable to the effects of leading questions, especially ones that are repeated frequently (Clarke-Stewart et al., 1989; Goodman & Clarke-Stewart, 1991). Preschoolers' recollections also are especially susceptible to stereotypes about the people involved in the events (Leichtman & Ceci, 1995). The vulnerability to leading questions extends to events involving their own bodies, including ones with sexual overtones (Bruck et al., 1995; Ornstein et al., 1992; Poole & Lindsay, 1995). Asking children to form visual images of a suspected crime that did not occur can lead to their saying and believing that the imagined events happened (Foley et al., 1994; Parker, 1995). On the other hand, having them draw what they remember about an event, without specifying the particulars, adds to the validity of their verbal reports (Butler et al., 1995). These findings provide useful guidance concerning how the legal system should elicit testimony from children.

A final substantial class of practical contributions concerns schooling. Studies using the cutoff design have demonstrated that a one-year difference in age of entry into school does not influence how much first graders learn about math or reading (Bisanz et al., 1995; Morrison et al., 1996). Studies of mathematical and scientific misconceptions have demonstrated that children often have systematic incorrect views that must be disconfirmed for learning to occur. This has been demonstrated for areas as diverse as understanding of the shape of the earth (Vosniadou & Brewer, 1992), the trajectories of falling objects (Kaiser et al., 1986), the speeds of moving objects (Levin et al., 1990), the magnitude of decimal fractions (Resnick et al., 1989), and the long subtraction algorithm (VanLehn, 1990). Promoting phonological awareness by teaching children to identify the separate phonemes within words has been found to enhance their later success in reading (Bradley & Bryant, 1983; Byrne & Fielding-Barnsley, 1995; Vellutino & Scanlon, 1987), as have teaching phonological recoding skills (Adams, 1990; Lovett et al., 1994) and comprehension monitoring (Palincsar et al., 1993; Rosenshine & Meister, 1994). Writing has been found to benefit from use of word processors (Bangert-Downs, 1993), and problem solving to benefit from mediated instruction, in which applications of computer-programming concepts to other types of problems are emphasized (Klahr & Carver, 1988; Lehrer & Littlefield, 1993). In short, research on children's thinking is contributing to solutions of practical problems as well as to theoretical understanding of cognitive development.

Future Issues

How can understanding of normal development be used to help children whose development is abnormal? A recent study suggests that at least in one case, that of *language-learning impairments*, techniques aimed at improving basic processing capacities can be useful.

Approximately 5 percent of children develop oral language unusually slowly, despite having nonverbal IQ scores in the normal range. Rapid processing of auditory information poses special problems for these children. This hinders their understanding of typical speech, which demands rapid discriminations among sounds. The problem extends beyond speech to interfere with their ability to distinguish among other types of sounds, such as quick sequences of tones (Merzenich, Schreiner, Jenkins, & Wang, 1993; Tallal, Miller, & Fitch, 1993).

Tallal et al. (1996; see also Merzenich et al., 1996) reasoned that exposing children with language-learning impairments to speech that was especially easy to understand, and then gradually moving in the direction of typical speech, might help their comprehension. They used a computer algorithm to produce the modified speech. The algorithm prolonged speech sounds by 50 percent, but in a way that left them sounding quite natural. It also increased the volume of the most rapidly changing elements within speech (the consonant sounds) to call attention to them.

In two experiments, 5- to 10-year-olds whose mean nonverbal IQs were around 100 but whose verbal abilities lagged far behind were exposed to a four-week training procedure (Tallal et al., 1996). The training procedure was intense: three hours per day, five days per week in the lab; one to two hours per day, seven days per week, of homework. During this time, children received extensive exposure to the computer-modified speech in games and stories involving audiocassettes, computer software, and CD-ROMs. The games were designed to encourage children to discriminate rapidly among sounds. Central within this training were two computer games. In one, children heard two brief tones in succession and needed to determine whether their pitches both rose, both fell, rose and then fell, or fell and then rose. In the other, children were presented a target phoneme (e.g., *buh*) and need to identify if it was the first or the second of two similar sounds that were then presented in rapid succession (e.g., *buh-duh*). As children improved at this game, the duration of each consonant was shortened, the time between the two stimuli was shortened, and the amplification of the consonant relative to the vowel was reduced.

This intense training produced marked improvements in the language-impaired children's ability to understand normally paced fluent speech. They became able to better discriminate between similar-sounding words, to obey longer and more grammatically complex auditory commands, and to evaluate the grammaticality of statements (which requires detection of brief sounds such as *ed* and *s* endings). On speech-discrimination and language-comprehension tests, their performance at the end of the study was comparable to that of children without language impairments. The improvements were far greater than those of a control group of language-impaired children who received training of the same general form but with natural, unmodified speech.

This research is new, and further tests are needed before its contribution can be fully evaluated. Nonetheless, it illustrates the types of practical benefits that we can gain from increasing our understanding of children's thinking.

SUMMARY

The development of perception, language, memory, conceptual understanding, problem solving, and academic skills have a great deal in common. Important unities exist in the issues, empirical findings, and mechanisms that produce changes in all aspects of children's thinking.

The largest issues in the study of children's thinking are "What develops?" and "How does development occur?" Four commonly advanced hypotheses about what develops are basic capacities, strategies, metacognition, and content knowledge. Each of these types of changes contributes to cognitive improvements in many areas and at many ages. An important goal for future research is to provide data that directly examines changes while they are occurring. Such data are critical for formulating better theories of cognitive development.

Four change processes that seem to be especially large contributors to cognitive development are automatization, encoding, generalization, and construction of new strategies. Among the greatest future challenges in the study of these change mechanisms is to determine whether there are change mechanisms that only operate in particular periods of life, or whether the same mechanisms produce learning at all ages.

Infants and toddlers are far more competent thinkers than is immediately apparent. Impressive perceptual and conceptual competence are apparent in the first year of life, as are general-purpose learning mechanisms. A key goal is to formulate models that demonstrate how the same child could generate both the impressive competence and the equally impressive incompetence that are so pervasive in early development.

Differences between the thinking of young children and adults no longer seem as huge as they once did. The narrowing has come from both directions. Young children have a variety of previously unsuspected capabilities. Adults think less rationally and scientifically than once was believed. In general, there is no single age at which children acquire a cognitive capability. Rather, understanding gradually increases over a prolonged period.

Existing knowledge about a topic exerts a pervasive influence on the acquisition of new knowledge. It increases the amount that children learn from particular experiences and also influences what they learn, by leading them to focus on the material most likely to prove important. A major current challenge is to specify the role of high-level knowledge structures, such as theories of biology and psychology, and to determine whether they differ in fundamental ways from local knowledge, such as understanding of baseball.

Development of intelligence involves changes both in the structure and functioning of the brain and in the efficiency with which cognitive resources are used. Neural development includes substantial increases in the size of the brain, shifts in the contributions of different parts of the brain to given behaviors, and decreasing plasticity to react to the effects of injuries to one part of the brain by relocating its typical functions to an undamaged area. Improvements in deployment of cognitive resources involve forming representations that are increasingly complete, flexible, and robust. Individual differences in intelligence appear to be much more complex than reflected in the traditional index of intelligence, the IQ. People seem to have multiple intelligences, and may excel in one area while being unexceptional in others.

Children's thinking develops within a social context of parents, peers, teachers, and the society in general. These social agents influence what children think about, the degree to which they acquire various skills, and their attitudes and values. The social world also influences motivation to think about some things rather than others. Cultural beliefs and values, as well as individual talents and interests, influence the content that children think about and the way in which they think about it.

Increasing understanding of children's thinking is yielding practical applications as well as theoretical understanding. The practical applications include diagnoses and treatments of perceptual problems, means for eliciting accurate legal testimony, and instructional techniques for improving learning of academic subjects. Recently developed methods for helping children with language-learning impairments illustrate that increased understanding of child development is yielding practical benefits as well as deeper understanding of children.

RECOMMENDED READINGS

Dweck, C. S., & Leggett, E. L. (1988). A sociocognitive approach to motivation and personality. *Psychological Review, 95,* 256–73. This article presents an intriguing theory of how people's ideas about the nature of intelligence influence their reactions to experience.

Gardner, H., Kornhaber, M. L., & Wake, W. K. (1996). *Intelligence: Multiple perspectives.* A stimulating and well-written survey of alternative approaches to intelligence, with an emphasis on Gardner's multiple intelligences approach.

Kuhn, D. (Ed.) (1995). Development and learning—Reconceptualizing the Intersection. Special issue of *Human Development,* (November–December, 1995), *38,* 293–379. This special issue of the journal *Human Development* presents the perspectives of 10 leading thinkers regarding the relation between learning and development. The differences in

perspectives illustrate strikingly how much this issue is still "up for grabs."

Munakata, Y., McClelland, J. L., Johnson, M. H., and Siegler, R. S. (in press). Rethinking infant knowledge: Toward an adaptive process account of successes and failures in object permanence tasks. *Psychological Review,* Reconciling infants' competence and incompetence is one of the primary needs for advancing understanding of infant cognition. This article illustrates one way in which this goal can be achieved.

Renninger, K. A., Hidi, S., and Krapp, A. (Eds.) *The role of interest in learning and development.* Hillsdale, NJ: Erlbaum. Children's interests influence what they do and how well they do it. This volume includes 17 chapters describing research on how interest influences children's and adults' behavior, as well as a number of interesting ideas about how it exercises its effects.

References

ABBOTT, K., LEE, & FLAVELL, J. H. (1996). *Children's understanding of intention*. Unpublished manuscript, Stanford University, Stanford, CA.

ACREDOLO, C. & HOROBIN, K. (1987). Development of relational reasoning and avoidance of premature closure. *Developmental Psychology, 23*, 13–21.

ACREDOLO, C.A., & O'CONNOR, J. (1991). On the difficulty of detecting cognitive uncertainty. *Human Development, 34*, 204–23.

ACREDOLO, L. P. (1978). The development of spatial orientation in infancy. *Developmental Psychology, 14*, 224–34.

ACREDOLO, L. P., ADAMS, A., & GOODWYN, S. W. (1984). The role of self-produced movement and visual tracking in infant spatial orientation. *Journal of Experimental Child Psychology, 38*, 312–27.

ADAMS, M. J. (1990). *Beginning to read: Thinking and learning about print*. Cambridge, MA: MIT Books.

ADAMS, R. J. (1987). An evaluation of color preference in early infancy. *Infant Behavior and Development, 10*, 143–50.

ADOLPH, K. E. (1995). A psychophysical assessment of toddlers' ability to cope with slopes. *Journal of Experimental Psychology: Human Perception and performance, 21*, 734–50.

AGNOLI, F. (1991). Development of judgmental heuristics: Training counteracts the representativeness heuristic. *Cognitive Development, 6*, 195–217.

AHN, W.-K., KALISH, C. W., MEDIN, D. L., & GELMAN, S. A. (1995). The role of covariation versus mechanism information in causal attribution. *Cognition, 54*, 299–352.

AITKEN, S., & BOWER, T. G. R. (1982). Intersensory substitution in the blind. *Journal of Experimental Child Psychology, 33*, 309–23.

ALIBALI, M. W., & GOLDIN-MEADOW, S. (1993). Gesture-speech mismatch and mechanisms of learning: What the hands reveal about a child's state of mind. *Cognitive Psychology, 25*, 468–573.

AMES, G. F., & MURRAY, F. (1982). When two wrongs make a right: Promoting cognitive change by social conflict. *Developmental Psychology, 18*, 894–897.

AMSEL, E., GOODMAN, G., SAVOIE, D., & CLARK, M. (1996). The development of reasoning about causal and non-causal influences on levers. *Child Development, 67*, 1624–1646.

ANDERSON, M. (1992). *Intelligence and development: A cognitive theory*. Oxford, England: Blackwell.

ANGLIN, J. M. (1977). *Word, object, and conceptual development*. New York: W. W. Norton.

ANGLIN, J. M. (1986). Semantic and conceptual knowledge underlying the child's words. In S. A. Kuczaj & M. D. Barrett (Eds.), *The development of word meaning*. New York: Springer-Verlag.

ANGLIN, J. M. (1993). Vocabulary development: A morphological analysis. *Monographs of the Society for Research in Child Development, 58* (10, Serial No. 238).

ANISFELD, M. (1984). *Language development from birth to three*. Hillsdale, NJ: Erlbaum.

ANTELL, S. E., & KEATING, D. P. (1983). Perception of numerical invariance in neonates. *Child Development, 54*, 695–701.

ARTERBERRY, M. E., CRATON, L. G., & YONAS, A. (1993). Infants' sensitivity to motion-carried information for depth and object properties. In C. E. Granrud (Ed.), *Visual perception and cognition in infancy*. Hillsdale, NJ: Erlbaum.

ASHMEAD, D. H., DAVIS, D. L., WHALEN, T. & ODOM, R. D. (1991). Sound localization and sensitivity to interaural time differences in human infants. *Child Development, 62,* 1211–226.

ASLIN, R. N. (1993). Perception of visual direction in human infants. In C. E. Granrud (Ed.), *Visual perception and cognition in infancy.* Hillsdale, NJ: Erlbaum.

ASLIN, R. N., & DUMAIS, S. T. (1980). Binocular vision in infants: A review and a theoretical framework. In L. P. Lipsitt & H. W. Reese (Eds.), *Advances in child development and behavior.* New York: Academic Press.

ASLIN, R. N., JUSCZYK, P. W. & PISONI, D. P. (in press). Speech and auditory processing during infancy: Constraints on and precursors to language. In W. Damon (Series Ed.) & D. Kuhn & R. S. Siegler (Vol. Eds.), *Handbook of child psychology: Vol. 2: Cognition, perception & language.* (5th ed.). New York: Wiley.

ASTINGTON, J. W. (1991). Intention in the child's theory of mind. In D. Frye & C. Moore (Eds.), *Child's theories of mind.* Hillsdale, NJ: Erlbaum.

ASTINGTON, J. W. (1993). *The child's discovery of the mind.* Cambridge, MA: Harvard University Press.

ASTINGTON, J. W., & GOPNIK, A. (1988). Knowing you've changed your mind: Children's understanding of representational change. In J. W. Astington, P. L. Harris, & D. R. Olson (Eds.), *Developing theories of mind.* New York: Cambridge University Press.

ASTINGTON, J. W. & GOPNIK, A. (1991). Theoretical explanations of children's understanding of the mind. *British Journal of Developmental Psychology, 9,* 7–32.

AU, T. K., & LAFRAMBOISE, D. E. (1990). Acquiring color names via linguistic contrast: The influence of contrasting terms. *Child Development, 61,* 1808–23.

AU, T. K., SIDLE, A. L., & ROLLINS, K. B. (1993). Developing an intuitive understanding of conservation and contamination: Invisible particles as a plausible mechanism. *Developmental Psychology, 29,* 286–99.

AVIS, J., & HARRIS, P. L. (1991). Belief-desire reasoning among Baka children: Evidence for a universal conception of mind. *Child Development, 62,* 460–67.

AZMITIA, M. (1996). Peer interactive minds: Developmental, theoretical, and methodological issues. In P. B. Baltes & U. M. Staudinger (Eds.), *Interactive minds: Life-span perspectives on the social foundations of cognition.* New York: Cambridge University Press.

AZMITIA, M., & MONTGOMERY, R. (1993). Friendship, transactive dialogues, and the development of scientific reasoning. *Social Development, 2,* 202–21.

BACKSCHEIDER, A. G., SHATZ, M., & GELMAN, S. A. (1993). Preschoolers' ability to distinguish living kinds as a function of regrowth. *Child Development, 64,* 1242–57.

BADDELEY, A. (1986). *Working memory.* Oxford: Oxford University Press.

BADDELEY, A. D., & HITCH, G. J. (1974). Working memory. In G. Bower (Ed.), *The psychology of learning and motivation: Advances in research and theory* (Vol. 8). New York: Academic Press.

BADIAN, N. A. (1983). Dyscalculia and nonverbal disorders of learning. In H. R. Myklebust (Ed.), *Progress in learning disabilities, Vol 5.* New York: Stratton.

BAHRICK, H. P., BAHRICK, P. O., & WITTLINGER, R. P. (1975). Fifty years of memory for names and faces: A cross-sectional approach. *Journal of Experimental Psychology, 104,* 54–75.

BAI, D., & BERTENTHAL, B. I. (1992). Locomotor status and the development of spatial search skills. *Child Development, 63* 215–26.

BAILLARGEON, R. (1987). Object permanence in 3½- and 4½-month-old infants. *Developmental Psychology, 23,* 655–64.

BAILLARGEON, R. (1993). The object concept revisited: New directions in the investigation of infants' physical knowledge. In C. E. Granrud (Ed.), *Visual perception and cognition in infancy.* Hillsdale, NJ: Erlbaum.

BAILLARGEON, R. (1994). How do infants learn about the physical world? *Current Directions in Psychological Science, 3,* 133–40.

BAKER, L. (1994). Fostering metacognitive development. In H. Reese (Ed.), *Advances in child development and behavior* (Vol. 25). San Diego: Academic Press.

BAKER, L., & ANDERSON, R. L. (1982). Effects of inconsistent information on text processing: Evidence for comprehension monitoring. *Reading Research Quarterly, 17,* 281–94.

BAKER, L., & BROWN, A. L. (1984). Metacognitive skills and reading. In P. D. Pearson (Ed.),

Handbook of reading research, Part 2. New York: Longman.

BAKER-SENNET, J., Matusov, E., & ROGOFF, B. (1992). Sociocultural processes of creative planning in children's playcrafting. In P. Light & G. Butterworth (Eds.), *Context and cognition: Ways of learning and knowing.* New York: Harvester Wheatsheaf.

BAKER-WARD, L., & ORNSTEIN, P. A. (1988). Age differences in visual-spatial memory performance: Do children really out-perform adults when playing Concentration? *Bulletin of the Psychonomic Society, 26,* 331–2.

BAKER-WARD, L., ORNSTEIN, P. A., & HOLDEN, D. J. (1984). The expression of memorization in early childhood. *Journal of Experimental Child Psychology, 37,* 555–75.

BALDWIN, D. A. (1991). Infants' contribution to the achievement of joint reference. *Child Development, 62,* 875–90.

BALDWIN, D. A. (1992). Clarifying the role of shape in children's taxonomic assumption. *Journal of Experimental Child Psychology, 54,* 392–416.

BALDWIN, D. A. (1993a). Early referential understanding: Infants' ability to recognize referential acts for what they are. *Developmental Psychology, 29,* 832–43.

BALDWIN, D. A. (1993b). Infants' ability to consult the speaker for clues to word meaning. *Journal of Child Language, 20,* 395–418.

BALTES, P. B. (1997). On the incomplete architecture of human development: Selection, optimization, and compensation as foundation of developmental theory. *American Psychologist, 52,* 366–380.

BANGERT-DOWNS, R. L. (1993). The word processor as an instructional tool: A meta-analysis of word processing in writing instruction. *Review of Educational Research, 63,* 69–93.

BANIGAN, R. L., & MERVIS, C. B. (1988). Role of adult input in young children's category evolution: An experimental study. *Journal of Child Language, 15,* 493–504.

BANKS, M. S., ASLIN, R. N., & LETSON, R. D. (1975). Sensitive period for the development of human binocular vision. *Science, 190,* 675–77.

BARON-COHEN, S. (1991). The development of a theory of mind in autism: Deviance and delay? *Psychiatric Clinics of North America, 14,* 33–51.

BARON-COHEN, S. (1994). How to build a baby that can read minds: Cognitive mechanisms in mindreading. *Cahiers de Psychologie Cognitive, 13,* 513–52.

BARON-COHEN, S., LESLIE, A. M., & FRITH, U. (1985). Does the autistic child have a theory of mind? *Cognition, 21,* 37–46.

BARSALOU, L. W. (1985). Ideals, central tendency, and frequency of instantiation as determinants of graded structure in categories. *Journal of Experimental Psychology: Learning, Memory and Cognition, 11,* 629–54.

BARTLETT, E. J. (1982). Learning to revise: Some component processes. In M. Nystrand (Ed.), *What writers know: The language, process, and structure of written discourse.* New York: Academic Press.

BARTSCH, K., & WELLMAN, H. M. (1995). *Children talk about the mind.* New York: Oxford University Press.

BAUER, P. J. (1995). Recalling past events: From infancy to early childhood. *Annals of Child Development, 11,* 25–71.

BAUER, P. J., & MANDLER, J. M. (1989a). Taxonomies and triads: Conceptual organization in 1- to 2-year-olds. *Cognitive Psychology, 21,* 156–84.

BAUER, P. J., & MANDLER, J. M. (1989b). One thing follows another: Effects of temporal structure on 1- to 2-year-olds' recall of events. *Developmental Psychology, 25,* 197–206.

BAUER, P. J., & MANDLER, J. M. (1992). Putting the horse before the cart: The use of temporal order in recall of events by one-year-old children. *Developmental Psychology, 28,* 441–52.

BAYLEY, N. (1969). *Bayley scales of infant development.* New York: Psychological Corporation.

BEAL, C. R. (1988). Children's knowledge about representations of intended meaning. In J. W. Astington, P. L. Harris, & D. R. Olson (Eds.), *Developing theories of mind.* Cambridge: Cambridge University Press.

BEAL, C. R. (1990). The development of text evaluation and revision skills. *Child Development, 61,* 247–58.

BEAL, C. R., & BELGRAD, S. L. (1990). The development of message evaluation skills in young children. *Child Development, 61,* 705–12.

BECK, I. L., & McKEOWN, M. G. (1984). Application of theories of reading to instruction. *American Journal of Education, 93,* 61–81.

BEHL-CHADHA, G., EIMAS, P. D., & QUINN, P. C. (1995, March). *Perceptually driven superordinate categorization by young infants.* Paper presented at the meeting of the Society for Research in Child Development, Indianapolis.

BEILIN, H. (1977). Inducing conservation through training. In G. Steiner (Ed.), *Psychology of the 20th Century,* (Vol. 7, *Piaget and beyond*). Zurich: Kindler.

BEILIN, H. (1983). The new functionalism and Piaget's program. In E. K. Scholnick (Ed.), *New trends in conceptual representation: Challenges to Piaget's theory*? Hillsdale, NJ: Erlbaum.

BELL, M. A., & FOX, N. A. (1992). The relations between frontal brain electrical activity and cognitive development during infancy. *Child Development, 63,* 1142–63.

BENSON, J. B., AREHART, D. M., JENNINGS, T., BOLEY, S., & KEARNS, L. (1989, April). Infant crawling: Expectation, action-plans, and goals. Paper presented at the biennial meeting of the Society for Research in Child Development, Kansas City, MO.

BENTIN, S., HAMMER, R., & CAHAN, S. (1991). The effects of aging and first grade schooling on the development of phonological awareness. *Psychological Science, 2,* 271–74.

BEREITER, C., & SCARDAMALIA, M. (1982). From conversation to composition: The role of instruction in a developmental process. In R. Glaser (Ed.), *Advances in instructional psychology* (Vol. 2). Hillsdale, NJ: Erlbaum.

BEREITER, C., & SCARDAMALIA, M. (1987). *The psychology of written composition.* Hillsdale, NJ: Erlbaum.

BERG, C. A. (1989). Knowledge of strategies for dealing with everyday problems from childhood through adolescence. *Developmental Psychology, 25,* 607–18.

BERKOWITZ, M. W., & GIBBS, J. C. (1985). The process of moral conflict resolution and moral development. In M. W. Berkowitz (Ed.), *New directions for child development: Peer conflict and psychological growth.* San Francisco: Jossey-Bass.

BERLIN, B., & KAYE, P. (1969). *Basic color terms: Their universality and evolution.* Berkeley: University of California Press.

BERMEJO, V. (1996). Cardinality development and counting. *Developmental Psychology, 32,* 263–68.

BERTENTHAL, B. I. (1993). Perception of biomechanical motions by infants: Intrinsic image and knowledge-based constraints. In C. E. Granrud, (Ed.), *Visual perception and cognition in infancy.* Hillsdale, NJ: Erlbaum.

BERTENTHAL, B. I., CAMPOS, J. J., & KERMOIAN, R. (1994). An epigenetic perspective on the development of self-produced locomotion and its consequences. *Current Directions in Psychological Science, 5,* 140–45.

BERTENTHAL, B. I., & CLIFTON, R. K. (In press). Perception and action. To appear in W. Damon (Series Ed.) & D. Kuhn & R. S. Siegler (Vol. Eds.), *Handbook of child psychology: Vol. 2: Cognition, perception & language* (5th ed.). New York: Wiley.

BERTENTHAL, B. I., & Pinto, J. (1993). Complementary processes in the perception and production of human movements. In E. Thelen & L. Smith (Eds.), *Dynamic approaches to development: Vol 2. Applications.* Cambridge, MA: Bradford Books.

BEST, C. T. (1995). Learning to perceive the sound pattern of English. In C. Rovee-Collier & L. Lipsitt (Eds.), *Advances in Infancy Research.* Norwood, NJ: Ablex.

BEST, C. T., HOFFMAN, H., & GLANVILLE, B. B. (1982). Development of infant ear asymmetries for speech and music. *Perception & Psychophysics, 31,* 75–85.

BIALYSTOK, E., & HAKUTA, K. (1994). *In other words: The science and psychology of second-language acquisition.* New York: Basic Books.

BILLMAN, D., & SHATZ, M. (1981). A longitudinal study of the development of communication skills in twins and unrelated peers. Unpublished manuscript, University of Michigan, Ann Arbor.

BISANZ, G. L., VESONDER, G. T., & VOSS, J. F. (1978). Knowledge of one's own responding and the relation of such knowledge to learning. *Journal of Experimental Child Psychology, 25,* 116–28.

BISANZ, J., & LeFEVRE, J. (1990). Mathematical cognition: Strategic processing as interactions among sources of knowledge. In D. P. Bjorklund (Ed.), *Children's strategies: Contemporary views of cognitive development.* Hillsdale, NJ: Erlbaum.

BISANZ, J., MORRISON, F. J., & DUNN, M. (1995). Effects of age and schooling on the acquisition of elementary quantitative skills. *Developmental Psychology, 31*, 221–36.

BJORKLUND, D. F., & COYLE, T. R. (1995). Utilization deficiencies in the development of memory strategies. In F. E. Weinert & W. Schneider (Eds.) *Memory performance and competencies: Issues in growth and development*. Hillsdale, NJ: Erlbaum.

BJORKLUND, D. F., & GREEN, B. L. (1992). The adaptive nature of cognitive immaturity. *American Psychologist, 47*, 46–54.

BJORKLUND, D. F., MUIR-BROADDUS, J. E., & SCHNEIDER, W. (1990). The role of knowledge in the development of strategies. In D. F. Bjorklund (Ed.), *Children's strategies: Contemporary views of cognitive development*. Hillsdale, NJ: Erlbaum.

BLADES, M., & SPENCER, C. (1994). The development of children's ability to use spatial representations. *Advances in child development and behavior*, Vol. 25. New York: Academic Press.

BLAYE, A., LIGHT, P., JOINER, R., & SHELDON, S. (1991). Collaboration as a facilitator of planning and problem solving on a computer based task. *British Journal of Developmental Psychology, 9*, 471–83.

BLEWITT, P. (1983). Dog vs. collie: Vocabulary in speech to young children. *Developmental Psychology, 19*, 601–609.

BLOOM, K. (1990). Selectivity and early infant vocalization. In J. T. Enns (Ed.), *The development of attention: Research and theory*. BV North-Holland: Elsevier Science Publishers.

BLOOM, K., RUSSELL, A., & WASSNBERG, K. (1987). Turn taking affects the quality of infant vocalizations. *Journal of Child Language, 14*, 211–27.

BOHANNON, J. N. II., & STANOWICZ, L. (1988). The issue of negative evidence: Adult responses to children's language errors. *Developmental Psychology, 24*, 684–89.

BOMBA, P. C., & SIQUELAND, E. R. (1983). The nature and structure of infant form categories. *Journal of Experimental Child Psychology, 35*, 294–328.

BONVILLIAN, J. D., ORLANSKY, M. D., & NOVACK, L. L. (1983). Developmental milestones: Sign language acquisition and motor development. *Child Development, 54*, 1435–45.

BORKOWSKI, J. G., CARR, M., & PRESSLEY, M. (1987). Spontaneous strategy use: Perspectives from metacognitive theory. *Intelligence, 11*, 61–75.

BORKOWSKI, J. G., JOHNSTON, N. B., & REID, N. K. (1987). Metacognition, motivation, and the transfer of control processes. In S. J. Ceci (Ed.), *Handbook of cognitive, social, and neuropsychological aspects of learning disabilities, Vol. 2*. Hillsdale, NJ: Erlbaum.

BORNSTEIN, M. H. (1978). Chromatic vision in infancy. In H. W. Reese & L. P. Lipsitt (Eds.), *Advances in child development and behavior: Vol. 12*. New York: Academic Press.

BORNSTEIN, M. H. (1989). Sensitive periods in development: Structural characteristics and causal interpretations. *Psychological Bulletin, 105*, 179–97.

BORNSTEIN, M. H., SIGMAN, M. D. (1986). Continuity in mental development from infancy. *Child Development, 57*, 251–74.

BOSCOLO, P. (1995). The cognitive approach to writing and writing instruction: A contribution to a critical appraisal. *CPC, 14*, 343–366.

BOWER, T. G. R., & WISHART, J. G. (1972). The effects of motor skill on object permanence. *Cognition, 1*, 165–72.

BOWERMAN, M. (1980). The structure and origin of semantic categories in the language-learning child. In M. Foster & S. Brandes (Eds.), *Symbol as sense: New approaches to the analysis of meaning*. New York: Academic Press.

BOWERMAN, M. (1982). Starting to talk worse: Clues to language acquisition from children's late speech errors. In S. Strauss (Ed.), *U-shaped behavioral growth*. New York: Academic Press.

BRADLEY, L., & BRYANT, P. E. (1983). Categorizing sounds and learning to read—A causal connection. *Nature, 301*, 419–21.

BRAINE, M. D. S. (1959). The ontogeny of certain logical operations: Piaget's formulation examined by nonverbal methods. *Psychological Monographs, 73*, (Whole No. 475).

BRAINE, M. D. S. (1971). The acquisition of language in infant and child. In C. E. Reed (Ed.), *The learning of language*. New York: Appleton-Century-Crofts.

BRAINE, M. D. S. (1976). Children's first word combinations. *Monographs of the Society for Research in Child Development, 41* (1).

BRAINERD, C. J. (1978). The stage question in cognitive developmental theory. *Behavioral and Brain Sciences, 1*, 173–213.

BRAINERD, C., & ORNSTEIN, P. A. (1990). Children's memory for witnessed events: The developmental backdrop. In J. Doris (Ed.), *The suggestibility of children's recollections: Implications for eyewitness testimony*. Washington, DC: American Psychological Association.

BRAINERD, C. J., & REYNA, V. F. (1990). Gist is the grist: Fuzzy-trace theory and the new intuitionism. *Developmental Review, 10*, 3–47.

BRAINERD, C. J., & REYNA, V. F. (1995). Learning rate, learning opportunities, and the development of forgetting. *Developmental Psychology, 31*, 251–62.

BRAINERD, C. J., REYNA, V. F., HOWE, M. L., & KINGMA, J. (1990). The development of forgetting and reminiscence. *Monographs of the Society for Research in Child Development, 55*, (Serial No. 222).

BRANSFORD, P. W. (1979). *Human cognition. Learning, understanding and remembering*. Belmont, CA: Wadsworth.

BRENNAN, W. M., AMES, E. W., & MOORE, R. W. (1966). Age differences in infants' attention to patterns of different complexity. *Science, 151*, 354–56.

BRETHERTON, I. (1984). Representing the social world in symbolic play: Reality and fantasy. In I. Bretherton (Ed.), *Symbolic play: The development of social understanding*. New York: Academic Press.

BRETHERTON, I., MCNEW, S., & BEEGHLY-SMITH, M. (1981). Early person knowledge as expressed in gestural and verbal communication: When do infants acquire a "theory of mind"? In M. Lamb & L. Sherrod (Eds.), *Social cognition in infancy*. Hillsdale, NJ: Erlbaum.

BRIARS, D., & SIEGLER, R. S. (1984). A featural analysis of preschoolers' counting knowledge. *Developmental Psychology, 20*, 607–18.

BRONSON, G. W. (1974). The postnatal growth of visual capacity. *Child Development, 45*, 873–90.

BROWN, A. L. (1976). Semantic integration in children's reconstruction of narrative sequences. *Cognitive Psychology, 8*, 247–62.

BROWN, A. L. (1989). Analogical learning and transfer: What develops? In S. Vosniadou & A. Ortony (Eds.), *Similarity and analogical reasoning*. New York: Cambridge University Press.

BROWN, A. L., BRANSFORD, J. D., FERRARA, R. A., & CAMPIONE, J. C. (1983). Learning, remembering, and understanding. In P. H. Mussen (Ed.), *Handbook of child psychology: Cognitive development, Vol. 3*. New York: Wiley.

BROWN, A. L., & CAMPIONE, J. C. (1972). Recognition memory for perceptually similar pictures in preschool children. *Journal of Experimental Psychology, 95*, 55–62.

BROWN, A. L., & DELOACHE, J. S. (1978). Skills, plans, and self-regulation. In R. S. Siegler (Ed.), *Children's thinking: What develops?* Hillsdale, NJ: Erlbaum.

BROWN, A. L., KANE, M. J., & ECHOLS, K. (1986). Young children's mental models determine analogical transfer across problems with a common goal structure. *Cognitive Development, 1*, 103–22.

BROWN, A. L., & SCOTT, M. S. (1971). Recognition memory for pictures in preschool children. *Journal of Experimental Child Psychology, 11*, 401–12.

BROWN, J. S., & Burton, R. B. (1978). Diagnostic models for procedural bugs in basic mathematical skills. *Cognitive Science, 2*, 155–92.

BROWN, R., & MCNEILL, D. (1966). The "tip of the tongue" phenomenon. *Journal of Verbal Learning and Verbal Behavior, 5*, 325–37.

BRUCHKOWSKY, M. (1992). The development of empathic cognition in middle and early childhood. In R. Case (Ed.), *The mind's staircase: Exploring the conceptual underpinnings of children's thought and knowledge*. Hillsdale, NJ: Erlbaum.

BRUCK, M. (1990). Word-recognition skills of adults with childhood diagnoses of dyslexia. *Developmental Psychology, 26*, 439–54.

BRUCK, M. (1992). Persistence of dyslexics' phonological awareness deficits. *Developmental Psychology, 28*, 874–86.

BRUCK, M., CECI, S. J., FRANCOEUR, E., & RENICK, A. (1995). Anatomically detailed dolls do not facilitate preschoolers' reports of a pediatric examination involving genital touching. *Journal of Experimental Psychology: Applied, 1*, 95–109.

BRUNER, J. S., & KENNEY, H. J. (1966). On relational concepts. In J. S. Bruner, R. R. Olver, & P. M. Greenfield (Eds.), *Studies in cognitive growth*. New York: Wiley.

BRUNER, J. S., OLVER, R. R., & GREENFIELD, P. M. (1966). *Studies in cognitive growth*. New York: Wiley.

BULLOCK, M., & GELMAN, R. (1979). Preschool children's assumptions about cause and effect: Temporal ordering. *Child Development, 50*, 89–96.

BUSHNELL, I. W. R., SAI, F., & MULLIN, J. T. (1989). Neonatal recognition of the mother's face. *British Journal of Developmental Psychology, 7*, 3–15.

BUTLER, S., GROSS, J., & HAYNE, H. (1995). The effect of drawing on memory performance in young children. *Developmental Psychology, 31*, 597–608.

BUTTERWORTH, G. (1991). The ontogeny and phylogeny of joint visual attention. In A. Whiten (Ed.), *Natural theories of mind: Evolution, development and simulation of everyday mindreading.* Oxford: Basil Blackwell.

BYRNE, B., & FIELDING-BARNSLEY, R. (1995). Evaluation of a program to teach phonemic awareness to young children: A 2- and 3-year follow-up and a new preschool trial. *Journal of Educational Psychology, 87*, 488–503.

BYRNES, J. P. (1988). Formal operations: A systematic reformulation. *Developmental Review, 8*, 66–87.

BYRNES, J. P., & OVERTON, W. F. (1986). Reasoning about certainty and uncertainty in concrete, causal, and propositional contexts. *Developmental Psychology, 22*, 793–99.

CAMPBELL, J. R., CONNOLLY, C., BOLOGH, R., & PRIMAVERA, L. (1984, April). Impact of ethnicity on math and science among the gifted. Paper presented at the annual meeting of the American Educational Research Association, New Orleans, LA.

CAMPIONE, J. C., & BROWN, A. L. (1984). Learning ability and transfer propensity as sources of individual differences in intelligence. In P. H. Brooks, R. Sperber, & C. McCauley (Eds.), *Learning and cognition in the mentally retarded.* Hillsdale, NJ: Erlbaum.

CAMPOS, J. J., BERTENTHAL, B. I., & KERMOIAN, R. (1992). Early experiences and emotional development: The emergence of fear of heights. *Psychological Science, 3*, 61–64.

CANFIELD, R. L., & HAITH, M. M. (1991). Young infants' visual expectations for symmetric and asymmetric stimulus sequences. *Developmental Psychology, 27*, 198–208.

CANFIELD, R. L., & SMITH, E. G. (1996). Number-based expectations and sequential enumeration by 5-month-old infants. *Developmental Psychology, 32*, 269–79.

CAPODILUPO, A. M. (1992). A neo-structural analysis of children's response to instruction in the sight-reading of musical notation. In R. Case (Ed.) *The mind's staircase: Exploring the conceptual underpinnings of children's thought and knowledge.* Hillsdale, NJ: Erlbaum.

CAREY, S. (1978). The child as word learner. In M. Halle, J. Bresnan, & A. Miller (Eds.), *Linguistic theory and psychological reality* Cambridge, MA: MIT Press.

CAREY, S. (1985). *Conceptual change in childhood.* Cambridge, MA: MIT Press.

CAREY, S., & GELMAN, R. (Eds.) (1991). *The epigenesis of mind: Essays on biology and cognition.* Hillsdale, NJ: Erlbaum.

CARPENTER, T. P., CORBITT, M. K., Kepner, H. S., LINDQUIST, M. M., & REYS, R. E. (1981). Results from the second mathematics assessment of the National Assessment of Educational Progress. Washington, DC: National Council of Teachers of Mathematics.

CARR, M., KURTZ, B. E., SCHNEIDER, W., TURNER, L. A., & BORKOWSKI, J. G. (1989). Strategy acquisition and transfer among American and German children: Environmental influences on metacognitive development. *Developmental Psychology, 25*, 765–71.

CARRAHER, T. N., CARRAHER, D. W., & SCHLIEMANN, A.. D. (1985). Mathematics in the streets and in schools. *British Journal of Developmental Psychology, 3*, 21–29.

CARVER, S. M., & KLAHR, D. (1987). Assessing children's LOGO debugging skills with a formal model. *Journal of Educational Computing Research, 2*, 487–525.

CASE, R. (1978). Intellectual development from birth to adulthood: A neo-Piagetian approach. In R. S. Siegler (Ed.), *Children's thinking: What develops?* Hillsdale, NJ: Erlbaum.

CASE, R. (1985). *Intellectual development: A systematic reinterpretation.* New York: Academic Press.

CASE, R. (1989, April). *A neo-Piagetian analysis of the child's understanding of other people, and the internal conditions which motivate their behavior.* Paper presented at the biennial meeting of the Society for Research in Child Development, Kansas City, MO.

CASE, R. (1992a). *The mind's staircase: Exploring the conceptual underpinnings of children's thought and knowledge.* Hillsdale, NJ: Erlbaum.

CASE, R. (1992b). The role of the frontal lobes in the regulation of cognitive development. *Brain and Cognition, 20,* 51–73.

CASE, R., & Griffin, S. (1990). Child cognitive development: The role of central conceptual structures in the development of scientific and social thought. In C. A. Hauert (Ed.), *Developmental psychology: Cognitive, perceptuomotor and neuropsychological perspectives.* Amsterdam: North Holland.

CASE, R., & Okamoto, Y. (1996). The role of central conceptual structures in the development of children's numerical, literacy, and spatial thought. *Monographs of the Society for Research in Child Development* (Serial No. 246).

CASE, R., Sandieson, R., & Dennis, S. (1987). Two cognitive developmental approaches to the design of remedial instruction. *Cognitive Development, 1,* 293–333.

CASELLI, M. C., BATES, E., CASADIO, P., FENSON, J., FENSON, L., SANDERL, L. & WEIR, J. (1995). Cross-linguistic lexical development. *Cognitive Development, 10,* 159–99.

CASTLES, A., & COLTHEART, M. (1993). Varieties of developmental dyslexia. *Cognition, 47,* 149–80.

CAULEY, K. (1985). The construction of logical knowledge: A study of borrowing in subtraction. Paper presented at the American Educational Research Association, Chicago, IL.

CAVANAUGH, J. C., & PERLMUTTER, M. (1982). Metamemory: A critical examination. *Child Development, 53,* 11–28.

CECI, S. J. (1989). On domain specificity . . . more or less general and specific constraints on cognitive development. *Merrill-Palmer Quarterly, 35,* 131–42.

CECI, S. J. (1990). *On intelligence . . . more or less: A bio-ecological treatise on intellectual development.* Englewood Cliffs, NJ: Prentice Hall.

CECI, S. J., & BRUCK, M. (1993). The suggestibility of the child witness: A historical review and synthesis. *Psychological Bulletin, 113,* 403–39.

CECI, S. J., & BRUCK, M. (in press). Child psychology in practice: Children's testimony. In W. Damon (Series Ed.) & I. Sigel & K. A. Renninger (Vol. Eds.), *Handbook of child psychology, Vol. 4: Clinical psychology in practice.* (5th ed.). New York: Wiley.

CECI, S. J., LOFTUS, E. W., LEICHTMAN, M., & BRUCK, M. (1994). The role of source misattributions in the creation of false beliefs among preschoolers. *International Journal of Clinical and Experimental Hypnosis, 62,* 304–20.

CHALL, J. S. (1979). The great debate: Ten years later, with a modest proposal for reading stages. In L. B. Resnick & P. A. Weaver (Eds.), *Theory and practice of early reading.* Hillsdale, NJ: Erlbaum.

CHANG, F. L., & GREENOUGH, W. T. (1984). Transient and enduring morphological correlates of synaptic activity and efficacy change in the rat hippocampal slice. *Brain Research, 309,* 35–46.

CHANGEUX, J. P. & DEHAENE, S. (1989). Neuronal models of cognitive functions. *Cognition, 33,* 63–109.

CHEN, Z. (1996). Children's analogical problem solving: The effects of superficial, structural and procedural similarity. *Journal of Experimental Child Psychology, 62,* 410–31.

CHEN, Z., CAMPBELL, T., & R. POLLEY (in press). From beyond to within their grasp: Analogical problem solving in 10- and 13-month-olds. *Developmental Psychology.*

CHEN, Z., YANOWITZ, K. L., & DAEHLER, M. W. (1995). Constraints on accessing abstract source information: Instantiation of principles facilitates children's analogical transfer. *Journal of Educational Psychology, 87,* 445–54.

CHI, M. T. H. (1978). Knowledge structures and memory development. In R. S. Siegler (Ed.), *Children's thinking: What develops?* Hillsdale, NJ: Erlbaum.

CHI, M. T. H. (1981). Knowledge development and memory performance. In J. P. Das & N. O'Conner (Eds.), *Intelligence and learning.* New York: Plenum Press.

CHI, M. T. H., & KLAHR, D. (1975). Span and rate of apprehension in children and adults. *Journal of Experimental Child Psychology, 19,* 434–39.

CHOMSKY, N. (1972). *Language and mind* (enlarged edition). New York: Harcourt Brace Jovanovich.

CHUGANI, H. T., & PHELPS, M. E. (1986). Maturational changes in cerebral function in infants determined by [18]FDG positron emission tomography. *Science, 231,* 840–43.

CHUGANI, H. T., PHELPS, M. E., & MAZZIOTTA, J. C. (1987). Positron emission tomography study of human brain functional development. *Annals of Neurology, 22*, 487–97.

CLARK, E. V. (1973). What's in a word? On the child's acquisition of semantics in his first language. In T. E. Moore (Ed.), *Cognitive development and the acquisition of language.* New York: Academic Press.

CLARK, E. V. (1978). Strategies for communication. *Child Development, 49*, 953–59.

CLARK, E. V. (1993). *The lexicon in acquisition.* Cambridge: Cambridge University Press.

CLARK, E. V. (1995). Later lexical development and word formation. In P. Fletcher & B. MacWhinney (Eds.) *The handbook of child language.* Cambridge, MA: Blackwell.

CLARKE-STEWART, A., THOMPSON, W., & LEPORE, S. (1989, May). *Manipulating children's interpretations through interrogation.* Paper presented at the Biennial Meeting of the Society for Research on Child Development, Kansas City, MO.

CLAVADETSCHER, J. E., BROWN, A. M., ANKRUM, C., & TELLER, D. Y. (1988). Spectral sensitivity and chromatic discriminations in 3- and 7-week-old human infants. *Journal of the Optical Society of America, 5*, 2093–105.

CLEMENT, J. (1982). Algebra word problem solutions: Thought processes underlying a common misconception. *Journal for Research in Mathematics Education, 13*, 16–30.

CLIFTON, R. K., MUIR, D. W., ASHMEAD, D. H., & CLARKSON, M. G. (1993). Is visually guided reaching in early infancy a myth? *Child Development, 64*, 1099–110.

COHEN, L. B. (1972). Attention-getting and attention-holding processes of infant visual preference. *Child Development, 43*, 869–79.

COLE, M., SCRIBNER, S. (1974). *Culture and thought.* New York: Wiley.

COLOMBO, J. (1993). *Infant cognition: Predicting childhood intellectual function.* Newbury Park, CA: Sage.

COLOMBO, J. (1995). On the neural mechanisms underlying developmental and individual differences in visual fixation in infancy: Two hypotheses. *Developmental Review, 15*, 97–135.

COLOMBO, J., O'BRIEN, M., MITCHELL, D. W., ROBERTS, K., & HOROWITZ, F. D. (1987). A lower boundary for category formation in preverbal infants. *Journal of Child Language, 14*, 383–85.

COONEY, J. B., SWANSON, H. L., LADD, S. F. (1988). Acquisition of mental multiplication skill: Evidence for the transition between counting and retrieval strategies. *Cognition and Instruction, 5*, 323–45.

COOPER, R. P., & ASLIN, R. N. (1990). Preference for infant-directed speech in the first month after birth. *Child Development, 61*, 1584–95.

CORMAN, H. H., & ESCALONA, S. K. (1969). Stages of sensorimotor development: A replication study. *Merrill-Palmer Quarterly, 15*, 351–61.

CORRIGAN, R. (1975). A scalogram analysis of the development of the use and comprehension of "because" in children. *Child Development, 46*, 195–201.

CORRIGAN, R. (1988). Children's identification of actors and patients in prototypical and non-prototypical sentence types. *Cognitive Development, 3*, 285–97.

CORRIGAN, R., & ODYA-WEIS, C. (1985). The comprehension of semantic relations by two-year-olds: An exploratory study. *Journal of Child Language, 12*, 47–59.

COURAGE, M. L., & ADAMS, R. J. (1990). Visual acuity assessment from birth to three years using the acuity card procedures: Cross-sectional and longitudinal samples. *Optometry and Vision Science, 67*, 713–18.

COYLE, T. R., & BJORKLUND, D. F. (1996). The development of strategic memory: A modified microgenetic assessment of utilization deficiencies. *Cognitive Development, 11*, 295–314.

COYLE, T. R., & BJORKLUND, D. F. (1997). Age differences in, and consequences of, multiple- and variable-strategy use on a multitrial sort-recall task. *Developmental Psychology, 33*, 372–380.

CRISAFI, M. A., & BROWN, A. L. (1986). Analogical transfer in very young children: Combining two separately learned solutions to reach a goal. *Child Development, 57*, 953–68.

CROWLEY, K., & SIEGLER, R. S. (1993). Flexible strategy use in young children's tic-tac-toe. *Cognitive Science, 17*, 531–61.

CULTICE, J. C., SOMERVILLE, S. C., & WELLMAN, H. M. (1983). Preschooler's memory monitoring: Feeling-of-knowing judgements. *Child Development, 54*, 1480–86.

CZIKO, G. (1995). *Without miracles: Universal selection theory and the second Darwinian revolution.* Cambridge, MA: MIT Press.

DAMASIO, A. R., & DAMASIO, H. (1992). Brain and language. *Scientific American, 117*, 89–95.

DAMASIO, H., & DAMASIO, A. R. (1989). *Lesion analysis in neuropsychology*. London: Oxford University Press.

DAMON, W., & PHELPS, E. (1988). Strategic uses of peer learning in children's education. In T. Berndt & G. Ladd (Eds.), *Children's peer relations*. New York: Wiley.

DANEMAN, M., & TARDIF, T. (1987). Working memory and reading skills reexamined. In M. Coltheart (Ed.), *Attention and performance XII: The psychology of reading*. Hillsdale, NJ: Erlbaum.

DANNEMILLER, J. L, & STEPHENS, B. R. (1988). A critical test of infant pattern preference models. *Child Development, 59*, 210–16.

DARWIN, C. (1877). A biographical sketch of an infant. *Mind, 2*, 286–94.

DASEN, P. R. (1973). Piagetian research in central Australia. In G. E. Kearney, P. R. deLacy, & G. R. Davidson (Eds.), *The psychology of aboriginal Australians*. Sydney: Wiley.

DAVIDSON, J. E. (1986). The role of insight in giftedness. In R. J. Sternberg & J. E. Davidson (Eds.), *Conceptions of giftedness*. New York: Cambridge University Press.

DAVIDSON, J. E., & STERNBERG, R. J. (1984). The role of insight in intellectual giftedness. *Gifted Child Quarterly, 28*, 58–64.

DEAN, A. L., CHABAUD, S., & BRIDGES, E. (1981). Classes, collections, and distinctive features: Alternative strategies for solving inclusion problems. *Cognitive Psychology, 13*, 84–112.

DECASPER, A. J., & FIFER, W. P. (1980). Of human bonding: Newborns prefer their mothers' voices. *Science, 208*, 1174–76.

DECASPER, A. J., & SPENCE, M. J. (1986). Prenatal maternal speech influences newborns' perception of speech sounds. *Infant Behavior and Development, 9*, 133–50.

DELOACHE, J. S. (1987). Rapid change in the symbolic functioning of young children. *Science, 238*, 1556–57.

DELOACHE, J. S. (1989). The development of representation in young children. In H. W. Reese (Ed.), *Advances in child development and behavior, Vol. 22*. New York: Academic Press.

DELOACHE, J. S. (1991). Symbolic functioning in very young children: Understanding of pictures and models. *Child Development, 62*, 736–52.

DELOACHE, J. S. (1995). Early understanding and use of symbols: The model model. *Current Directions in Psychological Science, 4*, 109–113.

DELOACHE, J. S., & BURNS, N. M. (1994). Early understanding of the representational function of pictures. *Cognition, 52*, 83–110.

DELOACHE, J. S., CASSIDY, D. J., & BROWN, A. L. (1985). Precursors of mnemonic strategies in very young children's memory. *Child Development, 56*, 125–37.

DELOACHE, J. S., MILLER, K. F., & PIERROUTSAKS, S. L. (in press). Reasoning and problem solving. In W. Damon (Series Ed.) & D. Kuhn & R. S. Siegler (Vol. Eds.), *Handbook of child psychology: Vol. 2: Cognition, perception & language*. (5th ed.). New York: Wiley.

DELOACHE, J. S., RISSMAN, M. D., & COHEN, L. B. (1978). An investigation of the attention-getting process in infants. *Infant Behavior and Development, 1*, 11–25.

DEMARIE-DREBLOW, D., & MILLER, P. H. (1988). The development of children's strategies for selective attention: Evidence for a transitional period. *Child Development, 59*, 1504–13.

DEMETRIOU, A., EFKLIDES, A., & PLATSIDOU, M. (1993). The architecture and dynamics of developing mind. *Monographs of the Society for Research in Child Development, 58* (5–6), Serial No. 234.

DEMPSTER, F. N. (1981). Memory span: Sources of individual and developmental differences. *Psychological Bulletin, 89*, 63–100.

DEMPSTER, F. N. (1992). The rise and fall of the inhibitory mechanism: Toward a unified theory of cognitive development and aging. *Developmental Review, 12*, 45–75.

DEMPSTER, F. N. (1993). Resistance to interference: Developmental changes in a basic processing mechanism. In R. Pasnak & M. L. Howe (Eds.), *Emerging themes in cognitive development*, (Vol. 1). New York: Springer.

DENNIS, S. (1992). Stage and structure in the development of children's spatial representations. In R. Case (Ed.), *The mind's staircase: Exploring the conceptual underpinnings of children's thought and knowledge*. Hillsdale, NJ: Erlbaum.

DEVALOIS, R. L., & DEVALOIS, K. K. (1975). Neural coding of color. In E. C. Carterette &

M. P. Friedman (Eds.), *Handbook of perception, Vol. 5.* New York: Academic Press.

DE VILLIERS, J. (1995). Empty categories and complex sentences: The case of wh-questions. In P. Fletcher & B. MacWhinney (Eds.), *The handbook of child language.* Cambridge, MA: Blackwell.

DEVRIES, R. (1969). Constancy of generic identify in the years three to six. *Monographs for the Society for Research in Child Development, 34* (Whole No. 127).

DIAMOND, A. (1985). Development of the ability to use recall to guide action as indicated by infants' performance on AB. *Child Development, 56,* 868–83.

DIAMOND, A. (1990). Rate of maturation of the hippocampus and the developmental progression of children's performance on the delayed non-matching to sample and visual paired comparison tasks. *Annals of the New York Academy of Sciences,* 608.

DIAMOND, A. (1991). Neuropsychological insights into the meaning of object concept development. In S. Carey & R. Gelman (Eds.), *The epigenesis of mind: Essays on biology and cognition.* Hillsdale, NJ: Erlbaum.

DIMANT, R. J., & BEARISON, D. J. (1991). Development of formal reasoning during successive peer interactions. *Developmental Psychology, 27,* 277–84.

DOBSON, V. (1983). Clinical applications of preferential looking measures of visual acuity. *Behavioral Brain Research, 10,* 25–38.

DODWELL, P. E. (1960). Children's understanding of number and related concepts. *Canadian Journal of Psychology, 14,* 191–205.

DROMI, E., (1986). The one-word period as a stage in language development: Quantitative and qualitative accounts. In I. Levin (Ed.), *Stage and structure: Reopening the debate.* Norwood, NJ: Ablex.

DRUMMEY, A. B., & NEWCOMBE, N. (1995). Remembering versus knowing the past: Children's explicit and implicit memories for pictures. *Journal of Experimental Child Psychology, 59,* 549–65.

DUFRENSE, A., & KOBASIGAWA, A. (1989). Children's spontaneous allocation of study time: Differential and sufficient aspects. *Journal of Experimental Child Psychology, 47,* 274–96.

DUNBAR, K., & KLAHR, D. (1988). Developmental differences in scientific discovery strategies. In D. Klahr & K. Kotovsky (Eds.), *Complex information processing: The impact of Herbert A. Simon.* Proceedings of the 21st Carnegie-Mellon Symposium on Cognition. Hillsdale, NJ: Erlbaum.

DUNN, J. (1988). *The beginnings of social understanding.* Oxford: Basil Blackwell.

DUNN, J., BROWN, J., SLOMKOWSKI, C., TESLA, C., & YOUNGBLADE, L. (1991). Young children's understanding of other people's feelings and beliefs: Individual differences and their antecedents. *Child Development, 62,* 1352–66.

DURKIN, D. (1966). *Children who read early.* New York: Teachers College Press.

DURKIN, D. (1974/75). A six-year study of children who learned to read in school at the age of four. *Reading Research Quarterly, 10,* 9–61.

DWECK, C. S. (1991). Self-theories and goals: Their role in motivation, personality and development. In R. Dienstbier (Ed.), *Nebraska symposium on motivation, 1990* (Vol. 36). Lincoln: University of Nebraska Press.

DWECK, C. S., & GOETZ, T. E. (1978). Attributions and learned helplessness. In J. H. Harvey, W. Ickes, & R. F. Kidd (Eds.), *New directions in attribution research, Vol. 2.* Hillsdale, NJ: Erlbaum.

DWECK, C. S., & LEGGETT, E. L. (1988). A social-cognitive approach to motivation and personality. *Psychological Review, 95,* 256–73.

DWECK, C. S., & LICHT, B. G. (1980). Learned helplessness and intellectual achievement. In J. Garber & M. E. P. Seligman (Eds.), *Human helplessness: Theory and application.* New York: Academic Press.

EATON, W. O., & RITCHOT, K. F. M. (1995). Physical maturation and information processing speed in middle childhood. *Developmental Psychology, 31,* 967–72.

ECHOLS, C. (1993). *Attentional predispositions and linguistic sensitivity in the acquisition of object words.* Paper presented at the Biennial Meeting of the Society for Research in Child Development, New Orleans, LA.

EDELMAN, G. (1987). *Neural Darwinism: The theory of neuronal group selection.* New York: Basic Books.

EFKLIDES, A., DEMETRIOU, A., & METALLIDOU, Y. (1994). The structure and development of propositional reasoning ability: Cognitive and metacognitive aspects. In A. Demetriou

& A. Efklides (Eds.), *Intelligence, mind, and reasoning: Structure and development*. Amsterdam: North-Holland.

EIMAS, P. D., & QUINN, P. C. (1994). Studies on the formation of perceptually based basic-level categories in young infants. *Child Development, 65*, 903–17.

EIMAS, P. D., SIQUELAND, E. R., JUSCZYK, P., & VIGORITO, J. (1971). Speech perception in infants. *Science, 171*, 303–6.

ELKIND, D. (1961a). Children's discovery of the conservation of mass, weight, and volume: Piaget replications Study II. *Journal of Genetic Psychology, 98*, 219–27.

ELKIND, D. (1961b). The development of quantitative thinking: A systematic replication of Piaget's studies. *Journal of Genetic Psychology, 98*, 37–46.

ELLIOTT, E. S., & DWECK, C. S. (1988). Goals: An approach to motivation and achievement. *Journal of Personality and Social Psychology, 54*, 5–12.

ELLIOTT-FAUST, D. J. (1984). The "delusion of comprehension" phenomenon in young children: An instructional approach to promoting listening comprehension monitoring capabilities in grade three children. Unpublished doctoral dissertation. London, Ontario: University of Western Ontario, Department of Psychology.

ELLIS, S., DOWDY, B., GRAHAM, P., & JONES, R. (1992, April). *Parental support of planning skills in the context of homework and family demands*. Paper presented at the meeting of the American Education Research Association, San Francisco, CA.

ELLIS, S., KLAHR, D., & SIEGLER, R. S. (1993, March). *Effects of feedback and collaboration on changes in children's use of mathematical rules*. Paper presented at the meeting of the Society for Research in Child Development, New Orleans, LA.

ELLIS, S., & ROGOFF, B. (1986). Problem solving in children's management of instruction. In E. Mueller & C. Cooper (Eds.), *Process and outcome in peer relationships*. Orlando, FL: Academic Press.

ELLIS, S., & SCHNEIDERS, B. (1989, April). *Collaboration on children's instruction: A Navajo versus Anglo comparison*. Paper presented at the biennial meeting of the Society for Research in Child Development, Kansas City, MO.

ELLIS, S., & SIEGLER, R. S. (1994). Development of problem solving. In R. J. Sternberg (Ed.), *Handbook of perception and cognition: Vol. 12. Thinking and problem solving*. New York: Academic Press.

ELLIS, S., & SIEGLER, R. S. (1997). Planning and strategy choice, or why don't children plan when they should? In S. L. Friedman & E. K. Scholnick (Eds.), *Why, how, and when do we plan: The developmental psychology of planning*. Hillsdale, NJ: Erlbaum.

ELMAN, J. L. (1993). Learning and development in neural networks: The importance of starting small. *Cognition, 48*, 71–99.

ELY, R., & GLEASON, J. B. (1995). Socialization across contexts. In P. Fletcher & B. MacWhinney (Eds.) *The handbook of child language*. Cambridge, MA: Blackwell.

FABRICIUS, W. V. (1988). The development of forward search planning in preschoolers. *Child Development, 59*, 1473–88.

FABRICIUS, W. V., & HAGEN, J. W. (1984). Use of causal attributions about recall performance to assess metamemory and predict strategic memory behavior in young children. *Developmental Psychology, 20*, 975–87.

FABRICIUS, W. V., & WELLMAN, H. M. (1993). Two roads diverged: Young children's ability to judge distance. *Child Development, 64*, 399–414.

FAGAN, J. F. (1984). The intelligent infant: Theoretical implications. *Intelligence, 8*, 1–9.

FAGAN, J. F., & SINGER, L. T. (1983). Infant recognition memory as a measure of intelligence. In L. P. Lipsitt (Ed.), *Advances in infancy research, Vol. 2*. Norwood, NJ: Ablex.

FANTZ, R. L., FAGAN, J. F., & MIRANDA, S. B. (1975). Early perceptual development as shown by visual discrimination, selectivity, and memory with varying stimulus and population parameters. In L. B. Cohen & P. Salapatek (Eds.), *Infant perception: From sensation to cognition*. New York: Academic Press.

FARAH, M. J., MONHEIT, M. A., & WALLACE, M. A. (1991). Unconscious perception of "extinguished" visual stimuli: Reassessing the evidence. *Neuropsychologia, 29*, 949–58.

FARRAR, M. J., & GOODMAN, G. S. (1992). Developmental changes in event memory. *Child Development, 63*, 173–87.

FAY, A. L., & KLAHR, D. (1996). Knowing about guessing and guessing about knowing:

Preschoolers' understanding of indeterminacy. *Child Development, 67,* 689–716.

FELDMAN, D. H. (1995). Learning and development in nonuniversal theory. *Human Development, 38,* 315–21.

FERNALD, A. (1992). Meaningful melodies in mothers' speech. In H. Papousek, U. Jurgens, & M. Papousek (Eds.), *Origins and development of nonverbal vocal communication: Evolutionary, comparative, and methodological aspects.* Cambridge: Cambridge University Press.

FERNALD, A., TAESCHNER, T., DUNN, J., PAPOUSEK, M., BOYSSON-BARDIES, B. D., & FUKUI, I. (1989). A cross-language study of prosodic modifications in mothers' and fathers' speech to preverbal infants. *Journal of Child Language, 16,* 477–501.

FERRETTI, R. P., & BUTTERFIELD, E. D. (1986). Are children's rule-assessment classifications invariant across instances of problem types? *Child Development, 57,* 1419–28.

FERRETTI, R. P., BUTTERFIELD, E. C., CAHN, A., & KERKMAN, D. (1985). The classification of children's knowledge: Development on the balance-scale and inclined-plane tasks. *Journal of Experimental Child Psychology, 39,* 131–60.

FIELD, D. (1987). A review of preschool conservation training: An analysis of analyses. *Developmental Review, 7,* 210–51.

FIRTH, I. (1972). Components of reading disability. Unpublished doctoral dissertation, University of New South Wales, Kensington, N. S. W., Australia.

FISCHER, K. W. (1980). A theory of cognitive development: The control and construction of hierarchies of skills, *Psychological Review, 87,* 477–531.

FISCHER, K. W. (1987). Relations between brain and cognitive development. *Child Development, 58,* 623–32.

FISCHER, K. W., & BIDELL, T. (1991). Constraining nativist inferences about cognitive capacities. In S. Carey & R. Gelman (Eds.), *The epigenesis of mind: Essays on biology and cognition.* Hillsdale, NJ: Erlbaum.

FISCHER, K. W., & FARRAR, M. J. (1988). Generalizations about generalization: How a theory of skill development explains both generality and specificity. In A. Demetriou (Ed.), *The neo-Piagetian theories of cognitive development: Toward an integration.* Amsterdam: North-Holland (Elsevier).

FISCHER, K. W., & GRANNOTT, N. (1995). Beyond one-dimensional change: Parallel, concurrent, socially distributed processes in learning and development. *Human Development, 38,* 302–14.

FISHER, C., HALL, D. G., RAKOWITZ, S., & GLEITMAN, L. R. (1994). When is it better to receive than to give: Structural and conceptual cues to verb meaning. *Lingua, 92,* 333–75.

FITZGERALD, J. (1987). Research on revision in writing. *Review of Educational Research, 57,* 481–506.

FIVUSH, R., & HAMMOND, N. R. (1990). Autobiographical memory across the preschool years: Toward reconceptualizing childhood amnesia. In R. Fivush & J. A. Hudson (Eds.), *Knowing and remembering in young children.* Cambridge: Cambridge University Press.

FLAVELL, J. H. (1970). Developmental studies of mediated memory. In H. W. Reese & L. P. Lipsitt (Eds.), *Advances in child development and behavior, Vol. 5.* New York: Academic Press.

FLAVELL, J. H. (1971). Stage-related properties of cognitive development. *Cognitive Psychology, 2,* 421–53.

FLAVELL, J. H. (1982). On cognitive development. *Child Development, 53,* 1–10.

FLAVELL, J. H. (1984). Discussion. In R. J. Sternberg (Ed.), *Mechanisms of cognitive development.* New York: W. H. Freeman.

FLAVELL, J. H., BEACH, D. R., & CHINSKY, J. M. (1966). Spontaneous verbal rehearsal in a memory task as a function of age. *Child Development, 37,* 283–99.

FLAVELL, J. H., FLAVELL, E. R., & GREEN, F. L. (1983). Development of the appearance-reality distinction. *Cognitive Psychology, 15,* 95–120.

FLAVELL, J. H. FLAVELL, E. R., GREEN, F. L., & KORFMACHER, J. E. (1990). Do young children think of television images as pictures or as real objects? *Journal of Broadcasting and Electronic Media, 34,* 399–417.

FLAVELL, J. H., FRIEDRICHS, A. G., & HOYT, J. D. (1970). Developmental changes in memorization processes. *Cognitive Psychology, 1,* 324–40.

FLAVELL, J. H., GREEN, F. L., & FLAVELL, E. R. (1986). Development of knowledge about the appearance-reality distinction. *Monographs of* the *Society for Research in Child Development, 51* (Serial No. 212).

FLAVELL, J., & MILLER, P. (in press). Social cognition. In W. Damon (Series Ed.) & D. Kuhn & R. S. Siegler (Vol. Eds.), *Handbook of child psychology: Vol. 2: Cognition, perception & language* (5th ed.). New York: Wiley.

FLAVELL, J. H., MILLER, P. H., & MILLER, S. A. (Eds.). (1993). *Cognitive development* (3rd ed.). Englewood Cliffs, NJ: Prentice Hall.

FLAVELL, J. H., ZHANG, X.-D., ZOU, H., DONG, Q., & QI, S. (1983). A comparison between the development of the appearance-reality distinction in the People's Republic of China and the United States. *Cognitive Psychology, 15,* 459–66.

FODOR, J. (1992). A theory of the child's theory of mind. *Cognition, 44,* 283–96.

FOLEY, M. A., HARRIS, J., & HERMAN, S. (1994). Developmental comparisons of the ability to discriminate between memories for symbolic play enactments. *Developmental Psychology, 30,* 206–17.

FORMAN, E. A., & MACPHAIL, J. (1993). Vygotskian perspective in children's collaborative problem solving activity. In E. A. Forman, N. Minick, & C. A. Stone (Eds.), *Contexts for learning: Sociocultural dynamics in children's development.* Oxford: Oxford University Press.

FRAIBERG, S. (1977). *Insights from the blind: Comparative studies of blind and sighted infants.* New York: Basic Books.

FRAISSE, P. (1982). The adaptation of the child to time. In W. J. Friedman (Ed.), *The developmental psychology of time.* New York: Academic Press.

FREUD, S. (1953). Three essays on the theory of sexuality. In J. Strachey (Ed.), *The standard edition of the complete psychological works of Sigmund Freud, Vol. 7.* London: Hogarth.

FRIEDMAN, S. L., SCHOLNICK, E. K., & COCKING. R. R. (1987). Reflections on reflections: What planning is and how it develops. In S. L. Friedman, E. K. Scholnick, & R. R. Cocking (Eds.), *Blueprints for thinking: The role of planning in cognitive development.* New York: Cambridge.

FRIEDMAN, W. J. (1990). *About time: Inventing the fourth dimension.* Cambridge, MA: MIT Press.

FRIEDMAN, W. J. (1991). The development of children's memory for the time of past events. *Child Development, 62,* 139–55.

FRIEDMAN, W. J. (1995). Arrows of time in infancy: The representation of temporal invariances. Unpublished manuscript, Oberlin College.

FRIEDMAN, W. J., GARDNER, A. G., & ZUBIN, N. R. E. (1995). Children's comparisons of the recency of two events from the past year. *Child Development, 66,* 970–83.

FRITH, U. (1989). *Autism: Explaining the enigma.* Oxford: Basil Blackwell.

FRY, A. F., & HALE, S. (1996). Processing speed, working memory, and fluid intelligence: Evidence for a developmental cascade. *Psychological Science, 7,* 237–241.

FRYE, D., BRAISBY, N., LOWE, J., MAROUDAS, C., & NICHOLLS, J. (1989). Young children's understanding of counting and cardinality. *Child Development, 60,* 1158–71.

FRYE, D., ZELAZO, P. D., BROOKS, P. J., & SAMUELS, M. C. (1996). Inference and action in early causal reasoning. *Developmental Psychology, 32,* 120–31.

FUSON, K. C. (1988). *Children's counting and concepts of number.* New York: Springer-Verlag.

FUSON, K. C., & KWON, Y. (1992). Korean children's understanding of multidigit addition and subtraction. *Child Development, 63,* 491–506.

GALOTTI, K. M., & KOMATSU, L. K. (1989). Correlates of syllogistic reasoning skills in middle childhood and early adolescence. *Journal of Youth and Adolescence, 18,* 85–96.

GALOTTI, K. M., KOMATSU, L. K., & VOELZ, S. (1997). Children's differential performance on deductive and inductive syllogisms. *Developmental Psychology, 33,* 70–78.

GARDNER, H. (1983). *Frames of mind: The theory of multiple intelligences.* New York: Basic Books.

GARDNER, H. (1991). Assessment in context. In B. R. Gifford & M. C. O'Connor (Eds.), *Changing assessments: Alternative views of aptitude, achievement, and instruction.* Boston: Kluwer.

GARDNER, H., KORNHABER, M. L., & WAKE, W. K. (1996). *Intelligence: Multiple perspectives.* Fort Worth, TX: Harcourt Brace College Publishers.

GARDNER, W., & ROGOFF, B. (1990). Children's deliberateness of planning according to task circumstances. *Developmental Psychology, 26,* 480–87.

GARNER, R., & REIS, R. (1981). Monitoring and resolving comprehension obstacles: An investigation of spontaneous text lookbacks among upper-grade good and poor comprehenders. *Reading Research Quarterly, 16,* 569–82.

GAUVAIN, M. (1995). Thinking in niches: Socio-cultural influences on cognitive development. *Human Development, 38,* 25–45.

GAUVAIN, M., & ROGOFF, B. (1989). Collaborative problem solving and children's planning skills. *Developmental Psychology, 25,* 139–51.

GEARY, D. C. (1990). A componential analysis of an early learning deficit in mathematics. *Journal of Experimental Child Psychology, 49,* 363–83.

GEARY, D. C. (1994). *Children's mathematical development: Research and practical implications.* Washington, DC: American Psychological Association.

GEARY, D. C. (1996). The problem-size effect in mental addition: Developmental and cross-national trends. *Mathematical Cognition, 2,* 63–93.

GEARY, D. C., BOW-THOMAS, C. C., & YAO, Y. (1992). Counting knowledge and skill in cognitive addition: A comparison of normal and mathematically disabled children. *Journal of Experimental Child Psychology, 54,* 372–91.

GEARY, D. C., & BROWN, S. C. (1991). Cognitive addition: Strategy choice and speed-of-processing differences in gifted, normal, and mathematically disabled children. *Developmental Psychology, 27,* 398–406.

GEARY, D,. C., FAN, L., & BOW-THOMAS, C. C. (1992). Numerical cognition: Loci of ability differences comparing children from China and the United States. *Psychological Science, 3,* 180–85.

GEARY, D. C., FAN, L., & BOW-THOMAS, C., & SIEGLER, R. S. (1993). Even before formal instruction, Chinese children outperform American children in mental addition. *Cognitive Development 8,* 517–29.

GELLATLY, A. R. H. (1987). The acquisition of a concept of logical necessity. *Human Development, 30,* 32–47.

GELMAN, R. (1982). Accessing one-to-one correspondence: Still another paper about conservation. *British Journal of Psychology, 73,* 209–20.

GELMAN, R. (1990). First principles organize attention to and learning about relevant data; Number and the animate-inanimate distinction. *Cognitive Science, 14,* 79–106.

GELMAN, R., & GALLISTEL, C. R. (1978). *The child's understanding of number.* Cambridge, MA: Harvard University Press.

GELMAN, R., MECK, E., & MERKINS, S. (1986). Young children's numerical competence. *Cognitive Development, 1,* 1–29.

GELMAN, R., & WILLIAMS, E. (in press). Constraints on thinking and learning. In W. Damon (Series Ed.) & D. Kuhn & R. S. Siegler (Vol. Eds.), *Handbook of child psychology: Vol. 2: Cognition, perception & language.* (5th ed.). New York: Wiley.

GELMAN, S. A., & COLEY, J. D. (1990). The importance of knowing a dodo is a bird: Categories and inferences in 2½-year-old children. *Developmental Psychology, 26,* 796–804.

GELMAN, S. A., COLEY, J. D., & GOTTFRIED, G.. M. (1994). Essentialist beliefs in children: The acquisition of concepts and theories. In L. A. Hirschfeld & S. A. Gelman (Eds.), *Mapping the mind: Domain specificity in cognition and culture.* New York: Cambridge University Press.

GELMAN, S. A., & KREMER, K. E. (1991). Understanding natural cause: Children's explanations of how objects and their properties originate. *Child Development, 62,* 396–414.

GELMAN, S. A., & TAYLOR, M. (1984). How two-year-old children interpret proper and common names for unfamiliar objects. *Child Development, 55,* 1535–40.

GELMAN, S. A., & WELLMAN, H. M. (1991). Insides and essences: Early understandings of the non-obvious. *Cognition, 38,* 213–44.

GENTNER, D. (1988). Metaphor as structure mapping: The relational shift. *Child Development, 59,* 47–59.

GENTNER, D. (1989). The mechanisms of analogical transfer. In S. Vosniadou & A. Ortony (Eds.), *Similarity and analogical reasoning.* London: Cambridge University Press.

GENTNER, D., RATTERMAN, M. J., MARKMAN, A., & KOTOVSKY, L. (1995). Two forces in the development of relational similarity. In T. J. Simon & G. S. Halford (Eds.), *Developing cognitive competence: New approaches to process modeling.* Hillsdale, NJ: Erlbaum.

GENTNER, D., & STEVENS, A. (Eds.). (1983). *Mental models.* Hillsdale, NJ: Erlbaum.

GENTNER, D., & TOUPIN, C. (1986). Systematicity and similarity in the development of analogy. *Cognitive Science, 10,* 277–300.

GHOLSON, B., EMYARD, L. A., MORGAN, D., & KAMHI, A. G. (1987). Problem solving, recall, and isomorphic transfer among third grade and sixth grade children. *Journal of Experimental Child Psychology, 43,* 227–43.

GIBSON, E. J. (1994). Has psychology a future? *Psychological Science, 5,* 76–92.

GIBSON, J. J. (1966). *The senses considered as perceptual systems.* Boston, MA: Houghton Mifflin.

GIBSON, J. J. (1979). *The ecological approach to visual perception.* Boston: Houghton-Mifflin.

GINSBURG, A. (1978). *Visual information processing based on spatial filters constrained by biological data.* Unpublished doctoral dissertation. University of Cambridge, Cambridge, England.

GINSBURG, G. P., & KILBOURNE, B. K. (1988). Emergence of vocal alternation in mother-infant interchanges. *Journal of Child Language, 15,* 221–35.

GINSBURG, H. P. (1989). *Children's arithmetic: How they learn it and how you teach it* (2nd ed.). Austin, TX: Pro Ed.

GLACHAN, M., & LIGHT, P. (1982). Peer interaction and learning: Can two wrongs make a right? In G. Butterworth & P. Light (Eds.), *Social cognition: Studies of the development of understanding.* Chicago: University of Chicago Press.

GLENBERG, A. M., & EPSTEIN, W. (1987). Inexpert calibration of comprehension. *Memory & Cognition, 15,* 84–93.

GOLDFIELD, B., & REZNICK, J. S. (1990). Early lexical acquisition: Rate, content, and the vocabulary spurt. *Journal of Child Language, 17,* 171–83.

GOLDIN-MEADOW, S.. ALIBALI, M. W., & CHURCH, R. B. (1993). Transitions in concept acquisition: Using the hand to read the mind. *Psychological Review, 100,* 279–97.

GOLDIN-MEADOW, S., & MORFORD, M. (1985). Gesture in early child language: Studies of deaf and hearing children. *Merrill-Palmer Quarterly, 31,* 145–76.

GOLDMAN, S. R., PELLEGRINO, J. W., & MERTZ, D. L. (1988). Extended practice of basic addition facts: Strategy changes in learning disabled students. *Cognition and Instruction, 5,* 223–65.

GOLDMAN-RAKIC, P. S. (1987). Development of cortical circuitry and cognitive function. *Child Development, 58,* 601–22.

GOLEMAN, D. (1993, April 6). Studying the secrets of childhood memory. *The New York Times,* pp. C1, C11.

GOLINKOFF, R. M., HIRSH-PASEK, K., LAVALLEE, A., & BADUINI, C. (1985). What's in a word? The young child's predisposition to use lexical contrast. Paper presented at the Boston University Conference on Child Language, Boston, MA.

GOLINKOFF, R. M., HIRSH-PASEK, K., MERVIS, C. B., FRAWLEY, W. B., & PARILLO, M. (1995). Lexical principles can be extended to the acquisition of verbs. In M. Tomasello & W. E. Merriman (Eds.), *Beyond names for things: Young children's acquisition of verbs.* Hillsdale, NJ: Erlbaum.

GOLINKOFF, R. M., SHUFF-BAILEY, M., OLGUIN, R., & RUAN, W. (1995). Young children extend novel words at the basic level: Evidence for the principle of categorical scope. *Developmental Psychology, 31,* 494–507.

GOODALE, M. A., & MILNER, A. D. (1992). Separate visual pathways for perception and action. *Trends in Neuroscience, 15,* 20–25.

GOODMAN, G. S., & CLARKE-STEWART, A. (1991). Suggestibility in children's testimony: Implications for child sexual abuse investigations. In J. L. Doris (Ed.), *The suggestibility of children's recollections.* Washington, DC: American Psychological Association.

GOODMAN, G. S., HIRSCHMAN, J. E., HEPPS, D., & RUDY, L. (1991). Children's memory for stressful events. *Merrill Palmer Quarterly, 37,* 109–58.

GOODNOW, J. J. (1962). A test of milieu differences with some of Piaget's tasks. *Psychological Monographs, 76* (Whole No. 555).

GOPNIK, A., & ASTINGTON, J. W. (1988). Children's understanding of representational change and its relation to the understanding of false belief and the appearance-reality distinction. *Child Development, 59,* 26–37.

GOPNIK, A., & MELTZOFF, A. (1994). Minds, bodies, and persons. In S. Parker, M. Boccia, & R. Mitchell (Eds.), *Self-awareness in animals and humans.* New York: Cambridge University Press.

GOPNIK, A., & SLAUGHTER, V. (1991). Young children's understanding of changes in their mental states. *Child Development, 62,* 98–110.

GORDON, B., ORNSTEIN, P. A., CLUBB, P. A., NIDA, R. E., & BAKER-WARD, L. E. (1991, October). *Visiting the pediatrician: Long term retention and forgetting.* Paper presented at the annual meeting of the Psychonomic Society, San Francisco, CA.

GOSWAMI, U. (1992). *Analogical reasoning in children.* Hillsdale, NJ: Erlbaum.

GOSWAMI, U. (1995a). Analogical reasoning and cognitive development. In H. Reese (Ed.), *Advances in Child Development and Behavior, Vol. 26.* New York: Academic Press.

GOSWAMI, U. (1995b). Transitive relational mappings in 3- and 4-year-olds: The analogy of Goldilocks and the Three Bears. *Child Development, 66,* 877–92.

GOSWAMI, U., & BROWN, A. (1990). Higher-order structure and relational reasoning: Contrasting analogical and thematic relations. *Cognition, 36,* 207–26.

GOUGH, P. B., & HILLINGER, M. L. (1980). Learning to read: An unnatural act. *Bulletin of the Orton Society, 30,* 171–96.

GRAHAM, F. K., LEAVITT, L. A., STROCK, B. D., & BROWN, J. W. (1978). Precocious cardiac orienting in human anencephalic infants. *Science, 199,* 322–24.

GRAHAM, T., & PERRY, M. (1993). Indexing transitional knowledge. *Developmental Psychology, 29,* 779–88.

GRANNOTT, N. (1993). Patterns of interaction in the co-construction of knowledge: Separate minds, joint efforts, and weird creatures. In R. Wozniak & K. W. Fischer (Eds), *Development in context: Acting and thinking in specific environments,* (Vol. 2). Hillsdale, NJ: Erlbaum.

GRAY, E. (1993). *Unequal justice: The prosecution of child sexual abuse.* New York: MacMillan.

GREENBERG, D. J., & O'DONNELL, W. J. (1972). Infancy and the optimal level of stimulation. *Child Development, 43,* 639–45.

GREENFIELD, P. M., & SMITH, J. (1976). *The structure of communication in early language development.* New York: Academic Press.

GREENOUGH, W. T., BLACK, J. E., & WALLACE, C. S. (1987). Experience and brain development. *Child Development, 58,* 539–59.

GRIFFIN, S. A., CASE, R. & SANDIESON, R. (1992). Synchrony and asynchrony in the acquisition of children's everyday mathematical knowledge. In R. Case (Ed.), *The mind's staircase: Exploring the conceptual underpinnings of children's thought and knowledge.* Hillsdale, NJ: Erlbaum.

GRUBER, H. E., & VONECHE, J. J. (1977). *The essential Piaget: An interpretive reference and guide.* New York: Basic Books.

GUTTENTAG, R. E. (1984). The mental effort requirement of cumulative rehearsal: A developmental study. *Journal of Experimental Child Psychology, 37,* 92–106.

GUTTENTAG, R. E. (1985). Memory and aging: Implications for theories of memory development during childhood. *Developmental Review, 5,* 56–82.

HAGEN, J. W., HARGROVE, S., & ROSS, W. (1973). Prompting and rehearsal in short-term memory. *Child Development, 44,* 201–4.

HAITH, M. M. (1980). *Rules that infants look by.* Hillsdale, NJ: Erlbaum.

HAITH, M. M. (1993). Future-oriented processes in infancy: The case of visual expectations. In C. E. Granrud, (Ed.) *Visual perception and cognition in infancy.* Hillsdale, NJ: Erlbaum.

HAITH, M. M. (1994). Visual expectations as the first step toward the development of future-oriented processes. In M. M. Haith, J. B. Benson, R. J. Roberts, Jr., & B. F. Pennington (Eds.), *The development of future-oriented processes.* Chicago: University of Chicago Press.

HAITH, M., & BENSON, J. (in press). Infant cognition. In W. Damon (Series Ed.) & D. Kuhn & R. S. Siegler (Vol. Eds.), *Handbook of child psychology: Vol. 2: Cognition, perception & language.* (5th ed.). New York: Wiley.

HAITH, M. M., BERGMAN, T., & MOORE, M. J. (1977). Eye contact and face scanning in early infancy. *Science, 198,* 853–55.

HAITH, M. M., HAZAN, C., & GOODMAN, G. S. (1988). Expectation and anticipation of dynamic visual events by 3.5-month-old babies. *Child Development, 59,* 467–79.

HAITH, M. M., WENTWORTH, N., & CANFIELD, R. L., (1993). The formation of expectations in early infancy. In C. Rovee-Collier & L. P. Lipsitt (Eds.), *Advances in infancy research.* Norwood, NJ: Ablex.

HALE, S. (1990). A global developmental trend in cognitive processing speed. *Child Development, 61,* 653–63.

HALE, S., BRONIK, M. D., & FRY. A. F. (1997). Verbal and spatial working memory in school-age children: Developmental differences in susceptibility to interference. *Developmental Psychology.*

HALFORD, G. S. (1982). *The development of thought*. Hillsdale, NJ: Erlbaum.

HALFORD, G. S. (1984). Can young children integrate premises in transitivity and serial order tasks? *Cognitive Psychology, 16*, 65–93.

HALFORD, G. S. (1993). *Children's understanding: The development of mental models*. Hillsdale, NJ: Erlbaum.

HALFORD, G. S. (1995). Learning processes in cognitive development: A reassessment with some unexpected implications. *Child Development, 38*, 295–301.

HARNISHFEGER, K. K., & BJORKLUND, D. F. (1994). Individual differences in inhibition: Implications for children's cognitive development. *Learning and Individual Differences, 6*, 331–55.

HARRIS, J. F., DURSO, F. T., MERGLER N. L., & JONES, S. K. (1990). Knowledge base influences on judgments of frequency of occurrence. *Cognitive Development, 5*, 223–33.

HARRIS, P. L. (1991). The work of the imagination. In A. Whiten (Ed.), *Natural theories of mind*. Oxford, England: Basil Blackwell.

HARRIS, P. L. (1992). From simulation to folk psychology: The case for development. *Mind & Language, 7*, 120–44.

HASHER, L., & ZACKS, R. T. (1984). Automatic processing of fundamental information: The case of frequency of occurrence. *American Psychologist, 39*, 1372–88.

HATANO, G. (1989, April). Personal communication.

HATANO, G. (1990). Commentary: Toward the cultural psychology of mathematical cognition. *Monographs of the Society for Research in Child Development, 55* (1-2, Serial No. 221), 108–15.

HATANO, G., MIYAKE, Y., & BINKS, M. G. (1977). Performance of expert abacus calculators. *Cognition, 5*, 57–71.

HATANO, G., & OSAWA, K. (1983). Digit memory of grand experts in abacus-derived mental calculation. *Cognition, 15*, 95–110.

HATANO, G., SIEGLER, R. S., RICHARDS, D. D., INAGAKI, K., STAVY, R., & WAX, N. (1993). The development of biological knowledge: A multi-national study. *Cognitive Development, 8*, 47–62.

HEIBECK, T. H., & MARKMAN, E. M. (1987). Word learning in children: An examination of fast mapping. *Child Development, 58*, 1021–1034.

HELD, R. (1993). What can rates of development tell us about underlying mechanisms? In C. E. Granrud (Ed.) *Visual perception and cognition in infancy*. Hillsdale, NJ: Erlbaum.

HERMER, L. & SPELKE, E. S. (1994). A geometric process for spatial reorientation in young children. *Nature, 370*, 57–59.

HICKLING, A. K., & GELMAN, S. A. (1995). How does your garden grow? Early conceptualization of seeds and their place in the plant growth cycle. *Child Development, 66*, 856–76.

HIRSH-PASEK, K., & GOLINKOFF, R. M. (1996). *The origins of grammar: Evidence from early language comprehension*. Cambridge, MA: MIT Press.

HITCH, G. J., & McAULEY, E. (1991). Working memory in children with specific arithmetical learning disabilities. *British Journal of Psychology, 82*, 375–86.

HITCH, G. J., & TOWSE, J. N. (1995). Working memory: What develops? In F. E. Weinert & W. Schneider (Eds.), *Memory performance and competencies: Issues in growth and development*. Mahwah, NJ: Erlbaum.

HOLYOAK, K. J., & THAGARD, P. (1995) *Mental leaps*. Cambridge, MA: MIT Press.

HOVING, K. L., SPENCER, T., ROBB, K. Y., & SCHULTE, D. (1978). Developmental changes in visual information processing. In P. A. Ornstein (Ed.), *Memory development in children*. Hillsdale, NJ: Erlbaum.

HUDSON, J. A. (1990). The emergence of autobiographical memory in mother-child conversation. In R. Fivush & J. A. Hudson (Eds.), *Knowing and remembering in young children*. Cambridge: Cambridge University Press.

HUEY, E. B. (1908). *The psychology and pedagogy of reading*. Cambridge, MA: MIT Press.

HUME, D. (1911). *A treatise on human nature*. (Original work published 1739–1740). London: Dent.

HUMPHREY, G. K., DODWELL, P. C., MUIR, D. W., & HUMPHREY, D. E. (1988). Can blind infants and children use sonar sensory aids? *Canadian Journal of Psychology, 42*, 94–119.

HUMPHREY, G. K., & HUMPHREY, D. E. (1985). The use of binaural sensory aids by blind infants and children: Theoretical and applied issues. In F. Morrison, & C. Lord (Eds.), *Applied developmental psychology, Vol 2*. New York: Academic Press.

HUNT, J. M. (1961). *Intelligence and experience.* New York: Ronald Press.

HUTTENLOCHER, J., & BURKE, D. (1976). Why does memory span increase with age? *Cognitive Psychology, 8,* 1–31.

HUTTENLOCHER, J., JORDAN, N. C., & LEVINE, S. C. (1994) A mental model for early arithmetic. *Journal of Experimental Psychology: General, 123,* 284–96.

HUTTENLOCHER, J., & NEWCOMBE, N. (1984). The child's representation of information about location. In C. Sophian (Ed.), *Origins of cognitive skills.* Hillsdale, NJ: Erlbaum.

HUTTENLOCHER, J., NEWCOMBE, N., & SANDBERG, E. H. (1994) The coding of spatial location in young children. *Cognitive Psychology, 27,* 115–47.

HUTTENLOCHER, P. R. (1979). Synaptic density in human frontal cortex-developmental changes and effects of aging. *Brain Research, 163,* 195–205.

HUTTENLOCHER, P. R. (1990). Morphometric study of human cerebral cortex development. *Neuropsychologia, 28,* 517–27.

HUTTENLOCHER, P. R. (1994). Synaptogenesis, synapse elimination, and neural plasticity in human cerebral cortex. In C. A. Nelson (Ed.) *Threats to optimal development. The Minnesota symposia on child psychology, Vol. 27.* Hillsdale, NJ: Erlbaum.

ILG, F., & AMES, L. B. (1951). Developmental trends in arithmetic. *Journal of Genetic Psychology, 79,* 3–28.

IMAI, M., & GENTNER, D. (1993). *Linguistic relativity vs. universal ontology: Cross-linguistic studies of the object/substance distinction.* Paper presented at the Chicago Linguistic Society, Chicago, IL.

IMAI, M., GENTNER, D., & UCHIDA, N. (1994). Children's theories of word meaning: The role of shape similarity in early acquisition. *Cognitive Develpment, 9,* 45–75.

INAGAKI, K., & HATANO, G. (1987). Young children's spontaneous personification as analogy. *Child Development, 58,* 1013–20.

INHELDER, B., & PIAGET, J. (1958). *The growth of logical thinking from childhood to adolescence.* New York: Basic Books.

INHELDER, B., & PIAGET, J. (1964). *The early growth of logic in the child: Classification and seriation.* London: Routledge.

INHELDER, B., SINCLAIR, H., & BOVET, M. (1974). *Learning and the development of cognition.* Cambridge, MA: Harvard University Press.

JACKSON, N. E. (1988). Precocious reading ability: What does it mean? *Gifted Child Quarterly, 32,* 200–4.

JACKSON, H. E., DONALDSON, G. W., & CLELAND, L. N. (1988). The structure of precocious reading ability. *Journal of Educational Psychology, 80,* 234–43.

JACKSON, N. E., DONALDSON, G. W., & MILLS, J. R. (1993). Components of reading skill in postkindergarten precocious readers and level-matched second graders. *Journal of Reading Behavior, 25,* 181–208.

JAKOBSON, R. (1981). Why "mama" and "papa"? *Selected writings: Phonological studies.* Paris: Mouton.

JAMES, W. (1890). *The principles of psychology.* New York: Holt, Reinhart, and Winston.

JENKINS, J. M., & ASTINGTON, J. W. (1996). Cognitive factors and family structure associated with theory of mind development in young children. *Developmental Psychology, 32,* 70–8.

JENSEN, A. R. (1993). Test validity: *g* versus "tacit knowledge." *Current Perspectives in Psychological Science, 2,* 9–10.

JOHNSON, C. N. (1988). Theory of mind and the structure of conscious experience. In J. W. Astington, P. L. Harris, & D. R. Olson (Eds.), *Developing theories of mind.* New York: Cambridge University Press.

JOHNSON, J. S., LEWIS, L. B., & HOGAN, J. C. (1995, March). *A production limitation in the syllable length of one child's early vocabulary: A longitudinal case study.* Paper presented at the Biennial Meeting of the Society for Research in Child Development, Indianapolis, IN.

JOHNSON, J. S., & NEWPORT, E. L. (1989). Critical period effects in second language learning: The influence of maturational state on the acquisition of English as a second language. *Cognitive Psychology, 21,* 60–99.

JOHNSON, K. E., & MERVIS, C. B. (1994). Microgenetic analysis of first steps in children's acquisition of expertise on shorebirds. *Developmental Psychology, 30,* 418–35.

JOHNSON, M. H. (in press). The neural basis of cognitive development. In W. Damon (Series Ed.) & D. Kuhn & R. S. Siegler (Vol. Eds.), *Handbook of child psychology: Vol. 2: Cognition, perception & language.* (5th ed.). New York: Wiley.

JOHNSON, M. H., & GILMORE, R. O. (1996). Developmental cognitive neuroscience: A biological perspective on cognitive change. In R. Gelman & T. Au (Eds.), *Handbook of perception and cognition: Perceptual and cognitive development,* (Vol. 13). Orlando, FL: Academic Press.

JOHNSON, M. H., & KARMILOFF-SMITH, A. (1992). Can neural selectionism be applied to cognitive development and its disorders? *New Ideas in Psychology, 10,* 35–46.

JOHNSON, M. H., & MORTON, J. (1991). *Biology and cognitive development: The case of face recognition.* Oxford, U.K.: Blackwell.

JOHNSON, M. H., POSNER, M. I., & ROTHBART, M. K. (1994). Facilitation of saccades toward a covertly attended location in early infancy. *Psychological Science, 5,* 90–93.

JOHNSON-LAIRD, P. N. (1983). *Mental models: Towards a cognitive science of language, inference, and consciousness.* Cambridge: Cambridge University Press.

JOHNSON-LAIRD, P. N., OAKHILL, J. V., & BULL, D. (1986). Children's syllogistic reasoning. *Quarterly Journal of Experimental Psychology, 38A,* 35–58.

JORDAN, N. C., LEVINE, S. C., & HUTTENLOCHER, J. (1995). Calculation abilities in young children with different patterns of cognitive functioning. *Journal of Learning Disabilities, 28,* 53–64.

JORM, A. F., & SHARE, D. L. (1983). Phonological recoding and reading acquisition. *Applied Psycholinguistics, 4,* 103–47.

JUEL, C. (1988). Learning to read and write: A longitudinal study of fifty-four children from first through fourth grade. *Journal of Educational Psychology, 80,* 437–47.

JUSCZYK, P. W., CUTLER, A., & REDANZ, N. (1993). Preference for the predominant stress patterns of English words. *Child Development, 64,* 675–87.

JUSCZYK, P. W., LUCE, P. A., & CHARLES LUCE, J. (1994). Infants' sensitivity to phonotactic patterns in the native language. *Journal of Memory and Language, 33,* 630–45.

JUSCZYK, P. W., ROSENER, B. S., CUTTING, J. W., FOARD, F., & SMITH, L. B. (1977). Categorical perception of non-speech sounds by two-month-old infants. *Perception & Psychophysics, 21,* 50–54.

KAIL, R. (1984). *The development of memory in children, 2nd edition.* New York: Freeman.

KAIL, R. (1986). Sources of age differences in speed of processing. *Child Development, 57,* 969–987.

KAIL, R. (1988). Developmental functions for speeds of cognitive processes. *Journal of Experimental Child Psychology, 45,* 339–64.

KAIL, R. (1991). Developmental changes in speed of processing during childhood and adolescence. *Psychological Bulletin, 109,* 490–501.

KAISER, M. K., MCCLOSKEY, M., & PROFFITT, D. R. (1986). Development of intuitive theories of motion: Curvilinear motion in the absence of external forces. *Developmental Psychology, 22,* 67–71.

KALISH, C. W. (1996). Preschoolers' understanding of germs as invisible mechanism. *Cognitive Development, 11,* 83–106.

KARMILOFF-SMITH, A. (1979). Micro- and macrodevelopmental changes in language acquisition and other representational systems. *Cognitive Science, 3,* 91–118.

KARMILOFF-SMITH, A. (1986). Stage/structure versus phase/process in modelling linguistic and cognitive development. In I. Levin (Ed.), *Stage and structure: Reopening the debate.* Norwood, NJ: Ablex.

KARMILOFF-SMITH, A. (1992). *Beyond modularity: A developmental perspective on cognitive science.* Cambridge, MA: MIT.

KATZ, H., & BEILIN, H. (1976). A test of Bryant's claims concerning the young child's understanding of quantitative invariance. *Child Development, 47,* 877–80.

KAY, D. A., & ANGLIN, J. (1982). Overextension and underextension in the child's expressive and receptive speech. *Journal of Child Language, 9,* 83–98.

KEARINS, J. M. (1981). Visual spatial memory in Australian aboriginal children of desert regions. *Cognitive Psychology, 13,* 434–60.

KEE, D. W., & HOWELL, S. (1988, April). Mental effort and memory development. Paper presented at the meeting of the American Educational Research Association, New Orleans, LA.

KEENAN, E. O. (1977). Making it last: Uses of repetition in children's discourse. In S. Ervin-Tripp. & C. Mitchell-Kernan (Eds.), *Child discourse.* New York: Academic Press.

KEIL, F. C. (1989). *Concepts, kinds, and cognitive development.* Cambridge, MA: The MIT Press.

KEIL, F. C. (1994). The birth and nurturance of concepts by domains: The origins of concepts of living things. In L. A. Hirschfeld & S. A. Gelman (Eds.), *Mapping the mind: Domain specificity in cognition and culture.* New York: Cambridge University Press.

KEIL, F. C., & BATTERMAN, N. (1984). A characteristic-to-defining shift in the development of word meaning. *Journal of Verbal Learning and Verbal Behavior, 23,* 221–36.

KELLMAN, P. J. (1988). Theories of perception and research in perceptual development. In A. Yonas (Ed.), *The Minnesota symposium on child psychology, Vol. 20: Perceptual development in infancy.* Hillsdale, NJ: Erlbaum.

KELLMAN, P. J., & SHORT, K. R. (1987). The development of three-dimensional form perception. *Journal of Experimental Psychology: Human Perception & Performance, 13,* 545–57.

KELLMAN, P. J., & SPELKE, E. S. (1983). Perception of partially occluded objects in infancy. *Cognitive Psychology, 15,* 483–524.

KENT, R. D., & MIULO, G. (1995). Phonetic abilities in the first year of life. In P. Fletcher & B. MacWhinney (Eds.), *The handbook of child language.* Cambridge, MA: Blackwell.

KERKMAN, D. D., & SIEGLER, R. S. (1993). Individual differences and adaptive flexibility in lower-income children's strategy choices. *Learning and Individual Differences, 5,* 113–36.

KERMOIAN, R., & CAMPOS, J. J. (1988). Locomotor experience: A facilitator of spatial cognitive development. *Child Development, 59,* 908–17.

KLAHR, D. (1978). Goal formation, planning, and learning by preschool problem solvers or: "My socks are in the dryer." In R. S. Siegler (Ed.), *Children's thinking: What develops?* Hillsdale, NJ: Erlbaum.

KLAHR, D. (1982). Nonmonotone assessment of monotone development: An information processing analysis. In S. Strauss (Ed.), *U-shaped behavioral growth.* New York: Academic Press.

KLAHR, D. (1985). Solving problems with ambiguous subgoal ordering: Preschoolers' performance. *Child Development, 56,* 940–52.

KLAHR, D. (1989). Information-processing approaches. In R. Vasta (Ed.), *Annals of child development, Vol. 6: Six theories of child develop-ment: Revised formulations and current issues.* Greenwich, CT: JAI Press.

KLAHR, D. (1992). Information processing approaches to cognitive development. In M. H. Bornstein & M. E. Lamb (Eds.), *Developmental psychology: An advanced textbook* (3rd ed.). Hillsdale, NJ: Erlbaum.

KLAHR, D., & CARVER, S. M. (1988). Cognitive objectives in a LOGO debugging curriculum: Instruction, learning, and transfer. *Cognitive Psychology, 20,* 362–404.

KLAHR, D., FAY, A. L., & DUNBAR, K. (1993). Heuristics for scientific experimentation: A developmental study. *Cognitive Psychology, 25,* 111–46.

KLAHR, D., & ROBINSON, M. (1981). Formal assessment of problem solving and planning processes in children. *Cognitive Psychology, 13,* 113–48.

KLAHR, D., & WALLACE, J. G. (1976). *Cognitive development: An information processing view.* Hillsdale, NJ: Erlbaum.

KLEMMER, E. T., & SNYDER, F. W. (1972). Measurement of time spent in communication. *Journal of Communication, 22,* 142–58.

KOBASIGAWA, A., RANSOM, C. C., & HOLLAND, C. J. (1980). Children's knowledge about skimming. *Alberta Journal of Educational Research, 26,* 169–82.

KOLB, B., & WHISHAW, I. (1996). *Fundamentals of human neuropsychology* (3rd ed.). San Francisco: Freeman.

KOONTZ, K. L., & BERCH, D. B. (1996). Identifying simple numerical stimuli: Processing inefficiencies exhibited by arithmetic learning disabled children. *Mathematical Cognition, 2,* 1–23.

KOTOVSKY, L., & BAILLARGEON, R. (1994). Calibration-based reasoning about collision events in 11-month-old infants. *Cognition, 51,* 107–29.

KRAUSS, R. M., & GLUCKSBERG, S. (1969). The development of communication: Competence as a function of age. *Child Development, 40,* 255–66.

KRESS, G. (1982). *Learning to write.* Boston, MA: Routledge & Kegan Paul.

KREUTZER, M. A., LEONARD, C., & FLAVELL, J. H. (1975). An interview study of children's knowledge about memory. *Monographs of the Society for Research in Child Development, 40* (Whole No. 159).

KRUGER, A. C. (1992). The effect of peer and adult-child transactive discussions on moral reasoning. *Merrill-Palmer Quarterly, 38*, 191–211.

KUCZAJ, S. A. (1977). The acquisition of regular and irregular past tense forms. *Journal of Verbal Learning and Verbal Behavior, 16*, 589–600.

KUCZAJ, S. A., (1978). Why do children fail to overregularize the progressive inflection? *Journal of Child Language, 5*, 167–71.

KUCZAJ, S. A., II. (1983). "I Mell a Kunk!" Evidence that children have more complex representations of word pronunciations which they simplify. *Journal of Psycholinguistic Research, 12*, 69–73.

KUCZAJ, S. A., II. (1986). General developmental patterns and individual differences in the acquisition of copula and auxiliary be forms. *First Language, 6*, 111–17.

KUCZAJ, S. A., II, BORYS, R. H., & JONES, M. (1989). On the interaction of language and thought: Some thoughts on developmental data. In A Galletly, D. Rogers, & J. A. Sloboda (Eds.), *Cognition and the social world*. New York: Oxford University Press.

KUHN, D. (1989). Children and adults as intuitive scientists. *Psychological Review, 96*, 674–89.

KUHN, D. (1995). Microgenetic study of change: What has it told us? *Psychological Science, 6*, 133–39.

KUHN, D., AMSEL, E., & O'LOUGHLIN, M. (1988). *The development of scientific thinking skills*. Orlando, FL: Academic Press.

KUHN, D., GARCIA-MILA, M., ZOHAR, A., & ANDERSEN, C. (1995). Strategies of knowledge acquisition. *Monographs of the Society for Research in Child Development, 60*, Serial No. 245.

KUHN, D., & PHELPS, E. (1976). The development of children's comprehension of causal direction. *Child Development, 47*, 248–51.

KUHN, D., SCHAUBLE, L., & GARCIA-MILA, M. (1992). Cross-domain development of scientific reasoning. *Cognition and Instruction, 9*, 285–327.

KUN, A. (1978). Evidence for preschoolers' understanding of causal direction in extended causal sequences. *Child Development, 49*, 218–22.

KUNZINGER, E. L., & WITTRYOL, S. L. (1984). The effects of differential incentives on second-grade rehearsal and free recall. *The Journal of Genetic Psychology, 144*, 19–30.

KURTZ, B. E., SCHNEIDER, W., CARR, M., BORKOWSKI, J. G., & RELLINGER, E. (1990). Strategy instruction and attributional beliefs in West Germany and the United States: Do teachers foster metacognitive development? *Contemporary Educational Psychology, 15*, 268–83.

LACASA, P., & VILLUENDAS, D. (1989). Adult-child and peer relationships: Action, representation, and learning process. In H. Mandl, E. de Corte, N. Bennett, & H. F. Friedrich (Eds.), *European Research in an International Context, Vol. 2.1: Social and cognitive aspects of learning and instruction*. Oxford: Pergamon Press. (Reprinted from *Learning and Instruction*).

LAMB, M. E., & CAMPOS, J. J. (1982). *Development in infancy: An introduction*. New York: Random House.

LANDAU, B., SMITH, L. B., & JONES, S. (1992). Syntactic context and the shape bias in children's and adults' lexical learning. *Journal of Memory and Language, 31*, 807–25.

LANGE, G., & PIERCE, S. H. (1992). Memory-strategy learning and maintenance in pre-school children. *Developmental Psychology, 28*, 453–62.

LANGLOIS, J. H., RITTER, J. M., ROGGMAN, L. A., & VAUGHN, L. S. (1991). Facial diversity and infant preferences for attractive faces. *Developmental Psychology, 27*, 79–84.

LANGLOIS, J. H., ROGGMAN, L. A., & MUSSELMAN, L. (1994). What is average and what is not average about attractive faces? *Psychological Science, 5*, 214–20.

LANGLOIS, J. H., ROGGMAN, L. A., CASEY, R. J., RITTER, J. M., REISER-DANNER, L. A., & JENKINS, V. Y. (1987). Infant preferences for attractive faces: Rudiments of a sterotype? *Developmental Psychology, 23*, 363–69.

LASKY, R. E., SYRDAL-LASKY, A., & KLEIN, R. E. (1975). VOT discrimination by four- to six- and a half-month-old infants from Spanish environments. *Journal of Experimental Child Psychology, 20*, 215–25.

LEBLANC, R. S., MUISE, J. G., & BLANCHARD, L. (1992). Backward masking in children and adolescents: Sensory transmission, accrual rate and asymptotic performance. *Journal of Experimental Child Psychology, 53*, 105–14.

LEE, S., STIGLER, J. W., & STEVENSON, H. W. (1984). *Beginning reading in Chinese and Eng-*

lish. Unpublished manuscript. University of Michigan, Ann Arbor.

LEFEVRE, J., BISANZ, J., & MRKONJIC, J. (1988). Cognitive arithmetic: Evidence for obligatory activation of arithmetic facts. *Memory & Cognition, 16*, 45–53.

LEFEVRE, J., & KULAK, A. G. (1994). Individual differences in the obligatory activation of addition facts. *Memory & Cognition, 22*, 188–200.

LEFEVRE, J., KULAK, A. G., & BISANZ, J. (1991). Individual differences and developmental change in the associative relations among members. *Journal of Experimental Child Psychology, 52*, 256–74.

LEFEVRE, J. A., SADESKY, G. S., & BISANZ, J. (1996). Selection of procedures in mental addition: Reassessing the problem-size effect in adults. *Journal of Experimental Psychology: Learning, Memory, and Cognition, 22*, 216–30.

LEGERSTEE, M. (1991). The role of person and object in eliciting early imitation. *Journal of Experimental Child Psychology, 51*, 423–33.

LEHRER, R., & LITTLEFIELD, J. (1991). Misconceptions and errors in LOGO: The role of instruction. *Journal of Educational Psychology, 83*, 124–33.

LEHRER, R., & LITTLEFIELD, J. (1993). Relationships among cognitive components in LOGO learning and transfer. *Journal of Educational Psychology, 85*, 317–30.

LEICHTMAN, M. D., & CECI, S. J. (1995). The effects of stereotypes and suggestions on preschoolers' reports. *Developmental Psychology, 31*, 568–78.

LEMAIRE, P., BARRETT, S. E., FAYOL, M., & ABDI, H. (1994). Automatic activation of addition and multiplication facts in elementary school children. *Journal of Experimental Child Psychology, 57*, 224–58.

LEMAIRE, P., & SIEGLER, R. S. (1995). Four aspects of strategic change: Contributions to children's learning of multiplication. *Journal of Experimental Psychology: General*, 83–97.

LEMIRE, R. J., LOESER, J. D., LEECH, R. W., & ALVORD, E. C. (1975). *Normal and abnormal development of the human nervous system*. New York: Harper & Row.

LENNEBERG, E. H. (1967). *Biological foundations of language*. New York: Wiley.

LEONARD, L. B. (1995) Phonological impairment. In P. Fletcher & B. MacWhinney (Eds.) *The handbook of child language*. Cambridge, MA: Blackwell.

LEPOFSKY, D. (1980, November). Consumer corner: Edited transcript from a speech. Wormald International, Sensory Aids Report.

LESGOLD, A., IVILL-FRIEL, J., & BONAR, J. (1989). Toward intelligent systems for testing. In L. B. Resnick (Ed.), *Knowing, learning, and instruction: Essays in honor of Robert Glaser*. Hillsdale, NJ: Erlbaum.

LESGOLD, A., RESNICK, L. B., & HAMMOND, K. (1985). Learning to read: A longitudinal study of word skill development in two curricula. *Reading Research: Advances in Theory and Practice, 4*, 107–38.

LESLIE, A. M. (1982). The perception of causality in infants. *Perception, 11*, 173–86.

LESLIE, A. M. (1987). Pretense and representation: The origins of "theory of mind." *Psychological Review, 94*, 412–26.

LESLIE, A. M. (1988). Some implications of pretense for mechanisms underlying the child's theory of mind. In J. Astington, P. Harris, & D. Olson (Eds.), *Developing theories of mind*. New York: Cambridge University Press.

LESLIE, A. M. (1991). The theory of mind impairment in autism: Evidence for a modular mechanism of development? In A. Whiten (Ed.), *Natural theories of mind: Evolution, development and simulation of everyday mindreading*. Oxford: Basil Blackwell.

LESLIE, A. M. (1994). ToMM, ToBy, and agency: Core architecture and domain specificity in cognition and culture. In L. Hirschfeld & S. Gelman (Eds.), *Mapping the mind: Domain specificity in cognition and culture*. New York: Cambridge University Press.

LEVIN, I. (1977). The development of time concepts in children: Reasoning about duration. *Child Development, 48*, 435–44.

LEVIN, I. (1982). The nature and development of time concepts in children: The effects of interfering cues. In W. J. Friedman (Ed.), *The developmental psychology of time*. New York: Academic Press.

LEVIN, I. (1989). Principles underlying time measurement: The development of children's constraints on counting time. In I. Levin &

D. Zakay (Eds.), *Time and human cognition: A life-span perspective.* The Netherlands: Elsevier.

LEVIN, I., & DRUYAN, S. (1993). When sociocognitive transaction among peers fails: The case of misconceptions in science. *Child Development, 63,* 1571–91.

LEVIN, I., & KORAT, O. (1993). Sensitivity to phonological, morphological, and semantic cues in early reading and writing in Hebrew. *Merrill-Palmer Quarterly, 39,* 213–32.

LEVIN, I., SIEGLER, R. S., & DRUYAN, S. (1990). Misconception about motion: Development and training effects. *Child Development, 61,* 1544–57.

LEVIN, I., WILKENING, F., & DEMBO, Y. (1984). Development of time quantification: Integration and nonintegration of beginnings and endings in comparing durations. *Child Development, 55,* 2160–72.

LEWIS, C. (1994). Episodes, events, and narratives in the child's understanding of mind. In C. Lewis & P. Mitchell (Eds.), *Children's early understanding of mind: Origins and development.* Hillsdale, NJ: Erlbaum.

LEWIS, C., FREEMAN, H. H., HAGESTADT, E., & DOUGLAS, H. (1994). Narrative access and production in preschoolers' false belief reasoning. *Cognitive Development, 9,* 397–424.

LEWKOWICZ, D. J., & TURKEWITZ, G. (1981). Intersensory interaction in newborns: Modification of visual preferences following exposure to sound. *Child Development, 52,* 827–32.

LIBEN, L. S. (1987). Information processing and Piagetian theory: Conflict or congruence? In L. S. Liben (Ed.), *Development and learning: Conflict or congruence?* Hillsdale, NJ: Erlbaum.

LIBERMAN, I. Y., SHANKWEILER, D., FISCHER, F. W., & CARTER, B. (1974). Explicit syllable and phoneme segmentation in the young child. *Journal of Experimental Child Psychology, 18,* 201–12.

LICHT, B. G., & DWECK, C. S. (1984). Determinants of academic achievement: The interaction of children's achievement orientations with skill area. *Developmental Psychology, 20,* 628–36.

LITTSCHWAGER, J. C., & MARKMAN, E. M. (1994). Sixteen- and 24-month-olds' use of mutual exclusivity as a default assumption in second label learning. *Developmental Psychology, 30,* 955–68.

LILLARD, A. S. (1993). Pretend play skills and the child's theory of mind. *Child Development, 64,* 348–71.

LILLARD, A. S., & FLAVELL, J. H. (1992). Young children's understanding of different mental states. *Developmental Psychology, 28,* 626–34.

LINDBERG, M. (1991). A taxonomy of suggestibility and eyewitness memory: Age, memory process, and focus of analysis. In J. L. Doris (Ed.), *The suggestibility of children's recollections.* Washington, DC: American Psychological Association.

LINDBERG, M. A. (1980). Is knowledge base development a necessary and sufficient condition for memory development? *Journal of Experimental Child Psychology, 30,* 401–10.

LITTLEFIELD, J., DELCLOS, V. R., BRANSFORD, J. D., CLAYTON, K. N., & FRANKS, J. J. (1989). Some prerequisites for teaching thinking: Methodological issues in the study of LOGO programming. *Cognition and Instruction, 6,* 331–66.

LOCKE, J. L. (1983). *Phonological acquisition and change.* New York: Academic Press.

LOCKE, J. L. (1995). Development of the capacity for spoken language. In P. Fletcher & B. MacWhinney (Eds.), *The handbook of child language.* Cambridge, MA: Blackwell.

LOCKE, J. L., & PEARSON, D. M. (1990). Linguistic significance of babbling: Evidence from a tracheostomized infant. *Journal of Child Language, 17,* 1–16.

LOVELL, K. (1961). A follow-up study of Inhelder and Piaget's *The growth of logical thinking. British Journal of Psychology, 52,* 143–53.

LOVETT, M. W., BORDEN, S. L., DELUCA, T., LACERENZA, L., BENSON, J. J., & BRACKSTONE, D. (1994). Treating the core deficits of developmental dyslexia: Evidence of transfer of learning after phonologically- and strategy-based reading training programs. *Developmental Psychology, 30,* 805–22.

LURA, A. R. (1973). *The working brain.* New York: Basic Books.

LYNCH, M. P., & EILERS, R. E. (1992). A study of perceptual development for musical tuning. *Perception and Psychophysics, 52,* 599–608.

MACLEAN, M., BRYANT, P., & BRADLEY, L. (1987). Rhymes, nursery rhymes and reading in early childhood. *Merrill-Palmer Quarterly, 33,* 255–81.

MACNAMARA, J. (1982). *Names for things: A study of human learning.* Cambridge, MA: MIT Press.

MACWHINNEY, B. (1989). Competition and connectionism. In B. MacWhinney & E. Bates (Eds.), *The crosslinguistic study of sentence processing.* New York: Cambridge University Press.

MACWHINNEY, B. (1996). Lexical connectionism. In P. Broeder & J. M. J. Murre (Eds.) *Models of language acquisition: Inductive and deductive approaches.* Cambridge, MA: MIT Press.

MACWHINNEY, B., & CHANG, F. (1995). Connectionism and language learning. In C. Nelson (Ed.), *Basic and applied perspectives on learning, cognition, and development: The Minnesota symposium on child psychology, Vol. 28.* Mahwah, NJ: Erlbaum.

MACWHINNEY, B., & LEINBACH, A. J., (1991). Implementations are not conceptualizations: Revising the verb learning model. *Cognition, 29,* 121–57.

MACWHINNEY, B., LEINBACH, J., Taraban, R., & McDonald, J. (1989). Language learning: Cues or rules? *Journal of Memory and Language, 28,* 255–77.

MADOLE, K. L., & COHEN, L. B. (1995). The role of object parts in infants' attention to form-function correlations. *Developmental Psychology, 31,* 637–48.

MANDEL, D. R., JUSCZYK, P. W., & PISONI, D. B. (1995). Infants' recognition of the sound patterns of their own names. *Psychological Science, 6,* 314–17.

MANDLER, J. M., & McDONOUGH, L. (1996). Drinking and driving don't mix: Inductive generalization in infancy. *Cognition, 59,* 307–35.

MANIS, F. R., CUSTODIO, R., & SZESZULSKI, P. A. (1993). Development of phonological and orthographic skill: A 2-year longitudinal study of dyslexic children. *Journal of Experimental Child Psychology, 56,* 64–86.

MANIS, F. R., SEIDENBERG, M. S., DOI, L. M., McBRIDE-CHANG, C., & PETERSON, A. (1996). On the bases of two subtypes of developmental dyslexia. *Cognition, 58,* 157–95.

MARATSOS, M. (in press). Some problems in grammatical acquisition. In W. Damon (Series Ed.) & D. Kuhn & R. S. Siegler (Vol. Eds.), *Handbook of child psychology: Vol. 2: Cognition, perception & language.* (5th ed.). New York: Wiley.

MARATSOS, M., & MATHENY, L. (1994). Language specificity and elasticity: Brain and clinical syndrome studies. In L. W. Porter & M. R. Rosenzweig (Eds.), *Annual Review of Psychology, Vol. 45.* Palo Alto, CA: Annual Reviews Inc.

MARCHMAN, V. (1992). Constraints on plasticity in a connectionist model of the English past tense. *Journal of Cognitive Neuroscience, 5,* 215–34.

MARCHMAN, V., & BATES, E. (1994). Continuity in lexical and morphological development: A test of the critical mass hypothesis. *Journal of Child Language, 21,* 339–66.

MARCHMAN, V., MILLER, R., & BATES, E. A. (1991). Babble and first words in children with focal brain injury. *Applied Psycholinguistics, 12,* 1–22.

MARCUS, G. F., PINKER, S., ULLMAN, M., HOLLANDER, M., ROSEN, T. J., & XU, F. (1992). Over-regularization in language acquisition. *Monographs of the Society for Research in Child Development, 57* (4), Serial No. 228.

MARINI, Z. (1984). The development of social and physical cognition in childhood and adolescence. Unpublished doctoral dissertation, University of Toronto.

MARINI, Z. A. (1992). Synchrony and asynchrony in the development of children's scientific reasoning. In R. Case (Ed.), *The mind's staircase: Exploring the conceptual underpinnings of children's thought and knowledge.* Hillsdale, NJ: Erlbaum.

MARINI, Z. A., & CASE, R. (1989). Parallels in the development of preschoolers' knowledge about their physical and social worlds. *Merrill-Palmer Quarterly, 35,* 63–88.

MARINI, Z., & CASE, R. (1994). The development of abstract reasoning about the physical and social world. *Child Development, 65,* 147–59.

MARKMAN, E. M. (1979). Realizing that you don't understand: Elementary school children's awareness of inconsistencies. *Child Development, 50,* 643–55.

MARKMAN, E. M. (1987). How children constrain the possible meanings of words. In U. Neisser (Ed.), *Concepts and conceptual development: Ecological and intellectual factors in categorization.* Cambridge, MA: Cambridge University Press.

MARKMAN, E. M. (1989). *Categorization and naming in children: Problems of induction.* Cambridge, MA: Cambridge University Press.

MARKMAN, E. M. (1992). Constraints on word learning: Speculations about their nature, origins and domain specificity. In M. R. Gunner & M. P. Maratsos (Eds.), *Modularity and constraints in language and cognition: The Minnesota symposium on child psychology.* Hillsdale, NJ: Erlbaum.

MARKMAN, E. M., & WACHTEL, G. F. (1988). Children's use of mutual exclusivity to constrain the meaning of words. *Cognitive Psychology, 20,* 121–57.

MARKOVITS, H. (1993). The development of conditional reasoning: A Piagetian reformulation of the mental models theory. *Merrill-Palmer Quarterly, 39,* 131–58.

MARR, D. B., & STERNBERG, R. J. (1986). Analogical reasoning with novel concepts: Differential attention of intellectually gifted and nongifted children to relevant and irrelevant novel stimuli. *Cognitive Development, 1,* 53–72.

MARSCHARK, M., & WEST, S. H. (1985). Creative language abilities of deaf children. *Journal of Speech and Hearing Research, 28,* 73–78.

MARSCHARK, M., WEST, S. A., NALL, L., & EVERHART, V. (1986). Development of creative language devices in signed and oral production. *Journal of Experimental Child Psychology, 41,* 534–50.

MASATAKA, N. (1992). Pitch characteristics of Japanese maternal speech to infants. *Journal of Child Language, 19,* 213–24.

MASUR, E. F., MCINTYRE, C. W., & FLAVELL, J. H. (1973). Developmental changes in apportionment of study time among items in a multitrial free recall task. *Journal of Experimental Child Psychology, 15,* 237–46.

MATZ, M. (1982). Towards a process model for high school algebra errors. In D. Sleeman & J. S. Brown (Eds.), *Intelligent tutoring systems.* New York: Academic Press.

MAURER, D., & MAURER, C. (1988). *The world of the newborn.* New York: Basic Books.

MAYER, R. E., LEWIS, A. B., & HEGARTY, M. (1992). Mathematical misunderstandings: Qualitative reasoning about quantitative problems. In J. I. D. Campbell (Ed.), *The nature and origins of mathematical skills.* Amsterdam: North-Holland.

MCCALL, R. B., APPLEBAUM, M. I., & HOGARTY, P. S. (1973). Developmental changes in mental performance. *Monographs of the Society for Research in Child Development, 38* (Serial No. 150).

MCCALL, R. B., & CARRIGER, M. S. (1993). A meta-analysis of infant habituation and recognition memory performance as predictors of later IQ. *Child Development, 64,* 57–79.

MCCALL, R. B., KENNEDY, C. B., & APPLEBAUM, M. I. (1977). Magnitude of discrepancy and the distribution of attention in infants. *Child Development, 48,* 772–86.

MCCARTHY, D. (1954). Language development in children. In L. Carmichael (Ed.), *Manual of child psychology.* New York: Wiley.

MCCLELLAND, J. L. (1995). A connectionist perspective on knowledge and development. In T. J. Simon & G. S. Halford (Eds.), *Developing cognitive competence: New approaches to process modeling.* Hillsdale, NJ: Erlbaum.

MCCLOSKEY, M., & KAISER, M. (1984). The impetus impulse: A medieval theory of motion lives on in the minds of children. *The Sciences.*

MCDONOUGH, L., & MANDLER, J. M. (1994). Very long-term recall in infants: Infantile amnesia reconsidered. *Memory, 2,* 339–52.

MCFADDEN, G. T., DUFRENSE, A., & KOBASIGAWA, A. (1986). Young children's knowledge of balance scale problems. *Journal of Genetic Psychology, 148,* 79–94.

MCGILLY, K., & SIEGLER, R. S. (1989). How children choose among serial recall strategies. *Child Development, 60,* 172–82.

MCGILLY, K., & SIEGLER, R. S. (1990). The influence of encoding and strategic knowledge on children's choices among serial recall strategies. *Developmental Psychology, 26,* 931–41.

MCKEOUGH, A. (1992). A neo-Piagetian analysis of narrative and its development. In R. Case (Ed.), *The mind's staircase: Exploring the conceptual underpinnings of children's thought and knowledge.* Hillsdale, NJ: Erlbaum.

MELTZOFF, A. N. (1988). Infant imitation and memory: Nine-month-olds in immediate and deferred tests. *Child Development, 59,* 217–25.

MELTZOFF, A. N. (1990). Towards a developmental cognitive science. *Annals of the New York Academy of Sciences, 608,* 1–37.

MELTZOFF, A. N. (1995). What infant memory tells us about infantile amnesia: Long-term recall and deferred imitation. *Journal of Experimental Child Psychology, 59,* 497–515.

MELTZOFF, A. N., & MOORE, M. K. (1983). Newborn infants imitate adult facial gestures. *Child Development, 54*, 702–9.

MELTZOFF, A. N., & MOORE, M. K. (1989). Imitation in newborn infants: Exploring the range of gestures imitated and the underlying mechanisms. *Developmental Psychology, 25*, 954–62.

MELTZOFF, A. N., & MOORE, M. K. (1994). Imitation, memory, and the representation of persons. *Infant Behavior and Development, 17*, 83–99.

MENDELSON, M. J., & HAITH, M. M. (1976). The relation between audition and vision in the human newborn. *Monographs of the Society for Research in Child Development, 41* (Whole No. 167).

MENDELSON, R., & SHULTZ, T. R. (1976). Covariation and temporal contiguity as principles of causal inference in young children. *Journal of Experimental Child Psychology, 13*, 89–111.

MENN, L., & STOEL-GAMMON, C. (1995). Phonological development. In P. Fletcher & B. MacWhinney (Eds.) *The handbook of child language*. Cambridge, MA: Blackwell.

MERRIMAN, W. E., & BOWMAN, L. L. (1989). The mutual exclusivity bias in children's word learning. *Monographs of the Society for Research in Child Development, 54*, (Serial No. 220).

MERRIMAN, W. E., MARAZITA, J., & JARVIS, L. (1993). Four-year-olds' disambiguation of action and object word reference. *Journal of Experimental Child Psychology, 56*, 412–30.

MERRIMAN, W. E., SCOTT, P., & MARAZITA, J. (1993). An appearance-function shift in children's object naming. *Journal of Child Language, 20*, 101–18.

MERVIS, C. B. (1987). Child-basic object categories and early lexical development. In U. Neisser (Ed.), *Concepts and conceptual development: Ecological and intellectual factors in categorization*. Cambridge, MA: Cambridge University Press.

MERVIS, C. B., & BERTRAND, J. (1993) *Early language and cognitive development: Implications of research with children who have Williams syndrome or Down syndrome*. Paper presented at the 60th Anniversary Meeting of the Society for Research in Child Development, New Orleans.

MERZENICH, M. M., JENKINS, W. M., JOHNSTON, P., SCHREINER, C., MILLER, S. L., & TALLAL, P. (1996). Temporal processing deficits of language-learning-impaired children ameliorated by training. *Science, 271*, 77–81.

MERZENICH, M. M., SCHREINER, C. S., JENKINS, W. M., & WANG, X. (1993). Neural mechanisms underlying temporal integration, segmentation, and input sequence representation: Some implications for the origin of learning disabilities. In P. Tallal, A. M. Galaburda, R. R. Linas, & C. von Euler (Eds.) *Temporal information processing in the nervous system: Special reference to dyslexia and dysphasia*. New York: New York Academy of Sciences.

METZ, K. (1985). The development of children's problem solving in a gears task: A problem space perspective. *Cognitive Science, 9*, 431–72.

MILLER, G. A. (1956). The magical number seven, plus or minus two: Some limits on our capacity for processing information. *Psychological Review, 63*, 81–97.

MILLER, J. (1992). Development of speech and language in children with Down syndrome. In I. Lott & E. McCoy (Eds.), *Down syndrome: Advances in medical care*. New York: Wiley.

MILLER, K. (1989). Measurement as a tool for thought: The role of measuring procedures in children's understanding of quantitative invariance. *Developmental Psychology, 25*, 589–600.

MILLER, K., & GELMAN, R. (1983). The child's representation of number: A multidimensional scaling analysis. *Child Development, 54*, 1470–79.

MILLER, K. F., & BAILLARGEON, R. (1990). Length and distance: Do preschoolers think that occlusion brings things together? *Developmental Psychology, 26*, 103–14.

MILLER, K. F., & ZHU, J. (1991). The trouble with teens: Accessing the structure of number names. *Journal of Memory and Language, 30*, 48–68.

MILLER, K. F., SMITH, C. M., ZHU, J., & ZHANG, H. (1995). Preschool origins of cross-national differences in mathematical competence: The role of number-naming systems. *Psychological Science, 6*, 56–60.

MILLER, L. T., & VERNON, P. A. (in press). Developmental trends in memory capacity and speed of information processing. *Developmental Psychology*.

MILLER, P., & SEIER, W. (1994). Strategy utilization deficiencies in children: When, where, and why. In H. Reese (Ed.), *Advances in child development and behavior, Vol. 25.* New York: Academic Press.

MILLER, P. H. (1990). The development of strategies of selective attention. In D. F. Bjorklund (Ed.), *Children's strategies: Contemporary views of cognitive development.* Hillsdale, NJ: Erlbaum.

MILLER, P. H. (1993). *Theories of developmental psychology.* (3rd ed.). New York: W. H. Freeman and Company.

MILLER, P. H., WOODY-RAMSEY, J., & ALOISE, P. A. (1991). The role of strategy effortfulness in strategy effectiveness. *Developmental Psychology, 27,* 738–45.

MILLER, S. A. (1976). Nonverbal assessment of conservation of number. *Child Development, 47,* 722–28.

MOLFESE, D. L., & MOLFESE, V. J. (1979). Hemisphere and stimulus differences as reflected in the cortical responses of newborn infants to speech stimuli. *Developmental Psychology, 15,* 505–11.

MORGAN, J. L. (1996). A rhythmic bias in preverbal speech segmentation. *Journal of Memory and Language, 35,* 666–88.

MORRISON, F. J., GRIFFITH, E. M., & FRAZIER, J. A. (1996). Schooling and the 5–7 shift: A natural experiment. A. Sameroff & M. M. Haith (Eds.), *Reason and responsibility: The passage through childhood.* Chicago, IL: University of Chicago Press.

MORRISON, F. J., HOLMES, D. L., & HAITH, M. M. (1974). A developmental study of the effects of familiarity on short-term visual memory. *Journal of Experimental Child Psychology, 18,* 412–25.

MORRISON, F. J., SMITH, L., & DOW-EHRENBERGER, M. (1995). Education and cognitive development: A natural experiment. *Developmental Psychology, 31,* 789–99.

MORRONGIELLO, B. A., FENWICK, K. D., HILLIER, L., & CHANCE, G. (1994). Sound localization in newborn human infants. *Developmental Psychobiology, 27,* 519–38.

MORRONGIELLO, B. A., HUMPHREY, G. K., TIMNEY, B., CHOI, J., & ROCCA, P. T. (1994). Tactual object exploration and recognition in blind and sighted children. *Perception, 23,* 833–48.

MORSE, P. A. (1972). The discrimination of speech and nonspeech stimuli in early infancy. *Journal of Experimental Child Psychology, 14,* 477–92.

MOSHMAN, D. (In press). Cognitive development beyond childhood. To appear in W. Damon (Series Ed.) & D. Kuhn & R. S. Siegler (Vol. Eds.), *Handbook of child psychology: Vol. 2: Cognition, perception & language.* (5th ed.). New York: Wiley.

MOSIER, C. E., & ROGOFF, B. (1994). Infants' instrumental use of their mothers to achieve their goals. *Child Development, 65,* 70–79.

MUIR, D., ABRAHAM, W., FORBES, B., & HARRIS, L. (1979). The ontogenesis of an auditory localization response from birth to four months of age. *Canadian Journal of Psychology, 33,* 320–33.

MULLER, E., HOLLIEN, H., & MURRAY, T. (1974). Perceptual responses to infant crying: Identification of cry. *Journal of Child Language, 1,* 89–95.

MUNAKATA, Y., MCCLELLAND, J. A., JOHNSON, M. H., & SIEGLER, R. S. (in press). Rethinking infant knowledge: Toward an adaptive process account of successes and failures in object permanence tasks. *Psychological Review.*

MURRAY, F. B. (1987). Necessity: The developmental component in school mathematics. In L. S. Liben (Ed.), *Development and learning: Conflict or congruence.* Hillsdale, NJ: Erlbaum.

MURRAY, F., & ARMSTRONG, S. (1976). Necessity in conservation and nonconservation. *Developmental Psychology, 12,* 483–84.

MUSSEN, P. H., CONGER, J. J., KAGAN, J., & GEIWITZ, J. (1979). *Psychological development: A life-span approach.* New York: Harper & Row.

MYERS, N. A., CLIFTON, R. K., & CLARKSON, M. G. (1987). When they were very young: Almost threes remember two years ago. *Infant Behavior and Development, 10,* 123–32.

NADEL, L., & ZOLA-MORGAN, S. (1984). Infantile amnesia: A neurobiological perspective. In M. Moscovitch (Ed.), *Infant memory: Its relation to normal and pathological memory in humans and other animals.* New York: Plenum.

NAIGLES, L. G., & KAKO, E. T. (1993). First contact in verb acquisition: Defining a role for syntax. *Child Development, 64,* 1665–87.

NAUS, M. J., & ORNSTEIN, P. A. (1983). Development of memory strategies: Analysis, questions, and issues. In M. T. H. Chi (Ed.), *Trends in memory development research.* New York: Karger.

NEEDHAM, A., BAILLARGEON, R., & KAUFMAN, L. (in press). Object segregation in infancy. In L. P. Lipsitt & C. Rovee-Collier, (Eds.), *Advances in infancy research Vol. II.* Norwood, NJ: Ablex.

NEISSER, U., & WEENE, P. (1962). Hierarchies in concept attainment. *Journal of Experimental Psychology, 64,* 640–45.

NELSON, C. A. (1995). The ontogeny of human memory: A cognitive neuroscience perspective. *Developmental Psychology, 31,* 723–38.

NELSON, K. (1973). Structure and strategy in learning to talk. *Monographs of the Society for Research in Child Development, 38* (Whole No. 149).

NELSON, K. (1978). How young children represent knowledge of their world in and out of language. In R. S. Siegler (Ed.), *Children's thinking: What develops?* Hillsdale, NJ: Erlbaum.

NELSON, K. (1993). The psychological and social origins of autobiographical memory. *Psychological Science, 4,* 1–8.

NELSON, K., & HUDSON, J. (1988). Scripts and memory: Functional relationship in development. In F. E. Weinert & M. Perlmutter (Eds.), *Memory development: Universal changes and individual differences.* Hillsdale, NJ: Erlbaum.

NEVILLE, H. J. (1995a). Developmental specificity in neurocognitive development in humans. In M. S. Gazzaniga (Ed.), *The cognitive neurosciences.* Cambridge, MA: MIT Press.

NEVILLE, H. (1995b, June). *Brain plasticity and the acquisition of skill.* Paper presented at the Cognitive Neuroscience and Education Conference, Eugene, OR.

NEWCOMBE, N. (1989). The development of spatial perspective taking. In H. W. Reese (Ed.), *Advances in child development and behavior, Vol. 22.* New York: Academic Press.

NEWCOMBE, N., & FOX, N. A. (1994). Infantile amnesia: Through a glass darkly. *Child Development, 65,* 31–40.

NEWCOMBE, N., & Huttehl,ocher, J. (1992). Children's early ability to solve perspective-taking problems. *Developmental Psychology, 28,* 635–43.

NEWELL, A., & ROSENBLOOM, P. S. (1981). Mechanisms of skill acquisition and the law of practice. In J. R. Anderson (Ed.), *Cognitive skills and their acquisition.* Hillsdale, NJ: Erlbaum.

NEWPORT, E. L. (1982). Task specificity in language learning? Evidence from speech. In E. Wanner & L. R. Gleitman (Eds.), *Language acquisition: The state of the art.* Cambridge, MA: Cambridge University Press.

OAKES, L. M. (1994). The development of infants' use of continuity cues in their perception of causality. *Developmental Psychology, 30,* 869–79.

OAKES, L. M., & COHEN, L. B. (1990). Infant perception of a causal event. *Cognitive Development, 5,* 193–207.

OAKES, L. M., & COHEN, L. B. (1995). Infant causal perception. In C. Rovee-Collier & L. P. Lipsitt (Eds.), *Advances in infancy research, Vol. 9.* Norwood, NJ: Ablex.

OAKHILL, J. (1988). The development of children's reasoning ability: Information-processing approaches. In K. Richardson & S. Sheldon (Eds.), *Cognitive development to adolescence.* Hillsdale, NJ: Erlbaum.

OAKSFORD, M., & CHATER, N. (1994). A rational analysis of the selection task as optimal data selection. *Psychological Review, 101,* 608–31.

OCHS, E., & SCHIEFFELIN, B. (1995). The impact of language socialization on grammatical development. In P. Fletcher & B. MacWhinney (Eds.), *The handbook of child language.* Cambridge, MA: Blackwell.

OKAMOTO, Y. (1992). *A developmental analysis of children's processes for solving word problems.* Unpublished doctoral dissertation, Stanford University.

OLLER, D. K., & EILERS, R. E. (1988). The role of audition in babbling. *Child Development, 59,* 441–49.

OLSON, D. R. (1993, March). *What are beliefs and why can a four-year-old child but not a three-year-old child understand them?* Paper presented at the biennial meeting of the Society for Research in Child Development, New Orleans, LA.

OLSON, R. K., FORSBERG, H., & WISE, B. (1994). Genes, environment, and the development of orthographic skills. In V. W. Berninger (Ed.), *The varieties of orthographic knowledge I: Theoretical and developmental issues.* Dordrecht, The Netherlands: Kluwer Academic Publishers.

ORNSTEIN, P., GORDON, B. N., & LARUS, D. (1992). Children's memory for a personally experienced event: Implications for testimony, *Applied Cognitive Psychology, 6*, 49–60.

ORNSTEIN, P. A., MEDLIN, R. G., STONE, B. P., & NAUS, M. J. (1985). Retrieving for rehearsal: An analysis of active rehearsal in children's memory. *Developmental Psychology, 21*, 635–41.

ORNSTEIN, P. A., & NAUS, M. J. (1985). Effects of the knowledge base on children's memory strategies. In H. W. Reese (Ed.), *Advances in child development and behavior, Vol. 19*. New York: Academic Press.

OSHERSON, D., & MARKMAN, E. (1975). Language and the ability to evaluate contradictions and tautologies. *Cognition, 3*, 213–26.

OVERTON, W. F., WARD, S. L., NOVECK, I. A., BLACK, J., & O'BRIEN, D. P., (1987). Form and content in the development of deductive reasoning. *Developmental Psychology, 23*, 22–30.

PALINCSAR, A. S., & BROWN, A. L. (1984). Reciprocal teaching of comprehension-monitoring activities. *Cognition and Instruction, 1*, 117–75.

PALINCSAR, A. S., BROWN, A. L., & CAMPIONE, J. C. (1993). First-grade dialogues for knowledge acquisition and use. In E. A. Forman, N. Minick, & C. A. Stone (Eds.), *Contexts for learning: Sociocultural dynamics in children's development*. New York: Oxford University Press.

PANAGOS, J. M., & PRELOCK, P. A. (1982). Phonological constraints on the sentence productions of language-disordered children. *Journal of Speech and Hearing Research, 25*, 171–77.

PAPERT, S. (1980). *Mindstorms: Children, computers, and powerful ideas*. New York: Basic Books.

PARIS, S. G. (1975). Integration and inference in children's comprehension and memory. In F. Restle, R. Shriffrin, J. Castellan, H. Lindman, & D. Pisoni (Eds.), *Cognitive theory, Vol. 1*, Hillsdale, NJ: Erlbaum.

PARKER, J. (1995). Age differences in source monitoring of performed and imagined actions on immediate and delayed tests. *Journal of Experimental Child Psychology, 60*, 84–101.

PASCUAL-LEONE, J. A. (1970). A mathematical model for transition in Piaget's developmental stages. *Acta Psychologica, 32*, 301–45.

PASCUAL-LEONE, J. A. (1989). Constructive problems for constructive theories: The current relevance of Piaget's work and a critique of information processing simulation psychology. In H. Spada & R. Kluwe (Eds.), *Developmental models of thinking*. New York: Academic Press.

PERFETTI, C. A. (1984). *Reading ability*. New York: Oxford University Press.

PERLMUTTER, M., & LANGE, G. A. (1978). A developmental analysis of recall-recognition distinctions. In P. A. Ornstein (Ed.), *Memory development in children*. Hillsdale, NJ: Erlbaum.

PERNER, J. (1991). *Understanding the representational mind*. Cambridge, MA: MIT Press.

PERNER, J., RUFFMAN, T., & LEEKAM, S. R. (1994). Theory of mind is contagious: You catch it from your sibs. *Child Development, 65*, 1228–38.

PERRET-CLERMONT, A. N., & SCHUBAUER-LEONI, M. L. (1981). Conflict and cooperation as opportunities for learning. In W. P. Robinson (Ed.), *European monographs in social psychology* (Vol. 24). New York: Academic Press.

PERRY, D. G., & BUSSEY, K. (1979). The social learning theory of sex differences: Imitation is alive and well. *Journal of Personality and Social Psychology, 37*, 1699–712.

PERRY, M., CHURCH, R. B., & GOLDIN-MEADOW, S. (1988). Transitional knowledge in the acquisition of concepts. *Cognitive Development, 3*, 359–400.

PERRY, M., CHURCH, R. B., & GOLDIN-MEADOW, S. (1992). Is gesture/speech mismatch a general index of transitional knowledge? *Cognitive Development, 7*, 109–22.

PETITTO, L. A. (1992). Modularity and constraints in early lexical acquisition: Evidence from children's first words/signs and gestures. In M. Gunnar & M. Maratsos (Eds.), *Modularity and constraints in language and cognition: The Minnesota symposia on child psychology*. Hillsdale, NJ: Erlbaum.

PETITTO, L. A. (1995). In the beginning: On the genetic and environmental factors that make early language acquisition possible. In M. Gopnick & S. Davis (Eds.). *The biological basis of language*. Oxford: Oxford University Press.

PIAGET, J. (1946a). *The development of children's concept of time*. Paris: Presses Universitaires de France.

PIAGET, J. (1946b). *Les notions de mouvement et de vitesse ches l'enfant*. Paris: Presses Universitaires de France.

PIAGET, J. (1951). *Plays, dreams, and imitation in childhood*. New York: W. W. Norton.

PIAGET, J. (1952). *The child's concept of number*. New York: W. W. Norton.

PIAGET, J. (1954). *The construction of reality in the child*. New York: Basic Books.

PIAGET, J. (1969). *The child's conception of time.* New York: Ballantine.

PIAGET, J. (1970). *Psychology and epistemology.* New York: W. W. Norton.

PIAGET, J. (1971). *The construction of reality in the child*. New York: Ballantine.

PIAGET, J., & INHELDER, B. (1969). *The psychology of the child* (H. Weaver, Trans.). London: Routledge & Kegan Paul.

PIAGET, J., INHELDER, B., & SZEMINSKA, A. (1960). *The child's conception of geometry.* London: Routledge & Kegan Paul.

PIERROUTSAKOS, S. L. (1995, April). *When do infants grasp the nature of pictures?* Poster presented at the Biennial Meeting of the Society for Research in Child Development, Indianapolis, IN.

PILLEMER, D. B., & WHITE, S. H. (1989). Childhood events recalled by children and adults. In H. W. Reese (Ed.), *Advances in child development and behavior, Vol. 21.* New York: Academic Press.

PILLOW. B. H. (1988). The development of children's beliefs about the mental world. *Merrill-Palmer Quarterly, 34*, 1–32.

PINKER, S. (1984). *Language learnability and language development.* Cambridge, MA: Harvard University Press.

PINKER, S., & PRINCE, A. (1988). On language and connectionism: Analysis of a parallel distributed processing model of language acquisition. *Cognition, 28*, 73–193.

PLAUT, D. C., MCCLELLAND, J. L., SEIDENBERG, M. S., & PATTERSON, K. (1995). Understanding normal and impaired word reading: Computational principles in quasi-regular domains. *Psychological Review, 103*, 56–115.

PLUNKETT, K. (1996). *Connectionism and development: Neural networks and the study of change.* New York: Oxford University Press.

PLUNKETT, K., & MARCHMAN, V. (1993). From rote learning to system building: Acquiring verb morphology in children and connectionist nets. *Cognition, 48*, 21–69.

PLUNKETT, K., & SINHA, C. (1992). Connectionism and developmental theory. *British Journal of Development Psychology, 10*, 209–54.

POOLE, D. A., & LINDSAY, D. S. (1995). Interviewing preschoolers: Effects of nonsuggestive techniques, parental coaching and leading questions on reports of nonexperienced events. *Journal of Experimental Child Psychology, 60*, 129–54.

POOLE, D. A., & WHITE, L. (1993). Two years later: Effects of question repetition and retention interval on the eyewitness testimony of children and adults. *Developmental Psychology, 29*, 844–53.

POSNER, M. I., ROTHBART, M. K., THOMAS-THRAPP, L., & GERARDI, G. (in press). Development of orienting to locations and objects. In R. Wright (Ed.) *Visual attention.* New York: Oxford University Press.

PRATT, C., & BRYANT, P. E. (1990). Young children understand that looking leads to knowing (so long as they are looking through a single barrel). *Child Development, 61*, 973–82.

PRATT, M. W., KERIG, P., COWAN, P. A., & COWAN, C. P. (1988). Mothers and fathers teaching 3-year-olds: Authoritative parenting and adult scaffolding of young children's learning. *Developmental Psychology, 24*, 832–39.

PRESSLEY, M. (1995). What is intellectual development about in the 1990s? Good information processing. In F. E. Weinert & W. Schneider (Eds.), *Memory performance and competencies: Issues in growth and development.* Hillsdale, NJ: Erlbaum.

PRESSLEY, M., LEVIN, J. R., & GHATALA, E. S. (1984). Memory strategy monitoring in adults and children. *Journal of Verbal Learning and Verbal Behavior, 23*, 270–88.

PRESSON, C. G., & IHRIG, L. H. (1982). Using matter as a spatial landmark: Evidence against egocentric coding in infancy. *Developmental Psychology, 18*, 699–703.

PYE, C. (1992). The acquisition of K'iche' Maya. In D. Slobin (Ed.), *The crosslinguistic study of language acquisition, Vol. 3.* Hillsdale, NJ: Erlbaum.

QUINE, W. V. O. (1960). *Word and object.* Cambridge, MA: MIT Press.

QUINN, P. C., & EIMAS, P. D. (1995). Peceptual organization and categorization in young infants. In C. Rovee-Collier & L. P. Lipsitt (Eds.), *Advances in infancy research: Vol. 11.* Norwood, NJ: Ablex.

QUINN, P. C., EIMAS, P. D., & ROSENKRANTZ, S. L. (1993). Evidence for representations of perceptually similar natural categories by 3-month-old and 4-month-old infants. *Perception, 22,* 463–75.

RABINOWITZ, M., & CHI, M. T. H. (1987). An interactive model of strategic processing. In S. J. Ceci (Ed.), *Handbook of cognitive, social and neuropsychological aspects of learning disabilities, Vol 2.* Hillsdale, NJ: Erlbaum.

RABINOWITZ, M., & WOOLEY, K. E. (1995). Much ado about nothing: The relation among computational skill, arithmetic word problem comprehension, and limited attentional resources. *Cognition and Instruction, 13,* 51–71.

RACK, J. P., SNOWLING, M. J., & OLSON, R. K. (1992). The nonword reading deficit in developmental dyslexia: A review. *Reading Research Quarterly, 27,* 29–53.

RADZISZEWSKA, B., & ROGOFF, B. (1988). Influence of adult and peer collaborators on the development of children's planning skills. *Developmental Psychology, 24,* 840–48.

RAIJMAKERS, M. E. J., KOTEN, S. V., & MOLENAAR, P. C. M., (1996). On the validity of simulating stagewise development by means of PDP networks: Application of catastrophe analysis and an experimental test of rule-like network performance. *Cognitive Science, 20,* 101–39.

REESE, H. W. (1962). Verbal mediation as a function of age level. *Psychological Bulletin, 59,* 502–9.

REICH, P. A. (1986). *Language development.* Englewood Cliffs, NJ: Prentice-Hall.

RENNINGER, K. A., HIDI, S., & KRAPP. A. (Eds.). (1992). *The role of interest in learning and development.* Hillsdale, NJ: Erlbaum.

RENNINGER, K. A., & WOZNIAK, R. H. (1985). Effect of interest on attentional shift, recognition, and recall in young children. *Developmental Psychology, 21,* 624–32.

RESNICK, L. B., CAUZINILLE-MARMECHE, E., & MATHIEU, J. (1987). Understanding algebra. In J. A. Sloboda & D. Rogers (Eds.), *Cognitive processes in mathematics.* Oxford: Clarendon Press.

RESNICK, L. B., LEVINE, H. M., & TEASLEY, S. D. (1991). *Perspectives on socially shared cognition.* Washington, DC: American Psychological Association.

RESNICK, L. B., NESHER, P., LEONARD, F., MAGONE, M., OMANSON, S., & PELED, I. (1989). Conceptual bases of arithmetic errors: The case of decimal fractions. *Journal of Research in Mathematics Education.*

RIESER, J. (1979). Spatial orientation of six-month-old infants. *Child Development, 50,* 1078–87.

RIESER, J., & GARING, A. (1991, April). *It is not being-there that counts, it is what one has in mind: Constraints on school-age children's access to spatial knowledge.* Paper presented at the meeting of the Society for Research in Child Development, Seattle, WA.

RIESER, J. J., GARING, A. E., & YOUNG, M. F. (1994). Imagery, action, and young children's spatial orientation: It's not being there that counts, it's what one has in mind. *Child Development, 65,* 1262–78.

RIESER, J. J., HILL, E. W., TALOR, C. R., BRADFIELD, A., & ROSEN, S. (1992). Visual experience, visual field size, and the development of nonvisual sensitivity to the spatial structure of outdoor neighborhoods explored by walking. *Journal of Experimental Psychology: General, 121,* 210–21.

ROBERTS, K. (1988). Retrieval of a basic-level category in prelinguistic infants. *Developmental Psychology, 24,* 21–27.

ROBINSON, E. J., & ROBINSON, W. P. (1981). Egocentrism in verbal referential communication. In M. Cox (Ed.) *Is the young child egocentric?* London: Concord.

ROEDELL, W. C., JACKSON, N. E., & ROBINSON, H. B. (1980). *Gifted young children.* New York: Teachers College Press.

ROGOFF, B. (1990). *Apprenticeship in thinking.* New York: Oxford University Press.

ROGOFF, B. (1995). Observing sociocultural activity on three planes: Participatory appropriation, guided participation, and apprenticeship. In J. V. Wertsch, P. d. Rio, & A. Alvarez (Eds.), *Sociocultural studies of mind.* Cambridge, UK: Cambridge University Press.

ROSCH, E., & MERVIS, C. B. (1975). Family resemblances: Studies in the internal structure of categories. *Cognitive Psychology, 7,* 573–605.

ROSCH, E., MERVIS, C. B., GRAY, W. D., JOHNSON, D. M. & BOYES-BRAEM, P. (1976). Basic objects in natural categories. *Cognitive Psychology, 8,* 382–439.

ROSE, S. A., & FELDMAN, J. F. (1995). Prediction of IQ and specific cognitive abilities at 11 years from infancy measures. *Developmental Psychology, 31*, 685–96.

ROSE, S. A., FELDMAN, J. F., & WALLACE, I. F. (1992). Infant information processing in relation to six-year cognitive outcome. *Child Development, 63*, 1126–41.

ROSENGREN, K. S., GELMAN, S. A., KALISH, C. W., & McCORMICK, M. (1991). As time goes by: Children's early understanding of growth in animals. *Child Development, 62*, 1302–20.

ROSENSHINE, B., & MEISTER, C. (1994). Reciprocal teaching: A review of research. *Review of Educational Research, 64*, 479–530.

ROVEE, C. K., & FAGEN, J. W. (1976). Extended conditioning and 24-hour retention in infants. *Journal of Experimental Child Psychology, 21*, 1–11.

ROVEE-COLLIER, C. (1989). The "memory system" of prelinguistic infants. Paper presented at the Conference on the Development and Neural Bases of Higher Cognitive Functions, Chestnut Hill, PA.

ROVEE-COLLIER, C. (1995). Time windows in cognitive development. *Developmental Psychology, 31*, 147–69.

ROVEE-COLLIER, C., ADLER, S. A., & BORZA, M. (1994). Substituting new details for old? Effects of delaying postevent information on infant memory. *Memory & Cognition, 22*, 644–56.

ROVEE-COLLIER, C., EVANCIO, S., & EARLEY, L. A. (1995). The time window hypothesis: Spacing effects. *Infant Behavior & Development, 18*, 69–78.

RUECKERT, L., LANGE, N., PARTIOT, A., APPOLLONIO, I., LITVAN, I., LE BIHAN, D., & GRAFMAN, J. (1996). Visualizing cortical activation during mental calculation with functional MRI. *Neuroimage, 3*, 97–103.

RUSSELL, J. (1982). Cognitive conflict, transmission and justification: Conservation attainment through dyadic interaction. *Journal of Genetic Psychology, 140*, 283–97.

RUSSELL, J., JARROLD, C., & POTEL, D. (1994). What makes strategic deception difficult for children—the deception or the strategy? *British Journal of Developmental Psychology, 12*, 301–14.

SALAPATEK, P. (1975). Pattern perception in early infancy. In L. B. Cohen & P. Salapatek (Eds.), *Infant perception: From sensation to cognition*. New York: Academic Press.

SAPIR, E. (1951). The psychological reality of phonemes. In D. G. Mandelbaum (Ed.), *Selected writings of Edward Sapir*. Berkeley: University of California Press. (Article originally published in French, 1933.)

SAYWITZ, K., GOODMAN, G., NICHOLS, G., & MOAN, S. (1991). Children's memory of a physical examination involving genital touch: Implications for reports of child sexual abuse. *Journal of Consulting and Clinical Psychology, 5*, 682–91.

SCARDEMALIA, M., & BEREITER, C. (1984). Written composition. In M. Wittrock, (Ed.), *Handbook of research on teaching, 3rd edition*.

SCHACTER, D. L. (1987). Implicit memory: History and current status. *Journal of Experimental Psychology: Learning, Memory, and Cognition, 13*, 501–18.

SCHAUBLE, L. (1990). Belief revision in children: The role of prior knowledge and strategies for generating evidence. *Journal of Experimental Child Psychology, 49*, 31–57.

SCHAUBLE, L. (1996). The development of scientific reasoning in knowledge-rich contexts. *Developmental Psychology, 32*, 102–19.

SCHIEFFLEIN, B. B. (1990). *The give and take of everyday life: Language socialization of Kaluli children*. Cambridge: Cambridge University Press.

SCHLESINGER, I. M. (1982). *Steps to language: Towards a theory of native language acquisition*. Hillsdale, NJ: Erlbaum.

SCHNEIDER, B. A., TREHUB, S. E., & BULL, D. (1979). The development of basic auditory processes in infants. *Canadian Journal of Psychology, 33*, 306–19.

SCHNEIDER, W. (1985). Developmental trends in the metamemory-memory behavior relationship: An integrative review. In D. L. Forrest-Pressley, G. E. MacKinnon, & T. G. Waller (Eds.), *Cognition, metacognition, and human performance Vol. 1*. New York: Academic Press.

SCHNEIDER, W., & BJORKLUND, D. (in press). Memory. In W. Damon (Series Ed.). & D. Kuhn & R. S. Siegler (Vol. Eds.), *Handbook of child psychology: Vol. 2: Cognition, perception & language*. (5th ed.). New York: Wiley.

SCHNEIDER, W., GRUBER, H., GOLD, A., & OPWIS, K. (1993). Chess expertise and memory for chess positions in children and adults. *Journal of Experimental Child Psychology, 56*, 328–49.

SCHNEIDER, W., KORKEL, J., & WEINERT, F. E. (1989). Domain-specific knowledge and memory performance: A comparison of high- and low-aptitude children. *Journal of Educational Psychology, 81,* 306–12.

SCHNEIDER, W., & PRESSLEY, M. (1989). *Memory development between 2 and 20.* New York: Springer-Verlag.

SCHNEIDER, W., & SODIAN, B. (1988). Metamemory-memory relationships in preschool children: Evidence from a memory-for-location task. *Journal of Experimental Child Psychology, 45,* 209–33.

SCHOLNICK, E. K., & WING, C. S. (1995). Logic in conversation: Comparative studies of deduction in children and adults. *Cognitive Development, 10,* 319–46.

SEIDENBERG, M. S., & MCCLELLAND, J. L. (1989). A distributed, developmental model of word recognition and naming. *Psychological Review, 96,* 523–68.

SHAKLEE, H. (1979). Bounded rationality and cognitive development: Upper limits on growth? *Cognitive Psychology, 11,* 327–45.

SHAKLEE, H., & ELEK, S. (1988). Cause and covariate: Development of two related concepts. *Cognitive Development, 3,* 1–13.

SHARE, D. L., & STANOVICH, K. E. (1995). Cognitive processes in early reading development: A model of acquisition and individual differences. *Issues in Education: Contributions from Educational Psychology, 1,* 1–57.

SHATZ, M., & GELMAN, R. (1973). The development of communication skills: Modifications in the speech of young children as a function of listener. *Monographs of the Society for Research in Child Development, 38* (Whole No. 152).

SHIMOJO, S., BAUER, J. A., O'CONNELL, K. M., & HELD, R. (1986). Prestereoptic binocular vision in infants. *Vision Research, 26,* 501–10.

SHULTZ, T. R., ALTMANN, E., & ASSELIN, J. (1986). Judging causal priority. *British Journal of Developmental Psychology, 4,* 67–74.

SHULTZ, T. R., FISHER, G. W., PRATT, C. C., & RULF, S. (1986). Selection of causal rules. *Child Development, 57,* 143–52.

SHULTZ, T. R., SCHMIDT, W. C., BUCKINGHAM, D., & MARESCHAL, D. (1995). Modeling cognitive development with a generative connectionist algorithm. In T. Simon & G. Halford (Eds.), *Developing cognitive competence: New approaches to process modeling.* Hillsdale, NJ: Erlbaum.

SIEGAL, M. (1991). *Knowing children: Experiments in conversation and cognition.* Hove, England: Erlbaum.

SIEGAL, M., & PETERSON, C. C. (1994). Children's theory of mind and the conversational territory of cognitive development. In C. Lewis & P. Mitchell (Eds.), *Children's early understanding of mind: Origins and development.* Hillsdale, NJ: Erlbaum.

SIEGLER, R. S. (1976). Three aspects of cognitive development. *Cognitive Psychology, 8,* 481–520.

SIEGLER, R. S. (1978). The origins of scientific reasoning. In R. S. Siegler (Ed.), *Children's thinking: What develops?* Hillsdale, NJ: Erlbaum.

SIEGLER, R. S. (1981). Developmental sequences within and between concepts. *Monographs of Society for Research in Child Development, 46,* (Whole No. 189).

SIEGLER, R. S. (1986). Unities in strategy choices across domains. In M. Perlmutter (Ed.), *Minnesota symposium on child psychology, Vol. 19.* Hillsdale, NJ: Erlbaum.

SIEGLER, R. S. (1987a). Strategy choices in subtraction. In J. Sloboda & D. Rogers (Eds.) *Cognitive processes in mathematics,* Oxford: Clarendon.

SIEGLER, R. S. (1987b). The perils of averaging data over strategies: An example from children's addition. *Journal of Experimental Psychology: General, 116,* 250–64.

SIEGLER, R. S. (1988). Individual differences in strategy choices: Good students, not-so-good students, and perfectionists. *Child Development, 59,* 833–51.

SIEGLER, R. S. (1994). Cognitive variability: A key to understanding cognitive development. *Current Directions in Psychological Science, 3,* 1–5.

SIEGLER, R. S. (1996). *Emerging minds: The process of change in children's thinking.* New York: Oxford University Press.

SIEGLER, R. S., & CROWLEY, K. (1994). Constraints on learning in non-privileged domains. *Cognitive Psychology, 27,* 194–227.

SIEGLER, R. S., & JENKINS, E. A. (1989). *How children discover new strategies.* Hillsdale, NJ: Erlbaum.

SIEGLER, R. S., & RICHARDS, D. D. (1979). The development of speed, time, and distance concepts. *Developmental Psychology, 15,* 288–98.

SIEGLER, R. S., & ROBINSON, M. (1982). The development of numerical understandings. In

H. W. Reese & L. P. Lipsitt (Eds.), *Advances in child development and behavior: Vol. 16.* New York: Academic Press.

SIEGLER, R. S., & SHIPLEY, C. (1995). Variation, selection, and cognitive change. In T. Simon & G. Halford (Eds.), *Developing cognitive competence: New approaches to process modeling.* Hillsdale, NJ: Erlbaum.

SIEGLER, R. S., & SHRAGER, J. (1984). Strategy choices in addition and subtraction: How do children know what to do? In C. Sophian (Ed.), *The origins of cognitive skills.* Hillsdale, NJ: Erlbaum.

SIGMAN, M., COHEN, S. E., BECKWITH, L, & PARMALEE, A. H. (1986). Infant attention in relation to intellectual abilities in childhood. *Developmental Psychology, 22,* 788–92.

SILVER, E. A. (1983). Probing young adults' thinking about rational numbers. *Focus on Learning Problems in Mathematics, 5,* 105–17.

SIMON, T. J., HESPOS, S. J., & ROCHAT, P. (1995). Do infants understand simple arithmetic? A replication of Wynn (1992). *Cognitive Development, 10,* 253–69.

SIMON, T., & KLAHR, D. (1995). A theory of children's learning about number conservation. In T. Simon & G. Halford (Eds.), *Developing cognitive competence: New approaches to process modeling.* Hillsdale, NJ: Erlbaum.

SIMONS, D. J., & KEIL, F. C. (1995). An abstract to concrete shift in the development of biological thought. *Cognition, 56,* 129–63.

SINGER, N. G., BELLUGI, U., BATES, E., JONES, W., & ROSSEN, M. (1995). Contrasting profiles of language development in children with Williams and Down syndromes. In D. Thal & J. Reilly (Eds.), "Origins of Language Disorders." *Developmental Neuropsychology.*

SIQUELAND, E. R., & LIPSITT, L. P. (1966). Conditioned head turning in human newborns, *Journal of Experimental Child Psychology, 3,* 356–76.

SLATER, A., MATTOCK, A., & BROWN, E. (1990). Size constancy at birth: Newborn infants' responses to retinal and real size. *Journal of Experimental Child Psychology, 49,* 314–22.

SLEEMAN, D. H. (1985). Basic algebra revised: A study with 14-year-olds. *International Journal of Man-Machine Studies, 22,* 127–49.

SLOBIN, D. I. (1986). Crosslinguistic evidence for the language-making capacity. In D. I. Slobin (Ed.), *The crosslinguistic study of language acquisition.* Hillsdale, NJ: Erlbaum.

SMILEY, P., & HUTTENLOCHER, J. (1989). Young children's acquisition of emotion concepts. In C. Saarni & P. L. Harris (Eds.), *Children's understanding of emotion.* Cambridge: Cambridge University Press.

SMILEY, S. S. & BROWN, A. L. (1979). Conceptual preference for thematic or taxonomic relations: A nonmonotonic age trend from preschool to old age. *Journal of Experimental Child Psychology, 28,* 249–57.

SMITH, A. (1984). Early and long-term recovery from brain damage in children and adults: Evolution of concepts of localization, plasticity, and recovery. In C. R. Almli, S. Finger (Eds.) *Early brain damage - Vol. 2.* NY: Academic Press.

SMITH, L. B., JONES, S. S., & LANDAU, B. (1992). Count nouns, adjectives, and perceptual properties in children's novel word interpretations. *Developmental Psychology, 28,* 273–86.

SMITH, M.E. (1926). An investigation of the development of the sentence and the extent of vocabulary in young children. *University of Iowa Studies in Child Welfare,3* (Whole No. 5).

SMITH, N. V. (1973). *The acquisition of phonology: A case study.* Cambridge: Cambridge University Press.

SMITH-HEFNER, B. (1988). The linguistic socialization of Javanese children. *Anthropological Linguistics, 30,* 166–98.

SNOW, C. E. (1986). Conversations with children. In P. Fletcher & M. Garman (Eds.), *Language acquisition: Studies in first language development.* Cambridge: Cambridge University Press.

SNOW, C. E., & HOEFNAGEL-HOHLE, M. (1978). The critical period for language acquisition; Evidence from second language learning. *Child Development, 49,* 1114–28.

SODIAN, B. (1988). Children's attributions of knowledge to the listener in a referential communication task. *Child Development, 59,* 378–85.

SODIAN, B., ZAITCHIK, D., & CAREY, S. (1991). Young children's differentiation of hypothetical beliefs from evidence. *Child Development, 62,* 753–66.

SOJA, N. N., CAREY, S., & SPELKE, E. S. (1991). Ontological categories guide young children's inductions of word meaning: Object terms and substance terms. *Cognition, 38,* 179–211.

SOPHIAN, C. (1984). Developing search skills in infancy and early childhood. in C. Sophian (Ed.), *Origins of cognitive skills.* Hillsdale, NJ: Erlbaum.

SOPHIAN, C. (1987). Early developments in children's use of counting to solve quantitative problems. *Cognition and Instruction, 4,* 61–90.

SOPHIAN, C., & HUBER, A. (1984). Early developments in children's causal judgments. *Child Development, 55,* 512–26.

SOPHIAN, C., & STIGLER, J. W. (1981). Does recognition memory improve with age? *Journal of Experimental Child Psychology, 32,* 343–53.

SPEAR, N. E. (1984). Ecologically determined dispositions control the ontogeny of learning and memory. In R. Kail & N. E. Spear (Eds.), *Comparative perspectives on the development of memory.* Hillsdale, NJ: Erlbaum.

SPEER, J. R., & FLAVELL, J. H. (1979). Young children's knowledge of the relative difficulty of recognition and recall memory tasks. *Developmental Psychology, 15,* 214–17.

SPELKE, E. (1976). Infants' intermodal perception of events. *Cognitive Psychology, 8,* 553–60.

SPELKE, E. S. (1994). Initial knowledge: Six suggestions. *Cognition, 50,* 431–45.

SPELKE, E. S., BREINLINGER, K., MACOMBER, J., & JACOBSON, K. (1992). Origins of knowledge. *Psychological Review, 99,* 605–32.

SPELKE, E. S., PHILLIPS, A., & WOODWARD, A. L. (1995). Infants' knowledge of object motion and human action. In D. Premack, J. Premack, & D. Sperber (Eds.), *Causal cognition: A multidisciplinary debate.* Oxford: Clarendon.

SPELKE, E. S., & VAN DE WALLE, G. (1993). Perceiving and reasoning about objects: Insights from infants. In N. Eilan, W. Brewer, & R. McCarthy (Eds.), *Spatial representation.* Oxford: Basil Blackwell.

SPERLING, G. (1960). The information available in brief visual presentation. *Psychological Monographs, 74* (Whole No. 176).

SPRINGER, K., NGYUEN, T., & SAMANIEGO, R. (1995). Early understanding of age- and environment-related noxiousness in biological kinds: Evidence for a naive theory. *Cognitive Development, 11,* 65–82.

STANOVICH, K. E. (1986). Matthew effects in reading: Some consequences of individual differences in the acquisition of literacy. *Reading Research Quarterly, 21,* 360–406.

STARKEY, P. (1992). The early development of numerical reasoning. *Cognition, 43,* 93–126.

STARKEY, P., & COOPER, R. S. (1980). Perception of numbers by human infants. *Science, 210,* 1033–35.

STARKEY, P., SPELKE, E. S., & GELMAN, R. (1990). Numerical abstraction by human infants. *Cognition, 36,* 97–128.

STASZEWSKI, J. J. (1988). Skilled memory and expert mental calculation. In M. T. H. Chi, R. Glaser, & M. J. Farr (Eds.), *The nature of expertise.* Hillsdale, NJ: Erlbaum.

STERN, D. N., SPIEKER, S., & MACKAIN, C. (1982). Intonation contours as signals in maternal speech to prelinguistic infants. *Developmental Psychology, 18,* 727–35.

STERN, E. (1992). Spontaneous use of conceptual mathematical knowledge in elementary school children. *Contempory Educational Psychology, 17,* 266–77.

STERN, E. (1993). What makes certain arithmetic word problems involving comparison of sets so difficult for children? *Journal of Educational Psychology, 85,* 7–23.

STERNBERG, R. J. (1984). Mechanisms of cognitive development: A componential approach. In R. J. Sternberg, (Ed.) *Mechanisms of cognitive development.* New York: Freeman.

Sternberg, R. J. (1985). *Beyond IQ: A triarchic theory of human intelligence.* New York: Cambridge University Press.

STERNBERG, R. J. (1989). Domain-generality versus domain-specificity: The life and impending death of a false dichotomy. *Merrill-Palmer Quarterly, 35,* 115–30.

STERNBERG, R. J., & RIFKIN, B. (1979). The development of analogical reasoning processes. *Journal of Experimental Child Psychology, 27,* 195–232.

STICHT, T. G., & JAMES, J. H. (1984). Listening and reading. In P. D. Pearson (Ed.), *Handbook of reading research, Part 2.* New York: Longman.

STIGLER, J. W. (1984) "Mental abacus": The effect of abacus training on Chinese children's mental calculation. *Cognitive Psychology, 16,* 145–76.

STILES, J., & THAL, D. (1993). Linguistic and spatial cognitive development following early focal brain injury: Patterns of deficit and recovery. In M. Johnson (Ed.), *Brain development and cognition: A reader.* Oxford: Blackwell Publishers.

STIPEK, D. J. (1984). Young children's performance expectations: Logical analysis or wishful thinking? In J. G. Nicholls (Ed.), *Advances in motivation and achievement: Vol 3, The development of achievement motivation.* Greenwich, CT: JAI Press.

STOKOE, W. C., JR. (1960). Sign language structure: An outline of the visual communications system of the American deaf. *Studies in Linguistics, Occasional Papers, Vol. 8.*

STRAUSS, M. S., & COHEN, L. P. (1978). Infant immediate and delayed memory for perceptual dimensions. Unpublished manuscript. University of Illinois-Urbana.

STRAUSS, M. S., & CURTIS, L. E. (1984). Development of numerical concepts in infancy. In C. Sophian (Ed.), *The origins of cognitive skills.* Hillsdale, NJ: Erlbaum.

STRAUSS, S. (1972). Inducing cognitive development and learning: A review of short-term training experiments. I: The organismic-developmental approach. *Cognition, 1,* 329–57.

STRAUSS, S. (1982). *U-shaped behavioral growth.* New York: Academic Press.

STRERI, A., & SPELKE, E. S. (1988). Haptic perception of objects in infancy. *Cognitive Psychology, 20,* 1–23.

STRYKER, M. P., & HARRIS, W. (1986). Binocular impulse blockade prevents the formation of ocular dominance columns in cat visual cortex. *Journal of Neuroscience, 6,* 2117–33.

SULLIVAN, K., & WINNER, E. (1993). Three-year-olds' understanding of mental states: The influence of trickery. *Journal of Experimental Child Psychology, 56,* 135–48.

SURBER, C. F., & GZESH, S. M. (1984). Reversible operations in the balance scale task. *Journal of Experimental Child Psychology, 38,* 254–74.

TAGER-FLUSBERG, H. (1992). Autistic children's talk about psychological states: Deficits in the early acquisition of a theory of mind. *Child Development, 63,* 161–72.

TALLAL, P., MILLER, S. L., BEDI, G., BYMA, G., WANG, X., NAGARAJAN, S. S., SCHREINER, C., JENKINS, W. M., & MERZENICH, M. M. (1996). Language comprehension in language-learning impaired children improved with acoustically modified speech. *Science, 271,* 81–84.

TALLAL, P., MILLER, S., & FITCH, R. H. (1993). Neurobiological basis of speech: A case for the preeminence of temporal processing. In P. Tallal, A. M. Galaburda, R. R. Linas, & C. von Euler (Eds.) *Temporal information processing in the nervous system: Special reference to dyslexia and dysphasia.* New York: New York Academy of Sciences.

TEALE, W. H., & SULZBY, E. (1986). Emergent literacy: A perspective for examining how young children become writers and readers. In W. H. Teale & E. Sulzby (Eds.), *Emergent literacy: Writing and reading.* Norwood, NJ: Ablex.

TEASLEY, S. D. (1995). The role of talk in children's peer collaborations. *Developmental Psychology, 31,* 207–20.

TELLER, D. Y., MCDONALD, M. A., PRESTON, K., SEBRIS, S. L., & DOBSON, V. (1986). Assessment of visual acuity in infants and children: The acuity card procedure. *Developmental Medicine & Child Neurology, 28,* 779–89.

THATCHER, R. W. (1992). Development as a dynamic system. *Current Directions in Psychological Science, 1,* 189–93.

THELEN, E. (1995). Motor development: A new synthesis. *American Psychologist, 50,* 79–95.

THOMPSON, R. F. (1985). *The brain: An introduction to neuroscience.* New York: Freeman.

TOLMIE, A., HOWE, C., MACKENZIE, M., & GREER, K. (1993). Task design as an influence on dialogue and learning: Primary school work with object flotation. *Social Development, 2,* 183–201.

TOMASELLO, M. (1995). Commentary. *Human Development, 38,* 46–52.

TOMASELLO, M., & BARTON, M. (1994). Learning words in nonostensive contexts. *Developmental Psychology, 30,* 639–50.

TOMASALLO, M., KRUGER, A. C., & RATNER, H. H. (1993). Cultural learning. *Behavioral and Brain Sciences, 16,* 495–511.

TRABASSO, T., ISEN, A. M., DOLECKI, P., MCLANAHAN, A. G., RILEY, C. A., & TUCKER, T. (1978). How do children solve class-inclusion problems? In R. S. Siegler (Ed.), *Children's thinking: What develops?* Hillsdale, NJ: Erlbaum.

TRABASSO, T. & NICKLES, M. (1992). The development of goal plans of action in narration of a picture story. *Discourse Processes, 15,* 249–75.

TRABASSO, T., RILEY, C. A., & WILSON, E. G. (1975). The representation of linear order and spatial strategies in reasoning: A developmental study. In R. J. Falmagne (Ed.), *Reason-*

ing: Representation and process. Hillsdale, NJ: Erlbaum.

TRABASSO, T. & STEIN, N. (1995). Using goal-plan knowledge to merge the past with the present and the future in narrating events on line. In M. M. Haith (Ed.), *The development of future oriented processes*. Chicago, IL: The University of Chicago Press.

TRABASSO, T., SUH, S., PAYTON, P., & JAIN, R. (1994). Explanatory inferences and other strategies during comprehension: Encoding effects on recall. In R. Lorch & E. O'Brian (Eds.) *Sources of coherence in reading*. Hillsdale, NJ: Erlbaum.

TRABASSO, T., VAN DEN BROEK, P., & SUH, S. (1989). Logical necessity and transitivity of causal relations in stories. *Discourse Processes, 12*, 1–25.

TROSETH, G. L., & DELOACHE, J. S. (1996, April). *The medium can obscure the message: Understanding the relation between video and reality*. Poster presented at the Biennial Meeting of the International Conference on Infant Studies, Providence, RI.

TUDGE, J. (1992). Processes and consequences of peer collaboration: A Vygotskian analysis. *Child Development, 63*, 1364–79.

TVERSKY, B., & HEMENWAY, D. (1984). Objects, parts, and categories. *Journal of Experimental Psychology: General, 113*, 169–93.

UZGIRIS, I. C. (1964). Situational generality of conservation. *Child Development, 35*, 831–41.

VALENZA, E., SKIMON, F., & UMILTA, C. (1994). Inhibition of return in newborn infants. *Infant Behavior and Development, 17*, 293–302.

VAN DEN BROEK, P. (1989). Causal reasoning and inference making in judging the importance of story statements. *Child Development, 60*, 286–97.

VAN DER MAAS, H., & MOLENAAR, P. (1992). Stagewise cognitive development: An application of catastrophe theory. *Psychological Review, 99*, 395–417.

VAN GEERT, P. (1994). *Dynamic systems of development: Change between complexity and chaos*. Hemel Hempstead, Hertfordshe: Harvester Wheatsheaf.

VAN LOOSBROEK, E., & SMITSMAN, A. W. (1990). Visual perception of numerosity in infancy. *Developmental Psychology, 26*, 916–22.

VANLEHN, K. (1990). *Mind bugs: The origins of procedural misconceptions*. Cambridge, MA: MIT Press.

VARNHAGEN, C. K., MORRISON, F. J., & EVERALL, R. (1994). Age and schooling effects in story recall and story production. *Developmental Psychology, 30*, 969–79.

VELLUTINO, F. R., & SCANLON, D. M. (1987). Phonological coding, phonological awareness, and reading ability: Evidence from a longitudinal and experimental study. *Merrill-Palmer Quarterly, 33*, 321–64.

VENEZKY, R. (1978). Reading acquisition: The occult and the obscure. In F. Murray, H. Sharp, & J. Pikulski (Eds.), *The acquisition of reading: Cognitive, linguistic, and perceptual prerequisites*. Baltimore, MD: University Park Press.

VERSCHAFFEL, L., DE CORTE, E., & PAUWELS, A. (1992). Solving compare problems: An eye movement test of Lewis and Mayer's consistency hypothesis. *Journal of Educational Psychology, 84*, 85–95.

VIHMAN, M. M. (1992). Early syllables and the construction of phonology. In C. A. Ferguson, L. Menn, & C. Stoel-Gammon (Eds.), *Phonological development: Models, research, implications*. Timonium, MD: York Press.

VON HOFSTEN, C. (1982). Eye-hand coordination in newborns. *Developmental Psychology, 18*, 450–61.

VON HOFSTEN, C. (1993). Prospective control: A basic aspect of action development. *Human Development, 36*, 253–70.

VOSNIADOU, S., & BREWER, W. 1992). Mental models of the earth: A study of conceptual change in childhood. *Cognitive Psychology, 24*, 535–85.

VURPILLOT, E. (1968). The development of scanning strategies and their relation to visual differentiation. *Journal of Experimental Child Psychology, 6*, 632–50.

VYGOTSKY, L. S. (1934). *Thought and language*. New York: Wiley.

VYGOTSKY, L. (1962). *Thought and language*. Cambridge, MA: MIT Press.

VYGOTSKY, L. S. (1978). *Mind in society: The development of higher mental processes*. Cambridge, MA: Harvard University Press. (Original works published in 1930, 1933, and 1935.)

WAGNER, R. K., & TORGESON, J. K. (1987). The nature of phonological processing and its causal role in the acquisition of reading skills. *Psychological Bulletin, 101*, 192–212.

WALTON, G. E., BOWER, N. J. A., & BOWER, T. G. R. (1992). Recognition of familiar faces by newborns. *Infant Behavior and Development, 15*, 265–69.

WATERS, H. S. (1980). "Class news": A single-subject longitudinal study of prose production and schema formation during childhood. *Journal of Verbal Learning and Verbal Behavior, 19*, 152–67.

WATERS, H. S. (1989, April). Problem-solving at two: A year-long naturalistic study of two children. Paper presented at the Society for Research in Child Development Conference, Kansas City, MO.

WATERS, H. S., & ANDREASSEN, C. (1983). Children's use of memory strategies under instruction. In M. Pressley & J. R. Levin (Eds.), *Cognitive strategies: Developmental, educational, and treatment-related issues*. New York: Springer-Verlag.

WATERS, H. S., & TINSLEY, V. S. (1985). Evaluating the discriminant and convergent validity of developmental constructs: Another look at the concept of egocentrism. *Psychological Bulletin, 97*, 483–96.

WAXMAN, S. R. (1990). Linguistic biases and the establishment of conceptual hierarchies: Evidence from preschool children. *Cognitive Development, 5*, 123–50.

WAXMAN, S. R., & HATCH, T. (1992). Beyond the basics: Preschool children label objects flexibly at multiple hierarchical levels. *Journal of Child Language, 19*, 153–66.

WEBER, R. M. (1970). First graders' use of grammatical context in reading. New York: Basic Books.

WEINERT, F. E. (1986). Developmental variations of memory performance and memory related knowledge across the life-span. In A. Sorensen, F. E. Weinert, & L. R. Sherrod (Eds.), *Human development: Multidisciplinary perspectives*. Hillsdale, NJ: Erlbaum.

WEIR, R. W. (1962). *Language in the crib*. The Hague: Mouton & Company.

Wellman, H. M. (1988). The early development of memory strategies. In F. Weinert & M. Perlmutter (Eds.), *Memory development: Universal changes and individual differences*. Hillsdale, NJ: Erlbaum.

WELLMAN, H. M. (1990). *Children's theories of mind*. Cambridge, MA: MIT Press.

WELLMAN, H. M., & BARTSCH, R. (1988). Young children's reasoning about beliefs. *Cognition, 30*, 239–77.

WELLMAN, H. M. CROSS, D., & BARTSCH, K. (1986). Infant search and object permanence: A meta-analysis of the A-not-B error. *Monographs of the Society for Research in Child Development, 51* (3, Serial No. 214).

WELLMAN, H. M., & GELMAN, S. A. (1992). Cognitive development: Foundational theories in core domains. *Annual Review of Psychology, 43*, 337–75.

WELLMAN, H. M., & GELMAN, S. (in press). Acquisition of knowledge. In W. Damon (Series Ed.) & D. Kuhn & R. S. Siegler (Vol. Eds.), *Handbook of child psychology: Vol. 2: Cognition, perception & language*. (5th ed.). New York: Wiley.

WELLMAN, H. M., RITTER, R., & FLAVELL, J. H. (1975). Deliberate memory behavior in the delayed reactions of very young children. *Developmental Psychology, 11*, 70–87.

WELLMAN, H. M., & WOOLEY, J. D. (1990). From simple desires to ordinary beliefs: The early development of everyday psychology, *Cognition, 35*, 245–75.

WELSH, M. C. (1991). Rule-guided behavior and self-monitoring on the Tower of Hanoi disk-transfer task. *Cognitive Development, 4*, 59–76.

WERKER, J. F. (1989). Becoming a native listener. *American Scientist, 77*, 54–59.

WERKER, J. F., & DESJARDINS, R. N. (1995). Listening to speech in the 1st year of life: Experiential influences on phoneme perception. *Current Directions in Psychological Science, 4*, 76–81.

WERKER, J. F., GILBERT, J. H. V., HUMPHREY, K., & TEES, R. C. (1981). Developmental aspects of cross-language speech perception. *Child Development, 52*, 349–55.

WERNER, J. S. & SIQUELAND, E. R. (1978). Visual recognition memory in the preterm infant. *Infant Behavior and Development, 1*, 79–94.

WERTHEIMER, M. (1961). Psychomotor coordination of auditory-visual space at birth. *Science, 134*, 1692.

WHIMBEY, A. (1975). *Intelligence can be taught*. New York: Dutton.

WHITCOMB, D. (1992). *When the child is a victim* (2nd ed.). Washington, DC: National Institute of Justice.

WHITE, L., & GENESEE, F. (1992, October). *How native is a near native speaker?* Paper presented at the Boston University Conference on Language Development.

WHITEHURST, G. J., & SONNENSCHEIN, S. (1981). The development of informative messages in referential communication. Knowing when vs. knowing how. In W. P. Dickson (Ed.), *Children's oral communication skills.* New York: Academic Press.

WHITNEY, P. (1986). Developmental trends in speed of semantic memory retrieval. *Developmental Review, 6,* 57–79.

WILLATTS, P. (1990). Development of problem solving strategies in infancy. In D. F. Bjorklund (Ed.), *Children's strategies.* Hillsdale, NJ: Erlbaum.

WILLIAMS, K. G., & GOULET, L. R. (1975). The effects of cueing and constraint instructions on children's free recall performance. *Journal of Experimental Child Psychology, 19,* 464–75.

WIMMER, H., & PERNER, J. (1983). Beliefs about beliefs: Representation and constraining function of wrong beliefs in young children's understanding of deception. *Cognition, 13,* 103–28.

WINNER, E. (1988). *The point of words: Children's understanding of metaphor and irony.* Cambridge, MA: Harvard University Press.

WINNER, E., ROSENSTEIL, A. K., & Gardner, H. (1976). The development of metaphoric understanding. *Developmental Psychology, 12,* 289–97.

WOOD, D. (1986). Aspects of teaching and learning. In M. Richards & P. Light (Eds.), *Children of social worlds.* Cambridge: Polity Press.

WOODWARD, A. (1995, March). *Infant's reasoning about the goals of a human actor.* Paper presented at the biennial meeting of the Society for Research in Child Development, Indianapolis, IN.

WOODWARD, A. L., MARKMAN, E. M., & FITZSIMMONS, C. M. (1994). Rapid word learning in 13- and 18-month-olds. *Developmental Psychology, 30,* 553–66.

WOOLLEY, J. D. (1995). The fictional mind: Young children's understanding of pretense, imagination, and dreams. *Developmental Review, 15,* 172–211.

WOOLLEY, J. D., & BRUELL, M. J. (1996). Young children's awareness of the origins of their mental representations. *Developmental Psychology, 32,* 335–46.

WOOLLEY, J. D., & WELLMAN, H. M. (1993). Origin and truth: Young children's understanding of imaginary mental representations. *Child Development, 64,* 1–17.

WYNN, K. (1992a). Addition and subtraction by human infants. *Nature, 358,* 749–50.

WYNN, K. (1992b). Children's acquisition of the number words and the counting system. *Cognitive Psychology, 24,* 220–51.

WYNN, K. (1995). Infants possess a system of numerical knowledge. *Current Directions in Psychological Science, 4,* 172–77.

YOUNGER, B. (1993). Understanding category members as "the same sort of thing": Explicit categorization in ten-month infants. *Child Development, 64,* 309–20.

YOUNGER, B. A. (1990). Infant categorization: Memory for category-level and specific item information. *Journal of Experimental Child Psychology, 50,* 131–55.

ZABRUCKY, K., & RATNER, H. H. (1986). Children's comprehension monitoring and recall of inconsistent stories. *Child Development, 57,* 1401–18.

ZAITCHIK, D. (1991). Is only seeing really believing? Sources of true belief in the false belief task. *Cognitive Development, 6,* 91–103.

ZAWAIZA, T. R., & GERBER, M. (1993). Effects of explicit instruction on math word-problem solving by community college students with learning disabilities. *Learning Disability Quarterly, 16,* 64–79.

ZBRODOFF, N. J. (1984). *Writing stories under time and length constraints.* Unpublished doctoral dissertation, University of Toronto, Toronto.

ZELAZO, P. D., & SHULTZ, T. R. (1989). Concepts of potency and resistance in causal prediction. *Child Development, 60,* 1307–15.

ZEMBER, M. J., & NAUS, M. J. (1985, April). The combined effects of knowledge base and mnemonic strategies on children's memory. Paper presented at the biennial meeting of the Society for Research in Child Development, Toronto, Ontario.

ZENTALL, S. S., & FERKIS, M. A. (1993). Mathematical problem solving for youth with ADHD, with and without learning disabilities. *Learning Disability Quarterly, 16,* 6–18.

Author Index

Subject Index